THE BLACK ATLANTIC RECONSIDERED

THE BLACK ATLANTIC RECONSIDERED

Black Canadian Writing, Cultural History, and the Presence of the Past

WINFRIED SIEMERLING

McGill-Queen's University Press
Montreal & Kingston | London | Ithaca

ISBN 978-0-7735-4507-6 (cloth)
ISBN 978-0-7735-4508-3 (paper)
ISBN 978-0-7735-8187-6 (ePDF)
ISBN 978-0-7735-8213-2 (ePUB)

Legal deposit second quarter 2015
Bibliothèque nationale du Québec

Printed in Canada on acid-free paper that is 100% ancient forest free (100% post-consumer recycled), processed chlorine free

This book has been published with the help of a grant from the Canadian Federation for the Humanities and Social Sciences, through the Awards to Scholarly Publications Program, using funds provided by the Social Sciences and Humanities Research Council of Canada.

McGill-Queen's University Press acknowledges the support of the Canada Council for the Arts for our publishing program. We also acknowledge the financial support of the Government of Canada through the Canada Book Fund for our publishing activities.

LIBRARY AND ARCHIVES CANADA CATALOGUING IN PUBLICATION

Siemerling, Winfried, author
The black Atlantic reconsidered : Black Canadian writing, cultural history, and the presence of the past / Winfried Siemerling.

Includes bibliographical references and index.
Issued in print and electronic formats.
ISBN 978-0-7735-4507-6 (bound).–ISBN 978-0-7735-4508-3 (pbk.).–
ISBN 978-0-7735-8187-6 (ePDF).–ISBN 978-0-7735-8213-2 (ePUB)

1. Canadian literature – Black Canadian authors – History and criticism. 2. Canadian literature – History and criticism. 3. Blacks in literature. 4. Culture in literature. 5. History in literature. 6. Transnationalism in literature. I. Title.

PS8089.5.B5S53 2015 C810.9'896071 C2014-908224-X
C2014-908225-8

Set in 10.5/13.5 Minion Pro with Gotham
Book design & typesetting by Garet Markvoort, zijn digital

For Juanita De Barros
and for Henry Felix and Linus

CONTENTS

PREFACE

When I first immersed myself in contemporary black Canadian writing as well as earlier texts and testimony, I was surprised to learn that this important aspect of Canadian culture had not received more attention. Why had this material not been more central to previous literary theory and discussion in Canada? And why was it so conspicuously absent from diasporic critical conversations about the black Atlantic?

Some of the reasons will become apparent in this book's introductory chapter. Fortunately, a number of researchers have augmented the relevant scholarship since I first undertook my own project. This volume builds on their insights and discoveries in addition to the efforts of some critics, theorists, sociologists, and historians who were earlier pioneers in the field. The main purpose of this book is to contribute to the task of making the fascinating and rich body of black Canadian writing available to a much wider readership and for more extensive contexts of discussion. The plan for this work has been to bring together in one place a critical account of black writing in what is now Canada from its beginnings to the present, to place this material in its diasporic black Atlantic and hemispheric contexts, and to include both anglophone and francophone perspectives.

As a result, *The Black Atlantic Reconsidered* is a multi-dimensional study that can be read and used in many ways. Since this account argues for a close link between past and present and for an appreciation of the value of relational connections, I hope that you will read it in its entirety. Most of the material covered in this study, for instance, would seem relevant for courses in black Canadian cultural studies or Canadian literature and culture. Some courses, discussion groups, or scholars, however, might use the volume as background reading while focusing on particular sections in related contexts. A more general introduction to North American literature and culture, a period course, or an introduction to the black Atlantic, for example, might rely on this book to provide necessary contexts while foregrounding specific chapters in juxtaposition with other materials. The same strategy might work for courses in diaspora, postcolonial, border, and hemispheric studies, or in critical regionalism.

In my previous monograph, *The New North American Studies*, I used multiple areas of literary and cultural studies in comparative ways to explore North American cultural emergence. To understand the relationship between normative recognition and alternative, emergent re–cognition, I worked through theoretical issues related to W.E.B. Du Bois's concept of "double consciousness" and his ideas about "race." While the study covered a wide range of materials, it was thus also very much concerned with literary and cultural theory. The present volume is again wide-ranging – across diverse transnational black Canadas – and engages many important theoretical issues, especially around forms of memory and the social and narrative production of time and space. I have moved some of the theoretical discussions, however, into endnotes and have tried to avoid overly specialized language. The aim has been to keep the text as readable as possible while providing additional information in the notes.

For quick orientation, the appendix presents a dual timeline with works organized by year and author. Given the sheer wealth of material, this timeline cannot possibly be exhaustive but is meant to provide context for the works discussed. It is important to note that many of the earlier works, especially the slave narratives and other sources discussed in Part I, are freely available on the Internet. I have occasionally provided links and other relevant information in the notes. In a more systematic manner, much of this information is also offered in a companion website to the book, which can be accessed at www.blackatlantic.ca.

Toronto, November 2014

ACKNOWLEDGMENTS

My thanks go out to many friends and colleagues as well as the institutions and archives that have facilitated my research and helped to make this volume possible. Since accessibility is so important, McGill-Queen's University Press deserves my gratitude for making the book available not only in hardcover but also in a simultaneous paperback edition and at a reasonable price. McGill-Queen's is a good home for this volume because it has published other important books in the field (for instance, texts by Robin Winks and Frank Mackey). I previously benefited from the editorial wisdom of Kyla Madden when working on *Canada and Its Americas*, and I would like to thank her again for her unstinting support and patience, as well as copy editor Judith Turnbull for her careful and precise work on the manuscript and managing editor Ryan Van Huijstee for seeing it through production. The outstanding research assistance of Jay Rawding was invaluable in the latter stages of this project, and the equally excellent work of Joanna Daxell and Marie-France Lafaille was helpful earlier on. Another factor that often remains invisible is the time-consuming and demanding work of anonymous readers who vet and critique book proposals and completed manuscripts. Three anonymous readers offered detailed evaluations for the Award to Scholarly Publication Program (ASPP), which subsequently supported the book with a generous publication grant. I also benefited from readers' comments that helped me receive two standard research grants from the Social Sciences and Humanities Research Council of Canada (SSHRC) in 2005–09 and 2011–15; these grants made much of the archival and other research for this volume possible. Further useful comments came from anonymous evaluators for the Killam Research Fellowship, which placed the project on its "3 Alternates" list in 2008 (and thus among the top thirteen applications in a national competition across all disciplines). Thanks also to three readers who prepared instructive and supportive comments for Routledge and to that publisher for its offer to include the volume in a prestigious Routledge Research series (although without the guarantee of a paperback edition). Further intellectual and financial support came from another SSHRC project in which I participate, the Major Collaborative Research Initiative "Improvisation, Community, and Social Practice," directed by Ajay Heble. The impact of this context can be seen especially in chapter 5.

I am grateful to many individuals who helped in other ways. My students at the John F. Kennedy Institute in Berlin, the Université de Sherbrooke in Quebec, and the University of Waterloo have helped me to explore many aspects of the material in this volume. I would like to thank Lawrence Hill for coming to speak and read in one of these classes – a public session of a graduate course on neo-slave narratives in 2007 – for granting me an interview, and for many subsequent conversations and much useful information. Ruth Whitehead, an ethnologist for many years at the Public Archives of Nova Scotia, graciously gave me access to her collation and discussion of different versions of the "Book of Negroes." It has always been a pleasure to talk with Karina Vernon about black Canadian writing, and I owe her thanks for her part in recent collaborative work on a new research project and her wonderful assistance with some last-minute sleuthing on Alfred Shadd for the timeline in this book. I would also like to thank Leslie Sanders and James (Jim) Walker for occasional informal conversations that have been both enjoyable and informative. Patricia Godbout, the translator of my previous monograph, has taken a lively interest in this project, which has benefited in many ways from our ongoing intellectual conversation. Hortense Spillers, finally, is not only a Berliner, often to be found in the city where I first met her when we both taught at the John F. Kennedy Institute; she can also be named an honorary Canadian for singing our national anthem before hockey games against the United States and her sustained interest in black Canadian writing. My thanks go out to her for the many conversations over the years that have helped to shape my scholarship.

Throughout the writing of this volume, I have been affiliated with the W.E.B. Du Bois Institute for African and African American Research at Harvard, and I would like to thank its director, Henry Louis Gates, Jr, and the Widener Library and Houghton Library at Harvard for their precious support. Will Straw offered me affiliation with his department at McGill University, and the MacLennan Library provided me with access and writing space for over a year. Ulla Haselstein and Heinz Ickstadt invited me for summer teaching stints at the John F. Kennedy Institute of the Free University Berlin, where I had access to libraries and taught much of the material included in this book. Finally, the Faculty of Arts at the University of Waterloo helped with a start-up grant, and my department chair, Fraser Easton, with much-needed other support.

The Public Archives of Nova Scotia (PANS) afforded me access to their copy of the "Book of Negroes," prepared for Nova Scotia's Commissioner of Public Records. Curator Henry Bishop welcomed me to the Black Cultural Centre for Nova Scotia and its Africville exhibit in 2010. Spencer Alexander, the assistant curator of the Buxton National Historic Site & Museum, took time to show me the historic Buxton sites, including the school, church, and cemetery; the museum also allowed me to examine the Isaac Shadd diary and the Abraham D. Shadd ledger. Gwendolyn Robinson at the Heritage Room of the Chatham-Kent Black Historical Society gave me access to materials during a visit there in 2005, which I used also for a trip to the Uncle Tom's Cabin Historical Site at the former home of Josiah Henson in Dresden, Ontario. Librarians at the Baldwin Room of the Toronto Public Library helpfully guided me to the notebooks of Dr Anderson Ruffin Abbott and other materials, while the University of Waterloo's Dana Porter Library and the University of Toronto's Robarts Library were steady sources of books and materials, especially towards the latter part of the writing process.

I should also like to thank the many friends, colleagues, conference organizers, and department representatives who during my research invited me to speak about the subject matter of this volume. They include Jaap Lintvelt at the University of Groningen; Sabine Sielke at the University of Bonn; Walter Moser at the University of Ottawa; Martin Klepper at Humboldt University in Berlin; Marta Dvořák at the Université Sorbonne Nouvelle; Waldemar Zacharasiewicz at the University of Vienna; Patrick Imbert at the University of Ottawa; Jean-François Côté at the Université du Québec à Montréal; Marie Carrière at the University of Alberta; Jutta Zimmermann and Konrad Gross at the University of Kiel; Rebecca Caines and Ajay Heble at the University of Guelph; Hortense Spillers at Vanderbilt University; Heike Paul, Katja Sarkowsky, and Meike Zwingenberger at the Bavarian American Academy in Munich; Hans Bak, Frank Mehring, and Mathilde Roza at Radbout University Nijmegen in the Netherlands; André Dodeman and Elodie Raimbault at the Université Stendhal Grenoble 3; and Pilar Cuder Domínguez and Belén Martín Lucas from the universities of Huelva and Vigo in Spain. In addition to conferences of professional associations in Canada, the United States, and Europe, the departments of English at the University of Basel, Carleton University, Auckland University,

Concordia University, the University of Waterloo, and the University of Toronto have given me occasion to speak about black Canadian writing and its transnational connections.

Some sections of the book have appeared in earlier forms elsewhere. I would like to extend a special thank-you to Smaro Kamboureli, Christl Verduyn, Heather Smyth, Leslie Sanders, Hyacinth Simpson, and Marlene Goldman for their interest and editorial suggestions, and to the publishers of the following articles and chapters for their reprint permissions:

"Jazz, Diaspora, and the History and Writing of Black Anglophone Montreal." In *Critical Collaborations: Indigeneity, Diaspora, and Ecology in Canadian Literary Studies*, edited by Smaro Kamboureli and Christl Verduyn, 199–214. Wilfrid Laurier University Press, 2014

"Transcultural Improvisation, Transnational Time, and Diasporic Chance in Wayde Compton's Textual Performance." *West Coast Line* 63 (March 2009): 30–7

"Time-Spaces of the Black Atlantic: Yemaya, Diasporic Disruption, and Connection in Dionne Brand." Edited by Heather Smyth and Leslie Sanders, Special Issue on Dionne Brand, *MaComère* 14, nos 1–2 (2013–14): 12–42

"May I See Some Identification? Race, Borders, and Identities in *Any Known Blood*." *Canadian Literature* 182 (2004): 30–50

"Ethics as Re/Cognition: Oral Knowledge, Cognitive Change, and Social Justice in the Novels of Marie-Célie Agnant." Edited by Marlene Goldman, Special Issue on Ethics and Literature, *University of Toronto Quarterly* 76, no. 3 (2007): 838–60

Arsenal Pulp Press and Wayde Compton deserve my gratitude for permission to use a page image from *49th Parallel Psalm*, and the UK National Archives for permission to use two pages from the 1783 "Book of Negroes."

Finally, I reserve my biggest thanks for the end, and they go to Juanita De Barros. She instructed me in Caribbean history while at the same time finishing her own volume way faster than I did mine. She also let me borrow all her books (I guess I have to return them now). Thanks for great ideas, wonderful conversations, and making it all fun.

THE BLACK ATLANTIC RECONSIDERED

1

Introduction: Modernity and Canadian Time-Spaces of the Black Atlantic

Readers are often surprised to learn that black writing in what is now Canada is over two centuries old and that black recorded speech is even older.[1] Ranging from pamphlets, letters, sermons, editorials, and slave narratives to contemporary novels, plays, poetry, and non-fiction, black Canadian writing offers a rich body of literary output and cultural achievement.[2] A great part of this work concerns our present. Much of it, however, also reveals the role of Canada in the development of transatlantic modernity.

Early black testimony is sparse. It was produced under circumstances over which black subjects had little or no control. The words of those black individuals who endured slavery in what is now Canada are available to us only through court and missionary records.[3] A document like Guy Carleton's 1783 "Book of Negroes" provides a wealth of certain kinds of information but reveals only tantalizing glimpses of black lives en route to Nova Scotia. The first major instances of writing by black authors themselves date back to the late eighteenth century, created by black settlers and ministers who relate their experiences in Nova Scotia. In the nineteenth century, an effervescence of black Canadian writing was ushered in by fugitive slaves and free blacks from south of the border who joined earlier black settlers in what is now southern Ontario. The resulting body of writing, which developed dramatically after the passage of the United States Fugitive Slave Act in 1850, includes narratives of their experiences in slavery and accounts of their lives as free settlers, in addition to a variety of other non-fictional genres and at least one novel. This outpouring of black Canadian writing slowed in the 1860s after the abolition of slavery in the United States. A renewed major black literature began to take shape from the 1960s and 1970s onward, supported by increased immigration, especially from the anglophone and francophone Caribbean, and by a revival of black Nova Scotian writing. Black Canadian writing grew even faster from the 1990s to the present, accompanied by a rediscovery and development of other regional black archives on the prairies and in British Columbia. Black Canadian writers of today are finalists and winners of national and international prizes – including Canada's Governor General's Award, Giller Prize, and Griffin Poetry Prize and, internationally, the Commonwealth Writers' Prize and the Man Booker Prize.

These developments have produced growing interest in black Canadian writing. They also have considerable consequences for scholarship, where their critical potential has yet to be made fully visible. The study of Canadian literature intensified from the mid-1960s and 1970s but initially focused on claims for national recognition and other priorities. This internal dynamic failed to support an earlier scholarly attention to black Canadian writing. A faster internal differentiation – subsequently expedited by discussions about Canada's postcoloniality and the composition of its literary canon – could have facilitated an earlier visibility of black Canadian writing in national, North American, transatlantic, and hemispheric terms (which are all constitutive contexts for the slave narrative, for example). It could also have alerted diasporic discussions much earlier to factors of black Canadian specificity.

As the study of black Canadian literature and culture has matured nationally, however, it has become a site of auto-critique in Canadian literary studies and has begun to motivate some revisions of Canadian literary history (to which this volume hopes to contribute further). In addition, black Canadian writing is also rooted in a diasporic imagination that often engages in highly critical relationships with national perspectives. Despite this fact, theories of the black Atlantic and studies of the hemispheric reach of transatlantic slavery have routinely marginalized slavery and post-slavery in what is now Canada. Observable from Paul Gilroy's groundbreaking *The Black Atlantic* (1993) to recent volumes on hemispheric American studies, this tendency has often persisted despite Canada's substantial role as a stage for black diasporic experience.[4] Black slavery was a reality in New France (where indigenous slaves were also held) and then in the Canadas officially until 1834.[5] The Underground Railroad spurred an important production of black Canadian writing in the mid-nineteenth century. All of these black diasporic contexts cross and transcend national borders. Accordingly, black Canadian studies has a role to play in related transnational fields, where it can offer occasions of critical self-reflection and opportunities for renewal. Early black Canadian writing speaks to contexts of imperial expansion and competition, and partakes in the hemispheric witnessing of slavery.[6] Black Atlantic studies more generally, as the following chapters will make clear, can benefit from referencing diasporic routes and networks that include locations in New France and Nova Scotia in the eighteenth century and Upper and Lower Canada in the nineteenth.[7] Similar transnational possibilities and imperatives pertain to the relevance of contemporary black Canadian writing.

Much of the rich black literary production in Canada in the last few decades engages directly with diasporic contexts, inviting attention to both national specificity and transnational perspectives. Together with Canadian, American, and North American studies, critical perspectives in black Atlantic, diasporic, hemispheric, postcolonial, and border studies are thus presented with crucial openings for innovative transformation through the engagement with black Canadian literature and culture. This field itself explores both the historical dimensions of black Canada and the work of contemporary writers who enjoy a substantial international readership. Authors such as Dionne Brand, Austin Clarke, George Elliott Clarke, Esi Edugyan, Dany Laferrière, and Lawrence Hill have garnered well-deserved attention, but a closer look reveals a much larger number of relevant texts and authors (see appendix). These works constitute a rich and vibrant literature that rewards detailed and attentive inquiry and engagement.

This specific area of interest is part of wider black Canadian cultural studies. While I concentrate mainly on a rich corpus of writing, I also evoke some facets of black musics in Canada where appropriate. This area of cultural studies enjoys a growing critical appreciation but deserves further detailed scholarly attention, not only to gospel, blues, jazz, and hip hop but also, for instance, to calypso, steel pan, and reggae – a task that is beyond the scope of this study.[8] Among other art forms, the same is true of black Canadian cinema; it is referenced here below and occasionally in the following chapters, but a thorough scholarly accounting of this material is yet to come.[9]

In the next three sections, I will contextualize the more specific discussions of texts and writers that appear later in this volume. I begin with a brief account of the period from the 1960s to the 1990s. Black Canadian writing gave signs of a renewed presence in this period, and black Canadian studies set out to build more decisively on earlier efforts. These are the developments that have created the enabling ground for current inquiry. This brief section adumbrates a few lines of development and signals a good number of writers and contexts, many of which are discussed later in more detail.

One of the main concerns in this book is to explore black writing simultaneously in its specifically Canadian and diasporic black Atlantic aspects. This problematic is joined by another, equally important one, which I will begin to discuss in the next section: the importance of the past in many contemporary black texts. These works mediate earlier black contexts and antecedents that thus become intertextual reference points and factors in the present. I also survey here some contemporary literary and cultural theory about the presence of an often traumatic past in texts that deal with aggrieved communities.

In the third section, finally, I briefly look ahead to some of the main precursors, routes, and intertexts that writers from different contemporary black cultures in Canada have referenced. These writers invoke aspects of the past as sources for the present they create and for the future they envision. These networks illustrate how black Canada – and hence also Canada in general – is closely interwoven with so many other times and spaces of the black Atlantic. After these introductory considerations, chapters 2 to 5 delve into the detailed discussion of black Canadian works and contexts.

BLACK CANADIAN STUDIES AND THE BEGINNINGS OF THE SECOND BLACK CANADIAN RENAISSANCE

Marcel Trudel's ground-breaking *L'esclavage au Canada français* (1960)[10] and two major historical studies in English, Robin Winks's *The Blacks in Canada* (first edition in 1971) and James Walker's *The Black Loyalists* (1976), were important milestones in the development of black Canadian studies. They reminded readers of aspects of Canadian history that were all but forgotten in the excitement and burgeoning cultural nationalism before and after Canada's 1967 centennial. In this period, building on increased postwar attention to the development of Canadian culture and extending the advances in this regard after the Massey Report (1951),[11] Northrop Frye, Margaret Atwood, the contributors to the *Literary History of Canada* (1965), an insurgent group of francophone writers in Quebec, and many others were engaged in seminal efforts to craft the communal declarations of literary independence of both Canada and Quebec.[12] Some kinds of cultural difference and specificity were given consideration in policy interventions by the state. After the Royal Commission on Bilingualism and Biculturalism (1963–69), the government of Pierre Elliott Trudeau acknowledged French as an official language (1969) and the "contribution of other groups" through a policy of multiculturalism (1971). For many racially identified groups, however, formal and cultural recognition was barely on the horizon. Even worse, in a White Paper crafted in 1969 under Trudeau and his Indian Affairs minister (and later prime minister) Jean Chrétien, Canada's First Nations were slated for assimilation (Government of Canada 1969).[13] For Japanese Canadians, who had suffered internment during the Second World War, redress was not in sight until much later.[14] And while attention to race relations – especially after the murder of Martin Luther King – was riveted on the civil rights movement in the United States, and important scholarship there on black nineteenth-century leaders like Martin Delany, Henry and Mary Bibb, and Mary Ann Shadd paid some attention to their time in Canada,[15] "race" was not yet a prominent issue in the discussion of Canadian literature.[16]

There were nonetheless some clear signs to remind the wider public of the existence of black communities in Canada. In 1967, the Caribbean Cultural Committee started Caribana in Toronto as a Caribbean Canadian contribution to Canada's centennial, founding an annual celebration that would go on to become one of the largest festivals in North America (see Foster 1995). In October 1968, important black intellectuals and leaders, such as C.L.R. James, Stokely Carmichael (later Kwame Ture), and Walter Rodney, gathered in Montreal for the "Congress of Black Writers/Congrès des écrivains noires: Towards the Second Emancipation – The Dynamics of Black Liberation/Vers la seconde émanicipation – dynamique de la libération noire." The congress was mostly concerned with black American, Caribbean, and African themes, although on the opening day Nova Scotian Rocky Jones delivered a brief talk on "Canada and Her Black Community" (Austin 2013, 103–4). This meeting coincided with a protest by West Indian students at Montreal's Sir George Williams University who were in negotiations with the administration over what they felt were discriminatory grading practices by one of the instructors. In January 1969, they and other students finally occupied the university's computer centre and were accused of being responsible when a fire broke out that caused severe damage, although the real cause was never established.[17] Despite the public attention and newspaper coverage bestowed on these events, however, awareness of black Canadian history *per se* remained minimal outside of the concerned community itself.[18] Winks and Walker heralded foundational stories that were integral to Canadian history and in some regards supported Canada's cherished myths as a land of freedom and the Canaan of aggrieved black populations. They also carried inconvenient truths, however, that appeared awkward in the context of Canadian national celebrations.

Winks's volume narrates black Canadian history from its known beginnings in the early 1600s. The subjects therefore include not only the Underground Railroad and the Canadian Canaan but also slavery in New France and English Canada. Walker's study focuses on the black arrivals after the American Revolution and especially after the evacuation of New York in 1783. It tells the story of free Black Loyalists finding refuge in Nova Scotia from re-enslavement south of the new border, but also of slaves brought by their Loyalist masters. In addition, the poor treatment of black settlers in Nova Scotia prompted the first major back-to-Africa Atlantic crossing; despairing of broken land promises and racism in Nova Scotia, about a third of the erstwhile immigrants left for Sierra Leone in 1792.[19]

These stories nonetheless underline the fact that Canadian history is also black history (and that the black Atlantic history is also Canadian). Further, they make it clear that this has been the case from the very beginnings of what is now Canada. In the process, these examinations of the past demonstrate that black Canadian history exceeds comforting accounts of Canada as the Canaan and land of black freedom, cherished by many Canadians for their contrast with the neighbour to the south. These works also reveal the falseness of the idea of a unified, homogeneous Canadian blackness. Recounting the trajectories of different groups of black slaves, early settlers, and later arrivals over time and across Canadian space, these works show that these diverse trajectories constitute an important and foundational aspect of Canadian history, while they also illustrate transnational and diasporic histories that implicate Canada in hemispheric and transatlantic stories of modernity.

The Early Second Renaissance: 1960s–1990s

While these historians and a few other scholars signalled the value of Canada's black past, increased immigration from the Caribbean and Africa had begun to augment Canada's black population from the 1950s and 1960s onward (see chapter 4; Mensah 2010, 71–3; Walker 1984). With regard to literary production, however, not many black writers were able to publish – and especially reach a wider audience – during this period of Canadian cultural nationalism and excitement. A few texts nonetheless offered signs of activity on the ground and indicated future developments, as I will discuss in more detail in chapter 4. The first three anthologies of contemporary black Canadian writing appeared between 1973 and 1976.[20] A small number of individual authors succeeded in publishing their own volumes: Bajan Canadian writer Austin Clarke followed up on earlier short stories and the first volume of his Toronto trilogy, published already in the 1960s;[21] Frederick Ward's *Riverlisp* (1974) reincarnated aspects of Africville, the black Halifax community erased by urban renewal only a few years earlier;[22] and Dionne Brand published her first volumes of poetry at the end of the decade.[23] With the Black Theatre Workshop, a professional theatre company was incorporated in Montreal in 1972, followed by Toronto's Black Theatre Canada in 1973 (Moynagh 2005, x–xi; Bayne 2004; J. Henry 2004). In francophone Quebec, authors fleeing Duvalier oppression in Haiti began to create an entire literature, with Gérard Étienne already publishing in Quebec in 1966 (after earlier volumes in Haiti) and Anthony Phelps and Émile Ollivier in print or preparing first volumes by 1976, when Dany Laferrière arrived in Montreal. These developments heralded a second renaissance of black Canadian writing, with an array of new black cultures joining older black groups in print. The attention of Canadian literary criticism at that time, however, remained largely riveted on national literary and cultural emergence and different theoretical issues. Courses dedicated to black writing in Canada, past or present, were not part of the university curriculum.[24]

Throughout the 1980s, however, and especially towards the end of that decade, the pace of production accelerated. A few examples across a range of genres and media illustrate this point. Among further texts that documented black lives and history in Canada are *A Black Man's Toronto 1914–1980: The Reminiscences of Harry Gairey* (1981) and Makeda Silvera's *Silenced* (1983), an important collection of oral histories by West Indian Canadian women domestic workers.[25] Earlier francophone novels by Gérard Étienne and Émile Ollivier were joined by first works from Dany Laferrière and Joël des Rosiers. In English Canada, Austin Clarke continued to publish prodigiously throughout the decade,[26] while some previously unpublished black writers and also filmmakers stepped forward. Their works include volumes of poetry such as the Tobago-born Marlene NourbeSe Philip's *Thorns* (1980) and *Salmon Courage* (1983), Trinidadian Canadian Claire Harris's *Fables from the Women's Quarters* (1984), and George Elliott Clarke's celebration of black Nova Scotian community, *Saltwater Spirituals and Deeper Blues* (1983).[27] The early dub poetry recordings of spoken-word artist and poet Lillian Allen also appeared at this point.[28] In drama, other black Nova Scotians offered their first plays later in the decade, which saw Walter Borden's *Tightrope Time* (1986), Frederick Ward's *Somebody Somebody's Returning* (1988), and George Elroy Boyd's *Shine Boy* (1988). In film, Claire Prieto and Roger McTair's *Home to Buxton* (1987) and Prieto and Sylvia Hamilton's documentary about black women's lives in Nova Scotia, *Black Mother Black Daughter* (1989), appeared in the same period. Like directors Jennifer Hodge de Silva and Roger McTair's earlier film about black community and discrimination in Toronto's Jane-Finch area, *Home Feeling: Struggle for a Community* (1983), the latter film was produced for the National Film Board of Canada, where Canadian multicultural policies began to facilitate black filmmaking.[29] Another event deserving attention is the appearance of Lorris Elliott's pilot bibliography *Literary Writing by Blacks in Canada: A Preliminary Survey* (1988). It was the first significant scholarly attempt to gain bibliographical control over black literary production in Canada. It also appeared with the support of federal multiculturalism through the Writing and Publication Program (WPP), as did Dionne Brand's short story collection in the same year, *Sans Souci and Other Stories* (1988).[30]

Black Canadian writing crossed new thresholds in the 1990s, which helped its establishment as an emergent and dynamic field of study. Brand followed up with *No Language Is Neutral* in 1990, a breakthrough volume like George Elliott Clarke's *Whylah Falls* the same year. In 1991–92, Clarke stunned a largely unsuspecting audience with a two-volume anthology of black Nova Scotian writing, *Fire on the Water*, pairing earlier Nova Scotian texts with contemporary work. After Silvera's 1983 collection of West Indian Canadian oral histories, Brand transcribed narratives of black Ontario women in *No Burden to Carry* (1991). Covering the period from the 1920s to the 1950s, the volume is enormously important as an illustration of black women's professional and social lives in this period, including their role in church organizations and the Universal Negro Improvement Association (UNIA; see Marano 2010). In addition, Cheryl Foggo's black prairies memoir *Pourin' Down Rain* and Nova Scotian Maxine Tynes's *Woman Talking Woman* both appeared in 1990.

Together with the growing impact of earlier texts and authors, the appearance of numerous other new writers and artists in the 1990s signalled a relatively broad presence of black writing and culture in Canada as the decade progressed. These writers include Marie-Célie Agnant, André Alexis, Maxine Bailey, Wayde Compton, Cecil Foster, Lorena Gale, Lawrence Hill, Nalo Hopkinson, Sharon M. Lewis, Tessa McWatt, Rachel Manley, Suzette Mayr, Andrew Moodie, Pamela Mordecai, Stanley Péan, Althea Prince, Mairuth Sarsfield, Djanet Sears, and Olive Senior. In addition, filmmaker and producer Clement Virgo offered his first feature films, *Rude* (1995) and *Love Come Down* (2000).[31] In the following decade, further exciting new authors such as David Chariandy and Esi Edugyan made their appearance, and rapper and songwriter Drake released his breakthrough recording *So Far Gone* (2009). Anthologies such as Ayanna Black's *Voices* (1992), George Elliott Clarke's *Eyeing the North Star* (1997), Djanet Sears's two volumes of theatre, *Testifyin'* (2000, 2003), and Donna Bailey Nurse's *Revival* (2006) or Valerie Mason-John and Kevan Anthony Cameron's more recent *The Great Black North* (2013) continue to make established and – in the latter case – especially new black writers and spoken-word artists available to the wider public.[32]

This body of work began to be recognized when, in 1997, black Canadian writers first received Governor General's Awards (for Brand and Manley).[33] The intensification of the production, study, and recognition of black Canadian writing reached a stage that would later make George Elliott Clarke identify 1997 as a breakthrough moment (G.E. Clarke 2008). The following years saw important conferences and the first research volumes entirely dedicated to black writing in Canada,[34] while a debate between George Elliott Clarke and Rinaldo Walcott over cultural nationalism and diasporic perspectives animated much discussion in the field.[35] Together, these events signalled a rapidly maturing field. They also showed a growing awareness of the fact that black Canadian writing deserves and rewards sustained interest and attention.

THE PRESENCE OF THE PAST

Much contemporary black writing turns its gaze beyond the immediate present to the past.[36] After following the same course in the next two chapters, I will explore works mostly written since the 1990s that are preoccupied with "presenting" the past. These texts guide our interest towards the presence of the past and to our contemporaneity with some of its dimensions. While not all contemporary black Canadian writing deals directly or overtly with earlier periods, an intensive engagement with the past is a remarkably dominant and frequent topic. This is the case not only in migrant writing, which often looks back, but also in such explorations of local contexts as George Elliott Clarke's or Wayde Compton's engagements with black Nova Scotia and British Columbia. The intensification of black Canadian writing from the 1980s and 1990s onward often expanded the interrogation of the past as an active condition of the present and a useful resource for the future.

These works can be read with reference to a wider trend towards historical and historiographically conscious writing in Canada that has received substantial comment.[37] Yet while these black Canadian texts can be usefully related to other historical and historiographic metafiction in Canada and beyond, they also follow specific – and often different – strategies that speak to black struggles and intertexts, both past and present. They regularly reveal counter-discursive engagements with the past that exceed purely deconstructive aims; their strategies are often marked by their exploration of diasporic routes and roots, and a search for a usable past. These texts are also distinguished by their attention to particular earlier texts and traditions, contexts, linguistic registers, and hoped-for futures.

The past emerges in many forms and genres in contemporary black Canadian writing. It appears in the forms of memoir and autobiography, poetic reflection, dramatization in theatre, or the neo-slave narrative. One might also want to think here, comparatively, about forms of memorialization such as museum exhibits, plaques, and the preservation, presentation, and narrativization of historical black settlements and other black memory sites.[38] In each case, questions arise about the form and function of articulations of the past: What *is* the role of the past in these instantiations? Is the past produced as "history" in the sense of "being over"? Does it appear as finalized, with static borders, and as part of what Homi Bhabha once called "the transcendental, pedagogical Idea of history" (1990, 307)? Or is it presented as a factor that does work in the present? As a space of contestation within the present where transformation can be enabled and certain forms of agency made possible? Or, by contrast, does the past appear not just as inescapable but also as overwhelming and incapacitating? And how are we alerted to the fact that our perceptions of the past are framed through multiple mediations – which include our various positionalities and the ever-present perils of projection?[39] What role, in other words, do these narratives and stagings of the past offer to their readers in the present, and how do they implicate often vastly different audiences?

Remembering, articulating, and staging the past are complex and often difficult acts in any context, but they require additional considerations in diasporic narratives. In his influential essay "Cultural Identity and Diaspora" (1990), Stuart Hall argues that European imperialism and the subjugation of black people not only positioned them as other but "had the power to make us see and experience *ourselves* as 'Other'" (1990, 225). For Hall, one of the consequences of this crippling "inner expropriation of cultural identity" – analysed earlier by Fanon in *Black Skin, White Masks* – is that cultural identity is not recoverable ready-made; it is not available as "a fixed origin to which we can make some final and absolute Return" (226).

Given the experience of diasporic displacement and fragmentation, Hall notes that a process of healing can be supported by texts that "restore an imaginary fullness or plentitude, to set against the broken rubric of our past" (1990, 225). Beyond that option, however, cultural identity is also "a matter of 'becoming'"; it "belongs to the future as much as to the past" and is not "something which already exists, transcending place, time, history and culture" (225). In this perspective, then, the articulation of identity is an act of self-fashioning, a practice of enunciation that works with and through the materials that are the product of the past. Such articulation can, unfortunately, replicate and re-inscribe domination or translate it into a symptomatic presence. Out of the languages offered by the past, however, it can also forge its own speech – a way of "saying something"[40] that not only applies but also adapts, appropriates, and modifies the rules and rulings of history. This work of transformation both recognizes the past and recodes it in forms of cultural agency that can institute new beginnings. Hall captures this dual articulation by saying that "identities are the names we give to the different ways we are positioned by, and position ourselves within, the narratives of the past" (225).

Staging identifications and resistances, these enunciative processes are channelled by modes of cognition and narrativization that come with their own forms and points of entry: the past is thus "always constructed through memory, fantasy, narrative and myth. Cultural identities are the points of identification, the unstable points of identification or suture" made "within the discourses of history and culture" (Hall 1990, 226). What is perhaps lacking in this particular formulation is a reflection of how the use of given scripts or models can also change them. Such transformations are achieved in forms of practice that are also forms of improvisation over available script archives.[41] It is clear, however, that in these individual and collective self-mediations through myriad cultural and historical discourses and emplotments, "there is always a politics of identity, a politics of position, which has no absolute guarantee in an unproblematic, transcendental 'law of origin'" (226).

Tropes of origin and return are frequent features in migrant and diasporic cultures. They often structure entire texts, concern both time and space, and occur in much contemporary black Canadian writing. But Hall is not alone in pointing out that these figures can hardly lead to closure or unmediated identity. His observation that the "original 'Africa' is no longer there" (1990, 231), for instance, is echoed in related comments by Édouard Glissant (1989, 16). For both theorists, any "return" to Africa is part of more complex trajectories (Hall 1990, 231–2), a perspective captured also by Glissant in his notions of errantry and detour (discussed in chapter 4).

In addition to the spatial dimension of this problematic, a related detour and "diversion" pertains to history as a return to origins in time. This kind of "return" produces not sameness but *more*, that is, a more complex relation to the past. Instead of a recovery of the known and the expected, attempts to return in time and to beginnings produce routes and mediations that also revise, transform, and re-articulate the past. Numerous theoretical formations that seek to account for the past's mediated presence and its active role within an individual *and* communal present illustrate that observation. They concern the emplotment of both dominant and revisionary histories and our relation to the archive (see Antwi 2011, 15–18), but they also include renewed questionings of the relationship between memory and trauma, the role of witnessing and testimony, psychoanalytic discussions of mourning and melancholia, and explorations of haunting and spectrality. While many of these investigations concern the individual, they also pertain to contexts of communal, cultural, and historical memory (Halbwachs 1980; Assmann 2006), and are relevant to Hall's concern with "memory, fantasy, narrative and myth" in diasporic cultural identities and identifications. These modes of theoretical inquiry map the detours and re-routings by which the present continually reconstructs and projects forms of the past, to create forms of the future in the process. Their insights limit or refute ideas either of a clear pastness of the past or of its unmediated recovery in the present.

Within these affirmations of the importance of the past, however, there are substantial differences in how subjects and their agency are understood. How do these theoretical formations make space for the questions of active intervention and transformation that I evoked a moment ago, and how do they articulate their own politics of time consciousness? Together with the geopolitically and historically oriented diasporic reflections exemplified by Hall, Glissant, and so many others, another strand of exploration has proceeded from psychological and psychoanalytic models to examine individual dimensions of diasporic subjectivity. In the black tradition, Fanon springs to mind (as Hall points out) and before him certainly Du Bois, who transformed earlier philosophical and psychological thinking in his extremely rich idea of double consciousness.[42]

I want to examine here a few more recent developments, beginning with a critical review of the notion of melancholia that has been put forward with regard to aggrieved communities' relationships with foundational traumas in the past.[13] While this discussion is familiar to specialists, it is still useful as a background for contrasting differently accentuated approaches. Other areas of discussion considered in this section include the Canadian postcolonial gothic, black hauntologies, and the concept of witnessing as it is deployed by Ian Baucom in *Specters of the Black Atlantic* (2005). To make these latter discussions more concrete, I will conduct them with anticipatory reference to Lawrence Hill's *The Book of Negroes* (further discussed in chapter 4).

Past Speaking

A Symptomatic Presence of the Past: Melancholia and Its Discontents

Freud's essay "Mourning and Melancholia" (1917) has elicited substantial comment in psychoanalytical writing but also in literary and cultural criticism. This has been especially the case after Judith Butler's discussion of the essay in *Gender Trouble* (published in 1990, incidentally the same year as Stuart Hall's essay). Freud's text has especially attracted scholars who seek to theorize a dynamic and open-ended engagement with the past. Freud understands *mourning* in this essay as a finite process in which cathexis of the beloved object is abandoned: "when the work of mourning is completed the ego becomes free and uninhibited again" (Freud 1917, 244). In *melancholia*, by contrast, the lost object is not abandoned but interiorized and identified with the ego. Because of disappointment, it is harshly judged by another agency "split off from the ego" (246). This process explains for Freud the melancholic's self-reproaches, self-debasement, and disavowals.[44]

A few years later, Freud revises this hypothetical opposition in *The Ego and the Id* (1923). He suggests now that the internalization operated by melancholia may not be opposed to mourning. Instead, as Judith Butler summarizes this reorientation, it is the ego's only way to survive "the loss of its essential emotional ties to others" (1990, 58). As she explains later, Freud's new account even suggests that "there can be no ego without melancholia, that the ego's loss is constitutive" (1997, 171). For Butler, melancholia becomes the "normal" modus operandi of the heterosexual performance of gender, as the result of the child's forced abandonment of same-sex parent cathexis under normative pressures (1990, 57–65; 1997, 132–50).

From there, scholars like David Eng have made the case that the theory of melancholia can shed light on aggrieved constituencies who are marked by "a collective group memory of historical loss and continued suffering" (2000, 1276). Eng suggests that "melancholia as a theory of unresolved grief is useful for investigating the formation of not only gendered subjects but also a host of other minority group identities" (1276). In melancholia's attachment to objects of loss, Eng even locates a "nascent political protest" (1280). With David Kazanjian, he writes that "by engaging in 'countless separate struggles' with loss, melancholia might be said to constitute … an ongoing and open relationship with the past – bringing its ghosts and spectres, its flaring and fleeting images, into the present" (Eng and Kazanjian 2003, 4). For these theorists, finally, this process "generates sites for memory and history, for the rewriting of the past as well as the reimagining of the future" (4).

While some of the theoretical temptations of this line of thinking are obvious, I think there are also considerable costs and disadvantages associated with it. With their evocation of the "flaring and fleeting images" of the past, Eng and Kazanjian call up Walter Benjamin's idea of memory and history that has to be grasped in the present "as it flashes up in moments of danger" (Benjamin 1968, 255).[45] With their reference to ghosts and spectres, they also join other work inspired by Jacques Derrida's thinking about spectrality and hauntologies (discussed below), which tends to deconstruct strict oppositions between the past, the present, and the future. They do so for good reason: since immediate forms of "healing" or closure are unavailable to many groups aggrieved by trauma and social injustice, this interest in the psychological state of melancholia is motivated by a search for an un-finalized process that keeps the past alive to produce future change.

Investing Freud's psychological construct with deconstructive and potentially political hopes, however, comes with numerous problems. Freud himself admitted that his conceptualization was based on too small a sample. Even more problematical, in the course of the more recent theoretical argument, melancholia has shape-shifted much too easily from Freud's incapacitating condition to a potentially "political" and transformative concept. While the argument seeks to access the open-ended side of melancholia, it also glosses over parts of the defining core of Freud's idea of melancholia. It is true that Freud suggests that the reactions of melancholia "proceed from a mental constellation of revolt" (1917, 247), but he adds, decisively, that this constellation of revolt "has been, by a certain process, passed over into the crushed state of melancholia" (247). The step to Eng's view of melancholia "as nascent political protest" (Eng 2000, 1280) (or Ian Baucom's formulation of the "political possibilities of testimonial melancholy," examined below) has to skip the very transition that in Freud's description makes melancholia what it is.

This crucial elision is necessary for the deceiving slippage of melancholia from an incapacitating state to a transformative potential. In formulations that hope to find potentials for "nascent political protest" in melancholia, some of its central qualities are repressed. For example, the "devouring" and internalization of the lost object are *unconscious* and *disavowed* (this feature applies better to the decidedly non-insurgent white melancholia with respect to disavowed subaltern groups), and the "complaints" of the melancholic – while plaints about someone else – are directed against the self. Melancholia certainly signals an "ongoing" relationship with the past, as Eng and others suggest; it is less clear, however, how it facilitates also an "open" relationship with it (the other adjective used to suggest its transformative potential). Melancholia signals a problem but does not *per se* offer transformational forms of agency and engagement.[46]

More troubling, a wholesale *ascription* of melancholia to entire aggrieved populations is homogenizing, casts doubt on the "analysand" group's ability to understand and engage its predicaments, and gives comfort to assimilationist rhetorical strategies that serve the dominant. Anne Anlin Cheng, who applies the idea of melancholia to race in *The Melancholy of Race: Psychoanalysis, Assimilation, and Hidden Grief* (2001), notes that in important discourses about indigenous groups "the rhetoric of the 'melancholic Indian and his fate' serves to legitimize the future of the white conqueror" (14).[47] The use of melancholia as theoretical concept in contexts of uneven power thus raises uncomfortable questions. Who is served by the ascription of melancholia to others and to aggrieved communities in particular? To what extent does the ascription of melancholia, especially to minoritarian others, help to underwrite the self-constitution and self-consolidation of the dominant (and its views of a "healthy" norm)? And how does the elaboration of this Vienna-centric concept of melancholia speak to the conditions of contemporary black writing and other subaltern groups in Canada?

Beyond Melancholia: Transformations of the Canadian Postcolonial Gothic

Cheng pays close attention to how groups with different relations to power can be affected by a problematic relationship with the past. She thus diagnoses a "racial melancholia for the raced subject" owing to internalized subjugation (2001, 17),[48] but she also finds a dominant "American melancholia" (10) and "white racial melancholia" (12) that result from a self-constitution and self-affirmation through the disavowed exclusion of racial others.

This ascription of melancholia to the dominant seems pertinent when considering Cheng's ideas in a Canadian context. In Canadian critical race theory, Cheng's work has been examined by Lily Cho and Daniel Coleman. Cho points out that in Cheng's perspective the only options for the racialized subject are to remain bound by never-ending melancholia or to face assimilation and "healing" by giving up grief, grievance, and the attachment to memories of loss (2011, 123). While Cho nonetheless finds some use in a refurbished concept of melancholia, Coleman refers to alternative epistemologies that he finds in David Chariandy's *Soucouyant* (Chariandy 2007b; see chapter 4) and Lee Maracle's *Daughters Are Forever* (2002). He shares some of Cho's concerns about the unpalatable choices in Cheng's account; more radically, however, his examination leads him to wonder "who can afford the theory of melancholia" (2012, 59)? As Coleman points out, the theory of melancholia as a form of unconscious haunting may re-inscribe the status quo, and while it seems applicable to the dominant, it is unhelpful and potentially hurtful for aggrieved communities.[49]

A related problematic appears in Cynthia Sugars and Gerry Turcotte's *Unsettled Remains* (2009). This volume considers the unsettling presence of ghosts and hauntings in white Canadian settler culture. Like melancholia, ghosts can signal the presence of an unresolved past. In their introduction, Sugars and Turcotte evoke a legacy of "imperialism and globalization" that appears "in the form of unresolved memory traces and occluded histories" resulting from "the experience of colonial oppression, diasporic migration, or national consolidation." In literature, this legacy sprouts "ghosts or monsters that 'haunt' the nation/subject from without and within" (Sugars and Turcotte 2009, vii). For these reasons, they argue, "settler locations would seem to invite gothic figuration … in terms of subjective and national interiority and unsettlement." Given what we have just discovered about theories of melancholia in such contexts, however, there is relevance in their observation that this view of settler cultures is "admittedly, positioned from the perspective of a White settler rather than that of an Aboriginal subject" (viii).

Contemporary black Canadian texts have their own ghosts, but they are not those of white settler culture. Here, a different kind of haunting drives the turn to history and often stages a more overt presence of the past. Reading for melancholia can be pertinent for some black Canadian writing, but it implies the deciphering of a disavowal that mainly signifies through symptoms. In many black Canadian texts, however, historical haunting creates ghosts that speak more directly, inviting and provoking communication. They usually seek an engagement that exceeds the hopeless, "crushed," and inactive state of melancholia.

How does this kind of haunting function in these texts, and what are the consequences? Consider, for instance, some of the seminal texts of the last two decades. In Lorena Gale's *Angélique*, which premiered in 1998, the eponymous Montreal slave hanged in 1734 leaves the audience with a fiery appeal for future justice; instead of disavowal, self-doubt, and passivity, the text emphasizes Angélique's ability to make courageous decisions in adverse circumstances. In George Elliott Clarke's *Beatrice Chancy* (1999), another play about slavery in Canada, the heroine kills her oppressor – and another opponent – rather than herself, as the theory of melancholia might suggest. In Austin Clarke's *The Polished Hoe* (2002), Mary Mathilda finishes off – with conviction and no regrets – the bestial plantation manager and erstwhile lover who is also the father of her child. Neither Angélique nor Beatrice nor Mary Mathilda is best described in terms of melancholia.

The term works perhaps better with reference to Marie-Célie Agnant's eponymous character in *Le livre d'Emma* (2001; trans. 2006 *The Book of Emma*), who *does* commit suicide – which is a high risk for Freud's melancholic. As I argue in chapter 4, however, the point of that novel is the transformation of that character's story through the voice of a translator. Flore – whose name comes from a goddess associated with flowering, fertility, and the rebirth of spring – re-conceives her professional obligation to convey the story impartially to another audience in decidedly partial ways. In the process of listening and translation, she becomes a witness who draws non-melancholic conclusions from Emma's story that she passes on to us.

Agnant's translator-narrator thus shares similarities with Aminata, the main character and narrator in Lawrence Hill's *The Book of Negroes* (2007a). Like Flore (and also Emma), Hill's character is instrumental in carrying stories across cultures, time, and the black Atlantic, sometimes also by translating, like Agnant's narrator. Facing the terrors of transatlantic slavery, Aminata resolves to become a witness who will be able to testify. It is not clear at that point what audience or judge will ever hear her testimony, but as Hill remarks in an interview, her decision "is part of her emotional salvation" (in Siemerling 2013, 21).[50]

Like Agnant's translator, Hill's narrator will transform the hold of the past on the present. Aminata acts by translating loss into a path of self-transformation and help to others. Significantly, this process involves a shift in the balance between roots and routes. Feeling "only a determination to stay free" (L. Hill 2007a, 442), she decides to abandon her quest to return to the geographical roots of her homeland. Instead, she transforms loss into a black Atlantic route of witnessing. While Agnant's Emma chooses suicide to return home by a watery "chemin des grands bateaux,"[51] Hill's Aminata begins with the words: "I seem to have trouble dying" (1). From our later perspective, this remark evokes ghostly overtones, suggesting that neither she nor her story is dead even in our time.[52] But Hill does not couch her loss in melancholia or disavowal. Her non-return safeguards her freedom and produces transformations in the future.

Aminata becomes an interventionist and determined witness who conveys her own and others' experiences of slavery and the middle passage across the Atlantic. She shares her knowledge with audiences whom she encounters in her subsequent routing through the circum-Atlantic world, a trajectory that includes South Carolina, New York, Nova Scotia, Africa, and London. But she also imagines future audiences for her written testimony. Her narrative, she hopes, will release its potential when the time comes, translating her present into the future. There, it will turn her present and the past into someone else's affective present, producing identifications and, potentially, future change.

Hill thus decides to create a character who is a witness in the triple sense evoked by Jacques Derrida[53] – of being present at, surviving, and conveying to someone else the traumatic events she has experienced. Ian Baucom has adopted these distinctions – which Derrida developed with reference to the Holocaust – in the context of slavery and the middle passage. In *Specters of the Atlantic,* Baucom reasons that "to bear witness is not only simultaneously to observe, hold to, survive, and subsist beyond the event but to transmit to another this property of observing, holding, surviving. It is, therefore, to serialize the event and its affect and also to elongate its temporality to stretch its time along the line of an unfolding series of moments of bearing witness" (2005, 177). Baucom, then, delineates (with Derrida) how witnessing moves beyond the participant-witness to call on the listener or audience, and how individuals become witnesses to an event they have not personally experienced.[54]

Baucom's immediate subject is the British abolitionist Granville Sharp and his involvement in an incident that became a turning point in the British Empire's relationship to the slave trade – the Zong massacre in 1781. In this mass murder – the subject of many works of art, including Marlene NourbeSe Philip's *Zong!* (2008; see chapter 4)[55] – over 130 slaves died on the high seas, forced overboard from the slave ship *Zong.*[56] The shipowners successfully sued their insurers – for what they called a loss of property! Alerted by Olaudah Equiano, Granville Sharp used his formidable legal knowledge to support an appeal that brought the case before chief justice Lord Mansfield in 1783.[57] An immediate outcome of Sharp's intervention was Mansfield's ordering of a retrial.[58] In the long run, however, Sharp's "witnessing" contributed to the abolition of the slave trade in 1807, in support of which we see Lawrence Hill's Aminata in London.[59]

Aminata is a participant-witness of slavery and the middle passage, but she can also be seen as Sharp's fictional relation, in her own time and in ours. Like Sharp, she reminds the England of her time of the horrors of the trade. And both for her London audience and for us, her acts of witnessing and writing indeed "serialize the event and its affect" in a temporality that finally haunts and includes our own present and its future.

To what extent Hill's fictional narrator is a realistic character is another question. The novel is based on painstaking historical research, but it also takes significant liberties with the historical record. Revising the mostly male genre of the slave narrative from an interventionist and feminizing perspective, Hill makes a black female scribe a creator of the historical "Book of Negroes." While many aspects of Aminata's life are rendered in realistic fashion, she is also the fictional embodiment of a necessarily reimagined historical relation.[60] She is a figure who speaks to the gaps and absences of a disrupted, absconded, silenced, and otherwise unavailable past.

As a character who evokes a traumatic past, she can be connected with what Marianne Hirsch, in her work on the relation of the children of Holocaust survivors to their parents' memory, calls "postmemory."[61] While the time span bridged by Hill's character exceeds the intergenerational frame explored in Hirsch's studies, Aminata, too, illustrates "how the break in transmission resulting from traumatic historical events necessitates forms of remembrance that reconnect and reembody an intergenerational memorial fabric that has been severed by catastrophe" (Hirsch 2008, 109–10). Hirsch suggests that postmemorial work "strives to reactivate and reembody more distant social/national and archival/cultural memorial structures by reinvesting them with resonant individual and familial forms of mediation and aesthetic expression" (2008, 111).[62] This is indeed one of the tasks that Hill also strives to accomplish in his novel.

As a witness of slavery and the transatlantic slave trade, Aminata reembodies the memory of one of the most defining and foundational facts of modernity. Since the recording and transmission of such memories have often been impossible, neglected, impeded, or disrupted, and their legacies remain unresolved, she is also a spectre of the black Atlantic. Like Hamlet's ghost (who haunts Marx and Derrida's discussion of both), she appears to us with a request: to consider how her past is also relevant to our present. *The Book of Negroes* stages a hauntology that evokes the past but also questions its pastness as self-contained event. It undermines the idea of a present that comes simply after the past and is entirely separate and different from it.

How, after all, does Aminata – and how do so many other characters discussed in the chapters below – exist in time? The question of their ontology is related to Derrida's query in *Specters of Marx*: "What is the time and what is the history of a specter?" He wonders "whether the *spectrality effect* does not consist in undoing this opposition, or even this dialectic, between actual, effective presence and its other" (2006, 48).[63] Spectrality indeed suspends the idea of dialectical progress (or Hegelian "supersession"). In this realm, the either/or of past and present is "temporarily" confounded, opening the way for other inquiries. Like Granville Sharp, Aminata brings the past into a later court, that of the present and the future, where her witnessing asks for judgment, justice, and transformation.

The Practice of Relation: Shared Knowledges and the Accumulation of Time

In *Specters of the Atlantic*, Baucom refers to the transformative potential of Sharp's intervention as the "political possibilities of testimonial melancholy"

(2005, 259).[64] Although we understand the theoretical pathway leading to this formulation, it is arguably a problematic way to reference Sharp's active engagement. Many contemporary black Canadian texts are better understood as embracing the political and literary possibilities of testimony and witnessing *beyond* the inherently incapacitating limits of the idea of melancholia. Neither Aminata's attitudes nor Hill's act of witnessing belong to the registers of the melancholic – their holding on to the past through forms of conveyance and transfiguration are in many ways its active transformation.

I would suggest that Hill's protagonist can be read as a figure of what Édouard Glissant calls "relation" and *errance* (variously translated as errantry or errancy). As Glissant explains, in the poetics of relation "each and every identity is extended through a relationship with the Other" (1997b, 11).[65] In this context, "the thought of errantry is also the thought of what is relative ... The tale of errantry is the tale of Relation" (1997b, 18). As opposed to melancholia, these Glissantian terms stand for the potential of transformation.

In an earlier discussion, Baucom glosses Glissant's notion of relation indeed as "a word for an *antimelancholic* politics of memory, and a word for those new forms of culture, identity, and solidarity that emerge from even this most violent scene of Atlantic exchange" (2001, 67, emphasis added). The word "antimelancholic" disappears in the book version of that passage, which specifies that Glissant's "relation" refers to "those new 'transverse' forms of culture, identity, and solidarity that emerge from the act of holding to, enduring, relating, and avowing our (present's) relational complicity with modernity's most violent scenes of exchange" (Baucom 2005, 311).[66] Conscious awareness of relational connection undoes a basic condition of melancholia, the disavowal that masks its causes.[67] Glissantian "relation" speaks to much contemporary black writing in Canada. A conscious recall of the past is more frequent and defining here than its disavowal, and theories of melancholia apply better to the dominant culture and its disavowals of the historical reality of transatlantic and other forms of slavery in Canada.

Aminata effectively embodies Glissant's notions of errantry and relation, which see the violent events of slavery and the middle passage as both primordial events of modernity and foundational for a relational practice of new beginnings and community. Glissant emphasizes that the drowned slaves of the Atlantic, "the entire ocean, the entire sea ... make one vast beginning" (1997b, 6): "For though this experience made you, original victim floating toward the sea's abysses, an exception, it became something shared and made us, the descendants, one people among others. People do not live on exception. Relation is not made up of things that are foreign but of shared knowledge. The experience of the abyss can now be said to be the best element of exchange" (1997b, 8). As a witness in the triple sense evoked above, Aminata is a figure of that sense of shared knowledge and relation, imparting to her contemporaries, and to us, that "every time I have sailed the seas, I have had the sense of gliding over the unburied" (7). Hill's staging of her witnessing works with a sense of time that Glissant calls "the accumulation of sediments" (1997b, 33). In this perspective, "time does not pass … it accumulates" (Baucom 2005, 24, 34).

This vision disturbs the notion of a dialectical progression that would contain the past. Such Hegelian supersession or sublation (*Aufhebung*) is disputed by the uncertain temporality of Derridean spectrality. From within a Caribbean tradition, it has also been explicitly critiqued by Kamau Brathwaite's alternative concept of "tidalectics." Brathwaite's critical play on the Hegelian dialectic advances the notion of overlap and repetition, much like the cyclical back-and-forth motion of water (see the discussion of Wayde Compton's work below). This challenge to the idea of our modern times as progressing and progressive means a thorough recoding of the notion of any singular, absolute spirit of modernity. That notion is replaced by accounts of multiple, resistant, and living spirits and spectres of modernity (Du Bois offered a related, titular revision of Hegel's *Spirit* with his plural *Souls of Black Folk*). Another effect is that such alternative temporalities, by making space for other ways to speak the past, help to envision different futures, creating space for new hopes and transformation. Hospitable to alternative ways of seeing, these reorientations signal potentials for cultural agency. Figures like Hill's protagonist are artistic devices to reorder time and also space, as I will suggest in a moment. This intervention into the retelling and ultimately social reproduction of time and space is "relation" in action and a *practice* of relation.

The Truth of the Imagination

But there are some important caveats. In many respects, the material past remains unimaginable and has occurred independently of our conscious relation to it (though not *as* "past," a notion that in itself implies a relational perception). Any account of the past is relational, conceived from specific horizons of understanding. Perceptual position affects how we tell the story (the choice of emplotment), the selection of incidents and angles, and the omission or sidelining of others. Important and necessary concerns have also been expressed regarding our need to fill the silences caused by historical violence. Words and images seem to allow us to come "to terms" with the horror of events and experiences that ultimately, however, exceed any understanding and comprehension. Even worse, as Saidiya Hartman so eloquently demonstrates, there is a danger of language and images "reinforc[ing] the spectacular character of black suffering" (1997, 3). I will return to these concerns in the conclusion, but they immediately signal the provisional, subjective, and also potentially deceiving nature of any truth of the imagination, historical or poetic. While degrees of veracity and objectivity can be established, such warnings remind us that any "truth" also pertains to a specifically mediated and defined relation.

Many writers draw consequences in their formal decisions because of these concerns. Some texts thus seek to block our longing to make sense of senseless brutality and horror. They try to convey the experience of shock, incomprehension, and horror beyond language by working with textual difficulty and the systematic disruption of the comforts afforded by language and understanding. Marlene NourbeSe Philip's *Zong!* radically exemplifies such strategies (see chapter 4), raising important questions about the ethics and even legitimacy of representation.

How do we read a "successful" or moving rendering of suffering? What are the sources, in this regard, of the enormous success of a "representational" text like *The Book of Negroes*?[68] Is it owed mainly to superb writing and a historically grounded, dramatic story? Or what other mechanisms may motivate our interest? The novel portrays horrible incidents, cruelty, and injustice (and it destroys a number of specifically Canadian complacencies), but it also uses representational and narrative strategies that offer a certain amount of comfort to the reader. Perhaps the most important among them is the creation of an exceptional protagonist who invites strong reader identification – with all the attendant problems of projection and self-interest. Many novelists use all their skill, of course, to create precisely what Brecht so adamantly objected to as detrimental to our critical alertness (Brecht 1964, 179–205): identification with their characters. Its representational risks and problems notwithstanding, Paul Gilroy for one has vigorously defended "heterophatic identification" in his more recent *Darker than Blue: On the Moral Economies of the Black Atlantic* (2010, 66; see chapter 6). As these different perspectives illustrate, the spectrum of formal choices and aesthetic strategies remains a crucial area of critical inquiry and attention. Whatever its angle on representation, however, no textual strategy – including, as we will see, the one realized by the techniques and devices deployed in Philip's *Zong!* – can avoid the fact that *as* strategy it approaches, recognizes, and configures its subject on the ground of a particular imagination.

While created in conversation with the historical record, Hill's Aminata is imagined and to some extent has to be imagined. Even for those victims who survived slavery and the middle passage, the difficulties of bearing witness publicly were all but insurmountable. The vast majority of them left no testimony behind. Besides material circumstances that make slave testimony an exceptional possibility, the experience of trauma is another inhibiting factor that can exceed the capacity of mental representation. Cathy Caruth describes trauma "as the response to an unexpected or overwhelming violent event or events that are not fully grasped as they occur" (1996, 91). This situation produces the paradox "that the most direct seeing of a violent event may occur as an absolute inability to know it" (1996, 91–2). In addition, even where explicit testimony exists in the case of slavery, the context of its production imposes other problems and restrictions. Toni Morrison reminds us that the narrators of slave narratives had to avoid information, claims, and language that might have antagonized white readers who "could make a difference in terminating slavery" (1995, 88). In addition, they drew a veil over "their interior life" (91). In his tellingly titled *Impossible Witnesses*, Dwight A. McBride observes that "the theater of abolitionism" both enables and restricts "the moment of articulation" (2001, 5; see chapter 2). The filter of this apparatus conveys only what can be couched in "the language that will have political efficacy" (5). As a result of the historical constraints placed on slave narratives, writers like Toni Morrison have argued for the powers and resources of the imagination to step in and articulate forms of "truth" and a past that we know has existed and been experienced in ways that have not been recorded (Morrison 1995, 93). As Morrison writes, "the crucial distinction for me is not the difference between fact and fiction, but the distinction between fact and truth. Because facts can exist without human intelligence, but truth cannot" (93).[69]

While Morrison's *Beloved* (1987) often seeks to disorient the reader and employs numerous non-realistic techniques, it also has become a celebrated example of texts that seek to provide an alternative account by evoking the middle passage and slavery from the point of view of slaves. These works include what critics have labelled "neo-slave narratives." Ashraf Rushdy delineates the emergence of this genre out of the US context of the 1960s and 1970s[70] and defines it as adopting the narrative conventions and first-person point of view of ante-bellum slave narratives (1999, 3). Other critics use more inclusive definitions of the genre beyond first-person narratives (see V. Smith 2007). As Rushdy explains, neo-slave narratives stage and interrogate "the process through which a historical subject constitutes itself by employing or revising a set of ideologically charged textual structures (1999, 7). His comment resonates with Stuart Hall's remarks, cited above, about how diasporic subjects, moving from the past to the future, position themselves with respect to historically available discursive options.

Contemporary black Canadian writers also transform discursive scripts and identities – and indeed the past and our possible futures – by engaging in many different ways what Glissant calls relation. Their work creates a *practice* of relation that connects times, spaces, and texts in a "shared knowledge," extending, in Glissant's words cited earlier, separate identities "through a relationship with the Other." They exert cultural agency in their reading and "consumption" of historical texts and contexts that have been mostly mediated by hegemonic historiography. De Certeau's notions of practice and the tactics of consumption come to mind, described as "the ingenious ways in which the weak make use of the strong" (1988, xvii). These ideas also shed light on Aminata's relation to a dominant language like English, to writing, and to the knowledge these pathways offer for her own aims. They further aptly describe Hill's tactical recoding of the 1783 historical "Book of Negroes."

Other writers go further in their relation to the historical record. Such tactical practice usually means the creative use, appropriation, and transformation of available materials and conventions for politically motivated but often innovative and unforeseen ends. These improvisational tactics – and risks – are part of a social aesthetic that seeks to recode historical and aesthetic narratives that elide black contributions and perspectives.[71] Transforming hegemonic histories by adopting and adapting contexts and materials, the authors I discuss in chapters 4 and 5 recognize *and* reconstitute the past, in acts of narrative re/cognition that create a socially grounded re-production with a black Canadian difference.[72]

ANOTHER BLACK ATLANTIC: THE TIMES AND SPACES OF MODERNITY

As roots turn into routes, textual practices of relation transform time and space. Glissantian errantry alters perceptions of time and creates layered temporalities, while maps are overlaid by other maps in experientially grounded geographies. As Katherine McKittrick reminds us, "we produce space, we produce its meanings, and we work very hard to make geography what it is" (2006, xi). With their multi-dimensional recodings, the relational practices evident in much black Canadian writing generate new time-spaces and genealogies, as well as other possible futures of modernity.

As Glissant's notion of time as an "accumulation of sediments" desynchronizes modernity's temporality of progress, the concept of errantry remaps the imperial spatiality of modernity from multiple vantage points. In contrast to a poetics that represents the colonizing movement from the centre, or a later, reverse and reactive one from the margins back to the centre, Glissant conceives of a third stage. Here, "the poet's word leads from periphery to periphery." This trajectory "reproduces the track of circular nomadism" and "makes every periphery into a center; furthermore, it abolishes the very notion of center and periphery" (1997b, 29). To some extent this re-routed circuitry can be seen in Aminata's life, even if it takes place in times and spaces that are still largely ordained by empire. Her life crisscrosses the eighteenth- and early nineteenth-century black Atlantic in an errantry that defies and redraws the lines of a typical slave life of her time. She also maintains a wary distance from the world of British abolitionists, who would love to write her story with their immediate political goals in mind; instead, she insists on her own diasporic, "errant" experience and perspective. In the context of this black Atlantic trajectory, and along with other stations in her life, Canadian space emerges as a nodal point. It is one of the many relational centres of a huge circum-Atlantic network that connects the "non-peripheries" of Glissant's vision and poetics of relation, which also situate Hill's writing.

Intertextual Relations

Much black Canadian writing is similarly routed through new time-spaces that disturb the geographies and temporalities, the borders and sedimented histories, left behind by the hemispheric expansion of empires in the Americas. Relations are also multiple *within* Canadian contexts. George Elliott Clarke notes: "We are divided severally; we are not just black and Canadian but also adherents to a region, speakers of an official language (either English or French), disciples of heterogeneous faiths, and related to a particular ethnicity (or national group), all of which shape our identities" (2002a, 40). But not only the texts produced by black writers in Canada exceed Canadian national boundaries and space in their narratives and settings; the intertextualities of these diasporic works also go beyond any particular national tradition.[73] Several routes have been travelled with particular frequency, including those through the United States, the anglophone and francophone Caribbean, and the past in Canada itself.

Black writing in the United States is a presence through its long tradition, through the cross-border Canadian connections in the nineteenth century, through the many signal texts from the Harlem Renaissance to the present, and through the impact of the civil rights, black power, and black arts movements. This cultural wealth and neighbourly influence have occasioned significant declarations of black Canadian difference and independence (e.g., Alexis 1995; G.E. Clarke 1998b). But for writers trying to rearticulate the past, some of the works by US authors that excavate, imagine, and restore black pasts and genealogies have been particularly informative. Among those that come to mind are Alex Haley's *Roots* (1976) and Toni Morrison's *Beloved* (1987) – the latter being perhaps the most influential among those American writings that reflect on the silences and hauntings caused by slavery and the middle passage.

This set of resources and relations is joined by many other geographically identified intertextual routings. Given the origin of many black Canadian writers and the connections of the Commonwealth and the Francophonie, major relational factors have been anglophone and francophone Caribbean contexts. Among the many anglophone intertextual resources are thus such black Caribbean writers as Derek Walcott and Kamu Brathwaite; many francophone writers reach back to a tradition spanning from Aimé Césaire and the writers of *négritude* to Édouard Glissant and more recent proponents of *créolité*.

The presence of another context, however, is becoming more pronounced as contemporary black Canadian writing itself claims a wider stage. It includes black history, testimony, and writing in what is now Canada, from slavery in New France and Nova Scotia to subsequent developments in the nineteenth-century Canadas, Nova Scotia, and the colonies of Vancouver Island and British Columbia. It also comprises the twentieth-century destructions of Africville in Halifax and Hogan's Alley in Vancouver, and many other, less conspicuous events and incidents in Canada that have significantly altered black emotional geographies. This context evokes black Canadian histories together with the voices of black Canadians themselves. Earlier black writings in Canada – for instance, by travellers and ministers, fugitive former slaves, or the indefatigable educator, editor, and editorialist Mary Ann Shadd – are leaving their imprint on the imagination of later authors. Some of these writings reach further back to the lives of slaves in what is now Canada, whose traces occasionally appear in reports, newspaper ads, and other documents, but whose words have been reported only in very few exceptional cases. In chapters 2 and 3, I will discuss these antecedents of contemporary black Canadian writing in their own right; in subsequent chapters, I return to them as they resurface in more recent works.

The different time-spaces emerging from these contexts and their re/cognition in contemporary black Canadian writing contribute to a counter-modernity that Gilroy has evoked in *The Black Atlantic*. But they also change the influential map he has provided with that volume. They further underline that black Atlantic spirits of modernity challenge any singular perspective and account. Like other aspects of the black Atlantic, they defy the narratives of progress that begin with "discovery" and encode what Gilroy, in his more recent *Darker than Blue*, calls a "triumphalist tale." Among other problems, such narratives sideline the victimization of indigenous populations and racial struggles when they tell "the story of the moral and legal ascent of Europe and its civilisational offshoots" (Gilroy 2010, 55).[74] Gilroy's alternative genealogy of human rights refers to black voices that include David Walker, Frederick Douglass, Angelina Grimké, W.E.B. Du Bois, and Frantz Fanon, who should be part of any respectable and responsible narrative of human rights. He also narrates "Yet Another Modernity" (2010, 69–73), which includes the stories of Haiti, Liberia, and Ethiopia. In the following pages, I hope to demonstrate that accounts and genealogies of the black Atlantic also need to be routed through the times and spaces of what is now Canada.

PART I

Early Testimony and the Black Canadian Nineteenth Century

2

Slavery and Early Black Canadian Writing

Contemporary black Canadian writers have repeatedly evoked slavery. Yet there are no fully formed narratives by slaves in what is now Canada that could serve as antecedents.[1] The very lack of such accounts has prompted interventions of the fictional imagination, such as those by Lorena Gale, George Elliott Clarke, and others that I discuss in chapter 4. We have nonetheless some documents that record slave testimony, at least briefly and indirectly, as it was transcribed by missionaries or white officials for various reasons. Some of these sources have been utilized in literary works that seek to reimagine slavery in New France and under the British Empire. I will look at some of these forms of early testimony in New France and the historical "Book of Negroes" before turning to the first longer narratives by black subjects related to their experience in early Nova Scotia. The black Canadian nineteenth century is the subject of chapter 3.

SLAVERY AND EARLY TESTIMONY IN NEW FRANCE

African slavery in what is now Canada began in New France, where slavery was suffered by both black and indigenous subjects.[2] While it has been documented by historians, there are almost no records of enslaved subjects speaking themselves, let alone traces of their writing. Historians such as Marcel Trudel and Robin Winks tell us of an anonymous black person reported to have died of scurvy in Port Royal in 1606. The first name we have for a black individual in Canada is that of Mathieu de Coste (or de Costa), who was a servant of Port Royal's governor in 1608. The first black slave whose voice is recorded is Olivier Le Jeune. He lived in the first half of the seventeenth century in the city of Quebec. In the *Jesuit Relations* of 1632,

Father Le Jeune gives him a voice: "You say that by baptism I shall be like you: I am black and you are white, I must have my skin taken off then in order to be like you" (Thwaites 1897, 5:62; qtd in Winks 1997, 1). While Le Jeune presents this remark as a child's naivety and reproduces the passage without further comment (Trudel 2004, 14), Winks gives it a certain ontological weight (1997, 1). Most remarkable, however, is the very fact that a black voice was transcribed at all at this time, and in the first person, which was a rare exception.

In general, we have to rely on newspapers, letters, trial records, census reports, and other documents rather than on fully articulated narratives. One event that gives us at least indirect access to black testimony came about a century later. In 1734, when perhaps between forty and fifty black slaves lived in Quebec (Gay 2004, 29; Trudel 2004, 86),[3] the Montreal slave Angélique was tried and hanged for allegedly burning down the better part of Montreal. The trial documents offer a source that has found echoes in Lorena Gale's play *Angélique* and in other texts, songs, and films (see chapter 4). These court documents record the words of the accused slave in the third person, revealing her responses under interrogation. Despite this context, the transcriptions of the accused slave's testimony offer elements of a slave narrative, the most detailed account based on a slave's statements in eighteenth-century New France that we have.[4]

On 12 April 1734, two days after the fire, the imprisoned Marie Joseph Angélique was interrogated by Pierre Raimbault, "King's counsellor, lieutenant general at the Jurisdiction Royale de Montreal."[5] The transcription of her first interrogation begins with a short account of her life.[6] In translation, it reads: "Stated to be named Marie Joseph, aged twenty-nine years, born in Portugal / And to have been sold to a Flemish man who sold Her to the deceased Sieur de francheville, about nine years ago, where she has remained ever since" (1–2).[7] Questioned about an earlier escape across the St Lawrence River with a white indentured servant called Thibeault, she "stated that … they made it only as far as thirty leagues from here on Their Way to new England And from there To Her country of Portugal across from Madeira" (2). Asked how she responded to her mistress's later accusation of having laid the fire, she tells the interrogator to have answered: "Madame, although I may be Miserable, I Am not Wretched enough to do an act Like That" (4).

During the second interrogation, on 3 May 1734, Raimbault asked only leading questions, obviously presuming the prisoner's guilt. Why did she set the fire? Where did she start it? While she denied all allegations, she offered frank reasons for her earlier flight. One was the fear of being sold into harsher conditions of slavery, the apprehension "that She Was to Be Sent to the Islands [the West Indies]; And that for this Reason She had fled with the Said thibault in order to escape to New England" (5). More details of this attempt emerged during the following interrogation, on 6 May 1734: "They soon crossed the [frozen] River to Longeüil; that the said thibault Led Her to a Barn far from the Houses And took from There Five to Six bread loaves that the Said thibault had there Hidden, And from there Made their Way to Chemin de Chambly, then Entered the Woods and Remained there the Night And a portion of the Next Day And that in the fifteen Days of their Journey and encampment of one week in the Woods, They entered no Houses" (6).

Recorded in 1734 as part of an interrogation by the authorities of New France, the narrative anticipated in some of its elements the better-known narratives of later fugitive slaves, although these were often elicited under more conducive circumstances by more sympathetic listeners, usually in the service of the cause of abolition.

The reported account of Angélique remains an exception, however. The traces of other slave lives in New France have to be discovered elsewhere. François-Xavier Garneau, the most important nineteenth-century historian of French Canada, elided the existence of slavery in his *Histoire du Canada* (1845–48). This omission was not corrected until the fourth edition, issued by his son in 1882 (Winks 1997, 19). Documentary evidence and the work of other historians, however, shed some light on this chapter of black French Canadian history. It begins with Viger's above-mentioned *De l'esclavage en Canada* (1859) and is decisively advanced by Trudel's work from 1960 onward. More recently, black Montreal lives in the eighteenth and nineteenth century have been explored in two volumes by Frank Mackey (2004, 2010).[8] In *Done with Slavery*, he offers an appendix with ninety-four newspaper notices from 1765 to 1810 that concern the "sales of black slaves and the flights of black prisoners, ship deserters, servants, and slaves" (2010, 307). These are "verbal snapshots" that inform us "about their subjects' physical appearance, scars or injuries, linguistic and other abilities, habits, dress" and such details "that about one-fifth are scarred by smallpox, and about one-third speak, or can get along in, two languages or more" (2010, 307).

While black slaves were numerically less significant than in the slave economies to the south, they certainly contributed to the building of Quebec. Slave labour was employed by the clergy, members of the army, notaries, and doctors. Seventeen years after Angélique's death, the peace treaty between England and France in 1760 confirmed the continuation of slavery in Quebec under the English regime (Trudel 2004, 66, 123–42). Blacks in New France and after the British Conquest were mostly house slaves, considerably more expensive than Aboriginal slaves and, according to historians, therefore better treated than many slaves elsewhere (Winks 1997, 10–11, 15; Rhodes 1998, 29).

How slaves themselves may have felt about their lives, however, is suggested by the fact that they voted with their feet. As revealed by their owners' attempts to retrieve them, they fled in considerable numbers. In the *Quebec Gazette* between 1769 and 1794, for example, "advertisements for runaway slaves were more frequent … than were those for the sale of slaves" (Winks 1997, 15).[9] The first printers of Quebec, in fact, employed slaves themselves and had problems keeping them. In 1764, for example, William Brown and Thomas Gilmore founded the bilingual *Quebec Gazett–Gazette de Québec* as Quebec's first newspaper (see Audet). Brown, who remained the sole owner of the paper and its slaves after 1773, saw his slave Joe flee at least six times between 1777 and 1789, including once from prison (Trudel 2004, 161). "Wanted" ads for Joe must have appeared in the very paper he normally helped to produce. Despite his flights, the trained printer was obviously valuable enough for his master to incur considerable expenses to regain his services (Trudel 2004, 205–7).

Slavery in Lower Canada (as the former Province of Quebec was called after 1791) was rendered impracticable by the courts around 1800 (see chapter 3; Mackey 2004, 26–30; Mackey 2010, 36–78). Before that development, however, slave numbers first rose when Loyalists arrived with their slaves in 1783 (Trudel 2004, 86). This further chapter involving race and empire produced the most significant eighteenth-century influx of black subjects in what is now Canada. The 1783 flight of Loyalists, especially to Nova Scotia, produced a document that offers us the richest collection of recorded statements by black subjects at the time, at a moment when they were about to become Nova Scotians.

WRITING AND READING CARLETON'S "BOOK OF NEGROES"

The "Book of Negroes" is an extensive ledger created in two versions by British and United States officials in 1783; eleven years later it was reproduced for an administrator in Nova Scotia.[10] Also known as "Carleton's Book of Negroes," it contains the names of three thousand black individuals, evacuated from New York between April and November 1783 on 219 ships that were destined for Quebec, Germany, and England, but mostly bound for Nova Scotia (Hodges et al. 1996, xi; L. Hill 2007b, 22). This transnational, twice-written and then copied document (referenced in the very title of Hill's *The Book of Negroes*) is also a Canadian text – and, more specifically, a black Canadian text. Among other elements, the ledger offers a large number of transcribed black statements. As a collection of black testimony, it is an anthology of embryonic slave narratives. It also offers accounts by a large number of black individuals who were at the point of taking up residence in Canada.

The War of Independence and the Provisions for Peace

What were the circumstances that made this document possible? And why is it so important to a discussion of slave narratives and early black transnational and Canadian testimony? A prelude to its genesis was the 1772 *Somerset* decision by the English Court of King's Bench, which created a precedent for black liberation by the British. While in England with his Boston owner Charles Stewart, James Somerset decided to make himself unavailable to his master. He was recaptured and put on a ship to be sold in Jamaica, but a writ of *habeas corpus* gained him a trial. Chief Justice Lord Mansfield eventually ordered his release, arguing that English common law did not allow for slavery on English soil. Contrary to initial assumptions, hopes, and fears of friend and foe alike, the decision hardly meant the abolition of slavery. Among slaves in the colonies, however, it raised hopes for freedom, and some owners suspected it motivated fugitives to try to reach British ships (Schama 2008, 18, 44–55). Especially after the beginning of the War of Independence, slaves indeed began to leave their masters in substantial numbers, lured by the British, who were desperate to gain an advantage in the fighting. Virginia's last British governor, Lord Dunmore – ironically a slave owner himself – promised freedom to blacks who joined the British forces (Schama 2008, 7). In his famous 1775 proclamation, Dunmore requested that "every person capable of bearing arms … resort to His Majesty's standard," and he declared "all indented servants, Negroes, or others (appertaining to Rebels) free, that are able and willing to bear arms" (qtd in L. Hill 2007b). After a similar proclamation by General Howe the following year, General Henry Clinton went further in the 1779 Philipsburg Proclamation, promising freedom to all blacks who would join the British.

The proclamations caused many outraged white colonists to become rebels. But slaves joined Dunmore's Ethiopian Regiment by the hundreds, participating in a much wider slave exodus that would number many thousands (Hodges et al. 1996, xii–xiii; Schama 2008, 7). New York City, the British military headquarters occupied in 1776, would become the most important gathering place of these refugees from slavery. Twelve hundred blacks were counted there in a 1779 military census, "joined in 1782 by over fifteen hundred black loyalists evacuated from Savannah and Charleston" (Hodges et al. 1996, xiv).

As the rebels advanced, however, Boston was evacuated by the British in 1776, and New York's turn came with the peace treaty. The "Book of Negroes" indirectly owes its existence to a passage in Article 7 of the Provisional Peace Agreement, signed in November 1782. It stipulated that the British would forego "carrying away any Negroes, or other Property of the American Inhabitants" (qtd in Walker 199, 10; Winks 1997, 32).[11] As the erstwhile Quebec governor and now British commander-in-chief Sir Guy Carleton informed an incensed George Washington in May 1783, however, the British considered all blacks free who had served the British or lived within British lines for at least a year (Walker 1992, 10; Winks 1997, 31–2; Hodges et al. 1996, xi). To pacify his opponent, Carleton offered to establish a list of all removed individuals in order to facilitate subsequent claims, and a board to examine any disputes that might arise. Washington was left with no choice but grudging approval, and US representatives were appointed. The "Book of Negroes," together with a board of inquiry, came into existence (Walker 1992, 11; Hodges et al. 1996, xvii).

Documenting a historical black exodus from New York City, the "Book of Negroes" is a unique source for our understanding of the African diaspora in North America and for our comprehension of Nova Scotia and the beginning of Canada. Yet it is important to realize that this ledger indexes not only black freedom – as is usually emphasized – but also continued slavery or some form of indenture for most of the black subjects travelling to what is now Canada. Furthermore, where the inspection rolls do name free black Loyalists, the short corresponding remarks often encapsulate stories of their earlier slavery. Since many of the remarks render the statements of black subjects, these instances of reported speech make the document a collection of encapsulated slave narratives that have rarely been considered as such. Similar points can be made about a fifteen-page section that precedes the three separate "books" of the inspection roll of the "Book of Negroes." This section contains the minutes of the cases heard by the board of inquiry. The minutes also render black testimony in the form of reported or indirect speech, and like the inspection roll, they document both black freedom and continued bondage administered by the British.

Negotiating Freedom: The "Cases" in the "Book of Negroes"

The board heard cases by white claimants but also heard from blacks who were fighting for their freedom. What were the outcomes of these hearings? As historian James Walker summarizes, "the minutes of the board … recorded only 14 disputed cases.[12] Of these, two were decided in favor of the slaves, nine in favor of the masters, and three were referred to General Birch, as the claimants, being Loyalists, had no recourse to a board established to settle American claims" (Walker 1992, 11–12). The American Congress soon abandoned the procedure as ineffectual (Schama 2008, 152), but the majority of the cases resulted in continued slavery for the subjects concerned. Graham Russell Hodges, however, in his edition of the American version of the document,[13] also emphasizes the important fact that in some cases the board allowed the testimony of former slaves to stand up against the agents of their former masters (1996, xviii). This recognition of black speech is not unheard of, but it was still an entirely remarkable fact in 1783.

Black testimony, at times amounting to short slave narratives, was not only relevant but in several cases even seemed decisive. Some examples will illustrate that point. During its first meeting on 30 May 1783, the board sided twice with black individuals and in one case rendered a black man's claim in the minutes:

> A. Bartram, a Negro, complains that his Daughter Nancy is detained by Henry Rogers of Queen Street in order to send her to her former master in Connecticut.[14]
>
> It appears by a Certificate of Captain Nathan Hubbell that A. Bartram with his two Daughters Nancy and Flora came within the British lines in July 1779.
>
> A. Bartram demands his Daughter Nancy of Henry Rogers, as she came with him into the British Lines at the abovementioned time. (3)[15]

Significantly, not only was black speech recorded, but the linguistic performatives, "complains," and "demands," uttered by a black subject in 1783, commanded attention and were of consequence. The white opponent's words did not automatically prevail. The board noted that said Henry Rogers "could not produce any authority for detaining Bartram's daughter Nancy," and ordered her released (3). The board was dominated by British officers who presumably had little sympathy for American claims. But this outcome was hardly a foregone conclusion, as another case on the same day demonstrated. When Violette Taulbert "complains of being detained by David Campbell as a slave without sufficient authority" (4), the board decided against her, forcing her to remain in slavery.

A longer narrative by a former slave was recorded on 15 July, and it, too, seems to have had an impact on the decision. Samuel Doron[16] produced "a Certificate from General Birch dated 14th May last that he … 'came within the British Lines under the Sanction and claims the Privilege of the Proclamations respecting Negroes theretofore issued for their Security and Protection'" (7). While such a "Certificate" from the British designated official, Brigadier General Birch, ordinarily sufficed to grant passage to Nova Scotia,[17] the commissioners agreed only if the arrival within British lines had occurred before the signing of the Provisional Peace Agreement on 30 November 1782. Much to George Washington's chagrin, in General Guy Carleton's interpretation, black individuals were already free if they had crossed the line before the agreement, and were thus not to be returned as "Property" to Americans under Article 7.[18] Since in Doron's case the certificate was dated later, the black individual was called upon to speak for himself. The minutes record his narrative at some length: "Samuel Doron, the Negro, being desired to make his Defense says that in April 1778 he with Consent of his Mistress went on Board a Galley commanded by Captain Clarke in Order to come to New York. That he then belonged to Allida Teller the Claimants Mother who lived at Teller's Point in the County of West Chester and that the Claimant had some time before come within the British Lines and he the Negroe was charged with having assisted the claimant and was therefore ill used by the continental People in the Country and that was the Reason of his determining to come within the British Lines" (8–9).

Prompted by this account, an American commissioner inquired into the allegiance of the claimant. As his former slave indicated, he turned out to be a Loyalist. The board consequently declared the case to be outside its purview. Since the board adjudicated only cases that involved American ownership, it referred the decision "to the Commandant and the Police of the Garrison" (9). The testimony of the black subject carried weight in this sequence and helped to stall the claimant's request.

While Carleton often decided in favour of the black subjects, no Samuel Doron (or similar name) appears on the inspection roll of the "Book of Negroes." The claimant being a Loyalist, Doron may not have gone free. Or he might have decided not to board any ship to Nova Scotia for another reason. In the following case, on 24 July 1783, the board returned his children Peter and Elizabeth to slavery:

> Gerard Beekman claims two Negro children, one a Boy named Peter, the other a Girl named Elizabeth, lately embarked with their father to go to Nova Scotia and brought on Shore for Examination.
>
> The Claimant produces a Certificate from Pierre van Cortlandt Esq. … that in the year 1777 he gave the Wench (the Mother of the said Children, with her Children) to his Daughter Cornelia the Wife of the Claimant and upon Examination it appears that Samuel Doron (the Father of the Children) in April 1778 took them from the Home of the said Pierre Van Cortlandt and brought them to the City of New York where they have remained since. (10)

In its decision, the board showed that it was perfectly capable of separating a family, thus perhaps causing the father to forego passage to Nova Scotia in order to remain closer to his children. Stated in terse language, the decision revealed the board's immediate power over the life of slaves: "The Board are of Opinion that the Children ought to be delivered to the Claimant and he is hereby permitted to take and dispose of them as he may think proper" (10).

Similarly "a Negroe Woman named Betty" (10), although in possession of a Birch Certificate, was sent back to her master on 2 August 1783. In her testimony, the black woman unwittingly incriminated herself, confirming that she had fled slavery only after the signing of the Provisional Peace Agreement in 1782: "The Wench acknowledges that she was the Property of the Claimant and left him in April last The Board are therefore of Opinion that the Wench is the Property of the Claimant, and hereby directs her to be delivered to the Claimant or his Attorney to be disposed of by him at his Pleasure" (11).[19]

In contrast to Samuel Doron, two other former slaves are named on the inspection roll of the "Book of Negroes," their decision having been referred to the commandant. In both cases, black testimony motivated the commissioners' inquiry into the claimant's allegiance, resulting here in freedom. The instructive case of Judith Jackson has received some commentary. Claimed by one Jonathan Eilbeck, she was "brought on shore for examination" (11). Jackson's Birch Certificate was dated 5 June 1783, after the signing of the Provisional Peace Agreement. Her testimony, however, helped to identify the former owner as a British Loyalist, not an American: "The Wench … says that she was formerly the Property of the said John McLean who left the Country on Account of the War and went to England leaving her behind and that she went with the Army under General Leslie to Charlestown and came from thence to New York" (11). Since the claimant "declares himself to be a British Subject," the board again referred "the matter to the Commandant and Police of the Garrison" (12). Jackson was allowed to continue to Nova Scotia because she had left her owner earlier, as an entry on pages 144–5 of the inspection roll indicates; she had also been working for the Royal Artillery Department (RAD): "Judith Jackson, 54 years, ordinary Wench, RAD. Formerly slave to John Clain, Norfolk, Virginia; left him in early 1779" (Hodges et al. 1996, 197). A number of commentators have elucidated her fate further.[20]

Significantly, Jackson's entry is blank in another column, under the heading "Names of the Persons in whose Possession they now are." This blank space differentiates her entry from the second case, in which "William Farrer claims a Negro woman named Dinah Archey" (12). Dinah, too, was in possession of a General Birch Certificate (12), and her account offers another brief slave narrative: "She now acknowledges that she was formerly the Property of John Bains of Crane Island Norfolk County Virginia and that he sold her as he then said to the Claimant with whom she lived about three Years and until he was obliged to leave the country on account of the War and went to England leaving this Negroe Woman behind him and she further says that the said John Bains afterwards told her that he had never given the Claimant a Bill of Sale for her and compelled her to return to him where she remained until the Expedition up the Chesapeake Bay under Sir George Collier and General Matthews when she came with them to New York" (12).

As with Doron and Jackson, Dinah's narrative helped to reveal the claimant's allegiance to the British, causing referral "to the Commandant and Police of the Garrison" (12). Like Judith Jackson, Dinah appears on the inspection roll of the "Book of Negroes," though with the slightly different spelling of Archer for her last name (Hodges et al. 1996, 148). The entry shows her embarked on the ship *Grand Duchess of Russia*, bound for Port Roseway (which was renamed Shelburne later in 1783).[21] But another name, Ms Savage, appears next to hers, in the column under the heading "Names of the Persons in whose Possession they now are." The meaning of the phrase is not clear; as we will see, it often seems to indicate indenture.

Why are the testimonies in these protocols so relevant? Although produced under interrogation and rendered by scribes, they reveal narratives by black immigrants to Nova Scotia. These slave narratives share the circumstance of being transposed to paper according to preordained protocols with many "classical" slave narratives solicited and recorded by white abolitionists. As opposed to the supportive – if not always unproblematic – interview situation offered by abolitionists or other sympathetic inquirers, these accounts are given in a threatening and intimidating context and have immediate, life-determining consequences. These recordings of black testimony nonetheless show a wider array of possibility than, for instance, the much earlier interrogation protocols of Angélique.[22] While her questioners presupposed her guilt and asked mostly leading questions, the cases in the "Book of Negroes" involve moments of genuine discovery and at times offer surprising outcomes. In these proceedings, black testimony was given standing and sometimes allowed black subjects a degree of agency that would determine their future.[23]

These proceedings can be seen in relation to later British hearings, such as those recorded in the "Reports" of the fiscals and of the Protectors of Slaves of Berbice and Demerera-Essequebo (later Guyana) in the 1820s and 1830s,[24] or the 1837 investigation of the Jamaican apprenticeship system.[25] Both produced important bodies of black testimony.[26] What is striking here, however, is the early date, prior to the British abolition of the slave trade in 1807, and the fact that these few cases only preface an inspection roll of three thousand entries that renders, in abbreviated form, interviews with black subjects – slaves, former slaves, and many whose freedom was in the balance.

Incomplete Life Stories: The Inspection Roll

Like the cases at the beginning of the "Book of Negroes," the main inspection roll contains abbreviated narratives that entail freedom in some cases and slavery in others. Divided into three separate "books," its brief entries offer glimpses and incomplete life stories that remain to be fully researched and imagined. Nine columns divide the information for each

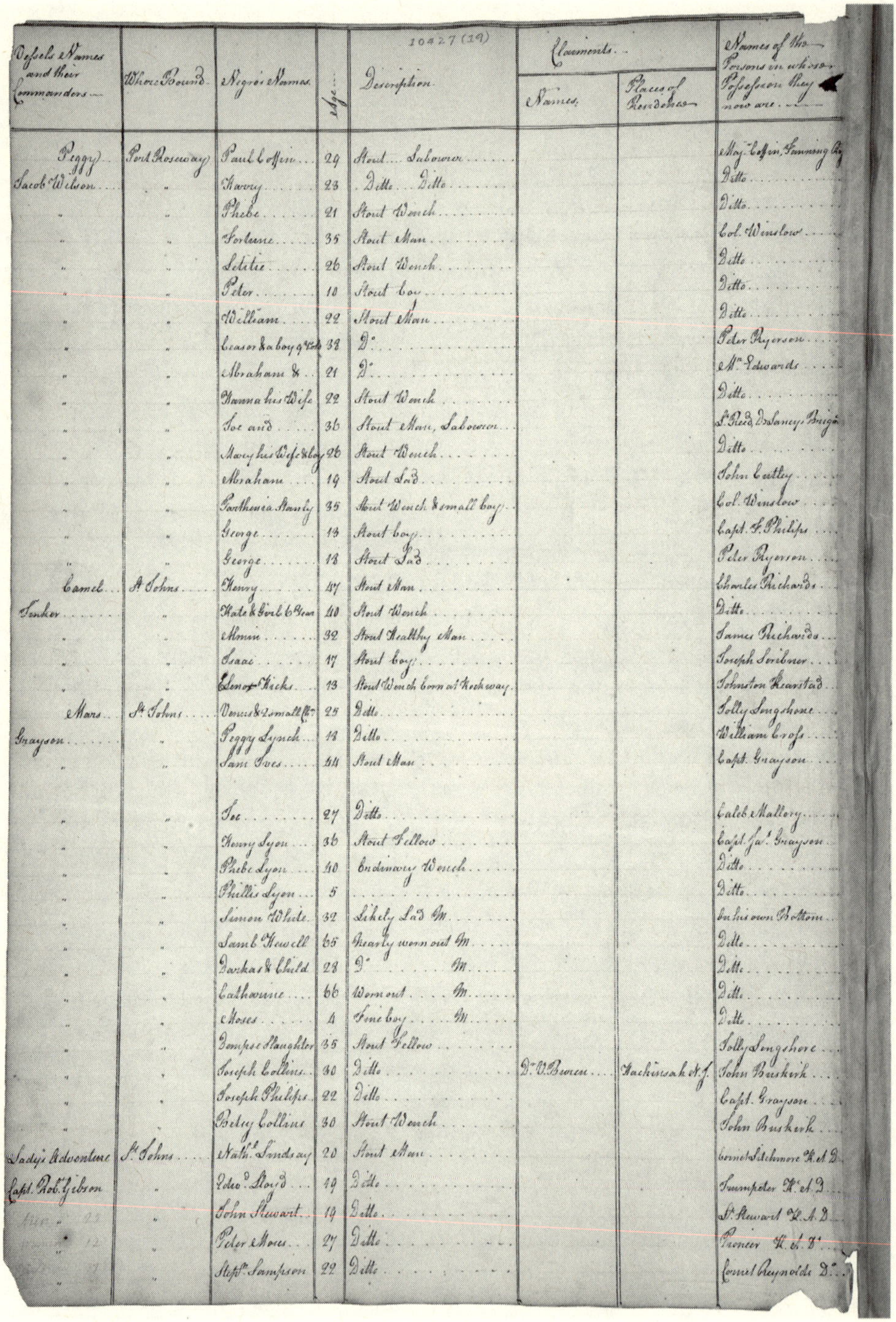

10427 (19)

Vessels Names and their Commanders	Whither Bound	Negroes Names	Age	Description	Claimants: Names	Claimants: Places of Residence	Names of the Persons in whose Possession they now are
Peggy	Port Roseway	Paul Coffin	29	Stout Labourer			Maj. Coffin, [illegible]
Jacob Wilson	"	Harry	23	Ditto Ditto			Ditto
"	"	Phebe	21	Stout Wench			Ditto
"	"	Fortune	35	Stout Man			Col. Winslow
"	"	Letitia	26	Stout Wench			Ditto
"	"	Peter	10	Stout Boy			Ditto
"	"	William	22	Stout Man			Ditto
"	"	Ceasor & a boy 9 Yrs	38	Do.			Peter Ryerson
"	"	Abraham &	21	Do.			Mr. Edwards
"	"	Hanna his Wife	22	Stout Wench			Ditto
"	"	Joe and	36	Stout Man, Labourer			J. Reid, Delancey's Brigd.
"	"	Mary his Wife & boy	26	Stout Wench			Ditto
"	"	Abraham	19	Stout Lad			John Cattley
"	"	Parthenia Stanly	35	Stout Wench & small boy			Col. Winslow
"	"	George	13	Stout Boy			Capt. F. Philips
"	"	George	18	Stout Lad			Peter Ryerson
Camel	St. Johns	Henry	47	Stout Man			Charles Richards
Tinker	"	Kate & Girl 6 Years	40	Stout Wench			Ditto
"	"	Amin	32	Stout Healthy Man			James Richards
"	"	Isaac	17	Stout Boy			Joseph Scribner
"	"	~~Lenor~~ Hicks	13	Stout Wench born at Rockaway			Johnston Kearstad
Mars	St. Johns	Venus & 2 small Ch.	25	Ditto			Solly Singshore
Grayson	"	Peggy Lynch	18	Ditto			William Cross
"	"	Sam Ives	44	Stout Man			Capt. Grayson
"	"	Joe	27	Ditto			Caleb Mallory
"	"	Henry Lyon	36	Stout Fellow			Capt. Jas. Grayson
"	"	Phebe Lyon	40	Ordinary Wench			Ditto
"	"	Phillis Lyon	5				Ditto
"	"	Simon White	32	Likely Lad M			On his own Bottom
"	"	Saml. Howell	65	Nearly worn out M			Ditto
"	"	Darkas & Child	28	Do. M			Ditto
"	"	Catharine	66	Worn out M			Ditto
"	"	Moses	4	Fine boy M			Ditto
"	"	Dempse Slaughter	35	Stout Fellow			Solly Singshore
"	"	Joseph Collins	30	Ditto	Dr. V. Bowen	Hackinsak N.J.	John Buskirk
"	"	Joseph Philips	22	Ditto			Capt. Grayson
"	"	Betsy Collins	30	Stout Wench			John Buskirk
Lady's Adventure	St. Johns	Nath. Lindsay	20	Stout Man			Cornet Litchmore K.A.D.
Capt. Robt. Gibson	"	Edwd. Lloyd	19	Ditto			Trumpeter K.A.D.
"	"	John Stewart	19	Ditto			J. Stewart K.A.D.
"	"	Peter Moses	27	Ditto			Pioneer K.A.D.
"	"	Stepn. Sampson	22	Ditto			Cornet Reynolds Do.

Pages from the 1783 ledger, "Book of Negroes." Courtesy of the National Archives, UK

Remarks.–

Property of Major Coffin purchased from Mr. Greenbree

Ditto

Ditto

Certificate from Genl. Birch, formerly the property of Isaac Warner of Philadelphia

Ditto ... freed by Mr. Deane of Jamaica Long Island

Ditto ... Ditto

Ditto ... free born in Montserrat

Property of Peter Ryerson with whom he is going to Nova Scotia

Property of Gideon White but allowed to go with Mr. Edwards to Nova Scotia

Free born on Staten Island, both of them having Genl. Birch's Certificate

His own property

Ditto

Came from Virginia with Lt. Col. Pennington of the Guards, formerly the property of Peter Rose

Free as per Certificate of her late Mistress, Mott

His own property

Formerly lived with Dennis Hagan in S. Carolina to whom he was Indented for 20 Years, bro't from thence by Capt. Gore 33d. Regt.

Formerly the property of Thomas Moore of Old Fairfield whom he left on Acct. of the Proclamation of Sir Wm. Howe.

Ditto ... Ditto ... Ditto

Formerly ye property of Williams at Tappan in New Jersey came in on Sir Wm. Howes Proclamatn.

Property purchased from Wm. Scribner of Setockett Long Island

Free, but Indented for 5 Years to Johnston Hearstead

Free Indented to him for 2 Years

Formerly the property of Mr. Lynch at Charles Town, Certificate from Genl. Birch

Sold to Capt. Grayson by Jonathan Eilbeck of New York who it does not appear had any right to sell him as he was the property of Captn. Talbot of Virginia from whence he was brought by ye Troops 5 Years ago & had a pass from Sir Hen'y Clinton wh. Mr. Eilbeck destroyed

His property as per Bill of Sale produced

Formerly to Andrew Lyon, Horse Neck New England, left him 3 Years past.

Formerly to James Lyon ... Ditto ... Ditto

Ditto ... Ditto ... Ditto

Born free Redding Connecticut

Ditto ... South Carolina

Ditto ... Ditto

Ditto ... Ditto Norwalk Connecticut

Ditto ... Ditto

Says he was born free, that he lived for some time with Dempsee Walls Norfolk Virginia

Formerly Slave to John Kipp New York Island, sold by Kipp to Doctr. Van Buren Hackinsak New Jersey whom he left 6 Years past

Ditto ... to Phill. Hawkins Jamaica West Indies, left him about 8 Years past.

Ditto ... to Nicholas Fortune Hackinsak New Jersey left him about 6 Years past.

Free born in the Grenades – Genl. Birch's Certificate

Formerly ye property of Ebenezar Cowley of Fairfield who gave him his freedom

Genl. Birch's Certificate says he was born free, but formerly lived with John Williamson Charles Town S. Carolina

Formerly the property of Genl. Balford of Hampton Virginia, says that at his Death got his freedom about 8 Years ago

Genl. Birch's Certificate, formerly ye property of Jno. Whitman of Charles Town S. Carolina who just before he died at N. York about 6 Years ago gave him his freedom in presence of Wm. Bryant.–

name. They contain: (1) the name of the ship and its captain; (2) the ship's destination; (3) the name of the black individual; (4) his or her age; and (5) a brief description, such as "stout fellow," "likely wench," or "worn out" (this column exceeds pure description by attributing putative value to individuals, although their occupation is usually omitted despite Carleton's instructions to include it) (Hodges et al. 1996, xlix–l). The next two columns, combined under the heading "Claimant," are for (6) the individual's name and (7) place of residence of American individuals seeking re-enslavement or redress, although this column is mostly empty.

This is not the case for a more enigmatic column (8) indicating "Names of the Persons in whose Possession they now are," which has created different interpretations and some confusion.[27] While the category of "Claimant" remains empty for most names, the "Possession" category is usually filled. Although it occasionally states that a person is travelling independently (on his or her "own bottom"), this column usually indicates relations ranging from free association to indenture and ownership, with the line between the last two often indistinguishable. Despite a certificate confirming their freedom, for instance, William and Hester Willis, listed in the "Book of Negroes" on board the ship *William* headed for the Bahamas, "were indentured to John Cameron at the point of departure. Later Willis had to purchase his wife from Cameron for £25" (Riley 2000, 141). As in many of the cases with Nova Scotian destinations discussed below, Cameron appears without further comment under "Names of the Persons in whose Possession they now are." In addition, finally, there is another, wider column for (9) "Remarks"; in the British version of the ledger, it takes up the entire opposite right-facing side of the ledger.[28] Like the "cases" that precede the inspection roll, these latter columns of "Claimant," "Possession," and "Remarks" are a space in which various kinds of life stories are adumbrated. The "Remarks" in particular contain information that in some cases amounts to brief narratives of freedom, often clearly based on information given by the black subject. In other cases, however, the concerned subjects are less fortunate.

Slavery in Nova Scotia

We have seen that black testimony about Canadian slavery is exceedingly scarce. The "Remarks" in the "Book of Negroes," however, contribute substantial information about masters and slaves moving north. Many of these entries tell stories of continued slavery in Canada. Despite Simon Schama's claim in *Rough Crossings* that the "Book of Negroes" "listed those who, as free men and women, were at liberty to go where they wished" (2008, 3), the inspection roll also indicates 366 individuals who went as slaves of white Loyalists to Nova Scotia, as summarized in Appendix 1 of the *Black Loyalist Directory* (Hodges et al. 1996, 221). The first ship to leave for the main new Loyalist settlement Port Roseway, the *Peggy*, thus carried Paul Coffin (29, stout labourer), Harry (23, stout labourer), and Phebe (21, stout wench). Under the rubric "Persons In Whose Possession They Now Are," we find "Major Coffin, Fanning's reg't," and the "Remarks" inform us that these individuals were the "Property of Major Coffin purchased from Mr. Greentree." Similarly, listed on the same ship are "Ceasor & a boy 9 years old, 30, stout man," with the remark "Property of Peter Reyerson with whom he is going to Nova Scotia" (7).

These black individuals were among the twelve hundred to two thousand slaves brought by Loyalists to Canada (Whitfield 2007, 1981). Given the emphasis on black freedom in scholarly writing about the period, historian Harvey Amani Whitfield wonders: "Why have historians focused on the freedom of the Black Loyalists instead of the continued enslavement of other African Americans? Why do we know much more about the Black Loyalists than black slaves?" (1980–1).[29] For him, "the typical experience of black migrants to the Maritimes after the Revolutionary War was not freedom, but rather slavery, re-enslavement, and other brutal forms of indentured servitude"; in fact, "slaveholding actually expanded and intensified in the Maritimes due to the Loyalist influx" (1981).[30] Whitfield comments on a good number of slave owners who appear with their slaves in the "Book of Negroes" (1983–4). As his enumeration indicates, slave ownership was common among different professions and did not exclude the clergy. A Reverend Beardsley thus sailed with Dinah, Scipio Bazeley, and Peter Beardsley, named as his property. Another young slave appears in the inspection roll as a gift by a reverend: "Sukey, 4, fine girl" as "[Property of Nathaniel Dickenson], present from the Rev. Mr. Badger" (Hodges et al. 1996, 59).[31]

As Marcel Trudel documents, slave owners in New France and later Lower Canada included not only merchants, bakers, butchers, bar and hotel owners, civil servants, parts of the military, doctors, notaries, and printers, but also the Church. The Jesuits and the Séminaire de Québec respectively held forty-six Aboriginal and thirty-one black slaves (2004, 123–42).[32] The Loyalist influx gave slavery a boost in Lower Canada; it expanded "rapidly after 1783 with the arrival of displaced settlers from the rebellious British North American colonies" (Winks 1997, 23). In fact, several ships noted in the "Book of Negroes" were destined for Quebec. On 10 July 1783, Abigail and Oliver Orser, fourteen and eleven years old respectively, travelled with Joseph Orser to Quebec on the ship *Camel*. For both we find the remark: "Appears to be said Orser's property." On the ship *Baker & Atlee* to Quebec, "Mary, 11, likely girl" is listed as "The property of Thomas Darling." The ship *Union* carried twenty-two-year-old Charity Umberston to Quebec, identified as "Samuel Umberston's property; proved by bill of sale"; while "Rosetta, thirty, stout wench," travelled on the ship *Blackett* with David Whitehill of Quebec, "His property having produced a Bill of Sale." On 6 September 1783, finally, the *Grace*, leaving for Quebec, had eight slaves on board; a thirty-year-old woman and her child are entered with the remark "Appears to be Peter Van Alsines's property."

The situation was complicated by the fact that certain designations seemed to hide slavery and the line between slavery and other forms of "possession" was not always clearly demarcated (Walker 1992, 21). Many slaves appear in documents as "servants." As Whitfield points out, "the few histories about slavery in Maritime Canada generally agree that the blacks listed as servants were, in fact, probably slaves" (2007, 1990n5; 2009, 80). Listings of the so-called Port Roseway Associates are an example of these difficulties.[33] In one of them, for instance, a Phil Ackland appears as arriving "in Shelburne with a woman, a child and a servant" (Szick et al.). The "Book of Negroes" shows Ackland twice. He appears under the rubric "Possession" for both the thirty-six-year-old Samuel Warner and thirty-five-year-old Sally Taylor (Hodges et al. 1996, 41). Sally Taylor is probably the person by the same name who appears in the "Muster Book of Free Black, Settlement of Birchtown, 1784" as twenty-nine years old (Port Roseway Associates, 138–9);[34] Samuel Warner, on the other hand, is not listed there. What their reality as "servants" of Phil Ackland may have been is hard to know.

The situation seems clear in the case of another white Loyalist settler. According to the above-cited Port Roseway Associates list, William Black "Arrived with a woman, a child and a servant" (Szick et al.). The "Book of Negroes" identifies him as slave owner in the entries for two ships bound for Port Roseway, the *Abondance*, with "Daniel, 13, stout boy, (William Black). Property of William Black" (Hodges et al. 1996, 153), and *Providence*, with "Bill, 26, stout fellow. William Black of Port Roseway, claimant. (William Black). Property of William Black" (40). In this case, the "Book of Negroes" disambiguates the meaning of the term "servant" in another document as clearly signalling the fact of slavery.

Indentured Black Subjects

A name appearing under the murky rubric "Names of the Persons in whose Possession they now are" often seems to indicate indenture. Only a few entries in the "Book of Negroes," however, state this clearly.[35] Most of these entries explicitly mention earlier manumission, but with a subsequent indenture of unidentified length or ranging from one to ten years. Cases of indenture were probably numerous, however, even where the fact was not mentioned. The background of Lt. Col. Isaac Allen would certainly make this plausible. He appears without further comment in that column for the first four entries of the "Book of Negroes" – George and Ann Black and the children Reuben and Sukey, all qualified as "Freed by Lawrence Hartshorne as certified." Citing the Loyalist Claims Commission[36] and other documents, Whitfield writes: "Colonel Isaac Allen of Trenton, New Jersey, owned a small farm of 120 acres on the Delaware River, a 'valuable piece of woodland' near Trenton of thirty-five acres, and other property. The land near the river included 'a Farm House and Barn with Orchards.' Allen possessed several 'servants' who laboured in his house and small farms" (2009, 65).

At least in Lawrence Hill's novelistic recreation (see chapter 4), the entries in the "Book of Negroes" concerning Allen are clearly interpreted as signalling indenture: "The Loyalist, Lieutenant Colonel Isaac Allen, said he had acquired the Negro as an indentured servant and was taking him to Saint John" (L. Hill 2007a, 292). With regard to the ship *Free Briton*, Hill's narrator mentions the thirty-four cases that also appear in the historical "Book of Negroes." Although this information does not appear in the original entries, he again adds that "every one … was an indentured servant." While Hill avails himself of more conspicuous artistic licence elsewhere, this small alteration seems warranted by the historical context.[37]

Free Black Immigrants and Their Embryonic Slave Narratives

The "Book of Negroes" is a record of Canadian slavery and indenture, but certainly also a record of Canadian freedom. Many entries contain accounts by black subjects that culminate in claims of freedom that are accepted by the British authorities. Even if couched in white officials' writing, these entries render the speech of former slaves. The "Book of Negroes" can be read accordingly, not only as a record of black migration and an index of Loyalist slavery and indenture, but also as an astonishing anthology of black testimony. The consequential acts of black speech and claims to liberty recorded in this ledger preface the subsequent, fully developed eighteenth-century Nova Scotian slave narratives explored below that mark the beginning of the Canadian line.

Instead of noting any kind of "Possession," twenty-seven of the entries indicate that the subject was travelling on her or his "own bottom." Entries under the rubric "Remarks" are typically accompanied by transcribed statements of self-proclaimed freedom accepted by the British. With no claimant present, these remarks are sometimes kept to a minimum. Six black travellers – namely Simon White, Lamb Hewell, Darkas and child, Catharine and Moses – are thus registered as travelling on their "own bottom" on the ship *Mars* to St John's; their claims to be free-born are recorded with the locations: "Born free, Redding, Connecticut," "Born free, South Carolina," and "Born free, Norwalk, Connecticut" (Hodges et al. 1996, 9). Similarly, Fonlove Jackson and her two children, Dinah and Ned, described as travelling on their "own bottom" on the ship *Providence* to Port Roseway, are entered as free-born "at Rhode Island" (39). Other independent travellers are inscribed in similar fashion, though for William Holchapan, 40, the remark includes his statement of having been baptized: "[Born free] and baptized in the year 1779 in the Parish of St. Paul's, London" (56). A somewhat longer story is recorded for Thomas Ogden, 29, travelling "on his own bottom" on the ship *London* to Port Roseway; his statement includes his claim of having responded to the British proclamation of freedom. While he had no certificate from General Birch, his claim was accepted (17). He seems to have been separated from Barbara Ogden, who similarly claims to have left the same master at the same time but is registered on a ship bound for Halifax (20).

Many of the entries that indicate a relation to a white settler – be it indenture or other – also transcribe statements of self-attested freedom, often explicitly as reported speech. Daniel Barber, on board the *Aurora* to St John's, thus "Says he was made free by Mr. Austin Moore of little York nigh 20 years ago" (Hodges et al. 1996, 5). The entry for Richard Stanley, listed on the *Peggy*, renders his statement that he was "formerly the property of Mr. Stoddard of Jamaica who he says at the time of his death made him free" (7). On the ship *Mary*, bound for Quebec, we find Phillis Duett, 46, who is in the "possession" of Matthew Peacock but "Says she was born free; that she lived as servant with James Duett at Pidee, South Carolina; that she left him about 3 years past" (74). Similarly, the entry for her daughter Judith Duett, 8, records that she "Says that she was born free; that she lived as a servant with James Duett of Pidee, South Carolina; that she left him about three years past" (74). Their relation to the white individuals mentioned in their entries remains uncertain.

In many cases, the possession of a "General Birch's Certificate" (or a "General Musgrave's Certificate") would signal that a similar narrative had been accepted by these officials. Such certificates might also encode black speech. With the exceptions that we have seen above, their possession had the same result as a statement during the interview for inscription in the "Book of Negroes." In the entry for Nancy Hill, 27, for instance, we read: "Says she is free and produces General Birch's Certificate to show it" (Hodges et al. 1996, 74). Overall, a substantial number of entries show or imply successful statements of self-claimed freedom and offer examples of black agency and self-determination.

In many respects, this was a remarkable fact in 1783. As mentioned earlier, the recording and acceptance of black testimony by British officials, and their willingness to act on it, can be seen in the context of the later fiscals' reports in Guyana in the 1820s and 1830s and the Jamaica Commission that followed James Williams's 1837 *Narrative*. These events, however, came after the abolition of the slave trade and of slavery respectively, following concerted abolitionist efforts and the creation of considerable public awareness. By contrast, 1783 was the year of the Zong case, in which black individuals were mainly discussed as chattel in the context of insurance law. The credence given to black testimony, the very same year, in the "Book of Negroes" can hardly be taken for granted.

While the "Book of Negroes" contains numerous stories of continued slavery in Canada, it is also a space where black testimony could inscribe decisive claims and turning points, such as manumission or the decision to leave a master. In many cases, this moment of narrative self-accounting offered a site of black self-affirmation and self-transformation. It is important to remember that these moments of transformational autobiographical intervention occurred when longer transcribed black narratives and black authorship – increasingly frequent in the nineteenth century – were still uncommon. Gustavus Vasa, known also by his African name Olaudah Equiano, was one of the most prominent free blacks in London at that time;

he triggered the Zong appeal with his visit to Granville Sharp (Hodges et al. 1996, xxix; Baucom 2005, 15; Schama 2008, 161; Thomas 2000, 94). Equiano's own famous narrative, however, would not be published until 1789, six years after the redaction of the "Book of Negroes." It was preceded by only a few other books written by black authors in Western languages.[38] Besides Phillis Wheatley's *Poems* (1773), these texts include the slave and Indian captivity narratives by Briton Hammon (1760) and Ukawsaw Gronniosaw (1770) and the Indian captivity narrative by the free black Methodist minister John Marrant (1785).[39] In 1783, only eleven years after the *Somerset* case, black testimony on a large scale and accepted with decisive consequences – as it often is in the "Book of Negroes" – was unusual in North America. Although severely constrained by the genre of the interrogative interview, early forms of the Canadian slave narrative thus took shape in the "Book of Negroes."

EARLY BLACK NARRATIVES, NOVA SCOTIA, AND MODERNITY

The Black Nova Scotian Accounts of John Marrant, Boston King, and David George

The "Book of Negroes" is a book of both administrative and personal accounting; it records geographical migration but also individual transformation. It offers a collection of life stories that are compressed into a few words, governed by the columns and categories that organize the ledger. With the arrival of these and other black diasporic newcomers,[40] Nova Scotia became a relevant site for those new and longer forms of black testimony that included most notably the slave narrative. While these forms offered new opportunities of black testimony and transformational self-affirmation, they were also subject to other constraints of material possibility, institutional context, generic facilitation, and audience expectation. Like the "Book of Negroes," they owed their existence to wider North American and black Atlantic contexts and spoke to them in turn.

Nova Scotia is connected to several eighteenth-century slave and captivity narratives, written by black community leaders who described the province in their memoirs or took up residence there. The Methodist minister John Marrant came to Nova Scotia in 1785 (Walker 1992, 71–2) after his *A Narrative of the Lord's Wonderful Dealings with John Marrant, A Black* had been published in London, transcribed by the Reverend William Aldridge. At the end of the text, he expresses his hope for safe arrival and success as a minister in Nova Scotia. Among the numerous editions of this popular Indian captivity narrative,[41] three appeared in Halifax between 1808 and 1813 (Gates 1988, 142). David George, a Baptist preacher and black Loyalist who had been evacuated from Charlestown, arrived in Nova Scotia in 1782. He became an important religious leader in Birchtown and Shelburne but left with twelve hundred others for Sierra Leone in 1792. His narrative, "An account of the life of Mr. David George, from Sierra Leone in Africa; given by himself in a conversation with Brother Rippon of London, and Brother Pearce of Birmingham," appeared in the *Baptist Annual Register* in 1793 in London. Boston King, another black Nova Scotian author, appears in the "Book of Negroes" in an entry for the ship *L'Abondance* bound for Port Roseway: "Boston King, 23, stout fellow. Formerly the property of Richard Waring of Charlestown, South Carolina; left him 4 years ago. GBC" (Hodges et al. 1996, 86). His work, "Memoirs of the Life of Boston King, a Black Preacher, Written by Himself during His Residence at Kingswood School," was composed in England and first published there in the *Methodist Magazine* in 1798. After his move to Sierra Leone, motivated by his wish to contribute to missionary work in Africa, he received further education in England at Kingswood School, established near Bristol by Methodist founder John Wesley in 1748.

Although recorded in England prior to, or after, their author's residence in Canada, the narratives by John Marrant, David George, and Boston King are related to important aspects of black Nova Scotian culture of the period. They reveal the lives and thoughts of these ministers, all of whom conveyed their religious convictions in their daily work in Nova Scotia. As preachers, their contributions were closely related to the other oral modes of black Nova Scotian culture at that time.[42] Their texts, written and published in England, however, share features with other modes of writing and with other eighteenth-century black narratives marked by similar literary and social contexts of production.

Like later slave narratives in the nineteenth century, their work relies on modes of facilitation that also impose formal and institutional constraints, preventing these texts from being transparent vehicles of unmediated narratives. White editorship and sponsorship motivated first by religious and then by abolitionist interests constituted defining factors in the production, publication, and dissemination of these accounts. "Typically the antebellum slave narrative carries a black message inside a white envelope," William L. Andrews remarks with respect to the prefatory assurances that were routinely offered by editors and sponsors seeking to guarantee the authenticity of the story and the probity of the black narrator (1998, 16). This very attempt to assure credibility, however, came with its own problems. As John W. Blassingame notes in his landmark volume *Slave Testimony* (1977), earlier scholarship often repudiates slave narratives as reliable sources because of the role of white editors. Blassingame thus feels compelled to examine both the character and the role of nineteenth-century white editors – and of later interviewers and transcribers – to prove *their* probity (1977, xvii–lxv). Even in the case of the most scrupulous editors, however, it was certainly true for antebellum slave narratives, as we have seen McBride observe (2001, 5), that the context of abolitionism marks a "discursive terrain" that includes "the co-mingling of abolitionist expectations with literary expectations and the objections of pro-slavers" (16).

As Philip Gould states, eighteenth-century black narratives share many features with these later texts but they also have their own characteristics. Evangelical Christian groups and then early Abolitionist societies often controlled their publication, shaping "the language and themes of the eighteenth-century slave narrative" and influencing "the genre's treatment of the black protagonist's physical and spiritual journey." The forms of the slave narrative that are better known today developed in the nineteenth century: "Not until the organization of more radical anti-slavery societies in America during the 1830s and 1840s, which now called for the immediate emancipation of slaves, did the genre turn its energies upon Southern plantation slavery" (Gould 2007, 12). Andrews makes a similar point with respect to a shift in genre affinities: "The earliest slave narratives have strong affinities with popular white American accounts of Indian captivity and Christian conversion in the New World. But with the rise of the anti-slavery movement in the early 19th century came a new demand for slave narratives that would highlight the harsh realities of slavery itself" (1998, 15).

David George's text is exceptional in that its opening graphically describes slaveholder brutality in nineteenth-century fashion. Like the narratives by Briton Hammon, Ukawsaw Gronniosaw, and John Marrant, though, it also belongs to the popular eighteenth-century genre of the Indian captivity narrative. Moreover, all but one of these narratives represent spiritual autobiographies and conversion narratives (Hammon's piety is never in question).[43] Marrant, who was not a slave, does not mention slavery. He relates his spiritual journey and Indian captivity, offering "the autobiographical story of a free black who converts to Christianity and later helps to convert several Cherokee Indians to the Christian faith" (Pierce 2007, 85–6). Boston King dedicates only the first part of his narrative to his slave experience and multiple escapes; the other three parts detail conversion experiences by his wife, himself, and other Nova Scotians. And although David George's first paragraph would fit in any nineteenth-century slave narrative, the Indian captivity tale is announced by the second paragraph. The narrative as a whole concentrates on George's spiritual journey and his work as a preacher, against the background of the War of Independence and his settler experience in Nova Scotia.

With respect to the black adoption of the genres of captivity narrative and spiritual autobiography, Yolanda Pierce speaks of a "common rhetorical strategy" that uses "conventional Anglo-American literary genres to tell unconventional African-American stories" (2007, 83). Genre is both constraining and enabling in this context. It can marginalize other forms of black expression but also allow for "strategic endeavors to counteract cultural and historical obliteration" (Thomas 2000, 157). While ambivalent in this regard, the adopted genres offer a space for hybrid and innovative self-translation. They open a contact zone that gives access to successful and even dominant channels of cultural conveyance, facilitating a "contract" with the reader that puts audience expectation to work and allows for recognition.

To what extent does the appropriation of the captivity narrative, a popular form directly related to white settlement, allow for the strategic emplotment of black self-expression? According to Annette Kolodny, "the single narrative form indigenous to the New World is the victim's recounting of unwilling captivity" (1984, 6; qtd in Pierce 2007, 84). The "Indian captivity narrative" – also referenced as Puritan, American, or colonial captivity narrative (Pierce 2007, 98n3) – pertains mainly to white settlers held captive by Indigenous "others." The captive settler subject reflects here on the ways and power of God under these trying circumstances.[44] It seems only fitting, however, that the form should be adopted and adapted by black authors experiencing various forms of captivity. Placed in a position homologous to that of white captives, they can occupy a position of similarity with the dominant culture. That situation allows access to the same repertoire of themes and tropes to evoke empathy, and shows black subjects in conversation with the same spiritual resources, relying on God and experiencing rescue as his gift. Marrant's narrative, among the most popular of the genre (Gates 1988, 142), offers an example of a black author successfully tapping this successful white genre. Its narrator appears in a position of moral and religious superiority to his Cherokee captors. The narrative thus permits Marrant to validate "his participation in the transcendental hemispheres of western culture and his appropriation of the discourse" by a process of "transference of cultural difference on to another subject" (Thomas 2000, 191).

In addition, Marrant invokes the conventions of the conversion narrative and the spiritual autobiography. Starting out as a musician, "I devoted [my life] to pleasure and drinking in iniquity like water; a slave to every vice suited to my nature and to my years" (Marrant, 2002, 50). But listening to George Whitefield, one of the co-founders of Methodism, Marrant is struck to the ground by the force of the preacher's invocation of God. He becomes a convert. Divine intervention and the power of the word are central to his narrative. Gates underlines its aural dimension, emphasizing Marrant's revision of the trope of the "Talking Book" that had been employed by earlier black writers (1988, 142–6).[45] Helen Thomas further points out that "the captivity framework of Marrant's *Narrative* pivots essentially upon the 'divine possession' or the gift of tongues" and his "appropriation of a divinely inspired language which 'delivers' him on separate occasions from the claims of his master and from the hands of the Cherokee Indians" (2000, 189).

The use of Christian typology (such as Israel's captivity and Exodus) is a common device in black cultural expression, but in particular the "discourse of the spirit" (Thomas 2000, 83, 167) seems relevant to Marrant's use of the conventions of the spiritual autobiography and conversion narrative. Popularized by "radical dissenting Protestantism" and emphasizing unmediated experience of the divine, "the discourse of the spirit enabled 'authorized' declarations of 'independence' which reached beyond the peripheries of religious orthodoxy" (Thomas 2000, 167). It is thus not entirely surprising that "the framework advanced by dissenting Protestant spiritual autobiographies found a continuum in the slave narratives which appeared in England during the latter half of the eighteenth century" (Thomas 2000, 168).

The advantages of generic channels such as the spiritual autobiography, the conversion narrative, and the captivity narrative comprise increased acceptance and recognition, but they come with certain restrictions and often a shift in emphasis. While genre familiarity "established an intricate rapport with its audiences' beliefs," the composite text resulting from the editor's interventions "shifted and dispersed the centre of the autobiographical text into a pluralised narrative, which sidetracked the issue of slavery or indeed racial miscegenation itself" (Thomas 2000, 187). Marrant's reliance on the powers of a proven genre, under the editorial influence of the Reverend William Aldridge,[46] had excellent reasons: his work "endorsed his career as an evangelical missionary" (Thomas 2000, 191) and paved the way for his mission to Nova Scotia. But to what extent did white institutional control, editorship, and conventions of genre obliterate rather than facilitate black expression in such narratives? Was there a voice in which the subaltern black subject could speak in the interstices of generic accommodation?

Thomas makes the case for that assumption, suggesting that the Protestant language of unmediated divine contact allows for a strong connection between African epistemologies and "the dynamics of radical dissenting Protestantism" (2000, 169). The "discourse of the spirit," for instance, is central not only to Protestant but also to several African epistemologies; the "ecstatic moment of spirit possession" plays thus a central role in the voodoo of Fon and Yoruba cultures and the obeah practised by Ashanti-Fanti tribes (170). Related religious forms as practised by slaves in the West Indies were effectively also known to British audiences when Marrant's text was recorded.[47] Thomas discovers "an articulation of African epistemologies within the continuum of the evangelical momentum" in Marrant's narrative (190). But she also detects a conflation of conversion and insurrection; reading the Scriptures after his conversion, Marrant refused to work for his master.

In Marrant's description, the spirit's presence is clearly felt as bodily possession and is often called forth by the preacher's voice. In the *Narrative*, Marrant is thus "struck to the ground, and lay both speechless and senseless near half an hour" (2002, 51). Later, "every word I heard from the minister was like a parcel of swords thrust into me" (51). In a moment singled out by Thomas for its disruptive "spiritual possession [that] exceeds that of the congregation" (2000, 189), Marrant finally is compelled "to halloo out in the midst of the congregation, which disturbing them, they took me away" (51). Bodily possession is thus indeed crucial to the *Narrative*; its presence is even more pronounced in Marrant's following work, his *Journal* ([1790] 2002a).

A Journal of the Rev. John Marrant, from August 18th, 1785, to the 16th of March, 1790 has been little noticed until its first reprint ever in 2002 (Brooks and Saillant). According to Joanna Brooks, it offers "the most extensive published account of black evangelism and community life in the eighteenth century" (Brooks 1999, 1). Marrant left for Nova Scotia in August 1785, ordained and sponsored by the Countess of Huntingdon. His journey responded to a letter from his brother, who indicated that the recently arrived black settlers in Nova Scotia desired strong black spiritual leadership. Marrant regularly records the direct bodily impact of spiritual possession in the *Journal*. These experiences include his minutes-long inability to speak in front of a congregation (2002, 104), the audiences' groaning, crying, and shouting, their bodies, overcome by the force of the spirit, "stretched out as though they were dead" (2002, 129). In addition to these descriptions of divine presence, divine intercession on behalf of Marrant is a frequent topic in the *Journal*. He thus describes a calming of the ocean and several encounters with death; he is saved from drowning and freezing, and from a bear he encounters (2002, 145–6). God is further on his side in an attack by the Arminian Wesleyans after he preaches (in keeping with the Calvinist Huntingdonian connection) that "there was no repentance this side of the grave; and thus inflamed the minds of the people" (Marrant 2002, 104). The *Journal* records the escalation of this conflict and his June 1786 run-in with the "old blind man who preaches for the Arminians" (2002, 124) – the leader of the Birchtown Wesleyans, Moses Wilkinson (see Walker 1992, 73; Brooks 1999, 9–10).

The *Journal* thus offers Marrant's spiritual vision together with intimate details of inter-denominational struggles in black Nova Scotia at the time. But it is an important and revealing text for many other reasons. Written to some extent as an accounting of his Nova Scotia mission for an audience back in England (Brooks 1999, 1), the text is also an important travel narrative that gives us insight into the daily life of Nova Scotians at this time. As an itinerant preacher, Marrant visited Birchtown, Shelburne, Halifax, Preston, and some locations that are no longer on maps of Nova Scotia. He records the poverty and hunger of the general population, the devastations of smallpox, and many other hardships witnessed throughout his travels.

Finally, Marrant's *Journal* is a document that records black agency. Marrant showed himself to be in direct contact with divine and spiritual power, and was capable of enabling that direct contact for others in ways that helped to build black community. He was further able to use his capacity to preach to reconnect with family and acquaintances from Charlestown, now across the Atlantic from England. In addition to his travels recorded in the *Narrative*, the *Journal* gives us not only an important black eighteenth-century travel narrative set within Nova Scotia; it also connects the province to the black Atlantic, which Marrant crossed on his way from London to Halifax, Birchtown, Shelburne, and other places in Nova Scotia, and from there to Boston and then back to London. The *Journal* thus provides an important example of both eighteenth-century black Canadian literature and transnational black self-expression. Like the "Book of Negroes" before it, it relates Canada to wide-flung connections and transformations at this moment of modernity that coincided with the acceleration of the Industrial Revolution after the peace of 1783.[48]

The same can be said for the slave and conversion narratives by Boston King and David George. King fled from his master to join the British in Charlestown; like George, he barely survived a smallpox epidemic. He was captured by the Americans and fled again, this time to New York. Here he describes the anxious scenes after the peace of 1783, "which diffused universal joy among all parties, except us, who had escaped from slavery, and taken refuge in the English army; for a report prevailed at New-York, that all the slaves, in number 2000, were to be delivered up to their masters, altho' some of them had been three or four years among the English" (B. King 2002, 217). As already mentioned, however, King would be registered in the "Book of Negroes." He arrived in Nova Scotia on the *L'Abondance* in 1783, together with the future Birchtown Methodist leader Moses Wilkinson (who, as we saw, gave Marrant considerable grief in the exercise of his office). While Wilkinson has left no text, King – in a dramatic fashion reminiscent of similar moments in Marrant's writing – describes his own wife's conversion during Wilkinson's preaching: "She was struck to the ground, and cried out for mercy: she continued in great distress for near two hours, when they sent for me" (B. King 2002, 218). Like Thomas, Cassandra Pybus relates such spiritual possession to previous African practices: "On his occasional visits to Birchtown, Freeborn Garrettson tried, with little success, to contain the 'enthusiasm' of the black Methodist congregation within accepted Wesleyan practice … he failed to appreciate that their raucous spiritual expression … reached back to a much older African past. The cultural practices that had nurtured the unregenerate self did not need to be abandoned in order for the followers of Daddy Moses to believe that they were reborn in God's grace" (2006, 147). Boston King himself experienced a first moment of conversion after a dream when he was still young (2002, 211). Only years later in Nova Scotia, however, he heard God's voice and "all my doubts and fears vanished away: I saw, by faith, heaven opened to my view; and Christ and his holy angels rejoicing over me" (221).

Like Marrant, King was an eloquent witness to the extreme hardship and poverty suffered by the population, especially during a famine and hard winters in the late 1780s – which forced many around him to indenture themselves and to "sell themselves to the merchants" (2002, 223). King himself survived as a carpenter and reluctant fisherman before becoming the Preston Methodist preacher in 1791. He was among those who joined the black exodus to Sierra Leone in 1792. While others left out of economic necessity, King states that his primary motive was the wish to convert Africans (2002, 228). After a dangerous crossing to Sierra Leone and the death of his wife from malaria shortly after their arrival, he opened a school, although he communicated with his students only through an interpreter and was met with little interest in religious conversion. In 1793, he was invited to England for further schooling. He spent two years at Kingswood school near Bristol, where he composed his narrative, before returning as a teacher to Sierra Leone.

Like that other world traveller, John Marrant, King offers an important contribution to early Canadian and black Canadian literature by portraying eighteenth-century Nova Scotia from a wider and transnational black perspective. His text is further relevant for early United States and transatlantic literature, since it is an important source for the black experience in the American War of Independence and the black missionary experience in Sierra Leone. In addition, his memoir testifies to his impressive ability as a black subject to exert agency under difficult circumstances. In ways that made him a community leader, he successfully engaged in risk-taking and self-transformation in his bid for self-determination and freedom. King's life is extraordinary in its black Atlantic, cosmopolitan reach, a trajectory over three continents that joins South Carolina, New York, and Nova Scotia to Sierra Leone and England.

Similarly, David George's life tells a black Atlantic story that connects Virginia, Nova Scotia, Sierra Leone, and England. Like Marrant's account, it contains a captivity narrative, and like King's text, it is a slave narrative. Like both of them, George offers mostly a spiritual autobiography and a story of self-transformation. As already mentioned, George's narrative is unusual and closer to typical later texts in its overt description of slaveholders' violence in its opening paragraphs. Historical conditions and his own initiative made him a pioneer in many ways. After a first escape from slavery and then Native captivity, he was sold again to white masters. He was still an illiterate slave when he was converted by another slave. In 1773, however, he became a cofounder of Silver Bluff Baptist Church in South Carolina, "North America's first black church" (Walker 1992, 74). Here he also began to preach. When his "Antiloyalist" (George 2002, 182) master forbade visits from the regular preacher (for fear of unwanted information reaching his slaves as the war approached), George began to minister himself to the community of over thirty, "the first slave in that position" (Walker 1992, 75).

In a manner later echoed by Frederick Douglass, he relied on white children to acquire literacy:

> I proceeded in this way till the American war was coming on, when the Ministers were not allowed to come amongst us lest they should furnish us with too much knowledge. The Black people all around attended with us, and as Brother Palmer must not come, I had the whole management, and used to preach among them myself. Then I got a spelling book and began to read. As Master was a great man, he kept a White school-master to teach the White children to read. I used to go to the little children to teach me a, b, c. They would give me a lesson, which I tried to learn, and then I would go to them, again, and ask them if I was right? The reading so ran in my mind, that I think I learned in my sleep as really as when I was awake; and I can now read the Bible, so that what I have in my heart, I can see again in the Scriptures. (George 2002, 181–2)

Despite George's excitement over this new possibility, the previous sentence also draws our attention to the primacy of the spoken word in his life and work. As D. Bruce Hindmarsh comments, "the oral and the personal was anterior to the written and the discursive elements in his experience. Indeed, George's phrase for many of his meetings with his people emphasized the oral context: they met 'to hear experiences'" (2005, 331).

We have the testimony of contemporaries attesting to George's impressive capabilities as an entrancing speaker (Walker 1992, 75–6). One is by Thomas Clarkson, who had never "heard the Psalms, sung so charmingly, in my life before" (qtd in Walker 1992, 75). When whites prevented George from preaching in Shelburne upon his arrival there, "I began to sing the first night, in the woods, at a camp … The Black people came far and near, it was so new to them: I kept on so every night in the week … and those poor creatures who had never heard the gospel before, listened to me very attentively: but the White people, the justices, and all, were in an uproar" (2002, 183). In his further career as a preacher, George would experience a fair share of antagonism. Whites resented his baptizing other whites, destroyed his house, and threatened him in his meeting house ("But I stayed and preached, and the next day they came and beat me with sticks, and drove me into a swamp" [185]). Blacks in Birchtown also resented him for proselytizing among other religious communities. Yet even when he temporarily lost the use of his frostbitten legs and had to be moved on a sledge, George persevered as a preacher and leader of his community.

In late 1782, George was among the first to arrive in Nova Scotia (Pybus 2006, 145). He was also a leader of the exodus of 1792. His name opens the "List of the blacks in Birch Town who gave in their names for Sierra Leone in November, 1791" (Walker 1992, 12). Like King, George describes the voyage to Africa in his account, and both continued preaching in Sierra Leone. Both were invited for a period to England,[49] where their narratives were recorded. Both took part in many of the turbulent events of the Sierra Leone settlement, first under John Clarkson as governor and then under the commercially oriented and reckless Sierra Leone Company.[50]

African Diaspora, Nova Scotia, and Modernity

The lives of these black diasporic subjects at the end of the eighteenth century link Nova Scotia with Virginia, South Carolina, New York, England, and often Sierra Leone in a web of black Atlantic circulation. Some of these texts document a back-to-Africa movement[51] that preceded projects like those of Martin Delany in the nineteenth century (discussed below) or Marcus Garvey in the twentieth. Intimately related to the abolitionist movement, they are foundational testimonies of a transnational and transcultural black Atlantic. As such, these narratives speak to a wide array of contexts and concerns that are crucial to modernity. As we have seen, these areas include their relationship to oral forms of testimony and literary forms such as spiritual autobiography and the captivity narrative. They concern early American and Canadian literature, but also the wider moment of Romanticism. Finally, these texts appear at a decisive stage of modernity, shortly after the American and around the time of the French Revolution, and emerge against the wider background of capital accumulation and imperial competition at this important moment of the Industrial Revolution.

In a fascinating chapter entitled "Romanticism and Abolitionism," Helen Thomas examines cross-fertilizations between spheres that allowed different discourses of captivity and freedom to interact and often draw on related resources. She highlights the important link "between the discourse of racial and gendered inequality in its employment of abolitionist rhetoric" that is provided by Mary Wollstonecraft, and she examines "the discourse of the spirit employed by Romantic writers, including Wordsworth, Coleridge and Blake" (H. Thomas 2000, 86) in relationship to "radical dissenting Protestantism"; this perspective strengthens a "juxtaposition between

Romantic writing and the autobiographical narratives by African slaves published in England" (83). While both groups performed "an inscription of a self-authorized sociohistorical self," their goals of liberation differ: "Whereas the language of radical dissenting Protestantism provided the Romantics with convenient tropes of metaphorical captivity and liberation, the narratives by the slaves registered the very real experience of transportation and enslavement and carried with them overt political messages of emancipation" (84).

The chapter demonstrates myriad links as well as telling erasures that connect the work of many now canonical Romantic writers with slavery and the slave trade. Thomas further points out that while Romantic authors in England often wrote for an intimate circle of friends and acquaintances, slave narratives "were on the whole aimed at a wider audience as a means of providing financial support for their authors and advancing abolitionist ideology" (84–5). Many of them "were immensely popular" (85). Their works were reissued in multiple editions on both sides of the Atlantic, as we have seen in the case of Marrant's *Narrative* (Gates 1988, 142; Gould 2007, 21).[52] Given the importance of these texts and contexts, Thomas points to revisionist scholarship that has "extended the study of Romanticism to the wider contexts of colonialism, education, racial policy, imperialist practice and international trade" (83).

The spiritual autobiographies, captivity, slave, and travel narratives authored by Marrant, George, and King also worry accounts of Canadian literature. The recognition of these works requires canonical change, and highlights the transnational roots of this national literature. Although these texts are relevant for any account of Canadian literature, their inclusion is mostly recent and occasional.[53] The timeframe of their publication coincides with that of the important travel and exploration narratives by Samuel Hearne (1795), George Vancouver (1798), and Alexander Mackenzie (1801).[54] Like some of these and the earlier exploration texts by Jacques Cartier, Samuel de Champlain, and the accounts in the *Jesuit Relations*, some of these black texts offer travel narratives and thematize encounters with First Nations populations.[55] As settler narratives, they precede the canonical texts by Catharine Parr Traill, Susanna Moodie, and other examples of early Canadian literature such as Oliver Goldsmith's "The Rising Village" (1825 and 1834) or Nova Scotia judge Thomas Chandler Haliburton's sketches beginning with *The Clockmaker* (1836).

Like many other travel and captivity narratives, of course, the narratives by Marrant, George, and King owe their publication to reader interest and other contexts in England. As itinerant, diasporic, and marginalized subjects, their authors may not seem promising candidates for prominent roles in Canadian national narratives. Like other authors published initially in England and later deemed canonical in Canada, however, they are Canadian pioneers who carve out their astonishing careers against incredible odds. Their story has a rightful place alongside other foundational figures. With respect to Harry Washington, the Africa-born slave of George Washington who joins the British, moves to Nova Scotia, and from there to Sierra Leone to become an elected community leader, Cassandra Pybus remarks: "An unlettered African man whom George Washington acquired … could have no role to play in the foundation narrative of the American Republic. Or could he? Surely, it is not utterly incongruous to set beside the story of the revered father of America an alternative story of the African man he had purchased to dig ditches. At the heart of both narratives lies a commitment to the transforming ideals of liberty and self-determination" (2006, xv). Similar remarks can be made about the role of these black Nova Scotian ministers with respect to Canada. In addition to working with oral testimony, they have left us written accounts of their experiences and of Nova Scotia that deserve a place in Canadian literary history.

The contextual relationships between Romanticism and early black narratives were close. These black texts also altered the relationship between Romanticism and early Canadian literature, usually envisaged with reference to the Canadian Confederation Poets publishing after 1880. In addition, and in keeping with the revisionist reflections on English Romanticism cited above, they placed important foundational moments of Canadian literature directly in contexts of imperial competition and expansion, which were intimately related to the growth of black diaspora. They brought early Canada into view as a node in transnational webs of transatlantic and hemispheric connections premised on contexts of slavery, race, and emancipation, inescapably interwoven with the foundational narratives of modernity.

The English interest in black subjects after the American Revolution – which facilitated the publication of the black Nova Scotian narratives – was thus related to contexts and developments that also helped prepare the ground for English abolitionism in the 1780s. These circumstances and events included Mansfield's 1772 decision against slavery on English soil, the 1775 Dunmore Proclamation promising freedom for black support in the American war, and finally the need, after the humbling British defeat against slaveholding colonies, to consolidate a battered national self-image through moral superiority. As Christopher Leslie Brown argues in *Moral Capital*, when Thomas Clarkson came to write *The History of the Rise, Progress, and Accomplishment of the Abolition of the African Slave Trade by the British Parliament* (1808), he provided an influential interpretation of the anti-slavery movement that was also a vindication of British morality and international leadership after a lost war. In Clarkson's interpretation of events, the "campaign for the abolition of the slave trade demonstrated and proved that civilized peoples, like the British, could achieve moral progress. British primacy in the war against barbarism reaffirmed the nation's place at the apex of refinement of virtue" (C.L. Brown 2006, 5). The "insistence on the selfless quality of British actions" provided even in the twentieth century "a compelling origin story for the modern empire as well as its ideological defense. It displayed Britain as the purveyor of civilization, justice, and order" (8). Brown shows that the actual motives and decisions by various actors in the years leading up to "the founding of the Society for Effecting the Abolition of the Slave Trade in 1787" (19) were complex and diverse. His consideration of "moral capital" complements other explanations of the anti-slavery movement, such as those by Eric Williams,[56] yet relates in important ways to North American contexts.

The idea that "material benefit might be sacrificed for moral satisfaction," Cassandra Pybus writes, marks a "significant shift in British thinking" (2006, 105). After Mansfield's decision in the *Somerset* case, British intellectuals were led "to an intensified self-scrutiny about the imperial enterprise, in which complicity in slavery was seen to have sullied the moral character of the nation. As tension with the American colonies mounted, these men began to articulate views about slavery that would distinguish the British from the slave-owning American colonists … The notion that slavery was an institution inconsistent with British law and repugnant to British sensibility was increasingly voiced as an index of national virtue, especially in the face of ignominious defeat. [Granville] Sharp went so far as to suggest that the disastrous war was a form of divine punishment for Britain's complicity in the slave trade" (Pybus 2006, 105).[57] Sharp received further ammunition for the abolitionist cause as events surrounding the Zong massacre strengthened the case for moral rather than economic perspectives on the slave trade. He subsequently took on an important role in the Committee for the Relief of the Black Poor.

The committee was founded in 1786 in response to the visible indigence and suffering of those black former allies in the war who found themselves in increasing numbers, not in Nova Scotia or other faraway parts of the

Empire, but in London. In this context, there originated a plan to found a settlement in Sierra Leone to alleviate their plight (Pybus 2006, 105–19); this was seen by others, however, as mainly an attempt to rid London of their presence.[58] After the near failure of the settlement and the foundation of the Sierra Leone Company in 1791, the request of Nova Scotian settlers for relocation – offered directly in a petition by their emissary Thomas Peters – solved the company's problem of finding new settlers (144–9).

Important chapters like the evacuation of blacks to Nova Scotia, as well as their subsequent part in the story of the "Province of Freedom" of Sierra Leone, can be understood in the light of genuine British support for black subjects and humanitarian philanthropy.[59] But they were also a response to a need for "moral capital" after the lost war and the 1783 Treaty of Paris. In any case, the desire for moral certainty and superiority that strengthened early abolitionism facilitated as well the self-determination and mobility of black constituencies like those settling or transiting Nova Scotia after the war. The accumulation of moral capital – closely related to the accumulation of financial capital before and during the Industrial Revolution[60] – was one of the links that made Canada part of an international, transatlantic, and hemispheric theatre in which imperial competition played out both materially and symbolically. This context included slavery, but it also included the abolition of the slave trade and eventually of slavery itself.

As part of this transatlantic and hemispheric story, John Graves Simcoe – a supporter of abolition as a British member of Parliament before his arrival in North America and then Upper Canada's first lieutenant governor – passed the 1793 Act against Slavery in the Upper Canada Legislative Assembly. He did so against the resistance of its slaveholding members. These developments helped to prepare the ground for the subsequent Underground Railroad; they influenced the course of Canada's nineteenth century and made it an important site of black experience and cultural expression. Despite the often racist realities that greeted blacks in eighteenth-century Nova Scotia and nineteenth-century Upper Canada alike, this context set the stage for the emergence of Canada's flattering self-image as a purely benevolent black Canaan.

3

The Black Canadian Nineteenth Century

Black Canadian writing in the nineteenth century continued to relate Canada to black Atlantic, North American, and hemispheric contexts. Increasingly a space for new black settlement, Canada was also a significant node in diasporic and imperial circulation that defined black transnational geographies and Canada's own national and cultural emergence. Like the eighteenth-century black works relating to Nova Scotia, the body of black writing that was produced in Upper Canada/Canada West in the nineteenth century belongs in any canon of black Atlantic or Canadian literature and culture. This work is important as a crucial space of black testimony and self-transformation. It also serves as a necessary corrective to the portrayal of blackness in other texts. I will first offer a brief survey of the period before abolition in 1834, then look at a now canonical settler writer like Susanna Moodie to show how the work of a non-black author is marked by the important black presence that helped to define Canada at that time.[1] Moodie's case is all the more intriguing because of her own past as an abolitionist editor in England. In the subsequent two sections I will discuss the heart of black Canadian writing in the nineteenth century. This work was produced in the years prior to and after the United States Fugitive Slave Act in 1850, an event that resulted in a significant increase of the black population in Canada. I cover a substantial number of authors and texts, paying particular attention to the writer, editor, feminist, educator, and cultural critic Mary Ann Shadd. She played a crucial role in this context after her arrival in Canada in 1850.[2]

As a consequence of the War of 1812, about 2,000 Black Refugees joined the existing black population in Nova Scotia (Winks 1997, 114–41; Whitfield 2006).[3] Few black texts, however, originated there in the nineteenth century.[4] Instead, developments in Upper Canada provided the background for a substantial production of black writing, which accelerated with the second Fugitive Slave Act in 1850. The most visible early legislative development was Simcoe's Act against Slavery in 1793, occasioned by the threat of the cross-border selling of slaves. But despite initially good intentions, the Act represented a compromise that "freed not one slave" (Winks 1997, 97). In Frank Mackey's words, "As originally envisaged by Simcoe, [it] was aimed at abolishing slavery; as adopted, its immediate aim was to stave off the moment of abolition" (2010, 77). Simcoe's Act determined that children born into slavery after 1793 were freed at the age of twenty-five. More importantly with regard to the migratory flows that it began to enable, the Act stopped the importation of slaves to Upper Canada (Winks 1997, 98). Any slave arriving in Upper Canada was now deemed free.

Less known than the subsequent Underground Railroad to Canada is a smaller reverse movement of the remaining Upper Canadian slaves to neighbouring Vermont, New York, Ohio,[5] and other free territories.[6] It contributed to the further decline of slavery in Canada. In Lower Canada, the courts began to render slavery impractical. According to one report, a Montreal court, transposing Mansfield's verdict creatively to the colonies, decided in 1794 that "slavery was not known by the laws of England and therefore discharged the Negro man" (Mackey 2004, 26). In particular Montreal Chief Justice James Monk, probably influenced by the *Somerset* case, during which he was in London (Mackey 2010, 48), repeatedly decided in favour of black subjects who contested their enslavement in courtrooms, beginning with the case of Charlotte in 1798 (Mackey 2004, 26–30; 2010, 36–78; Winks 1997, 100–2). While Lower Canada never legislated against slavery, the last slave sale took place in 1799. Slavery ended a few years later in the face of increasing flights and court-supported freedom of former slaves (Mackey 2010, 69–71).[7] By contrast, "slavery in Upper Canada, sanctioned by the statute of 1793, went on until the 1820s" (Mackey 2010, 71). Even before the official abolition of slavery in 1834, however, "the combination of legislative and judicial action had so severely limited its growth, applicability, and confidence as virtually to end the practice by the 1820s throughout the provinces" (Winks 1997, 110).

As a consequence, black immigration occurred in particular in areas closest to the border in Upper Canada, supported by some degree of protection from extradition.[8] In the 1820s, black immigrants brought tobacco to the area around Amherstburg, across the border from Michigan (Silverman 1985, 23–4). Events that threatened free blacks in the United States contributed to this migration.[9] One of these instances led to the first of several black settlements in Canada in the following decades, occasioning subsequent texts by two of the participants in this enterprise. When Cincinnati decided to enforce the Ohio black code in 1829 (Winks 1997, 155; Ripley 1986, 2:9), a group of blacks supported by Quakers founded the short-lived settlement of Wilberforce near London in Upper Canada. It would fail in 1836.

Israel Lewis, a former slave, an emissary of the Ohio group to Upper Canada, and then a disgraced collection agent for Wilberforce,[10] would publish *Crisis in North America: Slavery, War, Balance of Power, and Oregon* in Montreal in 1846.[11] Austin Steward, the president of Wilberforce, with whom Lewis jousted in court in 1833 over money and accusations of theft, later presented his side of that story in his own, substantial slave narrative, *Twenty-Two Years a Slave, and Forty Years a Freeman: Embracing a Correspondence of Several Years, While President of Wilberforce Colony, London, Canada West.*[12] Published in Rochester, New York, in 1857, the narrative attests to the realities of slavery and the dangers of re-enslavement in New York State, where in 1813 Steward left his master and later witnessed an extradition and an attempted re-enslavement in Rochester (chapter 14). When slavery ended in New York in 1827, he described happy celebrations that included making his own speech for the occasion. The Cincinnati race riots two years later and the subsequent black exodus, however, induced him to visit the new settlement in Canada, which consisted of "a few rude log cabins" (Steward 1857, 180) and, at his suggestion, was named Wilberforce.

Although "unaccountable gloominess and forebodings of evil took possession of my mind" (Steward 1857, 183), Steward moved his family there. In his narrative's first chapter – dedicated to his new life and entitled "Roughing It in the Wilds of Canada" – he describes clearing land for his farm and contending with wolves and bears. Much of what follows, however, is taken up with the description of troubles with Lewis and his associates, including attempts on Steward's life (chapter 29). Besides offering an account of the infighting and corruption that eventually led to the failure of the settlement (Winks 1997, 62–6),[13] Steward's text is also interesting ethnographically, since it works as a relay of other narratives. For instance, the text offers an encapsulated narrative by two other fugitives from Virginia, one that he claims to tell "as 'twas told to me" but actually delivers in the third person and with novelistic techniques in chapter 23. He also presents the often comic (though linguistically stereotyped) narrative of a Native who escaped slave-like treatment after being driven from his farm, a story that gives Steward occasion to express his thoughts of solidarity in the face of exploitation shared by blacks and Natives (chapter 26).[14]

Despite his own negative experiences, Steward describes Wilberforce and the new settlers' farming in this area as proof of the possibilities of black achievement under conditions of freedom (Steward 1857, 202). He also draws attention to the rights of blacks in Canada – such as to run for office – and he expresses satisfaction with being "elected township clerk, with all the responsibility of the office resting upon him and the same power given him as though he had been born in Her Brittanic Majesty's dominion, with a face as white as the driven snow" (261). From his vantage point in 1857, Steward would offer the following endorsement of Canada as a space of black self-transformation:

> The knowledge I have of the colored men in Canada, their strength and condition, would cause me to tremble for these United States, should a war ever ensue between the English and American governments, which I pray may never occur. These fugitives may be thought to be a class of poor, thriftless, illiterate creatures, like the Southern slaves, but it is not so. They are no longer slaves; many of whom have been many years free men, and a large number were never slaves. They are a hardy, robust class of men; very many of them, men of superior intellect; and men who feel deeply the wrongs they have endured. Driven as they have been from their native land; unprotected by the government under which they were born, and would gladly have died, – they would in all probability, in case of a rupture, take up arms in defense of the government which has protected them and the country of their adoption. England could this day, very readily collect a regiment of stalwart colored men, who, having felt the oppression of our laws, would fight with a will not inferior to that which actuated our revolutionary forefathers.
>
> And what inducement, I ask, have colored men to defend with their lives the United States in any case; and what is there to incite them to deeds of bravery? (Steward 1857, 321–2)

Indeed, Steward poses the question of moral capital, which we have seen delineated by Christopher Leslie Brown in the context of British abolitionism, and he connects abolition to sustainable claims of national integrity, black allegiance, and the possibility of war. A few years before Civil War erupts south of the border over slavery, Steward's comment underlines the extent to which the black Canadian nineteenth century was not only a site crucial for black possibility and Canadian national difference, but also integral to nineteenth-century North America as a whole. Black Canadian participation in the American Civil War was one of the concrete consequences of similar opinions, which Steward evidently shares with others.

It is perhaps remarkable that such a statement came not even thirty years after Steward's own first entry into Canada and his description of some destitute "fourteen or fifteen families" (Steward 1857, 185) huddled in a few log cabins in the woods. Steward was soon followed by others. In 1830, one year after the founding of Wilberforce, Josiah Henson entered Canada. He would become one of the leaders of another black settlement, at Dawn, and the author of one of Canada's most famous slave narratives (see the discussion of Henson below). In 1831, Thornton and Lucie[15] Blackburn fled from slavery in Kentucky; after their arrest in Detroit and escape to Canada two years later, they avoided extradition and later launched the first cab service in Toronto (Winks 1997, 169; Ripley 1986, 5; Frost 2007, 163–90). Their stories, however, emerged only later. The first edition of Henson's narrative did not appear until 1849, and no testimony by the Blackburns themselves exists; Karolyn Smardz Frost reconstructs their lives in a volume published in 2007. Despite these particular silences at the time, 1831 was a "watershed for abolitionism in the northern United States" (Frost 2007, xviii).[16] That year also saw the publication of two slave narratives co-authored by one of the most important writers of nineteenth-century Canada; she would move there in 1832.

A FORMER ANTI-SLAVERY EDITOR IN CANADA: SUSANNA STRICKLAND AND THE SLAVE NARRATIVES OF MARY PRINCE AND ASHTON WARNER

Susanna Strickland met John Wedderburn Dunbar Moodie, her future husband, in the home of Thomas Pringle, the secretary of the Anti-Slavery Society of England and editor of the *Anti-Slavery Reporter*. Here she also became the amanuensis of Mary Prince, a former slave from Bermuda, who was employed at this point by Pringle and whose narrative she readied for publication in 1831. The first meeting would lead Susanna Strickland Moodie to emigrate to the New World, where she became the quintessential chronicler of English Canadian settler experience; she would later be identified by Canadian literary history as one of its foundational figures. Her meetings and collaboration with Mary Prince, on the other hand, made her the immediate narratee (Whitlock 2000, 12) and partial shaper of the first published slave narrative in English by a woman. Susanna Strickland's role as amanuensis for Mary Prince and then for St Vincent–born Ashton Warner, whose slave narrative was also published in 1831 in London, is thus a thread in the web of Empire that connected the Caribbean, Canada, and London via routes of trade and travel as well as the black Atlantic. This thread also raises questions with respect to Moodie's subsequent work as one of Canada's foundational and canonical authors, the construction of Canadian whiteness, and the omission, until recently, of black connections in Canadian literary historiography.

Prince's account of her slave experience in Bermuda, Turks Island, and Antigua appeared three years before emancipation in the British Empire, and as a female slave narrative, it preceded by almost twenty years Sojourner Truth's *Narrative* (1850) and by thirty years Harriet A. Jacobs/Linda Brent's *Incidents in the Life of a Slave Girl* (1861).[17] It details her relatively unharmed childhood in Bermuda as well as her experience of multiple owners, brutal floggings, and sexual abuse. Prince gives an account of her work under appalling conditions in the salt ponds on Turks Island and then of her slave life in Antigua, where she joined the Moravian congregation and learned to read. Eventually her owners took her to London, where she realized she was technically free. She was also threatened by destitution, however, and re-enslavement if she returned home. Through the Moravian Society she connected with the Anti-Slavery Society and thus with Pringle, who eventually employed her. The society recognized the potential impact on other similar cases and petitioned Parliament, unsuccessfully challenging Prince's re-enslavement in Antigua should she return (see Sharpe 1996, 37; Whitlock 2000, 10–12; M. Ferguson 1997, 3–23). Prince's narrative was occasioned by the abolitionist campaign in England and thus evokes several black Atlantic contexts[18] and can be placed in relation to others. In a circum-Caribbean perspective, for instance, it appeared after the Spanish East Florida papers from 1784 to 1821 (see Landers 1999 and chapter 2) and Robert Wedderburn's *The Horrors of Slavery* (1824),[19] at the time of the 1820s and 1830s fiscals' reports, and a few years before Juan Francisco Manzano's *Autobiogafía de un esclavo* (1840) and James Williams's 1837 apprentice narrative that triggered the investigation and termination of the apprenticeship system.[20] Its year of publication, 1831, also saw the "largest slave rebellion in the British West Indies," the "Christmas Rebellion" led by Samuel Sharpe in Jamaica (Fisch 2007, xvii) and, in North America, Nat Turner's slave rebellion in Virginia,[21] two years after David Walker's militant *Appeal* called for armed resistance. In 1831, William Lloyd Garrison, inspired by Pringle's editorship of the *Anti-Slavery Reporter* (Sinanan in Fisch 2007, 66), also launched his own anti-slavery paper, *The Liberator*, and published what has been called the "first political manifesto written by a black woman" (M.W. Stewart 1987, 8). Influenced by Walker, "Religion and the Pure Principles of Morality, The Sure Foundations on Which We Must Build" (1831) was the first text by Maria W. Stewart, a free black woman considered "the first known African American female political writer as well as the first of her color to speak her mind on political matters to what was then called 'a promiscuous audience,' that is, an audience of men as well as women" (Andrews 2003, 3).

The year 1831 thus marked the publication of two pioneering texts by black women. While Stewart's text was written by Stewart herself, however, Prince's narrative was the result of her collaboration with Strickland and Pringle at the latter's residence in London, a context Gillian Whitlock calls the "writing scene at Claremont Square" (2000, 22). The outcome was a "hybrid quality of the text" (Whitlock 2000, 21). An increasingly substantive discussion has probed Prince's agency despite the constraints placed on the narrative by the necessities and conventions of abolitionist discourse and the English slave narrative.[22] In this particular case, some of the choices made in the published narrative are illuminated by alternative accounts of some of the incidents by Prince herself and by witnesses in a subsequent court case involving Pringle and Prince's owner. Sharpe, who contrasts the narrative with this material and other contexts, argues that slave tactics "are difficult to detect in the slave narrative, not only because they lack a language of their own, but also because they are overwritten by the moral discourse of the antislavery movement" (1996, 46). Referencing Toni Morrison's reminder about the omissions and "forgettings" in slave narratives necessitated by reader expectations (Morrison 1995, 91, qtd in Sharpe 1996, 32), Sharpe points out that instances of sexual abuse by Prince's owners are either omitted or transformed into accounts more acceptable to the readership of her narrative, such as Prince's refusal to wash her master on Turks Island (see also M. Ferguson 1997, 10). Further, Sharpe points to "a parallel narration of emancipation, beginning with [Prince's] religious conversion and ending with her appeal to English people" (Sharpe 1996, 40), which includes, however, also "more protracted and circuitous means by which Prince negotiated greater autonomy from her owners" (43). These attempts to increase her possibilities of agency ran counter to the "antislavery requirement to demonstrate that Prince was a decent and hardworking Christian woman" (42).[23] As a result, "much of the information Prince gave Strickland regarding her sexual relationships with free men was expunged from the published version of her *History* [*of Mary Prince: A West Indian Slave*]. Inasmuch as Pringle imposes silences upon Prince's sexual relations," Sharpe writes, "he effaces an unsavory aspect of slave culture that black women turned to their advantage" (44).[24]

Whitlock pays more particular attention to Susanna Strickland's role in the process of establishing the narrative. After all, Strickland was "in every sense Prince's foil: the white English woman who is able to embody the precepts of femininity, domestic respectability and innocent womanhood, an Englishness that casts Prince as 'the other woman'" (Whitlock 2000, 17). Strickland was also "a young, unmarried woman recently converted to Methodism," who appears to Whitlock as an "innocent scribe" (20). As we have seen, however, there were other reasons for the exclusion, or displacement, of certain elements, and Whitlock emphasizes that it was not in the narrative proper, but "in Pringle's supplementary materials that the issue of Prince's relationship with a white man in Antigua is discussed and rationalized … The amanuensis does not copy these sections of the text. The section which Prince and Strickland do produce together is a strictly policed first-person narration, with no sexually compromising material" (2000, 20).[25] However, not only did Strickland necessarily participate, either actively or as witness, in this aspect of shaping the content of the *History*; she also performed the primordial stage of its linguistic transformation from an oral testimony into a written slave narrative.

Pringle's introductory discussion of the editorial process states that "the narrative was taken down from Mary's own lips by a lady who happened to be at the time residing in my family as a visitor. It was written out fully, with all the narrator's repetitions and prolixities, and afterwards pruned into its present shape; retaining, as far as was practicable, Mary's exact expressions and peculiar phraseology. No fact of importance has been omitted, and not a single circumstance or sentiment has been added. It is essentially her own, without any material alteration farther than was requisite to exclude redundancies and gross grammatical errors, so as to render it clearly intelligible" (Prince 1997, 55). While the statement seeks to convey the impression of authenticity by stressing orality and immediacy ("from Mary's own lips"), the mention of "repetitions and prolixities" "afterwards pruned" and of the required exclusion of "redundancies and gross grammatical errors" points to the opposite and comes to join the indications of alteration at the level of content. We already know that despite Pringle's claim that "no fact of importance has been omitted," he himself in the "Supplement to the History of Mary Prince" discusses material that does not appear in the *History*. The subsequent court proceedings record Prince as saying that she "told all this to Strickland when that lady took down her narrative," and they note further that these "statements are not in the narrative published by the defendant [Pringle]" (Prince 1997, 148). If the content is thus subject to selection and emphasis, however, a process of filtering and transformation necessarily also takes place at the level of the signifier, as Pringle himself makes clear when he states that "*as far as was practicable*, Mary's exact expressions and peculiar phraseology" have been retained (emphasis added). As Midgley observes, "The result, with its standard English, ordered arrangement and selective exclusions, was well suited to appeal to the British public, but had doubtless lost some of the immediacy of Prince's original account" (Midgley 1992, 89).

In light of these indications, how literally can one take Susanna Strickland's own account of her role in composing the *History*? In a letter from late January 1831, she maintains that "I have been writing Mr. Pringle's black Mary's life from her own dictation and for her benefit adhering to her own simple story and language without deviating to the paths of flourish or romance." While she thus downplays, even effaces, her role as a co-creator of the text and claims her writing to be transparent with respect to Prince's account and language, Strickland nonetheless points to the omission of her contribution in the slightly ironic added sentence "Of course my name does not appear" (Moodie 1985, 57; qtd in Whitlock 2000, 18). Indeed, apart from Pringle's reference to his house visitor, the later mention of "this history, that my good friend, Miss S—, is now writing down for me" (Prince 1997, 94), and her naming in an appendix to the third edition,[26] Strickland's presence is not marked in the text.

She also often remains entirely invisible or largely unattended to in later critical commentary. Sandra Pouchet Paquet thus states that Prince's "narrative retains a qualitative uniqueness that is distinctly West Indian, distinctly a black woman's, and distinctly a slave's" (Paquet 1992, 131), and that the *History* "uses and privileges a black West Indian speaking voice" (133). At the same time, she alerts us to the restrictions of the editorial process and emphasizes that the text is "transcribed, pruned and edited for publication"

(133), citing Henry Louis Gates to say that such texts stand "at the crossroads of 'the black vernacular and the literate white text, of the spoken and written word, of oral and printed forms of literary discourse'" (Gates 1988, 131; qtd in Paquet 1992, 133). As Sharpe points out, however, this is a complex passage from oral to written, since "Prince probably spoke patois, the creolized speech of slaves that combined English, Spanish, French, and West African languages" (Sharpe 1996, 38).[27] Strickland employs a few techniques to evoke orality directly (such as quoted speech) but does not attempt here to imitate vernacular expression. Given the editorial comments by Pringle and the diction and language registers utilized in the text ("my obedience to her commands was cheerfully given" 58; "but oh! t'was light, light to the trials I have since endured," 58), it is not unproblematic to claim that we are in the unmediated presence of Prince's language. In the introduction to the 1997 edition, Ferguson does give Strickland a place, yet her comments on an "inimitable flair for language" concerning a passage "in Mary Prince's own words" (Prince 1997, 6) have the effect of making the transcribed language seem entirely transparent. While Prince by all accounts seems to have been entirely capable of effective linguistic self-affirmation in her interactions, at least an assumption of a "multi-accented" language is needed in the case of the transcribed *History*. The text's final direct appeal to the reader and to Prince's own experience of slavery justifies Ferguson's comment that "in the final persuasive oration, Mary Prince's lively style of speech comes into its own" (15). An editorial note introducing this passage (presumably by Pringle, though implying input by the transcriber Strickland), however, underlines conspicuously that various gradations of linguistic mediation have produced the very text we read: "The whole of this paragraph *especially*, is given *as nearly as was possible* in Mary's precise words" (93, emphasis added). Other passages, we infer, are given less directly in Prince's "precise words," and even this paragraph approximates them only "as nearly as was possible," begging the question what the criteria of possibility may have been and what a more literal transcription might have rendered.[28] We do not truly know Prince's account "in her own words." Even before being edited by Pringle, the text is already a result of both Prince's account and Strickland's writing, the outcome of what Arnold Krupat calls "bi-cultural composite authorship" (1983, 262), although that term says nothing about the inequality of power and the specific roles of the contributors.[29] This of course does not diminish the importance of Prince's *History*. It clearly implicates Strickland, however, in its composition. Giving Strickland credit for her work at the same time sharpens our attention to aspects of Prince's testimony that exceed, in terms of both content and expression, the limits of acceptability mediated by the "writing scene at Claremont Square" (Whitlock, 2000, 22).

Attention to Strickland's role in the production of the *History*, however, also raises questions about her subsequent writing career in Canada. Like Prince earlier, she became a migrant, transatlantic subject. Even if she had begun writing with a British audience in mind, she now had readers on both sides of the Atlantic. What trace does her experience with slavery leave in her new work? In a letter from April 1831, Prince is mentioned as a participant in Strickland's wedding to John Wedderburn Dunbar Moodie, prior to her departure from England: "Mr. Pringle 'gave me' away, and black Mary, who had treated herself with a complete new suit upon the occasion, went on the coach box, to see her dear Missy and Biographer wed." According to the same letter, she sent her correspondent "twenty copies of Mary's *History*, and 2 of *Ashton Warner*" with a request for dissemination, speaking also of her now diminished interest in literary pursuits (Moodie 1985, 60–1). Her departure, of course, only prefaced her extensive writing career in Canada. This stage of Strickland's work has been little examined, especially with regard to the convictions she would lay out so forcefully in her introduction to Ashton Warner's *Negro Slavery Described by a Negro: Being the Narrative of Ashton Warner, a Native of St. Vincent's* (1831), published this time under her name and editorship.

The story of Ashton Warner has some similarities with that of Prince, although he describes brutalities mainly not experienced by himself but committed against fellow-slaves. Believing himself free as a result of the manumission of his mother, but re-enslaved by a new estate owner, he escaped from St Vincent. Like Mary Prince, he was free in London, though left with a choice between destitution in England or re-enslavement under the Colonial Law at home. Also like Prince, he was able to have his narrative transcribed by Strickland, but he died in a hospital in London just before it appeared in print. The imprint of the "writing scene at Clarendon Square" also pertains to his narrative. As Pringle had done in Prince's narrative, Strickland intervenes repeatedly through the use of notes, especially to assure the reader that the words in particular passages are Warner's "own expressions" (Warner 1831, 43). In the introduction, we again find a statement concerning language that is similar to Pringle's in Prince's *History*; here, Strickland states that she has "adhered strictly to the simple facts, adopting, whenever it could conveniently be done, his own language, which, for a poor person in this condition, is remarkably expressive and appropriate" (Warner 1831, 15).

In other regards, however, Strickland's introduction is far less concerned than is Pringle's preface with assuring the audience about authenticity and much more concerned with delivering a direct anti-slavery message, regardless of her audience's possible reactions. The introduction opens with an aggressive attack on her social peers, charging "a very numerous class of well-educated persons" with "criminal ignorance" concerning "the system of slavery existing in our colonies" (Warner 1831, 2). Strickland admits having herself been, only months earlier, one of "the apathetical and deluded class I am now animadverting upon" and, owing to her trust in the popular press, having "never given the subject much serious thought, still less imagined that I was a sharer in a great national crime" (6). Her introduction amounts to a personal conversion narrative concerning slavery:

> The entire change in my own ideas, in regard to slavery, was chiefly effected by the frequent opportunities which Providence recently and unexpectedly threw in my way of conversing with several negroes, both male and female, who had been British colonial slaves, and who had borne in their own persons the marks of the brand and the whip, and had drank the bitter cup to its dregs. To their simple and affecting narratives I could not listen unmoved. The voice of truth and nature prevailed over my former prejudices. I beheld slavery unfolded in all its revolting details; and, having been thus irresistibly led to peruse the authentic accounts of the real character and effects of the system, I resolved no longer to be an accomplice in its criminality, *though it were only by keeping silence regarding it.*[30] (Warner 1831, 10–11, emphasis added)

What would become of this glowing commitment to the anti-slavery cause after this auspicious beginning and after her significant contribution to the publication of these two important slave narratives? In the same year, Moodie indeed published a story against slavery set in the Cape Colony, "The Vanquished Lion."[31] Her refusal to remain silent about slavery, however, may sound hollow to readers mainly familiar with Moodie's most heralded work, the Canadian settler narrative *Roughing It in the Bush, or, Life in Canada* (1852).[32] A certain split between Moodie's anti-slavery avowals in this passage and her later relative silence on the subject comes to join the "violent dualities" that Margaret Atwood locates later in the split between Moodie's commitment to, and rejection of, Canada.[33] Moodie does speak out against slavery in a few later works, though mostly briefly and in problematic ways. Critical interest in Moodie as a foundational figure of Canadian literature, with some notable exceptions, has either sidelined or entirely ignored the role of blackness in her work, together with the significance of that aspect of her writing for Canadian literature.

Blackness in Moodie's Canadian Texts

Slavery figures most extensively in "Richard Redpath," published in installments in the Montreal *Literary Garland* in 1843 and reprinted in 1854 in Moodie's *Matrimonial Speculations* (Moodie 1985, 88, 98n3; Thurston 1996, 97–9). Set in Jamaica under slavery, it strongly condemns the practice; yet the story raises questions about Moodie's convictions and her writing by thematizing slavery in a romantic comedy with blackface elements. The English title character and his brother, counselled by their impoverished father to renew the family fortunes by investing in Jamaica, lose their last goods in a shipwreck near the Jamaican shore and find themselves reduced to indigence. A number of elements in the story parallel Moodie's own settler predicaments. As John Thurston observes, in this period she is "preoccupied with plotting solutions to economic dilemmas related to her own" (1996, 95). The decline of fortune that leads to the brothers' Jamaican adventure (Moodie 1854b, 167–9) thus resembles the genteel poverty the Moodies sought to avoid by emigrating (Whitlock 2000, 51).[34] The loss of capital upon arrival similarly echoes further reversals suffered by the Moodies shortly after their arrival in Canada.[35]

The transposition of these elements has striking implications. With respect to a later text, George Elliott Clarke has interestingly suggested that, given "Moodie's status as midwife to Prince's *History*, it may be possible to read *Roughing It*, intertextually with Prince, as a displaced 'slave narrative' of a genteel, pioneer English woman, toiling in the bush country of Upper Canada" (G.E. Clarke 2005c, 13).[36] A similar suggestion can be made for "Richard Redpath," except here the setting is shifted to slaveholding Jamaica and the likening of white genteel poverty to slavery is literalized shamelessly. In the face of economic adversity, Richard transforms himself via blackface into a slave and convinces his brother to sell him on the market.[37] In the blackface comedy that ensues, replete with racialist stereotypes, Moodie also uses simulations of the black vernacular – avoided in her transcriptions of Prince and Warner but already present in "The Vanquished Lion" – as comic devices. The story relies on other stock conventions and nineteenth-century repertoires, including the figure of the tragic mulatto,[38] sentimentalism, the pirate adventure story, comic confusion and revelation of identities, followed by a happy ending and multiple marriages.

Moodie also references her London anti-slavery experience and *The History of Mary Prince* when the kindly paternalistic slaveholder in the story is petitioned by his daughter, Miss Betsy, for the newly acquired slave: "I wish, dear papa, you would give him to me" (1854b, 185). In her correspondence, Moodie sometimes uses an alliterating phrase as an epithet of familial benevolence to refer to her benefactor and Prince's employer: "Papa Pringle" (e.g., Moodie 1985, 41). The slaveholder is made into a semblance of Pringle when he not only grants freedom but also becomes the father-in-law of his white "slave." In addition, in her *History*, Prince relates that as a child she "was made quite a pet of by Miss Betsey, and loved her very much. She used to lead me about by the hand and call me her little nigger" (Prince 1997, 57). These references, then, invoke images of family and kindness as attenuating aspects of slavery.

Given Moodie's earlier transcription of narratives that describe the realities of slavery graphically, such light-hearted intertextual references – let alone her use of slavery to provide interest for her romance – are surprising. Thurston comments that the fact that "Richard's 'slavery' leads directly to marriage with his master's daughter" and other elements raise the suspicion "that Moodie had little understanding of slavery" (1996, 208n28). Such an explanation begs the question as to what Moodie's own understanding of the narratives of Prince and Warner might have been. How seriously might she have taken the experiences they describe?[39] A split is made apparent by the fact that the story both condemns slavery in highly rhetorical modes but, at the level of content, also dallies with pro-slavery discourse that lauds the generally benign and "family-like" character of slaveholding relationships. What seems clear is that Moodie was willing to exploit any aspect of her experience for commercial success at this crucial moment in her career. Able to devote more time to writing after leaving the backwoods and moving to Belleville in 1840, Moodie experimented there with forms that could integrate her new experiences and offer ways to entice white audiences with exotic and, she hoped, new elements. As Richard's brother muses with respect to the proposal that is the conceit of the story, "The scheme had at least novelty to recommend it" (Moodie 1854b, 174).

The split between racialist stereotype and abolitionist rhetoric is also notable through Moodie's use of racialist and at times clearly racist stereotyping in another context, her portrayal of a Jewish editor. Based on the real-life antagonism between Moodie and a Belleville editor whom she transposes here to Kingston, Jamaica, Moodie's portrayal has partially comic purposes but is also adversarial, racist, and unequivocally anti-Semitic; in Thurston's words, it makes her political enemy "the butt of gratuitous anti-semitism" (Thurston 1996, 98; Moodie 1985, 88–9).[40] Moodie's portrayal of blacks frequently also amounts to caricature and stereotype, but here it is conjoined with resounding anti-slavery passages. Researchers have explored similar combinations of abolitionism and racialist stereotypes in Harriet Beecher Stowe's *Uncle Tom's Cabin* (e.g., Tompkins 1985; Riss 1994, 2006); Moodie combines the same and other elements in "Richard Redpath" and, like Stowe, does not seem to judge this figuration as disjunctive.

While the stereotypical portrayal of blacks in her text relates to racialist assumptions shared by much of nineteenth-century liberalism,[41] what is more specific to Moodie as a writer of British extraction is her desire to distance Britain as much as possible from the practice of slavery. Robert Redpath thus declares, "I was born and brought up in London, where no slaves are suffered to be kept, and never saw Jamaica before in my life" (1854b, 172–3). Positioning herself in ways that speak only indirectly to the North American present, Moodie emphasizes early on that she is dealing with slavery as an event in the British past. Introducing the slave market and the stock scene of black family separation, chapter 4 of her narrative begins: "It is full fifty years ago since the events here narrated took place, and the horrid traffic in human flesh was still carried on with the greatest vigour in the West Indian Islands. That disgusting scene of human depravity, the slave market, was enough to tame the sparkling vivacity of the younger Redpath" (177). Richard Redpath is portrayed as the archetype of good-natured decency and as a man with a deep trust in humanity. His innocence is emphasized again just before this trust is temporarily shaken by his experience of the slave market:

> He had never studied human nature under one of its worst and most degraded forms. Here he beheld the pernicious effects produced by a bad and immoral system – a system contrary to all laws, human and divine – upon the minds of a people daily familiarized to acts of cruelty, injustice, and oppression; the disgusting exhibition of

> brute force triumphing over helpless ignorance, of Avarice filling her coffers at the expense of human suffering, utterly regardless of the tears and agonies of its victims.
>
> Abhorred slavery! Well is it for Britain that she has wiped off this foul stain from her national glory. And blessed, doubly blessed, to all time and through eternity, be the names of the great and good men, who stood unflinchingly forth to advocate the cause of an oppressed and unhappy race. Most noble of all modern reforms, was that bloodless triumph of reason and Christianity over the selfish, grasping avarice of the tyrant man! (Moodie 1854b, 178)

Moodie cannot be blamed for mincing words about the horrors of slavery. The auctorial comment in the second paragraph, though, is offered from a post-emancipation point of view that puts the British practice of slavery safely in the past. Her condemnation of slavery is not concerned with Britain's past participation in the slave trade or its consequences – such as the continuing practice of slavery south of the border from where she writes – but serves mainly to endorse British moral superiority. As we have seen earlier, Brown's discussion of Thomas Clarkson's influential account of the British anti-slavery movement shows that his vindication of British morality along similar lines served later to support claims for international leadership (C.L. Brown 2006, 5). Moodie's writing from a British North American colony about slavery fits into that framework. But to what extent did this shoring up of British moral superiority intervene in the battle against actual slavery that surrounded Moodie in Canada?

One might expect more explicit reference to the continued existence of slavery as Moodie settled into her renewed writing career. In a reprinting of the story as part of her volume *Matrimonial Speculations*, which appeared in 1854 and thus after the passage of the Fugitive Slave Act and its consequences for Upper Canada, Moodie clarifies in a preface only that the original publication in 1843 precedes "Mrs. Stowe's inimitable work 'Uncle Tom's Cabin.'" She adds that the text was based on a story a West Indian merchant told her in 1832 about events that would have taken place around the turn of the century. Moodie further suggests in this preface "presented to the British Public" that the story merely "may serve to while away the tedium of a 'juicy day'" (Moodie 1854b, 151).

"Richard Redpath" was first published in the 1840s and is thus one of Moodie's earlier publications written after she left England. In 1850, however, the Fugitive Slave Act presented a stark reminder of North American slavery. That year, reprints of Moodie's abolitionist poem "An Appeal to the Free" – originally published in 1830 in England – appeared in the *Literary Garland* (Thurston 1996, 59, 191n36). While an address to "Ye Children of Britain" might have also hailed Canadians in this new context, the reference to "such deeds as are done in the West" retained the poem firmly in the context of its creation in earlier British abolitionism.[42] More interesting are the new, autobiographical texts begun in the mid-1840s (Peterman 1983, 83), in which Moodie deals with her emigration and her experiences in Canada. One of these is "Trifles from the Burthen of a Life," published serially in the *Literary Garland* in 1851 (Thurston 1991, xx). Sending a longer version to her publisher that would appear as *Flora Lyndsay* in 1854,[43] Moodie informs him that it was originally written as the first part of *Roughing It in the Bush* (Moodie 1985, 130; qtd in Thurston 1991, xxi). "Trifles from the Burthen of a Life" deals in some passages with slavery and makes reference to *The History of Mary Prince*. Like "Richard Redpath" (also reprinted in *Matrimonial Speculations* in 1854), however, it displays the "caricaturing of blacks combined with a condemnation of slavery" (Thurston 1996, 209n28).

The main character defends the humanity of slaves against a slaveholding fellow traveller, the wife of a minister who maintains that if "they had immortal souls and reasoning minds, we should not be permitted to hold them as slaves. Their degradation proves their inferiority" (Moodie 1991, 227). Her further expression of concern that emancipation "will involve the West Indies Islands in ruin" prompts Moodie's protagonist to identify herself as the author of "The History of Mary P—." She defends its authenticity, but not without first delivering an impassioned response: "May He hasten their emancipation in his own good time. It were better that the whole group of islands were sunk in the depths of the sea than continue to present to the world a system of injustice and cruelty, that is a disgrace to a christian community – a spectacle of infamy to the civilized world. Nor think that the wise and good men, who are engaged heart and hand in this holy cause, will cease their exertions until their great object is accomplished, and slavery is banished from the earth" (228). As in "Richard Redpath," high-flying abolitionist rhetoric is conjoined here with a stereotyped and pejorative portrayal of a black individual. The first appearance of the interlocutor's slave is described in the following terms: "At this moment a young negro lad, fantastically dressed, and evidently very much in love with himself, strutted past." He is said to be swaggering along, "rolling his jet black eyes from side to side, and shewing his white teeth to the spectators, by humming some nigger ditty" (217). His owner is heard to say, "That boy is very pert … this is the effect of the stir made by the English people against slavery. The fellow knows that he is free the moment that he touches the British shores – I hope he will not leave me, for he saves me all the trouble of taking care of the children" (217). Yet the narrator herself only pities the children in the care of this "black imp," who remains the only black person portrayed in the text.

While *Richard Redpath* and "Trifles" refer to Caribbean slavery, somewhat familiar to Moodie through her dealings with Mary Prince and Aston Warner, subsequent texts begin to reflect the impact of slavery on her new Canadian surroundings, intensified by increased black immigration after 1850. Only one reference to these events appears in Moodie's best-known work, *Roughing It in the Bush* (1852). The sketch "The Charivari" is explicitly concerned with the experiences of immigration and cultural difference, including colonial practices such as the charivari.[44] Moodie's British-born neighbour begins an account of what amounts to a lynching with these words: "There was a runaway nigger from the States came to the village and set up a barber's poll, and settled among us. I am no friend to the blacks; but really Tom Smith was such a quiet, good-natured fellow, and so civil and obliging, that he soon got a good business" (Moodie 2007, 140–1). While ambivalence governs the account of this woman, who esteems the barber's civility despite her own racism, violence erupts when the barber marries a white woman. He is submitted to a charivari by some "young fellows" who, in the words of the neighbour, are "indignant at his presumption and her folly," with "some of the young gentlemen in the town" joining "the frolic" (141). Instead of being asked for ransom as is usual in a charivari, however, he is dragged out of his house and killed.

Criticism until recently has concentrated on Moodie's disapproval of the often violent and "heathenish" practice in the colony of the charivari as such (Thurston 1996, 152).[45] Moodie's sketch clearly thematizes the question of race, however, when the English-born neighbour's visit is immediately followed by the visit of an American neighbour. Yet it turns out that the issue of race is debated here mainly with reference to servants and class. It is used by Moodie against what she perceives as Yankee disrespect for her own class. When faulted for not eating with her white servants, Moodie counters this American republicanism attack on British class difference by blaming the American for not sharing her table with a black servant. In the ensuing debate about Christian behaviour and racial equality, Moodie seems to gain the moral high ground by deploying a superior interpretation of Scripture. In fact, though, she mainly succeeds in demonstrating her opponent's inconsistency: she too shuns her servant's company at the table. Cultural inferiority and class difference are the obstacles for Moodie, while it is race for the neighbour. The contrast seems to establish Moodie's British cultural and moral superiority, but without telling us what she herself would do with a black servant.

The sequence of these two episodes in the sketch is also relevant. The account of the lynching, partially submerged as one of several examples of colonial charivari violence, is immediately followed by the episode demonstrating American racial bigotry. While Moodie does not make the connection explicit, the sequential arrangement clearly conveys the impression that the second episode is a comment on the racial aspect of the first. Paradoxically, an incident of Canadian racism and racially motivated violence is here deployed by Moodie to reinforce her critique of American racism, helping her to express both her British resentment of the colony and her feelings of British North American superiority over Yankee republicanism. While she clearly rejects racial violence, her strategy seems mainly aimed at shoring up British moral capital. Yet the argument that Christian equality should transcend race becomes compromised and ambiguous when class enters into the equation.

Moodie's subsequent *Life in the Bush versus the Clearings* (1853) exhibits racial ambivalence that is directly occasioned by the reality of black immigration to Canada West, especially after 1850. The text contains two contrasting references to black fugitives from the United States. Moodie first offers her opinions on the consequences of the Underground Railroad, tellingly in the context of her chapter about the famous criminal Grace Marks (re-imagined later as the eponymous character of Atwood's *Alias Grace*). Contrasting peaceful Belleville with "Hamilton and Toronto, where daring acts of housebreaking are of frequent occurrence," Moodie engages in racist sensationalism and generalizations when faced with black immigration from the United States: "The constant influx of runaway slaves from the States has added greatly to the criminal lists on the frontier. The addition of these people to our population is not much to be coveted. The slave, from his previous habits and education, does not always make a good citizen. During the last assizes at Cobourg, a black man and his wife were condemned to be hung for a most horrible murder, and their son, a young man of twenty years of age, offered the sheriff to hang his own father and mother for a new suit of clothes. Those who laud the black man, and place him above the white, let them produce in the whole annals of human crime a more atrocious one than this!" (Moodie 1853, 214).

Another passage renders a visit to Niagara, but offers a very different picture. Moodie here lauds the accomplishments of black waiters, although they also seem to belong to the group of blacks from the United States she condemns earlier in a roundabout way:

> It would have done Mrs. Stowe's heart good to have seen the fine corps of well-dressed negro waiters who served the tables, most of whom were runaway slaves from the States. The perfect ease and dexterity with which they supplied the guests, without making a single mistake out of such a variety of dishes, was well worthy of notice.
>
> It gave me pleasure to watch the quickness of all their motions, the politeness with which they received so many complicated orders, and the noiseless celerity with which they were performed. This cost them no effort, but seemed natural to them. There were a dozen of these blacks in attendance, all of them young, and some, in spite of their dark colouring, handsome, intelligent looking men.
>
> The master of the hotel was eloquent in their praise, and said that they far surpassed the whites in the neat and elegant manner in which they laid out a table, – that he scarcely knew what he would do without them. (Moodie 1853, 348–9)

The black immigrant appears here as a servant who must rely on white approval and employment and thus occupies a non-threatening position that seems agreeable to Moodie. With this hierarchy intact, Moodie has no problems ascribing even superiority in fields related to the services performed, although she also uses stereotyped generalizations.

The scene perhaps also receives her approval because it serves to stabilize Moodie's own sense of middle-class whiteness in British North America, and it helps to allay her genteel pioneer's fears of downward social mobility. Moodie's discussions of servants in North America and their disregard for class difference, in "The Charivari" and elsewhere,[46] but also her own carrying out of tasks as a backcountry settler that in England she would have considered appropriate only for servants, suggest the sudden and undesired permeability of the mistress-servant dichotomy in her life. With her situation somewhat alleviated in the Belleville years when she wrote *Life in the*

Bush versus the Clearings, the Niagara tableau of cheerful black servants and "the politeness with which they received so many complicated orders, and the noiseless celerity with which they were performed," both contain her previously expressed fear of black immigration as socially disruptive and come to support her relational position of stabilized middle-class whiteness.

Clarke's suggestion that Moodie's writing evinces displaced elements of slave narratives (2005c, 13) would warrant further examination along the lines of Helen Thomas's readings of English romantics and their displacement of elements related to slavery and abolition.[47] Yet Clarke adds, "But such a 'stealth' reading must underline, again, the invisibility of the slave narrative in Canadian literature" (2005c, 13). We have seen important examples of Moodie representations of blackness[48] and of black border-crossers and immigrants from the United States; but what do the subjects portrayed have to say when they avail themselves of opportunities to render their settler experiences in print? After all, their experiences and writings, even more than Moodie's, provide insight into nineteenth-century Canada as a borderland of self-transformation in which, as Jane Rhodes has observed, "crossing the border was rarely an act of choice, and rather one of necessity" (2000, 178).

SLAVE NARRATIVES FROM ABOLITION TO THE FUGITIVE SLAVE ACT (1834–1850)

While the authors of slave narratives that speak of Canada have received some attention from historians and scholars of US literature, little attention has been paid to them until recently in Canadian literary contexts. They have been overlooked as authors of Canadian migrant and settler narratives and autobiographies, and indeed as Canadian nation-builders. It is a consequence of disciplinary focus and limitation that scholarship primarily concerned with US literature, despite all its hand-wringing over internationalization, has largely concentrated on these narratives only to the extent that they concern events south of the border. For Canadian literary studies, on the other hand, as George Elliott Clarke has put it, the "Canadian slave narrative is ignored as a genre of Victorian-era Canadian literature" partially because "North American slavery is so profoundly identified with the Great Republic that the slave narrative is eyed, in Canada, as … having only incidental and abstract engagement with British North America" (2005c, 7). It neither makes sense, however, to consider these border-zone testimonies of crossing and transformation in the isolated perspectives of subsequently emerged literary disciplines, nor is it meaningful to omit them from any of these fields, where they can serve as a site of disciplinary auto-critique. Clearly their production as relevant literary and documentary evidence invites us to reconsider some of the maps of nineteenth-century cultural expression in North America that remain predicated on whiteness.

Perhaps more importantly, however, these transnational texts speak to human and, here, specifically black hope, self-transformation, and possibility in the face of oppression and brutality. These texts, moreover, are indeed narratives of the border zone. They record shifting circumstances and perspectives on the self that are afforded by the transition from one set of conditions to another. Many of them also record a return of the escaped subject to the terrors of the slave territory in order to help others, be they family or, in some cases, strangers. The narrative of Moses Roper mentions proximity to his still-enslaved family as motivation for his settling in Canada; those of Lewis Clarke, Josiah Henson, and Henry Bibb all explicitly mention border-crossing rescue activities that carry the personal risk of re-enslavement. The life of Harriet Tubman, of course, while not recorded in a longer narrative by her, has become emblematic for this kind of engagement in the border zones.

The Narratives of Moses Roper and Lewis and Milton Clarke

In his introduction to *A Narrative of the Adventures and Escape of Moses Roper*, Ian Frederick Finseth notes that, after publication of the important slave narratives sponsored by British abolitionists in the eighteenth century and the successes of the movement in 1807 and 1833, "the primary battleground began to shift toward the United States" (2003, 25). Roper's narrative, written by himself at the age of twenty-one[49] and eventually going through "ten editions in twenty years, selling more than 20,000 copies" (Gould 2007, 24), was published first in London in 1837 and then in Philadelphia in 1838; that edition is hailed by Finseth as "an important reference point in a broader shift in antislavery publication toward an increasingly American readership" (2003, 33). William Andrews suggests that it is one of the works that are representative of the "beginnings of the classic fugitive slave narrative genre in the United States" (1986, 90).

Roper escaped North Carolina slavery and sailed first to England in 1835. He describes with calm but unrelenting directness the horrible violence he had experienced growing up under slavery. Shortly after his birth, his grandmother saved him from the hands of his master's wife, who wanted to stab him to death after learning "that I was white, and resembled Mr. Roper very much" (Roper 1848, 7). Together with his mother, he was sold shortly thereafter, but was then separated from her, flogged at age thirteen, and sold to numerous masters. Escaping several times, he was always brutally punished. While some readers, partly because of the seeming detachment of Roper's account, have critiqued his narrative as artless, Andrews points to his deployment of a typological – or what he calls "tropological" – mode in which former slaves project "their lives as secular figurations of scriptural *mythoi*" (1986, 62). Thus, in an important episode, Roper casts himself as Joseph – another former slave – hesitating to identify himself even to his own family. As Andrews suggests, Roper is pointing here, indirectly, not to the *black* but to the *white* side of his family that had betrayed him, and the reader is "exposed *by* the text" and implicated "morally in the role of the indifferent or estranging brother"; the text implies "metaphorically a standard of true brotherhood that can be appropriated by the reader" (95).

Early editions of Roper's narrative do not mention Canada. In an appendix to a later edition, however, he reports that he moved there in 1844 to remain closer to his family, still enslaved south of the border: "At the commencement of 1844, I left England with my family for British North America, and have taken up my future residence in Canada West, it being as near as I can get to my relations (who are still in bondage) without being again taken" (Roper 1848, 52). Roper returned several times to England to continue his extensive anti-slavery lecturing begun in the 1830s (Finseth 2003, 24). Preceding Frederick Douglass's narrative, Roper's account of perseverance in the face of multiple re-enslavements and brutal punishments not only provides "a powerful example of the indomitability of the human spirit" but also shows him in the process of becoming "the architect of his own destiny" (Finseth 2003, 29, 30). Canada seems to have become a safe staging ground for his further activities on behalf of his family, although no concrete activity on his part or escape of his family members to Canada is reported in the appendix or has come to light otherwise.

Several other black border-crossers, however, did report recrossing into the United States, often to engage in Underground Railroad activities on behalf of family members or others. One of them was Lewis Clarke, a Kentucky slave who escaped to Canada in 1841, despite the horror stories he had heard from slaveholders (Clarke and Clarke 1846, 40–1). His narrative, prefaced and transcribed by Boston minister Joseph C. Lovejoy and often using humour as a weapon against slavery (Andrews 1986, 138–9), only briefly reports that Clarke travelled to Canada and worked in Chatham

(39–43). He soon returned to the United States to find his escaped brother, Milton, in Ohio and to rescue his other brother, Cyrus, from slavery in Kentucky (48–59). Acknowledging his fears about returning to slave territory, he writes: "I knew it was dangerous, but I did not then dream of all that I must suffer in body and mind before I was through with it ... creeping round day and night ... in a den of lions, where, if one of them happens to put his paw on you, it is certain death, or something much worse" (48). Both the traumatic consequences of slavery and his own tremendous courage become apparent when he finds himself "again upon the soil on which I had suffered so much, I *trembled*, *shuddered*, at the thoughts of what might happen to me. My fears, my feelings, overcame for the moment all my resolution, and I was for a time completely overcome with emotion. Tears flowed like a brook of water ... I was now where every man I met would be my enemy" (49). His narrative was first published in 1845 and then again in 1846, together with that of his brother Milton. Clarke returned later to Canada to settle in Sandwich. He was one of the signatories of the "Report of the Committee on Emigration of the Amherstburg Convention" in 1853 (Ripley 1986, 270–5)[50] and was a co-founder of a "short-lived organization designed to aid fugitives in their transition to freedom" (277).

Josiah Henson, Dawn, and Black Education

Two other border-crossers who published important slave narratives between 1834 and 1850 also recrossed the Canada–US border to free family or fellow-sufferers and equally engaged in black Canadian institution-building designed to support fugitive slaves. Josiah Henson, as mentioned earlier, moved to Canada in 1830. He later took a leading role in the Dawn black settlement and its manual labour school, the British-American Institute, and its successor, the Chatham Wilberforce Educational Institute.

Henson's account is one of the best-known Canadian slave narratives. Through various editions, it displays the self-articulation and self-fashioning of a leading black Canadian in the nineteenth century, but also its mediation through abolitionist and commercial interests. Henson's life story first appeared in Boston in 1849 under the title *The Life of Josiah Henson, Formerly a Slave, Now an Inhabitant of Canada, as Narrated by Himself.* As the last part of the title intimates, the written version of Henson's narrative is the work of an amanuensis, the abolitionist and former Boston mayor Samuel A. Eliot. Henson himself describes the humiliating experience, soon after his arrival in Canada, of having to admit to his child that he could not read, although he subsequently acquired at least a rudimentary literacy (Henson 2003, 73–5). Increasingly identified – rightly or wrongly (see Winks 1997, 187–95) – as the model for Harriet Beecher Stowe's Uncle Tom, Henson was propelled to exceptional prominence. His text is a prime example of a slave narrative that becomes part of "commercial ventures" (Gould 2007, 23). The 1858 version, *Truth Stranger than Fiction: Father Henson's Story of his Own Life*, published by Stowe's Boston editor John P. Jewett, is more elaborate than the first edition,[51] contains chapter divisions, and is prefaced by Harriet Beecher Stowe herself. In an 1876 London edition, the narrative finally appears as *"Uncle Tom's Story of His Life": An Autobiography of the Rev. Josiah Henson (Mrs. Harriet Beecher Stowe's "Uncle Tom")*. The first Canadian edition – with the preface by Stowe and introductory notes by Wendell Phillips and John Greenleaf Whittier – was published in 1881 (Winks 2003, xxxi–xxxii).

Henson's story is important in its own right. He renders his conversion experience, for instance, and other important dimensions of his inner life by describing the thoughts he had in the face of moral and spiritual dilemmas. Henson explains why he decided to remain true to his master and not free a group of fellow-slaves when the occasion arose. He effectively succeeds in portraying himself as a reliable individual and blames his "unpardonable sin" of perpetuating slavery on his own ignorance, caused by "the degrading system under which I had been nurtured" (2003, 36–7). The climax of what Andrews calls the "morality play of Henson's life in slavery" (1986, 120) comes when he reflects on his temptation to kill his master while on a trip to be sold in New Orleans. At the decisive moment, he demonstrates that he values moral integrity and Christian redemption over his physical freedom. Henson's emphasis on his spiritual project of self-improvement commends him as trustworthy to the reader, as Andrews suggests, and Henson earns sympathy as a Franklinesque self-reliant individual who nonetheless looks out for others (121). The narrative thus delineates the various stages that slowly brought him to the realization that self-emancipation was necessary. He saw his fellow-slaves being sold and their families separated, he was cheated by his master while attempting to buy his freedom, and he was almost sold despite having saved the life of his master's son. The later editions include accounts of his Underground Railroad return trips into Kentucky to free others from slavery, and they expand significantly on his involvement and role in the Dawn settlement and the British-American Institute. He undertook numerous voyages on behalf of the settlement and its woodcutting operations, including a trip to the 1850/51 World Fair in

London, during which he met Queen Victoria. Crossing borders and waters like so many other black individuals and leaders in the eighteenth and nineteenth century, Henson led a life that illustrates the diasporic restlessness and mobility of the black Atlantic in many ways.

After Wilberforce, Dawn was the next in a series of black settlements in Canada prompted by the exodus from the United States. It was followed by William King's Elgin settlement in Buxton and then the Refugee Home Society (Pease and Pease 1963; Winks 1997; D.G. Hill 1981). Henson conceived of a black settlement project after his early experience in Canada. Dawn came into existence in 1842, beginning as a manual labour school. Established with the help of the "Lane rebel" Hiram Wilson and financially supported by the Quaker abolitionist James Cannings Fuller, the British-American Institute first opened its doors to twelve students.[52] Its mission was to serve the "Education Mental Moral and physical of the Colored inhabitants of Canada not excluding white persons and Indians" (Winks 1997, 180). The presence of the school helped to attract settlers to Dawn. The population eventually grew to over five hundred, and economic developments included the operation of saw- and gristmills and lumber sales (180). Despite its initial successes, however, the settlement ultimately failed because of inadequate management, infighting, and dubious accounting by several stakeholders. Wink's in-depth discussion of this process brings the inadequacies of Henson himself and of his narrative's version of these events to the fore (195–204). After the failure of Dawn, the proceeds from the sale of lands were used as endowment funds for the Wilberforce Educational Institute in Chatham (D.G. Hill 1981, 74).

One of the notable aspects of the British-American Institute was its emphasis on training in manual labour as the most pressing issue in black education at the time. Its curriculum was "to be conducted strictly on the manual labor system," and students "are to be trained thoroughly upon the full and practical discipline, which aims to cultivate the entire being, and elicit the fairest and fullest possible developments of the physical, intellectual, and moral powers" (Simpson 1970, 348; qtd in D.G. Hill 1981, 72). Henson's "demand for a primarily vocational school," as Heather Murray observes, "generated controversy in both his own time and since: did Henson underrate the intellectual capabilities of members of his own community, or was he simply alive to the hard realities and restricted possibilities that black settlers would face?" (2002, 63). Yet, the selection of manual labour training as the most appropriate program for black students contrasted with the vision promoted by the Presbyterian minister William King, who opened the Buxton Mission School as part of the Elgin settlement, initiated in 1849 and the most successful of the nineteenth-century black settlements in Canada.[53] At the Buxton Mission School, several "excellently trained young teachers from Knox Presbyterian College in Toronto gave the pupils a classical education" (D.G. Hill 1981, 83). The Buxton school produced a number of distinguished black leaders in Canada,[54] among them Dr Anderson Ruffin Abbott (discussed further at the end of this chapter). As "President of the Wilberforce Educational Institute from 1873 to 1880" (Abbott Papers, qtd in D.G. Hill 1981, 207), he promoted a literary and intellectual education, attracting "criticism not only from prejudiced whites sceptical of the intellectual abilities of the Black settlers but from members of his own community who considered his recommendations impractical, even impossible, for all but a small minority" (Murray 2002, 65). In the third chapter of *The Souls of Black Folk* (1903), W.E.B. Du Bois would famously critique the educational preferences for practical knowledge emphasized by Booker T. Washington, who served as the first principal at the Tuskegee Institute from 1881 onward. This better-known debate about black education in the United States was thus foreshadowed in the divergent practices and arguments that surrounded education in the black Canadian nineteenth century.[55]

Canada West and the Fugitive Slave Act of 1850: Harriet Tubman, Henry and Mary Bibb, and the North American Convention of Colored Freemen in Toronto

While questions of black education and settlement are posed by the "black utopias" – Wilberforce, Dawn, and the Elgin settlement – that sprang up in the 1830s and 1840s as a consequence of the black exodus to Canada, the plot would thicken with the Fugitive Slave Act in 1850. It updated and rendered more severe and consequential the first slave act, that of 1793, which had already "required that runaway slaves discovered anywhere in the United States and its territories be returned to their owners" (Frost 2007, 155). The Act was one of the five bills of the "Compromise of 1850," engineered by Kentucky senator Henry Clay in response to Southern furor over support for runaway slaves and intended to diffuse tensions between the North and the South. It effectively threatened both former slaves and free blacks alike. It was "not confined to state jurisdiction" and thus imperilled black "safety and freedom throughout the entire nation"; moreover, it arranged "legal fees for legal officers in the judging of fugitive slave cases" in such a way "that conviction of the Negro suspect was a more lucrative decision than his acquittal" (Pease and Pease 1963, 7). It also imposed stiff penalties for aiding fugitives and facilitated procedures to submit blacks to slavery.[56] As a consequence, it became "the single greatest impetus to African American migration to Canada during the antebellum period, effectively doubling the black population of what is now Ontario within a decade" (Frost 2007, 281). It has been estimated that the number blacks in Canada – ten thousand prior to 1850 – tripled in the following decade (Mensah 2010, 50; Krauter and Davis 1978, 44). According to the Anti-Slavery Society of Canada, there were already thirty thousand blacks in Canada in 1852, as Robin Winks reports in his summary of the various estimates, "How Many Negroes in Canada?" (1997, 484–96).

Harriet Tubman became one of the emblematic figures of this exodus and of the Underground Railroad in general. She escaped from slavery in 1849, the year Henson's first narrative was published. Tubman subsequently conducted numerous Underground Railroad expeditions. With Frederick Douglass's home in Rochester serving as one of the stops, many of these rescue missions ended in St Catharines in Canada. There, Hiram Wilson became a minister after his involvement with Dawn, and he provided a terminus for Tubman's operations (D.G. Hill 1981, 35–9). Sarah Bradford published an account of Tubman's life later in *Scenes in the Life of Harriet Tubman* (1869),[57] but Tubman herself provided a tantalizingly brief but concise narrative for Benjamin Drew's volume published in 1856 (to which we will return):

> I grew up like a neglected weed, – ignorant of liberty, having no experience of it. Then I was not happy or contented: every time I saw a white man I was afraid of being carried away. I had two sisters carried away in a chain-gang, – one of them left two children. We were always uneasy. Now I've been free, I know what a dreadful condition slavery is. I have seen hundreds of escaped slaves, but I never saw one who was willing to go back and be a slave. I have no opportunity to see my friends in my native land. We would rather stay in our native land, if we could be as free there as we are here. I think slavery is the next thing to hell. If a person would send another into bondage, he would, it appears to me, be bad enough to send him into hell, if he could. (Drew 2000, 30)

Tubman's opinions about slavery are crystal clear, as are her views on the ethics of enslaving other human beings; in her own life, she worked to effect the liberation of people from the living hell of slavery. Like Moses Roper, Lewis Clark, Josiah Henson, and, as we will see, Henry Bibb, she was among those who dared to return into slave territory to save others. The brief narrative published by Drew in 1856 was the first notice the public received of her existence, although her activities were previously known to a number of Underground Railroad stakeholders (Sernett 2007, 44). Strikingly, though, her brief 1855 account does not breathe a single word about frequent returns south – presumably so as not to endanger any railroad activities.

Franklin B. Sanborn's portrait of Tubman, published in an 1863 story in the Boston *Commonwealth*, introduces her as "Moses" to the wider public (Sernett 2007, 15, 46–7). According to Sanborn, her first rescue trip was undertaken in December 1850 to bring her niece from Baltimore to Philadelphia; then, in December 1851, she led a group for the first time to Canada West (56). There is some disagreement about the number of trips and rescued individuals. Sernett suggests that some of the often cited figures – nineteen trips and three hundred saved "passengers," for example – came from Sarah Bradford's account and the subsequent mythmaking surrounding Tubman. In his own accounting, the actual figures were perhaps closer to a dozen or so trips involving approximately seventy individuals (73–105). But it is clear that Tubman was an intrepid border-crosser and a daring Underground Railroad conductor. She was also noted by her abolitionist contemporaries for her capacity to hold any listener captive with her orally delivered accounts (48–54). The absence of written testimony about her conducting by Tubman herself only seems to have encouraged her later biographers' mythmaking.

Henry and Mary Bibb were two other important border-crossers who made Canada their base after the Fugitive Slave Act. These activists, while considering themselves expatriates rather than "permanent resident[s] of a new homeland" (Rhodes 2000, 178), played important roles in black Canadian organizing, publishing, education, and settlement. Henry Bibb, born in Kentucky of a white father and a slave mother, tells us that he was "educated in the school of adversity, whips, and chains" (Bibb 2005, xvii). Repeatedly, he escaped only to lose his freedom while pursuing liberty for his first wife and their daughter. He reached Canada for the first time in 1838 but was re-enslaved when he returned to the United States once again for his family. Free again, he eventually gave up his long and agonizing struggle for his family (Andrews 1986, 152–60). He recounts this decision towards the end of his influential *Narrative of the Life and Adventures of Henry Bibb, an American Slave*, which he published in 1849 while pursuing abolitionist activities in Detroit. The narrative mentions Canada, the "land of liberty" and "sweet land of rest" (Bibb 2005, 11), time and again as the motivation for his escape (e.g., 16–19, 22–9). Without offering any details, at some point Bibb asserts that, in fact, he "had been to Canada" (82).

It is only after the publication of his narrative and the passage of the Fugitive Slave Act in 1850, however, that he moves to Sandwich, Canada West, with his second wife, Mary, becoming a leading black organizer and editor. He was a founding member of the Anti-Slavery Society of Canada in 1851 (Frost 2007, 288); co-founded the Refugee Home Society north of Amherstburg, which bought and resold land to fugitives; and, with Mary Bibb, co-founded the *Voice of the Fugitive* (1851–53), Canada's first sustained black newspaper. Bibb's editorials promoted abolition, temperance, black education, and immigration to Canada (see Ripley 1986, 111n4; Stanton 2001). The *Voice of the Fugitive* also included accounts of refugee slave cases in the United States and of arrivals in Canada (Cooper 2000, 314). In addition, as we will see, the publication would serve as a platform in his feud with Mary Ann Shadd, who became increasingly critical of Bibb, the Refugee Home Society, and any form of black self-segregation in her own paper, the *Provincial Freeman*.

In two issues of the *Voice of the Fugitive* in August 1851, Henry Bibb called for a North American Convention to unite blacks in their fight against United States slavery and encourage black immigration to Canada. The gathering, which would take place at Toronto's St Lawrence Hall in September 1851, was one of the most important responses in Canada to the Fugitive Slave Act. While this response supported the black convention movement that had been underway since the 1830s, it began to shift the emphasis to black nationalism and was a clear expression of "emigrationism" to Canada.[58] The "Proceedings of the North American Convention," published in the *Voice of the Fugitive* on 24 September 1851 (repr. in Ripley 1986, 149–69), show that some of the most important abolitionists of Canada West and the northeastern United States were in attendance. They included Bibb, Henson, Martin Delany, and Toronto businessman Thomas Smallwood, who published his *Narrative of Thomas Smallwood (Coloured Man)* the same year; Hiram Wilson and the English abolitionist John Scoble were among the few white delegates. The convention minced no words, calling the "infamous fugitive slave enactment of the American Government … an insult to God, and an outrage to humanity, not to be endured by any people." While recognizing a dissenting minority that favoured continuing the fight within the United States,[59] the North American convention as a whole recommended emigration to Canada as the best chance blacks had "of making themselves and their offspring independent tillers of a *free soil*" (Ripley 1986, 152). It also held that the "establishment of exclusive churches and schools for colored people, contributes greatly towards the promotion of prejudice, heretofore unknown in the Canadas, and we do hereby recommend that all such organizations be abandoned as speedily as may be practical" (Ripley 1986, 155). The Garrisonian tenor of this recommendation would recur repeatedly in the writings of another major figure of the black Canadian nineteenth century, Mary Ann Shadd, who attended the convention with her father, the respected abolitionist Abraham D. Shadd (Rhodes 1998, 33–4; Frost 2007, 294–5). Shadd subsequently followed Henry Bibb's advice to open a school in Canada West, moving to Windsor in September 1851 (Rhodes 1998, 34–5, 234n22). Ironically, it was this very issue of resisting self-segregation that would lead to her eventual disagreements with Henry and Mary Bibb.

MARY ANN SHADD, CHATHAM, AND THE BLACK CANADIAN RENAISSANCE

The Black Canadian Renaissance

The texts and events discussed so far show the early contours of an "other" Canadian nineteenth century, one that remains underexposed especially in Canadian literary history (and is not perceived as such in US–related border studies or hemispheric studies). This nonetheless crucial domain is revealed and expressed in a literature that consists of black- and slavery-related texts of the period. The developments of the 1850s – including the Fugitive Slave Act and the 1857 *Dred Scott* Supreme Court decision, which denied citizenship to black Americans – vastly accelerated black immigration and brought some of the leading black intellectuals of the period to Canada. This migration led to an intensification of black and abolitionist activities, organization building, and publication activities. Earlier arrivals such as Josiah Henson were joined by Henry and Mary Bibb, the Shadd family, newspaper editor Samuel Ringgold Ward, emigrationist and black nationalist Martin Delany, and many others who moved to Canada in search of safety but also to promote transformation on a North American and ultimately hemispheric and transatlantic scale. The textual and cultural production facilitated by this concentration of highly motivated freedom-seekers in Canada, a group that included some of the best and brightest minds of the nineteenth century, was driven by a relentless desire for liberty and the unconditional appropriation of the full spectrum of human rights and possibilities, withheld by slavery and racial discrimination and their consequences. Collectively, the work of these writers, thinkers, and activists can rightly be called a Black Canadian Renaissance. This term signals a critical difference with regard to the "American Renaissance," a collocation mainly used to refer to a specific group of male white writers of the United States in the mid-nineteenth century; William Andrews has transposed that terminology to speak of a "parallel renaissance in Afro-American letters of the 1850s" in order to designate a critical counter-tradition, although his excellent discussion of Henson, the Bibbs, Ward, and other transnational black border-crossers of the nineteenth century quickly passes over their Canadian lives and often stops at the border.[60] I use the phrase "Black Canadian Renaissance" to signal a nineteenth-century effervescence of black writing and testimony that was transnational but written and rooted in Canada.[61]

This body of nineteenth-century cultural expression comprises a wide array of texts produced by former slaves and free blacks alike. These include slave narratives by Thomas Smallwood, the ministers Samuel Ringgold Ward and Jermaine Wesley Loguen, Austin Steward, Mahommah Gardo Baquaqua (who authored the only known longer Brazilian slave narrative while residing in Chatham), and over one hundred former slaves whose testimony was transcribed in Benjamin Drew's *A North Side View of Slavery*; the two newspapers, *Voice of the Fugitive*, edited by the Bibbs, and the *Provincial Freeman*, co-founded and edited by Mary Ann Shadd; Shadd's *A Plea for Immigration* and other writings; Martin Delany's texts of his Chatham period, among them the novel *Blake; or The Huts of America*; texts related to John Brown's raid on Harpers Ferry, such as the "Provisional Constitution and Ordinances for the People of the United States" and Osborne Anderson's *A Voice from Harper's Ferry*; and finally a large assortment of reports, pamphlets, letters, speeches, sermons, editorials, and other documents related to black experience and organization in Canada. Franklin Sanborn and Sarah Bradford's accounts of Tubman's life are related texts, as are, in more indirect ways, Harriet Beecher Stowe's *Uncle Tom's Cabin* and her novel *Dred*, based on William King and the Elgin settlement (see Levine 1997, 144–76).

The Black Canadian Renaissance thus signalled the production of an entire literature across diverse genres and with it an institution that included printers, editors, mechanisms of reprinting and plain pirating, implicit censorship by warring factions, authorization and authentification patterns, and a complex politics of reception and financial possibilities. To speak of a Black Canadian Renaissance is of course an interventionist act of strategic essentialism. Yet it helps to problematize both the notion of an American Renaissance – its exclusive concentration on white and male authors and willful forgetting of the transnational black and abolitionist dynamics of the period – and a number of discursive formations foundational to Canadian literary history, such as the concentration on prose by Haliburton, Traill, and Moodie, or a focus on the Confederation Poets.[62]

Mary Ann Shadd and Transformation: "We Can ... Change That Condition"

Early Interventions

Mary Ann Shadd stands out as a transformative figure in her own time. She is also key to reconfiguring the North American mid-nineteenth century from a perspective that includes the Black Canadian Renaissance.[63] She links a number of developments and other writers who were crucial to this cross-border transnational context. The daughter of prominent free black abolitionists, Shadd grew up in Wilmington, Delaware, and Westchester, Pennsylvania, near Philadelphia.[64] She set up her first school while still a teenager in Delaware (Rhodes 1998, 19). After her move to Canada, her emigrationist manifesto *A Plea for Emigration* and her editorship – as the first female black North American in that role – of the *Provincial Freeman* made her an active and visible participant in the debates about black priorities and strategies at a time when women were often not even allowed to be delegates at black conventions. Continuously challenging and overcoming limitations imposed by nineteenth-century gender roles, Shadd grew into a key player in the black Canadian 1850s context. She collaborated with a number of other leading intellectuals of her time, including Samuel Ringgold Ward and Martin R. Delany, and later edited the only account by a survivor of John Brown's raid on Harpers Ferry, Osborne Anderson. Although we have no full-blown autobiographical narrative that might have placed her earlier on the same plane as the better-remembered black authors who produced such accounts, her extraordinary role and career link her with Douglass and especially Delany, two of the "representative men" (Levine 1997, 1–17) and key figures vying for black leadership at the time.

Some of Shadd's most important convictions were visible early on. She entered the world of abolitionist publishing with two documents, a letter to Frederick Douglass printed in the *North Star* and her pamphlet *Hints to the Colored People of the North*. Both appeared in 1849 and thus prior to the Toronto convention, which would determine her subsequent career. Her letter to Douglass responds to his call for opinions about the situation of free blacks.[65] Shadd's opening words announce an orientation that marked her, at this point, as a "local" cosmopolitan, but in retrospect they can be interpreted as an earnest of her readiness to tackle any material and ideational limits that obstruct black liberation, equality, and progress: "Though native of a different State, still in anything relating to our people, I am insensible of boundaries" (Ripley 1991b, 4:31).[66] Equally significant, Shadd shows little respect for traditional black authority, including the black church. It must have come as a surprise to Douglass's readers to see a young black woman launching an all-out attack on black clergy:

> The influence of a corrupt clergy among us, sapping our every means, and, as a compensation, inculcating ignorance as a duty, superstition as true religion – in short, hanging like millstones about our necks, should be faithfully proclaimed … it does really seem to me that our distinctive churches and the frightfully wretched instruction of our ministers – their gross ignorance and insolent bearing, together with the sanctimonious garb, and by virtue of their calling, a character for mystery they assume, is attributable more of the downright degradation of the free colored people of the North, than from the effect of corrupt public opinion; for, sir, not withstanding the cry of prejudice against color, some think it will vanish by a change of condition, and that we can, despite this prejudice, change that condition. (Ripley 1991b, 4:32)

The black church would be a frequent target of Shadd's subsequent writing.[67] Her critique in this passage of black, internal self-colonization, however, clearly prioritizes black self-reliance, responsibility, and agency in overcoming oppression and prejudice. This dual emphasis would place Shadd firmly in an early black nationalist genealogy (F.J. Miller 1975, 94, 105–6; Rhodes 1998, xii), while at the same time making her a leading voice for the transcendence of colour lines, anticipating the perhaps inescapable but productive dualities of later black leaders like Du Bois.[68]

Shadd thus agreed with Henry Highland Garnet's proposal for "a Convention without distinction of caste … because by exchanging views with those who have every advantage, we are materially benefitted. Persons likely to associate with our people in such manner, are generally educated people, and possessed of depth of sentiment" (Ripley 1991b, 4:32). At the same time, however, she insists that "individual enterprise and self-reliance are not sufficiently insisted upon," expressing values that are later emphasized by Marcus Garvey or Malcolm X. Following ideas formulated earlier by Lewis Woodson, Shadd privileges agriculture as the most promising field of black enterprise: "Do you not think, sir," she addresses Douglass, "that we should direct our attention more to the farming interest than hitherto? … The estimation in which we would be held by those in power, would be quite different, were we producers, and not merely, as now, consumers" (32).[69] Critiquing the church's counselling of passivity in this world and hope for redemption in another, and rejecting dependence on whites, Shadd thus suggests that "the possibility of bringing about the desired end ourselves, and not waiting for the whites of the country to do so, should be impressed on the people" (33). But she is also impatient with the convention movement: "We … have been assembling together and whining over our difficulties and afflictions, passing resolutions on resolutions to any extent; but it does really seem that we have made but little progress, considering our resolves. We have put forth few practical efforts to an end." Four years after Marx notes, in the eleventh thesis on Feuerbach, that it is necessary not to interpret the world differently but "to change it," Shadd postulates that "we should do more, and talk less" (32).[70]

Shadd's idea of practice also includes a notion of theoretical critique as practical engagement. This emphasis comes to the fore time and again in her later editorials. In *Hints to the Colored People of the North*, Shadd proclaims it her "duty to myself … to expose every weakness, to exclaim against every custom that helps prolong our day of depression."[71] In the short passage that we have of the pamphlet, she denounces conspicuous black consumption and the display of sartorial wealth as social mimicry that most blacks cannot really afford: "We thought, in connection with professional men, as the whites had such, we should, as they do, make a grand display of ourselves; we should have processions, expensive entertainments, excursions, public dinners and suppers, with beneficial institutions, a display of costly apparel, and churches on churches, to minister to our vanity." For Shadd, coming herself from a relatively prosperous family but obviously educated in a tradition of thrift and hard work, such social scenes were reason for "our true friends [to be] sad at heart because of our weakness – this 'grasping at straws.'" Rhodes suggests that Shadd overlooks the social significance of such communal celebration and proposes that her condemnation "can be interpreted as a form of internalized racism" (1998, 23). Nevertheless, it is clear that effective transformation and change were of prime importance for Shadd.

Emigrationism and Canada

Shadd's decision to move to Canada in 1851 indicated her willingness to take decisive action. The Fugitive Slave Act of 1850 represented such a significant deterioration for blacks – even for free blacks in the northern United States – that it produced reactions from the entire spectrum of black opinion. In many cases, it led to a radicalization of positions, including coming to see violence as a legitimate response to the threat of personal danger and abduction into slavery. The law also gave new urgency to the debate about emigrationism, which we have seen play a role in eighteenth-century Nova Scotia and British abolitionist involvement in Sierra Leone. As a potential destination for US blacks, Sierra Leone was explored by James McKenzie, secretary of the African Society of Providence, in 1795–96 and later by Paul Cuffe, a mixed indigenous black Quaker and businessman, in 1811 (Park 2001, 9; F.J. Miller 1975, 15–53; Walker 1992, 284). These efforts failed.[72] The subsequent project of the American Colonization Society (established in 1816) to settle free blacks in the newly founded Liberia – and especially black resistance to this attempt – determined the shape of an early emigrationist debate (Ripley 1991a, 3:6–7). As Floyd Miller summarizes, "Whatever the exact mixture of benevolence and racism which characterized the Colonization Society at this time, most Afro-Americans viewed the organization as a deportation society whose members believed both in black inferiority and in the necessity of ridding the country of its free black population in order to preserve the institution of slavery" (1975, 54).[73] Emigrationism lost further steam with the Garrisonian turn, in the 1830s, from gradualist to immediatist positions on the abolition of slavery in the United States (F.J. Miller 1975, 90; Ripley 1991a, 3:8–12). Ripley points out that the "organized black abolitionist movement," of which Mary Ann's father, Abraham Shadd, became an important proponent, "grew out of the battle against colonization" (1991, 3:7).

As opposed to African colonization, however, emigration to Canada – although rejected by many black leaders (such as Douglass) as relinquishing the battle in the United States[74] – became not only an option but often a necessity after the Fugitive Slave Act. Henry Bibb thus touted Canada and Toronto as the location for a convention not only because of their proximity to the United States, but also in the name of safety: "We are satisfied that there is no spot in the United States where it would be safe or expedient to attempt to hold such a Convention. Under the existing state of things it would greatly endanger the liberty of thousands of self emancipated persons who would gladly meet with us on such an occasion. On the other hand, Canada is emphatically the only land of safety on the American continent for hunted refugees. She … protects the colored man in the enjoyment of that liberty with which he is endowed by the great Author of his existence" ("Call for a North American Convention," *Voice of the Fugitive*, 27 August 1851, 1). In addition, as opposed to African and other colonization projects that effectively removed free blacks from the struggle against slavery, emigration to Canada came to be seen by many black thinkers as a strategic move in the struggle for freedom in North America. Miller summarizes the position that had already been taken by Lewis Woodson in 1839: "To those who continued to reject any form of emigration and to insist upon the necessity of staying in the United States, at least partly on the grounds that free blacks must remain to aid those in bondage, Woodson replied that he would not conform to a policy he considered to be sheer folly … Woodson explained that free blacks who moved to Canada and the British West Indies would not be abandoning their brethren in chains. On the contrary, '*a colony of our choice*' … would also serve as an agent of liberation through the use of economic power" (F.J. Miller 1975, 100–1).

Shadd's distinction between emigration to Canada and African colonization was most emphatically expressed in her 1855 Philadelphia debate against J.C. Wears. The correspondent reporting the event in the *Provincial Freeman* (who signs with C.W.) describes the latter as "an unflinching opponent of emigration to Canada, or elsewhere." The article emphasizes Shadd's view that Canada was a site of human rights and black empowerment that projected a similar potential across the border while foiling African colonizationists who hoped for the removal of free blacks from North America:

> As to the slave and the fugitive being left in his chain and forsaken, she argued that it would be quite the reverse; taking the position that

> the colored man's increase of character, wealth, influence, education, &c., in Canada, where his manhood would be recognized, would afford opportunities to aid to a far greater extent than could be done under present circumstances; while poor, and unprotected, being obliged to fill menial occupations, with but poor pay, taxed heavily to support schools, public institutions, State and General Government; while Common School privileges are withheld, the right of franchise denied! without being allowed the slightest liberty or say, in making the laws by which he is ruled; besides being hourly exposed to the infamous fugitive slave law, and countless other outrages. With regard to colonization, her position was, that emigration would be just the antidote for that vile scheme. Though the colonizationists wanted to get rid of the black man, they had no wish or idea of his going to Canada, where he would occupy precisely the same position enjoyed by the whites, socially, politically, and religiously. Under those circumstances, their doctrines and aims would all be brought to naught.
>
> Also, by emigrating, she held up the idea, that in the event of the colored man's gaining power, being on the confines of the slave territory, he might, in a *time* of *need, be on hand to settle accounts with his oppressors*. ("For the Provincial Freeman," *Provincial Freeman*, 22 December 1855)

Shadd thus reiterated in 1855 a number of themes that recurred again and again in the debate of the 1850s, including the theme of the dual role of free blacks in Canada as living proof of the possible self-sufficiency and even prosperity of emancipated slaves and as a menacing Sword of Damocles over the United States. The very fact, however, that Shadd – a woman – was accepted as a debater at a public meeting signalled her reputation at this point, only a few years after her first published texts and her *A Plea for Emigration*.

A Plea for Emigration – *Shadd's Emigrationist Manifesto, Delany, and the Early 1850s*

Shadd's *A Plea for Emigration or Notes of Canada West, in its Moral, Social and Political Aspect: With Suggestions Respecting Mexico, West Indies and Vancouver Island, for the Information of Colored Emigrants* appeared in June 1852. An emigrationist manifesto, a settler guide, and an account of Canada

West, the text addresses primarily a black US audience. It was published in the same year that another settler narrative addressed a mainly British audience, Moodie's future Canadian classic *Roughing It in the Bush, or, Life in Canada*. As we have seen, Moodie mentions black immigration in only one chapter, in an account of a lynching. Also appearing in 1852 was the *First Annual Report* of the Anti-Slavery Society of Canada, founded in the previous year in response to the Fugitive Slave Act and the anti-black campaign by Edwin Larwill in Chatham.[75] Both Shadd's guide and the report describe various black communities and institutions in Canada; these accounts and the testimony of the earlier black narratives bearing on Canada challenge the elision of black experiences and writing in many previous accounts of mid-nineteenth-century Canadian life and letters.[76]

Shadd's call for black emigration from the United States, however, was also an explicit judgment on the United States that mapped out other Americas. Her text came at the height of the American Renaissance, with *its* simultaneous celebration and questioning of the United States. Shadd's reflection on blacks' emancipation and full participation in citizenship and democracy appeared two years after Hawthorne held the US Puritan past up to scrutiny in *The Scarlet Letter* (1850), one year after Melville's musings on democracy in *Moby Dick* (1851), and three years before Whitman would sing his America in *Leaves of Grass*. While some of the writers consecrated by F.O. Matthiessen's foundational *American Renaissance* (1941) dealt with blackness and slavery[77] – witness Emerson's and Thoreau's opposition to slavery, Queequeg's presence aboard the *Pequod* in *Moby Dick*, Melville's 1855 treatment of a slave revolt in "Benito Cereno,"[78] or Whitman's membership in the Free-Soil Party[79] – and while Matthiessen's account emphasizes the "devotion to the possibilities of democracy" (1941, ix) that united these writers, his pantheon does not include any black (or female) authors. It was later US literary revisionism that worked to recuperate the "repressed" of the American Renaissance.[80] The recovery of the slave narratives of Frederick Douglass and Harriet Jacobs as vitally important texts of the period occurs in this context, but also of Harriet Beecher Stowe's *Uncle Tom's Cabin* (1852).

In a black Canadian context, however, Stowe's novel is relevant not only as a literary response to slavery and the Fugitive Slave Act, but also as a text about emigrationism, intervening in a debate in which Shadd played a central role.[81] Beyond George Harris's flight to Canada, the question of emigration as a free choice is presented at the end of Stowe's novel by his decision to move with his family to Liberia.[82] This second step in his migration, although it is fleshed out only in Harris's epistolary explanation of his decision, provoked a substantial response from black intellectuals at the time, including an exchange of letters between Frederick Douglass and Martin Delany and a strong condemnation in the *Provincial Freeman*. The differences between these responses are instructive. The writer in Shadd's *Provincial Freeman* clearly supports her anti-colonizationist views in critiquing the character of George Harris: "The manner in which Mrs. Stowe disposes of him, and the words she puts into his mouth, as reasons for his going to Liberia, always struck us as a piece of needless and hurtful encouragement of the vile spirit of Yankee Colonizationism." Both Stowe and Douglass are assessed critically here, and Stowe's plot decision is even seen to align her with the "Slaveocrats": "Uncle Tom must be killed, – George Harris exiled! Heaven for dead negroes! – Liberia for living mulattoes! Neither can live on the American Continent! Death or banishment is our doom, say the Slaveocrats, the Colonizationists, and, – save the mark, – Mrs. Stowe!" (C.V.S., "George Harris," 22 July 1854). Douglass is attacked for his emphatic support of *Uncle Tom's Cabin* and the contradiction implied by that support with respect to his own anti-colonizationist position. An imaginary reader of Douglass charges him that

> that book of your idolatory … contains one of the strongest and best-put arguments for the colonization of yourself and the people of your race on the shores of Liberia that the world has heard for many a day. You might very well stand, Mr. Douglass, for Mrs. Stowe's George Harris; your complexion is alike, your intelligence is similar, your sense of wrong, and your mode of expressing it are sufficiently akin; but George Harris favours colonization, which you denounce as a 'nefarious scheme,' and determines to go thither, while you determine to stay here; and fortifies his determination by reasons and arguments which you, Mr. Douglass, and none of your co-laborers can refute or answer. (C.V.S., "George Harris," 22 July 1854)

Douglass is also criticized by Delany with respect to Stowe's novel. In an 1853 exchange of letters with Douglass (in Levine 2003, 224–37), Delany expresses his regret that Douglass promotes Stowe's work and ideas rather than those of a black leader – presumably Delany himself: "Why, in God's name, don't the leaders among our people make suggestions, and *consult* the most competent among *their own* brethren concerning our elevation?" (Levine 2003, 225). Delany of course had just published, to deafening silence from the anti-emigrationist Douglass, *The Condition, Elevation, Emigration, and Destiny of the Colored People of the United States*. Delany's text appeared in April, "several weeks after the publication of *Uncle Tom's Cabin*" (Levine 2003, 189).[83] Shadd's publication of *A Plea for Emigration, or, Notes on Canada West* followed in June 1852 (Rhodes 1998, 43). Her manifesto and settler guide were thus an integral part of a heated debate on emigration, especially relevant since she had previously been in direct contact with the main protagonists. As we have seen, Shadd published earlier in Douglass's *North Star*, and its co-founder Delany (associated with the paper until June 1849) was present at the Toronto convention (Sterling 1971, 160; Rhodes 1998, 33); he briefly acknowledges her *Hints* in his 1852 *Condition* (and will later work with her and the *Provincial Freeman* in Chatham).[84]

Shadd's place in this network underlines the fact that her role as an activist and author is crucial both to the "other" Canadian nineteenth century, signalled by the Black Canadian Renaissance, and the erstwhile repressed "other" side of the American Renaissance. This dual significance further points to an important connectedness and mutual implication of the two contexts. The extension of democracy that was signalled, for critics like Matthiessen, by the American Renaissance, was intimately linked to black writing in Canada. Indeed, Mary Ann Shadd, Martin Delany, and many other black authors wrote and worked in a Canadian context for such an extension of democracy and citizenship in all of North America. Since their labours are equally part of Canadian history, however, the trans-border and black Atlantic lives of many of these leading nineteenth-century black intellectuals also underline my claim that the bases of Canadian literary history are in need of revision.

Shortly after the publication of Delany's *Condition, Elevation, Emigration, and Destiny*, Shadd's *A Plea for Emigration* tackles a number of similar issues but often gives a very different analysis. These contrasts result from divergent views of how (and where) to achieve black "elevation" and self-transformation. Shadd sees these aspirations best served by the possibilities of black achievement and integration formally offered by British law in Canada; for Delany, "America's first 'Black Nationalist'" (Ullman 1971, ix), hope lay in black control in a separate political entity. The analyses outlined by Shadd and Delany in 1852 thus resulted in different strategies and geopolitical maps.

Delany also discusses the Canadas, albeit only in one chapter. He refers to his tour of Canada West in the autumn of 1851 and is positive about its climate and agriculture. But he objects to emigration to Canada on political grounds, because of "a manifest tendency on the part of the Canadians generally, to Americanism," which would open the door to US annexation. For Delany, "there is not a shadow of doubt" of such an outcome, "and our brethren should know this in time" (Delany 2004, 189).[85] Shadd did not share this opinion, but characterizes Canada as a safe haven under British protection.

Shadd adduces the "increasing desire on the part of the colored people, to become thoroughly informed respecting the Canadas … since that the passage of the odious Fugitive Slave Law has made residence in the United States to many of them dangerous in the extreme" (1852, iii).[86] Black US subjects were threatened not only by the Fugitive Slave Act and a "pro-slavery administration," she suggests, but also by the Colonization Society, which proposed to resettle free blacks in Africa. Delany also opposes the society, but his interest in Africa leads him to give a fairly extensive review of Liberia (chapter 18, Delany 2004, 177–88). Shadd, though, beyond condemning the society's attempts to have free blacks removed to Liberia, opposes any idealization of Africa with biting irony and cliché: "Tropical Africa, the land of promise of the colonizationists, teeming as she is with the breath of pestilence, a burning sun and fearful maladies, bids them welcome; – she feelingly invites to moral and physical death, under a voluntary escort of their most bitter enemies at home" (iii).

Shadd presents "British America," by contrast, as "a country equal, in extent, at least, to the United States" (5). She praises the fertility and the climate of Canada West, in particular, and collates detailed information from Frederick Widder's *Catechism of Information for Intending Emigrants of all Classes to Upper Canada* (1948), William Cattermole's *Emigration. The Advantages of Emigration to Canada …* (1831), and other sources.[87] Shadd discusses vital settler information under section titles like "Soil, Timber, and Clearing Lands," "Grains, Potatoes, and Turnips," and "Domestic Animals, Fowls and Game." Apparent objectivity, however, comes with clear valuation. Her landscape description can take on the tone of the tourist guide (Rhodes 43), and Shadd emphasizes "the superiority of many products" (1852, 7) or suggests that "the soil is unsurpassed by that of Kentucky and States farther south" (9). Her conclusion is unequivocal: "I firmly believe that with an axe and a little energy, an independent position would result in a short period" (10).

The true gist of Shadd's text, however, shines forth when she moves to social contexts. In sections on work, churches, education, and settlements, she repeatedly stresses integration and the absence of racial distinction after pointing out that, in a recently settled country like Canada, "there is much to do, and comparatively few for the work"; she goes on to claim that "no man's complexion [is] affecting his business. If a colored man understands his business, he receives the public patronage the same as a white man. He is not obliged to work a little better, and at a lower rate – there is no degraded class to identify him with, therefore every man's work stands or falls according to merit, not as is his color. Builders and other tradesmen, of different complexions, work together on the same building and in the same shop, with perfect harmony, and often the proprietor of an establishment is colored, and the majority or all of the men employed are white" (15–16). Shadd's account of the racial climate in Canada West is readily contradicted by other sources, such as the narrative by Samuel Ringgold Ward (see below; Silverman 1985), although Ward also emphasizes the possibility of legal redress for blacks in Canada. Instead of the often racist reality she had surely also experienced after a few months in Canada, however, Shadd seems determined to impress an ideal on potential black immigrants that is theoretically possible under Canadian legislation.[88] Her optimism can perhaps be attributed to a hope for a self-fulfilling prophecy, facilitated by massive black immigration, education, and self-sufficiency as the best antidotes to racism.

The subsequent topics of churches, schools, and settlements are also discussed with an emphasis on the absence of segregation. Shadd thus notes how in Toronto churches "the presence of coloured persons, promiscuously seated, elicited no comment whatever" (17). The black church, however, which earlier we have seen severely criticized by Shadd, also existed in Canada. Shadd admits that the "number of coloured persons attending the churches with whites constitutes a minority, I think. They have their 'own churches'" (17). Adding a Canada-specific component to her critique, she reiterates her previous attacks on the black church: "In her bosom are nurtured the long-standing and rankling prejudices, and hatred against whites, without exception, that had their origin in American oppression, and that should have been left in the country in which they originated" (18). If these institutions were necessitated by oppression in the United States, Shadd argues, they only re-inscribe limiting divisions that are obstacles no longer necessary in Canada. Similar issues recur in her discussion of education. "There are no separate schools" (19), Shadd states categorically. "At Toronto and in many other places, as in the churches, the colored people avail themselves of existing schools," she continues, before admitting, "but in the western country, in some sections, there is a tendency to 'exclusiveness.'

The colored people of that section petitioned, when the School Law was under revision, that they might have separate schools" (19). Shadd then quotes the 1850 Separate School Act to show that it offered choice; in reality, the Act was quickly used by whites to "justify racial segregation" (Rhodes 1998, 37).[89]

In her discussion of black settlements in Canada, Shadd concentrates again on segregation. She asserts that exclusive settlements encouraged "the attempt to identify colored men with degraded men of like color in the States … and as a consequence, estrangement, suspicion, and distrust would be induced" (22). Although Dawn and Elgin were de facto black settlements, Shadd defends them by arguing that they do not explicitly exclude white settlers (22). The Refugee Home Society, on the other hand, a settlement founded to sell land exclusively to fugitive slaves, is severely condemned by Shadd. Her critique launched her feud with Henry Bibb, the administrator of the society and the editor and printer of the *Voice of the Fugitive* (which became the society's official organ),[90] although Shadd later mentions both Bibb and his paper approvingly.[91] The dispute with Henry and Mary Bibb contributed to the closing of Shadd's school in Windsor in 1853;[92] at the same time, these differences motivated Shadd to publish her own paper, the *Provincial Freeman*. The venture had its beginnings in a meeting in 1852 (Rhodes 1998, 70), and the first issue appeared in March 1853.

Soon after her arrival in Canada, Shadd's arguments in *Plea* pitted her against the Bibbs and the *Voice of the Fugitive*, but with her preference for Canada and her insistence on racial integration, she also opposed important positions held by Delany. These differences also appeared in the geopolitical mappings envisaged by the two writers with regard to black emigrationist possibilities. For Delany, Canada would be an excellent choice for black settlers were it not for the threat of US annexation. Shadd, after reviewing political rights and giving a positive account of the "Thirty Thousand Colored Freemen of Canada" (1852, 30–4), comes to the conclusion that "no settled country in America offers stronger inducements to colored people" (36). While *Plea* is dedicated to this argument, the text does consider other possible sites for black emigration at the end. Here, Shadd's conclusions clearly differ from those of Delany in the several chapters he dedicates to the same exercise (Delany 2004, 177–203). Shadd's thoughts on resistance to slavery are focused on the protective force of the British Empire. She objects to the British West Indies, and in particular Trinidad and Jamaica, if blacks were only to go there to be employed on plantations; but she endorses black landownership in these locations because it would help to consolidate the protection afforded by the British Empire: "The vicinity of those islands to the Southern United States makes it necessary that they should be peopled by colored men, and *under British protection*; in short, that they should be British subjects" (1852, 36–7). Settlement of blacks in Jamaica is for her another way of strategically protecting Cuba and Haiti against United States expansionism (37). Similarly, Vancouver Island passes muster because it is under British protection and could be a check against "the encroachments of [American] slavery on free soil" (43). But Shadd excludes Mexico and Latin America, anticipating an imminent US takeover of the former, and rejecting the latter because of a lack of religious freedom and a dependence on "popery."

Delany, on the other hand, charted a different course. His direct connection with Douglass's anti-emigrationist *North Star* ended in 1849, though he is on record as opposing emigration as late as the 1851 Toronto convention (Ripley 1986, 152–3; in Levine 2003, 187–8). When penning *Condition* shortly thereafter, however, he concludes that emigration from the United States was necessary.[93] Rejecting Liberia and Canada, Delany points to Latin America as preferable location for black emigration: "Central and South America, are evidently the ultimate destination and future home of the colored race on this continent" (2004, 193). As a logical consequence, he reiterates an earlier call for blacks to learn Spanish.[94] At the same time – and his visceral dislike for Liberia notwithstanding – Delany continued to be interested in Africa; *Condition* thus also contains an account of an earlier plan for an East African expedition to explore additional emigration possibilities.

In her editorials for the *Provincial Freeman*, Shadd initially battled Delany's emigrationist views. When Delany announced a National Emigration Convention in Cleveland, Ohio, in 1854, black leaders such as Frederick Douglass objected that emigration weakened the anti-slavery forces in the United States. The *Provincial Freeman* published the announcement on 25 March 1854 but commented that the call did not include Canadians because it referred only to delegates from individual states (D., "The Emigration Convention"). The next issue, on 15 April 1854 contained Delany's request for a correction, but the same commentator now insisted that blacks in Canada had already "crossed the Rubicon" and therefore did not need an emigrationist convention. In the same issue, Mary Ann Shadd opposed

Delany's call much more directly in her editorial titled "A Word about, and to Emigrationists." While Delany initially identified "the West Indies, Central and South America, and the Canadas" as possible emigration destinations, the latter was later dropped when Delany argued that racial sympathy would welcome black emigrationists: "The West Indies, Central and South America – the majority of which are peopled by our brethren, or those identified with us in race, and what is more, *destiny* on this continent – all stand with open arms and yearning hearts, importuning us in the name of suffering humanity to come."[95] Shadd would have none of it; she maintained that racial solidarity was trumped by economic motives: "A man's dark color is no proof against prejudice. Should you labor for a livelihood, complexional identity will not save you. You will find colored nabobs as thick as hope, who will dispute every inch of ground with you, on the score of your pecuniary 'inferiority.' Colored men are as merciless as other men, when possessed of the same amount of pride, conceit and wickedness … Who would wish to be part of their exclusive nation; if one could be found outside of Central Africa, or inside of Hayti?" In particular, Delany's imperial assumption that any chosen destination was free to be settled and his for the taking met Shadd's justified ridicule:[96] "Know you not that men are there before you? Central and South America, Central Africa and Egypt, if you please, have as many great men now as they know what to do with. The black men of those countries want men to trim up their cane fields, at 3s 3d per day at the most, and find yourself. You can trim your own fields in Canada by paying 7s 6d an acre for the land, or another man's if you have not energy enough to have fields of your own, at better pay than that." Extending her negative assessment of Africa in *Plea* now to "Central America and other hot places," she describes them as problematic because of heat, illness, unpleasant animals, and a potentially hostile reception.[97] She rejects Delany's call for a separate black nation in favour of integration in a Canada that she daringly recodes as a "Colored British nation": "You *cannot* be a whole African Nation here brethren, but you can be *part* of the Colored British nation. This nation knows no one color above another, but being composed of all colors, it is evidently a *colored* nation. An integral part of this nation you can be, looking as tall or as short as your aims or efforts make you – nothing under the sun to prevent you" ("A Word about, and to Emigrationists," 15 April 1854).[98] Shadd's relationship with Delany changed as he repeatedly portrayed Canada as at least a temporary emigrationist solution; he finally moved with his family to Chatham, Canada West, in 1856, becoming a collaborator for the *Provincial Freeman*.

The Provincial Freeman: *Shadd, Gender, Ideology, and Transformation*

The *Provincial Freeman* was founded partially owing to Shadd's disagreements with Henry and Mary Bibb. A preparatory public meeting in late 1852 was promptly attacked in the *Voice of the Fugitive* as Shadd's machination to disguise her project as a communal one (Rhodes 1998, 70–1). The first issue appeared in March of 1853[99] and was followed by weekly deliveries from March 1854 onward; the last known issues of the paper date from January and June 1859 (see Rhodes 1998, 122, 129). Like most black papers at the time, the *Provincial Freeman* promoted abolitionism, temperance, and racial uplift; its hallmark was the simultaneous insistence on black self-reliance and opposition to self-segregation. The paper thus attacked Delany's call for black nationhood, critiqued Bibb's segregated Refugee Home Society, and denounced his "begging" for supposedly helpless fugitives. Shadd's belief in black agency and individual responsibility, which as we have seen she expressed from very early on, led to her fight against the image of helpless blacks in Canada. This rejection of passivity was also evident in her transgression of nineteenth-century concepts of a "women's sphere" that subjected respectable women, whether black or white, to a "cult of true womanhood" requiring submissiveness (Yee 1992, 40–59).[100] Shadd's editorship of the *Provincial Freeman* alone signalled change, marking an important moment in publishing and black representation in the mid-nineteenth century.[101] Shadd's irrepressible drive for freedom and active black self-transformation finally also produced a kind of *ideologiekritik* that reflected on the mental barriers to freedom among free blacks in Canada. While Henry Bibb saw in Canada only a temporary home for exiled US blacks, Shadd's *Provincial Freeman* offered an important stage for reflection on black specificity and transformation under the conditions of freedom in Canada.

Gender boundaries were at stake when the *Voice of the Fugitive* charged Shadd on 15 July 1852 with "having said and written many things which we think will add nothing to her credit as a lady." As Rhodes comments, this reprimand seemed to suggest that women "should be seen and not heard" (1998, 54). This was hardly Shadd's idea of black intervention and the public sphere. Launching the *Provincial Freeman* shortly thereafter, Shadd navigated potential gender prejudice by collaborating initially with Samuel Ringgold Ward, who was identified as editor on the masthead of the first issue, which appeared in Windsor, Canada West, on 24 March 1853. The publisher of two earlier abolitionist papers in the United States (*True*

American 1847–48 and *Impartial Citizen* 1849–51), Ward was cited earlier by Shadd in *Plea* (M.A. Shadd 1852, 33, 35). Threatened with prosecution for his anti-slavery activities,[102] he fled to Canada and became an agent for the Anti-Slavery Society of Canada. During one of his tours, a visit to Shadd's school in Windsor led to their further collaboration. Like Shadd, Ward had issues with Delany[103] and took her side against Bibb and the Refugee Home Society (Rhodes 1998, 60–1). Although Ward left shortly thereafter on a tour to England, never to return to Canada (though writing about it in his autobiography, as we will see below), the paper continued publication under his nominal editorship until October 1854. "M.A. Shadd" herself appears even thereafter only as "Publishing Agent," although hers is the only name signing the "Prospectus" at the head of each issue.

In August 1854, she finally disambiguated her initials and gender for the readers, "as we do not like the Mr. and Esq., by which we are so often addressed" (26 August 1854). When she was forced to relinquish control of the paper at the end of June 1855, she indicated gender prejudice towards a female editor as one of the reasons. On 9 June, she had already written of "Editors of the unfortunate sex" who, despite all their work, seemed to cause readership antagonism towards the paper "because obnoxious persons have it in charge." Announcing arrangements to "secure for the *Freeman* a gentleman editor," Shadd suggested that this step was necessary for women associations and other support groups to step up their fundraising efforts on behalf of the paper: "The ladies will be pleased, and assist to sustain it, which they will not do while a *colored* female has the ugly duty to perform" ("To our Readers West," *Provincial Freeman*, 9 June 1855). On 30 June, in a piece titled "Adieu," she names the Reverend William P. Newman as new editor.[104] She addresses the paper's "enemies" in a famous passage that encouraged other black women to pick up where she has left off: "It is fit that you should deport your ugliest to a woman. To colored women, we have a word – we have 'broken the Editorial ice,' whether willingly or not, for your class in America; so go to Editing, as many of you as are willing, and able, and as soon as you may, if you think you are ready."

Gender was a preoccupation elsewhere in the paper as well as in Shadd's writing. Discussing a lecture by Lucy Stone on "Women's Rights," the *Freeman* thus notes on 17 March 1855 that "in Toronto, with the strong attachment to antiquated notions respecting woman and her sphere, so prevalent, she was listened to patiently, applauded abundantly." The following year, when Shadd was prevented from speaking because of her gender during a fundraising tour for the *Freeman* in the Chicago area, she suggests that the "advocates of Women's Rights should go there, as the citizens are so conservative on the question, as not to tolerate lectures from women" ("A Short Letter," *Provincial Freeman*, 8 March 1856). Joining other proponents of not just racial but also gender equality, Shadd expresses her opinion clearly in the manuscript of a sermon that she may have delivered in Chatham in 1858 (Ripley 1986, 388). She prefaces her condemnation of slavery in the second half of the sermon with exhortations to treat men and women equally. Referring to Christian injunctions such as "to love the neighbor as ourselves," she notes that they "proscribe neither nation nor sex" (388). She refers to the "woman of every nation or clime in whose Soul is as Evident … the image of God as in her more fortunate contemporary of the male sex" (388–9) and insists that the "spirit of true philanthropy knows no sex." Finally, she reminds listeners that "the Sabbath [was] made for man and woman if you please as there may be those who will not … accept the term man in a generic sense" (389).[105] Throughout its existence, the *Provincial Freeman* carried commentary on issues such as women's rights, work, and education, and often reprinted relevant articles from other papers.[106]

Besides slavery, racial prejudice, and gender inequality, Shadd and others writing for the *Provincial Freeman* repeatedly targeted pernicious mental attitudes that blacks had internalized because of oppression and the denial of equality, recognition, and citizenship in the United States.[107] The denial of humanity through slavery, slaveholder propaganda, and racial prejudice was for them responsible for some of the problems of black progress even under British law and conditions of formal freedom. For Shadd, the transformation from slave life and the absence of human rights to freedom and full civic participation thus entailed more than emigration to Canada – which she so insistently advocated. It also required individual change. One of the challenges was to overcome forms of divided consciousness that were rooted in mental reflexes and identity formations imposed by ideologies of slavery and inequality. While tactics of self-protection and resistance were necessary and useful under oppression, they now required transformation so as not to limit forms of freedom. This work of analysis and critique is a burden assumed in many of Shadd's editorials.

In *Plea*, Shadd had already charged that black proponents of separate schools and churches "perpetuate, in the minds of the newly arrived emigrant or refugee, prejudices, originating in slavery, and as strong and objectionable in their manifestations as those entertained by whites toward them" (M.A. Shadd 1852, 33). In an important January 1857 editorial entitled "Obstacles to the Progress of Colored Canadians," Shadd suggested that free blacks in Canada often replicated divisions caused by slavery in the United States. She rebuked them "for their great indifference to their interests" and "the treachery, want of confidence and down right wickedness one towards the other." Shadd felt that a process of deprogramming is necessary to overcome negative mental conditioning inculcated by slavery and prejudice:

> In the United States, in slavery, the great aim of their oppressors was to destroy confidence the one in the other – to under-value one another in their person and pursuits; at the same time that they inculcate fear of the master, or the person of white complexion, to make him also the idol, the centre of homage, the one to be looked up to, to be clothed and fed by, though the very food to be furnished them, whether moral or other, should poison in the taking. Many in coming to Canada, have but fled from the sting, the bitterness of the dose, the direct result of the relation of master and slave, but not at all from these other evils which are as clearly concomitants of the relation.

While blacks in Canada had the opportunity to exist differently, Shadd claims that the kind of individual who would previously have betrayed fellow-slaves for personal gain, "brutalized as he is, has many a counterpart in these Provinces among colored men." She cites disunity, quarrels, and dysfunctional institutions; especially with regard to the "begging system" of collecting goods and money on behalf of the supposedly helpless free blacks of Canada, she deplores "this business of degrading an entire people, back almost to their [first] estate, as fast as British law could make men of them." Instead of aspiring "to be a nation of beggars" even under British Rule, Shadd wants free blacks in Canada to surge ahead as fully integrated and increasingly prosperous citizens: "Instead of each cry, ignorance, servility, we want to see confidence, intelligence, independence" (Shadd, "Obstacles to the Progress of Colored Canadians," *Provincial Freeman*, 31 January 1857; repr. in Ripley 1986, 360–3).

Such analyses of specifically Canadian black conditions, tasks, and possibilities find a complement in the analyses of specifically Canadian forms of racism – usually elided by Shadd – that were offered by Samuel Ringgold Ward, the nominal founding editor of the *Provincial Freeman*.

Samuel Ringgold Ward's Description of the Black Communities in Canada

Ward arrived in Canada as a consequence of his active opposition to the Fugitive Slave Act. In a speech at Boston's Faneuil Hall in April 1850, Ward eloquently opposed the coming law: "This is the question, Whether a man has a right to himself and his children, his hopes and his happiness, for this world and the world to come. That is the question which, according to this bill, may be decided by any backwoods postmaster in this State or any other." Ward justified physical resistance and announced that "crises as these leave us to the right of Revolution, and if need be, that right we will, at whatever cost, most sacredly maintain" (Ripley 1991b, 4:50, 51). When the self-emancipated former slave William "Jerry" McHenry was arrested under the Fugitive Slave Act in Syracuse, Ward addressed the crowd; like his friend the Reverend Jermaine Wesley Loguen, he was subsequently accused of being implicated in McHenry's rescue (Ripley 1986, 2:180n2). Loguen would later describe the event in his 1859 *The Rev. J.W. Loguen, As a Slave and as a Freeman: A Narrative of Real Life*, which recounts his experience of slaveholders' brutality and describes at length his escape to Canada in the mid-1830s. Openly advertising his role as an Underground Railroad conductor in Syracuse from 1841 onward and in participating in the Syracuse vigilance committee, Loguen had to return at least temporarily to Canada after the "Jerry" case. Ward also had to flee to Canada, where he contributed to the *Voice of the Fugitive* and became involved with the *Provincial Freeman*.

Writing to Henry Bibb after his arrival in Canada, Ward reports that his own paper, the *Impartial Citizen*, "breathed its last, after a lingering illness of the spine and obstructions, impurities and irregularities of the circulation. *Resquiat in pace*!" (*Voice of the Fugitive*, 5 November 1851; repr. in Ripley 1986, 177). After referring to the "Jerry" case as the reason for his move to Canada, Ward focuses his sharp intelligence, as in many of his subsequent texts, on "Canadian Negro Hate." His being denied cabin passage on a boat from Montreal to Kingston and other incidents lead him to comment: "The boast of Englishmen, of their freedom from social negrophobia, is about as empty as the Yankee boast of democracy."[108] Ward is optimistic, however, that "universal agitation … will rid our beloved adopted country of this infernal curse," and promises his active contribution (Ripley 1986, 179). In another letter to Bibb a few weeks later, he emphasizes the importance of Canada as a strategic location in the fight against slavery. Successes in Canada would limit talk of Liberia and refute theories of black inferiority; they would also stop persecution in the northern states and soften slavery in the South for fear of "driving us where we can be freemen to the fullest extent" (*Voice of the Fugitive*, 19 November 1851; repr. in Ripley 1986, 182). Ward subsequently writes in George Brown's Toronto *Globe* in July 1852 to correct a biased account of an incident involving blacks in St Catharines (repr. in Ripley 1986, 215–16) and contributes a much longer analysis of "Canadian Negro Hate" in the *Voice of the Fugitive* later that year. Here he exposes Edwin Larwill's racist interventions in Chatham (and Larwill's opposition to William King's Elgin settlement, mentioned earlier). He also names taverns, steamer captains, ministers, and schools that discriminate against blacks. In the process, Ward distinguishes Canadian racism as meaner and gratuitous when compared with "Yankee" racism. Yet, since neither the civil law nor the Church in general upheld Canadian racism, Ward suggests that "Canadian Negro Hate can not be eternal." His main fear – and here it becomes clear why he would be a natural ally for Mary Ann Shadd – was that blacks would exacerbate prejudice because of "separate and distinct black churches, schools and preachers" ("Canadian Negro Hate," *Voice of the Fugitive*, 4 November 1852; repr. in Ripley 1986, 224–8).

Shadd's choice of Ward in response to the general public's expectation of a male editor was thus not surprising when she launched the *Provincial Freeman*. Ward's "Introductory" to the first issue presents the *Freeman* as a temperance and anti-slavery paper that is beholden to no party; immediately following the "Introductory," however, a letter by Ward critiques the Refugee Home Society for reasons almost identical to those often adduced by Shadd – namely, that comparable or better lands could be purchased more cheaply directly from the government and that the society misrepresented free Canadian blacks as helpless and needy.

In his third contribution to the issue, Ward continues his earlier analysis – in the *Voice of the Fugitive* – of the black condition and racism in Canada in comparison with the United States. He begins with a short history of the unsuccessful US attempts, from 1825 onward, to have fugitive slaves extradited, concluding that Canada indeed offered self-emancipated black subjects "all the rights and immunities of the British subject." Turning to daily realities, however, he insists on the continuation of anti-slavery work in Canada in the face of continued support for slavery by a number of groups there. These included former slave-drivers from the South, former slaveholders from the West Indies, slave owners by marriage and inheritance, and other pro-slavery Yankees and Canadians who expressed their opinions freely. These circumstances, Ward stresses, necessitated his writing for the *Provincial Freeman* and his activities as lecturer for the Canadian Anti-Slavery Society ("Relations of Canada to American Slavery," *Provincial Freeman*, 24 March 1853; repr. in Ripley 1986, 228–31).

His lecture tours for the society allowed him to produce a brief survey of black communities in Canada West, also published in the opening issue of the *Provincial Freeman* under the title "A Recent Tour." As we will see, this kind of survey was usually produced to demonstrate emancipated blacks' capacity to thrive in freedom and constituted a genre of travel report on the black Canadian mid-nineteenth century that often included accounts by the former slaves themselves.[109] Ward describes black meetings, organizations, and the progress of black individuals, and portrays the black communities in Hamilton, St Catharines, London, Chatham, and Buxton. He rejoices over the economic progress in all of the communities visited, finds less-than-expected racism in St Catharines and London, and lauds the economic and educational achievements, absence of begging, and absolute temperance in the Elgin settlement. His emphatic conclusion is that black freedom led to black prosperity – pro-slavery statements to the contrary notwithstanding: "Our tour satisfied us abundantly that the colored people of Canada are progressing more rapidly than our people in the States – that the liberty enjoyed here makes different men of those once crushed and dispirited in the land of chains" (*Provincial Freeman*, 24 March 1853; repr. in Ripley 1986, 256–60).

Ward offers an extended account of these communities in chapter 4 of his *Autobiography of a Fugitive Negro; His Anti-Slavery Labours in the United States, Canada, and England*, published in 1855 in London.[110] A substantial portion of Ward's narrative, which also describes the events of the "Jerry" case, is dedicated to his time in Canada. It details his identification with Canada upon arrival and describes the beauty of the St Lawrence River in the autumn, experienced on a steamer trip from Montreal to Kingston. Ward insists again, however, on the need to fight prejudice and pro-slavery sentiment in Canada. He thus offers another version of his earlier analysis of racism in Canada (S.R. Ward 1855, 137–40) but also lauds impartial judges who upheld the law. Ward claims to be unaware of any case in which their duty would have been neglected, suggesting that racism in Canada was mostly restricted to the lower classes (149–50). Attacking the racist portrayal of blacks in Haliburton's Sam Slick sketches (156–7),[111] Ward underlines the ingenuity, perseverance, and value of black immigrants who succeeded in fleeing slavery (159–68). He allows, though, for the destructive influences of slavery, indeed admitting his fear of transmitting even to his descendants negative traits caused by his "slave origin. It is among my thoughts, my superstitions, my narrow views, my awkwardness of manners. Ah, the infernal impress is upon me, and I fear I shall transmit it to my children, and they to theirs!" (170). These concerns, however, hardly diminished the value and "True Heroism" (169) of those who succeeded in overcoming slavery: "All I claim for the Negro settler is, that as a slave, a fugitive, and a freeman, he is equal to other poor immigrants, superior to many, and from among the very best of his own class; and that, take him all in all, he is just such a man as our new country needs – a lover of freedom, a loyal subject, an industrious man" (170). After describing the skills and daring in the successful escapes he was familiar with, Ward further underscores the value of black immigrants with his report on the most important black communities in Canada West.

In comparison with the United States, very few blacks in Canada were household servants while a considerable number were "porters, carters, cabowners" and "small shopkeepers" (191). Ward is particularly proud of the number of excellent black "mechanics and artisans" (192). Adding to his first report in the *Voice of the Fugitive*, he also gives an account of the Dawn settlement with its now defunct trade school. Citing many individual success stories (including that of Josiah Henson), he hails the settlement's "present success and its prospective prosperity" (199), but he also critiques younger blacks for their lack of engagement in the community and deplores the fact that not all lands were actively cultivated (193–9). He is impressed with the achievements of Chatham's substantial black community, noting that three blacksmiths as well as other qualified skilled labourers were black. But he also deplores the exceptionally strong racism in the community and singles out the steamer trip between Chatham and Windsor as a site of discrimination against blacks (202). Ward also takes issue with a lack of black resistance to racism and black self-segregation in Chatham. He is only entirely positive when he describes the Elgin settlement in Buxton, citing the prosperity, temperance, and education of its settlers as providing a model. In concluding his survey of black communities, however, he adds "that I do not think that exclusive settlements for coloured people are to be considered desirable. Experiments have been made; they have proved triumphantly successful: now we need no more of them" (218). Like Shadd, Ward is critical of segregated black settlements, schools, and churches in

Canada; while they may have been justified in the United States, he sees them as an obstacle to black elevation in Canada.

Interestingly, Ward ends by considering the strategic significance of Canada's free black population for other contexts. He asks how long the South could afford the "drain of her most energetic men, the very lifeblood of the country, year after year" (219), and he refutes Delany's argument based on the threat of US annexation. Annexation did not come about in the War of 1812 when a small black Canadian population fought it; Ward argues that the now more numerous blacks would fight annexation again (220). Predicting that the "onward progress of the Canadian Negro shall exhibit the workings of American despotism, and British freedom" (221), he ascribes a model function to this segment of the continent's black population: "The coloured people of Canada, as a whole, are the most moral and upright of our race in America" (222). Ward thus concludes this section of his autobiography by emphasizing the crucial role of Canada's black communities in a wider context. They were living proof of the rich potential of free black communities, denied by the pro-slavery forces that kept the United States in their thrall. In this valuable snapshot of Canada West, taken in the years before 1855, Ward suggests that the importance of Canada's black population as a model must make it a central concern for abolitionists everywhere because it strengthens their claims: "This very important population may go on improving, and, by improving, reflect honour upon our race and justify the institutions under which it is their blessing and privilege to live" (224).

Recording Black Economic and Emotional Geographies of Canada West: The Accounts of Benjamin Drew, William Wells Brown, and Samuel Gridley Howe

A few years after the Fugitive Slave Act, Ward was not alone in recognizing the importance of the free black communities in Canada West to a wider discussion of possible black futures. In the same year that he published his autobiography in England, Benjamin Drew toured Canada West, sponsored by the Canadian Anti-Slavery Society. A few years later, in 1861, William Wells Brown, in his "The Colored People of Canada," would describe in very positive terms many of the same communities visited by Drew, even though Brown's account was published in the journal of the Haytian Emigration Bureau, for which he travelled. In 1864, Samuel Gridley Howe's report on the free black population of Canada, written for the American Freedmen's Inquiry Commission, revisited the ground previously covered by Drew.

Drew particularly sought to counter the pro-slavery view set forth in Nehemiah Adam's 1854 *A South-Side View of Slavery* – itself partially a critique of Stowe's *Uncle Tom's Cabin*.[112] The imperative to critique slavery and demonstrate the benefits of freedom for blacks was all the more urgent after the 1854 Kansas-Nebraska Act opened the possibility of further slave states being created in the United States, potentially tipping the balance between free and slave states. One of Drew's specific goals was to demonstrate to Americans that former slaves could become valuable and independent citizens once they enjoyed freedom. In the introduction to his *A North-Side View of Slavery; The Refugee: or The Narratives of Fugitive Slaves in Canada*, published by J.P. Jewett in 1856, Drew thus announces that he would visit black fugitives in Canada and "advise them that their good conduct and success in life may have an important bearing on the destinies of millions of their brethren, colored and white, in this country, who have the misfortune to be descended from slave mothers" (2000, 15).[113] Drew's project, he states, would be "to collect, with a view to placing their testimony on record, their experiences of the actual workings of slavery – what experience they have had of the condition of liberty – and such statements generally as they may be inclined to make, bearing upon the weighty subjects of oppression and freedom" (15).

Drew's methodology has been criticized. As Tilden G. Edelstein points out, his sample consisted of "mostly young men from border states" with few house servants and "only sixteen women"; in addition, African heritage and issues like miscegenation or voting are elided in the narratives elicited and transcribed by Drew as he sought to avoid issues "that would disturb many northerners" (2004, xiv–xv). As with all transcribed slave narratives, the possible areas here of shaping by the interviewer/transcriber include pre-structuring the accounts by questions, subsequent selection, and the choice of linguistic register. Like most transcribers of slave narratives, Drew sought to maximize the impression of authenticity conveyed by his ethnographic transpositions from orality to writing: "While his informants talked, the author wrote: nor are there in the whole volume a dozen verbal alterations which were not made at the moment of writing, while in haste to make the pen become a tongue for the dumb" ("Author's Preface," n.p.). Yet Edelstein accurately comments that Drew's transcriptions were "transmuting the language of the fugitive into educated prose. Selected for the task partly because of his interest in folk language and folk wit, he nevertheless failed to record African-American imagery and dialect" (xvi).

Despite these reservations, the result of Drew's ethnographic endeavour, undertaken mainly with the goal of influencing public opinion in the United States, not only was a systematic portrayal of the black settlements and especially the conditions of the black population in Canada West, but also offered the most extensive anthology that we possess of slave narratives recorded in Canada. Drew transcribed the statements of over one hundred former slaves and provided introductory descriptions of fourteen black communities visited in his travels, among them St Catharines, Toronto, London, Chatham, Buxton, Dresden/Dawn, Windsor, Sandwich, and Amherstburg. While the interviews varied in length, not surprisingly a number of themes recurred. The experience of violence, family separation, and the fear of being sold south were often mentioned. With respect to Canada, the repeated subjects were the availability of education, the undesirability of begging, and the absence of alcohol in black communities.

The largest group Drew interviewed was in St Catharines, the first stop on his tour from the East to the West, his guide being Hiram Wilson. Wilson, a co-founder of Dawn, now preached and accommodated fugitives in this border city, which was often the first port of call for self-emancipated black immigrants. In one of the twenty-three interviews, George Johnson tells Drew: "I arrived in St. Catharines about two hours ago" (Drew 2000, 52). Like many of the other informants, Johnson tells Drew that "the slaves were always afraid of being sold South" (52); he also speaks of the mistreatment of a fellow-slave who "received five hundred and fifty lashes for striking the overseer … two months after, I saw him lying on his face, unable to turn over or help himself" (54). Johnson then describes details of his escape and journey to Canada, and like many other informants, he contributes to the condemnation of slavery recorded by Drew: "I think that slavery is not the best condition for the blacks. Whipping and slashing are bad enough, but selling children from their mothers and husbands from their wives is worse" (53–4). St Catharines' Underground Railroad conductor Harriet Tubman is much more direct in her brief account. She states flatly that "slavery is the next thing to hell" (30). Another woman concurs, withholding her name even in Canada: "I look upon slavery as the worst evil that ever was. My life has been taken from me in a measure by it" (31–2). William Johnson opens his narrative with another simple but evocative condemnation: "I look upon slavery as I do upon a deadly poison" (29). James Adams, to cite one more example, ends the lengthy narrative of his flight: "I look upon slavery as the most disgusting system a man can live under. I would not be a slave again, except that I could not put an end to my own existence, through fear of the punishment of the future. Men who have never seen or felt slavery cannot realize it for the thing it is. If those who say that fugitives had better go back, were to go to the South and *see* slavery, they would never wish any slave to go back" (28).

What emerges from the narratives of these black Canadian settlers is not only a collective witnessing of white degradation and institutionalized violence in their country of origin, but also the co-presence of a new-found sense of relative safety, optimism, and determination with an emotional geography of traumatic haunting. The Reverend Alexander Hemsley thus offers the beginning of a study of slave trauma drawn from his personal experience: "I would as lief meet serpents as some people I know of in the States. If I were to meet them, my fighting propensities would come up. To meet one here, I would not mind it; there I would be afraid of the ghost of a white man after he was dead. I am no scholar, but if some one would refine it, I could give a history of slavery, and show how tyranny operates upon the mind of the slaves. I have dreamed of being back on my master's farm, and of dodging away from my master; he endeavoring to get between me and the land I was aiming for. Then I would awake in a complete perspiration, and troubled in mind. Oh, it was awful!" (39–40). Hemsley's comments join other condemnations of US slavery that Drew so abundantly records, but he comments also on his and others' economic progress in Canada, another central concern of Drew's volume. His economic progress helped him eventually feel at home in his new surroundings: "I rented a house, and with another man took five acres of cleared land, and got along with it very well. We did not get enough from this to support us; but I got work at half a dollar or seventy-five cents a day and board myself. We were then making both ends meet. I then made up my mind that salt and potatoes in Canada, were better than pound-cake and chickens in a state of suspense and anxiety in the United States. Now I am a regular Britisher" (39). In a similar vein, William Grose speaks about his and other immigrants' economic progress; he expresses optimism, pointing to a change of habits and a new-found sense of purpose in his former fellow-slaves:

> I have been through both Upper and Lower Canada, and I have found the colored people keeping stores, farming, etc., and doing well. I have made more money since I came here, than I made in

the United States. I know several colored people who have become wealthy by industry – owning horses and carriages, – one who was a fellow-servant of mine, now owns two span of horses, and two as fine carriages as there are on the bank. As a general thing, the colored people are more sober and industrious than in the States: there they feel when they have money, that they cannot make what use they would like of it, they are so kept down, so looked down upon. Here they have something to do with their money, and put it to a good purpose. (87)

During further travels, Drew collected more narratives in Toronto. He focused on the black inhabitants' prosperity[114] and racial integration in churches and schools, reporting that "colored youths are attending lectures in the University" (94). Continuing his interviews through Hamilton and Galt (part of today's Cambridge, Ontario) and then London[115] and Queen's Bush (north of today's Kitchener, Waterloo, and Guelph, and extending to Lake Huron),[116] Drew made his way to Chatham, Buxton, and Dawn, the important black settlements also visited by Samuel Ringgold Ward.

Like William Wells Brown, who saw many of the same communities in 1861, Drew noted the visibility of the black community in Chatham. It constituted close to a quarter of the town's population, the largest percentage of any Canadian town at that moment: "Here, indeed, more fully than anywhere else, the traveller realizes the extent of the American exodus. At every turn, he meets members of the African race, single or in groups; he sees them building and painting houses, working in mills, engaged in every handicraft employment: here he notices a street occupied by colored shopkeepers and clerks: if he steps into the environs, he finds the blacks in every quarter, busy upon their gardens and farms" (234). Brown would later write in his travel report titled "The Colored People of Canada": "In my walk from the railroad station to the hotel, I was at once impressed with the fact that I was at Chatham, for every other person whom I met was colored" (1986, 470). Drew mentions the 1852 arrival of the Great Western Railway as a decisive takeoff moment for the town (railroad construction was also one source of income for new arrivals). He was particularly impressed by the black self-help "True Band" associations that sought to improve schools, provide for the sick and destitute, and thereby work against the "begging" system. They also adjudicated disputes internally without recourse to the official justice system (236–7). Like the other narratives transcribed by Drew, those collected in Chatham often speak of previous experience in the United States and condemn slavery, but they also confirm the potential for economic progress in Chatham, and comment on other aspects of life in Canada. Philip Younger, for example, takes note of idleness on the part of some but proudly itemizes the relative wealth of others: "We are placed in different circumstances here – some drag along, without doing much, – some are doing well. I have a house; I have taken up fifty acres of land, and have made the payments as required; I have other property besides. Here is Henry Blue, worth twelve thousand dollars; Syddles, worth a fortune; Lucky, worth a very handsome fortune; Ramsay, a great deal of land and other property, at least twelve thousand dollars; all these were slaves at some time" (250). Henry Blue himself remarks: "Every thing goes well with me in Canada. I have no reason to complain" (270). Edward Hicks comments on his more modest circumstances: "I have been here about six years. I like Canada well, – I am satisfied with it. I have got a little property together, worth some two thousand dollars" (269). Isaac Griffin states, "I have lived in Canada one year. I find the people laboring well generally: as industrious as any men. The law is the same for one as another. We have our meetings and gatherings here, and have no trouble at all" (285).

Often hidden behind these statements of progress and contentment – in Chatham and elsewhere – is a reality of racism that we have seen condemned by Ward and that William Wells Brown mentions explicitly in his description of London: "Canada has so long been eulogized as the only spot in North America where the Southern bondsman could stand a freeman … that I was not prepared to meet the prejudice against colored persons which manifests itself wherever a member of that injured race makes his appearance" (1986, 466). Among Drew's Chatham interviewees, Thomas Hedgebeth is one of the few to mention racism: "In regard to Canada, I like the country, the soil, as well as any country I ever saw. I like the laws, which leave a man as much freedom as a man can have, – still there is prejudice here. The colored people are trying to remove this by improving and educating themselves, and by industry, to show that they are a people who have minds, and that all they want is cultivating" (279–80). Drew discusses racism explicitly in his introduction to the Chatham narratives (234–5), but his black respondents seem to have made strategic decisions about what they would discuss, often choosing to place selective silences over topics such as racial prejudice and discrimination in their narratives.

In the only five narratives from the Elgin settlement in Buxton, however, racism is mentioned repeatedly. Mrs Riley describes her erstwhile desire to return home because of racism in Canada (299). R. van Branken notes:

"Among some people here, there is as much prejudice as in the States, but they cannot carry it out as they do in the States: the law makes the difference" (305). The greater courage here to speak out against racism seems due to the settlers' relative independence and their financial and social security. Drew, like Ward before him, notes the model character of the settlement, with its good schools, high level of black land ownership, and the "independent air and manner" of its residents (297). As Brown would write a few years later, "There are now nearly 600 persons in this settlement, all of whom have comfortable homes, and are characterized by a manly, independent air and manner. Most of these people were slaves at the South, and came into Canada without a single dollar" (1986, 475). In Buxton, the value of education for their children (which included Latin and Greek) is cited by Isaac Riley: "My children can get good learning here" (298). Henry Johnson puts the reasons for his decisions succinctly: "I left the States for Canada, for rights, freedom, liberty. I came to Buxton to educate my children" (307).[117] Both Drew and Brown also discuss Dawn. The former mentions the prosperity of black farmers in the area, but also reports the dilapidated state of Dawn, which gives "an unfavorable and melancholy impression to the mind" (310). Brown more categorically states with respect to the Dawn Institute: "No place in the Western province has excited more interest, or received a greater share of substantial aid, as this association, and no place has proved itself less deserving" (1986, 477).[118] Both writers continued their tour further west to the Underground Railroad destinations across from Detroit, including Amherstburg, Colchester, and Windsor, which gave Drew occasion to discuss Bibb's Refugee Home Society. While Drew admits some dissatisfaction among the settlers there, he notes that the society and its officers and agents "possess the entire confidence of the American public" (325). Brown, however, produces a scathing account of the various conditions imposed by the society and its black settlers (1986, 478–9).

While Brown sprinkles his generally positive comments with a few more critical observations, the overall tenor of the narratives transcribed by Drew is unequivocal: free black citizens in Canada were doing well, implicitly providing a model for possible solutions in the United States. Not surprisingly, when the US government sought guidance on the possible post-abolition conditions of blacks in the United States, Drew's volume was a relevant source of information. Samuel Gridley Howe's 1864 account *The Refugees from Slavery in Canada West: Report to the Freedman's Inquiry Commission*, thus relied heavily on the information gathered by Drew, surveying many of the same places he had visited and referencing a number of the narratives in his collection. Howe added interviews with about another dozen black settlers.[119] A number of other texts further present accounts of black immigrants' self-emancipation and escape, such as those by William Troy[120] and William Still.[121] Troy's *Hair-Breadth Escapes from Slavery to Freedom* (1861) offers a narrative of his life in the first chapter, while the rest of the text is dedicated to the stories of about thirty slaves attempting their escape. Most of them succeeded, and many moved to Troy's communities in Amherstburg and later Windsor. William Still, whose substantive compilation *The Underground Railroad* was published in Philadelphia in 1872, also visits black Canadian communities in 1855 and reports positively on them. Besides other materials, *The Underground Railroad* includes correspondence – and often the narratives – of over six hundred fugitive slaves, many of them settling in Canada.

These accounts help to document the lives and communities of one of the most substantial groups of immigrants in nineteenth-century Canada. They afford us insight into an aspect of Canada that is often marginalized but is crucial to any approach to the period. The slave narratives, black life writing, travel accounts, and testimony, published independently or collected in works like those by Drew or Howe, constitute an important archive of Canadian immigrant and settler writing and give us vital access routes to the history of Ontario and Canada. The black nineteenth-century communities and the texts related to them have significant national implications, but they are also relevant in transnational perspectives. Many of the black writers and leaders of the period exemplify the criss-crossing routes of the black Atlantic, travelling between North America, Central America, the Caribbean, England, and in some cases Africa. In addition, as we have seen in Ward's address to an English and international audience, black nineteenth-century Canada was relevant for transatlantic abolitionist and anti-racist thinking at the time because it offered a model that validated abolitionist claims, especially those about the abilities of free black subjects to achieve progress and secure economic independence. Finally, it is important to remember that the black Canadian nineteenth century also constitutes a chapter in the story of hemispheric slavery and anti-slavery struggle – as is directly evident in the narrative by Baquaqua discussed below or in the hemispheric reach of emigrationist discussions exemplified by Delany and others. Nineteenth-century black Canada was transnational, however, not only as a border zone between countries and the different human-rights geographies that generated numerous border-crossing stories, but also as a black geopolitical location crucially important to the United States in the years between the Fugitive Slave Act and the Civil War. Chatham, where Mary Ann Shadd moved the *Provincial Freeman* in 1855, became an international crossroads and black capital in this respect, the domicile of Martin Delany from 1856 onward, for instance, and the site of John Brown's constitutional convention.

Chatham and Brazilian Slavery: Mahommah Gardo Baquaqua

Chatham, as we have seen, was a central destination for Ward, Drew, and William Wells Brown, and became the residence of a number of black leaders. When Brown visited in 1861, he described Mary Ann Shadd as the "most intelligent woman I have met in Canada" (1986, 474), and called Delany, freshly returned from Africa and London, "the ablest man in Chatham, if not America" (472). Delany's case illustrates the transnational cross-roads that traversed Chatham (we will pick up the earlier thread that connected Delany with Shadd below), but first let us take a brief look at the narrative of another Chatham resident that highlights Canada as a black hemispheric location.

Mahommah Gardo Baquaqua moved to Chatham in 1854 (Law and Lovejoy 2007, 62). After having been abducted from West Africa into Brazilian slavery, he had escaped while in New York, travelled to Haiti, and later received some schooling in upstate New York. Brazilian slavery was practised on a massive scale and not abolished until 1888.[122] Known slave narratives and testimony from Brazil, however, are relatively rare, mainly because of a late abolitionist movement and severe repression (Krueger 2002, 172).[123] The only known fully articulated slave narrative is Baquaqua's *An Interesting Narrative. Biography of Mahommah G. Baquaqua, A Native of Zoogoo, in the Interior of Africa. (A Convert to Christianity.) With a Description of That Part of the World; Including the Manners and Customs of the Inhabitants*, published in Detroit in 1854 when Baquaqua lived in Chatham.[124] I cite here the text that was republished in a critical edition by Robin Law and Paul Lovejoy in 2003.

Baquaqua's narrative contains ethnographic information about West Africa and its practice of slavery. He describes multiple captivities in wars, his enslavement through deception, then the march to the coast and his first encounter with whites. The traumatic memory of murders and suffering on the slave ship, he tells the reader, "will never be effaced from my memory; nay, as long as memory holds her seat in this distracted brain" (Law and

Lovejoy 2003, 153). Sold in Pernambuco, Baquaqua experienced further cruelty, learned Portuguese, and finally escaped from a sea trader while in New York. He was baptized during a stay in Haiti and subsequently attended a school in New York. But racism there made him leave for Canada, where he claims to have immediately acquired British citizenship (191).[125]

Co-written with the Unitarian minister Samuel Downing Moore, the first part of the narrative is mostly in the third person with direct quotations from Baquaqua, while the second part is generally narrated in the first person.[126] The collaboratively produced text exhibits the generic instabilities of auto/biography and raises again questions of voice and control. We do not know whether the text came into existence in Michigan, where Moore resided and the book was published (under Baquaqua's copyright), or in Chatham, where Baquaqua lived at this point in his life (Law and Lovejoy 2003, 7–11). But it is relevant that at the very end of his narrative he cites his new surroundings in Canada as reason for its genesis. Being "kindly treated by all classes where I went," Baquaqua writes, he was "thankful to God that I enjoy the blessings of liberty, in peace and tranquility, and that I am now in a land where 'none dare make me afraid'" (191). In this context, Chatham was a place that facilitated the production of his narrative: "Being thus surrounded by friends, and enabled to enjoy the blessing of peaceful freedom, I came to the conclusion that the time had arrived when I might with propriety commit to paper all that has been recounted in this work" (191–2).[127]

Chatham in the Later 1850s: Martin Delany, Mary Ann Shadd, and John Brown

In 1855, one year after Baquaqua's arrival, the significance of Chatham as a black centre was underlined when Mary Ann Shadd moved the *Provincial Freeman* there from Toronto. Shadd describes Chatham as "a grand central point for the Counties of Kent, Essex, Lambton, and Middlesex," noting that it was located in close proximity to the black settlements of Buxton and Dawn (Rhodes 1998, 100–2). In early 1856, Shadd was followed by Martin Delany, perhaps the best-known emigrationist of the day and the "first and foremost black nationalist" (Ullman 1971, 172). His presence made Chatham not only North America's black fugitive capital but also its black emigrationist capital.

Prior to moving there, Delany kept Canada steadily in view. Surveying potential emigration destinations in his keynote address at the 1854 National Immigration Convention in Cleveland – titled "Political Destiny of the Colored Race on the American Continent" – Delany repeats his earlier warning about the United States' annexation of Canada (in Levine 2003, 276). Yet he also notes that in Canada West "climate, soil, productions, and the usual prospects for internal improvements, are equal, if not superior, to any northern part of the continent." Delany indeed felt compelled "to recommend, that, for the present, as a temporary asylum, it is certainly advisable for every colored person, who desiring to emigrate, and is not prepared for any other destination, to locate in Canada West" (275). Reporting a year later to the National Board of Commissioners established at the convention, Delany notes that "our people are flocking into this beautiful country, and substantially settling themselves down by becoming possessors of the soil, as loyal British subjects. There is more real estate owned at this time by the colored people of the Canadas … then by all the balance of the colored people in North America together" (289).

It was not until February 1856 that Delany himself finally moved to Chatham. While Sterling cites education possibilities for his children as one of the reasons Delany chose to move there (1971, 159–60), Ullman suggests that it was imperative for Delany to remove his emigrationist organization from the growing insecurities in the United States: "If there was to be any consideration of a hemispheric plan, the National Board of Commissioners could not function anywhere in the United States. The Constitution of the organization required that all of its officers reside in the same area as the president. In effect, Delany's move transferred the entire organization to Canada" (Ullman 1971, 176–7).[128] With that decision, the role of Chatham as an essential intellectual and organizational hub of black North American resistance entered a new phase. This role was further reinforced by the aggravated conditions for blacks after the *Dred Scott* Supreme Court decision of 1857, which essentially denied blacks any citizenship rights and sent even free blacks into limbo; this led to growing black militancy and a need for alternative solutions.

With Delany's arrival, Shadd and her Chatham associates in turn modified their previous resistance to his emigrationist positions, which had generally favoured destinations elsewhere. The *Provincial Freeman* greets the "arrival of our esteemed and talented friend, Dr. M.R. Delany" (22 February 1856), lauds his achievements, and informs readers about the opening of Delany's medical practice in Chatham. In contrast to her condemnation of the 1854 Emigration Convention, Shadd encourages her readers to attend the 1856 Cleveland Emigration Convention in a *Provincial Freeman* editorial on 5 July 1856. Her wording, however, rather than being explicitly supportive of Delany's specific nationalist goals, suggests the desirability of a strategic emigrationist coalition in the face of anti-emigrationist opposition.[129] Delany, on his part, continues his quarrels with Douglass, deriding him in the pages of the *Provincial Freeman* one week later for his belated – and for Delany ill-intentioned – attention to Shadd and the Canadian community in the *Frederick Douglass' Paper* (in Levine 2003, 291–4).

Although Delany missed the Cleveland convention on account of illness (Delany 2004, 241), he was confirmed as president of the National Board of Commissioners. Given the new collaboration with the Shadd camp, it is not surprising that Mary Ann Shadd's brother Isaac attended (and was appointed to the National Board of Commissioners). Mary Ann (now Cary) became one of the eight corresponding editors of the *Afric-American Repository*, a publication planned to showcase black literary and scientific work and achievement. Chatham was retained as the new headquarters of the National Board of Commissioners, and the *Provincial Freeman* became the official emigrationist organ.[130] Chatham's status as the emigrationist, literary, and intellectual capital of the Black Canadian Renaissance was further confirmed by the fact that some of Delany's most important texts and initiatives were written or launched there. Based in Chatham, Delany would become involved with, or imagine, the transformation of black geographies on national Canadian, North American, hemispheric, and transatlantic scales. While carrying out his duties as president of the National Board of Commissioners, Delany began almost immediately to support a local political candidate in the struggle against racism in Chatham and Canada West.[131] John Brown came to Chatham to request help from Delany and the black Canadian community, and it was here that Delany wrote part of his novel about hemispheric black insurgence, *Blake; or The Huts of America: A Tale of the Mississippi Valley, the Southern United States, and Cuba*. Finally, while in Chatham, Delany launched an African expedition (at the same time as Livingstone was on the continent) and wrote his *Official Report of the Niger Valley Exploring Party*. These wide-ranging black diasporic connections and projections suggest the extent to which the Black Canadian Renaissance is a story of both national and transnational dimensions, rooted in Canada and the particular circumstances of Canada West at the time but simultaneously defined by North American, hemispheric, and black transatlantic dimensions.

As Delany pursued his projects – which often involved him in struggles with Douglass and others over black leadership (see Levine 1997) – Chatham offered him personal safety, access to a black newspaper, and support from the substantial anti-slavery community in Canada West. In the second half of the 1850s, from his strategically central position in Canada, Delany explored – in rapid succession and often simultaneously – North American, hemispheric, and African scenarios of black insurrection and/or self-governance and independence. With a novel about hemispheric black insurgence on the go, Delany planned an African expedition as he awaited news about John Brown's plans in the United States.

Delany and John Brown

The story of John Brown and the "Chatham convention" is well known, although some of the crucial details are missing and the significance of his stay and Delany's role have been interpreted in very different ways. Brown arrived in Chatham in April 1858, after his violent interventions in Kansas in May 1856[132] and prior to his raid on the US arsenal at Harpers Ferry in 1859. Delany acceded to his request to convene and co-chair a meeting of trustworthy opponents of slavery. According to Delany's own account, however, given later to his biographer Frances Rollin Whipper, Brown's plans divulged in Chatham did not concern Harpers Ferry, but an alternative to the Underground Railroad, the "Subterranean Pass Way" (SPW) to Kansas. Whipper cites Delany: "His scheme was nothing more than this: To make Kansas, instead of Canada, the terminus of the Underground Railroad … and there test, on the soil of the United States territory, whether or not the right to freedom would be maintained where no municipal power had authorized" (Rollin 1868, 87).[133] As the biographer stresses, Delany "further stated that the idea of Harpers Ferry was never mentioned, or even hinted in that convention. Had such been intimated, it is doubtful of its being favorably regarded" (88). Given Brown's secrecy in general,[134] it is indeed not unlikely that Brown withheld any specific plans – if they existed at the time – during the Chatham meetings – even from individuals such as Delany.[135]

The significance of Chatham as a kind of black North American capital at the time is underlined by the fact that Brown's "official" project was to seek ratification there of his "Provisional Constitution and Ordinances for the People of the United States." This document consists of forty-eight articles composed during Brown's visit to Frederick Douglass's house in Rochester in January and February 1858 (Quarles 2001, 38–9). He also came to Chatham in the hope of selecting officers for a provisional government, although it was not very clear what role such a government would play.[136]

Its function was ostensibly to safeguard the values of the Declaration of Independence that were endorsed in the Preamble. These values were seen to be violated by the barbarity of slavery and the exclusion of those who, by the *Dred Scott* Supreme Court decision, "are declared to have no rights which the white man is bound to respect." Article 46 of Brown's "Provisional Constitution" states explicitly that the aim was not to overthrow the United States government: "The foregoing articles shall not be construed so as in any way to encourage the overthrow of any State government, or of the general government of the United States, and look to no dissolution of the Union, but simply to amendment and repeal. And our flag shall be the same that our fathers fought under in the Revolution." It is not clear what Brown's goals might have been at this point. According to Delany, Brown also spoke of a military invention that could defend a community against attack. Was the aim, then, simply to establish protected anti-slavery communities in Kansas under a semi-autonomous status that could serve to correct the errors of the actual United States and lead them back to the principles of the Declaration of Independence?

In his biography, written at a time when he was a major in the United States Army, Delany asserts that this was indeed the project that he and the Chatham convention supported during Brown's 1858 visit. Kansas, where Brown had fought against slavery, was seen as "the proper place for his vantage-ground … Hence the favor which the scheme met of making Kansas the terminus of the Subterranean Pass Way, and there fortifying with these fugitives against the Border slaveholders, for personal liberty, with which they had no right to interfere" (Rollin 1868, 88). Delany, in his rendering of the project, sought to absolve himself and others from any activity punishable under US law, but also to demonstrate his interest in forms of separate self-governance. The idea of such a mode of government would explain the function and purpose of the "Provisional Constitution": to "avoid the charge against them as lawless and unorganized, existing without government, it was proposed that an independent community be established within and under the government of the United States, but without the state sovereignty of the compact, similar to the Cherokee nation of Indians, or the Mormons. To these last named, references were made, as parallel cases, at the time. The necessary changes and modification were made in the constitution, and with such it was printed" (Rollin 1868, 89).

Article 46 was the only item of the "Provisional Constitution" – signed by those in attendance and printed a few days later by William Howard Day in

St Catharines, Canada West – that occasioned substantial discussion. The request of allegiance to the US flag met with some resistance from those who had risked their lives fleeing to Canada to escape the power it symbolized (Sterling 1971, 172; Levine 1997, 182). Indeed, it was strange that Brown made such a request in Canada and sought legitimization from a Canadian community. According to Delany, it was Brown's need for a "general convention or council" to give his plans legitimacy that brought him to Canada, and with "these [plans] I found no fault, but fully favored and aided in getting up the convention" (Rollin 1868, 86). Canada West had clearly become the staging ground and preferred location for modelling and anchoring black transformation on a larger scale.

Complicating Brown's visit was that fact that his mission – if at least not simply explained as a recruiting mission for Harpers Ferry[137] – led him to Chatham for some of the reasons that also explained Delany's presence there: the need for a black community and an administrative body that could legitimize his projects and were outside the reach of the jurisdiction in which black freedom and citizenship were denied by slavery, the Fugitive Slave Act, and the *Dred Scott* Supreme Court decision. As a result, Chatham in 1858 harboured two "governments-in-waiting": Delany's own National Board of Commissioners and Brown's "Provisional Government." As the "Journal of the Provisional Constitutional Convention" reveals, the latter remained incomplete – John Brown was elected commander-in-chief and only a few other officers were appointed. It did not reconvene before the events of Harpers Ferry put an end to the undertaking.

Notably, the position of president could not be filled during the meetings. According to the "Journal," several candidates declined or were struck off the list because their acceptance was unlikely.[138] It is reasonable to assume that Delany's name was put forward, for, at least in Sterling's often awkward semi-fictional reconstruction, "Martin Delany shook his head when eyes turned to him" (1971, 173). There were a number of reasons why Brown had problems filling his slate. The Canadian participants might have been interested in supporting his cause but were not necessarily willing to get involved in Brown's entirely US-centred project. In addition, the prospect of being an elected officer in a project of insurrection might have been daunting. As for Delany, his plan for an African expedition was already well under way at this moment. Although in his own account he agreed to become "president of the permanent organization of the Subterranean Pass Way, with Mr. Isaac D. Shadd, editor of the Provincial Freeman, as secretary" (Rollin 1868,

89) – he declined other forms of involvement in Brown's plans, "as his attention and time were directed entirely to the African Exploration movement, which was planned prior to his meeting Captain Brown" (89).

While Sterling and Ullman accept Delany's account, Levine assumes that Brown must have been unaware of Delany's African project; he thus charges Delany with a certain duplicity in his dealings with Brown (1997, 183). Whether one believes Delany's version or not, it is clear that he was not interested in ceding control to other leadership figures, be it Frederick Douglass or John Brown. The same can be said for African colonization, long rejected by Delany as the project of the African Colonization Society and some of its pro-slavery minions, but attempted by himself at the end of the 1850s. At least in his novel *Blake; or The Huts of America* – completed it seems just before his journey to Africa – the role of commander-in-chief was reserved for his partially autobiographical hero.[139] As Sterling notes, here and elsewhere in the novel are "echoes of the John Brown convention, as the Rebels drew up plans for a Provisional Government and elected Henry Blake commander-in-chief" (1971, 181).

Delany's Blake; or The Huts of America

Delany's *Blake; or The Huts of America* was written, according to most estimates, between 1852 and 1858, with changes possibly made in 1861.[140] A number of critics assume that most of the book was completed after Delany moved to Chatham in 1856.[141] *Blake* is an intensely transnational text, with its eponymous hero's travels in the United States, Canada, Cuba, and Africa mirroring the transnational, hemispheric, and transatlantic implications of slavery and the fight against it. Especially after seminal studies by Gilroy (1993), Sundquist (1993), and Levine (1997), the transnational dimensions of the text have produced numerous critical analyses.[142] In his magisterial *To Wake the Nations*, a massive rewriting of US literary history organized around questions of race and the contributions of black culture, Eric Sundquist suggests that "*Blake*, whatever its weaknesses in narrative structure and characterization, is among the most compelling statements of black transnationalist ideology in the nineteenth century" (1993, 206). Paul Gilroy, who considers Delany "vital" (1993, 19) to the concerns of his foundational *The Black Atlantic*, asserts that the "affirmation of the intercultural and transnational" in *Blake* destabilizes the "opposition between national and diaspora perspectives"; the novel "locates the black Atlantic world in a webbed network, between the local and the global" (29). Gilroy sees Delany as a writer who shifts attention from "the relationship of identity to roots and rootedness" to a perspective that sees "identity as a process of movement and mediation that is more appropriately approached via the homonym routes" (19).

Delany turned to a novelistic expression of his transnational vision of black culture and resistance in the period of growing acrimony between him and the more United States–focused Douglass. Robert Levine, who has examined in detail the long process in which Delany and Douglass vied for political leadership, sees in *Blake* "an allegorical account of Delany's quest for leadership and community" that also "means to combat and expose the limits of the U.S. nationalism espoused by blacks aligned with Douglass" (1997, 190). Delany's first step of actual emigration led him to Canada, where, as we have seen, one of his initial gestures was to attack Douglass in the pages of the *Provincial Freeman* for his previous disregard for the black Canadian context. The status of Chatham and Canada West, however, oscillated for Delany. As with Baquaqua and so many others, Chatham and Canada West offered a relatively secure space that facilitated literary production; in the novel and in Delany's own life, however, Canada – as, ultimately, in Stowe's *Uncle Tom's Cabin* – served only as an enabling way station en route to other destinations. Delany's *Blake* nonetheless became Canada's first black novel and, according to Gilroy, "the fourth novel written by a black American" (1993, 27), joining other texts that inscribed the black Canadian nineteenth century in black hemispheric and Atlantic networks.

Blake is routed through a good number of texts and contexts crucial to the fight against slavery in the unpredictable antebellum period.[143] While some of its "ideas and verse" date back to Delany's 1846–48 *North Star* period (Sundquist 1993, 183),[144] it is generally assumed that *Blake* originated partially as a response to a novel much admired by Douglass, *Uncle Tom's Cabin.*[145] We have seen Delany peeved, in 1853, when Douglass showcased Stowe's novel. Leadership aspirations aside, Delany would have been displeased with George's final move to Liberia in the novel (though this is not mentioned in his exchange with Douglass). More significantly, Uncle Tom's submissive attitude, which is motivated by religion, and Stowe's ascription of intelligence and ability to George's mixed race are subject to revision in Delany's novel; Delany epigraphically cites lines by Stowe that have "the Lord of Ages" commit to "right the wrong," but his hero is proudly black, of "unmixed blood" (Delany 1970, 260), and the leader of a rebellion. And

Canada represents, not a stop before being shipped to Liberia by the American Colonization Society, but an episode in the protagonist's move towards black revolution and an independent black nation in Cuba.

Delany revises the portrayal of black leadership figures in two texts that, like *Blake*, feature a slave revolt on a slave ship, Douglass's "The Heroic Slave" (1853) and Melville's "Benito Cereno" (Sundquist 1993, 183).[146] He also offers an alternative to the leadership characters in Stowe's novel *Dred* (1856), which features a white figure modelled on William King, who takes his slaves to freedom in Canada, and the death of a maroon leader modelled on Nat Turner (whose "Confessions" Stowe appends to her novel).[147] While black leaders in Stowe's and Melville's texts go down to defeat, the insurgent messianic style of Delany's hero "far outstrips the language that Frederick Douglass would attribute to [his protagonist] Madison Washington" (Sundquist 1993, 206). Furthermore, Delany probably draws on a number of slave narratives,[148] and as we have seen, the Chatham convention with Brown may also have left traces in *Blake*.[149]

Opening with a meeting between US and Cuban businessmen in Baltimore, Delany's novel focuses on the transnational functioning of slavery from the very first page. The purpose of the meeting is to refit a trade vessel for use as a slave ship. In its new incarnation, the *Merchantman* will be fittingly renamed later, in Delany's parody of the US national emblem, as the *Vulture*. Another premise of the novel is immediately introduced: the abolition of the slave trade in the United States in 1808 has not changed anything. With bitter sarcasm, Delany has the Americans tout Baltimore as headquarters of their operation and praise the city as "having done more for the encouragement and protection of the trade than any other known place" (Delany 1970, 3).[150] The American partners further agree, we learn later, that Cuba should be annexed and "compelled to submit to the United States" (62). Delany reserves his second chapter for his other main premise: Northern and Southern interests collude in underwriting the continued slave trade. One of the business partners, a Natchez slave dealer, receives assurances from a Northern visitor that "we can have no interests separate from yours … in our country commercial interests have taken precedence of all others, which is a sufficient guarantee of our fidelity to the South" (4). The visitor's husband, like Stowe's senator, is shown as an active cog in the machinery of the Fugitive Slave Act; he is the judge who "tried the first case under the Act" (4).[151] The Southern slave dealer is convinced: "I yield the controversy. You have already done more than we of the South expected" (4). Delany thus delivers quickly on the prospectus by Thomas Hamilton, the editor of the *Anglo-African Magazine*, which advertises in January 1859 that the novel "shows the combined political interests that unite the North and the South" (qtd in Sterling 1971, 184). The prospectus further announces that the novel reveals a "formidable understanding among the slaves throughout the United States and Cuba" (qtd in Sterling 1971, 184). In response to the transnational tentacles of slavery, this resistant network begins to unfold in the novel when the Northern visitor buys one of the household slaves as a servant for her country seat in Cuba. The ensuing stock scene of family separation, in which children and parents, husband and wife are torn apart, is familiar from *Uncle Tom's Cabin*. The reaction, however, is much more radical in Delany's novel. While Stowe's character George accepts the use of violence in immediate self-defence, a transnational revolutionary leader is born in *Blake*. Henry[152] travels first through the US South to plant the seeds for massive insurrection, takes part of his family to Canada, and then rescues his wife in Cuba. His origins as Cuban-born Henrico Blacus are revealed in a meeting with a re-found relative, Placido, a Cuban revolutionary poet (in real life executed in 1844).[153] Employed on the very ship whose transformation from trade vessel to a slaver opens the novel, Blake now sails to Africa hoping to take over the ship and its black cargo and initiate a black uprising in Cuba. Instead, he witnesses hundreds of ill and dying slaves thrown overboard as the slave ship successfully eludes a British pursuer – a revolting scene of mass murder that echoes the Zong massacre of 1781. Blake's plans for a Cuban uprising proceed nonetheless with the help of Placido. Chapter 74 – the last chapter we possess – leaves the reader in suspense on the eve of the revolution. The effect of the unresolved ending is "to suspend the course of revolution in a crisis comparable to the historical moment at which *Blake* first appeared" (Sundquist 1993, 220).[154]

Chapter 33 of *Blake*, entitled "Happy Greeting," is of particular interest, since it is set in Canada, where Delany resided during much of the composition of *Blake*. The chapter begins with the protagonist, who has escaped slave catchers, crossing the river into Windsor; at its end, we see the "runaway leader … at the Windsor depot, from whence he reached the Suspension Bridge at Niagara en route for the Atlantic" (157). In contrast to other texts that make Canada the endpoint of the journey, or to "the typological figuring in *Uncle Tom's Cabin* of Canada as heaven" (Levine 1997, 199), Delany places this chapter in the middle of the text. The penultimate chapter of part 1, it marks the ending of one stage and the beginning of the protagonist's revolutionary undertaking in Cuba (and his transatlantic voyage on the *Vulture*).

Delany sets up his revision of earlier portrayals of the Canadian Canaan by replaying, at the beginning of the chapter and couched in a somewhat stereotyping vernacular, an archetypal scene of black fugitive arrival in Canada:[155] "'Is dis Canada? Is dis de good ole British soil we hear so much 'bout way down in Missierppi?' exclaimed Andy. 'Is dis free groun'? De lan' whar black folks is free! Thang God a'mighty for dis privilege!' When he fell upon his hands and knees and kissed the earth" (Delany 1970, 152). The chapter indeed offers all the positive elements of black progress associated with Canada: "the enlarged hopes of future Prospects in the industrial pursuits of life" (153), "the purchase of fifty acres of land with improvements suitable," and the chance "to provide for the schooling of the children" (155). The novel also makes Canada the scene of family reunion and a triple marriage, signs of a happy ending that are set against the backdrop of freedom and safety: "But Andy was free – being on British soil – from the bribes of slaveholding influences; where the unhallowed foot of the slavecatcher dare not tread; where no decrees of an American Congress ... could reach" (153).

This, however, is not *Blake*'s main message about Canada, and not its ending. The chapter also contains a long explanation of why, for Delany, the Canadian Canaan signifies not closure, but the need for other solutions and further transformation. After Andy kisses the ground, the narrator comments: "Poor fellow! he little knew the unnatural feelings and course pursued toward his race by many Canadians ... He little knew that while according to fundamental British Law and constitutional rights, all persons are equal in the realm, yet by a systematic course of policy and artifice, his race with few exceptions in some parts, excepting the Eastern Province, is excluded from the enjoyment and practical exercise of every right, except mere suffrage-voting – even to those of sitting on a jury as its own peer, and the exercise of military duty" (152–3). The comment on military duty seems contradicted by an evocation of blacks fighting Patriotes in the 1837 Rebellion, but Delany clearly warns against the racism of "those too pretending to be Englishmen by birth, with some of whom the blacks had fought side by side in the memorable crusade made upon that fairest portion of Her Majesty's Colonial Possessions, by Americans in disguise, calling themselves 'Patriots'" (152).[156] Despite Mary Ann Shadd's claims to the contrary in *Plea*, Delany rightly points to Canadian racism as a powerful fact. Samuel Ringgold Ward's analyses and the Larwill campaign against Elgin are among the many indicators of realities often repressed in abolitionist writings[157] but evoked with force by Delany: "He little knew the facts, and as little expected to find such a state of things in the long-talked of and much-loved Canada by the slaves. He knew not that some of high intelligence and educational attainments of his race residing in many parts of the Provinces, were really excluded from and practically denied their rights, and that there was no authority known to the colony to give redress and make restitution on the petition or application of these representative men of his race, which had frequently been done with the reply from the Canadian functionaries that they had no power to reach their case" (153). In contrast to Delany's narrator, Samuel Ringgold Ward lauds the work of the judiciary in upholding the law, but his account of Canada West also contains numerous breaches that indicate the reality of racist prejudice and practical exclusion. *Blake* underlines these circumstances with an episode in which "a few of the most respectable colored ladies of a town in Kent County, desirous through reverence and respect, to see a British Lord Chief Justice on the Bench of Queen's Court, taking seats in the gallery of the court house assigned to females and other visitors, were ruthlessly taken hold of and shown down the stairway by a man and 'officer' of the Court of Queen's Bench for that place" (153). Knowledge of such facts and incidents, the narrator avers, would quickly show the black immigrant the limits of Canada as a space of freedom and fulfillment: "An emotion of unutterable indignation would swell the heart of the determined slave, and almost compel him to curse the country of his adoption" (153).

In *Blake*, Canada is not a space in need of perfection, but a fundamentally flawed, temporary solution that can nonetheless facilitate other possibilities.[158] This is the position Delany had formulated – with slight differences – in *Emigration* in 1852, in his 1854 convention speech "Political Destiny," and then in his 1855 report "Political Aspects of the Colored People of the United States." Delany's novel cites prejudice and blacks' limited control over their lives in Canada as reasons why the quest for black redemption must continue elsewhere. Part 1 thus "ends by pointing to a conventional narrative closure and then disclosing the actual conditions that make such closure impossible" (Ernest 1995, 228n23). On the level of plot, closure is denied by Henry's dual quest for the freedom of his wife in Cuba and an independent black nation.

Blake is an important text in the corpus of the Black Canadian Renaissance. Partially written in Chatham, it speaks in important ways to the unfulfilled promise of Canada. One of the first black novels in the North American corpus, it revises the trope of the Canadian Canaan as a point of arrival and closure, dominant in abolitionist discourse at the time, and subsequently in the Canadian imagination and historiography. Instead,

Delany casts mid-nineteenth century Canada as part of a network of black hemispheric and black Atlantic routes and connections. Levine remarks: "As suggested by the series of Blake's border crossings – from the United States to Canada, back to the United States, and then on to Cuba – the black community has no fixed boundaries, though its 'political destiny' would appear to be in 'America'" (1997, 200). This last remark may pertain to *Blake*, but for Delany himself the preceding comment about boundaries was at least equally pertinent. As noted earlier, while Delany engaged with Brown's US-related project in 1858 and worked on *Blake* with its plot involving a hemispheric uprising, he had already reactivated his African expedition and emigration plans outlined in the appendix to *Emigration* in 1852.[159] Indeed, as his letter to William Lloyd Garrison in February 1859 suggests, Delany issued the serially-published *Blake* in book form to finance his African venture (Levine 1997, 178–9). His experiences from that voyage found their way into the novel, whose second part was published after his return. In *Blake*, the border town Windsor relates Canada West to black diasporic routes and emigrationist circuitry that include the United States and the Caribbean. After his trip to Africa and London, Delany returned to nearby Chatham – then his black Atlantic home – giving several lectures in dashiki there (Gilroy 1993, 20) and probably preparing the *Official Report of the Niger Valley Exploring Party* for printing.[160]

Osborne P. Anderson, Shadd, and *A Voice from Harper's Ferry*

While Delany was in Africa, John Brown struck at Harpers Ferry. In the aftermath of the attack, on 17 October 1859, a number of black leaders sought safety in Canada,[161] creating further North American implications for Chatham. As discussed above, the often-made assumption that Brown fully shared his plans at the Chatham convention is less than safe. There are "reasons to believe that Brown did not at this time announce unambiguously the full scope of his revolutionary plan[s]": some financial supporters might be alienated, for instance, and support for such plans from Chatham blacks was uncertain: "Indeed the black attendants had exercised a good deal of independent judgment" (von Frank 2006, 154). While black participants from the Chatham area supported Brown's "Provisional Constitution," only one, Osborne P. Anderson, would eventually join Brown in September 1859 at the Kennedy farm, where Brown assembled his group a few miles north of Harpers Ferry.[162]

A free black who attended Oberlin College before he moved to Chatham in 1850, Anderson was the printer of the *Provincial Freeman* from 1857 to 1858 and was present at the Chatham convention (Ripley 1986, 428).[163] After surviving the engagement at Harpers Ferry, Anderson eulogized Brown in a speech in Toronto in 1860, an occasion that also served to collect funds for the publication of his account of the raid (Ripley 1986, 425–6). In 1861, Anderson's *A Voice from Harper's Ferry: A Narrative of Events at Harper's Ferry; with Incidents Prior and Subsequent to its Capture by Captain Brown and His Men* was published in Boston. Details of this narrative have been contradicted by pro-slavery writers. In addition, in his biography of John Brown, Oswald Villard expresses doubts about the narrative's description of Anderson's escape (1910, 445–6, 685), although Jean Libby later attempts to explain some of the apparent discrepancies (1979, 151–4).[164] In his book on John Brown in 1909, W.E.B. Du Bois calls Anderson's the "best account of the raid by a participant" (2001, 239). Anderson's text was probably produced in Chatham, though little is known about the actual writing of it.[165] It is generally assumed, however, that Mary Ann Shadd participated in the writing of the text, as ghost writer, compiler, or editor,[166] playing a substantial role in the preparation of the text as she was accused of by Virginia's governor Henry A. Wise (Winks 1997, 268).[167]

In the preface to *A Voice from Harper's Ferry*, Anderson cites his "own personal experience … as the only man alive who was at Harpers Ferry during the entire time" to authenticate the account, promising a "plain unadorned, truthful story." It is not entirely certain, however, whether one hears the voice of Anderson or Shadd in passages like the following, which uses biblical typology to link freedom movements from Moses to Brown: "There is an unbroken chain of sentiment and purpose from Moses of the Jews to John Brown of America; from Kossuth, and the liberators of France and Italy, to the untutored Gabriel, and the Denmark Veseys, Nat Turners and Madison Washingtons of the Southern American States. The shaping and expressing of a thought for freedom takes the same consistence with the colored American – whether he be an independent citizen of the Haytian nation, a proscribed but humble nominally free colored man, a patient, toiling, but hopeful slave – as with the proudest or noblest representative of European or American civilization and Christianity" (O.P. Anderson 1861, 2–3). *A Voice from Harper's Ferry* links Brown to past leaders, but it is also written for the future. While it provides details of events before Harpers Ferry and during the actual fighting, it withholds other information with references to future action.[168] The preface thus states that "as his plans were not consummated, and as their fulfillment is committed to the future no one to whom they are known will recklessly expose all of them to the public gaze" (4). And later, when Anderson justifies escaping what had become a hopeless battle, he avers that "it was better to retreat while it was possible, as our work for the day was clearly finished, and gain a position where in the future we could work with better success, than to recklessly invite capture and brutality at the hands of our enemies" (46). While Anderson is concerned with defending himself against possible charges of desertion (see Libby 1979, 152–3), the main thrust of the account is to vindicate the enterprise and even to show its potential for success in the future.

The text manages to validate Brown's leadership – rejecting, for example, criticism that blacks were reduced to playing minor roles in the raid[169] – while hinting that Brown himself may have caused an unnecessary defeat. When Brown learned that a search of the Kennedy farm was imminent, he initiated the attack on Harpers Ferry earlier than planned. For Anderson, however, not the lack of further reinforcements but Brown's subsequent decision to tarry longer than agreed at Harpers Ferry was fatal: "This tardiness on the part of our brave leader was sensibly felt to be an omen of evil by some of us, and was eventually the cause of our defeat. It was no part of the original plan to hold on to the Ferry, or to parley with prisoners; but by so doing, time was afforded to carry the news of its capture to several points, and forces were thrown into the place, which surrounded us" (O.P. Anderson 1861, 38). Yet even here, Anderson insists that Brown's humanity in dealing with prisoners led to his downfall.

A Voice from Harper's Ferry contradicts Southern accounts that seek to minimize the military potency of the attack and to downplay black readiness for revolt. Anderson thus stresses the indeed deadly efficiency of the insurgents during the fight.[170] He also takes great care to underline courageous black participation in the uprising, demonstrating that slaves and other blacks were ready for insurrection. Libby cites "the controlled Southern version of frightened slaves and their reported unanimous refusal to fight with Brown's forces," suggesting that it "was in the interest of all factions at the time to minimize the role of local blacks in the raid" (1979, ii). In the words of *A Voice from Harper's Ferry*, "There was seemingly a studied attempt to enforce the belief that the slaves were cowardly, and that they were really more in favor of Virginia masters and slavery, than of their freedom" (O.P. Anderson 1861, 59). In response, Anderson sings the courage of black fighters throughout the text and honours their deaths in battle. Finally, his last chapter is entirely dedicated to slave participation in military efforts, which effectively signalled further insurrectional potential: "The truth of the Harper's Ferry 'raid' … in regard to the part taken by the slaves … demonstrates clearly: First, that the conduct of the slaves is a strong guarantee of the weakness of the institution, should a favorable opportunity occur; and, secondly, that the colored people, as a body, were well represented by numbers, both in the fight, and in the number who suffered martyrdom afterward" (60). While Brown patiently engaged in discourse with his prisoners, "hundreds of slaves were ready, and would have joined in the work" (60); this work, the closing suggests, would be completed at a later date, and the consequences of Brown's work would "eventually dissolve the union between Freedom and Slavery" (62). In a sense, Anderson's prediction would come true, given the role of Harpers Ferry as a factor that precipitated the Civil War.

FROM THE MID-1860S INTO THE TWENTIETH CENTURY

Together with Delany's *Blake*, Anderson's *A Voice from Harper's Ferry* is one of the last major black Canadian texts from the period that saw the beginning of the Civil War in 1861, Lincoln's Emancipation Proclamation of 1863, the outcome of the war, and the Thirteenth Amendment of 1865, which abolished slavery.[171] A number of black Canadian residents left to fight in the Union Army, while others returned to the United States after the war. Delany began to raise volunteers for a Massachusetts black regiment in 1863. He moved with his family to Ohio in 1864, becoming the first black major in the Union army in February 1865 (Sterling 1971, 230–51).[172] Part of the Shadd family remained in Canada, but Mary Ann followed Delany's invitation to become an army recruiter, and her brother Abraham enlisted in 1863 (see Ripley 1986, 520–2). Osborne Anderson, while operating like Josiah Henson from Canada, also served as an army recruiter, dying in 1872 in Washington. Like him, Mary Ann Shadd and Delany would remain in the United States after the war. As we will see in a moment, though, the number of black Canadian residents who moved from Canada to the United States because of the outcome of the war and the achievement of emancipation remains subject to debate.

Although at a slower rate than previously, Canadian slave narratives and other texts related to black life in Canada continued to appear in the 1860s and later. Slave narratives included the 1861 text by William Troy mentioned earlier and, in the same year, an account by Lavina Wormeny, a child of free parents who was enslaved in Washington and arrived in Montreal after multiple escapes and arrests.[173] Samuel Gridley Howe's report was published in 1864 and William Still's compendium in 1872. Former Maryland slave Jim Henson's much later narrative, *Broken Shackles*, documents the presence of fugitives further north in Canada West, in Owen Sound near Georgian Bay. It was published in 1889 by transcriber John Frost (under the pseudonym of Glenelg).

Two other known slave narratives from Canada come from the West Coast, where black British Columbian writing (see chapter 5) is documented in Wayde Compton's anthology *Bluesprint* (2001). William H.H. Johnson's *The Horrors of Slavery*, published in 1901 in Vancouver,[174] is disparagingly called by Winks "a potpourri of the fieriest of abolitionist tracts" (1997, 291), but black historian Dorothy Williams reads it as a sign of resistance against the racism experienced by blacks who remained in Canada after the Civil War (2005, 42). The story of Sylvia Stark, transcribed by her daughter Marie Stark Wallace, narrates her family's journey from Missouri to Salt Spring Island off the coast of Vancouver. Mifflin Gibbs, finally, is one of the prominent members of the community of free California blacks that comes to British Columbia in 1858; in *Shadow and Light: An Autobiography with Reminiscences of the Last and Present Century*, published in 1902, he recounts his life in Canada.[175]

In addition to these published documents, other texts and literary activities remain less visible and accessible. Over a dozen black literary societies demonstrated the "literary-society ideal in the southwestern part of the province," in some cases well into the twentieth century (Murray 2002, 73–4). Prominent examples of black writing in this context are the unpublished notebooks of Anderson Ruffin Abbott, whom I mentioned earlier with regard to debates over black education in Canada West. Abbott studied at Knox College together with Samuel Ringgold Ward before training at the School of Medicine in Toronto. He became "the first Canadian-born Black doctor and served as one of eight Black surgeons in the Union Army during the American Civil War" (D.G. Hill 1981, 206). In a sketch of his life, Abbott notes that he practised medicine in Chatham after the war, presided over the Wilberforce Educational Institute from 1873 to 1880, and served as "President of Chatham Literary & Debating Society" (Abbott Papers, qtd in D.G. Hill 1981, 207). He delivered the society's inaugural address in 1875 and contributed to newspapers, including the *Chatham Planet*, the *Dundas Banner*, the Boston *Colored American Magazine*, the *Anglo-American Magazine*, and the New York *Age*.[176] His notebooks from the years 1898–1913 contain essays and sketches ranging across biology, astronomy, history, economics, literary figures such as Browning and Tennyson, and many issues related to black culture and history in Canada, including "The Future of the Negro," "Negro Emigration (to Africa)," "The Elgin Settlement," "Colour Prejudice in Canada," "Niagara Movement & Booker T. Washington," and "History of Negro Immigration to Canada." In addition, a number of entries and addresses for the Grand Army of the Republic (GAR), an organization of Union Army veterans, highlight the participation of this Toronto-born black Canadian in the American Civil War. While Abbott practised medicine after the war not only in Chatham and Dundas but for a few years also in Chicago, he returned to Toronto for the last part of his life, from 1897 to 1913.

Abbott's life demonstrates that black Canadian life and culture continued after the Civil War, the departure of a number of US–born Canadian blacks notwithstanding. Much of white Canadian public opinion, however, has interpreted the leaving of some as tantamount to an end of any black presence at the time in Canada. The moral capital earned through Canada's role in the Underground Railroad has been happily pocketed in this perspective, while continuing black Canadian life has been cast as somehow exterior to the nation. As Winks writes, when "the fugitives returned to the United States at the end of the Civil War, Canadians congratulated themselves on succor well given and on a growing problem well avoided," ascribing black departures to the climate or homesickness rather than to any problems in Canada (1997, 231). Alongside such denial, the continuing black presence in Canada was seen as an anomaly: "Although many Negroes remained behind, they somehow were not thought to be Canadian Negroes, for one always anticipated that they too would follow their brethren to the United States" (232). Winks pointedly asks how one is to think about "the British North American attitude toward Negroes when all were assumed to be fugitives?" (234).

As the historian and curator Adrienne Shadd observes, the long black presence in Canada has been mostly "written out of our history and obliterated from the Canadian psyche in general" (A. Shadd 2001a, 11). While the Underground Railroad contributed to Canada's positive self-image, after "1865 Black Canadians disappear from view. It is as if they have fallen off their precariously held perch on the edge of a steep Canadian cliff" (A. Shadd 2001b, 296). In a more recent study of black Canadian culture and resistance from 1870 to 1955, Sarah-Jane Mathieu comments that "throughout the Jim Crow era (1877–1954), Canadians … saw blacks as an immigrant problem, conveniently ignoring that blacks have been in Canada since the early 17th century; in 1931, 80% of the nearly 20,000 blacks in Canada were in fact born there" (Mathieu 2010, 6).[177] Perceiving black Canada as always foreign, "Canadian imagination and historiography persistently framed African Canadians through the lens of recent immigration, erasing their investment in the formation of the Canadian nation-state" (6–7).

But the assumption that most mid-nineteenth-century black Canadians were fugitives from the United States, as well as the story that the majority of them joined a great black exodus from Canada after the American Civil War, has been challenged as a myth. While noting that few blacks left the Maritimes in these years, even Winks still guesses that "perhaps two-thirds of those in the Canadas, more recently arrived and often with family ties in their former homes, moved in reverse down the Underground Railroad" (Winks 1997, 289). Yet in 1998, Rhodes took another look at such guestimates: "Most scholarship has contended that the war depleted the black male population and contributed to the beginning of an exodus of blacks back to the United States … More recently, this argument has been countered with evidence that suggests only a small number of blacks in Canada were propelled across the border during this period" (1998, 154). In particular, she points to Michael Wayne's reassessment of census numbers, which speak against such a mass migration south (Rhodes 1998, 249n48; Wayne 1995). Working from the original handwritten schedules of the 1861 census, Wayne shows that these numbers – rather than the figures in the published report that have been dismissed as improbably low by most historians – are indeed compatible with figures that can be found in, or deduced from, the texts by Howe and Drew discussed above.[178] Allowing for some undercounting and cases of "passing" (especially in Toronto), he arrives at "maybe 22,500 or 23,000" blacks in Canada West in 1861 (470). This number is higher than the entirely unlikely published census numbers, but substantially lower than the roughly 40,000 often accepted in their lieu – for instance, by Winks (1997, 240). When compared with the 1871 census numbers (generally accepted to be more reliable than the earlier ones), this figure contradicts the often-made assumption that "fully two-thirds of the black population had left the province by the end of the decade" (Wayne 1995, 470). Instead, Wayne concludes that "the black population of Canada West decreased by about 20 per cent during the period 1861 to 1871," which "hardly amounts to an exodus. Apparently an overwhelming majority of blacks chose to remain in the province after the Civil War" (471). This finding highlights the myth of an absence of black life in Canada after the mid-1860s as a blinkered if perhaps convenient idea.

With respect to another popular assumption – that most blacks in Canada were fugitives – Wayne persuasively argues that the "manuscript census tells a different story" (1995, 472). In 1861, over 40 per cent of blacks were Canadian-born and new arrivals were often "free immigrants" rather than "fugitive slaves" (472). Free blacks had better opportunities to get to Canada than slaves did, and they also had many reasons to leave the United States (472). They were increasingly threatened by abduction after the Fugitive Slave Act, and almost "all Northern states imposed substantial legal disabilities on blacks," causing "several thousand blacks from the free states" to emigrate (478). In Wayne's final analysis, only "slightly under 20 percent of all the blacks in the province were fugitives" (474).[179] Such detailed work with the 1861 manuscript census is not only of interest to historians; it crucially corrects popular notions about the black presence in Canada. For Wayne, perhaps "the most unfortunate consequence of the prevailing view is that it tends to perpetuate the nineteenth-century perception of blacks as outsiders. If most blacks were fugitives ... and if the overwhelming majority returned to the United States after the Civil War, then clearly they were not truly part of the Canadian immigrant experience" (480).

The tendency to marginalize black Canada as an anomaly that disappeared with the Civil War ignores not only the majority of black Canadians who remained in the country, but also the arrival of further black immigrants after the war: "between 1870 and 1914 ... more than 5000 African-Americans and West Indians ... came to the dominion" (Mathieu 2010, 12). During the First World War, West Indians arrived in Halifax and Saint John, and hundreds "worked in the coal mines around Sidney, Nova Scotia, where they prospered" (Winks 1997, 334). Especially with the collapse of Reconstruction in 1877 and the concomitant beginning of Jim Crow laws in the United States, many blacks again looked north for salvation. Jim Crow laws in the United States picked up where the previous various "black codes" left off. They were eventually sanctioned by the 1896 United States Supreme Court decision known as *Plessy vs Ferguson*, which upheld segregation under its infamous "separate but equal" diktat.[180] In addition, as Mathieu points out, "lynching peaked between 1889 and 1899" (2010, 29).[181]

When Anderson Abbott resigned from his new position as medical superintendent at Provident Hospital in Chicago in 1897, he cited "business reasons" (O. Thomas 1998). One cannot help but note, however, that his decision came shortly after *Plessy vs Ferguson*.[182] Others arrived in Canada around this time in search of land, misreading Canadian attempts to recruit – as it turned out – white settlers: "The perfect timing of Canada's homesteading campaign in 1896, in the wake of the *Plessy* decision, seemed like a godsend to many Southern African Americans … the Canadian Department of Immigration noted a marked increase in African Americans requesting information on immigration to the dominion. Prospective black settlers wrote from a total of thirty-one states, including every southern and midwestern state" (Mathieu 2010, 29). Canadian immigration officials soon multiplied the obstacles. Yet as the Oklahoma immigrants from 1909 to 1911 demonstrated,[183] even these signs of racial discrimination did not deter black arrivals until they were stopped by Canada's first-ever immigration ban "singling out a racial group for unqualified exclusion" (57). It was signed by Laurier shortly before his government fell in 1911.

The subsequent Borden government admitted limited numbers of black immigrants to Canada, mostly entertainers and those in the service professions – domestics and sleeping-car porters. The latter group in particular came to play a conspicuous role. Recruited by railroad companies, "young black male workers – especially sleeping car porters – constituted the largest class of black immigrants admitted into Canada between 1911 and the early 1960s" (Mathieu 2010, 58). The Grand Trunk Railway brought Pullman sleepers to Canada in 1870, staffed from the beginning by black porters. Highly respected as breadwinners in their communities, and in contrast to the image and white expectation of black subservience, black porters and other railway employees "utilized the rails and the mobility that it afforded them, forging transnational social and political alliances" through "unions, Freemason temples, churches, and the press" (5). As I will show in more detail in chapter 5, black porters were behind the development of the black anglophone community in Montreal from the 1890s onward. Black families also settled near train stations in other cities, such as Winnipeg and Vancouver.

Because of black porters' importance in black communities, their lives have found a certain degree of representation in writing and film. In *A Black Man's Toronto 1914–1980: The Reminiscences of Harry Gairey* (1981), the Jamaica-born Gairey relates the story of his life in Toronto from 1914 onward and of his career as a porter after 1936. A co-founder of the Negro Citizenship Association in 1951 (Gairey 1981, 32), he also participated in a 1954 Toronto meeting with Jamaican prime minister Norman Manley prior to the launch of the West Indian Domestic Scheme a year later (35).[184] In *My Name's Not George* (1998), the porter, activist, and later citizenship judge Stanley G. Grizzle remembers his life and role in the Brotherhood of Sleeping Car Porters. Writer Frederick Ward (see chapter 5) narrates the black porters' fight for recognition and professional advancement in director Selwyn Jacob's National Film Board documentary *The Road Taken* (1996). In the same film, pianist Joe Sealy – like so many other Canadian jazz greats the son of a porter – offers reminiscences of his father's life. Finally, to note two examples in fiction, the father of the protagonist in Lawrence Hill's first novel, *Some Great Thing* (1992), is a former porter obsessed with black history who runs a porters' home in Winnipeg (1992, 5, 44–6); and a porter and his porter son play important roles in Mairuth Sarsfield's novel *No Crystal Stair* (1997), set in 1940s Montreal.

Black churches and social and political organizations are sources of correspondence, accounts, sermons, and oratory that are continuing forms of black writing and rhetoric.[185] A number of black newspapers appeared in the first two-thirds of the twentieth century (Winks 1997, 390–412). But the reminiscences and portrayals I have just cited emerge later. Earlier black lives and communities are also retrieved, for instance, in oral histories such as Daphne Marlatt and Carole Itter's 1979 *Opening Doors: Vancouver's East End* and Dionne Brand's 1991 *No Burden to Carry: Narratives of Black Working Women in Ontario, 1920s to 1950s*. After the outpouring in the nineteenth century, a resurgence of black Canadian writing occurred only after the increase in Caribbean immigration from the mid-1950s on and the liberalization of Canada's immigration policy in 1967. Wayde Compton notes that in the years 1904–69 "it appears no book-length work was published by a black person in B.C. – sixty-five years out of a 144-year history of presence in the province" (2001, 27). With reference to this remark, George Elliott Clarke observes, as noted earlier, that "in Nova Scotia too between 1798 and the 1960s, black 'writers' published mainly a few religious works" (2003a, 78). A renewed, more substantial black Canadian literary output would have to wait until the latter third of the twentieth century.

PART II

The Presence of the Past

4

Slavery, the Black Canadian Nineteenth Century, and Caribbean Contexts in Contemporary Black Canadian Writing

A second wave of black Canadian writing emerged from the 1960s and 1970s onward. These works comment on the present, but they often also make use of earlier black texts and contexts, including black Canadian literature and history. These texts demonstrate that contemporary black Canadian literature did not appear *ex nihilo* in the 1960s, without history or extraneous to Canada's traditions. They also complicate notions of Canadian literature as white or recently multicultural through immigration. Black Canadian literature is diasporic and transnational and thrives on interaction with black and other writing elsewhere, but from the eighteenth century onward, it has also been one of the foundational threads in the literature of what is now Canada. With the exception of First Nations culture and orature, a black tradition is as homegrown and resident as any other cultural tradition in Canada (and while a number of black writers are foreign-born, they share that trait with many canonical Canadian authors). The texts I discuss in the following chapters entertain critical conversations with the past. Many of them relate more specifically to black Canadian history, its tribulations, and cultural achievements. Geographically, linguistically, and otherwise diverse, these texts are vital strands in what Africadian[1] author George Elliott Clarke calls the "heterogeneous and polyglot discourse" (2002a, 332) of black Canadian literature since the 1960s.

Who are these authors, and what are some of the early landmark texts? While I can concentrate on only a few writers, it is useful to recall some of the names and developments mentioned in the introduction. Austin Clarke, announcing the strong Caribbean contribution to the second Black Canadian Renaissance, arrived from Barbados in 1955 and began to portray the life of "Caribbean Canadians" in the novels of his Toronto trilogy. The first volume, *The Meeting Point*, was published in 1967, the year of the Canadian centennial; it was followed by *Storm of Fortune* in 1973 and *The Bigger Light* in 1975. In the mid-seventies, Dionne Brand's first volumes came out, and a number of anthologies began to make black Canadian writing more visible. These included Camille Haynes's *Black Chat* (1973), Liz Cromwell's *One Out of Many* (1975), Harold Head's *Canada in Us Now* (1976), and Lorris Elliott's *Other Voices* (1985). They were followed by Ayanna Black's *Voices: Canadian Writers of African Descent* (1992), and George Elliott Clarke's *Fire on the Water: An Anthology of Black Nova Scotian Writing* (1991, 1992) and *Eyeing the North Star* (1997). By the 1980s, and especially the 1990s, the publication pace of individual authors had accelerated. After the mid-nineteenth-century developments in black writing, both Canadian-born writers and arrivals from elsewhere were contributing again – and on a larger scale – to an impressive black cultural production in Canada.

This effervescence extended to francophone Quebec. As briefly mentioned earlier, refugees from Duvalier oppression made Montreal one of the most important cities of the Haitian diaspora. The versatile Anthony Phelps returned to Quebec after his imprisonment in Haiti and an earlier stay in 1964, portraying Haiti in several novels[2] and winning the Casa de las Americas prize with a volume of poetry, *La bélière caraïbe* (1980). Gérard Étienne, arrested and tortured under Papa Doc Duvalier, also arrived in Montreal in 1964 (living later in Moncton, NB, until his death in 2008) and transformed trauma into literature. Émile Ollivier, too, arriving in Quebec in 1965 via Paris and the winner of numerous awards, wrote diaspora between the political violence of Haiti and Canadian exile. Other literary heavyweights of the following generation include the perhaps best-known – and most translated – writer of that group, Dany Laferrière, as well as the poet Joël des Rosiers[3] and Marie-Célie Agnant.[4]

The year 1997 was an exceptionally strong one for anglophone black Canadian literature, later prompting George Elliott Clarke to see here "the sudden arrival of African-Canadian Literature" (2008). At that point, of course, an entire corpus of important work in English had already been produced by black authors – to name just a few: Austin Clarke, Frederick Ward, Cecil Foster, Makeda Silvera, George Elliott Clarke himself, Dionne Brand, Marlene NourbeSe Philip, and André Alexis (all discussed later). But Clarke was right to point to the many highlights of that year. They included the first Governor General's Awards to be won by black English-Canadian writers (Dionne Brand for *Land to Light On* and Rachel Manley for *Drumblair*); a volume of essays by Marlene NourbeSe Philip; an important study of black Montreal by Dorothy Williams; and a novel about black Montreal by Mairuth Sarsfield. In addition, 1997 saw the publication of Clarke's own path-breaking anthology *Eyeing the North Star*, the first productions of his play *Beatrice Chancy*, and Djanet Sears's play *Harlem Duet*, as well as Lawrence Hill's second novel, *Any Known Blood*. A number of these texts will be considered in some detail below.

QUESTIONING BLACK CANADIAN HISTORY: LORRIS ELLIOTT'S "ANGÉLIQUE" FRAGMENT

While the rich production of the time is diverse in style and content, a deepened dialogue with the past is one of its characteristic hallmarks. In many cases, this engagement translates into a powerful preoccupation with black Canadian antecedents. A significant example is Lorris Elliott's contribution to his own anthology *Other Voices* in 1985, "The Trial of Marie Joseph Angélique – Negress and Slave" (1985, 55–64). This fragment of a play is relevant not only because it shows a Caribbean Canadian writer in conversation with black Canadian history, but also because Elliott underlines our contemporaneity with the past by making its interrogation a subject of the play.[5]

Elliott stages this questioning with a twist. In addition to the eponymous protagonist (whose historical counterpart we will meet again below), he introduces another black woman drawn from subsequent Canadian history, Mary Ann Shadd. This character appears disoriented as she encounters slavery in Canada. Her reaction to the first appearance of Angélique, who addresses her partially in French, resembles an encounter with a ghost: "(startled) Huh! What? Who are you, good woman?" (58). As Shadd seeks to find her bearings, the ghost-like Angélique asks her difficult questions. She is clearly conversant with the issues of Shadd's lifetime: "*Colonisation!* You wish for it, *n'est-ce pas?*" Does Shadd really want to settle in this country where she, Angélique, was brought against her will? And has she heard of the Code Noir? Elliott's Shadd answers in the negative but advises that "such practices have long been declared unlawful in this country" and that in "Canada today … all men … and women too are free." Angélique, however, insists that "this land … is no place to settle in" (60).

Elliott's short fragment achieves a number of effects. Reminding us that black Canadian history is multilingual, it also introduces us to the black mid-nineteenth century and earlier slavery in Canada. Canadian self-imaging as benevolent safe haven from US slavery takes comfort from the

Underground Railroad and figures like Shadd. The ghostly irruption and unexpected presence of Angélique signals something else: conflicted terrain that emerges from historical questioning. Emotional geographies and identitarian certainties are probed and opened up to interrogation; historical distance is transformed by a scene of haunting and disorientation. Elliott's short passage offers the outline of a hauntology that denies forgetting and complicates other forms of closure, preparing the ground for possible transformation.

Elliott's Angélique does not seek empathy and pity. Instead of those classical theatrical affects, she asks for reflection and a form of witnessing. She seems to claim that the past is over: "Do not feel pity for me … what you'll now hear and see, I have already suffered. *Adieu, ma chère*" (61). But is she really gone? Pity can lead to cleansing and a sense of closure, but this Angélique returns – a *revenante* – with undecidable, ghostly qualities. She is history in all its evocative complexity, both past and yet disturbingly present: "I am here before you now … only to counsel against *colonization* here in Canada. Seek other homes" (61). Her unhomely haunting denies closure, the end of a journey, *nostos*. Most importantly, this ghost is "here," not only before Shadd, but also before the readers of the play. The spectre of Angélique questions Shadd's views of Canada. And when she leaves, led away by her executioner, we could ask with Elliott's Shadd: "O journey … is this true? … is this Canada?" (65).

Related forms of dis-closure are the subject of the chapters that follow. They explore engagements with the past and transformations of the time-spaces of Canada and the black Atlantic in more recent black Canadian writing. I begin with the contemporary fictional recall of some of the earlier black texts we encountered at the end of chapter 3 and then examine works that stage Canadian slavery as a question for the present. Finally, I widen geographic reference to include black Canadian writing that deals with hemispheric slavery. From the end of chapter 4 through chapters 5 and 6, I discuss other and often more localized historical events and formations that mark black emotional geographies in Canada and appear in contemporary artistic articulations of black subjectivity.

Thus, in chapter 4, I first concentrate on the re-articulation of the black Canadian nineteenth century in Lawrence Hill's *Any Known Blood*, then look at Hill's use of earlier black Canadian and black Atlantic history in *The Book of Negroes*. I next examine how slavery in Canada speaks in later writing that thematizes Angélique and in George Elliott Clarke's *Beatrice Chancy*. In subsequent sections, I consider how writers of the Caribbean

Canadian diaspora engage times and spaces here and elsewhere as formative elements of contemporary black subjectivities that pertain also to Canada. After a discussion of theoretical constructions of Caribbeanness and their relation to the Canadian context, I explore writings by Cecil Foster and Makeda Silvera about Caribbean Canadian farm and domestic workers and look at the presence of Caribbean slavery in works by Austin Clarke. I then discuss the evocation of the infamous 1781 slave massacre on the high seas in Marlene NourbeSe Philip's *Zong!* and examine in some detail Dionne Brand's inventories of slavery's legacies across black Atlantic and Canadian times and spaces. I conclude the section by considering the portrayal of second-generation Caribbean Canadians in works by Brand, David Chariandy, and André Alexis.

In the following section, I turn to francophone Caribbean times and spaces in Quebec. I discuss the portrayal of the intergenerational conveyance of oral knowledge in Marie-Célie Agnant's novel *La dot de Sara*, her treatment of the legacies of slavery in *The Book of Emma*, and her concern with the consequences of the Duvalier dictatorship in Haiti. This topic is an ineluctable presence in the work of the other francophone authors considered here, Gérard Étienne and Émile Ollivier, and plays a role in Dany Laferrière's novelistic meditations on the enigma and (im)possibility of return.

In chapter 5, I move the discussion to other black geographies in Canada, beginning with black anglophone Montreal, jazz, and legendary Caribbean-descended Montreal musicians such as Oscar Peterson and Oliver Jones. In the rest of the chapter, I reflect on the Africadian Renaissance and writings motivated by the demise of Africville in Halifax; I also discuss a number of texts from the black Canadian prairies, and close with a consideration of black British Columbia and the work of Wayde Compton.

All of these texts relate to the issues that I have raised in the introduction. They concern our contemporaneity with the past, cultural memory, haunting, and transformation; more generally, they relate to the black Atlantic and the affirmation of a modernity that most decidedly is also black. These texts pose an array of questions that challenge established ways of knowing and cultural conveyance. Whose past is it that we are invited to consider relevant to a communal present? What are the responses made possible by fiction to historically silent and silenced stories, to absent and repressed testimony, and to disrupted chains of transmission? What are the possibilities and limitations of literary genre in this respect? And how does one deal with the radical otherness of a past that is necessarily also "our" past? To add another important question to this incomplete list: from these pasts in the midst of our present, what possible relations can be gleaned between the ravages of trauma, actively engaged counter-memories, and positive identifications in the present?

BLACK CANADIAN HISTORY AND LAWRENCE HILL'S *ANY KNOWN BLOOD* AND *THE BOOK OF NEGROES*

A good place to begin looking for answers to some of these questions is the work of Lawrence Hill. History is central in Hill's earlier non-fiction work[6] and an important theme in his first novel. In *Some Great Thing* (1992), a black reporter with an interestingly allusive first name, Mahatma Grafton,[7] explores race and French/English linguistic difference in Winnipeg. Hill's second novel, *Any Known Blood*, appeared in 1997, a year we have seen marked by a rich output of black Canadian writing. The again allusively named protagonist Langston Cane V[8] seeks to find out about his own mixed race and family by travelling extensively in time and space, across generations and the Canada–US border. Like *The Book of Negroes*,[9] Hill's subsequent novel, *Any Known Blood* responds not only to black history in general but, more specifically, to textual antecedents from the first Black Canadian Renaissance and earlier periods.

Any Known Blood: Revising and Re-appropriating the Canadian Slave Narrative

As suggested by its title, the protagonist's name, and epigraphs, *Any Known Blood* is a multi-generational family novel[10] about mixed race.[11] It is also about passing and identity, and more specifically about a process of identification that leads through an exploring, recounting, and claiming of a family history that is intricately intertwined with an equally reclaimed black Canadian and US history.[12] In this context, Hill's novel charts a path from indecision and ambivalence to a narrativized past, to community, and to an ability to act in the present. This journey allows the protagonist to overcome his isolation and personal failures.[13] Most significantly, this process of identification finds its crucial turning point in his encounter with a forebear's slave narrative. Hill's creation of this neo-slave narrative engages critically with black Canadian and US history and revises the sometimes limiting ways by which black lives have been transmitted. My focus here will be on this fictional recuperation of the past, which recasts black narratives from both sides of the border to allow for agency in the present.

Partly to assert his own identity against his race-conscious but also domineering father, the protagonist initially dissembles his racial identity.[14] He plays a "game of multiple racial identities" by identifying himself to others as "part anything people were running down" (2), be it Jewish, Cree, or Zulu. When he does settle on one identity in his application for a government speech writer position for which "only racial minorities need apply," he successfully claims the position as an Algerian. Langston Cane V's acts of passing afford him not only a job but also a certain degree of pleasure, freedom, and self-determination (that can be achieved despite the anxieties of discovery).[15] His passing comes at a cost, however, bringing disappointment to others but also keeping Langston Cane V himself in a state of instability and ambivalence that comes to a head in a self-provoked crisis.[16] This moment initiates his decision to undertake a journey of self-discovery by researching and writing the history of his family across geographical, generational, and racial borders. While travelling in the United States, Langston Cane V does not want to pass; on the contrary, he seeks identification and wants his "race clearly marked" (119).[17]

Langston Cane V's journey to the United States in search of racial identification necessitates a parenthetical discussion of the role of black United States culture for black Canada that goes beyond the obvious connections of diasporic transnationalism. Hill's cross-border stories evoke a pervasive black Canadian theme: the importance of black United States culture north of the border. In his essay "Borrowed Blackness," for instance, André Alexis critiques the presumption of an archetypicality of black American experience, evinced in an interlocutor's opinion that "no experience I might have in Canada could bring me closer to an understanding of real Black experience, that black Canadians were not Black enough" (1995). George Elliott Clarke, in his now canonical essay "Contesting a Model Blackness" (1998, repr. in. 2002a), also dismisses a US "model blackness," pointing to diverse and heterogeneous black Canadian affiliations; yet he also cites Diane Jacobs's "On Becoming Black Canadian," a poem that similarly rejects the idea of an insignificant African Canadian experience but also evokes a catalytic potential of border crossing: "Strangely it was in the U.S.A. / that I truly became a black Canadian. / In an attempt to rebut American Blacks' assumption / that being Canadian was an aberration. / That Canadian Blacks had no history" (Jacobs 1996, 71–2; qtd in G.E. Clarke 2002a, 41).

In Hill's novel, Langston Cane V's disidentified self at first seems to have taken the advice given to Alexis, "that in order to discover my 'Black self' I should move to the United States" (Alexis 1995).[18] Yet Hill's novel as a whole turns in quite different directions. Dealing with the lives of five generations of Langston Canes on both sides of the border, the text is packed with both actual and imagined aspects of black Canadian history. Searching for his cross-border family roots, Hill's protagonist certainly delves into black American history and encounters those positive qualities of black American culture that Clarke describes as prominent in black Canadian perceptions: "For African Canadians, *African America* signifies resistance, vitality, joy, 'nation,' community, grace, art, pride, clout, spirituality, and *soul*" (G.E. Clarke 2002a, 39). Yet Hill does not romanticize any such thing as *African America* – nor does he condemn it; his engagement with aspects of black American culture is creative and includes, as we will see, some re-appropriation of black Canadian history.

Hill's text is an example of historiographic metafiction – fiction about fiction that also reflects critically on the process of historiographic conveyance.[19] He delivers cross-cultural experiences and historical exploration through the writer Langston Cane V, who works on the novel and family history that we read. The novel also uses or mentions writings by Langston Canes I–IV. The narrator finds not only documents about Langston Cane II and III and their achievements (they were Baltimore church ministers and model community members like his own father), but also a manuscript by the first Langston Cane. In this journal and neo-slave narrative – which offers a most captivating voice in the novel and which George Elliott Clarke has called "masterful" (2002a, 312) – Hill creates a much more ambiguous figure and a questionable candidate for identification. This multiple-border-crosser is surrounded by family history rumours about his possible connection with John Brown, a link that leads us to some of the Canadian nineteenth-century narratives discussed earlier.

Any Known Blood also employs local and family history gleaned through oral history. As Hill notes in the acknowledgments, his sources include "more than twenty interviews" (1997a, 507) about family history taped with his father (author of *The Freedom Seekers*), Daniel G. Hill, and "many hours" of interviews with Oakville local historian Alvin (B. Aberdeen) Duncan "about the history of his family and other blacks in Oakville" (508).[20] With the fictive manuscript of Langston Cane I taking up most of the latter part of the novel (429–94), however, Hill invents a fugitive slave narrative that is in direct conversation with a body of Canadian and United

States nineteenth-century slave and other black narratives, including those contained in Benjamin Drew's *The Narratives of Fugitive Slaves in Canada*, Osborne Anderson's *A Voice from Harper's Ferry*, passages from *Life and Times of Frederick Douglass* (1881), and Douglass's 1881 speech on John Brown at Storer College in Harpers Ferry.[21]

"A more textured, layered humanity": The Neo-Slave Narrative of Langston Cane I

Langston Cane II, being handed the narrative by an individual claiming to be his father (L. Hill 1997a, 423, 426–7), doubts its authenticity and passes it on only at the end of his life, stating that he finds "parts of it blasphemous and immoral" and thus did not "share it with my family" (427). And indeed the story that follows is a neo-slave narrative with a twist, which often does not fit the pattern of the black paragon individual; it hardly matches the exemplary lives of Langston Cane II and III, the ministers and black achievers who are held up as role models to Langston Cane V by his father.[22] With the statement "I was born in Virginia in 1828" (429), the narrative opens typically enough, although the next sentence immediately hints at Langston Cane I's independent spirit; he repudiates the notion that he was "born a slave, for I do not care for the word" and insists his freedom was stolen. Then some more unusual elements begin to appear: he admits hating his mother, who visits him a few times at night after having been sold (429), and he exceeds the limits of classical slave narratives by offering graphic descriptions of a black woman's beauty and, later, of his sexual promiscuity. In addition, he also states that he is an atheist, not out of ignorance, but by conviction (432). His abilities as a rat catcher allow him to enter the master's house and gain access to his first reading materials (430). They are also of use to him in the slave resistance and retribution activities that are part of the narrative; for instance, when an old slave who shot an overseer for whipping a female slave is killed (433–4), Langston Cane I freely admits killing that overseer with rat poison.

Hill's neo-slave narrative thus either shirks a number of the conventions of historical slave narratives or engages them critically, often radicalizing the content beyond the limits that existed at the time of their composition. Frederick Douglass will appear in person later in the narrative, but earlier episodes evoke passages from his narratives. Threatened by his second owner if he is caught learning to read, Cane I, like Douglass, thanks his owner for instructing him by interdiction. Yet, while Douglass uses his master's lecture on the liberating consequences of black literacy to understand the relationship between knowledge and power, Cane's version is both more crude and comprehensive. Reading is not the only forbidden fruit made more appealing here; severe punishment is also threatened "if he caught me stealing, or fornicating, or drinking whiskey. I thanked him, in my mind, for tipping me off about the good things in life, and made a vow to taste them all" (435–6).[23] Douglass also comes to mind in the next paragraph, in which we learn of the stalemate between Cane and his master, reminiscent of the one Douglass achieves after resisting the brutal Covey; here, Cane holds the slaveholder "off with a garden hoe. He left me alone after that" (436). Yet where Douglass is critical mainly of slaveholder religion, noting other doubts about religion cautiously and late in the narrative,[24] Cane is more direct a few pages into his narrative: "In the near dark, I learned to read. I read the Bible, cover to cover. I read it all, and I must say, I didn't believe a word of it" (437).

Cane's narrative also differs from Douglass's in that it thematizes the crossing into Canada. Hill, for instance, offers what reads like a parody of Josiah Henson's account of his own arrival in Canada (discussed in chapter 3). Henson tells us that "I threw myself on the ground, rolled in the sand, seized handfuls of it and kissed them, and danced around, till, in the eyes of several who were present, I passed for a madman" (2003, 69–70). Cane I describes his fellow fugitive's similar behaviour with considerable distance: "Upon landing on the shores of Canada, Paul Williams made a sight of himself. Down on his knees, rolling in the water and sand and debris from the Oakland Harbor, calling out, Lord Almighty, Lord Have Mercy, and so forth" (L. Hill 1997a, 447). His own reaction differs markedly: "Personally, I was dirty enough, after four weeks of running, and I didn't care to get any of that sand or water on me. And as for the Lord – well, if it made Paul Williams feel better to think there was one, that was fine with me. But I think the Bible is just a scheme to keep negroes from slitting their masters' throats" (447). He himself, of course, has already dispatched a slave overseer when young, and here his narrative also contrasts sharply with Henson's elaborate explanation of why he *does not* kill his master's son when the occasion arises.[25]

As a border-crossing narrative, Langston Cane I's account can also be read with reference to the black Canadian nineteenth century and against the narratives collected by Benjamin Drew. Cane I arrives via the Underground Railroad, being almost betrayed by a dissembling minister but helped by Quakers; trusting captain Robert Wilson, he admits knowing of the Fugitive Slave Act (443).[26] Hill also has him visit the Toronto "North American Convention of Negroes" in 1851 (462); while no mention is made of Martin Delany, Mary Ann Shadd, or Henry Bibb, he learns of Bibb's *Voice of the Fugitive* (463, 464, 466). Like many of the subjects whose lives were recorded by Drew, Cane I comments positively on the opportunities for finding work and making a living in Canada West. Yet his account differs in many respects from theirs, and it becomes clear that Hill works against the often stereotypical formulae available to fugitives under the literary and abolitionist-controlled conventions of the nineteenth century. Hill portrays instead a less-than-perfect, but complex and possibly more true-to-life, individual; Cane I wrestles not only with slavery and racism but also his own limitations. While Drew's narratives emphasize time and again the speakers' uniform condemnation of alcohol, Cane makes no secret of the fact that he likes a drink when the subject of temperance is evoked at the Toronto convention: "Some people talked about temperance and the worship of God and other measures to lift up the race. They nearly ran me out of the conference for arguing that we didn't need any lifting up and that if a man – colored or not – wanted whiskey, it was his own business" (462).

Conformity and adherence to protocols of black respectability – as we remember, the weighty expectation also imposed on his descendant Cane V – are not among Cane I's priorities. He comments for instance on the black community of Chatham: "I didn't care for it. There were too many colored folks, too close together, each one making sure the other was praying enough" (463). Much of this attitude, it becomes clear, has to do with his need to break with any patterns of coerced conformity and enforced physical labour reminiscent of slavery: "And they were all farming … I didn't like the idea of bending down over growing plants and breaking my back to pick them. The whole thing made me think of the Virginia plantation where I was born" (463).[27] His words echo earlier comments about certain types of labour. Cane's aversions, however, extend not only to the black community and church, but also to conjugal and parental obligations. They also feed his promiscuity: "But I seemed to want to destroy the conventions of my life" (469). Accused of bigamy, Hill's anti-hero leaves town when John Brown calls in search of participants for his undertaking.

Without diminishing the historical importance of Brown's actions, Hill presents a critical fictive portrayal of him. Captain Robert Wilson throws Brown out of his house, predicts his defeat, and calls him mad and patronizing (381–3, 472–3).[28] Hill states in the book's acknowledgments that this dialogue is entirely fictive (512); yet he suggests elsewhere that "it seemed truthful and right to depict Robert Wilson, a great man himself who rendered tremendous services to blacks … as still essentially a conservative person himself … He was scandalized, as most of the people were, by the very idea of John Brown's raid" (in Siemerling 2013, 13). While Hill further suggests that "many normal, striving black people also would have … wanted to put as much distance as humanly possible between themselves and this man's trouble" (in Siemerling 2013, 13), Cane I eventually follows Brown, although not for heroic reasons alone. Hill here draws on sources of the black Canadian nineteenth century that include, in particular, the narrative of Osborne Anderson. As we have seen, it is the only account of the raid by a participant. Like Anderson, Cane I attends the Chatham convention in May 1858, but unlike Anderson, he remains distanced and critical of Brown. To Brown's assertion that "slavery is a sin against God," Cane responds that it is "a sin against man" (466). According to Cane, only the plan to "free Negroes from the plantations" was discussed in Chatham, not Harpers Ferry. Even on that basis, however, Cane judges him to be unrealistic: "John Brown had never lived on a plantation, and he didn't know colored folks … They would take one look at him and declare him mad" (467).

Given his own troubles, Cane nonetheless follows Brown and hears him divulge his now modified plans in a meeting with Frederick Douglass; learning that Brown wants to attack Harpers Ferry, the fictional Douglass, too, declares Brown mad and rejects his appeal, which was recorded by the historical Douglass in his *Life and Times*: "When I strike, the bees will begin to swarm, and I shall want you to help hive them" (L. Hill 1997a, 475–6; Douglass 1881, 325). Despite his own reservations, however, Cane can "find no way to abandon Brown's mission honorably" (476). Hill here utilizes aspects of Osborne Anderson's narrative for his own purposes. Like Anderson, Cane joins Brown at the Kennedy farm as the only black Canadian participant in the raid. Anderson, despite his much more respectful tone towards Brown, is also doubtful about his efficiency in battle (as we have seen), and notes that "I could not help thinking that at times he appeared somewhat puzzled" (O.P. Anderson 1861, 36). Hill's Cane similarly notes that "John Brown looked confused" (L. Hill 1997a, 488). Like Anderson, he will decide to abandon a hopeless battle[29] and escape before it is too late. He thus survives what Douglass once called the "perfect steel-trap" of Harpers Ferry.[30] Unlike Anderson, however, who is eager to defend his decision, Cane is not concerned with justifying his desertion. On the contrary, after the first casualty turns out to be a black man shot by one of Brown's men, he admits that he has "no more fight" in him, even that he probably "never had any in the first place" (488). In general, Cane I shows much less respect for Brown and his plans than the reverent Anderson does, and unlike Anderson's description of the preparations at the Kennedy farm (Anderson 1861, 24–32), his report describes a near revolt against Brown during the preparations. There is no pretension to heroic action in Hill's character, but rather a willingness to admit to his shortcomings.[31] While Hill makes use of Osborne Anderson's narrative, he avers that he "did not model Cane closely on Anderson." Instead, he is interested in "imagin[ing], as a novelist, how a black man would perceive being a foot soldier in a white man's attack on slavery in the United States … What would a black man feel about all this? How would he feel being led by a white man against slavery in the United States?" (in Siemerling 2013, 12).

Another way of looking at this character can be gleaned from Hill's review a year later of Russell Banks's *Cloudsplitter* (1998), which portrays John Brown through the eyes of his son Owen. Both narrators initially follow Brown, yet leave the scene at crucial moments and live to tell the tale (Banks 1998, 744–6; L. Hill 1997a, 491). While Hill's narrator, like the historical Osborne Anderson, comes to his own conclusions and is capable of independent action, the Owen Brown conceived by Russell Banks remains caught in the trap, not of Harpers Ferry, but of his father's will.[32] Where Hill's Langston Cane moves quickly and independently in the present, Banks's Owen Brown remains immobilized by the past: "For a long while, as if I could not, I did not move" (Banks 1998, 745). Hill observes that Banks has "chosen to tell the story from the vantage point of the main character's son, Owen," which "brings the reader within intimate reach of … the gap between a man's public victories and private failures" (L. Hill 1998, 64). And within this question of literary technique emerges for Hill the issue that looms large in Langston Cane V's predicaments of identity: the issue of generational position and identification. "What emerges from Owen's first-person account," Hill asserts, "is a sad memoir of how he was unable to create a life for himself under the shadow of a domineering, charismatic father" (64). While Owen Brown has escaped Harpers Ferry, his identity remains strangely shackled to the internalized will and law of the father.[33] Hill's Langston Cane I, though his identity and freedom would seem to be circumscribed even tighter because he is black, not only succeeds in crossing boundaries drawn by North American political and racial geography, but also defies the "paternal" authority of John Brown and an identification that would ascribe him the role of victim in the very process of resistance to victimization and United States slavery.

Hill's neo-slave narrative, transgressing the normative expectations imposed by the historical limits of the classical slave narrative, thus creates an anti-hero – or perhaps, more accurately, an individual who is neither entirely good nor bad. Such "refusal to deify" black forebears, as Jennifer Harris claims, is "defiantly irreverent in its insistence on humanizing subjects in sometimes less than flattering ways" (2004, 371). Hill thus approaches black Canadian history with a poetics of fiction that rejects normative expectations in the name of believable and instructive imagination and dramatization. As a novelist, he maintains, "my job is to create a believable, dramatic, interesting person who seems to reflect a vital aspect of the human experience … I have to be interested in human character, not in role modeling" (in Siemerling 2013, 14). Instead of the hero Langston Cane I that his descendant has been invited to admire, Langston Cane V, while exploring his family and black Canadian history, discovers "a flawed individual" (14). Hill points out that this fact "is liberating for him" (14). At the end, Langston Cane V feels "strangely connected to Langston the First" (L. Hill 1997a, 497). His identification becomes possible because he discovers that his forebear, like him, "didn't fit in. I love him for his mixture of weakness and dignity" (L. Hill 1997a, 497).[34] Despite his shortcomings, of course, Cane I is often courageous and capable of critical self-evaluation and, above all, action. In Hill's words, he is "a flawed individual who tries to be heroic and whose life has elements of heroism: he has survived the most oppressive childhood, lost his mother, survived slavery, fled through the Underground Railroad with great personal risk, came to Canada, and set up a life. He is just not wired to become suddenly a model citizen … Langston Cane V finds this liberating, and indeed it helps him and allows him to embrace his own humanity" (in Siemerling 2013, 14).

Langston Cane V's willingness to confront the contradictory complexity of history enables him to bring family members together, while his father's fear of compromised family history has kept them separated.[35] The critical interrogation and dramatization of history – and the portrayal of acts of individual decision-making that are often incompatible with the perfect lives of model characters – facilitates understanding and community, despite imperfection: Langston Cane V's act of telling the family story "brings his family together" (in Siemerling 2013, 10). Similarly, in Hill's novelistic dramatization of the relationship that Langston Cane V develops with his forebears and the first Langston Cane, we discover Hill's proposition about a productive look at history through fiction – in this case an effective appropriation of black history by contemporary black Canadian fiction. Hill's neo-slave narrative in *Any Known Blood* thus imagines the lives of black nineteenth-century Canadians outside the boundaries of the literary forms and conventions in which they were encased and which have often constituted our main access routes to their realities. "This more textured, layered humanity also enters into the fray in *The Book of Negroes*," Hill states; "it is the complexity of the absence of absolute right and wrong in these books" (in Siemerling 2013, 14).

Crossing Borders

This "complexity" exceeds the limits of propriety that circumscribe nineteenth-century black narratives; in addition, as we will see again in *The Book of Negroes*, the lives portrayed by Hill are not contained by any national boundaries. There is nonetheless a nationally circumscribed component to Hill's texts; while *Any Known Blood* seeks to unite black experience across national boundaries (Siemerling 2013, 16), Hill insists on a located black Canadian context and problematic that provide the starting point of the novel and mark the ending, a border crossing. Here, Cane V's Aunt Mill reclaims her Canadian citizenship – all but forgotten during her life in Baltimore – and claims as well all the other travellers in the car as her family, independently of the degree of "any known blood."[36] Her act has more integrative power symbolically and practically than the laws of a country whose official she thus deceives at the border. Her "conducting" on this (rail)road trip permits both Cane V's US lover Annette and his African friend Yoyo to cross illegally into Canada and is achieved by her identification of, and with, a "family" of many stripes and colours: "There was Yoyo, who was as dark as dark got, and a good deal darker than Mill. There was Annette, who was of a medium complexion, and then there was me – Zebra Incorporated" (400).

Yet while Hill ends this novel with a border official wishing this group "a safe trip home" (505), he also makes it clear that there is no unproblematic Canadian "national" family (or model) available for homecoming. In an article entitled "Black Like Us, Eh?," he writes: "Canada is not nearly as integrated as we like to think" (1997b). Instead – as he demonstrates in virtually all of his writings – there are stories about black Canadian history and lives to tell. The article includes an emphatic summary: "Let's celebrate our own stories during Black History Month, says Canadian novelist Lawrence Hill, not those from south of the border."[37] Hill himself hardly objects to "American content" *per se* in the films he discusses here; rather, among other things, he objects to the way they are received by Canadian audiences. Reiterating a familiar problematic, Hill worries "that Canadians often develop a second-hand, borrowed impression about what it means to be black in Canada from the American experience."

In light of such comments, one has to nuance a remark by Rinaldo Walcott: "Writing against a nationalist culture that assumes a reading of Canada as distinct from the U.S., Hill's text seems to suggest that it is impossible to make sense of some aspects of black Canadian history without a serious and sustained consideration of the place of the U.S. in that history" (2003, 67). While the second claim is self-evident – especially given the role of nineteenth-century black history and texts in Hill's novel – both *Any Known Blood* and Hill's connected memoir *Black Berry, Sweet Juice: Growing Up Black and White in Canada* do emphasize the specificities of black Canadian racial and emotional geographies. In addition, the historical dimension of *Any Known Blood* operates through situated references to the past, utilizing numerous texts from the Black Canadian Renaissance from a decidedly situated vantage point, one that appropriates them for black Canadian literature and history while demonstrating their border-crossing and transnational characteristics. As Moynagh puts it, "the transnational imaginary at work" in such "African Canadian texts has to do with embedded, place-specific, material, and historical relationships that nonetheless operate across national borders" (2010, 154).

The Book of Negroes

Hill's *The Book of Negroes* (2007a) broadens many of the strategies selected in *Any Known Blood.* It reaches even further back in history and extends further out in geography. It thus relies on Carleton's historical "Book of Negroes" as well as on some of the black Nova Scotian texts discussed in chapter 3. Like many of these texts, it crosses national borders in a diasporic reach that places Canadian locations directly in the context of a far-flung black Atlantic. In addition, the novel extends some of the formal choices made at the end of *Any Known Blood.* It thus delivers the entirety of the story in the form of a neo-slave narrative told in the first person. And like the previous work, *The Book of Negroes* fleshes out, humanizes, and imagines black diasporic lives whose voices have been muted or silenced by the protocols, narrative conventions, and documents made available by history.

Hill's text brings these voices to life in a way that reflects processes of recognition and naming from a positionality in the present. Like the previous novel, *The Book of Negroes* is a metafictional work in which the storyteller's and writer's present alternates with narrations set in the past. Here, however, the narrated and narrating subjects coincide. We encounter Aminata Diallo in her old age in 1802 in London, where she reflects on her life. At the same time, she is concerned with maintaining control over her story. Her testimony is coveted by her abolitionist hosts – among them William Wilberforce – who want to convince King George III and the British Parliament that it is time to end the slave trade in the British Empire.[38] The abolitionists' desire to shape the story according to political needs is repeatedly at odds with Aminata's own ideas. Hill's novel is thus concerned not only with the remarkable story Aminata has to tell, but also with the politics of the slave narrative and with the acts of storytelling, witnessing, and writing. These acts of conveyance are portrayed at many levels in the novel; they include the writing and reading of the historical 1783 "Book of Negroes" and Aminata's own story, which becomes *The Book of Negroes.*

Hill has Aminata tell her story, which includes the fate of others who perished during the middle passage and in slavery, in different languages and circumstances. She thus offers her account repeatedly, both orally and, eventually, in writing. The narrative begins in Africa,[39] where Aminata grows up bilingually in a village called Bayo, in what is now Niger. She speaks both her mother's Bamanankan and her father's Fulfulde,[40] but her father teaches her a few phrases in Arabic from the Qur'an. In addition, she learns the art of midwifery from her mother. Her parents are killed when she is kidnapped by Africans as a child, and she is marched in a coffle to the coast.[41] After surviving the middle passage, she works as a slave on a Carolina indigo plantation and escapes her second owner in 1755 in New York, just before the British surrender of the city. She leaves with the British for Nova Scotia in 1783. Here, her itinerary joins that of the historical Black Loyalists (this includes her return to Freetown in Sierra Leone, Africa) before she sails for England at the behest of the abolitionists.

Witnessing, Community, and Recognition: The Djeli

The Book of Negroes tells a story about black diaspora that makes language, witnessing, and writing some of its central concerns. As Aminata is forced onto the slave ship, she comes to understand that the spirits and protections of her homeland "can do nothing for any of us out on the water" (L. Hill 2007a, 54), but she hopes that if she succeeds in returning, she will be allowed to become "a *djeli*, or storyteller" (55). This hope, which eventually comes true, implies a transgression of the traditional boundaries of knowledge and the limits of authorized conveyance. Her father is "not supposed to show his daughter how to read and write a few lines in Arabic" (56), but he breaks the gender-based rules that traditionally govern access to writing in her society. Now her desire to become a storyteller transgresses the rules governing her society's oral knowledge transmission, which require that "to become a *djeli*, you had to be born into a special family … It was said that when a *djeli* passed away, the knowledge of one hundred men died with him" (55). The unprecedented trauma of entering the slave ship, however, seems to require her to witness and potentially to testify: "I sought comfort by imagining that I had been made a *djeli*, and was required to see and remember everything. My purpose would be to witness, and to prepare to testify" (55–6). She later states that her experiences are shared by those "who still scream out in the middle of the night"; others, however, "cannot know what we endured if we never find anyone to listen" (56). This last remark speaks of a need to make suffering and trauma known, and it also speaks of the importance of sharing that knowledge with others in a form of communication, community, and recognition that holds the promise of some form of redemption. In Aminata's understanding, these acts of inclusion also concern those who have met deaths that would remain unrecorded otherwise: "In telling my story, I remember all those who never made it through the bullets and the sharks and the nightmares, all those who never found a group of listeners, and all those who never touched a quill and an inkpot" (56–7). The telling of her story constitutes an act of recovery necessitated by a past that is not over but continues to accumulate its weight in the present. In Aminata's mind, ocean crossings remain associated with a sense of haunting. At the end of her life, she recalls, using a phrase that titles the book's chapter about the middle passage ("We glide over the unburied," 55–95): "Every time I have sailed the seas, I have the sense of gliding over the unburied" (7).

Aminata's use of language, reiteration, and eventual re-inscription makes her a figure of mediation, transmission, and transformation who can create community, hope, and redemptive recognition. During the middle passage, her knowledge of several languages gives her the power to bring community into being. The ship's doctor recognizes her ability to facilitate his communication with different slave groups and has her chains removed (58–9). She thus hears the captives in the ship's hold call out "in a frenzy of languages," pleading for "water, food, air, light" in Arabic, Fulfulde, Bamanankan, and other languages and dialects she can decipher often only partially.

Hill makes the need to be recognized, known, and remembered central in a passage from which he later draws the title of the US edition of the novel:

> "Please. Say it. Say my name."
> "Chekura," I said.
> "Someone knows my name. Seeing you makes me want to live." (66)

Similarly, other captives in the ship's hold "repeated my name and called out their own as I passed. They wanted me to know them. Who they were. Their names. That they were alive, and would go on living" (66). As a consequence, Aminata comes to remember most of the enslaved individuals on the ship by name, and she can carry out one of the primordial tasks related to a community and its story: the naming of its members. She performs this task of enumeration and safekeeping in their midst: "I began to sing a song while we danced, naming all the people I saw. I tried to name every single face, and give the name of the person's home village" (50).

A similar mode of surreptitious communication – which the crew mistakes for *only* singing – allows the slave leader to prepare an insurrection (81). Its failure, however, causes more captives to be killed, in addition to those thrown overboard daily because of their weakness from exhaustion and disease (89–92). Aminata's story also records the suffering that the slave trade inflicts on slavers. They too are in ill health, and many die: "The toubabu [white] sailors looked just as ill. I saw many dead seamen thrown overboard without ceremony" (93). While these and other shocking elements of her story will bolster her testimony against future slave trade, Aminata's acts of witnessing have an immediate impact on the present situation of the captives, offering a sense of community and meaning at a time when most other resources of hope have vanished.

The Scene of Testimony and Writing

Aminata's story and testimony are later delivered to other audiences that afford specific opportunities but, in some cases, impose particular constraints. They include Aminata's husband in New York after a long separation; listeners in Nova Scotia such as the minister Moses Wilkinson (318–19); African audiences encountered on a trip from Sierra Leone to find her native village (which almost ends in her re-enslavement) (446–7); and, finally, future audiences Aminata will imagine when she writes her story at the end of her life (103). The immediate audience of that account, however, consists of the abolitionists who have brought her to London for their own purposes. Each of the first three "Books" of Aminata's story, and *The Book of Negroes,* are thus introduced by a section that recounts her interaction with the London abolitionists, while the fourth and last "Book" concludes with one.

Aminata carefully notes the impact that different audiences have on her. Her official testimony in Parliament, for instance, leaves her "exhausted" (460) because of the absence of audience participation and community. By contrast, "when I had told my stories night after night in the village far in the interior of Sierra Leone, the people had made me feel admired. With their laughter and interjections, and with the drinks and the food that they urged me to take, they had made me feel as if I were surrounded by family" (460–1). Her African audiences pose questions, react, and comment, while the parliamentary committee only listens; her abolitionist hosts, however, seek to control her story.

The first sign comes shortly after she arrives in London, narrated in a section dated 1802 that is placed at the end of the book. One of the abolitionists tells her that "we will interview you and write a short account of your life, including the abuses you suffered in the slave trade" (451). Aminata, who has read and admires the narrative written by Olaudah Equiano[42] – but has arrived too late to meet him still alive in London (454) – insists that she herself will "write the story of my life" (455). The abolitionists' concern is that the "slightest inaccuracy or inattention to detail could be fatal to our cause" (451). They worry in particular about contact with the London poor (once defended by Equiano): "There can't be a whiff of suggestion that your story has been influenced by the blacks of London. This would do our cause great damage, as they are not well regarded here" (455). Like their historical counterparts, these abolitionists covet the value of "authenticity" (455), but strangely and paradoxically, they seek to ensure authenticity through the use of a ghostwriter, or at least "guidance" (455). Yet Aminata insists: "My life. My words. My pen. I am capable of writing" (455). When the abolitionists "insist on correcting 'allegations that cannot be proved'" in the completed text (469), she lets them know, at the very end of the novel, "that my story is my story and it will be published by the one who lets my words stand" (469).[43]

As she points out in the opening London section of the novel, "And I am writing this account. All of it. Should I perish before the task is done, I have instructed John Clarkson, one of the quieter abolitionists but the only one I trust, to change nothing" (4).[44] Among the reasons for this insistence are

Aminata's objections to fighting only the slave trade and not slavery itself – although the abolitionists tell her that any "talk of outright abolition will unite planters, shippers, traders and insurers. Can I not see that it is men of property who vote in Parliament?" (100–1). Aminata, however, avers that she "cannot speak against the slave trade without condemning slavery." She is convinced that "their way is better than the alternative, but their way is not enough" (101). As opposed to the tactical considerations that see her narrative as a tool within a parliamentary equation, Aminata considers her witnessing and writing in ways that imply another temporality as well as healing and redemption.

Early in the novel, Aminata calls her life "a ghost story" (4). Yet, if there is haunting, it implies not passive melancholia, but transformation and appropriation of the present and the future. As Hill explains in conversation, Aminata's life is a "horror story" in the sense that, to an African child abducted in the eighteenth century, white slavers must have appeared "like ghosts: they are completely unknown, they are otherworldly, they represent in her imagination the most evil manifestation imaginable" (in Siemerling 2013, 20). Moreover, Aminata's story itself has ghostly qualities, since she has come back from a place "that few ever return from" (in Siemerling 2013, 21). The reality of her words about the past, however, lies in the present and in the future. To see herself in the role of a storyteller "is part of her emotional salvation … The tribulations she has endured … are translated into something valuable from her own cultural viewpoint: to be a djeli incarnate and to share her experiences" (in Siemerling 2013, 21). As I suggested in chapter 1, Aminata's decision to choose such a vantage point gives her an ability to act and provides emotional support in the present. The advantages and promises of her chosen positionality are reinforced by the concrete hopes that connect her acts of testimony and writing to the future.

This orientation to the future is clearly announced in the title of the London section that introduces Book III (set in 1803): "And my story waits like a restful beast" (99). This section reflects explicitly on the power of language and narrative. Aminata makes it clear that writing opens a time frame that allows her story to be told because it can be heard and received by another, future audience, without being curtailed by the limits imposed by possible recognition by her current addressees: "The abolitionists may well call me their equal, but their lips do not yet say my name and their ears do not yet hear my story. Not the way I want to tell it" (101). Instead of that story, she seems to imply, the abolitionists are only prepared to hear *their* version of the story, a reflection of their own needs and desires in the present. By contrast, Aminata's conception of her written testimony and autobiography is directed towards the future. It is a powerful being that will release its potential in its own time: "But I have long loved the written word, and come to see in it the power of the sleeping lion. This is my name. This is who I am. This is how I got here. In the absence of an audience, I will write down my story so that it waits like a restful beast with lungs breathing and heart beating" (101).

This horizon reaches beyond the abolition of the slave trade to that of slavery itself and seems not even limited to that context. Hill's orchestration of transformative temporalities implicates future acts of recognition and includes us as the readers of *The Book of Negroes*. The time of our reading is transformed from a look at the past into an affective present, which comes to life in further acts of witnessing and testimony: "If I live long enough to finish this story, it will outlive me. Long after I have returned to the spirits of my ancestors, perhaps it will wait in the London Library. Sometimes I imagine the first reader to come upon my story … One of these people will find my story and pass it along. And then, I believe, I will have lived for a reason" (103).

As the three sections set in London at the end of Aminata's life demonstrate, throughout the rendering of its spell-binding story of enslavement, diaspora, and freedom, one of the novel's recurrent themes is the tension between the different discursive needs that shape a story. Hill shows Aminata time and again claiming the power of language, story, and writing. She has to claim that power even if – or, perhaps better, because – she has to wrest control over her life story from benevolent abolitionists. Aminata's conscious realization of the power and joy that comes with the ability to give testimony orally and in writing is an intricate part of the story she has to tell. This primordial theme of *The Book of Negroes* applies not only to her own life story, but also to her part in the writing of the historical 1783 "Book of Negroes" and to the role she plays in the rendering of black lives as part of a communal exodus as portrayed in the novel.

Writing the "Book of Negroes"

When Aminata comes to New York in 1775, her multiple linguistic competencies extend not only to Fulfulde, Bamanankan, Arabic, and a Gullah dialect, but also to a variety of English dialects and writing skills, including bookkeeping. A mixed-race overseer secretly begins to teach her some

English reading and writing at the indigo plantation where she works at first (154–5) and where she embarks on reading the Bible. Solomon Lindo, her second owner, instructs her in doing sums, bookkeeping, and other aspects of economics;[45] he also discusses Exodus as understood in Judaism, Christianity, and Islam with her (199–205).[46] His wife becomes her writing teacher, allowing her to acquire business writing skills while she works in Charles Town (207). Here, she reads newspapers, Swift, and Voltaire (207), and eventually she sees maps of Africa. Their uncertain geographies and lack of detail confirm to her that white representations cannot account for the Africa she knows – and certainly not for her own experience of it: "I now felt, more than ever before, that these people didn't know me at all" (213). This insight will remind her at every turn of the necessity to become the author of her own story. She arrives with Solomon Lindo in New York one year before the outbreak of the American Revolution (240), on the *Queen Charlotte* – a ship named after a queen rumoured to have some African ancestry and thus hinting at the possibility of black sovereignty.[47] At this point, Aminata has already decided that she will seek personal independence and that this trip "would be my Exodus" (229).

Historically, Fraunces Tavern in New York would later be the site of Washington's farewell to his officers after the British evacuation of New York; it was owned by the man who became the steward of Washington's New York and then Philadelphia households, West Indian black Sam Fraunces. The tavern also becomes a prominent part of the scene and context in which Aminata, too, declares her independence, and it signals her exodus through writing. As Lindo steps away for business, Aminata inscribes her own name to register at this historical site that will later be associated with United States freedom: "I wrote my name into the registration book: *Aminata Diallo*. I took it as a good sign that I was free to write my own name in New York City. The mere act of writing it, moving smoothly, unerringly with the quill in the calligraphy that Mrs. Lindo had so patiently taught me, sealed a private contract that I had made with myself. I have now written my name on a public document, and I was a person, with just as much right to life and liberty as the man who claims to own me. I would not return to Charles Town" (243–4). This personal declaration of independence is soon enough followed by her physical exodus, which Hill shows in conscious parallel with the American Revolution. "Never again shall we be slaves" (252), she hears on her second day in New York from a Patriote ransacking a house after the battles at Lexington and Concord. While the Patriote speaks figuratively, and explicitly excludes real slaves from this liberation project, Aminata uses the turmoil to hide in the woods on "April 23, 1775, and I had taken back my freedom" (255).

Aminata finds herself teaching other black New Yorkers (258–65), preparing them for similar possibilities, when she reads Lord Dunmore's proclamation promising freedom to all black slaves and servants of Rebels who will join the British to fight (268). As we have seen in chapter 2, and as Aminata duly notes, the proclamation addresses itself only to potential soldiers and thus men (268). She much more happily teaches her students the words of Henry Clinton's 1779 Philipsburg Proclamation, which promises "*To every Negro who shall desert the Rebel Standard, full security to follow within these lines, any occupation which he shall think proper*" (279–80). In 1782, however, as Aminata is herself in the employ of the British as midwife, she has to read another document to the black community following the British surrender. The Provisional Peace Treaty and in particular its Article 7 cause panic – as we have seen in Boston King's "Memoirs," discussed in chapter 2 – with its interdiction of "carrying away any Negroes or other Property of the American Inhabitants" (282–3). Yet Aminata also learns of Carleton's interpretation that self-emancipated and other free individuals having served the British for at least one year are not viewed as American "property" any longer. And she is asked to play a role in the plans to evacuate blacks along with other Loyalists to Nova Scotia: "You will help us register them. In due time, you will collect names, ages, and how they came to serve the British" (286).

With this crucial turn, Hill again validates the principle underlying so many of the passages in *The Book of Negroes* that are concerned with language, testimony, and writing: the necessity to express views and tell stories – or, here, history and (her)story – from socio-historically specific vantage points. He also underlines the urgency for Aminata to appropriate and articulate her own history and that of other black diasporic subjects. Hill's own appropriation of imperial and black diasporic, Canadian, and US history thus does not only make a black subject, Aminata, a translator and a mediator of the statements, claims, and encapsulated life stories offered by blacks to the interrogating British and American officials; more than that, Hill makes her one of the scribes – and in many cases an author – of the 1783 "Book of Negroes." In Hill's novel, Aminata becomes a chronicler of the black exodus to Nova Scotia, a *djeli* of one of the most important chapters of black Canadian beginnings.

Initially, Aminata's task is to elicit information, translate, and "relay answers to the officers" (290), who, in the case of past service for the British, produce "tickets" – the equivalent of the historical Birch Certificates – that will afford access to the ships. Although this is a life-deciding interrogation, Aminata's intermediary role as the one who elicits and receives these stories of black diasporic subjects allows for a sense of community and recognition, recalling her similar function of repeatedly enunciating the names of the distressed black community during the middle passage. Listening to black life stories again helps her to overcome isolation: "Each person who stood before me had a story every bit as unbelievable as mine" (291). To allow the interviewees to realize their inscription in a communal story, Aminata performs in each case the act of a modern-day *djeli* who translates the written record back into orality: "I showed them the tickets, read out the names and made sure they saw that their names had been recorded" (291).

Hill gives Aminata an even more active and determining role in his fictional transformation of the writing of the "Book of Negroes" itself (291–302). During the inspection of the ship *Spring* – the first vessel recorded in Carleton's original document – Aminata is asked to function as a scribe. Hill thus gives a black subject, instead of a white official, the task of writing the "Book of Negroes." At the same time, he begins to revise the myth of the "Book of Negroes" being a document of black freedom only. The first individuals Aminata is asked to register, to her surprise and dismay, are "slaves and indentured servants … the property of white Loyalists" (292). As mentioned in chapter 2, Hill here interprets the relationship recorded under the rubric "Names of the Persons in whose Possession they now are" as indenture, not benevolent protection. His first white Loyalist in this context is the one who heads that column in the historical document, Isaac Allen (L. Hill 2007a, 292), whose background is discussed by Whitfield (2009, 65). Hill dramatizes the original entry, as it appears in the historical record, by supplementing it with further context.

In Hill's novelistic staging of the creation of the historical record, the black person's story is silenced by Allen, who incidentally uses the words of the devil: "The colonel began to interview a Negro who stammered uncontrollably, but a white Loyalist stepped forward and said: 'He's mine'" (292). Not surprisingly, after registering further such individuals on the ship *Free Briton* – a name consistent again with the historical document, but ironic in this context – Aminata asks, "Is 'indentured' another word for slave?" (295). As seen in chapter 2, Hill ensures disambiguation of the category of "Possession" with the slight addition of "Ind to" to the historical record otherwise cited verbatim of, for instance, "*Sarah Johnson, 22, squat wench, quadroon. Ind to Donald Ross*" (295). Hill comments similarly on other entries containing Ross's name, such as by adding that he "brought five indentured servants with him on that ship" (295).

Further supplementary revision by Hill concerns not the content, but the act of writing and recording itself. He thus augments data otherwise repeated verbatim from the historical "Book of Negroes" with the presence of the supervising army official and, in his particular appropriation of the historical record, of Aminata as the actual scribe: "Following the colonel's instructions, I began to write in the ledger. In the first column, *George Black*. Next to it, *35*. And then I wrote the name of the owner or indenturer, *Lt. Colonel Isaac Allen*. In a final column, I wrote how he came to be freed before taken into indenture. *Freed by Lawrence Hartshorne, as certified*" (293). Having introduced this context of enunciation – the scene of question and answer and of reporting, interpretation, and transcription – Hill further accentuates the process of revisionary appropriation. Often, the procedure is entirely carried out by Aminata: "When the colonel grew impatient with the Negroes' accents, I took over the questioning and scrivening" (293). Hill also attributes some moments of largesse to the scribe, in particular the acceptance of such self-emancipatory statements as "*Says he came behind the British lines three years ago*"; the British colonel "was wearying of details and the American inspectors were growing bored, so I dashed out the entry as I saw fit" (294).

Hill's staging, however, also draws attention to likely tensions and contestations implicit in each entry. This dimension is elided in a historical document that can name black diasporic subjects, but that also silences their full stories by substitution and erasure. Hill shows Aminata's desire to give more ample detail: "I liked writing names in the Book of Negroes, recording how people had obtained their freedom, how old they were and where they had been born: South Carolina, Georgia and Virginia, Madagascar, Angola and Bonny. I wanted to write more about them, but the ledger was cramped and Colonel Baker pressed me to rush through the lineups" (294–5). Aminata also registers her dislike of short descriptive phrases "such as *stout wench, marks on face, stout fellow, pitted with pox, likely fellow, ordinary fellow, worn out, one-eyed, lusty wench, incurably lame, little fellow, likely boy* and *fine child*," stating that she doesn't "care for the descriptions" (295). They are chosen for brevity but hide so much more complex and relevant stories about these individuals that we – like Hill – in most cases must imagine.

While most ships leave from New York for Nova Scotia, some sail to Quebec, England, and Germany. Here, Hill tells one of the other stories eclipsed by the brevity of the historical entries, rendering (with very slight revision) the following entry: "*David, 10, likely boy, Germany is residence of claimant, M. General Kospoth. The boy goes with the General who got him at Philadelphia. The boy can give no account with whom he formerly lived*" (296).[48] Hill elaborates the entry by partially adding a historical background and partially imagining the story: "The colonel made me write it that way, but David had spoken with me briefly, on board the *Hind*, and he told me that General Kospoth and his Hessians had made off with him and a number of other slaves belonging to a tobacco farmer" (296–7). Some of the stories behind such entries, which Hill chooses in order to exemplify the need for further narrative and explanation, are slowly beginning to surface through historical research.[49] Here again he imagines the final shape of the ledger entry as the result of decisions between actors with different interests: "'Just keep it simple, Meena,' Baker said, dictating the response" (296–7).

Beyond the entries recorded in the Inspection Rolls of the "Book of Negroes," Hill's revisionary process extends to the transcript of the hearings of the Board of Inquiry. As we have seen in chapter 2, the transcript gives substantially more space to black testimony than do the Inspection Rolls of the "Book of Negroes" proper. Hill, however, intensifies the staging of black experience here, making the case of Aminata herself the subject of a hearing held at Fraunces Tavern, historically the meeting place of the board but also Aminata's refuge in the novel. Aminata, "*In Possession of General Birch Certificate*" (303), can document her service for the British. Like other cases discussed in chapter 2, however, she is hauled off the ship that she boarded and is compelled to face a claimant before the board at Fraunces Tavern.

While the case transcriptions are perhaps more eloquent than the short entries of the Inspection Rolls, they are still mute with respect to the emotions, fears, and hopes of the black subjects. Their fate is decided after a brief exchange of claim and counter-claim and the swift decision of an official. Showing the procedure from Aminata's perspective, Hill dramatizes the personal trauma of this moment. For Aminata, the claim means separation from her husband after both had boarded a ship to freedom and had felt safe from re-enslavement. Hill also uses the scene to imagine Solomon Lindo's remorse. He thus adds the element of guilt to the spectacle of greed and fraud that occasionally surfaces even in the historical transcript. When Aminata's first owner seeks to claim her despite a subsequent sale, Lindo appears to present proof of his own ownership. Guilt-ridden and seeking – in vain – forgiveness, however, he does not claim his "property" but rather lets Aminata go free (311). In Hill's handling of the incident, Lindo appears as a *deus ex machina*, but it is clear that for Hill these hearings – beyond their recorded content – put also the white claimants and their motivations on trial.

In addition, the very nature of these hearings is submitted to our – and history's – judgment. While Aminata waits for her decision, she is forced to listen, with heightening anxiety, to cases in which other former slaves are handed back to their previous owners. Carleton's interpretation of Article 7 of the Provisional Peace Treaty may seem courageous from some historical perspectives, but the very act of subjecting black lives to this kind of life-deciding hearing is seen as scandalous when looked at from a perspective such as Aminata's: "I despised the Americans for taking these Negroes, but my greatest contempt was for the British. They had used us in every way in the war. Cooks. Whores. Midwives. Soldiers. We had given them our food, our beds, our blood and our lives. And when slave owners showed up with their stories and their paperwork, the British turned their backs and allowed us to be seized like chattel" (307). Hill thus underlines the ambivalent nature of the historical document, which records both freedom and continued slavery. He complicates any simple and mythological comparison of the "Book of Negroes" with a biblical book of exodus from oppression. Such caveats are further emphasized when Aminata, narrowly escaping re-enslavement herself, flees with the last British ship out of New York to Shelburne, Nova Scotia.

Nova Scotia, the Promised Land?

"Was this the promised land"? (312). Hill begins his portrayal of the reception of Black Loyalists in Nova Scotia with this hopeful, yet also anxious, question as Aminata steps off the ship in Shelburne (initially named Port Roseway). This section of the novel, however, dismantles many popular assumptions and complacencies about early Canada as a haven for blacks mistreated south of the nascent border. Near the black community of Birchtown, where Aminata finds shelter, she encounters overt racism in Shelburne (313). She sees advertisements offering rewards for runaway slaves (321), and she discovers that even small offences committed by blacks receive harsh punishment, including hangings (323). She observes that "if you came to Nova Scotia free, you remained free" but "if you came to Nova Scotia as a slave, you were bound just as fast as our brothers and sisters in the United States" (321). Aminata finds work in Shelburne as a typesetter and as help for a white family. Hill takes care to describe the hard times for everyone there, which have been documented in historical sources. His main concern, though, is to imagine that particular experience from a black perspective (337). Aminata thus witnesses a race riot break out when disbanded and impoverished soldiers attack blacks, whom they perceive as competition for scarce jobs.[50] They kill a number of Black Loyalists,[51] and Birchtown is vandalized (340). While her white employers give her shelter, one of them also flees Shelburne and steals Aminata's last child.

In addition to creating this portrait of race relations in late eighteenth-century Shelburne, Hill seeks to flesh out the life of the black community, especially in Birchtown. We have seen this community described in the account by the Shelburne Baptist David George, the *Memoirs* of Boston King, and the journal by John Marrant. Hill, however, focuses on a black leader who did not leave his own account, the Methodist preacher Moses Wilkinson. Also known as Daddy Moses, Wilkinson is listed in the 1783 "Book of Negroes" and is described as "blind & lame." Despite his physical disabilities, the result of smallpox, he was an energetic and influential community leader whose meeting house served the Birchtown community (Walker 1992, 73). He would later be a leader of the exodus to Sierra Leone. Wilkinson is a subject in the *Memoirs* by Boston King, whose wife was Wilkinson's first Birchtown convert and who himself started out as a preacher in his community. He also appears in Marrant's journal in an episode about this itinerant Calvinist preacher's hostile disagreement with Wilkinson over matters of faith (see chapter 2). In Hill's portrayal, however, Wilkinson is the first black person to welcome Aminata and to offer her help and shelter. Perhaps equally important, the open ear he lends her encourages her to tell her story for the first time in Nova Scotia (318–19). He subsequently turns up as a community leader who courageously stands up to the wrath of the white population, who threaten to kill him and who destroy his meeting place and home during a riot.[52]

Hill recounts the suffering experienced by the black community during the race riots, but also the struggle for justice led by the Black Loyalist Thomas Peters. Hill again has Aminata write part of a historical document (353), in this case Peters's "Memorial," a document that was taken up by abolitionists in England and eventually led to the British offer to relocate black

Nova Scotians to Sierra Leone.[53] Aminata plays a role similar to the one she had in New York, reading first the offer of the Sierra Leone Company to the black Nova Scotians (355), then taking notes for Thomas Clarkson when he comes to Birchtown and speaks in Daddy Moses's meeting house to the black settlers; she subsequently becomes Clarkson's assistant (358, 360). The former slave Aminata values her freedom above all, yet eventually she comes to the conclusion that Nova Scotia is but a station on the way to a promised land. Early on, she is forced to observe: "I had less food and fewer comforts than at any other time in my life" (322). Although she is able to earn a living for a while, she loses her youngest child and her livelihood after the race riot. With twelve hundred other Black Loyalists, exasperated by racism and broken promises over land, she sails back to Africa in 1792 in search of a better life in Freetown, Sierra Leone. From there, she will later leave for London to support the fight against slavery. As suggested in chapter 1, her life thus underlines the idea of diasporic routes and errantry rather than a literal return to her geographic roots, and a shift from a rendering of imaginary homelands to the idea of witnessing, self-articulation, connection, and relation.

During her travels, Aminata tells her story repeatedly, to different audiences and under varying circumstances. She tells it in New York privately to her husband and then under questioning to the officer who determines access to the ships. She shares it in Nova Scotia with the preacher Moses Wilkinson and others. She offers it to Africans in the villages surrounding Sierra Leone, then to the abolitionists and a parliamentary committee in London. Finally, she records it in her written autobiography. In each case, she insists on her own story, one that often defies the formal conventions and thematic restrictions requested. Hill thus makes her resist the very limits that have caused significant silences and omissions in the transmitted written black narratives that we have from that period. In that process, not only does Aminata become the fictive scribe – and at times the content-shaping author – of parts of the "Book of Negroes," but, through her persona, Hill revises a larger book of black diaspora constituted by the hitherto prevailing accounts of the black Atlantic in the late eighteenth century.

The black Nova Scotian experience becomes part of a vividly remembered and imagined black Atlantic story not only of diasporic migration and trauma, but also of self-determination, courage, and hope. Aminata tells this story for her own and for others' personal emotional salvation at the time, but also as a testimony that "waits like a restful beast" in our contemporary present. Hill thus produces a counter-narrative of modernity that revises and refocuses the accounts of foundational accumulation of white wealth in the New World. His story includes both white barbarism and especially the black labour upon which that New World was built, whether on an indigo plantation in South Carolina or in the Nova Scotia settler town of Shelburne. Shelburne's decline, Hill points out, coincided with the departure of much of its labour force when the black settlers left for Sierra Leone (L. Hill 2009, 325).[54]

Hill's text also does not omit the fact that many Nova Scotia blacks were slaves. As opposed to Aminata and the Sierra Leone migrants, they were not free to go. As we have seen, Aminata repeatedly notes the presence of slaves who are brought by Loyalists on the ships from New York. Yet Hill's text concentrates on the story of free Black Loyalists who continue onward to Sierra Leone, on Aminata's acts of witnessing, and on the abolitionist scene at the imperial centre. While *The Book of Negroes* puts Nova Scotia on the map of fiction that imagines the black Atlantic in the eighteenth century, and while it counteracts any notion of early Canada as a racially unproblematic Canaan, the imaginative reconstruction of Canadian slavery is more centrally the focus of the texts that are discussed in the next section.

CANADIAN SLAVERY AND BLACK CANADIAN WRITING: LORENA GALE AND GEORGE ELLIOTT CLARKE

Slavery is the subject of a number of black Canadian texts that imagine, witness, and remember numerous diasporic black Atlantic routes and settings. Imagining slavery in what is now Canada through imaginative literature, however, is a task begun especially by texts reflecting on the fate of Montreal slave Angélique, such as Lorena Gale's play about her (first produced in 1998), and by George Elliott Clarke's verse drama and opera *Beatrice Chancy* (1999) about slavery in Nova Scotia. Gale's play is set in Montreal in 1734, while Clarke evokes Nova Scotia's Annapolis Valley in 1801, barely a decade after the Black Loyalists portrayed by Hill left the province for Sierra Leone. Like so many of the other texts about slavery under discussion here (e.g., Hill's *The Book of Negroes*, Dionne Brand's work, or Marlene NourbeSe Philip's *Zong!*), these works insist that the past reality of transatlantic black slavery is still part of our present. It lives on in its consequences as a foundational fact of modernity, even if it is repressed by institutionalized forms of memory and knowledge reproduction.

Canadian slavery, little remembered, points to a public amnesia and a delusional "lack of ghosts" that block access to a deeper historical consciousness and hide the full extent of Canada's role in black Atlantic networks and connections. While historical records offer some information, the resources of literary writing allow imagining vital realities beyond the traces left by history. Clarke works from the historical fact of slavery in Nova Scotia, and he makes a historical figure such as Nova Scotia governor John Wentworth a character in his text. His eponymous slave character, though, is imagined, even if she is an individual responding to historically determined circumstances. Gale and other authors concerned with Angélique can rely on a historical figure as their central character, but they have to negotiate the silences created by the very sources that seem to speak of the subject. The only testimony available by Angélique herself consists of transposed statements given under interrogation, and her fate has come down to us through court documents and other sources that belong to a white colonial archive.

Imagining Angélique

Montreal slavery is not an unknown fact, but until recently it has tended to be voluntarily forgotten or unevenly remembered. As seen in chapter 2, François-Xavier Garneau's seminal *Histoire du Canada* (1845–48) thus omitted the fact of slavery in New France until its fourth edition in 1882 (Winks 1997, 19). Slavery – suffered by blacks and indigenous peoples alike – received its first systematic treatment with Marcel Trudel's work beginning in the 1960s, which was not always greeted with enthusiasm in Quebec,[55] and has been elucidated more recently by Maureen Elgersman (1999) and Daniel Gay (2004) and in two volumes by Frank Mackey (2004, 2010). Despite the silences and continuing widespread ignorance concerning slavery in Quebec, Angélique is an exception. Her trial testimony, discussed above, potentially creates openings within cultural memory and its representation, as well as within the discursive reproduction of public space (see McKittrick 2006, 91–119). At the same time, her case also represents significant risks of critical foreclosure and "museumification." Romanticized readings seem one danger. As George Elliott Clarke puts it, "the image of her figure (hanging, then burning), martyred in the cause of liberty, *is* irresistible" (2002b). And while fictional characters can create emotional investments, they can also vampirize history, feeding on the past but leaving significant aspects of it lifeless in the present. Another disabling gesture, finally, is to declare the past over. Such pedagogical containment hides the lively potential of Hill's "sleeping beast" behind an accumulation of facts that simulates closure.

Lorris Elliott's 1985 play fragment addresses some of these issues by staging the questioning of history itself and by showing nineteenth-century black educator, author, and editor Mary Ann Shadd in dialogue with Angélique. Gale's play *Angélique* accentuates this interrogation of history even further. The Montreal slave is also the subject of francophone novels composed by Paul Fehmiu Brown (1998) and white Québécoise author Micheline Bail (1999), a song by Faith Nolan, a movie from 1999 (G.E. Clarke 2002b; 2006, xv), and another film released in 2010, *Black Hands: Trial of the Arsonist Slave*. In 2006, Afua Cooper devotes a monograph to the topic and Katherine McKittrick a book chapter; around this time, Angélique also gains increased francophone attention in exhibits and other media.[56] While the potential of her case to widen interest in New France slavery and help transform dominant narratives of Quebec's past remains to be seen, Angélique seems to be able to forestall closure. As the "Book of Negroes," Trudel's *Dictionnaire*, Mackey's accounts of black life in Montreal, and many other sources demonstrate, countless other stories and contexts within New France and Quebec await attention, inviting writers to rise to the occasion.

Angélique's ability to attract attention is due in part to the fact that her story remains productively unstable, especially around the question of guilt. Whether the historical Angélique was in fact guilty is more than questionable. After all, fires were a common occurrence in the eighteenth century, when towns like Montreal were mostly built of wood. In 1721, a fire destroyed more of Montreal than the forty-five houses and the convent that went up in flames in 1734.

In light of the few known facts, one might assert Angélique's innocence. Yet despite the many indications of a race-based witch hunt, other commentators and researchers leave the question of guilt open, a decision that invites repeated inquisitive participation. One example is the adoption of Angélique by the project tellingly called *Great Unresolved Mysteries of Canadian History*. There is another way, however, of dealing with Angélique's presumed guilt. Here, the choice is to assume – or to leave the possibility emphatically open – that Angélique intentionally committed arson but to justify her incendiary action as understandable, necessary, or revolutionary. As opposed to the courtroom drama of the wrongly accused, the scene shifts here to the court of history. The option is effective in terms of literary drama, but a number of facts militate against the likelihood of Angélique being a female Montreal Nat Turner. Open insurrection by the perhaps forty or so black slaves among the five thousand inhabitants of Montreal at the time is hard to imagine, especially since most of them were house slaves living individually in their owners' residences, unlike Southern field slaves (McKittrick 2006, 110–12).

An individual act of sabotage was possible, given her intention to flee across the frozen river "to new England And from there To Her country of Portugal across from Madeira" (first interrogation). Even her owner, though, the widow Mme de Couagne, avers in her statement on 14 April 1734 that "she cannot However suspect ~~that~~ the said Negress had Set the fire because there were none in the Chimneys of the House" (Juridiction royale de Montréal 1734).[57] As Clarke points out, before this accusation she was inconspicuous and even if "she did set a fire to consume her mistress's mansion, then it was to cover her flight – into the arms of her white lover, Claude Thibault, a fact that complicates her status as a Canadian slave rebel" (2002b, 42).

From another perspective, however, the actual origin of the fire is less important than the accusation and its consequences, which speak to the issue of race and slavery in Montreal and New France, leaving an archival trace that creates a breach in dominant historiography. Whether guilty or not, her accusation and condemnation "confirmed," and at the same time contained, the fears of a white colonial population, compounded by the repressed guilt caused by slavery. The trial also allowed the colonial elite to reinforce racial boundaries it deemed necessary to sustain. Angélique's case sheds light on the entire period and can potentially help to evoke the anonymous lives and deaths of countless other black subjects in New France. As in the case of the Zong massacre, it was a court case that produced documents that left a trace for posterity. These documents facilitate a process of unceasing witnessing that brings wider contexts into view and that continues into the present.

As Lorris Elliott's treatment of the subject indicates, one of the challenges in this respect is to evoke Angélique as a sign of a continued process of questioning, one that interrogates not a black culprit but a chain of historiography and the conveyance of presumed facts determined by colonial and then national perspectives. Such an interrogation makes later ways of reading and interpreting that historiography one of its subjects. The past exists for itself, independently of our reading; because of its consequences, however, it also belongs to our contemporary present. For us, it continues either unrecognized or in acts of witnessing, reading, and interpretation.

Witnessing and Temporality

This active relationship is staged literally in the most influential literary treatment of the topic to date, Lorena Gale's play *Angélique.*[58] First published in excerpts, then workshopped from 1995 onward, it premiered in 1998 and was published in book form in 2000.[59] Despite the substantial investment by the artistic community, as documented by its workshop and publication history, it was not produced in Canada after its 1998 premiere.[60] For Alan Filewood, its commercial risk for Canadian institutional theatre lies in the fact that it is a "genuinely radical statement that uses the moment of performance to destabilise the narratives that have historically secured Canadian nationhood" (2001, 280–1).

From the beginning, Gale uses a number of devices to emphasize that her treatment of Angélique and slavery is also, emphatically, a play about reading and about the narrativization of Angélique in Canadian national history. The *dramatis personae* introduces "Marie Joseph Angélique: A slave, in a Canadian History book" (Gale 2003, 7).[61] Gale then indicates the "Time" of the play as consisting of two levels; however, they are interchangeable: "The present and 1730s. Then is now. Now is then" (7). The meaning of this elliptic statement develops in the play at various levels. The first scene applies it directly to the act of reading. The stage directions call for "the sound of African drumming. The featureless silhouette of a woman dancing with a book against a backdrop of red, oranges and yellow, suggestive of flames." At the same time, the stage directions specify a voice-over "building in a rapid repetitive delivery" (9). The content of the voice-over is the shortened version of the incident as it is summarized in Canadian history, impersonal except for the specification of race: "And in seventeen thirty-four a Negro slave set fire to the City of Montreal and was hanged." The repetitions consist of shorter and shorter versions of this sentence, omitting more and more words at the beginning, until we are left with a single word at the end: "hanged."

The sound of drumming suggests an accented reading of the "sentence" of history that condemns a negro slave for the burning of Montreal. It evokes the endless repetition of that sentence as it is reiterated, time and again, by colonial and national history, but also submits the sentence to a rhythm of African drumming, shortens it, and reduces it to its final, brutal consequence in one word. That word, "hanged," now isolated and freed from the sentence of history, becomes available for another contextualization throughout the play. Its imagined reader could be the "woman dancing with a book" whom we see against a backdrop of colours that suggest fire. This female reader interacts in new ways with the history book account of Angélique. She does so in a dance of history and interpretation with a new outcome, guided by another temporality that is suggested by African drums, producing repetition with a difference. Or could she be an incarnation of Angélique herself, having come to life? A modern-day incarnation who has escaped the book that normally contains her, taking control and dancing with the object that now helps to channel other versions of her story?

From the next scene on, Gale's play offers a reading of that initial sentence that begins to fill in its many silences and punctuate it by staging scenes that provide another witnessing. As Gale indicates in a general staging note, "what can be explored is the concept of witnessing. As servants and slaves are essentially invisible, experiment with who sees what, who knows what" (7). The play thus invites the audience to reflect imaginatively on how another Montreal can be witnessed, one that is not available through standard historiography. This form of imaginative witnessing would take into account the daily lives and emotional geographies of black slaves and other servants at the time. The play also makes it clear that instead of focusing on the single "sentence of history" that is quoted at the beginning, a plurality of perspectives arises as many of the characters in the play observe each other. Often they do so in the shadows and unbeknownst to the observed subject, thereby complicating any monolithic from of counter-memory.

As the monoperspectival account of history is replaced by a multiperspectival orchestration of knowledges, we are invited to witness stagings that imagine degrees of power, control, and subjugation. These relations pertain to the mighty, the oppressed, and those in-between, all also involved in conflicts with potential equals and allies. In addition, we are asked to consider different temporalities of witnessing. How would the past have looked to different actors at the time? Whose past makes it into our present? And how would it look if it was part of our present?

After the single-sentence introduction of "a negro slave" in the history book opening, Angélique herself appears in the second scene, first "in shadows" and as the subject of her master's monologue, but possibly also in the act of listening. In the following scene, she "directly addresses the audience as documentary" (11), now a speaking subject who provides information on her object-self from a later perspective. She is accompanied by her mistress's voice "as commentary" (11). This presentation lets us witness an aspect of the power politics of slavery: her renaming in relation to her white owners. As she presents herself as "Angélique … Marie Joseph," her mistress explains the latter part as her own act of naming, "After my sister, Marie Joseph de Couagne." Prompted by Angélique's repetition of her other name, her mistress is unable "to speak the name of her dead daughter" (11). Angélique's next comment abruptly highlights the contradiction between the self-delusional representation of slavery as familial affiliation (by which the "peculiar institution" traditionally seeks to represent itself to itself and others) and the stark reality: "Negro slave born around 1710. Baptized in Montreal June 28, 1730. Hung in Montreal June 21, 1734" (11). In this cryptic and stark biography, we never learn her real, earlier name.

With a light change, we are transported to a present in the past. Different temporalities of witnessing are further emphasized with the already-mentioned instruction of temporal equation: "Then is Now. Now is Then." The co-presence of period and modern clothing and the presence of a vacuum "deluxe machine," lighters, cars, and computers remind us that the past that has been evoked through "documentary" and "commentary" is also present in a dual sense: for the characters themselves, whose concerns in their present are signalled by markers of "dailiness," but also for us, if we pay attention. By insisting on both perspectives – one that acknowledges the pastness of the past and the modes of conveyance that signal and control it, the other an insistence on the presence of the past – Gale's play forces the viewer to struggle with a simultaneity of distance and proximity, of difference and sameness. It ultimately remains undecidable: we have to acknowledge both perspectives as being present at the same time.

After citing the initial history book sentence that "contains" Angélique's life and death, Gale's play contrasts it with a staging that begins with another figure, François Poulin de Francheville. The buyer of Angélique, he is shown as the protagonist in a play of colonial and sexual power relationships (which is also staged in Clarke's *Beatrice Chancy*). Gale presents him as a "Donald Trump on a roll," a commercially successful member of the New France elite who understands that, after the fur trade, the next opportunity is the production of iron. He is able to afford a slave as a display of luxury and wealth, but also to gratify his sexual desires.

Witnessing here is again multiple as individuals observe each other and as we look at the monstrous sexual politics of slavery. We witness Angélique express her hopes for a life in which hard work will result in "reasonable peace" (13), but we also see both her new indentured co-worker and her new employer looking on from their own perspectives: "*CLAUDE and FRANÇOIS* witness" (13). Furthermore, when Angélique's hopes are dashed by her owner's sexual advances, Gale's stage directions indicate that, along with us, "CLAUDE and THÉRÈSE witness" (14). As the slave is dispossessed of her hopes, we also see the female owner witnessing her own dispossession. The scene is further witnessed by the indentured servant, who will later dispossess Thérèse of her slave.

Instead of adjudicating a slave's guilt for a fire, we are asked to witness slavery as a sexual politics of rape and reproduction that has terrible repercussions. While Gale stages Angélique's forced coupling with another slave, a comment about her "awfully fair child" (23) suggests that it was fathered by her owner. As a consequence, Angélique smothers the child (27). The wife is left with her rage about her husband's infidelity (30–1), which will eventually lead to Angélique's sale – and thus perhaps the fire. Instead of the "sentence of history," we are presented with a more detailed and historically textured geography of (white) crime, power, suffering, and tragedy. "Angélique," initially a signifier of the Montreal fire, is thus re-inscribed as a symbol of the brutal realities of slavery in New France – pronouncements about differences with Southern field slavery notwithstanding. The result is a reconstituted historical problematic that redirects our present sense of the past and of the way history is written. The play calls on the audience to respond as reconstructed witnesses of complex geopolitical, gendered, and racial relationships, not as recipients of a schoolbook text.

Alliances and Agency

The sexual politics of slavery are shown to undermine important forms of resistance in the play, among them a politics of female and racial alliances. At the end of Act I (41–2), Gale indicates a possible alliance between slave and mistress after the master's death. This possibility is precluded by Thérèse's memory of her envy of and her economic need to sell the slave. The sound of drumming, heard at the very beginning, recurs later to suggest possibilities – and failures – of alliances of resistance.[62] The other radically dispossessed group evoked in the play is indigenous slaves, called "Panis." in New France (see chapter 2). The Panis Manon appears in the historical record of Angélique's case, accusing her of making an incriminating statement before the fire that Gale transposes into the play: "She said, you really don't want to laugh? You see Mme de Francheville … She won't have a house to sleep in" (62; II.15).[63]

Gale, however, reads this historically documented accusation as the outcome of a failed possible alliance undermined by the sexual politics of slavery. Like Angélique at the beginning, Manon is first introduced by the motif of drums: "Another drum beating to a corresponding African rhythm joins with the first. They do not clash. They complement ... The women work and sing. All the while getting closer and closer. Freer and freer" (30; 1.12). Here, it is Thérèse who interrupts the possible alliance, but we learn later that it is destroyed by Angélique's forced coupling with a fellow-slave, which has deprived Manon of her lover (51–2). The failure of an alliance of the oppressed is further explored in a later scene. Manon denies any commonality with Angélique, and the latter accuses her of having "forgotten the way" (54–6). Eventually, Manon will be among Angélique's accusers (62). The third possible alliance explored by Gale is between Angélique and the indentured Claude. It is an association between two oppressed individuals across race that fails during their flight. Claude abandons Angélique, leaving her to be recaptured and returned to Montreal.

As we witness the crumbling of possible alliances, Gale invites us to ponder the question of Angélique's agency in terms of open acts of resistance – such as the setting of a fire. Gale does not exclude that possibility. As Filewood points out, Gale does not show Angélique starting the fire, but "she shows us how she might have" (2001, 286). Filewood is right, since Gale certainly portrays a potentially insurrectionary spirit. Before her master's death, Angélique secretly spits in his drink with the incantation: "Mistah buckra / he get sick / he tak fever / he be die / he be die" (38). Further, told by her mistress that she will be sold yet again, Angélique says to herself: "YOU BITCH ... I'LL KILL YOU BEFORE I HAVE ANOTHER MASTER! I'LL KILL YOU" (53). On the other hand, Gale's rendering of the hearsay "evidence" of the historical court record (the stage directions speak of the "specious and ridiculous eyewitnesses often seen on many sensational news programs" [63], and a four-year-old is the only one blaming Angélique directly [64]) does not entirely support the idea that Gale wants to convince us of an Angélique incendiary in her own time. That interpretation is also contradicted in another scene[64] and by a remark in Angélique's closing monologue: "If thought is sin / then I am guilty /... But though I am wretched, / I'm not wicked" (70). Translating here from the transcript of the historical Angélique's trial, Gale chooses to give credence to her statement of innocence during the first interrogation.[65]

The play does not conclude with the idea of insurrection, but rather with the historically recorded failure of Angélique's flight. As she is captured and dragged away, a voice-over resumes the history book reading that replaces Angélique on a stage that is now empty (II.xxii, 67–8). As her torture is described by several characters, Angélique re-enters in a return of the scene of reading, taking and closing the book (69). Her final monologue evokes a historical primacy of spirit over matter and truth over "twisted history" (70):

> Set my spirit free.
> The Truth cannot be silenced.
> Someday,
> someone will hear me
> and believe …
> I didn't do it.
>
> Until then …
> *Drums start beating softly and grow.*
> I'm going home. (70)

Possible alliances in her own time failing, she announces an alliance with another, later present, made possible by our witnessing. Referencing the moment of the play's performance, her belief that "Someday, / someone will hear me" becomes an injunction that implicates the audience as witness and as host of her return from the realm of the ancestors where she will reside "Until then."

Thus, it seems fair to argue that Gale envisions the role of Angélique not as a revolutionary agent of insurgency, but in a dialogic role, as a witness herself who also requires our witnessing. The audience thus channels her return, not as a ghost, but as a meaningful sign that gives access to the constitution of our own modernity and thus of ourselves. Her reappearance offers an occasion to create a breach in Canadian self-representation as the heterotopia of a slavery-marked United States. As George Elliott Clarke points out in his foreword to Afua Cooper's *The Hanging of Angélique*, "The price of this self-flattering self-portrait is public lying, falsified history, and self-destructive blindness" (2006, xiii).

After *Angélique*, beyond Black Angels: George Elliott Clarke's *Beatrice Chancy*

George Elliott Clarke does his own part in dispelling the myth of a slavery-free Canada. In *Beatrice Chancy* (1998/1999),[66] he makes slavery in Nova

Scotia's Annapolis Valley his subject, engaging another side of the black Nova Scotian context Lawrence Hill engages in *The Book of Negroes*. While Hill's protagonist witnesses the slaves who were brought to Nova Scotia by the Loyalists, the novel concentrates on the free Black Loyalists, many of whom left Nova Scotia again in 1792; together with the remaining free blacks, however, Nova Scotian slaves stayed behind in the province.[67]

In his treatment of Nova Scotian slavery, Clarke follows Lorena Gale in linking his eponymous heroine to the present. Their texts offer grounds for instructive comparison. Gale's Angélique punctures the settler myths of New France. Clarke's protagonist is, like Angélique, a victim of the sexual politics and violence of slavery but worries a foundational anglophone narrative of Loyalists maintaining in Canada the superior moral and political values trampled by the American Revolution. Clarke's *Beatrice Chancy*, however, also serves to imagine a different, more radical response to slavery in black Canadian writing.

Angélique and Beatrice

Angélique is mentioned in both the libretto and the drama version of *Beatrice Chancy*. In the introductory "Charge" of the libretto, Clarke allows that "slavery is an unpalatable, perhaps even un-Canadian, subject." Yet he feels "compelled to recall the fate of Marie-Joseph Angélique, an African slave in Nouvelle-France who, in 1734, started a fire that incinerated a good part of the fledgling town of Montréal, and who was subsequently imprisoned, tortured, and hanged" (1998a, 63). In the verse drama version, Angélique is the first dedicatee. Together with the name of the title, she opens a continual flow of intertextual references that make the play a complex citational weave. These intertextual evocations allow Clarke to appropriate, cannibalize,[68] and indigenize (Moynagh 2002, 99) European high and Gothic "low" literary sources, but they also let him honour black Canadians in the past, and combat "the mass ignorance about the conduct of slavery in the British North American colonies" (G.E. Clarke 1999, 7).

Angélique thus shares the opening dedication with Lydia Jackson, another black victim of slaveholder sexual abuse. These figures adumbrate a wide spectrum of black agency and resistance, interpreted somewhat differently by Gale and Clarke. While Gale seems to place Angélique's incendiary potential more with an audience in our present than in the colonial past, Lydia Jackson employed a substantial and impressive range of means of resistance in her own black Nova Scotian time. Maureen Moynagh has convincingly argued that she is "Beatrice Chancy's historical correlate" (2002, 106).[69] Clarke's Beatrice Chancy, however, is closer to an indeed violent Angélique. While the uncertain potentiality of a violent slave response to slavery in Canada – part of the fascination exerted by the historical Angélique – is somewhat tempered in Gale's play, it is fully realized in Clarke's text.

Like slavery itself, Clarke's Beatrice Chancy is overtly violent. She disturbs the image of African Canadian slaves as the more peaceful counterparts of their southern neighbours – no Nat Turner here! – which seems to give credence to its problematic corollary: the discourse of a "milder form" of slavery in Canada. Important differences between practices of slavery notwithstanding, Clarke points out that "stubbornly … slavery is slavery" (1999, 7). In the end, none of its victims are ever safe from the harshest forms of brutality, a truth Harriet Beecher Stowe illustrates in *Uncle Tom's Cabin* by moving from "milder" forms of slavery to her protagonist's brutal demise. Clarke makes this point in the context of a black Canadian literary tradition; in important aspects, he revises and radicalizes the story of slavery in Canada as told by Gale's play before him. His white colonial household tyrant Francis Chancy compounds the crimes of Gale's François Poulin de Francheville. He destroys his marriage by forcing sex not only upon his acquired slave, Beatrice's mother, but also on their daughter. By having his protagonist raped by her own father and owner, Clarke rips the veil from the fiction of slavery as "family" – asserted in Southern discourses of slavery as benign tutelage (and suggested in Gale's play, where the slave is given the family name).

The response of Clarke's Beatrice differs from that of Gale's Angélique. Clarke's heroine is more openly revengeful than Gale's Angélique, showing a degree of agency and overtly violent resistance that is only hinted at in Gale's play. Her Angélique spits secretly into her rapist owner's drinking water while saying a death incantation, but she says in the end that her wishes differ from her deeds. Clarke's Beatrice Chancy, by contrast, takes the dagger from her hesitant fellow-slave and plunges it into her father's body. She does not hesitate to kill an overseer in front of the authorities (1999, 126–9, 137). And while *Beatrice Chancy* is set around Easter, there is neither resurrection in her own time nor religious salvation: she acknowledges that she has abandoned God as He has abandoned her: "Don't utter that name. I want nothing more to do with Him" (1999, 94).[70] In this respect, she mirrors her victimizer's abandonment of any morality as sanctioned by religion: "Oh God if You do breathe … / If You do judge! / Too late. All's resolved now" (1999, 83). Unlike Gale's Angélique, who states that "though I am wretched, / I am not wicked" (70), any moral superiority of Beatrice Chancy does not reside in her renunciation of violence. On the contrary, she responds to violence with violence, adopting brutality in response to her brutal oppression. Clarke's Beatrice is "chanced" in evocation of Beatrice Cenci, who was hanged in Rome in 1599 for a patricidal response to her incestuous rape, and then immortalized by earlier writers. Clarke's conception of her is illuminated especially by his comments on Shelley's drama *The Cenci*.[71] As he avers in the libretto's "Charge": "I was enraptured by Shelley's play, especially by his depiction of his heroine, Beatrice Cenci, who orchestrates – coolly, rationally – the bloody demise of her diabolical father, Francesco. For Shelley, Beatrice is a revolutionary, a light that annihilates tyranny … Beatrice metes out a radical justice that shames a corrupt, gold-driven society. She becomes a martyr for liberty" (1998a, 63).

In Clarke's "Canadianized" and "Africadianized" version (1998a, 63), Beatrice's trajectory from innocence and endurance to violent revenge follows that of her Italian model in many aspects. Clarke's Beatrice initially reacts to her father's assault, not coolly but, according to a stage direction, by speaking "*(Wildly)*" (1998a, 71; 1999, 90). Noting "the connection between the *wild* and the Gothic" in his reading of Shelley's play as a Gothic slave-narrative, Clarke points out that Shelley's Beatrice "is often bidden by bracketed stage directions to speak 'wildly.'"[72] She first does so in response to her father's tyrannical behaviour in general and then "to stress the shock of the sexual assault effected by her father." It is only after her decision to kill the tyrant that "her speech calms" (2000c, 172).

Morality and Revolt

While she will risk hanging for her decision to break the law and kill her father, Beatrice finds some peace according to another kind of law and ethics. In his reading of Shelley's Beatrice, Clarke finds a morality of revolt (albeit not of revolution) that is as justified in one perspective as it is reprehensible in another. He thus delineates Beatrice's "moral progress – or decline," which leads "from a policy of passive resistance to her father to one of active instrumentation of his demise" (2000c, 176). As Clarke puts it, Beatrice learns "the useful truth that corrupt and absolute power can only be checked by a correspondingly vicious opposition, not by naïve appeals to 'humanity' or 'morality'" (2000c, 170–1). Is there a point when resistance – even violent resistance – to injustice becomes necessary, legitimate, and even morally superior? For Clarke, Shelley's play "raises up for debate the severe problem of whether the oppressed may employ violence – virtuously – to oppress their oppressors" (2000c, 174). Clarke's answer to this question as a writer seems positive. In a comment on his own play, he describes his version of Beatrice as "a heroine who exudes both the painful smell of a damaged flower and the victorious, pure April scent of a justified killer" (2000a, 18).

There is an important caveat, however, that ultimately distinguishes the weapons of a poet from those of murderous revenge and revolt. Clarke makes it clear that "Beatrice revolts, but she foments no real revolution. (Assassins never do)" (2000c, 181).[73] Successful revolts may win battles, not wars; Beatrice, like Angélique, is executed. For both characters, the ultimate truth and victory do not pertain to their own time. These can only come in courts of history, where the characters serve as witnesses, and being witnessed become part of, and participants in, such later times. One vehicle for this possibility is literature; as Clarke states, "My poetry must come of anger – / Or nothing from it comes" (2000a, 21).

It is thus important to note that for Clarke the Italian noble woman's violent, quasi-Leninist pragmatism has direct implications across different time periods. Forcing "a confrontation between power and a powerlessness that must put on power or be destroyed" (2000c, 173), Clarke tells us, Shelley uses "an episode of authoritarian injustice and insurrectionist justice from the Italian Renaissance as a test case for like situations in his own time" (173). This connection between the past and Shelley's present extends even further, as Clarke explains: "*The Cenci* is projected not just to the past, but to a future of continued, liberationist struggle" (181). It is only cogent, then, to ask how Clarke himself uses this case of renaissance resistance to tyranny, redeployed through Shelley's Gothic romaticism, for "like situations in his own time" (173).

Putting the Audience to Work

Clarke's invocation of Beatrice Cenci in his play about slavery and slave resistance in Canada – revising and radicalizing Lorena Gale's Angélique – is also a story for our times. In one sense, this is clear from his introductory section in the verse drama, entitled "On Slavery in Nova Scotia," where he writes: "A mass ignorance exists about the conduct of slavery in the British North American colonies – including ceded Québec – that remained loyal to Britain during and following the raid and the American Civil War that birthed both the United States and – a few generations later – Canada" (1999, 7). One of the purposes of Clarke's play, we thus infer, is to instruct.

Yet beyond offering simply a reminder of past violence, Clarke's text has other interventionist goals in the present. As Katherine Larson has shown, Clarke engages the reader through a wealth of peritextual elements within the text – such as epigraphs and stage directions – that often establish a connection with the reader and the present; together with the epitext beyond the volume (such as author interviews), these elements are part of a wider paratext whose "strategic function" is to "provide a guiding framework for the reader" (Larson 2006, 103).[74] Larson thus finds that the various peritextual elements position "the events of the verse drama within a context evoking the resistance of Acadians, slaves, Black women, Black artists, and poetry itself";[75] beyond this thematic aspect, the stage directions and epigraphs in particular "resist generic and linguistic categorization and containment" and thus "consistently mirror and enter into dialogue with the themes and events explored in the drama itself" (107).

Indeed, it quickly becomes apparent that an important part of the play is to be acted out, not simply on the stage, but in the reader's head. As Larson points out, many of the stage directions are "impossible to stage" (2006, 113), citing for instance the peritextual comment "*Invisible shovelfuls of dirt thud upon the scene – as if those present were being buried alive – like ourselves*" (G.E. Clarke 1999, 91). One could also adduce the following stage direction that sends the reader to a reference work to produce, again, a scene mentally that is explicitly not visible in the play: "*Unseen, Chancy's body sprawls, shocked – like the subject of David's* Marat assassiné" (128). As a final example, consider this task given to the reader: "*to conceive of her inquisitors, think of swine*" (139). Clarke's text reveals itself to be more than a blueprint for the stage by demanding to be read as poetry; as Moynagh points out, "stage directions scan, descriptions of the characters are similarly poetic, there are photographs scattered through the volume, and the arrangement of the words on the page is frequently key to meaning" (2002, 101). These strategies are part of a postmodern repertoire of border blurring that makes the line between text-receiver and text-producer porous, emphasizing the active role of a reader in the production of the text.

But Clarke's art also puts the reader to work in ways that have to do with the impact of language on an audience. Discussing the play, he sees it as an "envisioning of the blues, the furious corporeality of oppression, as if every line were a bullwhip lashing flesh" (2000a, 15). The motivation for charging language with such violence lies in the memory of perpetrated violence, but also in a "rage, coming out of the slavery that is history" (15). Against a history that operates *now* by obliterating the violence of slavery and the past, Clarke thinks of language as an inescapable and aggressive force in the present. He thus begins to "dream an opera of pain: a nasty work that could jet blood and saliva in amnesiacs' faces" and function as "a re-enacted news story about colonial crime, lust and greed" (16). Such re-enactment of the past as "news story" – reminiscent of Lorena Gale's invocation of the O.J. Simpson case in her play about Angélique – puts his *Beatrice Chancy* squarely in the present.

For Clarke, it also means that his language has to convey a similar traffic between different times and language layers. As he states, "I had to quarrel with language" (2000a, 18). A host of literary texts, past and present, and a variety of other discursive resources, such as movies, songs, print news, and overheard jokes, are evoked, and the inspirations for Beatrice's lines not only include Romanticism and Gothicism but also range from "blues songs to newspapers, from slave narrative to Shakespeare, from Italian *bel canto* to the trash talk of Jerry Springer's confessional harpies" (18). And while he selects "vulgar, uglified verbs to picture the violation that is *Beatrice Chancy*" (19), all of these often unconventional choices are part of his "maximist" poetics in which "*everything can be poetry*" (18). They become part of a beauty Clarke describes as "a quality productive of tumult and crises and revolution, I mean, really, of art" (23). As we have already seen, these investments in language strive for an engagement with the audience in the here and now – an engagement that is at times confrontational, difficult, and challenging; yet, as Clarke observes, "No true art or science … exists independently of an audience" (23).

Not Over Yet: The Future of the Past

Clarke's treatment of history and time similarly implicates the audience in the present consequences of the past. He reminds us that, for him personally, one of the implications of the past is that he "will never know the furthest origins of my African heritage. I do know that it was disrupted by a ship and ruptured by chains" (1999, 8). But he also uses an epigraph to the "Colophon" at the end to suggest that the events represented in his play – though set in 1801 and thus presumably in the past – speak to a past that is not over. The colophon – meaning literally "summit" or "finishing touch" (*Canadian Oxford Dictionary*) – is a place that usually offers technical information on the book, and that here, in fact, offers a poeticized comment about the typeface, printing, and paper. It thus tells us what materials the book is made of. Clarke offers this "finishing touch" in the epigraph about the material we have in front of us: "And if the African belief is true, then somewhere here with us, in the very air we breathe, all that whipping and chaining and raping and starving and branding and maiming and castrating and lynching and murdering – all of it – is still going on" (158).

Clarke's choice for an epigraph is revealing. The citation is from David Bradley's novel *The Chaneysville Incident* (1981), where it is preceded by this passage: "For if European knowledge is true, then death is cold and final, and one set of our ancestors had their very existence whipped and chained and raped and starved away, while the other set – a larger proportion than any of us would like to admit – forever burns in Hell for having done it to them" (Bradley 1981, 213; qtd in Pavlić 1996, 174). This is the predicament of the mulatto/a, often without knowledge of – or constrained to abandon belief in – half of his or her ancestry for positive identification. It is very directly part of the predicament of Beatrice Chancy, who suffers all of the violence in this description at the hands of her white father.[76] As Bradley's protagonist realizes, this is not "some dialectical battle between African thesis and European antithesis," since both are part of the victimized subject's inheritance; Beatrice thus has to "amputate" part of her ancestry in order to regain a sense of herself. In Bradley's novel, as Edward Pavlić suggests, such predicaments can be negotiated only in a way of thinking in which "apparent contradictions need not be resolved in synthesis" (1996, 169), exemplified by Yoruba aesthetics in which time, too, does not move in dialectical progress but is seen in a "syndetic model of accretion" (1996, 167–8);[77] time in this model does not pass, it accumulates.[78]

Clarke's Beatrice Chancy, it is true, kills and is killed in turn, a historical progress that eliminates first the criminal and then the revenging agent or "justified killer." The play thus shows us that "death is cold and final" for both Beatrice Chancy and her father. Yet Clarke chooses not to cite the passage containing this phrase, with its reference to "European knowledge" and epistemology; instead, in his "finishing touch" that tells us about the "materiality" of his own book, Clarke selects the second part of the passage to stay with the reader at the end, which speaks about the African belief that "somewhere here with us, in the very air we breathe, all that ... is still going on" (Bradley 1981, 313; qtd in Clarke 1999, 158).

The ways in which this is so include more than the interrupted genealogy that Clarke cites at the beginning;[79] the past is also present in the various embodiments of racism partially grounded in this history, from the erasure of Africville to twenty-first-century racist incidents such as the February 2010 cross burning in Poplar Grove, Nova Scotia.[80] And furthermore, "all that … is still going on" in an internalized self-perpetuating violence that Clarke thematizes, as we will see, in his next works about his murderous and murdered cousins, George and Rufus Hamilton, who were whipped as children by their father. Finally, the past is paradoxically also present in the very silences that deny its existence – in what Clarke calls "the slavery that is history" (2000a, 15). The repressive energies extended to regional or national narratives that elide parts of our historical inheritance contribute to marginalization and hamper fights against present-day racism. In the realm of literature and culture, such cultivated oblivion curtails the possibilities of art to intervene critically in processes of cultural transformation and social justice.

Writing Violence: "Reader, love this. I promise only further murders and executions"

Clarke's Africadian transformation of Beatrice Cenci worries self-imposed literary limits with respect to the portrayal of slavery and racial violence in Canada. Writing about Angélique in 2002, he notes that "prison memoirs and antiexecution protests are *underrepresented* in Canadian literature,"[81] although the history of African Canadian "conflict with white Canadian law enforcement and the judiciary … should mandate the creation of a race-conscious creative literature of crime and punishment" (2002b, 30). *Beatrice Chancy* responds to this mandate, and in his discussion of that text, Clarke prepares his audience: "Reader, love this. I promise only further murders and executions" (2000a, 21).

Racism and race-related violence in Canada are present throughout Clarke's work. The evocation of Lydia Jackson is an example from his early *Saltwater Spirituals and Deeper Blues* (1983). This was followed by the literary transfiguration of the 1985 shooting of Graham Cromwell in "Weymouth Falls Suite" (1989)[82] and Clarke's related breakthrough verse novel and play *Whylah Falls* (1990, 1999).[83] Central to this work – according to Clarke a "falling into consciousness" of black Nova Scotian community and speech (in A. Compton 1998, 139)[84] – is the section that deals directly with the incident, "The Martyrdom of Othello Clemence." Cromwell is directly named as one of the dedicatee's of the play version of *Whylah Falls* (5).[85] *Beatrice Chancy* is another step in this continued preoccupation with race and violence in Nova Scotia. Clarke's promise of "further murders and executions" seems to refer directly to other texts that followed, such as *Execution Poems* (2001b) and the subsequent novel *George & Rue* (2005b).[86]

The subject of *Execution Poems* is the 1949 hanging of two first cousins of Clarke, George and Rufus Hamilton, introduced here as "George & Rue: Pure, Virtuous Killers" (12). This poem title echoes Beatrice's epithet "a justified killer" (2000a, 18) and recalls Clarke's discussion of employing violence "virtuously – to oppress the oppressors" (2000b, 174). While Beatrice kills her rapist father-owner, though, George and Rue murder an innocent man. Their oppressor is hunger, as Geo underlines in "Ballad of a Hanged Man": "But I ain't going to hear my child starve" (2001b, 13). In addition, their deed is conditioned by a childhood full of violence (2001b, 15–17). Rue links this violence to the past, as a long-lasting effect of slavery: "The blow that slew Silver came from two centuries back. / It took that much time and agony to turn a white man's whip / into a black man's hammer" (35).[87] While his brother counters with a more short-term view of economic necessity,[88] Clarke, in the section headings of his novel *George & Rue* (2005b), maintains the concatenation of violence that begets violence, crime, and death by law: "Whip" (1), "Hammer" (111), and "Rope" (151).

Bradley's passage about the persistence of violence takes on particular pertinence here, since it applies literally to Clarke's cousins. As he reveals in an interview, they "had been beaten with a bullwhip" by a father perpetuating a behaviour of domestic abuse that "predated me by decades – or centuries." Here, Clarke makes the connection with the violence of slavery:

> I learned … that the Hamilton clan had come to Nova Scotia from a vicious plantation in Georgia during the War of 1812. This information convinced me that the violence that George and Rufus Hamilton inflicted upon their white victim in Fredericton, New Brunswick, in 1949, was rooted, perhaps, in the violence of slavery itself, carried forward in the family, although in a different country and a new century after leaving the United States. Arguably, because their slave ancestors were abused by white masters and overseers, the Hamilton parents extended this oppression to their own flesh and blood. They had learned only too well the lesson that blackness is evil and black people worth nothing. Thus, the brothers' attack on Silver was a continuum of the violence they had both imbibed. Their eventual execution evinces the truth that they inhabited a punitive (white) universe. (Kyser 2007, 867)

The story of *George & Rue* is thus also the story of this concatenation of violence, from slavery to black violence to retribution by the law. This context underwrites Clarke's interest in black crime and his call for a body of writing in Canada that deals with it adequately.

Racially motivated unequal punishment by the law is one of the concerns in this context, but, for Clarke, adopting a contextual view of crime is an equally important task of literature. With regard to the colour-motivated inequality before the law, it is no coincidence that Clarke dedicates his essay on Angélique to the Hamilton brothers; in it, he sets out the fact that "twenty-three percent of all persons convicted in capital cases were hanged in Canada, but fifty percent of all blacks so convicted were hanged" (2002b, 38).[89] As for George and Rue, he believes "that the judge, knowing the racist feelings against the Hamiltons, proceeded with their death sentences out of fear of provoking a lynch-mob reaction should such not occur" (Kyser 2007, 869). In a section entitled "Crypt" at the end of *George & Rue*, Clarke emphasizes his point about racial inequality before the law by offering a parallel case, also in 1949: two white perpetrators killed a cab driver and robbed a bank in Montreal; they were sentenced to death but had their sentences "commuted to life in prison. George and Rue – black – had no such white luck" (2005b, 214). The context that facilitates such judicial inequalities, however, comprises other aspects that require observation and attention, as Clarke makes clear in a justification of his project: "There remained socio-political attitudes, respecting 'Coloureds' in the Maritimes, in the 1940s and earlier, that merited examination, especially given that these attitudes helped to imprison black people in illiteracy, poverty, and unemployment (all excellent conditions for creating criminals and killers)" (Kyser 2007, 868–9).

Earlier in "Crypt" – a title that denotes a place of last rest and remembrance – Clarke questions the silencing and elision of these black lives that seem to "merit no poetry, no laurel, no ballads, no statues, no headstones, no memory, no existence" (2005b, 213).[90] His volume, of course, provides all that as well as a more worthy resting place than the brothers' graves in "unmarked corners of two Fredericton cemeteries" (213). Given potent and onerous stereotypes about black violence, Clarke's decision to create poetry, ballads, memory, and existence for the brothers – killers after all – hardly goes without saying. Yet Clarke points out that his aim in portraying the violence of George and Rue's father, for instance, "was not to surrender to stereotypes, but to indulge in (social) realism" (Kyser 2007, 866). Together with inequalities before the law and other continuing forms of disenfranchisement, the concatenation of violence from slavery to the present is part of what Clarke calls, just before "Crypt," "*the 'Black Acadian' Tragedy of 'George and Rue'*" (2005b, 207).

Against any demands for the exclusive portrayal of exemplary black lives, Clarke thus insists on the right and necessity to also portray black crime. While Lorena Gale entertains the very real possibility of Angélique's innocence, Clarke asks more bluntly, "Must I – as writer – bear the burden of presenting only black angels, just because white society demonizes black people? To answer that rhetorical question, I say I can't assume that responsibility" (Kyser 2007, 866). While the treatment of black crime and white punishment has been limited for various reasons in Canadian writing, Clarke argues, "The erasure of *le captif noir canadien* in African-Canadian literature is problematic, for the Canadian state has hanged – and the Canadian people have lynched – recoverable 'heroes.' Their narratives, if unearthed, could bare the 'clandestine' racism of Canadian authority and popularize the resistive strategies of African-Canadian communities" (2002b, 37). As this remark makes clear, the portrayal of "resistive strategies" is relevant because it recodes violent lives but also keeps originary white violence in view; an insistence on the former means a refusal to minimize the latter. Clarke's Beatrice responds to slaveholder violence; his George and Rue react to a violence that springs from social conditions originating, to an important degree, in slavery. To minimize the response is to minimize the true crime – slavery and its consequences into the present.

ANGLOPHONE CARIBBEAN CANADIAN WRITERS AND THE LEGACIES OF THE PAST

George Elliott Clarke writes out of a long history of Africadian experience and cultural expression, while Lawrence Hill, the son of United States immigrants to Ontario, includes stories based on his own background in his work. African Caribbean Canadian writers draw on other culturally specific antecedents and experiences. Their works evoke the complex legacies of slavery and alert us in many other ways to the presence of the past. Working and publishing largely out of Canadian contexts (see Clarke 2005a), however, these writers routinely reference Caribbean times and spaces, issues of a "deterritorialized diaspora,"[91] and experiences of immigration, life, and racism in Canada. Like the other texts discussed so far, which implicate what is now Canada in the transnational times and spaces of slavery and the black Atlantic, these works articulate extended time-spaces and foster the migration of histories. They create narratives of the in-between and of the in-several-places-at-once. In so doing, they establish hybrid sites of relation, contesting from diasporic transnational angles unequal relationships that are governed by geography, race, class, gender, and sexuality.

To speak of these works as African Caribbean *Canadian* writing means to isolate one particular aspect of texts that also belong to other national and more generally Caribbean contexts.[92] It is impossible to contain them within a single national designation, and they exceed narrowly defined national histories and boundaries that would belong only to either Canada or the Caribbean. At the same time, they have actively transformed Canadian time-spaces and emotional geographies. Insisting on Caribbean specificity, these texts have opened critical cultural spaces that help audiences critique and dismantle Canadian complacencies. They have also withstood and rearticulated narrowly defined notions of immigration and migrant writing beyond the purely integrative confines of a Canadian multicultural embrace. Such multicultural perspectives tend to see the migrant subject as a seamless supplement to the "sameness" of Canadian diversity within Canadian borders. Instead, many of these texts show the necessity of navigating "Canada" as an often hostile, restrictive, and racist negation of "Caribbeanness." In this process, however, these works have also helped to adumbrate a "Canada" that has been productively Caribbeanized. How, then, have ideas of Caribbeanness begun to include, relate to, and transform the times, spaces, and emotional geographies of Canada? And how have they managed to do so in ways that reconfigure Canada as part of a hemispheric and black Atlantic perspective perceived from the vantage point of the Caribbean?

As Michael Bucknor and Daniel Coleman explain, the two-pronged category "Caribbean Canadian" signals "the processes of mutual exchange and influence between these two very different geopolitical categories without erasing the radical unevenness not just between them but within them" (2005, xv). Cheap Caribbean labour in Canada and Canadian corporate activities in the Caribbean contribute to an uneven, often exploitative chiasmus that links North and South economically: "Private remittances flow to the Caribbean, while corporate remittances flow to Canada" (xviii). These asymmetrical exchanges join other processes of globalization and migration that create "'first-world zones' in formerly 'developing' countries and 'third-world zones' in supposedly 'first-world' nations" (Braziel and Mannur 2003, 10–11; qtd in Bucknor and Coleman 2005, xv). Such transactions add to existing fault lines and internal differentiation within both Canada and the Caribbean. Regional, cultural, and linguistic differences mark Canada, while the Caribbean consists of "discreet island states" with different "colonial, political, and economic histories" that, for Bucknor and Coleman, "resist collective generalization" (xv).

Caribbeanness and Caribbean Canadian Time-Spaces

Despite such multiplicity, Caribbean thinkers have sought to articulate an "Antillanité" or "Caribbeanness" (e.g., Glissant 1989, 139; 1997a, 426) or what Michael Dash calls a "regional ethos" (1998, 9). They have often done so in the footsteps of Cuban thinker José Martí and his New World–centred, US-wary appeal for "Our America." Martí's compatriot, the novelist Alejo Carpentier, thus conceptualized a more localized "New World Mediterranean" in the 1940s (Dash 1998, 11). To such a European-derived image signalling a land-bound universe, however, Édouard Glissant has opposed a double, janus-faced idea of the Caribbean. This idea is both marked by a "Caribbean opacity" (Dash 1998, 199) and articulated in relation to the Americas, with which the Caribbean is connected rhizomatically, simultaneously their beginning and their outcome. In *Le discours Antillais* in 1981, Glissant observes: "La mer des Antilles n'est pas le lac des États-Unis. C'est l'estuaire des Amériques" (1997a, 427; "The Caribbean Sea is not an American lake. It is the estuary of the Americas" [Glissant 1989, 139]); in 1995, he saw the Caribbean also as "une sorte de préface au continent américain" (1995, 12). While Glissant does not mention Canada here (though he has things to say about Montreal and Quebec elsewhere), these articulations of a Caribbean relationally connected to the wider Americas – defining them and being defined by them – have implications for how one might read the idea and practice of Caribbean Canadian writing.

Glissant's insistence on "opacity" signals the need to respect local specificity. It rejects universalizing tendencies that would supersede or sublimate Caribbean difference, be it difference from Europe or within the New World.[93] As Dash puts it, Glissant seeks "to theorize an otherness that cannot be contained or appropriated" (Dash 1998, 11). Diversity, then, respects and operates through relation, not via the appropriation, negation, and sublation operated by universalisms.[94] Like Stuart Hall, who sees diasporic experience defined "by the recognition of a necessary heterogeneity and diversity" but also as "a conception of 'identity' which lives with and through, not despite, difference" (1990, 235), Glissant excludes neither "nation" nor the larger term "Caribbeanness." The category of "nation" remains necessary as an expression of the local and its opacity, but it is understood in relation to the larger term: "L'antillanité … nous arrache de l'intolérable propre aux nationalismes nécessaires et nous introduit à la Relation qui aujourd'hui les tempère sans les aliéner" (Glissant 1997a, 426–7; "Caribbeanness … tears us free from the intolerable side proper to nationalisms and introduces us to the thought of Relation that now tempers them without estranging them").[95]

The key to conjugating such identities is the notion of relation. Glissant thus casts the Caribbean more generally as multiple relation: "Qu'est-ce que les Antilles en effet? Une multi-relation" (1997a, 426–7; "What is the Caribbean in fact? A multiple series of relationships" [Glissant 1989, 139]). This view signals the abandoning of statically conceived sameness; relational identities thus are forms of "becoming" rather than of "being" (Dash 1998, 11).

Glissant's view, which has implications for other New World identities, is specifically contingent on the black Atlantic and on the middle passage, which, in contrast to white settler cultures, made the exportation and replication of identitarian certainties impossible. While this circumstance exposes diasporic black cultures in the New World to the dangers of seeking to imitate the dominant, it also signals their potential to function as sites of becoming and creation and of critique and difference. In his essay "Le Retour et le détour," Glissant insists on the fact that the consequences of the slave trade, which cut African diasporic populations off from earlier knowledges and certainties, necessarily implied particularity and prevented "toute ambition d'un universel généralisant" (1997a, 41; "any attempt at universal generalization" [1989, 14]). The initial impulse of "return" partakes of "l'obsession de l'Un" (1997a, 44; "the obsession with a single origin" [1989, 16]). It comes too late, however: the original point of departure in Africa cannot be recaptured. Instead of an unmediated identity articulated as a return "au rêve d'origine" ("to the longing for origins"), Glissant thinks of a more complex, augmented return that ideally leads back "au point d'intrication" (1997a, 56–7; "to the point of entanglement" [1989, 26]). This more complex "return" is mediated by multiple detours.

Before (re-)routing this consideration of detours and multiple, augmented returns through Caribbean Canadian times and spaces, I want to return here briefly to Stuart Hall's "Cultural Identity and Diaspora." As we have seen, Hall similarly complicates unmediated notions of Caribbeanness. He questions the idea that identity is an existing essence readily available for "excavation" and rediscovery: "Is it only a matter of unearthing that which the colonial experience buried and overlaid, bringing to light the hidden continuities it suppressed? Or is a quite different practice entailed – not the rediscovery but the *production* of identity. Not an identity grounded in archeology, but in the *re-telling* of the past?" (1990, 224). Like Glissant, for whom the disruptions of slavery and the middle passage signify also "one vast beginning" (1997b, 6), Hall names "precisely the experience of a profound discontinuity" as the shared connection of the Caribbean (1990, 227). For Hall, the break of the middle passage is one of the most striking reasons the past is only available in mediated fashion: it "continues to speak," but it is always "constructed through memory, fantasy, narrative, and myth" (226).

In the case of the Caribbean, the "*re*-telling of the past" is for Hall subject to three major "presences" (which also have consequences for an understanding of the Caribbean Canadian): those of Africa, Europe, and an America understood as the New World (1990, 230). The African presence, the "site of the repressed" (230), requires "symbolic journies" that are "necessarily circular" (232) but never promise a simple return. Since the "original 'Africa' is no longer there" (231), the African presence has to be accessed "'by another route': what Africa has *become* in the New World, what we have made of 'Africa': 'Africa' as we re-tell it through politics, memory, and desire" (232). This route, then, "takes place" in the form of complex, multiple "returns" that lead through "Africa." Ultimately, "Africa" is here, not a goal, but a mediation on the way to a "home" that is a process and engagement in the present. By contrast, the European presence, which "has positioned the black subject within its dominant regimes of representation" (233), needs to be "re-placed." The goal is "that, finally, we can place it … rather than being forever placed by it" (233). The third presence, that of the New World, is the "space where the creolisations and assimilations and syncretisms were negotiated" and a place of "many, continuous displacements" (234).

In his own version of what Glissant calls "errance" (errantry or errancy), Hall thus sees "the Antillean as the prototype of the modern or postmodern nomad, continually moving between centre and periphery" (1990, 234). In *The Repeating Island*, Antonio Benítez-Rojo has extended this consideration in a more explicitly postmodern perspective on Caribbean space, which he sees as "having neither a boundary nor a center" (1996, 4).[96] The intervening presences cited by Hall and the detours noted by Glissant "take place" all over the world through migratory routes and times and spaces: "Thus the Caribbean flows outwards past the limits of its own sea with a vengeance, and its *ultima Thule* may be found" in far-flung places like Bombay, Gambia, Bali, Bristol, or "Bordeaux at the time of Colbert" (Benítez-Rojo 1996, 4). One might add Toronto, Montreal, Hamilton, and so many other sites in Canada. In the processes of increasing the de-territorialization of Caribbean culture(s) signalled by these spatial conceptualizations, movement to and from any of these locations takes on seemingly endless, circular, and rhizomatic forms of continual detour. As Bucknor and Coleman (2005, i–xiv) point out with reference to the emphasis on movement theorized by James Clifford and Paul Gilroy, the diasporic search for roots often translates into narratives of routes, observable also in the work of Caribbean Canadian writers.

In the texts of Caribbean-descended writers, Canadian times and spaces appear not just as problems or impediments; they also become extensions of the Caribbean and its issues. As a result, Canada has been effectively contextualized and "Caribbeanized" in wider hemispheric and black Atlantic contexts by Caribbean Canadian writers. Yet these perspectives work also to release and realize a certain "Canadianness" beyond the more parochial and stubborn limits of that term. One can note that Canada, at least rhetorically and until recently, has itself aspired to something like the often-cited view of the Caribbean as a "union of the diverse" (Benítez-Rojo 1996, 2), indeed to the realization of Glissant's notion of a "multi-relation." With regard to the particular "contact zone" of the Caribbean Canadian, of course, Canada is mostly a "European presence." Yet as a site of multiple racial, ethnic, and linguistic encounters, Canada is also to some extent a "creolized" and hybrid version of that European presence, and part of Hall's "présence Americaine" as "'New World' or *Terra Incognita*" (1990, 230). As Hall points out, this is where new possibilities appear and further creolizations occur.

Caribbean Canadian contact zones and their (dis?)connections provide a critical space within Canada that could hold it to some of its own professed ideals and ideas. They also emphasize a relational aspect that from the outset has governed what is now Canada, defined by a modernity marked by the logic of empire and the black Atlantic. In this sense, the Caribbean Canadian not only signals a bilateral contact zone of economic and cultural interaction; it also opens onto a wider and more encompassing perspective that sees *both* Canada and the Caribbean constituted by a larger context of modernity and the black Atlantic. This perspective allows transnational, black Atlantic, and hemispheric contexts to sharpen our view of national specificities.

The porous, multiple, and non-linear time-spaces of the black Atlantic and their consequences for the circulation of mediated identities in the Americas have produced sophisticated reflections on corresponding aesthetic choices and artistic form. In his essay "The Novel of the Americas," Glissant's considerations of space and time are useful with regard to a number of the Caribbean Canadian works I want to consider shortly. With regard to temporal relations, Glissant observes a "tortured sense of time" owing to "a chronology that has become obscure, when it is not completely effaced for all kinds of reasons, especially colonial ones" (1989, 144). As a consequence, the "American novelist ... finds himself struggling in the confusion of time" (144).[97] Time thus often represents a disconcerting challenge for writers of the Americas: "We do not see it stretch into our past ... but implode in us in clumps, transported in fields of oblivion where we must, with difficulty and pain, put it all back together if we wish to make contact with ourselves and express ourselves" (145).[98] As we will see, time is indeed often complex for Caribbean Canadian writers who face an array of layers of historical time that refuse easy synchronization. Glissant further links temporal and spatial disruption, since "this exploded, suffered time is linked to 'transferred' space" (144), and remarks that "space in the American novel seems to me open, exploded, rent" (145).[99] These observations about temporal dimension are pertinent to many of the Caribbean Canadian works considered below. Spatial disruption is not always readily apparent at the surface of some of these works. The novels by Austin Clarke and David Chariandy that I discuss, in fact, are set, at least on one level, in remarkably closed spaces. These are thrown wide open, however, in their temporal descent into other times and spaces. Finally, Glissant's attention to questions of linguistic relation and hybridity deserves to be noted here. He often reflects on creolized transformations of language and on the intersection of the oral and the written (e.g., 1995, 31; 1997a, 330–1; 1989, 100–1).[100] The significance of orality, francophone Creoles, and "blackened English" – already encountered above – will recur in several texts below, for instance in Agnant's novels and Austin Clarke's *The Polished Hoe.*

The following pages open a number of windows on the time-spaces of the Caribbean Canadian and its various intersections. I begin with Cecil Foster's novel *Slammin' Tar* (1998) and Makeda Silvera's interviews with domestic workers in *Silenced* (1983). These two texts give voice to those who marked increased West Indian immigration because of Canadian labour needs after the Second World War; this change was signalled by the 1955 West Indian Domestic Workers Scheme and the 1966 Caribbean Seasonal

Agricultural Workers Program, by immigration policy modifications in 1962 and 1967, and later by a 1973 policy allowing visas for temporary workers (Mensah 2010, 70–2).[101] As we will see, Austin Clarke – the most important early Caribbean Canadian writer – is also a chronicler of these Caribbean Canadian experiences. As in Foster's novel about seasonal workers, however, lines of memory run deeper in Clarke's work. In a text like *The Polished Hoe*, they eventually reach back to slavery.

Marlene NourbeSe Philip's *Zong!* – the subject of the following section – and numerous texts by Dionne Brand also take us back to transatlantic slavery as a fact that has made and now haunts the present. Brand returns to slavery as a foundational fact of modernity and a condition of post-slavery black diasporic subjectivities in works such as *No Language Is Neutral* (1990), *In Another Place, Not Here* (1996), *At the Full and Change of the Moon* (1999), and *A Map to the Door of No Return* (2001). In her Toronto novel *What We All Long For* (2005), her recurring theme of intergenerational conveyance extends to the second generation of immigrants in Toronto and to the relation to their parents' past. The question of a second generation's encounter with the memories of its foreign-born elders is also the central theme of an essay by David Chariandy (2004) and his first novel, *Soucouyant* (2007b).

The extraordinarily diverse and productive field of anglophone Caribbean Canadian writing, beyond these and other authors discussed earlier or in subsequent chapters – Lorris Elliott, André Alexis, Claire Harris – comprises numerous other important creators.[102] In addition, black Caribbean Canadian writing also comprises a rich francophone, mostly Haitian-Québécois literary production. Later in this chapter, I will thus discuss the work of Marie-Célie Agnant; in *La dot de Sara* (1995), she has written about the intergenerational struggle about values made problematic by migrancy and immigration, here for instance regarding the role of Creole. Her second novel, *Le livre d'Emma* (2001), carries the presence of the past back to slavery and offers another treatment of the concatenation of violence that is also addressed by George Elliott Clarke, Austin Clarke, and Dionne Brand. In this novel, however, she considers such seemingly inexorable determinism as a motivation for life-affirming decisions in the present. Agnant's third novel, *Un alligator nommé Rosa* (2007), points to another historical marker that constitutes an important antecedent considered relevant by many francophone Caribbean Canadian writers: engagement with the consequences of the Duvalier regime, which is also an important theme in the work of Gérard Étienne and Émile Ollivier. In addition, Ollivier and Dany Laferrière have produced important treatments not only of the diasporic existence between the Caribbean and Canada following exile from Haiti under the Duvalier regime, but also of the trope of return.

Caribbean Canadian Farm and Domestic Workers: "Like Nothing Ever Change"

Agricultural Workers on Edge: Cecil Foster's Slammin' Tar

Cecil Foster's novel *Slammin' Tar* (1998) is not his first novel[103] and neither does it come early in the Caribbean Canadian corpus. In portraying the lives of participants in the Caribbean Seasonal Agricultural Workers Program (which began in 1966), however, it introduces readers to early aspects of an increased Caribbean presence in Canada, one driven by economic motives – those of the Canadian state and of those who provide their labour – that in related forms continue to this day.[104] The novel also demonstrates Benítez-Rojo's above-cited contention that "the Caribbean flows outwards past the limits of its own sea with a vengeance" (1996, 4). Although set mostly in a claustrophobic cabin on the significantly named Edgecliff Farm in southwestern Ontario, the novel supports Glissant's notions of an "open, exploded, rent" space, of parallel yet asynchronous times, and the "presences" of Africa, Europe, and the New World; in some passages of the novel, these presences are seen to reach far back in a very long history of Caribbean labour migration and remind us, as E.D. Chamberlin put it succinctly, that "slavery shaped the West Indian" (1993, 1). The title of the novel thus picks up, in a vernacular guise, on the "running" of earlier fugitives, transporting their story into our asphalted times.[105]

The novel signals contemporary spatial dimensions of diasporic routes by opening, not on Bridgetown Wharf in Barbados (as in Foster's memoir *Island Wings*), but at the Grantley Adams International Airport, "the beginning and ending of so many journeys and dreams" (Foster 1998, 1). The unreliable trickster narrator of the novel, Brer Anancy, later uses the image of the boat to describe a shared Canadian farm cabin, offering it as a sign of enduring stability in the workers' journey through their Canadian experience. Given the novel's occasional evocation of slavery, however, the trickster's evocation of this particular chronotope as a sign of safe predictability is suspicious from the beginning: "This cabin definitely has its own rhythm … As the captain tells Brer Anancy in that loveable yarn about becoming a sailor, on a boat, there is a place for everything, but everything must be in its place always. That way there are no problems on the high seas, in the storm of life. Everything and everyone in its right place. No unexpected changes. No surprises. Just predictability" (223).

These views about place and space are not unchallenged in the novel. The hopes of many characters seem concentrated on breaking out of the restricted Canadian time-space of labour and confinement that keeps "everything and everyone in its right place." This spatial restriction is enforced practically by winter, disease, and the farm workers' long working hours, but more generally by the Canadian government's refusal to grant landed immigrant status, which would make a permanent life and family reunion – and eventually citizenship in Canada – possible.[106] The prospect of "running" – that is, evading the program and immigration officers and starting a "free," albeit illegal, life in Canada – is thematized repeatedly, but is dismissed as unrealistic by the narrator and by some of the workers: every attempt in the past has ended in the fugitive's apprehension and in aggravated circumstance for everyone else on the program.

The main evasion – at least temporarily and mentally – from these constraints is provided by the game of dominoes. A competition with workers from other farms offers one of the few occasions of excursion and egress, and, for the winning team, culminates in a visit to the jazz festival in Toronto. Together with Bajan food and dominoes, music and the city signal alternatives to an enclosed existence in the Canadian rural setting of the novel.

Letters coming (or not) from the Caribbean are the other line of connection with the outside. Their delivery – a recurring scene in the novel – produces a marked change of rhythm in the cabin. With their arrival, the workers who've received them – silently and individually – re-enter their Caribbean life. While the letters seem to connect Caribbean and Caribbean Canadian times and spaces, they also reveal the distances and a-synchronicities. Winston – the youngest and newest member of the crew – does not receive letters; nor does Johnny – the oldtimer and leader of the men. When Johnny finally does receive a letter, he first forgets to read it and then learns of bad news (343, 418, 423). As we find out, letters can be signs of trouble back home in the Caribbean. Life there goes on without the workers and sometimes behind their back.[107] Conversely, when the farm falls on hard times, the letters from the Caribbean are answered not by hapless men at a loss about what to say, but by the farmer's wife instead.

If the letters provide one tenuous connection across different times and spaces in the novel, the diaries kept by Johnny's grandfather Percy "back in 1902" in Panama (145) provide another. Despite the narrator's view that

Johnny, by reading these diaries, "enters a strange land and time" (141), the time-spaces and experiences in the diaries are hardly unfamiliar. Johnny realizes that his experience is part of a long line in Caribbean labour history: "Lots of things in [that diary] remind me of when I first came up here … Some o' the same things my grandfather went through in Panama and then my father in Cuba, I went through too. In fact, we still going through. Like nothin' ever change" (267).

Unfortunately, Johnny's conclusion takes on an even more sombre significance shortly afterwards, adding to the distressing connotations of the name of Edgecliff Farm. The diaries describe not only his grandfather's experience as a worker on the Panama Canal (145–7, 235–6), but also an explosion that killed sixty of his co-workers and turned out to have been an act of group suicide in the face of desperation (354–5). After Johnny reads the passage out loud to a co-worker who is sick, the suicide in the past is emulated in the present. Unable to continue working and thus to fulfill his financial obligations at home, the co-worker chooses death (358).

Here it is time to look at the garrulous narrator, Brer Anancy, whose comments on a task he dislikes – documenting events on the farm – provide a metafictional frame. The trickster spider has received this assignment from his often unsympathetic critic, Mother Nyame, after having failed in his job earlier in the century during the "New Negro Era" and the Harlem Renaissance.[108] Brer Anancy voices his dim view of these diaries, saying he feels uncomfortable "whenever I see people trying to dig too far into their past"; he also evokes "some poor fool who immersed himself into the study of history only to end up a bigger fool" (139). Given the outcome in this episode, his reservations are not entirely unfounded: the journal's deadly impact seems to clinch his case. Rising to rhetorical heights, Anancy feels called upon to "testify, to become a witness, to make a commentary, to tell it like it is" (361). Beginning with a loose paraphrase of Langston Hughes's "The Negro Speaks of Rivers" (361), he offers his credentials as a recorder of black suffering from the beginnings of time. This history ranges from the Euphrates and the Pyramids through the Door of No Return to the murders of Martin Luther King and Malcolm X, not forgetting events in Bridgetown and the Caribbean. Closing with the line of desolation from Hughes's "The Weary Blues," "*ain't got nobody in all this world*" (361–2), he blames the diaries and "all that stupidness from the past" for the worker's tragic death and Johnny's lack of leadership (362).

Foster thus packages his ultimately insurrectionary comment on the plight of Caribbean Canadian seasonal workers in the shape of a trickster story. Brer Anancy is indeed not to be trusted. His aversion to history, it turns out, mainly concerns competitors, be they these diaries or the upstart female storyteller Nyame has sent to shadow him.[109] Further warning comes when Brer Anancy uses the term "Anancy story." "What I am telling you ain't no Anancy story" (139), the narrator states emphatically, implying the very pejorative connotation of idle nonsense that he has condemned earlier.[110] We are thus repeatedly warned that Brer Anancy can easily lead the reader into a briar patch. His own disclaimer not to tell an Anancy story, for instance, introduces his suggestion that a preoccupation with history often blinds individuals to the emergence of a leader (139) – a blindness that has cruelly applied to him not once, but twice: first by failing to recognize Du Bois, then by misjudging the two leader figures in the group of workers.

The reader should have known better than to trust Brer Anancy's musings about "proper" space and place, and his comparison of the workers' cabin with the image of the boat, which suggests the importance of keeping things and people in their "right" place. With his focus on Johnny, whom he sees as the voice of reason in contrast to irresponsible ideas of "slammin' tar," he has yet again overlooked a crucial figure. This is young Winston, who opts to "jump ship." Instead of following immigration rules and returning to Barbados when the farm fails, he chooses to join the farmer's daughter in Toronto. With respect to "proper" places and confines, this interracial gambit puts paid to Brer Anancy's earlier warning against the affair, delivered with anti-miscegenation racist comments by Garvey (216–17).[111]

Worse for Brer Anancy, who has staked his authority on Johnny as the legitimate leader of the group, Johnny follows Winston. He leaves both Brer Anancy and observers back home in disbelief when he is "the one to run, to be slammin' tar" (433). The narrator admits defeat. Yet perhaps he tricks us one last time. The workers' decision to "jump ship" and to redefine Caribbean Canadian spaces by transgressing the confines assigned by officialdom, after all, answers Brer Anancy's own call earlier for the abandonment of self-imposed slavery. Laughing at Mother Nyame, who "spared no production costs" in recording the announcement of abolition (in 1833), he asks about these farm workers who now supposedly enjoy freedom: "Don't they look like the slaves that four or five generations earlier were the forebears of these men slipping into the dark?" (160). The main difference, he claims, is that the new slaves are victims of their *own* choices (and of their own interiorized hegemonic ideas): "Those slaves in my memory complained bitterly about lack of freedom and longed to go back home … They run away when they can and do so often … These people on Edgecliff Farm actually choose to be here … That is the major difference. Is there something so ingrained in the black man's psyche that … he will never be free? That he must still be looking for what even to this day we still call *Panama money* – selling our bodies and dreams in a foreign land for token remittances to send back home?" (161–2). Caribbeans' desire for economic betterment and education, it seems, leads them to places like Edgecliff Farm. Yet as Foster tells us, they also seek "to run away" from the restrictions imposed upon them, rejecting tricky warnings against "runnin'" and "slammin' tar." They seem to think little of the trickster Brer's vaunted stability and of the maintenance of a "proper" segregation of Canadian and Caribbean (Canadian) spaces and races.

Domestic Workers in Makeda Silvera and Austin Clarke

Foster leaves us to imagine the fate of his "fugitives," Winston and Johnny, whose lives presumably continue in Toronto. Caribbean Canadian workers in that city have been portrayed in other works, notably Austin Clarke's Toronto trilogy. Clarke's trilogy also shows another group of earlier arrivals, Caribbean Canadian domestic workers. This group is later the subject of Makeda Silvera's *Silenced: Talks with Working Class West Indian Women about Their Lives and Struggles as Domestic Workers in Canada*, first published in 1983.[112]

A lone research paper from the 1960s notes the lack of knowledge about the women who arrived under the 1955 West Indian Domestic Workers Scheme. The study reports indirect evidence of "the alienation and loneliness of these women and their difficulties in assimilating to the new Canadian scene" (F. Henry 1968, 83–4).[113] An earlier pilot study by the author, based on sixty-one interviews, however, finds that middle-class status was the typical background of these women, most of whom "were clerks, typists, teaching assistants and nurses' aides"; in addition, only a few had worked as domestics prior to coming to Canada, and "at least eight" of the sixty-one interviewed "had domestics working for them in their own family homes" (1968, 85). While the sample is not necessarily representative,[114] the results puncture class assumptions in Canada about Caribbean Canadian domestic workers at the time. Henry also emphasizes the disappointment and racism experienced by these women (1968, 83, 86–8). Yet despite their negative experiences, these domestic workers enjoyed a decisive advantage over the workers who arrived later on temporary work visas, such as those portrayed in Foster's *Slammin' Tar* or in Austin Clarke's *The Meeting Point*.

After having been pre-selected in the Caribbean, they received automatic landed immigrant status upon arrival in Canada (F. Henry 1968, 83).[115]

Henry's study provides valuable information, but it does not reproduce the interviews themselves. The later domestic workers' struggle for landed immigrant status is documented in a work that does provide their own narratives: Makeda Silvera's *Silenced*, published in 1983 and reissued with a new introduction in 1989.[116] Silvera emphasizes that oral history renders women's stories in their own words rather than in the registers imposed by their employers or officials; it can thus reflect cultural and personal nuances that disappear in questionnaires and surveys (1989, viii–ix).[117] It is for other reasons, however, that oral history is a useful and even necessary medium to relieve an "imposed muteness" (1989, viii) that evokes, in some of its aspects, echoes of earlier historical black silences.

The ten women offering their story in *Silenced* live in precarious circumstances. Admitted to Canada under temporary worker visas, their real names are withheld in the text "for fear of harassment and deportation" (1989, 3).[118] A particular vulnerability of these workers is that their visas are employer- and job-specific, with the requirement that any changes have to be reported to the authorities (8). While the "living-in" working conditions are often characterized by a lack of privacy (10) and "sexual harassment, long hours and low pay" (6), regulations are rarely enforced and contact with authorities is often problematic (10). One of the women, for example, refrained from complaining, since "if I go and complain they might tell me to go home" (59).[119]

Under these circumstances, the withholding of landed immigrant status creates an entire population of not just cheap but also uncomplaining and intimidated labour.[120] Temporary yet prolonged tolerance of this situation on the part of the concerned individuals is facilitated by often elusive hopes for landed immigrant status in the future (also thematized in Foster's novel). The aforementioned woman thus continues: "I am just sticking it out until I get my landed" (59). Another black woman in the text, also "trying to stick this out until I get my landed" (17), repeats the dream of this door-opening event like a magic formula, "When I get my landed …" (20, 21).

Silvera's volume thus gives voice to Caribbean Canadian individuals who exist and survive in existential uncertainty and often legal limbo. The lure of eventually gaining increased legal rights (if not immediate citizenship) and improved personal and economic freedom prevents their flight and "runnin.'" On the contrary, it fosters supposedly temporary acceptance of harsh circumstances and a hesitation to speak out against non-law-abiding employers. Another common corollary of such deferred and often disappointed dreams is a silence that leads to an absence of black lives and voices in writing and historiography. Silvera's use of oral history breaches that silence. As seen in *Slammin' Tar*, fiction provides another avenue to the inscription of otherwise invisible and silenced lives.

Silvera points out that, prior to her own oral histories, the "only available work that provided a feel of the reality of the life of Caribbean domestics were the novels by West Indian author Austin Clarke" (1989, viii). Clarke arrived from Barbados as a student in 1955, the very year the Domestic Workers Scheme was inaugurated, and he would begin to make Bajan and Caribbean Canadian contexts the subject of his writing from 1960 on.

His first novel, *The Survivors of the Crossing* (1964), is set in Barbados, yet its plot is set in motion by the lure of Canadian wealth and promise. A letter from a participant in the Canadian Seasonal Agricultural Workers Program is received in Barbados (A.C. Clarke 1964, 9–11); boasting about better working conditions in Canada, it triggers a revolt by Bajan plantation workers. The content of the letter corresponds to the pressure of having to hide misery in Canada (that is also present in Foster's *Slammin' Tar*); its sender, in fact, confesses that "I had to write that kind o' letter … I sorry to paint a technicolour picture o' the place, but … I couldn't let you know that up here in this country is the same slavery as what I run from back in the island" (1964, 91).

Such confessions notwithstanding, one of the characters, Boysie, has moved to Canada in Clarke's Toronto trilogy, where we encounter him among other Caribbean Canadians in *The Meeting Point* (1967) and *Storm of Fortune* (1973); he is then the central character in *The Bigger Light* (1975). Clarke also portrays Caribbean Canadians in his later novel *More* (2008), for instance, in some of the stories in *When He Was Free and Young and Used to Wear Silks* (1971), and in the short story collections *Nine Men Who Laughed* (1986) and *In this City* (1992). As Clarke explains in the introduction to *Nine Men Who Laughed*, most of the diasporic men in that collection "exist on the periphery of rewards, and suffer from unfair chastisements" in Toronto – though they may also live and bitterly laugh "in London, Paris, New York or Moscow" (1986, 1). In addition to portraying Caribbean Canadian masculinity (see Coleman 1998, 29–51), however, Clarke regularly depicts Caribbean Canadian women, domestic workers in particular.

With its rendering of great expectations and often dashed economic hopes, *The Meeting Point* offers an example of what Bruce Robbins has discussed as the postcolonial "au pair narrative" (1994, 143), as Sarah Casteel points out. The novel also performs "a powerful critique of this promise of self-fulfillment in the metropolis" (Casteel 2005, 116–17). Among other aspects of Caribbean Canadian Toronto,[121] Clarke also draws attention to the imperative force of legal status and the importance of landed immigrant papers. The main character, Bernice, and her friend Dots have arrived on the "domestic scheme" (A.C. Clarke 1967, 70) and thus have landed immigrant status. Dots's husband, Boysie, complains bitterly about having married her, not for love, but in the "specified time" (83) required by the scheme for a fiancé to become a landed immigrant (84). Bernice's sister Estelle, newly arrived in Canada, also wants citizenship "by hook or by crook" (112), but her desire for landed status is used by the employer of both sisters to avoid discussing his responsibility for her pregnancy (218). "Silence comes to dominate," David Chariandy notes about the consequences of this sleight of hand that profits from her hope for landed status, in his insightful discussion of the often treacherous role of recognition that is promised by state policies (2005, 158).

The workers and domestics shown by Foster, Silvera, and Clarke seek alternatives in Canada to their past lives and to an often unpromising future in the Caribbean. All too often, however, as Johnny realizes when reading his grandfather's diaries, it seems as though "nothing ever change" (Foster 1998, 167). Economic success sometimes seems possible (although for Boysie in *The Bigger Light* it can lead to despair), but more often a past of limited possibilities determines Caribbean Canadian lives, marked again by exploitability and few options. Clarke often portrays the lives of highly educated Bajans (like himself), but those who labour on farms and as domestics in these texts remain caught in chains of disenfranchisement that reach back to their Caribbean lives. In this regard, their existence is still connected with an even earlier past and forms of disenfranchisement that many of them see hardly (if at all) remedied by a post-emancipation plantation economy. As we have seen, a worker in Clarke's *The Survivors of the Crossing* comments on this continuity of oppression and exclusion that reaches from Bajan plantation realities both before and after emancipation to his Canadian Caribbean present: "In this country is the same slavery as what I run from back in the island" (1964, 91).

Connections between slavery and the continuing reality of exploitation are also voiced – with less than metaphorical connotations – in *The Meeting Point*: Bernice "always saw herself as a servant; a sort of twentieth-century slave" (A.C. Clarke 1967, 5; qtd in Chariandy 2005, 153). This view is further endorsed by Silvera when she comments that Caribbean Canadian domestic workers are "brought to Canada to work virtually as legal slaves" (1989, 5) and by Foster when he compares the workers on Edgecliff Farm with "the slaves that four or five generations earlier were the forebears of these men" (1998, 160).

As the times and spaces of Canada and the Caribbean intertwine and overlap, the offshoots of their roots in imperial modernity and the black Atlantic create a new tangle of Caribbean and Canadian lives in the present. In addition to the examination of contemporary Caribbean Canadian experiences, however, the interrogations of Canadian slavery we have encountered in Gale and Clarke (and, to a lesser extent, in Elliott and Hill) are joined by Caribbean Canadian reflections that may deal with the middle passage or slavery perpetrated in the Caribbean yet are now enunciated from the Canadian contexts of which they are a part, and in which readers are asked to come to grips with their disturbing implications. Among the various spectres of the past interrogated by Caribbean Canadian authors, slavery continues to maintain a primordial role in anglophone work in particular – as the texts I will now discuss by Austin Clarke, Marlene NourbeSe Philip, and Dionne Brand show; it is also an important subject for the francophone writer Marie-Célie Agnant.

Witnessing Empire: Austin Clarke's *The Polished Hoe*

In this context, I want to consider Austin Clarke's vernacular-steeped novel *The Polished Hoe* (2002). On the surface, this novel appears to work with classical restraints of time and space. Set entirely in a fictionalized 1940s, pre-independence Barbados – referred to as the "Island of Bimshire"[122] – the action of the novel takes place mainly during an evening and night in a plantation's Great House. Here, Mary-Mathilda, a descendant of slaves and the former mistress of the plantation manager, offers her life story and confession. She has just dispatched Mr Bellfeels, the plantation manager and also the father of her beloved son Wilberforce. To this end, she has used the hoe she first wielded working in the field as a young girl of seven or eight. She has committed the deed with "determination of mind." As she tells the constable, she started "to polish my hoe" three months earlier, and she is not "hiding from anybody. Not from the Law; not from God; not from my conscience" (A.C. Clarke 2002, 6).

However, as the past takes over the present – indeed, it seems chained to it by inexorable concatenations – the novel's haunting temporalities are joined by spatial, subterranean linkages between the Caribbean island, US slavery, and the general reach of the British Empire (or what Hall terms the "European presence"). In addition to evoking the connective network of hemispheric and Atlantic relations, explicitly voiced on the level of content, Clarke's novel implicates Canadian contexts in other ways. Published in Canada by one of the country's foremost authors, it addresses Canadian readers, if in some cases to their dismay.[123] The network of connective relations in which the work can be read, however, becomes clearer in the context of Clarke's other work and some of the texts I have just discussed. *The Polished Hoe* can be seen to provide a prequel of sorts – for instance, to Clarke's *The Survivors of the Crossing*, which connects a Bajan plantation rebellion and a Caribbean Canadian immigrant. Both the rebelling workers and the immigrant seek a reprieve from the oppressive presence of a past; this past has its ultimate roots (as Clarke argues loudly and clearly in *The Polished Hoe*) in the British Empire's New World reach and especially in its engagement in transatlantic slavery. The connective relations between Canada and the Caribbean intensify as we see inhabitants of Clarke's Bimshire and their descendants move north; the times and spaces of the Caribbean become those of Canada, as we have seen in the lives narrated in Foster's *Slammin' Tar*, Silvera's *Silenced*, and much of Austin Clarke's earlier work.

The Polished Hoe is concerned with the long-lasting forces of oppression, but it also perpetuates the reflection on violence – and its concatenation, from perpetrators of slavery to their victims and descendants – that we have seen in some of George Elliott Clarke's work. Like the protagonist of George Elliott Clarke's earlier *Beatrice Chancy*, Austin Clarke's main character in *The Polished Hoe*, Mary-Mathilda, is not afraid of committing a bloody deed; neither is she afraid of taking responsibility for killing a man who had quasi-proprietary power over her. On the contrary, she summons the police herself to take down her account. As in the case of George Elliott Clarke's subsequent *George & Rue*, although there is a murder, we are not reading a traditional detective story. In the words of one reviewer (that could apply to both works), the text "does not hinge on the suspense of who committed the crime, but rather on the 'why'" (Walcott-Hackshaw 2006, 680). The question of guilt is complicated, again, by contexts and historical legacies whose reading depends on point of view. Adjudication of guilt or relative virtue, as we have seen in the case of George Elliott Clarke, depends on community, place, and ways of seeing, which correlate with ways of speaking. Austin Clarke uses in *The Polished Hoe* what he will call, in a blurb for George Elliott Clarke's later *George & Rue*, "a brilliant 'blackened' dialect."

As opposed to her words cited above, much of Mary-Mathilda's narrative is rendered in stylized varieties of popular Bajan English. Austin Clarke's portrayal of the Island of Bimshire continues his earlier linguistic practice. As he states in conversation, "Once I began writing, it was clear to me that I would use the popular language. It gave authority; it made the work authentic" (H.N. Thomas 2006, 32). Clarke references the counsel of Frank Collymore, his former teacher and founder of the Barbadian literary magazine *Bim*, in which some of his early stories appeared (Algoo-Baksh 1994, 51, 60–1, 67). At the beginning of the 1960s, he offered Clarke critically important advice about the "use of Barbadian" or "nation language" (H.N. Thomas 2006, 32), suggesting that he concentrate on speech rhythms and only occasionally "bring in the misspelt word here and there, but not too often" (Algoo-Baksh 1994, 51).[124] Yet Clarke also points to important linguistic differences with respect to *The Polished Hoe*: "In this book the usage of dialect is not the pure [Barbadian]. I thought I could not do that because [Mary-Mathilda is] a woman who has moved up in social status … Her language would therefore have changed. But, since she's Barbadian and black, she would retain the essence. And that's the way she talks to the constable. When she talks to the sergeant the language is different" (Richards 2002).

Indeed, not only her language, but also her identity and her name change depending on context. The opening of the novel emphasizes this: "My name is Mary. People in this Village call me Mary-Mathilda. Or, Tilda, for short. To my mother I was Mary-girl … My surname that people 'bout-here uses, is either Paul, or Bellfeels, depending who you speak to" (A.C. Clarke 2002, 3). While the constable assures her that she is known and respected in the village as Miss Bellfeels, she lets him know that this "is not the name I want attach to this Statement that I giving you" (3).

Her confession, it turns out, is both a self-assertion and a legacy. An oral history that reaches back to the times of slavery, it also tells the story of her life and of the plantation that Sergeant Percy is not familiar with. Since the sympathies of the sergeant – once a potential lover – lie with Mary-Mathilda, he does not really want to hear the conclusion of her confession (40, 51). To gain time, he first sends the constable to interrogate Mary-Mathilda, who assures him that she knows stories about "the doings and happenings in this small Island of Bimshire" that are apt "to make your head curl" (36). These include incidents that reveal the bestiality of Bellfeels. He seems to have been responsible for the pregnancy of Clotelle, a sixteen-year-old girl who hanged herself from a tree earlier used for a hanging under slavery (13–15). We also learn that Bellfeels mutilated a young boy named Colborne (16) and that he shot Pounce for trying to steal "three sweet potatoes and four pulp-eddoes" (17). Bellfeels's crimes also include the rape of Mary-Mathilda's mother when she was sixteen (she only tells her daughter about it on her deathbed sixty-two years later) (37). Mary-Mathilda thus informs the constable early on that she is neither hiding her deed nor denying her intentions: "I was determined. And deliberate. Because I knew what my cause was. And I had a cause," beginning from the time she was sent to work on the plantation (8).

Inverting the signs of salvation, Clarke has the story of her downfall begin on an Easter Sunday "in the Church Yard of Sin-Davids Anglican Church." On that day, Bellfeels's gaze and riding-crop first inscribe the future on her body, as her mother silently stands by. Instead of Easter, she experiences a meeting with the Anti-Christ:

> "The sun was playing tricks in his face too. So, neither of the two of we could see the other person too clear. But he could see my face, because he was looking down.
>
> "Then, Mr. Bellfeels put his riding-crop under my chin, and raise my face to meet his face, using the riding-crop; and when his eyes and my eyes made four, he passed the riding-crop down my neck, right down the front of my dress, until it reach my waist. And then he move the riding-crop right back up again, as if he was drawing something on my body." (11)

In this parody of Easter, with Mary-Mathilda repeating in her mind the reverend's reading of "One, Sin-Peter, three, seventeen" (9),[125] Clarke conceivably plays with the conventional pun sun/son in the opening words of this passage.[126] But almost more cruelly, the often-cited passage from 1 Corinthians 13:12 comes to mind: "For now we see through a glass darkly; but then face to face: now I know in part; but then shall I know even as also I am known" (King James version). In this viciously ironic inversion, Mary-Mathilda espies not God, but the evil she will eventually kill, whereas Bellfeels's gaze seizes for the first time the woman he will later know in the biblical sense.

The allusion to impeded visibility also evokes Du Bois's famous metaphor of the veil in *The Souls of Black Folk.* As Shamoon Zamir has pointed out, in Hegel's *Phenomenology* the drawing aside of the curtain or the lifting of the veil signifies cognitive progress and marks the "moment that self-consciousness discovers itself behind natural appearance" (Zamir 1995, 135); in Du Bois's revision and inversion of Hegel, by contrast, the veil *descends* (Zamir 1995, 136) in a childhood moment of rejection that marks the child's entrance into race consciousness. This moment also signals the entrance into double-consciousness, "this sense of always looking at one's self through the eyes of others" (Du Bois 1986a, 364).

The moment when Mary-Mathilda is seized and defined by the gaze of this ostensibly white man[127] marks in many ways her entrance into a world of double-consciousness. This circumstance is suggested by her double surname – "either Paul, or Bellfeels, depending who you speak to" (A.C. Clarke 2002, 3) – and the dual linguistic registers she employs in different contexts.[128] It is also associated with the biblical notion of walking in darkness. Her decision to end her association with this realm of darkness is a moment of conversion. As she emphasizes at the beginning of her confessional testimony, she wants her experience to be known as an act of conversion: "A long time ago, before tonight, I decided to stop walking in darkness" (6). Her crime, it turns out, is also a moment of virtue, as she decides to abandon a life of sin and falsehood. We come to understand that she had few defences against entering into that sinful life as a child; it was a life of darkness and sin normalized and imposed upon her by the world she was forced to grow up in.

Mary-Mathilda's acquiescence to the wishes of Bellfeels is portrayed in many ways as a pact with the devil. Beelzebub intrudes upon her life in front of "Sin Davids Anglican Church" (9).[129] The moment occurs with her mother silently standing by, "voiceless, as if the riding-crop was Mr. Bellfeels finger clasped to her lips, clamped to her mouth to strike her dumb to keep her silence, to keep her peace" (11–12). As Mary-Mathilda understands, even as a child who knows nothing as yet of the history of slavery, the power that controls her mother – and herself – is made possible by a system of wealth that can exploit and dominate poverty, usually with impunity. This power maintains and feeds on a radical inequality akin to slavery that persists in plantation society. Mary-Mathilda thus associates that first encounter with Bellfeels with her conscious awareness of poverty: "From that Sunday morning, the meaning of poverty was driven into my head. The sickening power of poverty" (12). Her mother's complicity and her own later acquiescence are outcomes of a pact with the devil dictated by poverty and the power of Bellfeels.[130]

Mary-Mathilda recalls – while recounting her anger and the violence she imagined inflicting upon despots like Bellfeels, only rarely punished by acts of violence (60) – how it had been impossible to speak up for her own generation of women and those before her. And only on her deathbed, having finally spoken of how, at the age of sixteen, she had been raped by Bellfeels (37), does her mother find the words to speak of her silence of many years ago, charging Mary-Mathilda to "bear witness": "*You must never forget that Sunday afternoon in the Church Yard! And bear witness to how my mouth was stricken. But there is times when it is more better not to open your mouth than to speak a word*" (60). Using "her dying breath, to utter her last advice" (60), she thus projects her own life and testimony into the future by witnessing. To recall Baucom's rendering of Derrida, witnessing "is not only simultaneously to observe, hold to, survive, and subsist beyond the event but to transmit to another this property of observing, holding, surviving. It is, therefore, to serialize the event and its affect and also to elongate its temporality to stretch its time along the line of an unfolding series of moments of bearing witness" (Baucom 2005, 177). While Mary-Mathilda's great-grandmother uses medical skill from her native Africa "plus a lil touch of obeah and witchcraft" to deal with the immediate consequences of Bellfeels's rape (A.C. Clarke 2002, 38), the mother's account will move her daughter-turned-witness to act later: "That is why I did what I did" (39). Her conversion, "crime," and confession bear witness again, and they implicate further audiences in an "unfolding series of moments of bearing witness" (Baucom 2005, 177).

"A statement worth its salt": A Hoe and Circumstances "Make in Englund"

Mary-Mathilda's act of bearing witness constantly connects her own life with the Island of Bimshire, with its history, and especially with its unrecorded past, which reaches back to the time of slavery. At first glance, this tendency of her narrative seems to be at odds with her self-assigned task of accounting for the demise of Mr Bellfeels. Why indeed, in her statement to the police, is she giving "this history of my personal life, and the history of this Island of Bimshire, altogether, wrap-up in one" (20)? Her myriad digressions appear to impede the progress of her narrative. These "vertical" interruptions of what seems to be the main story, though, are central to the novel. They structure its very architecture and work in tandem with its vernacular registers. The novel as a whole responds to Mary-Mathilda's musings when she notes, "I am rambling again. I don't know what got-me-off on this topic, talking about the history of this place" (18).

As the narrative progresses, it becomes clear that her deed can only be accounted for contextually. It belongs to a social reality imprinted on both the protagonist and the community: "All our lives was branded by this Plantation" (18). As the language of branding suggests, it is the mark of slavery seared into the fabric of the community and individual lives that persists, long after formal abolition, in the presence of plantation society. Past slavery and the presence of its past are still legible in the economy of power that determines the community and the lives of its members. This context allows Bellfeels to inscribe his will on the body of Mary-Mathilda. The Easter churchyard scene of subjection (to use Hartman's phrase) comes again to the fore in Mary-Mathilda's long digression about a wishbone that she has carried for years on her body (20–7); it has served as a mnemonic device, reminding her daily of her "wish *never-ever* to forget Mr. Bellfeels; and how he moved the riding-crop over my entire body, as if he was taking off my clothes, and then taking off my skin" (22). In addition, the presence of the wishbone actuates a constant reiteration of her oath "to never forget to give him back" (22). Since Bellfeels's act is deeply connected with the power structure of the plantation, the village, and the past, Mary-Mathilda bears witness not only to the events in her own life, but also to that wider context. Ultimately, her testimony comes to include the lives of those who lived under slavery.

The kind of contextualism that is evident in Mary-Mathilda's narrative is supported, in a more legal sense, by the constable.[131] As she apologizes about the digression about the wishbone – which is her equivalent of a Catholic's rosary and a wealthy person's gold watch (27) – the constable expresses his interest in hearing about the history of the island. He argues that he is legally obligated to listen to this story, with its many vertical sidelines digging deep into unrecorded history: "To-besides," he observes, "we need to know the whole background to a person, for a Statement to be a statement worth its salt" (2002, 27).

Not only is the entire community visibly marked by its roots in slavery; the murder weapon, too, is directly linked with that past. Treating the constable to a long account of her polishing and sharpening the hoe (53–9), she points out that things made of the clammy cherry wood used for the handle of the hoe "last for generations." Indeed, the hoe has a long history: "Ma herself used the hoe she inherited from her mother, my gran … This is the same hoe I inherited from my Ma. Yes!" (53). Eventually, the shed where the hoe may be, or perhaps the hoe itself, leads her further back: "It is a relic from the slave days" (57).

Mary-Mathilda's long account of polishing the hoe includes reflections on the importance of tools, which she recalls from her Europhile and Oxbridge-educated son, named for the abolitionist Wilberforce. She renders his maxim, derived from Winston Churchill, as "*Give we the tools, and we will do the rest*" (55). Mary-Mathilda's own tool has taken care of Bellfeels and his phallo-imperial "tool" (382, 460–1). Instrumental in her personal moment of abolition, the hoe also answers "Englund," where it was made; it thus "speaks back" to the centre of empire across the Atlantic that has produced not only the historical Wilberforce and abolition, but also slavery and its continuing impact on Bimshire or Barbados. To the sergeant's observation that the tool "was made in Englund," Mary-Mathilda responds: "What isn't ... What isn't?" (453).

It is clear that this remark also comes to bear upon the murder itself, embedded as it is in the web of communal, colonial, and historical contexts and associations. The sergeant, who has written next to nothing so far, dutifully enters in his notebook protocol: "*Make in Englund ... Nota bene. Reference: the hoe blade! Important!*" (453). As he repeats this fact, "he says it as if it is an earth-shattering conclusion he has come to, the solution of a long, nagging problem to do with this case" (454). Indeed, not only the hoe, but also plantation society, Bellfeels, and Mary-Mathilda as a polished "hoe" or whore (118)[132] are in important ways products of empire and made in "Englund." Given that his own sexual aspirations were previously barred by poverty and Bellfeels's possession of Mary-Mathilda, Sergeant Percy's discovery may offer him a more personal revelation in addition to insight into the contextual determination and genealogy of her deed.

One further product "make in Englund," as Mary-Mathilda knows and Percy comes to realize, is the absence of knowledge about slavery in Bimshire. This silence is produced by an educational system based on British models. As she points out with reference to her son Wilberforce, in "all the years he went-school at Harrison College, one of the most reputed and best institutionals in the British Empire, not one Master who teached him ever mentioned to him a word about this History of the Laws of slavery! He left without knowing ... the history of himself" (191).[133] Sergeant Percy, for his part, who until now has believed that "there was never any slaves in Bimshire" and "wasn't taught nothing-so at Sin-Davis Elementary School" (351), is led to discover an unknown island when Mary-Mathilda takes him into the tunnels underneath the Great House. After the sergeant witnesses the panoptic view over the plantation from the upstairs bedroom and is made welcome on the ground floor, the underground part of the Great House introduces him to an unknown part of the island's topography. It reveals to him more clearly its roots in slavery as it is conveyed in Mary-Mathilda's stories: "The story that duplicates this strange underground journey [that] Sargeant is being made to take causes him to feel he is a foreigner, a stranger in a land in which he thought he had a straight course" (342). As Mary-Mathilda points out to him, although a member of the police force, he is "a stranger to the truth, to the history, and to the actions of the powerful in this Island" (348).

The first layer that is uncovered in this archaeological narrative concerns a rebellion for higher wages. Mary-Mathilda, however, immediately references earlier events during slavery: "If we had time … I could tell you the things that take place in this underground dungeon. And this don't have nothing to do with the times of slavery that Ma used to narrate to me, about when even more stranger things took place on this Plantation" (339). The narrative of the rebellion is framed by references to bloodshed, opening with the words, "Always blood being shed. And blood flowing" (339). It concerns the plantation workers' demand for "a couple-more-pennies-a-week, in wages" (339) and results in three of the leaders being handcuffed to the walls of the underground passage; they receive up to forty lashes, as in slavery times, until the "blood was all over this underground tunnel" (342). This flow of blood has seeped out in stories and conversation fissures: "Pieces of this history, this pageantry of blood, have leaked-out through various cracks and crevices" (342).

As Clarke has pointed out, his novel is not strictly historical, since it is more concerned with psychological dimensions.[134] It is thus not entirely clear when the rebellion took place, since the struggle for wages implies the post-emancipation period after 1834, while the Bimshire authorities link it to the 1831 Nat Turner rebellion in Southampton, Virginia (344–5). For Mary-Mathilda, the rebellion is mainly linked to her mother's memories of blood.[135] Significantly, the references to bloodshed tie this history of violence to her mother's rape by Bellfeels and to her own decision to act: "My God, the blood" is all she remembers her mother saying when, after the successful abortion, "the sin, and the stain, and the mistake, came out in the form of blood." Mary-Mathilda adds to that memory earlier: "But blood was always in our lives. Blood, and more blood … and that is why I did what I did" (39).

The chain of narrative transmission and the account of the rebellion point to slavery both in Bimshire and the United States. The names and narratives of Frederick Douglass and Booker T. Washington are familiar to Mary-Mathilda through the stories of her mother (346). In addition, slavery in Bimshire emerges as part of a hemispheric and transatlantic network involving both Bellfeels's and her own ancestors. Mary-Mathilda has thus been "told that the main branch o' Bellfeelses comes from Southampton in Englund, finally settling in South Carolina where they had five cotton and sugar plantations, populated with thousands of slaves" (354). Hence the Bimshire Bellfeelses, she reasons, were able to link local discontent with the Nat Turner insurrection in the United States. Her imagination gives a concrete dimension to the subterranean, transnational tentacles of slavery by linking them to her immediate surroundings underneath the Great House: "I won't be surprised if this little underground passage … doesn't have some link and terminal, some connection, to the United States of Amurca, travelling unknown to every person on this Island, under the Carbean Sea, and the Atlantic Ocean" (354). This network of oppression offers an ironic counter-image to the Underground Railroad and is mirrored by the diasporic lifelines of her forebears.

Her forebears' existence emerges through a chain of oral conveyance that constitutes a counter-network to the tunnels under the Great House. This subterranean connection exists below the surface of written history. It links Mary-Mathilda through her mother's stories to her grandmother, to slavery in the United States and Bimshire, and finally to Africa: "Ma told me that her mother, my great-gran, was a slave on this very Plantation. Ma didn't know where she come from, neither. Africa-somewhere. Or Charleston-South-Carolina. They sent all the rebelling slaves, following the Southampton Resurrection, I mean Insurrection, here to Bimshire, which has the reputation, Ma say Great-gran told her, of having the most cruel slave overseers and slave-drivers" (354–5). Mary-Mathilda's knowledge of her great-grandmother is unreliable,[136] reflecting a disrupted knowledge of her family's origins. Yet the matrilinear connection is emphasized repeatedly as strong and relevant: "Ma started her life here, too. My grandmother, Gran, started her life here, and before Gran, my great-gran, who was taken from a different place" (366). This genealogy represents a chain of transmission that Mary-Mathilda considers her inheritance, and she now wants to pass it on to others (a sequence we will see again in Agnant's *Book of Emma*).

Ultimately, this historical inheritance determines the context for her acts in the present. She tells the sergeant that she is presenting "a narrative told to me by Ma, which she heard from her mother, Gran, who I am sure, heard it told by my great-great-gran, and finally handed down to me. These narratives are the only inheritances that poor people can hand down to their offsprings … love. And bitterness. And blood. And anger. And all four, wrap-up in one narrative" (355). Despite a widespread reluctance to recognize the history of slavery in Bimshire, she points out, "the treatment that Ma tell me about that she suffer through, and what my great-great-gran went through, you would have to invent a new name for it, if not slavery" (356). These thoughts, it turns out, are integral to the moment she sits down and decides that "after all this years, she would choose this Sunday to correct all the injuries she had suffered, swollen through the passage of the years themselves"; they are part of the moment she "find the motive" for her deed in Bellfeels's actions and those before him, as they have come down to her "through the narrative of her mother's life, and the tales handed down from her great-great-gran's life from a time even before that" (359).

One of Mary-Mathilda's more poignant formulations about the presence of the past, however, comes much earlier in the text: "There is a time when your past takes over you, and takes over your present" (59). This thought presents in a nutshell the novel's large-scale portrayal of a contextual relation that links the present to the past. More specifically, it suggests that the historical legacy of slavery is unfinished business and that it can determine both black and white subjectivity long after slavery is over.

That outline of history as an accumulation of time, rather than as progress or dialectical supersession, rejoins the reflections that George Elliott Clarke offers with respect to *George & Rue*. Like him, Austin Clarke relates his protagonist's action to a contextual framework that reaches back to slavery. Poverty is one of the factors, but violence also occurs as a consequence of, or in response to, a continuity of violence initiated earlier by slavery. As George Elliott Clarke suggests, violence is inherited in George and Rue's family. Together with abject poverty, it causes victims to produce other innocent victims. In Austin Clarke's *The Polished Hoe*, the violence of slavery turns more directly against Bellfeels, who has inherited slavery's contempt for black lives. Sexual violence in particular links *The Polished Hoe* to George Elliott Clarke's *Beatrice Chancy*. And since black violence and revenge are clearly directed in these cases against a tyrant figure, the question of crime and virtue evoked by George Elliott Clarke is applicable also to Austin Clarke's novel. In the case of Mary-Mathilda, as Sergeant

Percy makes clear, nobody really wants to hear the murder confession that will see her punished. Yet she herself is not afraid of the law, and she considers that she has ceased to "walk in darkness." Mary-Mathilda makes a virtue of insisting that her account be known as a valuable inheritance. She wants it to be on record as the real history of the island and as a story of moral salvation to be conveyed to her community.

Mary-Mathilda's testimony offers what Sergeant Percy calls a "statement worth its salt," providing "the whole background to a person" (27). It bears witness to diasporic and transnational contexts beyond borders and across historical time. Many of the determining circumstances turn out to be, like the hoe and her Oxbridge-trained son's language, "make in Englund." Her oral testimony, though, never seems to be transcribed into a police report controlled by standard English or the *Oxford English Dictionary*. Clarke's linguistically de-colonized creation of her oral account insists on the dire legacies of slavery and speaks back to narratives of modernity promulgated by empire and its language.

In creating oral chains of transmission as a literary device for the inscription of black histories across diasporic, transnational black Atlantic spaces, *The Polished Hoe* joins other Caribbean Canadian texts that imaginatively counter the interruption or suppression of African knowledges and languages caused by slavery and colonial domination. Dionne Brand and Marie-Célie Agnant use similar devices, as we will see, also emphasizing female genealogies and lines of conveyance as sites of narrative resistance. The precarious relationship between silence, voice, and writing is crucial for marginalized cultures and the assertive inscription of non-hegemonic narratives. It can also raise difficult questions, however – as suggested in the introduction – when witnessing is possible only through the imagination.

A "story that cannot but must be told": Marlene NourbeSe Philip's *Zong!*

The relationships between silence, language, and the possibilities of witnessing are vital to Marlene NourbeSe Philip's writing.[137] Her 1991 volume *Looking for Livingstone: An Odyssey of Silence* begins with this epigraph: "For the ancestors / who have been silent for too long / and whose Silence is. Always." (5). These opening lines posit a complex temporality. The ancestors persist in the present, albeit as Silence. The very words that deplore as "too long" the absence of their voice suggest their transformative potential in the future. But the ancestors' Silence also "is." The presence and reality of this "always already there"[138] is emphatically hypostatized by the syntactically self-contained word "Always." This ontology articulates the simultaneity of a presence dynamically linked with absence, naming a potent critical negativity. This critical dimension will also mark *Zong!* (2008), her poetic performance of the necessity and necessary impossibility of bearing witness to the murders epitomized by the eponymous slave ship's name.

The word "silence" also appears in Philip's earlier volume *She Tries Her Tongue, Her Silence Softly Breaks* (1989).[139] Yet as she explains in the introductory essay,[140] besides silence, too much language can also be a problem. The language imposed on Africans by the slave trade thus came with attendant forms of alienated consciousness: "To speak another language is to enter another consciousness. Africans in the New World were compelled to enter another consciousness, that of their masters, while simultaneously being excluded from their own" (Philip 1989, 15). The problem of linguistic dispossession is shared by many other cultures divested of self-determination by imperialism; the linguistic disruption of African languages by the slave trade, however, signals an especially radical break. It led to an "almost absolute destruction and obliteration of African languages" which, "together with the accompanying act of renaming by the European … was one of the most devastating and successful acts of aggression carried out by one people against another" (15). Thus, in Philip's perspective, language often obviates rather than facilitates the expression of experience.[141]

Rhythms and "tonal accentuation" are for Philip among the elements of verbal expression "rooted in African languages" (1989, 17) that survived in African appropriations of English, thereby contributing to new linguistic forms that she refers to as "a demotic variant of English" or the "Caribbean demotic." Like Dionne Brand in this respect, she suggests that the "excitement for me as a writer comes in the confrontation between the formal and the demotic within the text itself" (18). Nonetheless, language for Caribbean writers "must always present a dilemma" (18). Even more radically, Philip stresses that the "language as we know it has to be dislocated and acted upon – even destroyed – so that it begins to serve our purpose" (19). From that position, the dilemma is more complex than the question of whether to write in standard or demotic English, or even in both. How does one destroy a language while at the same time using "language in such a way that the historical realities are not erased or obliterated, so that English is revealed as the tainted tongue it truly is" (19)? And how does one destroy a language and also heed Philip's "imperative that our writing begin to re-create our histories and our myths, as well as integrate that most painful of experiences – loss of our history and our word" (25)?

The texts that follow in *She Tries Her Tongue* thematize and enact this problematic. Philip employs deconstructive poetic techniques, using syntactic and spatial isolation and displacements on the page. She also makes language an explicit topic in sections like "Discourse on the Logic of Language," "Universal Grammar," "The Question of Language is the Answer to Power," and "Testimony Stoops to Mother Tongue." Her subsequent volume, *Looking for Livingstone: An Odyssey of Silence*, which she labels "a poem in poetry and prose" (in H.N. Thomas 2006, 200), offers an extended allegory – in the shape of a travel narrative and a linguistic pilgrim's progress – of working through forms of silence. A black character named "The Traveler" encounters cultures with different relationships to words and silence.[142] Eventually she encounters Livingstone, "an embodiment of British colonial agency and power" (D. Jones 2004, 201). He is also at the source of a torrent of European words about Africa that buries much of the continent under it (like the original name of the Victoria Falls, Mosi-oa-Tunya, "the Cloud that Thunders").

As Philip explains in a 2008 interview, "working through" the conjoined difficulties of language and silence in *She Tries Her Tongue* and *Looking for Livingstone* facilitated her move to the radical de-structuring of language that she undertakes in *Zong!*[143] She describes these writing experiences as "integral to getting to a place in 'Ferrum,' the last chapter in *Zong!*, where I can risk destroying language … For the first time in my writing life, I felt, this is my language – the grunts, moans, utterances, pauses, sounds, and silences" (in P. Saunders 2008, 71). The 1781 slave massacre committed on the *Zong* to collect insurance resulted not in a murder trial, but in a case brought by the shipowners against their understandably recalcitrant insurers. After the owners' initial victory, a court under Lord Mansfield ordered a new trial (which may never have taken place). The summary of that decision, commonly known as *Gregson vs Gilbert*, is reproduced at the very end of Philip's *Zong!* In the preceding essay, "Notanda," Philip cites her journal about the main premise of her project: "My intent is to use the text of the legal decision as a word store; to lock myself into this particular and peculiar discursive landscape in the belief that the story of these African men, women, and children thrown overboard in an attempt to collect insurance monies, the story that can only be told by not telling, is locked in this text.

In the many silences within the Silence of the text. I would lock myself in this text in the same way men, women, and children were locked in the holds of the slave ship *Zong*" (2008, 191).

The limitation imposed by the selection of this "word store" is not the only constraint governing her writing process. As Philip's concern with "not telling" indicates, *Zong!* is an exploration of the limits and ethics of the sayable, a project wary of false certainties of knowing and wary as well of the deceptive comforts of projection. For Jenny Sharpe, the text "does not tell the story that is missing from the archives so much as indicate the limits of its telling" (2013, 466). Philip notes, for example, that she was "uncomfortable" when she began reading a novel about the incident (presumably Fred d'Aguiar's *Feeding the Ghosts* [1997]): "'A novel requires too much telling,' I write, and this story must be told by not telling" (2008, 190). Earlier the essay speaks of the aim "to not tell the story that must be told," and it returns to this theme repeatedly. Modulations of the phrase include "a story that cannot be told" (190) (evoking Adorno's dictum about the impossibility of poetry after Auschwitz) but also "the story that must tell itself" (191). Philip's text is thus crucially concerned with the ethics of representing trauma. It raises the question, as Veronica Austen points out in her lucid examination of the stakes and strategies involved, "whether or not silence can, or even should, be overcome" (Austen 2011, 64); for Austen, Philip's project suggests not only "self-consciousness regarding the necessary limits to one's knowledge as the means through which past victims of trauma can be honoured yet their alterity respected," but also that "recovering grievable subjects is simply too important to shy away from the challenge and responsibility of ethical secondary witnessing" (67).

Philip is thus engaged in an arguably impossible attempt to use the words of the case, which she calls "the tombstone, the only public marker of the murder of those on board the *Zong*" (194).[144] In Sharpe's words, her "delicate task … involves using [the case's] language while refusing the sense of its meaning" (2013, 468). At the same time, however, she seeks to avoid not only the emplotment that the case offers but also any other perspective that she herself might impose. This concern is motivated by her fear – a classic deconstructive dilemma – of being caught in language that carries the historical implications we have seen her delineate earlier, of having to tell the story "in a language already contaminated, possibly irrevocably and fatally" (Philip 2008, 199). In her attempts to avoid "contaminated" discursive formations and the "sentence" of language, Philip considers, in a journal reflection on the use of word "materials," a motivated application of the poetic technique of random sampling to the case, here a "random selection that parallels the random selection of Africans" (192).

Philip emphasizes the danger of her need for sense-making. She notes that "there are two poems – the one I want to write and the one writing itself" (192); to make room for the latter, "my urge to make sense must be resisted" (193). As we will see, however, the text also reveals major elements that exhibit a clear resistance to that resistance (and ultimately a clearly and historically motivated intentionality that strives powerfully against randomness and an only formally motivated hermeneutics of linguistic suspicion). The most striking feature first noticeable for the reader is nonetheless the success of the techniques Philip employs "to not tell the tale that must be told" (193). She itemizes some of them: "mutilate the text as the fabric of African life and the lives of these men, women, and children were mutilated" (193). And further: "I murder the text, literally cut it into pieces, castrating verbs, suffocating adjectives, murdering nouns, throwing articles, prepositions, conjunctions overboard, jettisoning adverbs: I separate subject from verb, verb from object – create semantic mayhem" until she can proceed "like some seer, sangoma, or prophet who, having sacrificed an animal for signs and portents of a new life, or simply life, reads the untold story that tells itself by not telling" (193–4).[145]

These formal techniques result in "difficult" language and a text that indeed impedes any reader from imposing and projecting meaning too quickly on the text. On the other hand, Philip's image of the "seer, sangoma, or prophet" suggests traditional strategies of poetic self-authorization as vatic medium and conveyor of meaning, a channelling presence legitimized by higher forces and/or the past.[146] The power of that image, and the urgency of the task it implies, makes itself felt at the same time as the text experiments aggressively and progressively with linguistic fragmentation. What can be observed first in the text is a progressive deconstruction and de-structuring of language elements, from the poems "Zong! #1"–"Zong! #26" in the section "Os" and the unnumbered poems entitled "Zong! #" in the following section "Dicta" through the "four subsequent movements or books." As she writes in her journal, in these four books she goes beyond the use of the words used in the earlier part in their integrity. From a certain point in the writing process onward, she decides "to explode the words to see what other words they may contain. I devise a dictionary with a list of each of the 'mother words' followed by the words contained in that particular word … As I put the dictionary together, little dramas appear to take place in the margins of the text and so the poem continues to write itself, giving up stories and resulting in four subsequent movements or books – I think of these poems as the flesh – the earlier 26 poems are the bones" (2008, 200).

As Philip observes, the resulting poems "need a great deal of space around them" (2008, 194), and they also contain within them large spaces around individual phrases, words, or word fragments. In Philip's poetics, these silences are as relevant and as generative of meaning as the words on the page. As she points out, there is "a very fine balance between the text and the surrounding space" (in P. Saunders 2008, 73). Relation is "the organizing principle of relationship used in *Zong!*" (Philip 2008, 205). Philip attempts to let the story tell itself in the spaces, silences, and relations created in the break between, and within, broken syntagms and words. While she creates these spaces and relations herself in the writing process, the result tasks the reader to become a co-creator by "forcing the eye to track across the page in an attempt to wrest meaning from words gone astray" (Philip 2008, 198). Since this spatial poetics offers almost unlimited combinatory possibilities, meaning-making seems entirely contingent on each individual or collective act of reading.[147]

There are important textual elements that operate outside of this (il)logic of the text, however, that stabilize meaning partly through authorial intervention. Besides the section titles,[148] epigrams, and the explanatory essay "Notanda," there is another element by which Philip breaks her own rules, which is when she proceeds to an act of naming in order to impose individuality on the anonymity and silence of the drowned victims of the Zong massacre. Philip thus cites from a journal entry that very "early on I develop a need to know the names of the murdered" (2008, 194). After learning from James Walvin, the author of *Black Ivory*, that no names were kept, she receives from Ian Baucom (who works at this point on *Spectres of the Atlantic*) the list of a sales agent trading with the shipowners that reveals only minimal descriptions of each slave and no names.[149]

In the face of this anonymity, Philip creates a series of names that appear first in the section "Os" at the bottom of each page, separated from the rest of the poem (but also a part of it) by a centred line.[150] As the trained lawyer Philip explains, the "legal principle at the heart of the decision" is referred to as "ratio," whereas everything else becomes "obiter dicta" or simply "*dicta*," which is "what the Africans on board the *Zong* become – *dicta*, footnotes, related to, but not, the *ratio*" (2008, 199). While the names indeed appear in the section "Os" in a position resembling footnotes, Philip adduces another principle in her journal: "*Idea at heart of the footnotes in general is acknowledgement – someone else was here before – in* Zong! *footnote equals the footprint. / Footprints of the African on board the* Zong" (200).[151] In the section "Dicta," however, the space underneath the still present line at the bottom remains empty. Further names appear at the end of "Ferrum," the last of the four books and according to Philip the most fragmented section.[152] They are still underneath a black line, but now they appear in the middle of the page, written in cursive script and arranged in several lines (in a shape that a willful eye could interpret as a ship). In their solid, linear textuality, they seem to support the sparse fragments floating above them on the page (173).[153]

Despite Philip's endeavour to let the story tell itself, these acts of naming are part of a narrativity that is also emphasized by some of the epigraphs. Among these, one is taken from Ezekiel 37:7–10: "There was a noise and behold, a shaking … and the bones came together, / bone to this bone … the sinews and flesh came upon them … and the skin / covered them above … and the breath came into them … / and they lived, and stood upon their feet" (2008, 126). The epigraph thus seems to offer active guidance about how to approach the words and silences that follow – in contrast to any poetic intention to let the bones and flesh of the murdered slaves rise by their own force, out of the water and oblivion, in the spaces and silences of the poem.

A second epigraph on the same page is taken from St Augustine: "Praesens de praereritis [*sic*]. / The past is ever present" (126).[154] This epigraph complements an earlier one by St Augustine, introducing the section "Sal": "Non enim erat tunc. / There was no then" (58). Both epigraphs posit the presence of the past. The second one questions even more directly the very distinction between these categories of time – a temporality, as we have seen, that pertains also to Derrida's hauntologies and his question "whether the *spectrality effect* does not consist in undoing this opposition, or even this dialectic, between actual, effective presence and its other" (Derrida 2006, 48). Philip's own reading of Derrida's *Specters of Marx* "confirmed me in my earlier feelings that *Zong!* is a wake" (2008, 202). But if it is a wake, it is hardly one that takes leave of the dead. It rather serves as a hauntological evocation of their presence; it "is a work of haunting, a wake of sorts, where the spectres of the undead make themselves present" (201). In this sense, Philip cites, just before referring to Marx and Derrida, Baucom's *Specters of the Atlantic.* Baucom himself uses poems or parts of poems from *Zong!*

(or earlier drafts) as epigraphs to all of his chapters in part 2 of his study.[155] Especially the cited poems "*Zong!* #14" and "*Zong!* #24" highlight the undecidability between past and present. In his evocation of *Zong!* in the concluding paragraphs of *Specters of the Atlantic*, Baucom tellingly cites the beginning of "Zong! #4": "This is / not was" (Philip 2008, 7; Baucom 2005, 332). In turn, Philip in "Notanda" cites Baucom's argument of "an 'order of historical time' that does not so much pass as 'accumulate'" (2008, 208n26). This, I would argue, is the narrative that emerges, in mutual relation with the silences, spaces, and fragmentations, and in disruptions of the individual poems, through the surface of the textual spaces in Philip's *Zong!*

Dionne Brand: Witnessing and the Inventory

Dionne Brand evokes black Atlantic time-spaces and accumulative temporalities as alternatives to Eurocentric modernity in a number of works of prose and poetry, especially from the late 1980s to the early 2000s, that remain mindful of slavery. These works reconstitute the virulent reality of a dis-remembered past. Reconnecting disrupted lines of knowledge and conveyance, they overtly re-inscribe the past in the present. This process is related to a large-scale inventory of historical traces and deposits that Brand continues to compile, for instance, in further volumes of poetry such as *Land to Light On* (1997), *Thirsty* (2002), *Inventory* (2006), and her Griffin Prize–winning *Ossuaries* (2010).[156]

Brand has spoken about the necessity of such an inventory as one of the factors that motivates her writing: "In *Orientalism*, Said quotes Gramsci's conviction that 'the starting point for critical elaboration is the consciousness of what one really is, a product of historical process to date which has deposited in you this infinity of traces without leaving an inventory … Therefore it is imperative at the outset to compile such an inventory' … If I can choose and identify one of the reasons why I write, it is to address this Gramscian starting point, to address these traces deposited in me, both of imperial domination but also of race, class, and gender resistance to that domination."[157] Besides Marx and Gramsci, Brand relies on numerous other genealogies of resistance. These include Caribbean intellectual traditions and black Marxisms and feminisms, the Pan-African movement, the civil rights, black power, and black arts movements in the United States, as well as more local developments within her Toronto and Canadian community.[158] As with Philip and Clarke, the question of language and the means of conveyance prove vitally important here. Versions of the demotic are a crucial hinge in Brand's linguistic and literary practice, signalling a constant, often self-reflexive search for a language of witnessing and transformation.

Demotic Knowledge, Ancestors, Genealogy

Brand thus distinguishes between a "standard demotic" and one "that signifies the working class," but she also states her wish to deploy forms of the demotic "like a language rather than work it as an example of culture" (Butling 2005, 72).[159] In an interview with Pauline Butling, she mentions her short story "Blossom: Priestess of Oya, Goddess of Winds, Storms, and Waterfalls" (in *Sans Souci and Other Stories*, 1988) as one of the first examples of her use of the demotic. Here the demotic combines with African Caribbean spirituality as they become signs of resistance to the disruptions of diasporic dispersal. The eponymic immigrant from Trinidad turns to running a speakeasy-cum-obeah-house in Toronto. Her practice of obeah among other black immigrants prolongs certain functions of obeah under colonialism and slavery, where it channelled black self-determination and often resistance.[160] Blossom's transformation from an exploited to a self-employed and relatively autonomous subject occurs via possession by the Yoruba deity Oya, an "Afro-Atlantic orisha" and warrior-spirit of storm and lightning, but also of change and transformation, who also inspired Zora Neale Hurston (Cartwright 2006, 743–4; Gleason 1987). As a consequence of Oya's positive response to her invocations, Blossom "sleep exhausted and full of Oya warrior dance and laughing" but "live peaceful" (Brand 1988, 42). Brand's practice of the demotic throughout the story seems to parallel the character's own deployment of resistant tactics, as Blossom uses West Indian ancestral knowledge successfully to navigate a difficult Canadian environment and counteract some of the negative effects of her diasporic displacement.

Brand later varies her use of the demotic, observing that in her volume of poetry *No Language Is Neutral*, she "found a way to slip in and out of these two demotics with no compunction at all" (2005, 73). Significantly, the title poem first switches to a demotic register in its evocation of *slavery*. Brand will continue to explore the impact of slavery on post-slavery consciousness and language in later works that function both as witnessing and as part of her ongoing inventory of historical traces. The poem "no language is neutral" is seminal in this respect. Opening with the titular phrase (1990, 22), Brand begins by registering a critical awareness of her medium, intertextually recalling a passage by Derek Walcott; he writes in *Midsummer*: "No language is neutral; / the green oak of English is a murmurous cathedral / where some took umbrage, some peace, but every shade, all / helped widen its shadow" (LII). Brand is well aware of the shadow; as Susan Gingell observes, however, she "is more inclined to take umbrage than to find peace" (1994, 50).[161] Referencing Gingell, Leslie Sanders notes that instead of peace or shade, for Brand there is "only bitter history barely written, and when written at all, neither by women, nor about them" (2009, x). In the passage in question, the speaker evokes only a "history which had taught my eyes / to look for escape" (1990, 22), and thus two recurrent themes in Brand's work: the "malicious horizon" as merciless limit of earlier island slave flight[162] and the related wish "to fly gravity" – a figure of transformation and possibility connected also with slaves' longing for a return to Africa.[163] The poem then turns to the demotic as an explicit form of linguistic partiality and evokes *language* itself as technology of escape and retribution:

> … The malicious horizon made us the
> essential thinkers of technology. How to fly gravity,
> how to balance basket and prose reaching for
> murder. Silence done curse god and beauty here,
> people does hear things in this heliconia peace
> a morphology of rolling chain and copper gong
> now shape this twang, falsettos of whip and air
> rudiment this grammar. Take what I tell you. When
> these barracks held slaves between their stone
> halters, talking was left for night and hush was idiom
> and hot core. (1990, 23)

In the demotic, the poet tells us that silence "done curse god and beauty here." Silence and this "heliconia peace"[164] do not reveal religious and aesthetic grounding; instead, from a context of experience related to the demotic rather than to the dominant, "people does hear things": a haunting and a curse in a ghostly language, originating with the sounds and images of slavery that persist through time. A language of haunting thus arises out of the suffering of slavery. The sounds associated with slavery "rudiment this grammar," providing the first principles and incomplete beginnings of a language and knowledge that persist through silence into "now." Like the speech of slaves barred from daylight, it is a secret, hushed voicing that comes out of the night of a historical darkness.

This language is witnessed by Brand's own language. Her testimony combines a demotic that witnesses with a language that witnesses and frames it in turn. In addition, the poem tasks the reader to "take what I tell you." With this imperative, readers are implicated and mandated to make the subject their own and thus to become witnesses in turn. In the words of Derrida, they have "to be able to testify, in their turn, before their consciences or before others … to what they happened to be in the presence of: the testimony of the witness in the witness box" (qtd in Baucom 2005, 177). The beginning of this speech that needs to be witnessed, born out of the perversion of beauty and out of suffering, is sounded earlier: "To hate this, they must have been / dragged through the Manzinilla[165] spitting out the last / spun syllables for cruelty, new sound forming, / pushing towards lips made to bubble blood" (Brand 1990, 23).

But how is it that this language survives, that it is witnessed, that "people does hear things"? What is the subjective side of this haunting that primes such hearing "now"? The poem has already named "some damn memory half-eaten / and half hungry" (Brand 1990, 23) as one of the sources. On the beach of her childhood, the speaker remembers, "The smell of hurrying passed / my nostrils with the smell of sea water and fresh fish / wind, there was history which had taught my eyes to / look for escape" (22). Then the source of such synaesthetic knowledge is inventoried: "I learned to read this from a / woman whose hand trembled at the past" (22). While the link between that woman – presumably her mother[166] – and the time of slavery is not spelled out explicitly,[167] the poem reaches further back in the next section about slavery. It traces a genealogical line of information that leads back, if not directly, to slavery, as far back as to her great-grandmother: "When Liney reach here is up to the time I hear about" (24).

Without the poised ear of a witness, Liney's life, like the language of slavery, would be lost in silence. Without the poem's act of conveyance, it would go unrecorded and would be left out of the inventory: "Even she daughter didn't know but only / leave me she life like a brown stone to see" (24). Elements of her biography arise sparingly "in between" her own preoccupations and the stories she can elicit from Liney's 90-year-old son "and in between his own trail of conquests" (25): "In between, Liney, in between, as if your life could / never see itself" (26).

Brand's reflection on how historical traces are mediated continues into the era of photography. Brand reminds us of the silences even here. Her story "Photograph" in *Sans Souci* offers a loving portrait of an old woman, fondly remembered by the grandchild narrator but otherwise lost in the silences of history. This verbal portrait emerges ironically out of the silences of an "identity" card photograph taken on the occasion of independence.[168] Similarly, the poem "Blues Spiritual for Mammy Prater" is occasioned by "looking at 'the photograph of Mammy Prater an ex-slave, 115 years old when the photograph was taken'" (Brand 1990, 17). With the repeated assertion that "she waited" until photography was ready for her, the poem evokes the haunting presence of Mammy Prater. At the same time, the poem is also about the speaker and about the subject's self-constitution through history and the other. The speaker is held by the gaze of the old slave and responds to it with a feeling of mutual election, calling this relationship "a pact across a century." The act of recognition is carefully recorded in the last lines, "this moment of / my turning the leaves of a book / noticing, her eyes" (19). The former slave's eyes have power over the present, while the speaker derives emotional strength from this poetically imagined "pact across a century." The assertion of mutuality confirms the recognition of an ancestor and a subjectively meaningful past.[169]

Through these two ekphrastic texts, one can set the mediating and connecting aspects of the narrator's ancestor in "Photograph" and of the ex-slave Mammy Prater in this poem side by side. Both are part of the inventory that gives the later subject access to herself: in one case, as a person filled with the corporeal memories and mental images of her grandmother; in the other, as a subject held by the gaze of slavery and called upon to witness.[170] The juxtapositions and personalized conversations worked by Brand's poetics of relation give imaginative reality to the connections between events and subjectivities otherwise separated by the times and spaces of diaspora and the black Atlantic.

Beckoned by the Past: Slavery and the Inheritance of Namelessness in In Another Place, Not Here

Following "Blues Spiritual for Mammy Prater" and "no language is neutral," the legacy of slavery continues to emerge as a defining, deep layer in processes that Brand witnesses and imagines in an inventory she further pursues in the novels *In Another Place, Not Here* (1996) and *At the Full and Change of the Moon* (1999), as well as in the non-fiction *Map to the Door of No Return* (2001).[171] Her novel *In Another Place, Not Here* draws its title from a passage in *No Language Is Neutral* (33). It also shares important thematic consonances with the earlier work, including the complex emotional geographies between the Caribbean and Canada, lesbian love, and the invasion of Grenada.[172] Like the earlier work, the novel still finds, even in the present, "the hard, distinct, brittle smell of / slavery" (1990, 10). As Pamela McCallum and Christian Olbey observe about one of the locations (which resembles Austin Clarke's Bimshire in this respect), "More than a century after emancipation and the formal end of slavery, the village seems to be still suffused with the atmosphere of plantation economy and slave life" (1999, 163). They also note Brand's deployment of several conventions of the slave narrative identified by James Olney – namely, the description of work, the theme of flight, and the "omnipresence of the whip" (167). The political activist Verlia and the plantation worker Elizete thus fall in love while working in the cane fields; Verlia is characterized throughout in terms of movement, with a section narrated from her perspective opening with the announcement of her final escape: "Verlia, flying" (Brand 1996, 119); and Elizete is whipped by the man she tries to escape from (8). These themes connect the novel to important motives in the tradition of black writing.[173] In addition to that formal relation, the novel also makes a search for connection and genealogy the concern of its characters.

The title phrase of the first part, "Elizete, beckoned," is explained later as signalling a moment of adoption that also means the insertion into a tradition (45). Brand opens this section in the demotic without any framing comment, wanting to give a narrative independence to the "first person narrative of this woman who is a cane cutter" (Butling 2005, 74). Elizete seems to have no knowledge of her parents, having been brought up by an otherwise nameless "woman I was given to" (17 passim). She thus initially appears without a known past. The first two sections of her narrative, however, concern her learning about the woman's slave ancestor, Adela. Through Elizete's interest in this woman, whom she accepts as an ancestor, Brand creates a much more detailed "pact across time" than in the connection between speaker and subject in the poem about Mammy Prater.

As we learn in the first of two sections about Adela (18–25), she has responded to her forced dislocation with a rejection of names that has been handed down to Elizete, through a female line that almost ends with "the woman they give me to": "She say when she great-great-great-ma come here she was grieving bad for where she come from … she decide that this place was not nowhere and is so she call it. Nowhere" (1996, 18). Adela relies on obeah to kill her owner. Together with her original refusal of New World names, her curse persists through time: "even now" none of the slave owner's descendants "is ever happy with life" (18–9). The same is true for her own children, who have been forced upon her. As a consequence, "she mothered not a one. She only see their face as bad luck and grudge them the milk from her breast." Due to her charms against them, "all of she generations have a way so that nothing is right with them neither … each have some affliction" (18). Adela's response to displacement and enslavement is denial and a curse that continues through the ages: whatever "they bless on she curse. And that was she inheritance. And that is how I don't know the names of things" (19).

Adela's decision and Elizete's predicament speak to the wider disruption of memories, knowledge, and languages symbolized by the "door of no return" from the African shore to the slave ship: "Everything after the narrow passage to the new world, the tunnel to the ship where only one body could pass, everything after the opening … she lose" (21–2). As with some of the reactions to slavery portrayed in Morrison's *Beloved*, here too the response is a denial of any emotion: "her heart just shut" (22).

Elizete begins from this loss, an inheritance she seeks to reverse: "Where you see nowhere I must see everything. Where you leave all that emptiness I must fill it up" (24). This decision foreshadows an acknowledgment of the break as the source of a new beginning. It signifies, in fact, the need to create as much as to recreate – from traces and questions – the details, stories, and mental maps of a disrupted and absconded history. Brand will return to this problematic, also evoked by Glissant, in particular in *A Map to the Door of No Return*.

The duality of disruption and reconstruction recurs in different forms in the second section dealing with Adela (26–45). It opens with Elizete at the deathbed of the woman she has been given to. Elizete recalls later "her lack of surprise that the woman who took her wanted to go" (28).[174] She hears from the old woman that Adela "curse we" (31) and that she wants the entire line and that curse to end: "no more child for me" (37). Spirits have other ways to perpetuate the past, however. Elizete seems the "spitting image" of Adela and appears as a "Jumbie girl" to the woman she has been given to: "'I say I was the end of that woman, but they come and drop this child staring at me with she face' … As what couldn't be sent in blood no longer … Anything now would have to come from spirit" (31–2). Brand's narrative thus makes the point that spiritual and imaginative continuities exceed the disruptions of physical descent, just as Elizete's adoption of Adela as ancestor circumvents the gaps in the conveyance of history and knowledge wrought by both slavery and Adela's own response to it.

While the woman Elizete has been given to, who has inherited and handed down namelessness, wants genealogy to end, Elizete represents the opposite: a desire for naming, for history, for genealogy. She wants the old woman to become the voice of Adela, and she begins to place herself in the narrative about the slave ancestor by shifting pronouns: "She wanted her to talk about Adela, talk like Adela would talk … 'Yes. Leave is all I … she could think of …'" (35–6). In this double-voiced passage of alternating pronouns, the present mingles with the past, the seemingly history-less orphan communes with, adopts, and is possessed by the slave life emerging in the voice of the old woman: "Adela's voice hovered on their hot cold lips, the two of them" (37).[175] Adela, we come to understand, reappears in all kinds of newborns (40), while Elizete is among those who "needed history, something before this place, something that this place cut off" (41). She wants a form of knowledge that can reconnect her with the time before the middle passage and slavery, fill the void of absconded genealogy, and replace the dominant accounts of the past that have been enforced by slavery.

Absent from Western histories of progress, the experiences of the enslaved and the oppressed live on in other forms of temporality, residuality, haunting, or intuited presence. While time and knowledges are interrupted by the middle passage, the unresolved time after that traumatic break seems not to pass or to be past, but to stand still and accumulate for the descendants of slaves in Brand's novel: "They had surpassed the pettiness of their oppressors … who measured time in the future only and who discarded memory like useless news … So they saw everything. Heard everything, abandoned distance, abandoned time and saw everything … That is how they dealt in the thoughts of everyone who had existed for five hundred years, everyone who was brought here left here since Adela's time and left their thoughts in the air … And the living, they lived in the past or had no past but a present that was filled, peopled with the past. No matter their whims and flights into the future some old face or old look, some old pain would appear" (43–4). These temporalities remain outside of the narratives of discovery, settlement, and progress circulated as part of a story of modernity and the Americas, endlessly rearticulated by those who benefited from slavery. Disrupting the linear monologues of the historical victors, they unhinge Western time and continue to circulate past realities as part of the present, as continuing grievance and unshakable negative memories, but also as a potentially generous gift. Recognizing the unavoidable presence of the past despite her attempts to shake off her connections with it, the nameless old woman finally "beckon[s]" (45) the parentless Elizete and invites her into her house. This is an act of profound ambivalence on the part of the old woman, who wants to leave the negative aspects of the past behind. Realizing that the child may be the spirit of Adela returning, she does so reluctantly and only "after singing a song to show she [is] not afraid" (44). With that gesture, Elizete is also hailed by Adela and her story. Like the speaker in Brand's poem about Mammy Prater, she is beckoned by the past, which despite its desolations also contains for her the gift of a meaningful genealogy.

Time-Spaces of the Black Atlantic: Disruption, Connection, and Yemaya in At the Full and Change of the Moon *and* A Map to the Door of No Return

Elizete thus becomes a witness. Her life enters a temporality that elongates earlier diasporic events into the future. At the same time, her trajectory bridges spaces across parts of the black Atlantic. The earlier routes of empire are reconfigured here by mid-twentieth-century state labour stratagems and their attendant migratory paths, which bring Verlia's relatives – and then Verlia herself – to Canada. Elizete follows that route after losing her lover Verlia, who dies in the assault on St Vincent (the historical Grenada).[176]

With respect to this spatial dimension of *In Another Place, Not Here*, Rinaldo Walcott and others have emphasized how the novel, like *No Language Is Neutral* before it, reconfigures both Canadian and Caribbean nation spaces (R. Walcott 2003, 43–55).[177] Indeed, the characters exist both in and between those spaces. The Caribbean exists, and "takes place," in the characters' Toronto, just as the city becomes a determining factor in Elizete's emotional geography when she still lives in the Caribbean. Temporally, together with these connected and overlapping spaces, the past of one place becomes a past of the other. Experiences of the Caribbean can thus define an individual's present in Toronto via the diasporic realities and inheritances of the black Atlantic. In Elizete's Toronto, "the only thought coming to her was more names for Adela" (1996, 232). More generally, Brand relates and relays trajectories that – while they are also marked by plural national specificities – belong to the complex time-spaces of the black Atlantic.

Across these times and spaces, much of Brand's work orchestrates an ambivalent duality of disruption and connection. These explorations of silence and language are also related to such themes as the refusal of procreation or escape by death, on the one hand, and a renewal of genealogy and story on the other. These large-scale concerns (present also in Marie-Célie Agnant's *The Book of Emma*, discussed below) permeate *No Language Is Neutral* and *In Another Place, Not Here*; they also run through the extended neo-slave narrative in *At the Full and Change of the Moon*[178] and through the reflection of post-slavery subjectivity in *A Map to the Door of No Return: Notes to Belonging.*

One of the reasons for this duality is that, as Brand shows, intentional silence and even self-inflicted death are often acts of determined resistance, emphasizing both the agency of ancestors, even when brutally oppressed, and the need of the descendants to engage with this form of resistance and its consequences in the present. Adela refuses the "Nowhere" forced upon her and "set her mind to stopping her breath after that" (1996, 22). Her decision to "climb the silk cotton tree up there and fly all the way to Africa" appears in Elizete's mind at the same time Verlia's jump off the cliff is first mentioned (23), which at the end is referred to as "flying out to sea" (246).[179] Elizete, on the other hand, chooses a different path: "I could not put my foot in that darkness when the time come though I envy Adela" (23). Yet, while the nameless woman she has been given to curses Adela and wants Adela's curse to end, Elizete seeks out the ancestor's voice and incarnates it. This act of channelling and connection is a repetition with a difference, an anchoring in the past that wants to witness and speak it, but also revise it. In the face of an inherited namelessness that is born out of a rejection of imposed places, languages, and slavery, Elizete finds herself "dreaming up names all the time for Adela's things" (23), continuing, even in Canada, to imagine "more names for Adela" (232).

Brand gives more extensive geographical dimensions to the dual force and impulse of disruption and connection in her subsequent novel, *At the Full and Change of the Moon* (1999), with her creation of Marie Ursule and the "doubling of this ancestral figure in her daughter, Bola" (Cuder-Domínguez 2003, 69). The novel narrates diaspora on a large scale, from Caribbean slavery under the French and English and then across the times and spaces of post-slavery throughout the Americas and into Europe. It begins with a seemingly final act of resistance and refusal committed by the Creole-speaking Marie Ursule. She is a slave previously owned by Ursuline nuns who have moved from Guadeloupe to Martinique and then Trinidad (Brand 1999, 9). Now, under the British, she is owned by a certain de Lambert. Punished after an initial rebellion though not granted her wish to die (14), she learns from Caribs the deadly powers of the poisonous Woorara, which she uses in the mass suicide of eighteen slaves. Prior to this deadly act of self-determination, she "had vowed never to bring a child into the world, and so to impoverish de Lambert" (8). Marie Ursule thus shares with

Adela and her nameless descendant a determined self-affirmation through denial.

Her refusal to bear children, however, works only "until one day" when Bola is born, with eyes "startlingly open as if to say, 'I'm coming, Marie Ursule. Don't lay a harmful hand on me'" (8). Brand reverses here the theme of infanticide that is present, for example, in Morrison's *Beloved* and Agnant's *Le livre d'Emma*: Marie Ursule kills not the child but herself, sending Bola away to escape slavery and survive in maroonage.[180] Brand has described Marie Ursule's deed as an "act of great despair" but also as "both horrific and freeing in some kind of way," because "it releases the other characters into their own imagination" (Sanders and Walcott 2000). Kamena, who carries Bola away, is in search of the maroon community at a place called Terre Bouillante or, as Brand puts it in interview, of "another kind of Country, another citizenship, another beginning" (Sanders and Walcott 2000). Bola is left behind on the way; she ends up not in the interior, but at Culebra Bray. She finds the nuns who once owned her mother still hovering here, a ghostly presence of the past. At the same time, she discovers the sea, which is connected here with the future. This duality makes Bola a crucial figure at the crossroads. Her unusual nature is signalled immediately: "From the moment she was born her eyes saw too much. She was born with teeth, which was a sign of gifts or curses" (8). Bola's ability to perceive the nuns "more than a century" after their slaveholding days (38) is due to "the gift her mother had given her," which "makes Bola see beyond the conclusions that flesh can come to" (38). Despite their physical disappearance, the slaveholding nuns appear to her as part of the unresolved time of the black Atlantic: "There is time that is always happening. The time that is lost or forgotten or misplaced … and the time that is unresolved and therefore unmoving, held there by frail wills." The slaveholding Ursulines, we learn, "are buried in this time … Except, nothing dies. Nothing disappears with finality along this archipelago" (35–6).[181] Bola's perception of them thus partakes of the temporality we have encountered in *In Another Place, Not Here*.

Bola's gift, however, is Janus-faced; it points to the past and the future, but also inward and outward, like the liminal location of Culebra Bay itself.[182] On the estate itself, "everything is slow and hesitates" as it emerges dreamlike from the past in Bola and Kamena's imagination. But the sea has the opposite effect: "a step toward the sea and the rusting spray and wind begin abruptly, undoing the spell of the Ursulines" (41). Bola discovers the sea at Culebra Bay, but in fact from the beginning of the novel, she is identified with both the sea and the future: "Marie Ursule saw water in the child's eyes. So much water she dabbed it away, but more and more came. It wasn't tears. It was the sea … There in the sea, in the middle of Bola's eyes, Marie Ursule saw skyscrapers and trains and machines and streets … and she knew it was the future she was looking at" (45).

Moreover, Bola represents the other side of Marie Ursule's refusal to live. Ready to die, Marie Ursule tells her killers: "This is but a drink of water to what I have already suffered" (21). She compares death to the small comfort of a drink of water; Bola, however, is an ocean. Indeed, out of the mass suicide that ends almost all of her community, Marie Ursule sends Bola away with Kamena – "like sending messages, but not knowing their destination" (20). She sends out a new beginning associated with the ocean and the power of song: "she'd sent eyes like an ocean. She'd sent singing" (21).

While her mother shares part of her name with García Márquez's Úrsula, the matriarch who has several children and whose life spans centuries in *One Hundred Years of Solitude*, it is Bola who gives birth to many children and lives herself "in two centuries" (82).[183] The family tree that prefaces the text both responds to and is different from the one that prefaces García Márquez's famous novel.[184] The latter begins with a male Buendía, followed by his wife Úrsula underneath; two of their male and married sons secure the line that multiplies in Macondo. By contrast, the line that will people Culebra Bay and later Terre Bouillante (both isolated by long marches through a jungle like Macondo) is matriarchal, beginning with a single woman, Marie Ursule. It then traces the children of her only daughter, also single. Their number almost equals the seventeen slaves who perished together with her mother in a mass suicide, to some extent filling the void created by that event. Bola is a figure of lust and abundance who takes lovers as she pleases and has "filled the semi-circle with her children" (69). Most of the children remain nameless, to a degree echoing Adela's refusal to name the world; here, though, it is not refusal but the carelessness of a mother who "was not one for sadness" (69) and who identifies her children by descriptive phrases that resemble the names we have seen Elizete give to things; they appear in the family tree as "The one she made in the dry season" or "The one who was taken in a hurricane," but also as "The one unrecalled" and "The ones left in the sea." An echo of *One Hundred Years of Solitude* appears again with the repetition of the name Bola in the youngest generation.

While family trees suggest linearity, Bola's time works in several directions. There are elements in the temporal ebb and flow of *At the Full and Change of the Moon* that respond to the narrative architecture of *One Hun-*

dred Years of Solitude. Michael Ondaatje has observed that, from a certain point in García Márquez's novel, ghosts begin to replace dead family members; in addition, the book offers the reader a complex and non-linear temporality: "About halfway through the book you begin to feel that while you are still moving forward to the end you are simultaneously moving from midpoint to the beginning. Your consciousness is sliding both ways" (Ondaatje 1978, 30; see also Siemerling and Casteel 2010, 3–4). Brand seems to be following a related strategy in *At the Full and Change of the Moon*, which has been called a "de-centralized novel or, rather, short-story cycle" (Cuder-Domínguez 2003, 67). We encounter such a sense of time in Bola when she appears later as an old woman: "She lived now in the best of places, where everything happened at the same time ... All happening at the same time. In all of it the present was small and just a part" (Brand 1999, 83). Bola's consciousness is here a site of connection and translation, but also a place where flows can change direction and traditional separations disappear.

This reordering of time and the real has other counterparts in García Márquez's great novel. Both novels repeatedly narrate individual realities that seem madness to others, worry the line between dream and reality, and keep the present infused with the past. Like the mad José Arcadio in old age, Bola sits outside when she is "old and gone" (83). Startling her son with her almost forgotten presence, she laughs at his decision to go to war for the British. She is heard singing the taunting Creole song (82) that her mother had used to greet the Ursulines (11),[185] a song that is heard again when the ghost of Marie Ursule herself appears to a seemingly mad descendant (285). The last section of Brand's novel – finally, the titular "At the Full and Change of the Moon" – echoes the large-scale narrative conceit of *One Hundred Years of Solitude* when it questions and recodes beginnings and creation. We see Bola again in Culebra Bay, remembering Kamena's account of her own beginning: "Marie Ursule ... dropped you and me into her dream" (297). Causality and origin seem as much in abeyance as the flow of time and the ontological status of real beings and ghosts.

Yemaya and the Sea

Like the simultaneities in the aged Bola's mind, these oscillations question the temporalities and cognitive maps of Western modernity: the ideas of causality, linearity, and the unfolding of truth in the singular, a logic embodied in the expansion of empires and the subjugation of black bodies.

These forms of cognition are perturbed by registers also used in magic realism that pervade *At the Full and Change of the Moon*. The title of Brand's novel suggests other intertextualities that frame oscillation in terms of the sea.[186] Here, tidal change suggests not just the presence of Yemaya as the Yoruba mother of orishas and deity of waters and the sea, but also cognitive alternatives evoked in Caribbean and black Atlantic conversations that include such theoretical interventions as those by Kamau Brathwaite, Derek Walcott, and Édouard Glissant. In the following discussion, I will also reference Brand's *A Map to the Door of No Return*, which considers much of this context and the novel itself.

At the end of the novel, Bola recalls how Kamena "had recounted their life like a psalm. 'At the full and change of the moon. Everything gets measured here by the moon'" (1999, 296). Brand's title phrase is derived from an account by Thomas Jeffreys, the geographer of King George III, that seeks to guide ships approaching Trinidad, a point in the middle passage, through tides around the island. Brand explains, in terms we have also encountered in the discussion of Philip, that she cut his beautiful language "into pieces" for her novel (2001, 202). Her counter-discursive repurposing of an imperial account of navigation, tidal change, and time in the Caribbean can be related to other attempts at formulating alternative epistemological and cognitive principles. Elaine Savory describes Kamau Brathwaite's term "tidalectics" as a transfiguration of the subsuming drive of Western dialectics. Brathwaite uses that term to name a Caribbean-originated non-linear concept of time. It is related to the back-and-forth of the tides and is meant to suggest the new ways in which ideas and images combine and recombine continually (Savory 1994, 754).[187] Brathwaite is among the many writers repeatedly evoked by Brand in discussion (Butling 2005, 85; Sanders and Walcott 2000); the use of time in *At the Full and Change of the Moon* – even the book's very title – speaks to a sense of time, repetition, and reorientation that is expressed in tidalectics.[188]

Similarly, the religious dimension alluded to by the word "psalm" deserves attention from an African Caribbean perspective. Part of Marie Ursule's name links her to the virgin, an association furthered by the fact that no physical father appears for her daughter Bola in the family tree (Bola, like Elizete, seems to "come from spirit" [1996, 31–2]). In addition, Bola is a figure of life and resurrection, yet she is also an African Caribbean response to patriarchal Euro-Christianity. We have seen Brand's reference to Oya, "Goddess of Winds, Storms and Waterfalls," in her earlier short story collection *Sans Souci*; discussing post-slavery subjectivities in *A Map to the*

Door of No Return, Brand writes: "The religious ritual across North and South America and the archipelago of being inhabited by the gods, goddesses, and spirits of Africa may be another method of way-finding" (2001, 44). Bola's connection to the sea links her in particular to Yemaya, whom Brand discusses in *A Map to the Door of No Return* as "the goddess of the ocean" (2001, 172). Yemaya is also the patron deity of women, especially pregnant women, and the mother of orishas, among them Oya.

Brand has paid tribute to Yemaya in *A Map to the Door of No Return*. During a walk to the sea, she uses "a chorus of Yemaya's song" by the Cuban singer Celia Cruz[189] "to bow down to the vast ocean and contemplate my smallness and its majesty … The ocean and the planet it weeps around, these are the only powers I truly respect" (171). We have seen earlier that Bola is continually associated with the sea; other passages that link her more directly to Yemaya and other water orishas are numerous throughout the text.[190] Some of the associations with Yemaya are especially conspicuous in the last section, which shares its title with the novel as a whole, "At the Full and Change of the Moon." The section begins with Bola observing "showers of rain" joining the ocean and rain-heralding birds "appearing and disappearing" (294). Swimming out to a rock in the sea "to get a moment's peace from her children" (294),[191] her "dress balloon[s] around her like a raft" (294), evoking Yemaya's dress of seven layers that represent the oceans. Since all things coming from the ocean connect with Yemaya, Bola's "blowing her shell" (296) to warn the whales also belongs to this register. Finally, like Yemaya, Bola "loved them, these children strung out across the beach" (295); when faced with their complaints, however, she threatens to return to her own element with the closing words of the novel: "Or I'll go back in the sea" (299).

Bola and the sea are thus signs of both connection and disruption in the novel. Marie Ursule's daughter, like Yemaya, appears mainly as a life-creating force that connects her dispersed children. There is a second character named Bola, however. The latest born in the novel's generational tree, this Bola speaks to the disconnections among generations in the diaspora. Although her mother, Eula, longs for an uninterrupted genealogy,[192] she has moved through the United States to Toronto while leaving this second Bola behind in Trinidad. Eula is entirely alienated from her family, to the extent that she can write to her own "Dear Mama" only after the latter's death (236). In this "Blue Airmail Letter" to a deceased person, Eula highlights the disruptive force of diaspora when she writes about her daughter: "I hear you named her Bola. I hope you have never spoken to her of me …

Don't saddle her with a memory that is not hers" (250). As a consequence, Bola has mis-identified her grandmother as her mother. She will see but never read the blue airmail letter that contains the truth about her genealogy. Bola – in whose imagination her deceased (grand)mother is alive – throws it behind a wardrobe along with many other letters, "so that it would not make her unhappy to read it" (284).[193] What does keep Bola connected to her ancestors are her dreams and visions, which include Marie Ursule (285) and the first Bola (281). She is the last recipient of the older Bola's self-portrait, a piece of paper "with an ocean and a rock and a far shore and a figure standing on the rock" (283).[194] The second Bola will arrange the drawing on the floor in what amounts to a shrine for both her deceased grandmother and Yemaya: "I put fine dirt around it for sand and I polished around the sand as brilliant as the ocean might be and I left it there for our mother to swim to any time she wanted" (286–7). The ocean and Yemaya thus appear as figures of that connection across time in the imagination, but Bola's life is also marked by real disruption in the diasporic time-space of the black Atlantic.

Yemaya, the Door of No Return, and the Creation of New World Communality

In *A Map to the Door of No Return: Notes to Belonging* (2001), Brand's transgeneric meditation on the continuing psycho-historical consequences of the passage into slavery, water and the sea are crucial signifiers of both disruption and communality. With numerous sections entitled "Maps," the volume reflects on "cognitive schema" (16, 28) to negotiate routes and to "find our way successfully" in the diaspora.[195] Brand looks at the "Door of No Return," the passage from the slave castles on the African west coast to the slave ships, as a "place where all names were forgotten and all beginnings recast" (5). This passage circumscribes more generally for her the condition of black subjectivities in the Americas: "Our inheritance in the Diaspora is to live in this inexplicable space. That space is the measure of our ancestors' step through the door toward the ship … The frame of the doorway is the only space of true existence" (2001, 20).[196] This premise, which also determines Brand's portrayal of the dispersed later generations in *At the Full and Change of the Moon*, emphasizes the consequences of the "Door of No Return" in the present: "The door casts a haunting spell on personal and collective consciousness in the Diaspora … History is already seated in the chair in the empty room when one arrives" (25). At the same time, this space of ultimate disorientation and disruption also signifies communality and beginning: the door is "the creation place of Blacks in the New World Diaspora" (5). Brand's project, then – in this book subtitled *Notes to Belonging* – is to explore this passageway of loss and transformation as an ambivalent "site of belonging or unbelonging" (6).

The ocean and water are a continuation of the door as liminal and ambivalent space of disruption and creation. *Map* opens with the narrator's memory of experiencing a "tear in the world" (4) and a "moment of rupture" when her grandfather, as a consequence of the Door of No Return, fails to account for their family origins. The subsequent section, "Maps," is followed by a longer section, "Water," which again connects the narrator's life to historical dimensions of the black Atlantic. "Water is the first thing in my imagination" (6), Brand tells us, adding that as a child she could see (like Bola from Culebra Bay) "the mainland of South America" (6) and, to the east, "the immense Atlantic gaping to Africa" (7).

The extended description of the sea that follows recalls what Marie Ursule sees in Bola's eyes: "To look into this water was to look into the world … because the sea gave one an immediate sense of how large the world was, how magnificent and how terrifying" (7). The sea is both "feared and loved" (7) because it takes lives but it also brings food in abundance. Above all, the sea is all-encompassing and awe-inspiring. It "would forever be larger than me … It reduced all life to its unimportant random meaning. Only we were changing and struggling, living as if everything was urgent" (11). These lines foreshadow Brand's comments on Yemaya later in *Map*. The sea's indifference is there emphasized in an episode that ends with Yemaya's similar response: "I ask Yemaya why, what is it that we must live like that? She answers … 'So what'" (173–4). Her answer underlines the connection with Bola, whose response to her bickering children is similar at the end of *At the Full and Change of the Moon*. Towards the end of "Water," Brand ascribes to the ocean powers like those of Yemaya, who in some traditions is credited with protecting captives during the middle passage (Perez 2010, 207): "Our origins seemed to be in the sea. It had brought the whole of Guayaguayare there from unknown places, unknown origins" (Brand 2001, 12).

Brand closes the section by citing the title phrase of Derek Walcott's poem "The Sea Is History" (12). In his poem, Walcott delivers a parodic reading of the biblical and Western narrative of origin, progress, and modernity through the lens of suffering caused by slavery and the middle passage. In addition, the victims are asked to answer for the consequences of slavery, which has left them no history: "Where are your monuments, your battles, martyrs? / Where is your tribal memory?" A diasporic voice answers: "Sirs, / in that grey vault. The sea. The sea / has locked them up. The sea is History." In closing, however, the speaker reports that "in the salt chuckle of rocks / with their sea pools, there was the sound / like a rumour without any echo / of History, really beginning" (D. Walcott 1979, 25, 28). Walcott's poem suggests that the history of disruption and silence of black Atlantic lives – during and after slavery – needs to be articulated from sound into narrative (something Brand undertakes when she says that "falsettos of whip and air rudiment this grammar" in *No Language Is Neutral*). Brand's reading of the Door of No Return and its ensuing silences and conundra heeds that call for elaboration. In *A Map to the Door of No Return*, the loose arrangement of meditations on post-slavery diasporic subjectivity is a response to both the disruptions and the unifying condition suggested by the middle passage and the door, which we have seen Brand refer to as "the creation place of Blacks in the New World Diaspora." As we have also seen (in chapter 1), Édouard Glissant makes reference to the set of conditions evoked by Walcott and then Brand, saying that the middle passage "became something shared and made us, the descendants, one people among others" (1997, 8). For him, "the entire ocean, the entire sea … make one vast beginning" (6).

Like Walcott, Brand is among those who "hear things in this heliconia peace" (Brand 1990, 23). Her articulation of narrative and genealogy in *No Language Is Neutral*, out of a silence that "done curse god and beauty here," speaks to what Glissant terms a "vast beginning" (1997, 6). The need to create words – and a place in the present for the disruption and silences of slavery, dislocation, the middle passage, and its long-lasting and nefarious outcomes – motivates Elizete, in *In Another Place, Not Here*, to counter Adela's refusal to relate to her new surroundings: "Where you leave all that emptiness I must fill it up" (1996, 24). In *At the Full and Change of the Moon*, the generations of diasporic descendants that Bola creates respond in other ways to Marie Ursule's determined disruption of life under slavery.

This is not a narrative of restored plenitude, however. Yemaya's children remain governed by the ebb and flow of the sea, and its forces include both connection and disruption. This is clear in the sections of *At the Full and the Change of the Moon* that deal with Marie Ursule and Bola's diasporic descendants in the cities of New York, Toronto, and Amsterdam, and in Brand's intimation in *Map* that her city diasporic dwellers continue Kamena's "unending and … inevitably futile search for a homeland." Such a sheltering place is lost forever in Brand's novel: "this is what they give all cities; they inhabit temporariness, elsewhere – thinking of something they cannot remember but thinking furiously. The journey is the destination" (2001, 203). Brand's own text is part of the Gramscian inventory that Yemaya, the sea, and history have failed to create while depositing their "infinity of traces" in post-slavery subjects. It is part of the inventory that Brand continues to compile, often with regard to other concerns and genealogies, in her subsequent work on diasporic lives and their encounters, especially in the city.

Second-Generation Diasporas and the City: Brand, Chariandy, and Alexis

Brand's What We All Long For

Brand's Toronto is a site of transformations and encounters where diasporic emotional geographies are in motion, intersect, and jostle. Cultural memories and identity scripts are re-articulated, and personal hopes and histories revised. In the contact zones of the city, continuities between past and present are easily disrupted in the face of new ambivalences and resistances. In her Toronto novel *What We All Long For* (2005), Brand reflects more specifically on a "second generation," one step removed from the origins of its parents, negotiating cultural identity scripts in the city. This second generation may discover and explore its ancestral origins, reject them out of hand, or remain endlessly ambivalent. Brand shares an interest in this second generation's uncertainties and experiences with such authors as David Chariandy and André Alexis, who will be discussed briefly below.

In many of the texts by Brand that I have discussed, the discovery and conveyance of cultural genealogies is also mediated by the city. In "no language is neutral," Toronto is a place of arrival that overwhelms and disorients: "the concrete / building just overpower me, block my eyesight" (1990, 28). One of the responses is to search for connection and genealogy across time and space, leading back as far as to slavery and the middle passage. We have seen another newcomer to the city, Blossom, turn to vernacular spiritual genealogies by making obeah central to her emotional geography of the city. Brand then multiplies memory spaces in her novel *In Another Place, Not Here*, where Toronto becomes a site of both arrival and departure. Verlia takes the Toronto that is within her to the Caribbean, whence Elizete then comes to the city to look for traces of her lover's former life. She is looking for them – in vain – in the remembered and imagined spaces that have now become her own mediated past. *Land to Light On* shows

Brand navigating Toronto's racially rough hinterland (close to the setting of Moodie's *Roughing It in the Bush*), before she returns to the urban geography of Toronto, to Spadina, Church, or Gerrard, as a backdrop to urban lives and diasporic memories. In *Thirsty* (2002), the city finally becomes a subject of its own. References to specific places and streets accumulate as signs of a precise cityscape (full of trash, ugliness, and beauty, but also indifference). Against this background, we see the individual drama of a black man's death in a police shooting.[197] Such weaving of individual lives into the tapestry of an often uncaring city is also evident in Brand's list-making that names diasporic trajectories in the multiracial city: "The Filipina nurse bathes a body, the Vincentian courier delivers a message, the Sikh cab driver navigates a corner" (2002, 37); present already in *Map*, this practice is continued later in *What We All Long For*.[198]

In *A Map to the Door of No Return*, Brand refers to other diasporas as she reflects on the condition of post-slavery subjectivities. Different diasporic times and geographies overlap in the time-space of Toronto, signalling their continued presence within new lives. Brand notes that in "a new city there are ghosts of old cities … Ghosts try to step into life. Selam Restaurant, Jeonghysa Buddhist Temple, Oneda's Market, West Indian and Latin American Foods, Afro Sound, Lalibela Ethiopian Cuisine, Longo's Vegetable and Fruits, Astoria Athens Restaurant …" (110–11). Brand has spoken optimistically about a sense of possibility and transformation evident in this city where "people from all over the world make a living out of it"; fabulous "possibilities exist, things haven't been worked out, and we see the becoming of it. We're in the middle of becoming, we have these yet-to-become people" (Da Costa 2001, 2).

The "ghosts of old cities," however, can signal difficult investments and emotions: welcomed and venerated by some, they are unwanted by others. In *Map*, Brand notes the multiplicity of old allegiances and inside many transformations in the city, but she also observes another new element in a group that ranges across different diasporas – a second generation that often seems to have little relation to its family origins. In a Toronto courtroom, Brand's narrator thus notices that "defendants are Chinese, Hispanic, Portuguese, Italian, African/Caribbean, Vietnamese, Russian. But not really. None of them know these origins except through their parents or grandparents. They were all born in this city" (2001, 105). Brand also sounds the theme of intergenerational immigrant disappointment, as "the clerks who seem Caribbean in origin give each child a look of reprimand, as if they're disappointed in this bunch of children who have wasted their parents' sacrifice" (2001, 105–6).

These ideas (and the narrator's subsequent visit to the Mimico prison) are reworked more extensively in Brand's next novel, *What We All Long For* (2005), and some of them recur to a lesser extent in her subsequent novel, *Love Enough* (2014). An anchoring sense of origin or homeland is the preoccupation of the first generation of urban immigrants in *What We All Long For*; by contrast, the Canadian-born, second generation seek to exorcize their parents' ghosts. Not interested in ancestral homelands and disillusioned with their parents' hopes and choices,[199] their notion of arrival is continual movement, a mode of being Brand has ascribed to Kamena's diasporic descendants in the city: "The journey is the destination" (2001, 202–3). A sense of "kinetic electricity" (Brand 2005, 17) is epitomized by the bicycle courier Carla, Canadian-born but of Jamaican and Italian origin, who negotiates the city at high cycling speeds: "If she could have stopped she would have, but she was light and light moves" (29).

Like her friends Tuyen, Oku, and Jackie, whose parents come from Vietnam, Jamaica, and Nova Scotia respectively, she was "born in the city from people born elsewhere" (20). School has taught them that "they weren't the required race" (47), uniting them in a "friendship of opposition to the state of things" (19). Their parents' desire that they "fit in" exacerbates their sense of alienation; they seek to distance themselves from "the unreasonableness, the ignorance, the secrets, and the madness of their parents" (19). Their parents' relation to the past, in particular, seems to be fake – a fantasy – to the second generation. They want to hear "no more diatribes on what would never happen back home, down east, down the islands, over the South China sea, not another sentence that began in the past that had never been their past" (47). As a consequence, "they inhabited two countries – their parents' and their own" (20).

Brand stages the second generation's wrestling with cultural inheritance, obligation, and loyalty in relation to the parental generation, but also with regard to friends and siblings who hauntingly remind them of the potentially defining circumstances of their diasporic situatedness. Oku cannot bear his Jamaican-born father's expectations of filial academic achievement. In his quest for Jackie, however, who stubbornly insists on having a white partner, he does not want to appear "like so many burned-out guys" (265) in the Toronto social housing complex where her parents moved from Nova Scotia. Jackie herself has a multi-layered relationship with her parents and their social environment. She feels uncomfortable, for instance, with her mother's drinking and smoking when her friends visit (256). Despite this discomfort, she "hadn't left Alexandra Park. She owed a loyalty to her mother and father. That faithfulness didn't mean that she wanted to have it burn her as it had them. Hence, the white boy. Oku knew this logic" (265). While Jackie acknowledges her family, she seeks to ward off the spectre of the return of their social circumstances into her own life by denying, at least in Oku's eyes, his blackness in her own generation. While she will grant him favours occasionally, his vernacular request to "hook a brother up" fails to have the longed-for effect; instead it "lost her to him in that moment" (93).[200]

Carla and Tuyen are also marked by contradictory emotions with respect to brothers in the novel – in this case, physical siblings who signal the socio-historically determined risks of their particular diasporic situation. As Jennifer Blair points out, both of these brothers are associated in the text with childlike ghosts (2012, 55–9);[201] they are literally lost brothers who have disappeared in spaces of societal exclusion and invisibility, symbolized by a refugee camp in one case and a prison in the other. They are also both associated with socially determined crime and violence – issues also explored by George Elliott Clarke. Like Jackie, who keeps her own life distinct from both her family and her racial "brother" Oku, her second-generation friends Carla and Tuyen seek to appease, exorcise, or negotiate their relationship with these ghosts of a family past and a diasporic background that is perceived as a potentially dangerous burden.

Carla thus worries about her half-brother Jamal, a young black man who has been "implicated" (Brand 2005, 35) in a carjacking and who seeks to project "badness" (30). While Carla deplores Jamal's lack of judgment and his "inability to show loyalty or see himself as connected to people" (36), his fate preoccupies her intensely. She "dread[s] his phone calls" (33), which usually signify trouble. Visiting him in Mimico Prison and trying to arrange for his bail, she shows the very qualities Jamal lacks. While he is proud of his nickname "Ghost," she dryly observes that his "ghostliness didn't stop the police from finding him" (37). At times she wishes this ghostly burden to be gone: "Ghost, why don't you just disappear from my life" (37). There are many reasons why she might think this way: her half-brother drains her and exhausts her; and being mixed-race and light enough to pass (106) and rejecting her black father and stepmother, she has a number of emotive avenues open to her that might help her disassociate entirely from her brother. Yet the opposite is the case: "she felt rotten when she thought that"

(37). When asked by Tuyen about Jamal's troubles, "Why do you have to fix it?," she clearly claims him as family: "Because he's mine" (26). And so he is. At the very end of the novel, as we see Carla relaxed and looking forward to a life temporarily unburdened by responsibility for him, Jamal, seemingly forever driven by his chosen responses to the choices he has been offered – and like a ghost that cannot be exorcised – repeats the very acts that make him a ghost-like presence in Carla's life.[202]

Tuyen's response to what feels to her like a past-defined family burden seems to be the opposite of Carla's. Indeed, Tuyen feels betrayed when Carla employs the word "mine" with respect to her half-brother. Desiring Carla sexually and emotionally, she would perhaps rather see it applied to herself, but the possessive pronoun also expresses the sense of loyalty and obligation to a sibling she has been asked to have with respect to Quy (26), her lost brother who disappears as a young child when the family flees Vietnam by boat. Yet Tuyen wants to disassociate herself as much as possible from her family and from this phantom brother – forever present in her parents' thoughts – and to assign him to an irretrievably lost past that she wants to forget. She thus disapproves of her brother Binh's search for Quy, and she counsels forgetting instead of melancholia: "Why don't you let them forget instead of encouraging them?" (13). Her need to be unencumbered by family history and by what she perceives to be her parents' past is clear: "It's not my stuff, it's theirs" (13).

As with Carla and Jamal, however, it turns out that her family history, including this lost brother, is indeed hers. The Canadian-born Tuyen seems to refuse all things Vietnamese, including the language (employed exclusively by many employees and customers in her parents' Vietnamese restaurant in Toronto [26]). Yet this refusal comes with some ambivalence. In her art, Tuyen transfigures aspects of her cultural background into something new, but instead of Western art, she chooses a Chinese influence, an Asian culture adjacent to her culture of origin. Asked by Jackie whether her latest installation is "some ancient Vietnamese shit" (16), she responds furiously that "there is some ancient Chinese-Vietnamese shit that's my shit and I'm taking it. Okay?" When Carla insists, "I thought you were Vietnamese," Tuyen's reaction indicates that her friend has "ventured into a sensitive space" (16).

Indeed, all her artwork seems related to Chinese(-Vietnamese) culture: the *lubaio*, an installation structure that makes the longings of the city public (16–17, 150) and, as Chariandy has pointed out, a metaphorical equivalent to the novel itself (2007a, 826); the *hutoung*, her miniature of a

Chinese alleyway (24); and her "ornamental *wenshou* – monsters and lions, horses and fish, phoenixes – all magical animals" (24). Tuyen's transformative desire comes to the fore when she steals copies of letters written by her parents in their effort to find Quy, "from her mother's stack like a magical *wenshou*" (24); while she does not know what to do with these letters, she "held them like ornate and curious figures of a time past" (25).

This attempt at transfiguring and containing her lost brother in an ornamental figuration of the past is significant, yet it fails. Quy haunts her life and he will return. Signs of Tuyen's fear of that possibility emerge in the text even before she begins to realize that her brother Binh has brought a person to the city who is probably Quy (208, 227). Brand's chronological narrative of this return is doubled, it turns out, by another temporality, suggested and created by the novel's sophisticated narrative structure. We come to understand that Quy – without yet being named – has been there from the first pages of the novel (4), not only as an imagined figure of the past but, literally, as an embodied return of repressed history that has always already been there. While his own first-person narrative is dispersed in contrapuntal sections throughout the novel, Quy appears first as an unrecognized stranger crossing the city in the same subway, "jammed in a seat down the car" (4), where the reader is introduced to the equally as yet unnamed Tuyen, Carla, and Oku (2–3).

Lost and abandoned as a child, Quy experiences the degree zero of belonging, and Larissa Lai (2006; 2014, 209) has likened him to the *homo sacer* of Giorgi Agamben.[203] He grows up in the camp of Pulau Bidong, a "place where identity was watery, up for grabs" (Brand 2005, 9).[204] "When you look at photographs of people at Pulau Bidong you see a blankness. Or perhaps our faces are, like they say in places, unreadable" (8). Tuyen will dread and doubt the identity of this long-lost brother. Contemplating a picture she has snapped of her other brother and this as-yet-unknown man, she thinks his "face was like an angel or a ghost or a child" (224). She feels that she has made "some discovery that she was yet to understand. The two seemed both real and metaphoric" (224). Indeed, while she knows Binh from childhood and in his grown-up state, this other figure is both the innocent child known only from her parents' photographs and stories *and* an unknown stranger, who embodies an unknown diasporic life trajectory and a haunting past that has returned. On the one hand, Tuyen comprehends this diasporic Gothic as innocence when she sees "the face, innocent, as a ghost's"; at the same time, she "felt disoriented, drawn to the babyness of the face against the body springy as violence" (227). This violence, we learn through Quy's monologues, is real. It is an ever-present potentiality and the result of the choices life has offered him. Moral judgments seem to him irrelevant, even if they are positive: "Don't be sentimental. Don't ascribe good intentions. Who are you to judge?" (9). Brand shows Tuyen as harbouring very ambivalent feelings towards her lost, new-found sibling: "Quy gave her the creeps … It was all well and good to have a tragic story in the past, *but what if it returns*? What if it comes back with all it has stored up … The lost boy would have to have been sad, lonely, angry, hurt, angry" (300, emphasis added).

We learn that the lost sibling's name means "precious" (6, 301), a meaning strangely literalized in this text as his parents, in preparation for the family's fateful flight, have carefully stitched precious stones into his clothes (which are discovered and stolen by pirates [8]). His loss also weighs on them emotionally, though, causing them endless guilt and despair. The meaning of Quy's name further evokes the eponymous figure in Morrison's *Beloved*. As with *Beloved*, his return is marked by an insatiable greed to make up for lost life. Yet in this case, life has made him a ruthless criminal who envisages his newfound brother as target: "I know that I'm going to take him for everything he's got. It's the things that were mine, and he's got them double. He's got my mother and my father and my two sisters … He's got everything" (310).

Tuyen hopes that Carla can help her to see "the new apparition of her brother Quy as a blessing" (301). At the very moment she wants to share her doubts, however, she finds Carla beaming over her own brother's return from prison. But Brand does not offer a narrative of restored plenitude. As the trajectories of the two lost brothers meet in the reassertion of a brutal, violent, and relentless past (317), Brand tells us that Tuyen's – and our – hope for a "universe restored" (303) in which "everything would be fine" (304) has been illusory. The destructive force that spells out the realities of violent and oppressive historical legacies continues to co-exist with human longings for another, better life. The stage irony created by the novel's temporal structure permits the reader to be aware of the terrible forces of disruption that are about to descend again on Carla and Tuyen before they realize it. The last lines of the novel show us Carla, as yet unaware of what has already happened, longing for the sound of Tuyen's chiselling at her structure that records the city's many – and in some cases deadly – longings, an inventory not unlike Brand's own in *What We All Long For*.[205]

The past as diasporic Gothic appears here as an endless burden that determines many immigrant lives, but it also comes to drain an inventive second generation that seeks alternative routes, uncoupled from victimage and socially determined disenfranchised fates. While Brand herself is not a member of this second generation, her work, as Chariandy has observed, provides nonetheless "a crucial space in which to explore just how the second-generation visible minority subject can be imagined and represented" (2007a, 824).

Second-Generation Perspectives in Chariandy and Alexis

David Chariandy approaches this work from his own position as a writer "born in Canada to immigrants from Trinidad, a 'mixed' black mother and a dark-skinned South Asian father" (in Dobson 2007, 810). He himself has experienced the "generational identity and cultural dilemma" (810) that Brand so vividly depicts, that of a second generation that "possesses intimate and lifelong knowledge of Canada as a complex and sometimes outright painful space to grow up in as a visible minority"; Canada thus also "stands to inherit, consciously or not, the cultural legacies of their parents, legacies that ultimately stem from geographic spaces and contexts that the second generation may never have directly experienced to any real extent" (811).

The weight of these legacies – a haunting presence in Brand's novel despite Tuyen's efforts to discard them – is also at stake in the work of other second-generation Caribbean Canadian writers. Among these, as Chariandy points out in an essay dedicated to the subject, André Alexis figures prominently. Born (like Brand and Chariandy's parents) in Trinidad but having moved to Canada at age four, "he happens to be the first nationally and internationally prominent writer of African Caribbean heritage to have been socialized in Canada during most of the formative years of his childhood and early adulthood"; yet despite his ancestral connection and the use of some corresponding elements in his writing, he expresses "considerable reluctance about being described as a Caribbean or black writer" (Chariandy 2007a, 821).[206] Donna Bailey Nurse goes even further, suggesting that "very little African or Caribbean culture finds its way into *Childhood*" (qtd in Chariandy 1007a, 823), probably Alexis's best-known novel.[207]

By contrast, Chariandy's own first novel, *Soucouyant* (2007b), demonstrates emphatically the dynamic depth of the multi-layered time-spaces of Caribbean Canadian experience from a second-generation perspective. While two of the main characters in the novel are born, like he himself, in Canada and many of the immigrant mother's experiences have taken place there, Chariandy suggests that his title points also to a crucial "Caribbean-ness" and thus to another time and space (Tancock 2008, 3):[208] "I wanted my title to suggest that the protagonist of the novel, a second-generation Caribbean immigrant based in Canada, was engaging with a cultural legacy that seemed, *at least on the surface*, to be attached to a very different space, a legacy that seemed, at times, to be remote, otherworldly, and spectral, and yet hauntingly present at the time" (in Dobson 2007, 811, emphasis added). In his novel, he thus uses the "word and legend of the soucouyant to explore a particular generational condition, a particular state of sensing, but not really knowing one's origins" (811).

This seeming duality confounds distance and proximity, temporal remoteness and the present, and the clear separation between the second generation's experience and their parents' more or less known lives before they came to Canada. How writers of his generation navigate such ambiguous relations opens for Chariandy a new and a highly relevant field of inquiry.[209] In this context, the soucouyant, "a vampire-like spirit in the folklore of certain islands in the Caribbean" (in Tancock 2008, 2), offers a fascinating figure of cultural mediation that has also been evoked by other Caribbean Canadian authors.[210]

One of these writers is André Alexis. In the opening story of his collection *Despair and Other Stories of Ottawa* (1994), "The Night Piece," the youthful main character, Michael, attends a Trinidadian Canadian wedding, expressing his discomfort "with all of these people, family or friends of family, whom he seldom saw" (Alexis 1994, 14). In this environment, another guest tells him of a fateful encounter with a soucouyant – in Canada at that – "so far from where they usually apportioned death" (29). Winston – having answered an ad stating "Trinidadian preferred" because "although he'd lived most of his life in Canada, he was Trinidadian by birth" (17) – discovers that his employer is a soucouyant who drinks his blood at night. He comes to enjoy the nightly encounters, however, since the soucouyant, having sloughed off her "costume of flesh and skin" (27) of an old woman, appears to him in an erotically desirable form (32). What ensues is "an escalation of the conflict within: his desire for the Soucouyant deepened, as did his desperation to be rid of her" (33).

In the story, there is a telling correlation between Winston's second-generation status in Canada and the effects of his encounter with the soucouyant. We are told that he "loved his parents, and he was almost at ease in the country to which they'd come" (28). As his health declines, weakened by the vampire-like spirit from his parents' culture, we learn that his "condition had no name, unless you count *mal de pays*" (33). Winston is consumed, the story seems to suggest, by an attractive vampire who represents a morbid homesickness for his parents' culture. Just as Winston resents the soucouyant at first (and even wants to kill her with the help of salt), Michael resents having been importuned by the story, but for him, too, "it was too late" (37). In a dream, he sees Winston "*ecstatic*" in the soucouyant's house, and he ends up "looking for the Soucouyant" too (41).

Significantly, Michael encounters this story from his parents' culture at a wedding when he is 15. He subsequently experiences his own sexuality in connection with the image of the soucouyant (38).[211] This is a story, then, of a sexual and cultural awakening that is coded via the Caribbean and associated with danger, desire, disease, and death.[212] For Michael, this end of innocence comes with the experience of cultural difference or with an unsettling form of double or multiple consciousness: "Winston had broken Michael's faith in the unique world, and it upset him to feel the number of worlds that now existed at once" (41).

Chariandy, who finds mainly negative images of blackness and the Caribbean in the other stories in *Despair*, sees "Night Piece" as Alexis's "most complex and powerful representation of the ambiguous attitudes that the second generation of Caribbean descent may have towards their Caribbean cultural backgrounds" (2004, 87). Although Alexis "represents his Caribbean heritage as a blood-sucking vampire creature from Trinidadian folklore," the story also suggests "that it is an especially complex haunting, full of threat but also strangely seductive" (80–1). In particular, the Caribbean here "still literally haunts the lives of those who otherwise might consider themselves Canadian" (88).

If any such haunting is still present in Alexis's novel *Childhood* (1998), it has been largely displaced and seems to appear mostly in symptoms of denial. Several black characters practise a compulsive, genteel white Britishness or Canadianness, partially designed to ward off Caribbean hauntings in Canada. This paradoxical performance of Caribbean Canadianness puzzles, but also marks, the second-generation narrator and protagonist. His grandmother Edna MacMillan is prominent in the local Dickens Society (Alexis 1998, 29), and she instills in him hefty portions of the work of Canadian Confederation poet Archibald Lampman.[213] We first learn of her Trinidadian origin fifteen pages into the text and at the end of a very long footnote that offers the first hint of the narrator's racial origins (Sanders 2000, 176). The narrator later tells us that her "life, but for the two years in Trinidad, was lived in Petrolia, and Petrolia crushed everything else from her so thoroughly that I could not have guessed her origins were anything but Canadian" (29). Indeed, her "fanatic attachment to Lampman and Dickens" goes hand in hand with "her disapproval of anything that might link her to Trinidad" (Alexis 1998, 168).[214]

The more overtly ex-centric choices of Henry Wing, another of the narrator's custodians, prompts his puzzled question: "Why would a twentieth-century man, Trinidadian at that, choose to live in a Victorian setting ?" (168). The narrator comes to feel that Henry's overt preoccupations "reveal so little of his origin I have to come to think of them as a screen before his birthplace; not for others, for himself" (170). Like the grandmother, Henry Wing largely keeps his origins under wraps, with the exception of some culinary Caribbean habits that are temporarily tolerated but later give way to Canadian foodways and cabbage.[215] In general, as Leslie Sanders observes in her perceptive analysis of the novel, "Henry Wing performs the perfect colonial mimicry, albeit of a form of colonial presence long past" (2000, 181). To some extent, the stance of his custodians also appears in the second-generation narrator; Peter Hudson has described *Childhood* as the "novel of a phenotypically Black man who, for all intents and purposes, is white" (Hudson 2000, 192).

Earlier and elsewhere, Alexis has emphatically called for "black Canadian writing that is conscious of Canada," as opposed to US-inflected modalities (1995, 17). He has also defended, however, his "right to speculate on things that aren't directly to do with race" (Nurse 2003, 149). His often tongue-in-cheek representation of blackness leaves ample room for ambivalence in the novel; it can seem "to suggest that once the markers of the Caribbean are discarded or repressed, race is of no consequence in the Canadian landscape" (Sanders 2000, 184). Chariandy, who believes that such wishful thinking is illusory (2004, 87–8), notes that *Childhood* has proven to be controversial in this respect (2007a, 823–4). Caribbean Canadian haunting is hardly absent from the novel; however, it is sublated in the first-generation patterns of avoidance that the narrator ridicules to a degree but also imitates.

While Alexis portrays studied attempts at forgetting Caribbeanness, in Chariandy's text – although it is subtitled *A Novel of Forgetting* – "the soucouyant functions as a symbol of the pasts that each of the main characters have struggled to forget – pasts that continue to haunt these characters in shadowy or spectral forms" (in Tancock 2008, 2). The present of the novel is set in the late 1980s in the Toronto suburb of Scarborough, after the narrator returns to his mother's house from which he had fled earlier in desperation. His mother, Adele, a black woman born in Trinidad, moved to

Canada via the aforementioned domestic scheme and lost her husband in an industrial accident. She suffers from early dementia, which has driven the narrator and his brother away, and initially she does not recognize her son when he returns longing "for even so frightening a mother as she had become" (Chariandy 2007b, 33). As a medical leaflet once handed to his parents warns, however, the diagnosis of "*cognitive dementia*" can be misleading, since "*depression and certain post-traumatic states may produce false positives*"; especially when administered to "*uneducated and/or ethnic minorities,*" tests can be positive even when "*strictly speaking, cognitive dementia as discussed is not truly in effect*" (41).

As the narrator seeks to reconstruct aspects of her story, we learn in layered bits and pieces that Adele has indeed experienced trauma. We also come to understand that her forgetting is selective. While she forgets simple facts that are essential for daily life, she remembers certain words with a clarity that surprises her.[216] The narrator suggests that such moments point to a breach in self-protection (that pertains to both his mother and himself), since "forgetting can sometimes be the most creative and life-sustaining thing that we can ever hope to accomplish. The problem happens when we become too good at forgetting. When somehow *we forget* to forget … This is how we awaken to the stories buried deep within our sleeping selves or trafficked quietly through the touch of others" (32). Such an awakening occurs literally to the narrator after he has fled his mother's house – and her presence – to the city that, for him, is "a place of forgetting" (30); he is awoken by a roommate who hears him mumbling the word "soucouyant" (32) in his sleep. Eventually it becomes clear that the novel is not so much about forgetting as it is about forgetting to forget. It is also about the coding and deciphering of knowledge in a guise – or here a garment – that clothes it in the appearance of forgetting. That outer form may lend itself to dismissal by a second generation unfamiliar with forms of meaning-making that belong to their parents' cultural context.

Indeed, "Mother wasn't simply forgetting" (22). Adele's memory is surprisingly sharp in some details, reaching back beyond her own lifetime: "'Carenage,' she might say, almost surprised that she had done so" (22). This is the name of the fishing village to which her dispossessed family was moved to accommodate a US military base during the Second World War; yet she further remembers that it comes from a term for the removal of barnacles from Spanish ships to make them "smooth again after the trip from Africa" (23). She remembers this information from "an old woman … with long memory and the proper name of things" (23). The same woman told her that the ships were carrying "Ghosts" (182) and that the sea contains "endless floors of bone" (182).[217]

Adele also remembers words related to healing in the traditional knowledge conveyed by this woman (23), a sign that in some respects her capacity for cultural memory is sharp and exact. Chariandy continues this list of useful and specific knowledge with items that initially seem unrelated to such healing information; they concern forms of meaning he associates with her past: "Mother never deliberately explained to me her past, but I learned anyway. Of lagaboos, and douens, and other spectres of long-ago meaning" (23). Enters the titular spirit: "'Soucouyant,' Mother said aloud to herself one day … 'I saw one in the morning'" (23). She then confirms her son's understanding that a soucouyant "is an evil spirit. Someone who sucks your blood at night" (23).

Elements of the mother's soucouyant story recur in different forms throughout the text. As Chariandy explains, "a soucouyant, from the son's perspective at least, is a word that is simultaneously familiar and strange. It's a word, among many, that the son has heard his mother utter throughout his life, but that he doesn't completely understand; and his relationship to his cultural history is similarly doubled or ironic" (in Tancock 2008, 2). As a result, the "meaning of the title is indeed layered, and it emerges through an unruly process of re-scripting and deciphering on the part of the speaker" (in Dobson 2007, 811).

The next remembered name refers not to healing, but to a site of trauma related to Adele's mother. This event may have triggered Adele's complex relationship to remembering and may explain her clear remembering of means of natural healing: "'Chaguaramas … She loss she skin at the military base in Chaguaramas. She wore a dress of fire before it go ruin her'" (Chariandy 2007b, 24). Through subsequent reiterations and reconstitutions, we come to understand that these words render the perception and experience of a child. They have come to be the outer form of a memory that contains but also covers a traumatic event. This memory partially disguises the traumatic event, clothing it in imagery made available to the child by the legend of an evil figure in Trinidadian legend, the soucouyant.

The event – in which the five-year-old Adele semi-inadvertently transforms her mother into a ball of fire – caps a sequence of traumatizing childhood experiences, a sequence that shapes the child's perception of the final catastrophe. To support herself and Adele in new surroundings, Adele's mother has been working as a prostitute at the military base that has displaced them from their earlier home. Adele has seen strangers in the house and has associated the sounds from her mother's bedroom with "creatures who enter in the night and ravage the flesh" (184). She has further seen her mother wear "her costume for work" at home and discovered the "sloughed form on the floor, her mother's empty dress" (186) when the latter attempts to kill herself. Adele finally tries to disassociate herself entirely from this person who, for her, comes to represent the shape of evil: "'You not my mother. *You horror. All horror!*'" (189).

Adele finally escapes from her mother's house. She runs from the evil that she associates with her mother's dress, the "evil" (189) of her naked body and the brutalized sexuality that the dress does not cover but exposes. So much like the skin that hides a soucouyant, the outer form and signifier of the dress takes on its own life, a "horror" disassociated from the eclipsed humanity of her mother. At the military base, she finds a soldier who once offered her a lighter as a gift, but then she sees her "mother's chiffon gown, the image that she had fled since dawn ... A garment without a body, animated through terrible magics" (191). As a reified, inhuman being, the dress "flies toward her as if borne upon storm-winds" (191), then inexplicably sprouts a hand that holds Adele. In an ensuing confrontation with the soldiers, this being is brutally doused with gasoline and oil. Scared and wanting "to get away, somehow, from this creature and the entertained eyes around them," Adele flicks the lighter and "holds it to the loose corner of the white sleeve" (192–3). Only then does she discover, inside the growing flame and "visible now for the first time to Adele's eyes, a human form" (193).

This moment is the ultimate traumatic realization that her conscious memory cannot accommodate. It retains the child's perception, frozen in time, just before that terrible recognition. Maintaining the elements of dress and fire, the memory associates them with the soucouyant but inverts them inside out. Whereas the soucouyant appears as a ball of fire when not dressed in human skin, here the mother's dress signifies evil, and its hidden nature (and what it hides) is revealed when it turns into fire. The soucouyant has been turned inside out, it seems – until the mother's human form appears inside this terrible shape of fire. Memory has not further processed that traumatic experience, which is covered and conveyed in this outer form. As her son observes, "She told, but she never explained or deciphered. She never put the stories together. She never could or wanted to do so" (136). Her way of communication, as the son tries to explain earlier, is "a way of telling without really telling" (66).

The son's task is to try to undo – to the extent that this is possible – the effects of disassociation, lest he himself remain in the state of disassociation from his mother that her experience has caused. He consequently tries to reiterate the story in her presence and with her participation. His hope is to understand what happened, which necessitates his acquisition of another kind of knowledge, and cultural translation. But he also seeks to revisit and re-articulate together with his mother her seemingly incomprehensible memories – the signs of cognitive dementia perhaps, but possibly of trauma experienced in the form of a soucouyant – so that recognition can occur, connections can be voiced, and some kind of healing can begin. Indeed, his mother's complex (non-)memories have become his in more ways than one. He himself seems marked by the sign of the soucouyant, and just as Adele fled her mother's house, so he has fled hers. While he does not reject his mother, she has become monstrous to him and seems to suck the life out of him just as Adele's mother had out of her. He returns to her house in order to reverse the disassociation that the "specters of history" (183) have created not only between Adele and her mother, but also between Adele and him. The most literal incarnation of those spectres is the soucouyant, but other incarnations include the legacies of the entire social, political, and patriarchal history that led to the sexual exploitation of his grandmother at the military base located where her home village once stood, as well as the ensuing traces of suffering and disruption that have come down to Adele and then to her family and children.

Jennifer Bowering Delisle uses the notion of "postmemory," first developed by Marianne Hirsch with regard to the children of Holocaust survivors, to discuss the narrator's experience of this sequence of events and the memories and stories by which they are conveyed. Postmemory, for Hirsch, is "distinguished from memory by generational distance and from history by deep personal connection" (Hirsch 1997, 22; qtd in Delisle 2011, 6). Chariandy's narrator formulates his own version of similar distinctions. For him, "History is a rusted pile of blades and manacles," but he offers a striking image for the force of memory, suggesting it is a physical mark on the body: "Memory is a bruise still tender" (32). Tellingly, the formulation omits the word "like," claiming literal identity rather than similarity.

As Delisle observes, the image of the bruise connects the evocation of memory with the sign of the soucouyant in the novel; she leaves the victim – among the few signs of her work – with "a tell-tale bruise or mark on his skin" (Chariandy 2007b, 135; Delisle 2011, 5–6). The narrator not only mumbles the word "soucouyant" in his sleep, but after his mother's death, he also sports a "mysterious bruise" on his forehead (141). While the ontological status of the soucouyant remains uncertain in the text, the bruise is real. A rational explanation might see it as a somatic, outer representation of an interiorized, internal presence of the past.

In his discussion of the novel, Daniel Coleman defends the validity of traditional knowledge systems and beliefs as alternatives to Euro-American epistemologies (2012, 54). A "long-held set of community beliefs" (63) like the one evoked by the soucouyant, Coleman suggests, can help us see the narrator's situation in communal contexts (and temper, for example, a theoretical focus on melancholia).[218] Elements of spiritual cosmologies that address realms that exceed human control, he explains, can be devalued "if people for whatever reason no longer see them as essential to the workings of the more-than-human world and instead see them as tropes invented by the human mind" (2012, 61). This is the case for figures like the soucouyant; we can read them "downward" in terms of a secularized understanding[219] or "upward" "for their traces as descendants from fuller, dynamic spirit worlds" (61).

Chariandy seems careful to leave the status, or reality, of the soucouyant in abeyance. While the mother repeatedly claims to have seen a soucouyant, she also denigrates the story in a decisive moment: "Whatever you think you want with some old nigger-story?" (194). Her statement can be read as straight dismissal or as another willful disruption of her son's attempts to reconnect with her. In general, it seems true that Chariandy's novel is not in the business of disambiguating the ontological status of the soucouyant, but neither is it diminishing the experiential reality of the soucouyant or subtracting from its explanatory force. Chariandy employs the possibilities of fiction to maintain both "what-ifs?" without forcing a resolution between these potentialities.[220] The facticity of the bruise may be read as a psychosomatic symptom, but it might also suggest the soucouyant's reality in another realm. The soucouyant's power functions irrespective of literal truth; it is effective if it is believed in.

As such, the soucouyant signals a shared meaning, evoking shared cultural and historical legacies. It points to a bruise sustained at times without the immediate awareness of the bruised subject (who may not even be awake or historically present at the moment it is inflicted). Because the soucouyant is derived from a shared historical context, however, it also signals a memory and a knowledge that circulate both within and outside of any individual. As Delisle points out, another character in the novel, Meera, "is similarly marked by the sign of the soucouyant," a birthmark that is "one of the first things the narrator notices about her" (Delisle 2011, 14). Meera, who for reasons of her own has cared for the narrator's mother in his absence, repeatedly emphasizes her knowledge of a story that he has been seeking to reconstitute. Looking at a figure in the narrator's brother's notebook that seems to represent a soucouyant, she offers a remark that could refer both to the spirit and to its role in the family story: "'You don't have to tell me the story … I know'" (172).

Meera repeats the phrase on the novel's last page when the narrator mentions a ritual blessing by water; he received it as a young child on a trip to Trinidad but cannot consciously remember it. Meera tells him: "'I know … Your mother told me many times. She never forgot'" (196). With regard to remembering and forgetting, the roles of mother and son are strikingly inverted here. This reversal unites them in the experiences of both. In also emphasizing forgetting within this commonality, however, Chariandy is very careful not to end with a happily shared memory. Instead, it is the son who suffers from amnesia and who must be helped by the memories of his mother and Meera in order to articulate an important element in the story of his own life.

The novel thus refuses any recourse to a moment of *unmediated* return or recognition. It does not offer a redemptive fusion of memories between mother and son that would undo the disruptions wrought by history and personal experience (in this regard, the novel has affinities with the aforementioned theories of diaspora of Stuart Hall).[221] This point is emphasized in the novel through the mother's non-recognition of the son's last telling of her story (194–5). Yet the novel maintains the possibility of a communal knowing that occurs through a shared and constant re-articulation of diasporic experiences, and the processes by which individual subjects use language to make sense of such experience, together with others and in their own lives.

This seems the point of the final sentence of the novel, spoken by Meera. Echoing the earlier blessing that the narrator has just told her he cannot remember, she touches his face before the novel concludes: "'Eyestache,' she says" (196).[222] The utterance builds on a chain of signification that begins earlier in the novel and extends beyond it. It includes the "spot of blood. Not very large at all," that the narrator discovers on his mother's head after she has died (138) and the mysterious bruise that appears on his own head the day of the funeral. A child "looking at the bruise on my forehead … probes gently and then moves down to my eyebrows, tracing them with his thumb. His cool fingers before he pulls them away. 'Eyestache,' he says" (143–4). It is another blessing, one that brings cooling, but the child's simple perception says something else as well: analogous to the moustache as facial hair next to the mouth, the child's reference to the facial hair on the forehead as "eyestache" contextualizes the nearby bruise as another kind of mouth. The bruise reveals a hurt and is a "tell-tale sign" that bespeaks a past event. It signals the existence of a story to be told.

On the last pages, the narrator speaks of his seemingly disappointed hope that the time with his failing mother would have yielded something new, "something that we wouldn't have guessed otherwise. The freedom of meaning, the wild magic of existence. Geographies slipping into each other. Constellations wheeling above and seasons bleeding into each other so that some wintry neighbourhood can become tropical in an instant" (194). Some such combination and mutual translation across time and space, however, does occur in his final exchange of stories with Meera, with times and places switching back and forth between now and then, here and there. As they sit by Lake Ontario in the "house on the weathered edge of the Scarborough Bluffs," she recalls his mother's memories of his blessing by water on another shore, on a "beach near Mother's birthplace" in a "seaside village named Carenage" (195). Initially forgotten, the moment is now remembered, recognized, and symbolically reiterated with Meera's gesture of touching the narrator's face and her utterance of the word "Eyestache." With Meera's gesture, the utterance of the word evokes its association with a mysteriously sustained bruise whose story needs to be spoken. This re-articulation of memories circulates here within the orbit of a communally mediated and constituted second-generation memory. In the second-generation communality between Meera and the narrator, the memory voices, translates, and gives new interpersonal reality to the story – and to the presence of a culturally specific past – that is mediated by the sign of the soucouyant.

With reference to Sneja Gunew's theorizing about a form of belonging that is "assembled precariously out of the shards of individual lives and their 'imagined relations' to genealogies (private histories) and public events, that is, global or national histories" (Gunew 2004, 109), Delisle suggests that belonging based on such "shards" of memories – like the fractured bits and pieces Chariandy's narrator seeks to articulate and assemble – "inherited from both birthplace and ancestral homeland offers a way of thinking about second-generation identity in Canada" (Delisle 2011, 20). Yet *Soucouyant* the novel makes it clear that an element of what Glissant calls "opacity" (1995, 54) pertains to this practice of self-articulation that proceeds by translating the experience and memories of others across generational and geographic distance. As the novel suggests, we may never really know another person's experiences – or even entirely know ourselves – although it also indicates that we may know more about ourselves through others. *Soucouyant* shows a process of self-articulation that works as a relational mediation of the self through cultural and historical contexts, as well as through the presence and the perceived past of others.

While the performance of narrative self-remembering in *Soucouyant* occurs mostly in the space of one house (as with Austin Clarke's novel discussed earlier), we see how the process reaches out – in time and space – in ways that I have noted at the beginning of the discussion of Caribbean Canadian writing in the present chapter. The forces of disruption and connection that we have seen in other texts are also in operation here. They result in practices of re–membering time-spaces and emotional geographies of the black Atlantic in narrative performances that cannot undo the disjunctive realities of diaspora and generational distance, but that process them in new forms of self-articulation. Issues of intergenerational questioning and conveyance – and of the translation and re-articulation of culturally specific, vernacular knowledges across time, space, and the primordial abyss of the middle passage – are also at stake for the francophone Caribbean Québécois writer Marie-Célie Agnant, to whom we will now turn.

WRITING THE HAITIAN DIASPORA IN QUEBEC

Oral Knowledge and Intergenerational Transmission in Marie-Célie Agnant's *La dot de Sara* and *Le livre d'Emma*

Marie-Célie Agnant is one of many Haitian writers who have contributed to a substantial body of black francophone writing in Quebec. Like many of her compatriots, Agnant was directly marked by the Duvalier dictatorship when she arrived in Montreal in 1970.[223] Here she wrote and published poetry, short stories, children's books, essays, and several novels (Boucher and Spear 2013, 7–8).[224] In *La dot de Sara* (1995), her first novel, she draws on oral histories obtained through a research project on older Haitian women in Montreal that posed questions of intergenerational cultural conveyance among migrant women of colour, especially under the pressures of assimilation.[225] Her next novel, *Le livre d'Emma* (2001), deals again with the transmission of oral memory by women, but in this case it thematizes slavery. The novel reaches back to the moment of abduction in Africa and poses questions about the (im)possibilities of oral and alternative histories being heard within institutional Western contexts. Her subsequent novel,

Un alligator nommé Rosa (2007), examines the continuing trauma, even for exiles, of having experienced the dictatorship of Baby Doc Duvalier.

Agnant is one of the rare women in the Haitian Québécois corpus. She has repeatedly focused on the long-standing difficulty that women in Haiti – and in the diaspora – have in gaining access to writing and publishing. This problem of gender means that in the Haitian context women's voices often find expression mainly through orality.[226] This background finds its consequences in a number of aspects in Agnant's work. As commentators have observed, her texts often feature forms of the female storyteller or *griot* (Boucher 2005, 195; Proulx 2005, 35–6). This choice underscores the importance of women's access to public space via language while claiming Agnant's own right to transpose that access into writing and literary publication. In her collection of stories *Le silence comme le sang* (1997), such marginalized female figures speak in the silences under the Haitian dictatorship. In *La dot de Sara* and *Le livre d'Emma*, Agnant portrays the chains of conveyance that transpose black women's stories from the realm of orality into the public geographies of writing and literature. This theme is explicit in the latter novel, while in the first the addressee of the grandmother's stories is the eponymous grandchild who promises to make her grandmother's life and stories known through writing in the future.[227] In a sense, this is of course the text we are reading, written in the grandmother's first person.

Agnant's novel, however, also speaks to the disruption of oral memories. The transmission of these stories is complicated here by the fact that Sara's mother, Giselle – who has asked the grandmother to join them in Montreal – rejects the stories from Haiti that have begun to pass from grandmother to grandchild. Marianna, the grandmother, comes to understand that these stories are an heirloom ("dot"; 67) that she can offer to her granddaughter. In some stories, this inheritance consists of traditional lore from Haiti, which her daughter rejects as "histoires farfelues" ("weird stories"); [228] Marianna clearly expresses disappointment over her daughter's dismissal of this cultural heritage.[229] In other stories, Marianna remembers female genealogies that name the exceptional women in her past who knew how to survive against all odds. For Giselle, this chain of transmission seems but another liability in the diaspora, and she fails to endorse Marianna's assertion of similarities between her own grandmother, Aïda, and Sara: "Giselle affirme ne pas se souvenir d'elle" (14; "Giselle claims not to remember her"). Giselle's attitude is due to seemingly irreconcilable cultural references and a double consciousness.[230] Her ambivalences reveal a complex array of issues typically prominent in diasporic narratives, including migrancy, gender, and generational difference, assimilation and cultural memory, and bilingualism and linguistic normativity under pressures of assimilation. The question of Creole in particular becomes part of the generational drama in the novel: "Alors qu'à sa mère elle ne parle qu'en français, avec moi, Sara parle ma langue, celle de grand-mère Aîda. C'est avec ravissement que je l'entends me demander lorsqu'elle revient de l'école: 'Ki soloba ou kite pou mwen jodi a Ti Manm?' ('Quel bon petit repas m'as-tu laissé aujourd'hui, petite mère?')" (67–8; "While she speaks only French to her mother, with me, she speaks my language, that of grandmother Aîda. I am delighted to hear her ask me when she comes home from school: 'Ki soloba ou kite pou mwen jodi a Ti Manm?' ['What nice little meal did you keep for me today, mummy?']").[231] Agnant thus emphasizes in her own way that in the transmission of genealogies, situated knowledges, and oral memories, to use Brand's words, "no language is neutral."

Agnant makes the issue of Creole central to her subsequent novel, *Le livre d'Emma* (2001). The novel thematizes the transmission of oral memory reaching back to slavery and places particular emphasis on writing and translation. The black narrator, Flore, is a translator and a cultural interpreter who assists a white Montreal doctor in examining a Caribbean woman, Emma, who is accused of having murdered her child (16).[232] Flore's intervention is required because Emma, despite her fluent French (7), insists on communicating in her mother tongue only, which turns out to be Creole. Ignoring the doctor's questions, she offers long bursts of speech about the blue of the sea and the sky, about black skins, and about the madness that has come in the hold of slave ships (8). Agnant's novel turns around Flore's encounter with Emma and her stories and her translation and her transmission of them.

Despite initial difficulties,[233] Flore begins to identify with Emma. In the process, she creates *Le livre d'Emma*, the written account of a long chain of oral transmissions that has reached Emma through her grandmother's cousin Mattie and that relates experiences of abduction, slavery, and resistance. This was also the subject matter, it turns out, of Emma's own doctoral thesis on slavery, rejected in the old slave port of Bordeaux.

Emma insists that her stories speak of the "malédictions du sang." In Agnant's variation of Brand's theme of the ongoing curse and namelessness caused by slavery, Emma views these stories as attesting to a deterministic script that circulates in the body with the blood. The "curse in the blood" whose existence Emma asserts, initiated by slavery and the middle passage, leads her in the end to take "la route des grands bateaux" and to drown herself.[234] It is here, in the last pages of *Le livre d'Emma*, that Flore parts with the story. In a final re/cognition[235] of Emma's life and narrative, Flore emphasizes life and connection over death and separation: "Oui, me disais-je, Emma me met au monde, elle réinvente ma naissance. Elle est là pour mener à travers moi sa dernière lutte et se jouer du destin" (167; "Yes, I told myself, Emma is bringing me into the world; she is reinventing my birth. She is there to lead her last fight and to defeat destiny, through me" [2006, 204]).[236] Instead of an immutable fate, the narrator reads possibilities of human decision and valuation in Emma's story that call for choice and active interpretation.

Flore has earlier decided on a strong version of translation, interpretation, and retelling when she refuses to translate Emma's life into the "target" language[237] and normativity postulated by the mental institution that has hired her. Giving up the traditionally required distance of the translator (34–5), she decides: "finies les séances tranquilles au cours desquelles je parviens à garder … la distance nécessaire afin de retrouver … ma pleine et entière liberté. Avec Emma, je traduit non pas des mots, mais des vies, des histoires. La sienne, d'abord … Je traduis ensuite l'histoire d'une île, lambeau de l'époque coloniale, vestige de sa cruauté, de son inhumanité" (16–17; "no more of the peaceful sessions during which I am able … to keep the distance necessary to recover my complete and total liberty … With Emma, I am translating not words but lives, stories. Hers, first of all … I am also translating the history of an island, a scrap left over from the colonial period, a vestige of its cruelty, of its inhumanity" [2006, 19]). At the same time, Flore re/cognizes her own history, which has been eclipsed by dominant narratives and white normative understanding, the other side of her double consciousness: "Au fond de moi, une voix soufflé: 'Tôt ou tard, on trahit quelqu'un ou soit-même'" (21; "Deep down, a voice whispers: 'Sooner or later, one betrays oneself or someone else'" [2006, 27]).

This ethics of trans–lation (of "carrying across") takes sides in the quarrels of historiography. Indeed, Agnant's text presents three different versions of a "Livre d'Emma" that also thematize three different possible entries of slavery into writing and the historiography of modernity. These three books have entirely different relations with oral traditions and their rendering of slavery. One is Emma's dissertation, which has been denied entry into academic knowledge in written French, also the language of the former slavers. The second is constituted by the doctor's notes, an account presumably defined by dominant medical and legal norms, and is condemned by Emma.[238] Finally, Flore produces another account but finds herself initially suspected by Emma of reproducing the perspectives of white historiography.[239] Flore, however, hears and translates the historical subtext and identifies with Emma.[240] This identification also determines the form of her writing, although in the end she will take the liberty to read and to interpret the script conveyed by Emma in her own way. The transposition of Emma's counter-story (which has become partially her own), together with her own reflections, becomes the metafictional *Le livre d'Emma*, which Flore describes as the result of an act of listening: "J'écris … pour que vive à jamais ta voix, toi que personne n'a jamais écoutée" (34–5; "I am writing … so that your voice may live forever, you whose voice no one has ever listened to" [2006, 42]).

The institution that examines Emma fails to hear her story of the middle passage, slavery, and its historical legacy. The doctor MacLeod has left the room (147–8) when Flore hears Emma's account of slaveholder violence, rape, and resistance, which also contains elements that foreshadow Emma's own ending: "Plus tard, Kilima donna naissance à une fille qu'elle tenta de noyer, puis elle perdit la raison. Un jour, tout de blanc vêtue, elle entra dans l'océan et ne revint plus jamais. Elle avait pris le chemin des grands bateaux" (156; "Later, Kilima gave birth to a daughter whom she attempted to drown; after that she went mad. One day, dressed completely in white, she walked into the ocean and never came back. She had returned to the route of the big boats" [2006, 189]).[241] While Emma's narrative about Kilima offers neither an admission that she killed her own child nor a precise parallel with her life, it shares important elements with her own fate, including her eventual decision to "return home" by reversing the middle passage and "le chemin des grands bateaux." Emma insists on the present-day validity of her account as a foundational narrative of origins (Ndiaye 2004) that continues to determine the present: "Tout ce passé n'a de passé que le nom, Flore" (158; "All this past is past in name only, Flore" [2006, 192]). Indeed, the non-linearity of time is impressed upon Flore, who acknowledges the presence of the past when she describes a moment of storytelling and listening: "Le temps avait reculé depuis longtemps, je n'existait plus. Emma non plus … évoluaitent maintenant Kilima, Béa, Cécile" (148; "Time had been turned back long before; I no longer existed. Nor did Emma … there were now Kilima, Cécile, and Béa" [2006, 180]).

In the relationship between Emma and the narrator Flore, Agnant stages a dialogue that recognizes the historical legacy of slavery as ground for contemporary black subjectivities, but that also redefines the seemingly deterministic implications of that past. Flore opts for possibilities of agency and life that rewrite the script of continued, unavoidable malediction, recognizing herself in Emma but finding within this recognition a reason for life-affirming rebirth. In this respect, then, *Le livre d'Emma* does more than offer the transmission of repressed narratives of origin and slavery as violent foundational narratives of the Americas and modernity; it also proposes interventionist readings of such narratives to support active choices in the present. Agnant's novel, in fact, compares the narratives' possible reading and reception with the performativity of oral storytelling, and several metafictional moments in the text thematize this performativity.[242] The decisions Flore makes in her performance of interpretation – which are based on recognition but also create relative non-equivalences between "the book" and its readings – open spaces for self-determination, personal and political choice, and new beginnings.

The Trauma of Duvalier Repression and Impossible Returns: Agnant, Étienne, Ollivier, and Laferrière

Marie-Célie Agnant

Shortly after publishing *Le livre d'Emma*, Agnant stated in an interview that "la période de l'esclavage dans les romans haïtiens … est tout à fait absent, sinon refoulée" (Jurney 2003, 388; "the time of slavery is entirely absent or repressed in Haitian novels").[243] In her subsequent novel, *Un alligator nommé Rosa* (2007), she approaches another, more recent collective Haitian trauma that has proven in many respects to make speech difficult: oppression under Papa and Baby Doc Duvalier.[244] The titular character, Rosa Bosquet, is based on the historical figure Rosalie Bosquet, the right hand of François Duvalier and warden of Fort-Dimanche prison. In the novel, we encounter her as an old, paralyzed woman hiding in southern France. Laura, whom Rosa adopted in Haiti after her parents were murdered, has been looking after her until Antoine Guibert arrives, in the guise of a nurse responding to an ad. In reality, after forty years of searching he has finally located the murderer of his family and he is now looking for answers to his questions and some form of justice.

As Scott Lyngaas suggests, the novel engages several kinds of silence. One is "the silence of historical discourse on the Duvalier regime" (2011, 974), which Agnant pointedly addresses by choosing a historical figure as her title character. Another silence is that of Rosa, who chooses not to speak in the novel, although she is capable of doing so. While Antoine initially worries about Rosa's deafness or Alzheimer's disease (Agnant 2007, 30), the mass murderer who has also killed his family uses silence to foil his attempts to hear any explanation or sign of regret (Selao 2010, 22), let alone an apology (although by withholding food, he does succeed in making Rosa sign a written confession). The third silence, the one more explicitly dramatized in the novel, is Laura's. The adopted orphan will finally find the strength to begin articulating her own traumatic history in the presence of this newly arrived listener (Roth 2012, 203). Despite trying to stay away from Rosa, she also feels some kind of responsibility for her, so she has chosen passivity and silence while awaiting Rosa's death.

Antoine, however, knows from his own experience that silence is but an illusion here, "habité par une clameur douloureuse" (25; "inhabited by painful clamour"). His need for speech – his own, Rosa's, and Laura's – is thus part of "his own talking cure" (Lyngaas 2011, 974). Like Laura, he is haunted by Rosa. Even after Rosa becomes paralyzed, Laura continues to react nervously to her earlier habit of appearing unexpectedly (16). Antoine, while not a timorous man otherwise, has lived with a deep terror ever since his childhood that "commandant Rosa Bosquet" will suddenly appear in the night, a deadly weapon in hand (27). Surrounded by "une armée de spectres" (28; "an army of ghosts"), he is imprisoned by his past, unable to leave it behind: "Comment prétendre à une quelconque liberté?" (29; "How to pretend to any freedom whatsoever?"). It is particularly the image of his family's burning house (an image that we have seen evoked also by Agnant) that haunts him (32).

The ability to articulate and share their stories liberates neither him nor Laura. Within themselves "l'irrémediable débâcle, tous ces souvenirs … affluent, se pressent en un tumulte obsédant qui leur emplit le corps" (214; "the irreparable defeat, all those memories … rush and push in an obsessive tumult that fills their body"). Antoine knows that killing Rosa will not free him, but will only mean that he has joined Rosa as a killer. Voicing at times the desperate idea of leaving her simply to die in her bed or of setting her house on fire, Antoine is brought to reason by Laura (221–2). Still, there seems to be no solution to their dilemma: "Les voilà, une fois de plus, exilé, chacun dans sa souffrance" (222; "And again each of them is exiled in their suffering"). Though surrounded by the beauty of southern France, they recognize that life in the present remains impossible for them: "La vie est là, mais Antoine et Laura n'y sont pas. Côte à côte, ils se tiennent, orphelins de tout, sauf de leur mémoire" (160; "Life is there, but without Antoine and Laura. Side by side, they remain orphans of everything except their memory").

Unlike in Chariandy's novel, *Soucouyant*, here there is no "forgetting to forget": memory is constant, conscious, and traumatic; it also leaves its subjects feeling radically diminished and implacably governed by its determining force. While the result is not fatal – as in Emma's case in Agnant's previous novel – there is no instance in the book that would allow a perspective comparable to that of Flore, whose translation and articulation of Emma's narrative allows her life-affirming insights, affordable perhaps only from her position as a listener, which is closer to that of a second-generation witness.

Laura and Antoine finally abandon Rosa in a "mouroir" (232; "hospice").[245] The novel ends with news images of violence, however, and evokes again the image of the smoking remains of a violently destroyed home (235–6). Even though Laura and Antoine have left the physical body of Rosa behind and may have transformed their individual isolation into a company of sufferers, the novel's ending does not suggest that they have left their traumatic memories behind. Their exilic lives do not sever them from Haiti – from what Antoine calls a "pays de la démémoire" (215; "country of de-membrance" or "un-memory").

Gérard Étienne, Émile Ollivier, and Dany Laferrière

Other members of the Haitian diaspora in Montreal have similarly been trying to come to terms with Duvalier repression and its historical legacy. They have also attempted to sort out their own personal memories and relation to Haiti. Gérard Étienne's first novel, *Le nègre crucifié* (1974), is based on his own incarceration and torture at the hands of François (Papa Doc) Duvalier's henchmen, and it holds a particular place in that corpus.[246] As Franck Larack notes in the preface to the second edition, it is "la seule oeuvre littéraire haïtienne dont la trame est constitutée par la torture de l'auteur" (Étienne 1994, 14; "the only Haitian literary work whose framework is constituted by the author's torture").[247] In Étienne's own words, the text is "un réquisitoire littéraire" (1994, 9; "a literary indictment") of the regime and its methods.

This literary indictment is pursued with grotesque, absurd, and surrealistic images of violence. As the narrator awaits torture in his cell, he invents another character to distract himself from his predicament, but he also remembers and bears witness to the maiming, torturing, and killing of others (70). The text ends with the narrator's account of the last moments before his death (Étienne himself, during torture, was beaten into a coma [Redouane and Bénayoun-Szmidt 2011, 16]). The text is set entirely in Haiti, and Étienne has remarked that his stylistic choices are intended to shock Haitian intellectuals and writers and to challenge their lyrical prose that has no connection with "la sale réalité haïtienne" (Dumontet 2003, 211; "the dirty reality of Haiti"). At the same time, Étienne remembers and re-imagines torture and Duvalier's Haiti from a specifically Québécois exile.[248] As Clément Moisan and Renate Hildebrand have observed, the work "n'est pas étrangère au Québec des années 1960 et 1970, au moment où les événements d'octobre 1970 et les mesures de guerre ont lieu" (2001, 109; "is not foreign to the Quebec of the 1960s and 1970s, the time of the October Crisis and the War Measures Act"). Indeed, while Étienne himself has cited earlier Quebec classics like Anne Hébert's *Le torrent* (1950) and Marie-Claire Blais's *Une saison dans la vie d'Emmanuel* (1965) (Dumontet 2003, 212), his opening pages also evoke *Prochain episode* (1964), written by Hubert Aquin while imprisoned in a Montreal psychiatric institution after his arrest for gun possession and his public declaration of his public commitment to armed struggle for independence. Published in the very year that Étienne sought exile in Montreal, Aquin's novel also portrays an incarcerated revolutionary – betrayed by the country he tries to serve – deliriously inventing an alter ego for himself, free to roam the outside world in stark contrast to his own lack of mobility and power.

The imaginative cross-fertilization between Haiti and Quebec is explicit in *Un ambassadeur macoute à Montréal* (1979). With Haitian diplomatic representation in Canada[249] and his own Montreal arrival serving as background, Étienne's second novel features a poor black immigrant seeing the country of his chosen exile – a revolutionary and separatist Quebec ready to overthrow an oppressive religious past – threatened by a voodoo-wielding emissary of Haiti.[250] This grotesque figure has been invited by Quebec's reactionary forces to use his unnatural powers against the insurgents. The novel is set in the context of the 1970 October Crisis and the invocation of the War Measures Act. As Mireille LeBreton observes, when the "ambassadeur macoute" receives extraordinary powers from Canadian and Quebec authorities, the distance between Quebec and Haiti in the novel is "considérablement réduite" (2011, 62; "considerably reduced"). Étienne's Quebec is written here palimpsestically over a clearly visible Haitian ground and memory that powerfully shines through the northern surface.

Étienne's novel *La pacotille* (1991) has him again "faire la navette entre Port-au-Prince et Montréal" (Dumontet 2003, 213; "shuttle between Port-au-Prince and Montreal"), and his protagonists in *La romance en do mineur de Maître Clo* (2000) and *Vous n'êtes pas seul* (2001) struggle with their past and new, but difficult, lives in Montreal. On the other hand, in his novel *Une femme muette* (1983) and its rewritten version, *Au bord de la falaise* (2004), Étienne shows the reactionary "other" Haitian in Montreal. These texts feature a superficially successful but brutally patriarchal and dictatorial (and again voodoo-practising) husband and medical doctor who keeps his wife captive at home and then, with the help of a colleague, institutionalized in a psychiatric hospital.[251]

Literary criticism has often emphasized the plight of the displaced subject in Étienne's work. Joubert Satyre, for instance, repeatedly citing Simon Harel's sombre diagnoses of the migrant subject (Harel 2005), discusses several works by Étienne and Émile Ollivier under such headings as "Hallucinations" (2009, 96), "Folie" (97), "Cauchemars" (99) ("Hallucinations," "Madness," "Nightmares"). While this may pertain to many of the characters under discussion, it is interesting to note that Étienne maps his own artistic production from a very different perspective. With reference to sociolinguistic notions of additive and subtractive bilingualism, Étienne suggests that his is a productive case of "migrance additive" (Dumontet 2003, 218; "additive migrancy"). He avers that many of his works could not have been written without the critical distance made possible by Montreal and Moncton and, with respect to Quebec settings, by Haiti (218.) For that reason, he asserts that his "vraie culture littéraire a commencé à Montréal" (218; "real literary culture has begun in Montreal"). Étienne is thus on record as appreciating the artistic and creative possibilities of living between two cultures, although the Duvalier dictatorship and its brutality have evidently marked his characters.

The same is true, as Satyre points out, for the characters of Émile Ollivier (2009, 99). Ollivier's two long texts that make up *Paysage de l'aveugle* (1977), for instance, look at torture in Haiti and Montreal exile respectively. In his first novel, *Mère-Solitude* (1983), a family's story is closely interwoven with the history of Haiti. The decline and decimation of the Morelli family involves the resistance of his narrator's uncle to a massacre under the Haitian president Magloire and the hanging of his mother for killing Duvalier's chief of police. After the publication of his second novel, *La discorde aux cent voix* (1986), again set in Haiti (see Satyre 2012), Ollivier's literary attention shifted increasingly towards the context of diasporic lives and the Haitian community in Montreal (Klaus 2012, 39–40). The relationship between Haiti and Quebec becomes a constant preoccupation of Ollivier's characters and narrators, together with the longing for an impossible return.

In his novel *Passages* (1991), the tellingly named Normand Malavy[252] is surrounded by exiled compatriots who are "empoisonnés par l'obsession du retour au pays natal" (2002, 70; "imprisoned by the obsession of a return to their homeland"). They express their painful nostalgia in literary and cultural journals. As Satyre points out, the death of the main character in Miami – where he had gone from Montreal to assist Haitian boat people and to be closer to his native Haiti – prefigures the motif of an impossible return, which is more fully developed in *Les urnes scellées* (1995) (2009, 93). During an actual return, the protagonist Adrien Gorfoux realizes the distance between harsh realities and the idealized image he has created of Haiti during his absence. He decides to return to Montreal.

Ollivier himself has again described his own situation in more positive terms than these novels might suggest he would. In a 1983 newspaper article, he outlines the dual but not unhappy condition that he later summarizes in the phrase "Haïtien la nuit, Québécois le jour" (Jonassaint 1986, 88; "Haitian at night, Québécois by day").[253] He arrives at a tentatively positive conclusion: "Je m'amuse, même, par grands bouts, de ce double visage. Serais-je un schizophrène heureux?" (qtd in Gauvin 2012, 82; "I am even often amused by that double life. Could it be that I am a happy schizophrenic?").

In his posthumously published novel, *La brûlerie* (2004), he describes a group of Haitian Québécois intellectuals who, each in his or her own way, are responding to similar situations and questions. To a friend who dreams of writing about Montreal, the narrator suggests that "un vrai travail d'écriture sur Montréal devrait commencer par mettre en scène la parole nomade, la parole migrante, celle de l'entre-deux" (2004, 55; "a serious writing project about Montreal would have to begin by staging nomad speech, migrant speech, the speech of the in-between"). This is, indeed, what the novel does in recording the conversations of its characters in the cafés of Montreal's Outremont neighbourhood; as Lise Gauvin points out, the novel could be subtitled "des milles manières de vivre l'exil" (2012, 89; "The Thousand Ways of Living in Exile"). As a consequence, the reader encounters a spectrum of attitudes, from the sadly nostalgic, to the narrator, Jonas Lazard. In Gauvin's words, he has managed to turn the situation to his advantage and in the end "aura fait de son handicap, l'exil, non plus une fatalité mais l'occasion d'un nouveau départ" (2012, 90; "will have made out of his handicap, exile, not a fatal situation but the occasion for a new departure"). In the process, he has succeeded in fulfilling his own postulate with regard to writing about Montreal; in this city of what he calls the four solitudes of being English, French, immigrant, and black, such writing should "montrer comment notre présence bouscule, bariole, tropicalise le lieu montréalais" (2004, 56; "show how our presence shakes up, colours, and tropicalizes the site of Montreal").

One of the many other writers who have contributed to that task is Dany Laferrière, who, after his arrival in Montreal in 1976, began his steady stream of publications with *Comment faire l'amour avec un nègre sans se fatiguer* (1985).[254] Like Agnant, Étienne, and Ollivier, Laferrière also fled the Duvalier dictatorship, although that theme itself is less emphasized in his texts.

Laferrière's work reflects the consequences of his flight in publications that for the most part deal with North American life or offer memories of his childhood and adolescent life in Haiti. As Anne Marie Miraglia points out, texts like *Comment faire l'amour avec un nègre sans se fatiguer* and the subsequent *Cette grenade dans la main du jeune nègre est-elle une arme ou un fruit?* (1993) are set in Quebec and then in the United States, while what she calls Laferrière's nostalgic novels – such as *L'odeur du café* (1991) and several others – take place in the protagonist's memories. A third group, however, deals with a physical return to Haiti (Miraglia 2011, 81): besides a recent text about Laferrière's experience of the Haitian earthquake in 2010, *Tout bouge autour de moi* (2010), the works in this group include *Pays sans chapeau* (1996), occasioned by the end of the Duvalier dictatorship but above all by the death of the narrator's grandmother Da; and *L'énigme du retour* (2009), prompted by the death of the narrator's father in New York.

These last two works also offer a reflection on the ambiguities and the impossibilities of return – and to some extent perhaps also on the impossibilities of ever leaving. *Pays sans chapeau* draws its title from a Haitian way of naming the land of the dead; as Laferrière explains epigraphically, "personne n'a jamais été enterré avec son chapeau" (2006, 7; "nobody has ever been laid to rest with their hat on"). Chapter epigraphs in Creole further underline the Haitian language as a sign of the narrator's return. Nothing is simple, however, with either the narrator's return or the living and the dead. The dead are not really gone and are palpably present as soon as their names are invoked (37). The living often resemble the dead, or they are compared to the living dead and to the zombies in this country where death seems ubiquitous.[255] In addition, the narrator's visit to the land of the dead leaves him disappointed: its inhabitants and voodoo spirits – which are some kind of "dieux de classe moyenne" (256; "middle-class gods") complaining about their marriage – are not all that different from the beings who inhabit the "real" world.

The line between one world and the other also seems difficult to discern when it comes to the narrator's return to Haiti. As the text opens, the narrator is obviously pleased to be able to "parler d'Haïti en Haïti" (2006, 1; to "speak about Haiti in Haiti"); he asserts repeatedly: "Je suis chez moi" (2006, 11; "I am at home"). Things are more complicated, however. In this opening chapter, entitled "Un écrivain primitif," he vaunts an aesthetic of simply writing what he sees; he proceeds like a four-year-old child, reducing perceptions to simple nouns: bird, mango, children, ball, cars (14). Repeating the first chapter's title at the end, however, the narrator explicates his writing style with reference to a primitive Haitian painter. Asked by the *New York Times* why he never paints the pain and suffering around him, he attests that he paints "le pays que je rêve" (276; "the country that I dream"), having no need to dream the real one ("le pays réel"). The two realms, however, refuse this neat division.

Laferrière's book itself is divided in sections alternately entitled "le pays rêvé" and "le pays réel,"[256] yet often the two seem to work in an inverse sense. In the opening of the first "Dreamed Country" section, the previously happy scene under the mango tree has become treacherous and fraught with difficulty. The heat weighs heavily on the narrator, who is no longer used to it; the journey down south becomes a "plongée aux enfers" (36; "a fall into Hell"). A ripe mango has fallen and exploded close to the chair of the writer (36), who tries to speak again about his relationship "avec ce terrible pays" (37; "this terrible country"). The home ("chez moi") – which just a few pages ago seemed real – reveals itself as a dream that is interrupted by some decidedly less "homely" realities. Instead of the perceived timelessness of this home where initially he thought he recognized "chaque son, chaque cri, chaque rire, chaque silence" (11; "every sound, every shout, every laugh, every silence"), the narrator now observes a "movement incessant qui peut bien être trompeur et donner l'illusion d'une inquiétante immobilité" (38; "an incessant movement that could well be deceptive and give the illusion of a disturbing immobility"). Moreover, as Miraglia notes, he realizes that he cannot understand even basic details (2011, 89). The "home" he expected to return to was dreamed. The place he actually "returns" to has changed. And so has the narrator. He is now more "at home" elsewhere, although in a place that is equally fluid. What emerges, then, is a sense that the narrator lives not in a world where "here" and "there" – or "now" and "then" – can be easily identified or separated. Instead, his life creates a dialogic time-space in which these distinct mappings of experience are continually transformed.

A similar sense of identity and transformation also marks the aptly titled *L'énigme du retour* (2009). The narrator returns to Haiti with the intention of bringing his father's spirit home after his exilic death in New York. In this voyage, neither the remains of the father nor the narrator himself return to their home. And yet there is a homecoming of sorts, one that works through substitution. In an attempt to understand a man he barely knew, the narrator – in lieu of his father – returns "home," and in a further substitution, the image of Aimé Césaire and his writing is superimposed onto that of his father ("Césaire se superpose à mon père," 33). We learn that initially the narrator did not like Césaire's *Cahier d'un retour au pays natal*, the account of his own homecoming to the Caribbean. Now, however, the narrator never travels without the volume. Césaire's rage, poetry, and will to live in dignity now illuminate for him his father's subtle smile and speak to his own pain (60). There is no literal return to any roots or home for the narrator, as there never was one for his exilic father. Instead, his journey articulates and mediates identity as relational: it becomes understandable in the context of the complex and multiple "returns" and "detours" we have seen explicated by Stuart Hall and Édouard Glissant.[257] Unsurprisingly, the narrator of *L'énigme du retour* truly feels at home ("parfaitement chez moi") only between sips of rum and the pages of Césaire's famous book (2009, 33). This "return" by reading is coterminous with the act of writing that renders this journey between texts, times, and Canada, Haiti, and the United States as spaces of the black Atlantic.

Laferrière's narrative returns in time and space express and enact a relational self. They articulate the ever moving present in a continually changing perspective on the past; and they invoke times, spaces, and literary antecedents that mediate – or are fashioned as – the narrating subject's ancestors. Ollivier, we have seen, also suggests that a direct return to a time and place of the past is impossible, since any such attempt also creates a movement in a new direction. Like the texts by Étienne and Agnant that deal with trauma and the brutality of the Duvalier regime, those by Ollivier are marked by the unavoidable weight of the past. Yet the act of writing in another place and time – and a perspective that shuttles back and forth between erstwhile separate and distinct times and spaces – allows all of these writers to formulate different relations with the past.

The translational practice that turns history and the past into something new is made explicit in Agnant's *Le livre d'Emma*. The text portrays the deterministic force of the past but also stages – in Flore's acts of translation – a self-positioning with respect to past events and identity scripts. For Flore, such acts of choice offer forms of agency and freedom that are based on respect for – but also re/cognition of – the past. In *La dot de Sara*, Agnant shows how resistance can be directed against oral or marginalized knowledge not only by normative instances, but also by a second generation that has lost its connection with such knowledge. This disruption is also examined in the works by Chariandy and Alexis that I have discussed. All of these works are defined, however, by their engagement with a past that is an inevitable part of the present.

Le livre d'Emma, more specifically, shares with many of the other works a dual impulse. The novel posits the importance of a past that is marked by the dislocations of the middle passage and the legacies of slavery, but that also evokes a nourishing communality arising from that historical experience. This defining communality is deplored but is also understood as a potential source of strength and affirmation. Agnant's translator, like Aminata in Hill's novel, respects but also transforms the past's hold on the present. Similarly, we have seen Elizete build on and transform the stories of Adela that are transmitted to her, while Bola becomes the matriarch of a diasporic lineage founded on the disruptive violence that has determined her mother's life.

Lorena Gale's *Angélique* stages acts of witnessing and re-parses the "sentence of history" to foster transformation. The play's bold assertion that "Then is Now. Now is Then" (7) affirms that the often comforting separation between present, past, and future does not hold – an insistence it shares with works by Brand, Agnant, and Hill, and by George Elliott Clarke, Austin Clarke, and Marlene NourbeSe Philip. In whatever modality the insight in the presence of the past is cast – as witnessing, haunting, the perseverance of curses, or the magic realist commingling of the living with the dead – the temporalities created by these works want to have a word with Western narratives of progress. They expose, defamiliarize, and critique perspectives that facilitate obliviousness to the violence, dislocations, and exploitation of slavery and that forget their consequences as foundational realities of the Americas. These consequences have not entirely gone missing from historical accounts, but they have routinely been sealed off and packaged as resolved and safely contained in the past. In contrast to these tendencies to devalue the history of the black Atlantic and its constitutive role for the Americas, these works offer counter-narratives and alternative temporalities that stress, not the passing of time, but its accumulation in the present.

Other works, as we have seen, look to the black Canadian nineteenth century for ancestors. They ensure that this crucial aspect of Canadian history comes to life again and remains present in cultural discussion. These texts rework dominant perceptions and projections of both time and space. Whether one looks at the narratives that come out of Caribbean Canadian experiences, that reflect on the Africadian past and present, or that draw on the cross-border realities of the black Canadian nineteenth century, the wider counter-connectivity of the black Atlantic is present in all of these texts and their geographies and temporalities. In these works, the trade routes and realities of empire and the black Atlantic traverse and co-constitute what is now Canada. At the same time, the spaces and places of Canada become visible parts and nodes of the black Atlantic.

Other Canadian geographical and historical contexts have been recognized and reconstituted in contemporary black Canadian texts as antecedents, or blueprints, for the present and the future. Like the texts discussed so far, the works explored in chapter 5 incite cultural history to listen to the signals of contemporary black writing and its recuperation of black pasts and achievements.

5

Other Black Canadas

The diversity of black Canadian writing is underlined by contemporary authors who re/cognize other – specifically Canadian – regional histories as antecedents. Building on previous chapters, I will now explore some of these contexts. I will begin by adding to the Haitian story several other dimensions of black Montreal, moving from the city's early history (where we have witnessed Angélique's fate) to the beginnings of a more substantial anglophone black community in the late nineteenth century. Connections between diaspora and jazz will then appear in a discussion of Montreal jazz legends such as (Caribbean-descended) Oscar Peterson and Oliver Jones. I will also tell the story of a certain "blackening" of Quebec in its literature with the appearance of Montreal emotional geographies that have had no place in the classical literary portraits of the city.

The texts discussed in the following section on Africville and the Africadian Renaissance produce similarly (re)visionary effects. I touch again on the work of one of its contributing facilitators, George Elliott Clarke, and look at a host of other writers and cultural workers relevant to this particular context. In two concluding sections, I will first consider texts by Cheryl Foggo, Claire Harris, and Esi Edugyan that exemplify the diversity of black prairies writing and will then explore black British Columbia in particular through the work of Wayde Compton. These sections help to demonstrate further how transnational networks have traversed locally situated black writing in Canada. Moreover, the case studies of black anglophone Montreal and Wayde Compton's work highlight the impact of black musics in this context. The selections of case studies, authors, and works in this chapter require the obvious caveat – pertinent also to previous chapters – that they can hardly be exhaustive and have been governed by the relevance of these works to the main threads of the discussion; their number could have been substantially augmented in a longer study. While I have chosen what I think are some of the most important contexts, they, too, could easily be multiplied – and hopefully will be in future studies.[1]

I will begin, then, with Montreal's black anglophone community and jazz. The community originated towards the end of the nineteenth century in connection with railroad networks that brought increasing numbers of porters and redcaps to the city who eventually settled there. A good number of the black jazz musicians who later signalled the ascent of Montreal jazz, such as Steep Wade, Oscar Peterson, and Oliver Jones, came from railroad worker families. I will survey the (lack of) representation of these musicians' black Montreal neighbourhood in canonical Canadian novels and will then focus on Mairuth Sarsfield's portrayal of this locality in *No Crystal Stair* (1997). Like many of the texts I discuss, this novel articulates a local geography but finds resources in wider transnational black contexts, past works, and events.

THE BLACKENING OF QUEBEC: JAZZ, DIASPORA, AND THE HISTORY AND WRITING OF BLACK ANGLOPHONE MONTREAL

On 30 June 2009, Montreal jazz pianist Oliver Jones and singer Ranee Lee opened the thirtieth Montreal Jazz Festival in its new venue, L'Astral. After a premature retirement, Jones was returning to a festival that his presence had graced from its second year in 1981. His importance as a citizen of Montreal and a member of its black community, however, easily exceeds such widely advertised events. In April 2007, Jones headlined a benefit concert that was attended by Daisy Peterson, his former piano teacher. Due to illness, her brother Oscar – that other Montreal jazz legend – was represented by a large photograph on stage. The concert was a fundraiser to help reopen the former Negro Community Centre (NCC), founded in 1927, whose mission had been to "alleviate social and economic conditions among Blacks in Montreal" (NCC).[2] Oliver Jones had spent much of his time there as a child. Now he was back for a benefit that served as a vivid reminder of the strong, ongoing presence of one of Montreal's oldest black communities. The beginnings of this black anglophone community date back to the late nineteenth century. It was preceded by earlier blacks in Montreal such as the "oldtimers" of the Underground Railroad and, as we have already seen, the black slaves of Montreal.

The evening's celebration of black musical traditions, institutions, and community history evoked Montreal and Quebec cultural geographies that are rarely present in a wider public imaginary. In her 1984 memoir *Growing Up Black in Canada*, Carol Talbot uses the term "folk geography" to speak about "the 'felt' geography of a particular group [that] can indicate significant factors which will not be revealed by an orthodox scientific approach" (1984, 19). Cultural geographers such as Joyce Davidson and Christine Milligan have explored such "emotional geographies" in their field (Davidson and Milligan 2004, 523–32), and Katherine McKittrick (2006) employs the same approach in her discussion of Angélique. There are now many black communities in Montreal – such as the aforementioned Haitian diaspora – that have found literary expression and, in some cases, significant francophone reception. The pre-1960s black geographies of Quebec, however, have rarely been imagined with the depth that fiction could bring to their emotional contours. Canadian classics set in this space and time either elide such emotional geographies or treat them problematically. Pierre Nepveu's remark in his *Lecture des lieux* remains pertinent: "Lire Montréal, ce pourrait être, par exemple, raconter son histoire et réinventer en particulier son commencement" (2004, 49; "To read Montreal could mean, for instance, to tell its history and reinvent in particular its beginning").[3] Or perhaps one could say that it is time to wake up, not so much from the dream of the nineteenth century, as in Walter Benjamin's *Arcades Project*, but from the images of Montreal that were part of the national dream to finally put Canada and Quebec on the map against European and US cultures. This dream was partially realized by some of the most important novels of the mid-twentieth century, but the priorities and necessities of that dream and "the hoary battles of the national epic" (Simon 2006, 7) have eclipsed the more complex realities that have now come to the fore in more recent texts that afford other perspectives.

Black Spaces/White Novels: Hugh MacLennan, Gabrielle Roy, and Morley Callaghan

While I will briefly examine earlier moments, my main focus here is the period from the 1920s to the 1950s that included Montreal's jazz age. This era of the city's history was heavily marked by black cultural contributions that seem to be non-existent or at best problematic in Montreal geographies afforded by literary texts about the period. Consider, for example, three of the great canonical novels about 1940s and 1950s Montreal: Hugh

MacLennan's *Two Solitudes* (1945), Gabrielle Roy's *Bonheur d'occasion* (1945; translated as *The Tin Flute* [1947]), and Morley Callaghan's *The Loved and the Lost* (1951). MacLennan's *Two Solitudes* is a sweeping portrait of Quebec between the wars that also claims to reimagine Canadian national space. Montreal, Canada's most important city at the time, serves MacLennan in the first pages as a metonymic microcosm of modern industrial Canada, with its social and ideological practices governed by linguistic difference. Within this space, MacLennan writes, "two old races" meet, continuing to use an older nomenclature still evident in later documents (such as in the report of the Royal Commission on Bilingualism and Biculturalism in the 1960s),[4] in which the term refers to the anglophone and francophone white settlers of Canada respectively: "Two old races and religions meet here and live their separate legends, side by side. If this sprawling half-continent has a heart, here it is. Its pulse throbs out along the rivers and railroads; slow, reluctant and rarely simple, a double beat, a self-moved reciprocation" (2). The Quebec countryside of *Two Solitudes* is home to francophone agricultural labourers, working the fields for the inheritors of the seigneurial regime and under the ultramontane Catholic clergy. Montreal is the site of the francophone working poor and an anglophone industrial and merchant capital that reaches deep and aggressively into the traditional structures of the surrounding countryside for ever more resources of capital accumulation. But while the "two races" in Quebec, and specifically in Montreal, are charted in the Canadian national space that MacLennan weaves out of personal and "emotional geographies" (Davidson and Milligan 2004, 523), non-white characters remain invisible.

This is also the case in another "classic" portrait of Montreal that, like MacLennan's novel, appeared in 1945: Gabrielle Roy's *Bonheur d'occasion*. The absence here is particularly striking given that Roy's setting is more specifically working-class Saint-Henri in southwest Montreal – the home of a small but growing black community since the end of the nineteenth century. After arriving from Manitoba (via Europe) in 1939, Roy had taken a deep interest in Montreal as a meeting place of diasporas. For *Le bulletin des agriculteurs*, she wrote a series of reportages, entitled "Tout Montréal," that took note of the city's cosmopolitan population. Yet by the time she came to pen her portrayal of francophone working-class life in Saint-Henri, those signs of a multiracial Montreal were gone.[5] True, when Roy's protagonist Florentine Lacasse is invited to a party in a house on Place George-Étienne Cartier,[6] one of the quarter's prestigious addresses, a turn of the radio knob suddenly fills the room with "un air de jazz, furieux, à grands éclats de saxophone" (136).[7] The younger generation opts to dance, embracing swing as do so many white bands at the time. The originators of this music, though, are identified only when M. Létourneau, a member of the parents' generation and a "marchand d'objets de piété, d'ornements et de vin eucharistique" (133),[8] inquires pejoratively, "Qu'est-ce que c'est que cette danse de nègres?" (137).[9]

Roy's focus in the novel is Montreal's francophone working class, especially its women; even so, it is striking how she renders invisible another universe that existed at the same time in the same Montreal neighbourhood. Oscar Peterson grew up just a very short distance from this neighbourhood, drawing public attention from 1942 onward as a black musician in one of Montreal's popular white swing bands. Place Saint-Henri, at the very centre of the universe described by Roy, served as inspiration for his eponymous composition that became part of his *Canadiana Suite* (1964). The trains that continuously crossed Saint-Henri certainly loom large in Roy's novel, but she is more preoccupied with their noise and the coal dust they shower on the neighbourhood than with their travellers and destinations – or with the black porters and redcaps whose lives were as interwoven with North America's railroad networks as they were a part of Saint-Henri. Later, in 1955, in rendering her Saint-Boniface childhood context in the vaguely autobiographical stories of *Rue Deschambault* (*Street of Riches*, 1957), Roy writes about the black porters who boarded at her parents' and neighbours' houses. In "Les deux nègres," she notes her subjects' love of music; one of them is assigned to the Montreal–Halifax run, thus fleetingly evoking the city and neighbourhood that Roy portrays a few years earlier in such detail but without its black residents.

Black Montreal features prominently in Morley Callaghan's *The Loved and the Lost* (1951). The novel contrasts the affluent Westmount district with the rest of Montreal, describing the former as "a rock of riches with poverty sprawling around the rock" (166). Within this particular geography, the black jazz milieu of the Saint Antoine district is presented as the "other," dark side – and ultimately the downfall – of the white hero's quest for wealth and social standing in Westmount.[10] Black jazz, although an important theme here, ultimately serves as the background for a white character's unsuccessful search for meaning. Black Montreal and its music hold an ambivalent place in the novel; they may appear to threaten the social order, yet they hint at a utopian chronotope of otherness and interracial possibility. In any case, the perceptions of Callaghan's protagonist remain caught in primitivist stereotypes:

> Music came from the ground-floor open window, the music of a cello and a piano, and he could see three figures, one a Negro at a piano, another, who looked like a French Canadian, at the cello, and the third figure, the face hidden, was bending over the piano. The piano and the cello achieved an hypnotic effect in primitive counterpoint, repeating a simple theme over and over with curious discords; but it was the posture, the attitudes of the musicians as they played their solitary theme that held him spellbound: the cello twanged, the piano repeated the minor chords with a little variation, the musicians were held in their strange rapture, and there was nothing in the world for them but the lonely little theme and that one room in the cold night and their own intensity. (57)

Perhaps the figure with the hidden face is the place-holder for a position that Callaghan's protagonist considers to be his. The image conveys social intimacy even while withholding the readability of the face. The protagonist remains in the position of an observer. In Jim McAlpine's assertion of himself as Emersonian "independent man" and his quest for innocence – connoted repeatedly with the colour white in the novel – black Saint Antoine is used as background. Callaghan is "playing in the dark"; the neighbourhood and its blackness become here a space for what Toni Morrison calls the "projection of the not-me" and a "playground for the imagination" containing "a fabricated brew of darkness, otherness, alarm, and desire" that *pace* Morrison is *not* "uniquely American" (1990, 38). In *The Loved and the Lost*, blackness is construed along stereotypical significations, portrayed as exotic and ultimately as potentially murderous and destructive otherness.[11] The novel can therefore hardly convey a sense of Montreal and the Saint Antoine district as the home of everyday black lives that have long been part and parcel of the city and its history. We must look elsewhere for perspectives that bring black geographies and lives to the fore, and that heed Nepveu's injunction that "to read Montreal could mean … to tell its history and reinvent in particular its beginning."

Of Railroads, Trains, and Jazz: The Beginnings of the Black Anglophone Montreal Community

We have already looked at slavery in New France and Lower Canada and at its demise via the courts. On 1 August 1834, black Montrealers congregated to celebrate the abolition of slavery in the British Empire (Mackey 2004, 92–6). French Canada, and Montreal in particular, became Underground Railroad destinations, although the numbers of blacks coming across the border were much smaller than in Upper Canada. The slave narrative of Lavina Wormeny, as mentioned in chapter 3, is reported in the *Montreal Gazette* in January 1861. An earlier case has been minutely reconstructed by Gary Collison in *Shadrach Minkins: From Fugitive Slave to Citizen* (1997). Collison uses census slips, city directories, newspaper accounts, and other sources to document a slave's escape from Norfolk, Virginia, to Montreal. Despite spotty documentary evidence, Collison offers interesting conjectures about the size of Montreal's black community at the time: "But just how many African-Americans joined Shadrach Minkins in Montreal, or where they came from, is unclear. Although the *Gazette* argued that there were more than four hundred, the published census of 1861 indicated only 46 Black residents. Manuscript census slips, however, show 228, and since this figure almost certainly represents an undercounting, the actual numbers may have been fairly close to the *Gazette* estimate" (Collison 1997, 206).

Interestingly, by 1860 Shadrach Minkins had moved from the old city to what was then – and still is in Callaghan's novel – the Saint Antoine district in Montreal's southwest.[12] At the end of the nineteenth century, a larger black community began to develop there. From the 1920s onward, the area became one of the crucial geographies for the development of Montreal jazz. Just to the south, by the second half of the nineteenth century, the Lachine Canal emerged as the heart of Canada's industrial heartland: "iron works, flour mills, the Chemical and India Rubber Works, the Oil and Colour Works, the Candle Works, and the Canada Marine Works, among others" (Collison 1997, 205).[13] Canals extended the water routes that marked Canada's early economy so intensely. The Lachine Canal – the realization of dreams that had already developed under the French regime and an invaluable asset in controlling the Great Lakes trade and the hinterland – opened in 1825, the same year as the competing Erie Canal. It was built to circumvent the Lachine Rapids, which, since the days of Jacques Cartier and the search for Cathay,[14] had been a barrier and the final stop for ships sailing up the St Lawrence. In many ways, the rapids and the efforts to circumvent them "explain Montreal" (Desloges and Gelly 2002, 9). Part of a century-long international "canal craze" (9), the Lachine Canal allowed the more rapid transportation of goods. After 1846, it provided hydraulic power for flour and saw mills, grain elevators, foundries, nail factories, and other industries, while from 1893 onward it also provided electricity (129). The canal attracted numerous industries that together would become the centre of industrial Canada of the time.

Yet soon after they were built, the canals had to compete with railways as the most effective conveyors of goods and people. A few years after the Champlain and St Lawrence Railroad (Canada's first railway) was completed in 1836, the Montreal and Lachine Railroad was inaugurated in 1847 to bypass the Lachine Rapids – although it could not compete with the lower freight rates on the Lachine Canal (Tulchinsky 1977, 172). The twelve-kilometre track was soon incorporated into a large network of lines connecting Montreal to the western hinterland and to the Atlantic seaboard (Tulchinsky 1977, 127–200). A generation later, after the railways began hiring blacks as redcaps and porters – occupations that became one of the few reliable sources of income for black Montrealers – a larger black community began to develop in the Saint Antoine district. By the late 1850s, the Grand Trunk Railway connected Montreal with Toronto and Chicago (D.W. Williams 1997, 32); by the 1880s, the American Pullman Palace Car Company, the Grand Trunk Railway, and the Canadian Pacific Railway were employing black sleeping car porters, with the latter company doing so directly out of Montreal (Calliste 1987, 2; D.W. Williams 1997, 32–3). At first, many of these porters used Montreal only as a temporary home because of immigration restrictions (D.W. Williams 1997, 33). After this, the "period between 1897 and 1930 … marked the beginning of a genuine black community in Montreal. Major institutions such as the Union United Church (Union) in 1907, the Universal Negro Improvement Association (UNIA) in 1919, and the Negro Community Centre (NCC) in 1927 were established" (D.W. Williams 1997, 38). These landmark institutions, so crucial for the development of Montreal's black community, are often overlooked in the city's history.

The black community contributed in various ways to another important chapter of Montreal history – the development of jazz – although the acceptance of that musical genre by the community was hardly smooth. Many parents preferred lessons in classical music for their children. Some aspects of jazz and the associated show culture were often met with suspicion and rejection by respectable members of the community, in large part because of jazz's association with alcohol. While prohibition in the United States lasted from 1920 to 1933, Nancy Marrelli notes that "Quebec was the last Canadian province to get prohibition in 1918 and it was the first to repeal it, in 1919" (2004, 14). As Dorothy Williams remarks, this made Montreal attractive for many: "as a result of Prohibition, Montreal was *the* place to be"

(1997, 44). Prohibition favoured the development of jazz in Montreal: "From the 1920s until the early 1950s Montreal had an international reputation as a glamorous wide open city with a lively nightlife" (Marrelli 2004, 9). In his history of Montreal jazz, John Gilmore notes that "work for musicians was plentiful" (1988, 43). Many of the bands and venues, however, were exclusively white. Marrelli offers the following racial geography of Montreal jazz from the 1920s to the early 1950s:

> The Montreal club scene was one of complex race, class, and language relations, as well as territorial boundaries. The "downtown" clubs were on St-Antoine street, where many blacks lived because it was close to the railways where many of the men worked as porters ... There was an active music scene in the black community, although there was a long history of discrimination in the unions until the early 1940s, and mixed black and white bands were not common. At various times it was trendy to have black musicians and black shows, particularly in east-end clubs, but all-white policies were the rule in hotels and were common for uptown clubs in the early years. The downtown clubs usually had black musicians and entertainers and their patron policies were wide open. That's where you could almost always find great music, and it was where other musicians went to "jam" after their shows in theaters or clubs in other parts of town. (2004, 10–11)

Gilmore chronicles, after some earlier black entertainers, a "second wave of black musicians who had heard tales about the exciting city and ventured north ... By the end of the decade [the 1920s], it had drenched Montreal with talent and with the sounds of the latest black music" (1988, 43). Together with these musicians from elsewhere, home-grown talent like the pianists Steep Wade, Oscar Peterson, Oliver Jones, Joe Sealy,[15] and Milt Sealey (see M. Miller 2001, 178–9) – all sons of railway employees – became part of Montreal jazz history.

Steep Wade, Oscar Peterson, Jazz at "The Corner" – and Union United Church, the Negro Community Centre, and the UNIA

Particularly fascinating and influential – if historically elusive – is Steep Wade. Even though there are no recordings of his saxophone playing and very few of him on piano,[16] his influence on pianists like Peterson, Sealey,

Jones, and others is a matter of record. Born in Montreal in 1918, he began as an alto saxophonist and played with the Canadian Ambassadors, the "most successful of Canada's few black jazz bands active during the 1930s" (M. Miller 2001, 37). While his lifestyle brought him notoriety, he gained musical fame as the pianist for the mixed-race International Band from 1947 to 1949 (see Gilmore 1988, 141–54; M. Miller 2001, 207). This formation was led by Louis Metcalf, a trumpeter who had previously played with Duke Ellington, Jelly Roll Morton, and King Oliver in New York. They became the first band to try bebop on Montreal audiences. This incursion took place during their 1947–50 residency at the Café St Michel (Gilmore 1988, 115–40; M. Miller 2001, 136). This club and Rockhead's Paradise across the street became "The Corner," the internationally known headquarters of black Montreal jazz.[17]

This was where Oscar Peterson fell under the spell of Steep Wade. While still a teenager, Peterson had listened to Wade, among other musicians, at Rockhead's and was occasionally asked by him to fill in: "They used to sneak me in because I was under age at the time. Steep used to call me 'kid.' On different nights when he used to go for a walk or listen to someone else's music, he'd say 'Okay, kid, go on and play the show for me. I'll be back.' That's where I really served my jazz apprenticeship – in that environment" (Lees 1988, 42). At the Café St Michel as well, late at night after performing with his own trio at the Alberta Lounge between 1948 and 1950, Peterson listened to Wade and sat in with the Metcalf International Band to familiarize himself with bebop; later he would identify Wade as his "favourite pianist" (M. Miller 2001, 127). According to legend, Peterson's engagement at the Alberta Lounge (near the CPR's Windsor station) led to his appearance at Carnegie Hall and subsequent international career (Gilmore 1988, 109–10).

Peterson's career is part of jazz history. But his life, like that of Steep Wade and Oliver Jones, is also intricately linked to the black anglophone community in southwest Montreal, including institutions such as the Union United Church, the Negro Community Centre, and the Universal Negro Improvement Association. Peterson was born in 1925 next to the Union United Church on Delisle Street and was later married there (Lees 1988, 22). Oliver Jones played his first public boogie-woogie at one of the church's events when he was five years old (Sansregret 2005, 30). One day, across Atwater Avenue in Little Burgundy, Jones heard beautiful music through an open window and knocked at a door, which happened to be Peterson's. That is how, at the Negro Community Centre, Jones became one of

Daisy Peterson's students – she also taught her brother Oscar and Joe Sealy. In 1954, that centre moved to Coursol Street, where Jones was born, but he grew up on the intersecting Fulford Street (now called George Vanier), where the UNIA's Liberty Hall was located. While these locations are in what is now called Little Burgundy, for Jones they were all part of Saint-Henri: "I grew up in Saint-Henri," he confirmed during the intermission of a concert by Keith Jarrett at the 2007 Montreal Jazz Festival (a few days later, Jones would play the festival's closing concert). Jones's personal geography thus unites under that name of Saint-Henri the experiences of his childhood and a network of connections and lives that were part of Montreal's oldest substantial black community. The area roughly coincides with what was earlier called the Saint Antoine district; as the historian Dorothy Williams writes, it was "synonymous with the growth of the black community in the southwest core of the city of Montreal" (1997, 36–7).

We are fortunate to have documents such as Dorothy Williams's history and other accounts of wider segments of that community.[18] Jazz historians such as John Gilmore, Mark Miller, and Nancy Marrelli, together with a number of documentaries (e.g., *In the Key of Oscar*, *Oliver Jones in Africa*, *Crossroads – Three Jazz Pianists*, and *Show Girls*) have delineated aspects of the more public, visible, and audible side of black Montreal represented by jazz. Oliver Jones and the singer Ranee Lee still perform in Montreal. Recordings of Oscar Peterson, bassist Charlie Biddle, guitarist Nelson Symonds, and others form part of the unique musical and cultural contributions of that community. But strangely enough, as noted above, the community's presence has remained all but unheralded in literary portraits of Montreal.

Mairuth Sarsfield's No Crystal Stair *and Jazz*

One text that does focus on the black community of southwest Montreal of that era is Mairuth Sarsfield's historical novel *No Crystal Stair* (1997).[19] Opening in the spring of 1942, it is set – like Roy's *Bonheur d'occasion* and parts of MacLennan's *Two Solitudes* – against the background of the Second World War. With Callaghan's *The Loved and the Lost* (1951), it shares not just the city or – as with Roy's novel – the larger neighbourhood, but often the very streets and a subject crucial to both works: black Montreal jazz. While black Montreal and its culture serve as enabling background for white trajectories in Callaghan's novel, Sarsfield, by contrast, places black Montreal culture at the novel's centre, unfolds its inner workings and contradictions, and explores how it relates to other cultural groups. Musical and to some extent literary traditions are key to Sarsfield's project.

In Sarsfield's Montreal, many diasporas and cultures meet.[20] Black Montreal is itself international and heterogeneous. The novel's cast includes black characters from the Caribbean and the United States; it features fictive and historical participants in the Harlem Renaissance and famous black exiles who lived in Europe between the wars. Earlier black history in Quebec is evoked through references to slavery in Quebec City and the events surrounding Angélique in Montreal (86), while black Nova Scotian history surfaces briefly with the Jamaican Maroons shipped to Nova Scotia and the exodus of black settlers from there to Sierra Leone (87). A number of diasporic connections come up in regard to the protagonist's work environment (she works at the Westmount YMCA), yet at the novel's centre is the black community of the Saint Antoine district and its institutions: the UNIA, the Marcus Garvey Debating Society, and the Union United Church, a focal point of the community from the time of its founding in 1907 by railroad porters.[21] Dorothy Williams notes that in "the heyday of the UNIA in Montreal (1919–1928), people attended Union Church in the morning and UNIA social activities at Liberty Hall in the afternoon" that often featured a "focus on Pan-Africanism" (1997, 61). Sarsfield also refers variously to the Coloured Ladies Club (5 and passim),[22] Asa Philip Randolph's Brotherhood of Sleeping Car Porters union, the importance of the railway as purveyor of employment – and ultimately their connection with Montreal jazz.

Directly or indirectly, the railway influencs the lives of most of Sarsfield's black characters, connected as they are with work- and community-related aspects of black Montreal such as unions and, in particular, Garveyism. Marion Willow, the novel's protagonist, is the widow of a railroad redcap who was a McGill dentistry student. At "a Back to Africa rally in the old UNIA hall on Fulford Street" (Sarsfield 1997, 24), she meets Edmond Thompson, a Guyanese chemist turned Montreal railroad porter. Like him, she participates in the Marcus Garvey Debating Society. Thompson's attitudes reflect a dual strategy that was the choice of many Montreal porters at the time. In Marion Willow's thinking, "Above all, he was a true Garveyite. He believed, like she did, in the need for self-sufficiency for Black folks" (146). At the same time, however, this very Garveyite porter urges "his cricket-playing teammates … to join the American J. [*sic*] Phillip [*sic*] Randolph Movement to form a Pullman porters' union" (22). Randolph's racial integrationism stood in stark contrast to the self-segregation advocated by Garvey.[23] As Dorothy Williams points out, Garvey's anti-union message – strengthened by union racism and the very slow acceptance of blacks by many unions[24] – did not convince blacks in Montreal: "By the mid-thirties, Randolph was embraced and honoured by all but the staunchest Garveyites in Montreal" (1997, 59).[25] Sarsfield thus evokes accurately the contradictions – and also the productive transfigurations – of Garveyism in Montreal.

A comparable double strategy of black self-reliance and integration is adumbrated in Sarsfield's portrayal of jazz and the role of Oscar Peterson within it. The novel features the legendary Rockhead's Paradise and the Café St Michel at "The Corner," a location that is glossed here as the centre of "the nightlife around Montreal's Mountain Street, with its jazz entertainers and brown-skinned chorus girls imported from New York's Harlem. Both nightclubs were owned by former railway porters who, gossip contended, had made their initial nest eggs rum-running, in the decade when Prohibition in the United States made smuggling liquor across the border profitable" (Sarsfield 1997, 58).[26] Besides writers and entertainers from the United States (e.g., Langston Hughes, Sammy Davis, Jr), a number of Montreal musicians are mentioned, including Steep Wade (73, 142), Lou Hooper (137), Maynard Ferguson (135), Paul de Marky (137), and Johnny Holmes. What these musicians had in common was their connection with the Peterson family, and Daisy Peterson Sweeney and Oscar Peterson both appear briefly in the novel.[27] Given Sarsfield's dual strategy of emphasizing both black strength and lively interaction across racial boundaries, it is not coincidental that a longer passage staging a discussion of tradition and influence in terms of black cultural specificity turns around Oscar Peterson.

Peterson was trained in both classical and jazz piano. One of his important early solo concerts, at the Majesty's Theatre in Montreal in 1946 when he was age twenty, featured both classical and jazz pieces (Gilmore 1988, 107). From 1942 onward, Peterson played with the Johnny Holmes Orchestra – usually as its only black musician, which led to a few racist incidents.[28] Peterson continued to play in mixed bands throughout his career.[29] At the same time, he remained an icon of black Montreal's culture and community, which he credited with his success; at one point in his autobiography, *A Jazz Odyssey* (2002), he emphasizes the formative roles that the UNIA and Marcus Garvey's visit to Montreal played in his career.[30] This endorsement of a black cultural leader mostly associated with black nationalism might be surprising, but it hardly minimized Peterson's integrationist stance, illuminated strikingly by the dedication of one of his best-known compositions, "Hymn to Freedom," to Martin Luther King, Jr.[31]

In Sarsfield's *No Crystal Stair*, an early Oscar Peterson concert with the Johnny Holmes Orchestra – probably in the fall of 1942[32] – gives rise to a heated post-concert discussion among a racially mixed group of participants (135–9, 141–2). The debate mostly concerns influences on Peterson's style and pitches his right-hand arpeggio technique against his left-hand bass work. Affinities with Liszt[33] and Rubinstein strike a white commentator as significant; a black observer, however, sees Peterson as more "influenced by Duke Ellington's mastery of harmonic chords" and insists, "It's a soul thing" (141). This latter stance rejects recognition on the basis of whiteness as a norm. Emphasizing aspects of Peterson's technique that seem comparable to those of famous white musicians prevents a re–cognition of artistic possibility and excellence, eclipsing the specificity that makes Peterson's style different. Whiteness here "constitutes itself as a universal set of norms by which to make sense of the world" (Fiske 1994, 42; qtd in Lewis 2004, 140).[34] In the words of Sarsfield's character, "Here we go again: Ole Whitey's discovered him, so he must be for real" (Sarsfield, 1997, 142).

In this musicological debate staged by Sarsfield, the denial of difference is thus met by an insistence that Peterson's music expresses "race spirituality." This claim is countered in turn by a two-step protest: "You can't deny the European influence. Music doesn't have boundaries." The first statement is accurate in Peterson's case. The second seems a simple reiteration, yet in fact it denies difference and any kind of social aesthetics. Another character objects: "Yes, it does, and until Europe acknowledges the influence of jazz on its culture, there's no dialogue" (142).[35]

Significantly, this protest is voiced not by a black participant in the debate, but by a white Jewish woman. The discussion here switches to the issue of "passing," another important issue in the novel (Wegmann-Sánchez 2001, 147–54). Of the two women present, one is of mixed Russian and black Caribbean descent and passes as white, while the other is Jewish Canadian. Both women feel constrained to "pass" by dissimulating their "ethnic" names at work to fit in socially and professionally – Marushka and Sarita becoming Maria and Sara (142–3). The novel thus connects prejudicial pressures on racial and ethnic identities that lead to passing with the "whitening" of black jazz through forms of re/cognition that reaffirm Eurocentric vantage points. The insistence on black jazz as a constitutive element in

North American culture and on a "dialogue," by contrast, implies multiple vantage points and traditions.

Yet the novel goes out of its way to emphasize *as well* the influence of European music on Peterson's style, and it certainly does not deny cross-cultural influence. Similar issues are raised by some of the novel's intertextualities as well as by its theme of reading itself. Beginning with the title, which cites Langston Hughes's poem "Mother to Son" and its call for perseverance against harsh odds, the novel references a "Who's Who" of black culture, including, in addition to those already named, not only musicians and entertainers such as the Fisk Jubilee Singers, Bessie Smith, Cab Calloway, Duke Ellington, Sammy Davis Jr, Josephine Baker, and Paul Robeson, but also writers such as Frederick Douglass, W.E.B. Du Bois, Claude McKay, and Frantz Fanon. Some of the writers appear in an impassioned discussion about education, during which Marion Willow realizes that her bookish daughter's voracious reading of British and other white literature should be balanced by readings from the black tradition. *Anne of Green Gables*, however, also holds a special place in the novel; the daughter blasts an unfortunate playmate with "There's no poetry in your soul" (16), worries about the absence of "a kindred soul" (17), bemoans her plight as a demi-orphan (21), and reads *Rilla of Ingleside* (30). Sarsfield's novel focuses on the wealth of black geographies and traditions in Montreal while relying, at the same time, on intertextualities that are at least "double-voiced" (Gates 1988, xxiii), as demonstrated by its repeated references to the black tradition and the Harlem Renaissance but also to Lucy Maud Montgomery. A related strategy pertains, as we have seen, to the novel's discussion of jazz.

In Sarsfield's portrait of black Montreal culture of the 1940s, jazz is only one element – albeit a highly visible one. It constitutes a specific and remarkable contribution (among many) to Montreal history and culture. The debate about different cultural specificities and their dialogues takes on a wider meaning in that context. Evoking black jazz as a community-specific and culturally rooted yet cross-culturally receptive and influential matrix, Sarsfield's novel is relevant for its reimagining of the multiple emotional and imaginary geographies that constitute Montreal's history. This is underscored by the historical depth of the community it portrays. Jazz is a visible and audible sign of that community, whose rooted history is intertwined with the founding of modern Montreal in the nineteenth century and its earlier black history, which the novel cites back to Angélique and slavery in Montreal (86).

The role of black performers – and here, particularly, of Oscar Peterson – in Montreal jazz serves Sarsfield in her portrayal of black diasporic geographies as integral to Montreal and to Canadian culture. The novel stages an interculturally active version of multiculturalism, although black self-reliance and Garveyism play at least equally important roles. *No Crystal Stair* thus outlines a dual strategy. Instead of pitting opposite options against each other by insisting on *either* black nationalism *or* integration, it pursues multiple possibilities by emphasizing both black culture and its intercultural or transcultural options. The novel thus stages a "rooted cosmopolitanism" (Appiah 2005, 213–72) that rests in a culturally specific, grounded openness.

No Crystal Stair is part of a wider group of texts that make anglophone black Montreal come alive in literature. Also set in Little Burgundy is Ernest Tucker's 2006 crime novel *Lost Boundaries*, in which a black lawyer crosses racial boundaries in the name of justice, while his anglophone mother, very worried about the announcement of a referendum, seeks to solve the same murder case in her own way. Nigel Thomas's *Behind the Face of Winter* (2001), a Caribbean immigrant's coming-of-age story, is set in 1980s Montreal outside of Little Burgundy, but refers to the displacement of blacks from this neighbourhood by the new Ville-Marie Expressway (115). Little Burgundy is also home to his mother's congregation, which had "come to Canada looking for green pastures beside still waters; the Lachine Canal bordering their warehouse church was still enough" (184). In Tessa McWatt's novel *Out of My Skin* (1998), a black woman searches for her family history and discovers Montreal during the Oka standoff in 1990.[36] Cecil Foster has dedicated a chapter of his non-fiction *A Place Called Heaven: The Meaning of Being Black in Canada* to black suburban life in Montreal's Parc Agrignon; he has also been at work on a novel involving Montreal, the railroads, and jazz.[37] And George Elliott Clarke – whose jazz opera *Québécité* (2003) is provocatively set in Quebec City, one of the whitest cities in Canada, and whose Trudeau in the eponymous 2007 jazz opera is a regular at bassist Charlie Biddle's nightclub in Montreal – features plenty of jazz in *George & Rue* (2005b). Montreal appears here as the "fabulous Montreal" (18) that is Cynthy's black Nova Scotian dream getaway (18–23 passim), but is also the site of George's wartime enlistment and eventual jailing (75–82), remembered as "a burgh of cops and jail" (84). These often jazz-inflected black anglophone Montreals are joined, of course, by the much larger corpus in French that was discussed earlier.[38] All of these writers' heterogeneous black diasporic Montreals invite multiple rereadings of the city (a project that Pierre Nepveu and Gilles Marcotte's *Montréal imaginaire*, Nepveu's *Lecture des lieux*, and Sherry Simon's *Translating Montreal* have advanced in other respects). Together with Sarsfield's *No Crystal Stair* – or Oliver Jones's championing of community renewal through present-day musical interventions – they reinscribe black diasporas and local lives into the literary emotional geographies of Montreal.

AFRICVILLE AND THE AFRICADIAN RENAISSANCE

Restorative and interventionist cultural work has been the hallmark of the "Africadian" Renaissance.[39] Much of George Elliott Clarke's archival work has helped in the retrieval of earlier black Nova Scotian voices, brought together with contemporary Africadian writers in his two-volume *Fire on the Water: An Anthology of Black Nova Scotian Writing*. Clarke also references the black Nova Scotian past in his creative oeuvres from *Saltwater Spirituals* and *Whylah Falls* onwards; at the same time, he points to a "Great Void" (2002a, 109)[40] in Africadian writing after 1798, until a resurgence in the 1970s.

A driving force in this revival and creation of a diverse contemporary Africadian corpus has been the reinscription of the memory of Africville. The black Halifax neighbourhood began as a rural settlement, first documented in the mid-nineteenth century (Clairmont 2010a, 35–7). It was destroyed under the pretext of urban renewal between 1964 and 1970.[41] Insistent cultural memory work by writers, musicians, filmmakers, curators, and other artists has transformed this moment of rupture into a memory site and communal resource for renewed community building. Emphasizing the pattern of rupture and communal new beginnings, Clarke writes that the downfall of Africville resulted in "an upsurge in *national* feeling, pride, which, in turn, demanded a combative assertiveness. This reflex, engendered in the rubble of Africville, can be termed the Africadian Renaissance" (2002a, 117). This shift is facilitated by the active role of artists belonging to an educated "indigenous Black Nova Scotia middle class," who are "self-consciously Black" (Mannette 1990, 4; qtd in G.E. Clarke 2002a, 117). As Moynagh suggests, while "the former residents lacked the institutional resources to win the struggle over Africville, the middle-class artists and intellectuals who began to produce in ever greater numbers in the late 1970s and the early 1980s were gaining access to cultural institutions that enabled them to take up the task of contesting hegemonic representations of African-Nova Scotians" (1998, 19).

The process of the symbolic recuperation of Africville begins with Frederick Ward's *Riverlisp: Black Memories* (1974), a text that draws on conversations with former residents and makes effective use of the vernacular. Ward – *inter alia* an erstwhile student of Oscar Peterson's and a contributor to documentaries on Oliver Jones and other jazz pianists – uses here experimental techniques that include the citation of multiple, direct oral speech. These virtuoso vocal orchestrations have led George Elliott Clarke to compare Ward's style with jazz techniques.[42] At the same time, Clarke suspects that this "difficult" style may have contributed to Ward's hitherto slow reception (G.E. Clarke 2012, 192), and to his "inaudibility, his invisibility in the dull, bland canons of this northern confederacy" (197).

Riverlisp innovates not only with its voicings. Weaving in and out of residents' lives in Riverlisp – a place with recognizable Africville features – Ward also bends that most successful of Canadian genres, the short story cycle, to an oral style.[43] One of the speakers interrogated by the narrator – "just to git his tale" (1974, 13) – speaks about the fate of the local school: "We had our own school – education be important culture, you knows? – til year fore last when th government been cused of segregated schooling. Then they done tore our school down soon after that'" (14).[44] And we follow, through several sections, the fate of a bible-selling, jive-talking Jewish man, Micah Koch, in the midst of the community. This narrative thread mixes comedy with tragedy: "'Go tell you mother … I mean' – Micah's head slightly bowing with each word – 'go tells your mama somebody there to see her.' And to himself: yes, that's it. 'MAMA!' the boy yellin loud, 'THERE A WHITE MAN HERE TO SEE YOU.' And from way back in the house. 'A WHAT?' The man's voice from inside: 'Woman, what you done now?' The boy even louder: 'WHITE MAN!'" (F. Ward 1974, 29). The response of the woman of the house, confronted with Koch's knowledge that she does "not own the words of the Lord" (30), is as theatrically entertaining and linguistically multi-accented as this rendering of the opening encounter.

While the sales visit may have ended in humiliating defeat, we see Koch impress Mama Fuchsia more positively in an episode that tops any of Haliburton's renderings of the clockmaker's efforts: "His liquid words matched the liquid in her heart" (31). Comedy turns to tragedy, however, when Koch falls in love with Purella Munificance. Community vitriol leaves the interracial couple permanently affected, although Mama Fuchsia tempers the evil gossip and brings Koch as a repentant sinner into the black church community. Throughout, as Clarke suggests, *Riverlisp* "is speech – and reports on speech delivered in a spoken way" (2012, 199). In the process, it also offers a fictionalized, quasi-ethnographic account that inscribes memories of Africville, orchestrating and staging stylized speech acts inspired by some of its former residents.

Ward offers several poems that speak explicitly about Africville in his subsequent collection of poems, *The Curing Berry* (1983).[45] In "Dialogue #1: MAMA," we hear the voice of an Africville resident who reflects on "the day they come'd / from room to room I moaned some tween me teeth til moaning / and quiet yelpings be all I had left / Then come'd the knock. Me fear swelled up in me jaws" (F. Ward 1983, 19). While this passage could evoke any gruesome scene plucked from the history of persecution, the very last line of the poem links its Gothic horror to an incident associated with the relocation of the Africville residents: "THEY MOVED ME IN GARBAGE TRUCKS" (19).

Ward's "Dialogue #3: OLD MAN (TO THE SQUATTER)" (1983, 21) demonstrates a process that Moynagh calls the transformation of Africville into "a sign of community and resistance" (1998, 26). The poem shows Africville to be more than a place: "Africville / ain't a place. Africville is us … / You think they destroyed something. They ain't. They / took away the place. But it come'd round, though. Now that / culture come'd round" (1983, 21). As the speaker explains, the name of Africville is a social marker that identifies a group – sometimes also negatively: "If we say we from Africville, *we are Africville*. And we don't git / no job" (1983, 21). Conversely, however, such a statement of identity is also a performative speech act with positive consequences, creating a continued existence separate from the actual site itself.

For Moynagh, a similar impetus can be seen in Maxine Tynes's Africville poems in *Woman Talking Woman* (1990) – for example, in the following lines in her poem "Africville": "No House is Africville. / No road, no tree, no well. / Africville is man / woman / child" (Tynes 1990, 62; qtd in Moynagh 1998, 25). One could cite other lines from the same poem that illustrate – and perform – acts of identification that create the past settlement in the now empty Seaview Park as a reality that continues to exist between interlocutors in the present: "I am Africville / says a woman, child, man at the homestead site. / This park is green; but / Black, so Black with community. / I talk Africville / to you / and to you / until it is both you and me / till it stands and lives again / till you face and see and stand / on its life and its forever / Black past" (Tynes 1990, 62).[46] The physical Africville has been destroyed but, in Moynagh's words, it has "been reborn as the sign of a community and thereby lifted out of historical time" (1998, 25).

Like Ward's *The Curing Berry*, George Elliott Clarke's *Saltwater Spirituals* appeared in 1983. Its first section, "Soul Songs," celebrates aspects of Black Nova Scotian life and culture with poems named after the churches united in 1854 by Richard Preston in the African United Baptist Association. Among them is "Campbell Road Church," the old name of the Africville Seaview African United Baptist Church. As the poet and filmmaker Silvia Hamilton points out in the introduction, "George would have been barely six years old when the bulldozers began razing Africville" (in G.E. Clarke 1983, 5).[47] Hamilton, too, however, emphasizes the persistence of Africville beyond its physical existence: Clarke "takes us to the edge of Africville, a community doomed physically, but one whose true spiritual sense is ever strong in the heart of those who had called it home" (8–9). Clarke's "Campbell Road Church" itself seems elegiac. The poem contrasts the beauty of a sunrise over the harbour and Bedford Basin – observed "when it was easy to worship / benin bronze dawns" – with an alliterative phrase that (twice in the poem) brutally marks absence in the present: "none do now" (1983, 15). Yet any sense of a purely nostalgic or melancholic perspective is countered, in the second part of the poem, by a figure who replaces the erstwhile admiring worshiper of Africville beauty. A CN porter now "lusts for africville" and "rages to recall / the gutting death of his genealogy, / to protest his home's slaughter / by butcher bulldozers / and city planners molesting statistics" (15). Such rage trumps the mourning of nostalgia and the endless tribulations of melancholia: its vector towards an active reckoning is the gist, as we will see, also of subsequent developments facilitated by the cultural memory work of the Africadian Renaissance. Clarke subsequently contributes the lyrics for the song "Africville" composed by Delvina Bernard,[48] which is included on the recording *In My Soul* (1995) by her Halifax a cappella group Four the Moment. As Moynagh points out, these lyrics insist not only on the past, but also on the present and future of Africville: "Africville will never die / Africville has made us wise" (qtd in Moynagh 1998, 23).

Music heralded Africville's continued reality in other ways. Singer-songwriter Faith Nolan released her album *Africville* in 1986, and Joe Sealy's Juno award–winning jazz album *Africville Suite* was released in 1996. These musicians – together with a host of others – took part in a series of events that decisively helped to turn Africville from a regrettable but likely-soon-repressed example of misguided urban "renewal" into a symbol that "has become central in the new black consciousness of Nova Scotia" and "something to appreciate and identify with" (Clairmont 2010b, 76). Founded in 1983, the Africville Genealogical Society (AGS) hosted an "annual picnic and reunion each July in Seaview Park" (Kimber 2010, 82) and, with other stakeholders, organized an Africville exhibition at the Art

Gallery of Mount Saint Vincent University in Halifax in 1989.[49] In conjunction with the exhibition, two other events took place: an evening of readings and music and a conference. The former event featured Maxine Tynes, Faith Nolan, Four the Moment, Joe Sealy, and other musicians. It also offered an occasion for readings from Charles Saunders's "A Visit to Africville," a literary walking tour through the community in 1959, published first in the exhibition catalogue *Africville – A Spirit That Lives On* (1989) and then reprinted in *The Spirit of Africville* (1992) by the AGS.[50] Saunders's piece is unique in that it offers an occasion to learn in some detail about Africville's geography, customs, and individuals. The text helps convey the sense of a tightly-knit community to outsiders who never set foot in the settlement or who in the 1960s saw it only from the outside as the "Africville problem."

Such inside perspectives were also expressed in a conference associated with the exhibition that convened former residents – who it seems were never formally consulted prior to the city's relocation decision (O'Brien in Kimber 2010, 101)[51] – and black and white "decision makers" in the 1960s events. An account of the conference is provided in Stephen Kimber's contribution to *The Spirit of Africville* (2010, 79–104). Former residents, many of whom were children at the time of the bulldozing and destruction, such as Irvine Carvery (the president of the AGS), Clarence Carvery, Terry Dixon, and Linda Mantley, give moving accounts of their memories and losses. Testimony is also provided by members of the previous generation, such as Ruth Johnson, from an Africville-founding family; or Laura Howe, who reports how, one night at four o'clock in the morning, her son told her: "Mom, the church is gone" (Kimber 2010, 88).[52]

But the account of the conference also indicates issues that complicate purely nostalgic perspectives. It suggests that Africville's response to the city's brutal impositions may have signalled some acquiescence in the technocratic, thoughtlessly modernizing ideologies voiced by administrators and technocrats, and even evinced a certain degree of complicity. The testimony from "decision makers" includes not only that of Allan O'Brien – a city councillor (and later Halifax mayor) responsible for the relocation decision, who admits that in light of later insights he would have acted differently (Kimber 2010, 101) – it also includes accounts by those who negotiated on behalf of Africville, including Alan Borovoy, Gus Wedderburn, and Charles Coleman. Borovoy was head of the Ontario Labour Committee for Human Rights at the time and had been sent at the request of Africville resident and leader Joe Skinner. During a four-day visit to Halifax, Borovoy organized the Halifax Human Rights Advisory Committee (HHRAC), which in effect became the main contact for the city in the subsequent negotiations. Eventually, HHRAC unanimously accepted a report recommending "that Africville be cleared over a two- to three-year period" (Clairmont 2010b, 67). At a 1964 meeting arranged by HHRAC, even "thirty-seven of the forty-one Africvilleans present voted to accept it" (Clairmont 2010b, 68). In his 1989 conference comments, Borovoy maintains that there were no financial resources at the time to do anything more than arranging the best deal possible with the city under the circumstances (Kimber 2010, 97–8). As Clairmont points out, however, "as a leading proponent of civil liberties in Canada" at the time and as an outsider to Africville, it is "not surprising" that Borovoy "would emphasize that a 'black ghetto should not be subsidized' … and stress the importance of racial integration," perceiving "Africville to be a slum and relocation … virtually inevitable" (Clairmont 2010b, 64).

Gus Wedderburn, a black Halifax lawyer and member of HHRAC, stresses the poor conditions in Africville at the time.[53] He assures the conference audience that everything done was thought "to be in the best interest of everyone," but like O'Brien, he adds that from his current perspective he would have acted differently. Wedderburn even suggests that "the lands of Africville should be returned to the former residents or the descendants of Africville" (in Kimber 2010, 99). Finally, Charles Coleman, the minister of Seaview Baptist Church at the time and one "of Africville's most influential representatives during the relocation process" (Kimber 2010, 99), tells the audience: "We did what we had to because it seemed to be the best alternative for the choices before us" (99).

These statements raise difficult questions. These social actors were part of the *de facto* Africville leadership that responded to the city (Clairmont 2010b, 63–5). Were they clear-sighted realists who simply accepted the inevitable? Or were they blinded by Gramscian hegemony and technological and modernizing thought, agreeing with the city's evaluation (if not necessarily with its mode of proceeding)? And finally, is asking that very question – with the hindsight of a historical horizon after the civil rights movement and black nationalism – an act of naivety that disregards any possible historical dialectic and horizon of expectation at the time?

Perhaps not. Together with other Africville archival footage, the conference testimonies appear in *Remember Africville*, a 1991 National Film Board documentary by Shelagh McKenzie (one of the organizers of the 1989 conference). In his 1993 review of the film, George Elliott Clarke writes that "the film serves up the oral and visual confessions of the removed and their removers" (2002a, 288). He also notes that while "racism and City policies were external causes for the death of Africville, Africvillers and other Africadians did little, it seems, to slow or try to stop the relocation" (2002a, 292). Clarke's review serves as a site where he can reckon with a "regressive conservatism [that] paralyzed Africadian society" (2002a, 293) and with the church leaders: "The clergy ceded Africville, with hardly a whimper, to its enemies … Our leaders of the 1960s allowed themselves to be seduced into thinking of Africville as a slum rather than as a potentially strong Africadian community-neighbourhood in a prime location on peninsular Halifax" (294).[54] Clarke thus suggests the sway of hegemony as the cause of a loss of faith: "Africville was lost because we Africadians refused to sufficiently value our right to exist. If we had held fast to our faith … we would have laid our bodies before the bulldozers" (2002a, 294).[55]

Such assertions suggest a certain complicity on the part of the community – and thus seem the stuff of which not nostalgia, but drama – and perhaps insight – is made. In the process of a historically necessary response to the destruction of Africville, the Africadian Renaissance has articulated, as Moynagh observes, a unity that "sutures class divides and urban-rural splits" (1998, 31).[56] Yet some of the texts have also engaged in critical self-analysis. David Woods, who celebrates Africville in his poetry,[57] raises issues of complicity in his radio play *Part of the Deal* (CBC 1991). Here he replaces, for instance, the actual white social worker who negotiated with Africville residents for the sale of their properties with a young, educated *black* "Assistant Relocation Officer" (see Moynagh 1998, 30).

The question of divisions among Africvillers, down to disputes between couples and conflict within individuals is one of the subjects of George Elroy Boyd's *Consecrated Ground* (first produced in Halifax in 1999).[58] Woods has several connections with the play. It begins with "'Poem #1' from Joe Sealy's Africville Suite" (Sears 2003, 399), which is a reading of Wood's "Mood Indigo" (Moynagh 1998, 26). In the opening production in 1999, Woods played, of all things, the minister of the Africville Seaview Baptist Church, here called Reverend Miner.[59] Scenes 6–8 of Act I show the reverend in relation to his flock and his dealings with the relocation social worker, here a twenty-year-old white kid "fresh out of social work school" (G.E. Boyd 2003, 397).[60] Tom Clancy has landed the job because of political favours owed to his father (Act II, 4; G.E. Boyd 2003, 466), and he sees his assignment as a career opportunity; he hopes for "a book, maybe a master's thesis. Build a career based on what happens at this site" (435).[61] Reverend Miner tells Clancy that "it was agreed that I would help you bring your task to a swift and successful conclusion" (435). It turns out that while he "realize[s] the inevitable," his main concern is, "does the church stay?" (436). On the basis of Clancy's affirmative answer, the reverend proceeds to sell the necessity of relocation to his community: "Now they're going to develop this land and they're making financial offers ... And – we'll have the church right here in Africville" (438–9). When he realizes, after delivering his flock to the city, that he himself has been betrayed and that the church will be destroyed, he is brought to the limits of his faith (468–9). When Africville's most visible spiritual leader is forced to admit that he kept his meetings with the city secret (439), his gullible complicity with the city is exposed and his deception of the community revealed. A subsequent "conversion" finally allows him to break the city's self-serving laws in the interest of his community.

Another division dramatized by Boyd can be seen in the relationship between Clarice and her husband, Willem. Clarice has signed her Africville house over to Willem; it was built by the community after her grandfather's house was lost in a fire. Coming from a farm in Annapolis Royal, however, Willem has an attachment to Africville that hardly matches Claire's. He sees Africville largely in the terms proposed by the city. He wants to leave what he calls a "tired ol' shack" (480) and seek a better future for their newborn child. Willem signs the house away after the baby is killed by rats from the dump that the city has placed close to Africville. His decision is sealed by a financial offer made by the social worker in the same Seaview Baptist Church that supposedly symbolizes the principles of the Africville community (475). In the last scene, Willem interrupts his child's burial service to carry the casket outside and pour Africville soil over it. This ceremony contravenes the regulations of the city (which wants to minimize any attachments to Africville), but he persists in carrying out his wife's wishes. His own act of "conversion" to an appreciation of Africville facilitates that of the minister; in the midst of the work of bulldozers and shortly before the destruction of his church, the latter joins in the illegal but legitimate act and declares Africville consecrated ground (482–3).This recognition of value and of a connection that cannot be severed comes in response to the certainty of loss. It parallels the collective cultural declaration of the value of Africville that is made by the Africadian Renaissance. Had this collective identification occurred earlier, Clarke suggests, it could have saved the physical site of Africville (2002a, 294–5).

In the case of Africville, however, the dialectic of place and consciousness does not end here. It is true that the cultural work of the Africadian Renaissance with regard to Africville came well after the last resident, Aaron (Pa) Carvery, reluctantly left Africville on 2 January 1970 (Clairmont 2010b, 74), but the gathering force leading to the response was unmistakable. It began, to recall some of its markers, with Ward's *Riverlisp* in 1974 and his Africville poems in *The Curing Berry* in 1983, the year of Clarke's *Saltwater Spirituals* and, of supreme importance, the formal founding of the Africville Genealogical Society by Deborah Dixon-Jones, Linda Mantley, and Brenda Steed-Ross. The dynamic continued to build in the years leading to the 1989 exhibition and conference and its multiple sequels, including the 1992 follow-up *The Spirit of Africville*, published by the AGS, and Mackenzie's National Film Board documentary. The Africville section in Maxine Tynes's 1990 volume and Woods's poems and radio play attest to the insistent force of this cultural work, as do Boyd's *Consecrated Ground* and Sealy's *Africville Suite*. George Elliott's Clarke's anthology *Fire on the Water*, which in volume 2 includes many of the writers and texts just mentioned, participates actively in this context. This extended and communal memory work contributed to events "on the ground" that eventually went beyond the purely artistic aspect of the Africadian Renaissance.[62]

In 2001, after a series of promising developments and protests (AGS 2010, 121–2), the Halifax Regional Municipality finally began talks with the Africville Genealogical Society "on the question of compensation" (AGS 2010, 122). Federal heritage minister Sheila Copps subsequently travelled to Halifax "to declare the neighbourhood that had once been known as Africville a national historic site" and to unveil a plaque (AGS 2010, 122). Her visit raises many of the complicated questions associated with memorialization, especially when it occurs in the absence of any compensation for former residents or their descendents. Indeed, unless it helps to animate an active and rewarding community in the present, officially sanctioned memorialization risks being little more than a tranquillizing gesture that pacifies aggrieved individuals and absolves officialdom from any further action.

In the case of Africville, there have been many encouraging developments, including an apology, a settlement (AGS 2010, 121–6), and the building of a replica of Seaview Baptist Church with a museum. Despite a 2004 United Nations report that "urged Ottawa to consider reparations to former Africville residents" (AGS 2010, 123), however, the Halifax Regional Municipality refused to "negotiate on that issue"; it only began to move in other directions once the AGS had dropped such claims (AGS 2010, 123). On 24 February 2010, Halifax mayor Peter Kelly, on behalf of the city, apologized formally "to the former Africville residents and their descendants for what they have endured for almost 50 years, ever since the loss of their community" (Halifax Regional Municipality 2010). An agreement with the AGS – while not offering personal compensation and thus leaving a number of unsatisfied former residents and descendents vowing to fight on (AGS 2010, 125–6) – included land allotted on the former site of Africville and a financial commitment of three million dollars "toward the reconstruction of the Seaview United Baptist Church to serve as an Africville memorial … designed to honour the past, take action in the present, and plan for community-based improvements for the future" (Halifax Regional Municipality 2010, "News Release"). The Africville Church Museum was officially opened on 25 September 2011;[63] it is housed in the replica of the Seaview Baptist Church, which greeted the Africville annual reunion for the first time in 2012.

Regardless of the further consequence of these developments, the Africadian Renaissance impressively demonstrates the importance of particular local sites of black experience in Canada as they are mediated through the work of writers and other artists in the present. While it is not clear where the contestations around Africville and its communal reinventions will lead, Africville's relevance is striking as a site where past and present interact and define each other and together are translated into the future. In this regard, Africville may play an important and future inspirational role not only for Nova Scotia, but also for other places and contexts of black history and experience.[64]

DIASPORIC CROSSROADS AND THE BLACK PRAIRIES: CHERYL FOGGO, CLAIRE HARRIS, AND ESI EDUGYAN

Canada's black prairies, another important regional site, have been investigated in a groundbreaking study by Karina Vernon (2008). She reminds us of the immigration of 1,650 black pioneers during the years 1905–12 (many of them part of an exodus of Oklahoma blacks)[65] and subsequent arrivals. According to the 2001 census, Alberta alone had "a black population nearly *double* that of Nova Scotia," and together with Saskatchewan and Manitoba made the prairies the "second most densely populated black region" in Canada (Vernon 2008, 11). Vernon heralds a "significant new regional literary archive" (17), whose origins date back to 1873. She critiques the elision of blackness from earlier accounts of the Canadian prairies.

In addition to settlers and pioneers such as Alfred Schmitz Shadd (Mary Ann Shadd's brother), Vernon discusses the self-identified Blackfoot US immigrant Sylvester Long Lance, who felt safer in Alberta not acknowledging his partial blackness in his *Autobiography* (1928). She also looks at descendants of these earlier pioneers, such as Cheryl Foggo, and at a "second wave" of contemporary writers, such as Suzette Mayr, Claire Harris, Esi Edugyan, and a host of others.[66] Some of these writers, she points out, are also claimed by other contexts – for example, Claire Harris by a Trinidadian Canadian canon or Suzette Mayr by a "diasporic German Canadian" one (32–3). The result is a heterogeneous black prairies archive that builds on diverse diasporic trajectories. This diversity further unsettles any notions of homogeneous blackness in Canada – and any visions of whiteness habitually associated with the Canadian prairie provinces.

The setting of Suzette Mayr's *The Widows* (1998), for example, switches back and forth between Canada and Germany, enriching the black prairies corpus with unexpected crossings. Mayr's often hilarious novel mixes Annie Edson Taylor and the history of Niagara Falls with German postwar and later history, Kaffee-Klatsch-Kultur, and period pop idol Freddy. The text features a mixed-race couple in Edmonton. Dieter's wife, Rosario, appears to her German mother-in-law, Hannelore, as "half Mexican, half African, half Chinese, half Kanadian" (Mayr 1998, 17); after a visit to the pool in the Edmonton Mall, Hannelore finds herself wrestling with her granddaughter's "fine, frizzy hair" (15). Mayr's code-switching novel offers "engagements with the particular ways in which globalizing processes are lodging themselves in the prairie imagination" (Brydon 2008, 8). Together with many other texts, this novel contributes to a blackening of the province.[67]

I now want to concentrate on three texts – by Cheryl Foggo, Claire Harris, and Esi Edugyan – that engage with particular black diasporic histories and contexts and make the prairies the site of their encounter with the present. Like Mayr's *The Widows*, they demonstrate how black prairies writing participates in networks of diverse diasporic trajectories of the black Atlantic and thus contributes to the heterogeneous, yet connected, multiplicity of black Canadian literature. In the case of these texts, United States, Caribbean, and African contexts contribute to a multiple, black diasporization of the Canadian prairies, a setting not usually theorized in such perspectives.[68]

Listening to Black Prairies History: Cheryl Foggo's *Pourin' Down Rain*

Cheryl Foggo's autobiographical coming-of-age memoir *Pourin' Down Rain* (1990) is told from a present-day vantage point in Calgary. Beginning in

1958, it describes the narrator's mostly happy childhood that leads into a growing awareness of racism and her own blackness in a prairies context. Together with her own experiences, the narrator shares observations about her parents' community. We learn about its strategic use of linguistic codes, for instance,[69] and about events in the lives of relatives, such as the Second World War, the Great Depression, and experiences in later periods, especially in Calgary, Regina, and Winnipeg. We are thus introduced to "details of all the home spaces inhabited by four generations of her family" (Vernon 2004, 76). She discovers that her parents and grandparents "once lived in America" (7), almost at the same time as she learns about the term "Jim Crow." Her mother's assurance that "we don't have that kind of thing here" and that in-laws "came to Canada to get away from that" (6) contributes to the narrator's "growing belief that I was lucky to have been born in Canada" (7). This belief is bolstered by the story of her grandfather, whom she initially believes to be white. Born in Oklahoma as George Washington Smith, he joins the Canadian Army in 1919, lying to his commanding officer about his middle name; he is henceforth known as George Willis Smith. When he and his visibly darker wife visit relatives in Oklahoma, they are refused service in a restaurant. Following his example after this experience, the narrator vows not to "bother to darken America's doorstep" (10).

Later we learn that the grandfather leaves the Canada Packers plant in Regina after twenty years of work when he is bypassed for a promotion because of racism. The narrator feels that the incident prompts his rude awakening from any illusions he might have had about the absence of racism in Canada: "His former employers were as surprised by his expectation to be given a position of authority over White men as he was by their bigotry" (60). While her grandfather subsequently finds employment in Winnipeg with the Canadian Pacific Railway,[70] the narrator recounts an incident involving a threatening note found in her grandparents' mailbox at their new home there (62) and her own mother's experiences of work-related racism at the same time in Regina and then in Winnipeg (61, 62–3). As the narrator grows up, the incremental understanding of such incidents contributes to a slow realization: for the older generation, it is mainly a sheltering notion that the Oklahoma pioneers experienced the reward of racial equality on moving up north to Canada.

This learning process about the past coincides with the narrator's own increasing experience of racism as she gets older. Her perceptions are also sharpened by the civil rights movement south of the border: "Although the struggles of black Americans had very little impact on my day-to-day life, after 1966 I became less comfortable in my White World" (43). Part of this experience is visible in musical codes: two of her best friends "ridicule the black music and musicians" she introduces them to; she cannot help but feel that the vitriolic rejection of the music she loves "seemed to carry a message other than a simple dislike for a few songs" (44).[71] Moving towards adolescence, she feels that "barriers that seemed to have something to do with race were going up in relationships I had counted on" (44). Although only eleven years old in 1968 when Martin Luther King is murdered, she feels "changed by his death" and now more closely connected to the "toil of other Black people" (45). She finally decides to "no longer straighten my hair" (51), heeding James Brown's call to be "Black and Proud" (52). After a wounding interracial dating experience (53), she further concludes that "I was not black enough" (53). She abandons the belief "that Canada was a refuge from racism" and retreats from "what I perceived to be 'White culture.'" The result is a "drastically" reduced social circle (53). She renounces further interracial dating (66) and vows to "cry every night for the rest of my life before I'll marry a White man," a moment Foggo uses to discuss attitudes in her family towards – and incidents of – mixed-race marriage (66–9).[72]

Despite – and yet also through – her own experiences and the simultaneous apprenticeship made possible by the orally conveyed history of her family, the narrator comes to another realization. As she notes, this insight "may not be comprehensible to someone who has not lived as a peculiarity": "I belong in the world. I belong here in Western Canada where my family has lived and worked for four generations" (83). Towards the end of the book, her recognition is bolstered by a deepening of the historical narrative that now reaches back six generations to an African ancestor abducted into slavery. It includes the realization that she is the "descendant of American slaves" (91) and of some of the subsequent vagaries of race, freedom, and enslavement in her family (91–103). She is also aware of the history of the Oklahoma exodus (mentioned above) as lived by her ancestors. That past includes the loss of black voting privileges shortly after "the territories had been merged into a state called Oklahoma" (107), the Canadian promise of 160 acres of land "for the filing fee of ten dollars" (106), and her great-grandfather's belief in benevolent providence thus showing the way to Canada (107). Although this experience also contains the discovery of a negative response to – and systematic, state-sponsored Canadian race discrimination against – "every recognizable minority that lives here today" (110), the story of her family's triumph over all obstacles sustains the narrator's own sense of belonging and identity: "I was connected to history by them … I was what I was – Black, Canadian, one of my family – and so I shall always be" (117). While the account of her family reaches back to several slave narratives, it also offers an early-twentieth-century settler narrative that helps to sustain a black Western identity. Such a trajectory includes both diasporic consciousness of black Atlantic routes and the knowledge of settler roots. And as Vernon points out, it is the "legacy of the black pioneers – their writing, recipes, and family orature – not indigenizing metaphors" that a writer like Foggo uses "to achieve the sense of a long and continuous black presence on the prairies" (Vernon 2008, 182).

The Caribbean Prairies: Claire Harris's *Drawing Down a Daughter*

A very different black Calgary emerges in *Drawing Down a Daughter* (1992) by Claire Harris.[73] In the thoughts and dreams of the Caribbean-born narrator, the Bow River under her Calgary balcony mingles with the Lopinot of her Trinidadian youth. Through dreams, memories, and a great-aunt's stories, two geographical and cultural contexts join one another in a complex Caribbean Western Canadian time-space. At the same time, the text opens onto possible futures in dialogue with Caribbean and Canadian experiences of the past. In this process, dreams about others turn into realities of the self, endlessly dismantling such boundaries. The text performs continuous permutations of identity, creating variations of a self in flux, beyond itself and across distances of time and space.

In more concrete terms, the narrator's visions occur in dialogue with her unborn child. The confluence of two rivers and realities, associated initially with past and present, becomes here a site of creation and possibility, joined in the text by the amniotic fluids that will carry both the pregnant narrator and her daughter into the future: "**Daughter** to live is to dream the self / to make a fiction / … / … as we move together / on this swell of water / this swimming and whirling" (C. Harris 1992, 43).

Drawing Down a Daughter is a transgeneric and metafictionally self-reflective text. Not only the transitions between different times and places are seamless, but so, too, are those between prose and poetry, dream and reality, and "fact" and fiction. Slipping in and out of dreams, the narrator records her thoughts while writing and converses with her unborn daughter in a journal that will be a birthgift (set off in different type and marked by a lower-case first-person pronoun). The text begins with the narrator having an anguished dream about her own mother in Trinidad. In the dream, the mother refuses to leave her house – a house remembered in the dream as overgrown and rotting, a "green damp gloom" (7) – to join her daughter. Waking, the narrator notes that she is "dreaming the mother / dreaming myself dreaming the mother dream / potent as love / or hate / helpless as a daughter" (8). It becomes clear that she is not only dreaming, with ambivalence, *her* mother (and herself as daughter), but also *herself as mother* of a future daughter. She continues: "still and all for this your birthgift Child who / opens me" (8). Referring to herself in both the first and the third person, the narrator underlines this sense of transformation and becoming "other" to herself. She even states, "I prefer the third / person" (9). The unborn daughter opens her to another future.

The transformative "swimming and whirling" in the poem's present has similarly complex temporal aspects. Thoughts about a possible future are conjoined by conflicting experiences of the past. The narrator awaits the return of her husband, a third-generation African Canadian. He is travelling in the Caribbean, looking for a job and a future for the family there. Given his own past, he is concerned about the daughter's future experience of racism in Canada. Yet the narrator resolutely resists a return to the Caribbean. She is worried about being defined by the narrowness there, by her mother, and by the "tangled skeins of relationships" (71) that would await her in Trinidad. She tells her unborn daughter: "Baby we journey down dreamlines alone while your father searches islands 'a safe place for this daughter!' my mother's terrible love does not alarm him … at least Girl you'll be born here" (8).[74] The husband bases his position on his experience of racism in Canada: "I'm the third generation Canadian. There has to be something better for my child! … You didn't like being defined by your family, everyone knowing your business. I understand that. Have you any idea what it is to grow up defined by race?" (69). She, on the other hand, points out that "there is racism there too" and refuses categorically to move (71). She tells her unborn daughter: "I'm going to keep this father for you / as long as I can but don't count on it" (75).

Her concerns exceed being circumscribed by her Trinidadian family. Her reluctance has to do with the implications of gender, but she is concerned, first of all, about her professional possibilities: "she won't be able to hold out   she thinks of teaching   the career she's built   her writing   Child if he hauls us home your collage may never be published   remembers   certain calls   'have you ever thought to send us some thing Canadian   set here'" (15). The passage offers a telling indictment of an understanding of Canadian literature that would excise the Caribbean preoccupations of many Canadian writers.[75] Yet the narrator also "wonders whether their marriage would survive macho Trinidad" (74). Such concerns about gender patterns extend indirectly to the future of her daughter. A textual irony reveals this connection: awaking from a dream, she thinks: "are you there Girl / your daddy's looking to find a safe place / for your childhood and his" (15). The preceding dream, however, has just offered the first evocation of Burri (14) – a philanderer, as the text reveals later – who leaves a young girl, pregnant, to her fate by the Lopinot River in Trinidad. As the connection and irony dawn on the reader, the implication seems clear: growing up in the Caribbean may protect the daughter from the racism her father has experienced in Canada, but it is far less certain that it will protect her from experiences of gender that the narrator remembers from childhood and adolescence and that *she* is trying to leave behind.

But the dream only hints at the further permutations and juxtapositions that will unfold subsequently. It juxtaposes the two rivers that metonymically represent two cultural contexts and emotional geographies – one evoked as the river of her husband's childhood: "they scramble down the incline to river-edge and icy revelation: his childhood" (14). A tumble that she takes and her crying bring forth his "Baby   i'm sorry," which evokes, without transition or separating punctuation, a scene from Trinidad: "Bebe on the other side   by the Lopinot" (14), involving a young woman who is "sobbing hands cross over balloon belly suddenly empty" (14), breaking away from a man holding her "about the waist." As she "scrambles up rocks towards the ledge" she, too, takes a painful tumble. As her fall comes to a stop, the sequence continues, again without transition, with the first vision of Burri. We will only later understand that these images belong to the moment Burri walks away from his desperate lover after learning of her pregnancy. Spurning her idea of marriage, he lies about returning; he leaves through the bamboo by the Lopinot River, which he will have to cross on his way back to his car (50–2). At this point, however, we only read: "a man in bamboo tunnels   candy smile   gleaming shirt   Burri flings his jacket over a shoulder   moves his lean easy grace past them all   fine silver buckle glimmers   behind him old old woman steps   scattering words sentences paragraphs drawing down a daughter / she scrambles after …" (14; slash in the original).

The dream spins a web of myriad questions and connections. Has the narrator herself lost a child in her youth? Or does her motherhood in the present bring to mind a young Trinidadian girl suffering a fate that could have been hers – or her daughter's in the future? We learn later that the narrator indeed knew the girl Burri abandons (though she did not have an abortion). Other connections, however, are evoked by the phrase "behind him old old woman steps" and by the references to writing, which include the title of the book we read. These connections take on contours with the mention of another beautiful young woman, an accident, and La Diablesse. According to Trinidadian lore, La Diablesse is an old woman in the guise of a beautiful young girl; she lures men to their death. Could the old old woman be La Diablesse? Or could she be the old storyteller who mentions La Diablesse in a story she tells to a group of children (that includes, it turns out, our narrator in her youth)?

Or is she, perhaps, the narrator herself? And if so, "scattering words sentences paragraphs drawing down a daughter / she scrambles after ..." what? Burri and the connections with her current situation? The dreams and circumstantial details that create her text? Or perhaps facets of a self as it appears in relation to different contexts and others – a daughter, a poor pregnant girl in Trinidad, the man who has gotten her with child? Is she after a fluid "fact" that is, as a key passage has it later in the text, an "amalgam of variations of itself"? She once thought of introducing herself to Burri as "La Diablesse in waiting" (59); when younger, she was afraid of waking up as someone else she didn't want to be.

Burri's story is told in multiple versions later in a prose section. Ironically, it begins with the words "It is a matter of fact" (50–66).[76] Given the different accounts that follow, the source and authority of the subsequent "factual" information about the rendez-vous by the Lopinot are uncertain. As Burri leaves, all the markers are evoked that are associated with him in the first dream: the jacket over one shoulder, his "lean surefooted grace," the bamboo, his white shirt, and the "gleaming silver buckle" (52). But then the account is ruptured. The perspective shifts as we are introduced to an "old storyteller" who "has no truck with this simple form, with its order and its inherent possibility of justice" (52). She knows of "unseen presences, of interruptions, of rupture" (52), and she dramatizes the story for her audience of children (that we later come to understand includes her great-niece, our narrator). She provides comments and opens the sequence repeatedly to its possible alternatives and continuations. "Her tale," we hear, "is a celebration, and a binding of community. Her theme is survival in the current of riverlife" (52).

Like the reader, however, the children "lust after the story" (52). A small boy repeatedly "wants to get on with the story" (53). With interruptions that describe how the children respond like a chorus, we learn that Burri almost drowns when he crosses the Lopinot. He is saved by a beautiful woman on the other side who offers to take him to her family to save him from catching a cold. Unlike the jilted lover who wanted Burri to talk to her mother, she assures him that her mother will not be at home. As he lights a cigarette against her objections in the car, he sees her face slip, and presumably he recognizes La Diablesse: "He think: 'I ketch! Now is Lawd help me'" (57). Asked what will happen next, the children comment on the story. Some have not realized the implication of the slipping face, suggesting, "*You lucky, eh Burri, You lucky*"; others, like a vernacular Greek chorus voicing a community's normativity, shout, "*I woulda break you neck fuh you / de devil eat you, Burri*" (58). This is indeed what almost happens to him, although the storyteller, claiming to have received the information from Burri himself, only says that the girl disappears.

A short subsequent paragraph speaks of a child touching the storyteller's face, trying to sort out the horror of the slipping face. Then the passage continues enigmatically: "is it possible to be La Diablesse and not know it, she wonders" (58). The thought can hardly be attributed to the young child, so it seems reasonable to assume that the shifter "she" refers to her later self. The narrator here steps in with a self-reflexive comment, to suggest that what she meant to write as a straightforward fiction, with a little horror element, "has become an autobiography. Of sorts" (58). She remembers being told the story by the old woman (her great-aunt, it turns out) and of hearing it years later told to her father by a certain John Burian Armstrong, called Burri. Asked by him during this sole encounter whether she is Mr Williams's daughter, "it crossed my mind suddenly to say coldly, 'Not really, I'm La Diablesse in waiting'" (59).[77]

The associative permutations and extensions of identity continue as she overhears Burri Armstrong's account. He tells her father that the girl in the car gives her name as "'Mera,' … short for 'Ramera'" and that "to tell you the truth she look a lot like the girl I was seeing" (60–1), whose full name we learn later is Jocelyn Romero. Armstrong does not mention the slipping face, but he describes how, as he lights the cigarette, his car spins out of control and crashes, leaving him trapped until help arrives. While the car door is never opened, the girl is gone (61). Was she La Diablesse – here as an avenging incarnation of Jocelyn, a beautiful young woman disguising the "old old" one whose steps follow Burri – forcing his car off the road and into a wild crash, as if she is responding to the children's later call to "*break you neck fuh you / de devil eat you, Burri*"?

The narrator raises this latter possibility. As Burri Armstrong ponders the mysterious disappearance, he asks, "But if a thing like that could happen, what kind of world is this?" (61). The narrator continues: "What kind of world indeed! For Mr. Armstrong claimed to have had his amazing experience three years earlier. Four years after the night we had danced wildly … chanting: '*de devil eat you, Burri*'" (62).[78] In a *mise en abyme* of the text, she answers Armstrong's question a few lines later: "A world in which each fact like the legs of runners photographed at slow speed is an amalgam of variations of itself. Myriad versions of event reaching out of time, out of space, individual to each observer" (62). With respect to La Diablesse, she wonders, "Is it possible that the old lady bodying forth a world in that long ago August night gave it flesh?" (62). And clamouring with the other children for Burri's punishment, could it be that she was herself indeed "a Diablesse in waiting"?

The text leaves these and other questions unanswered, but it creates a strong sense of relational connection.[79] It also raises the distinct possibility that "utterance breathes life" (Beckford 2011, 199).[80] In this perspective, the anteriority of the past is reversed by storytelling that seemingly refers to the past but evokes events that will have happened in the future. Such performance of language contests the primacy of reality or "fact" over the narrative imagination and emphasizes the reality-creating powers of speech, staged here in the cross-over terrain of fiction and autobiography. In addition, the text explores not only the possibility that our self may appear to us in others, but also that others may foreshadow versions of our self. That self, then, appears as a complex "fact" that is articulated, in dreams and language, as an "amalgam of variations of itself" (62).

Within the second extended prose section in *Daughter*, this latter relation between self and other – and between the narrator and the seemingly past events in the story – is fathomed in an interpolated dream poem: "what is a dream *without revelation* / I watch as from a great distance above how *she* / *comes face to face with her self that other that* / in the dream *is glimmering* trailing not always there not all there sudden as dreams are sudden" (96). The "other," it turns out, is the young girl, Jocelyn Romero – before her encounter with Burri – who now also appears in Calgary as Enid Thomas, a name adopted to deceive Canadian Immigration.

As the section opens, the narrator emphatically claims not to be her: "She is not Enid Thomas. Let's make that clear" (95). Yet in fact, her own "autobiography" has also been the story of Jocelyn Romero, whom she encountered once when she was eight years old (105). Or perhaps better, her own story is also, *ex negativo*, that of *not being* Jocelyn. The additional aspect of class is added here to that of gender and of geography in the text: when she encounters Jocelyn – a relatively well-off child in Trinidad encountering a poor one – she realizes to her horror that she herself could be such a poor girl. The evocation of the incident communicates indirectly with the narrator's own possible future as a single mother, and with her daughter as a poor waif ("how you gonna wear 'poverty' a badge 'lower class' / eh! eh! girl chile we done you wrong!" 12). The narrator cries as a child when the young Jocelyn offers her a gift, and she has to be prompted to accept it. The reason is revealed in another narrative by the great-aunt: "She say Jocelyn just like she … She say it ain't have no difference. She could be Jocelyn, Jocelyn could be she … What if she wake up one morning and find she self Jocelyn? She ain't want to be poor" (105–6).

The narrator's preoccupation with Jocelyn, Burri, and La Diablesse is clearly connected with the narrator herself in the web or her dreams and thoughts. In this text, where dream and reality are intermeshed, she continually wakes up altered, as someone else. As the text progresses, these variations and permutations of identity continue to contribute to the "amalgam" of her self, created and articulated in relational self-mediation through the lives of others. Indeed, after the narrator has dreamed the name "Enid Thomas," her own act of searching for – and writing about – this person, whose reality she never doubts, finally intervenes in the life of a person by that name. This intervention, triggered by a dream and the imagination, has real, and even deadly, consequences. In the account of her great-aunt: "She got to interfere with Enid Thomas … pretending that anything she see is hers … she seeing changing it, you understand … that poor woman, Jocelyn" (97). Jocelyn had defined aspects of the narrator's life in Trinidad. The narrator is now not simply, as she believes, the "author of her own story"; she has also become the co-author of Jocelyn's destiny, as her research triggers a fateful intervention by the Canadian Immigration Department.

Harris's text is fiction. Susan Rudy, characterizing it as "liminal autobiography," points out that Harris "has never married" and "has no child. Yet on more than one public occasion, she has said that parts of *Drawing* – all the dreams except one, the story about Burri, the memories of her mother and Great Aunt's stories – are 'true.' She has even said of the book that it is her life" (Rudy 1996, 82).[81] This comment underlines that Harris's text, which in many ways can be called a fictive autobiography, relates to aspects of reality – which here comprises culturally specific, Trinidadian frameworks of interpretation.

Harris's narrator observes, "The fiction persists that autobiography is non-fiction. A matter of fact. The question, of course, is what is fact, what is reality? Though the myth of La Diablesse sticks to convention, the stories themselves are specific to a particular event" (62). Fictional connections can thus help to bring out or structure actual relation. The narrator emphasizes such a point when admitting to having tampered with what actually happened: "I'm trying for fact. A little artistic license here, a little there, and the next thing you know I'm writing history" (59). Harris's text thus constitutes work with language that functions on both sides of the presumable fact-or-fiction divide. In emphasizing fictional aspects of our patterns of perception, interpretation, and understanding, this textual work is an intervention in reality. At the same time, the process of writing articulates a relational identity, transforming the speaker's understanding of how her present connects with the past, how Calgary connects with the Caribbean, and how this understanding can inflect the lived time-spaces of the Caribbean Canadian black Atlantic.[82]

Many of the textual strategies I have just delineated – I think it may have become clear – belong to a postmodern repertoire. In the specific diasporic and black Atlantic context of Harris's text, however, I think these strategies also achieve a specifically postcolonial intervention that reaches beyond a politically disinterested postmodern destabilization and deconstruction of boundaries. In Caribbean Canadian terms, the text inscribes its "amalgamated" complex time-spaces in Western Canadian times and spaces, challenging thereby previous mappings of Western Canada as white. Instead of evoking nostalgia, the text creates a simultaneity of both contexts without anteriority or primacy in the amalgam of the present (or of the future, which the text leaves open). The scene of enunciation is staged in Calgary, mentioned by name and metonymically evoked throughout the text by the Bow, but the content – consisting of dreams, memories, stories, notebook entries, and the event of the ending – flows with few obstacles between "here" and "there." This poetic self-mediation continually accumulates possibilities, spaces, and temporalities, operating a widening and expanding of the self that draws on these erstwhile different contexts. They are conceived not as alternatives that exclude one another, but as composite parts and variations of a self that is open to many dimensions and possibilities.

In this respect, the text's conjoining of prose and poetry (two generic rivers, if you will) bears a meaningful relation to its rooting of diasporic presence. The generic interplay continually opens the diasporic sequence of events and geographies (a syntagmatic relation that Roman Jakobson famously associated more closely with prose [1987]) to the vertical or paradigmatic dimension of its simultaneous possibilities (seen by Jakobson as more typical of poetry). The Trinidadian past thus exists as co-presence in Calgary: the Calgarian present does not simply come after the narrator's life in Trinidad; it may in turn become the past of her Trinidadian future. In another refusal of unilinear sequence and causality, the daughter is present before she arrives; she is the source of, and thus also anterior to, the text that her future existence helps to create.

Harris highlights this relationship between linear sequence and the interruptions of possibility in the great-aunt's storytelling – which often takes time to meander and comment – and her audience of children whose "eyes lust after the story" (56). One little boy, in particular, who always wants to get on with the story, is a personified narrative-regulating element. At one point, he even "decides to assert control" (56) over the constant interruptions of the story. What flashes forth in these "vertical" interruptions and comments, however, is the depth of the great-aunt's oral knowledge. She makes connections with other realms of experience, is aware of unseen presences, and insists on a sense of rupture.[83] This knowledge offers a figuration of causality and temporality that contests the teleologies that the narrator at one point says are "Infected by Newton and the Church" (62).[84] As in Chariandy's evocation of the soucouyant, the story of La Diablesse comes to mediate the (self-)knowledge of the diasporic narrator. This form of knowing has an oblique and often critical relationship with the knowledge of Western modernity, which would claim to be more advanced and to be able to understand vernacular knowledge as superstition. Temporalities and spaces are hybridized in the text, but without dissolution of their elements or resolution; they concurrently enrich the text and its variations of the self.

Such a celebratory vision of diasporic space, however, needs to be placed within certain limits. Harris's own positive vision is outlined in a comment that (like remarks by Étienne and Olivier) sees diaspora as a space of possibility. In her essay "Poets in Limbo," she writes: "That the diaspora has made the world 'home' is our good fortune," and referencing Victor Turner, she adds that "liminality, the space between two worlds, is a place of paradox ... A potent space of creativity and fullness" (Harris 1986, 125; qtd in Zackodnik 1999, 187). Zackodnik cites this passage in support of her comment that throughout *Drawing Down a Daughter* "Harris sees diaspora as enabling a different sense of belonging or 'home'" (186–7). Also referencing Harris's comment on liminality, Rudy similarly suggests that *Drawing Down a Daughter* "consciously inhabits and reconfigures the potential of liminal space by imagining it as a space not of indeterminacy or meaninglessness but of pregnancy" (1996, 96n5). While I agree, it is important to note that Harris also problematizes this space of possible multiplicity in her subsequent verse novel, *She* (2000). Here, the Trinidad-born Penelope suffers from multiple personality disorder, which is related, in the text, to her diasporic position.[85] This further permutation can be seen as a consequence of Harris's relentlessly self-altering, curious, and critical textual strategies. Continually exploring other possible dimensions, this textual drive for critical negativity also investigates the other side of diasporic chance and creativity as yet another aspect of a "world in which each fact … is an amalgam of variations of itself" (62).

African Antecedents in Aster/Amber Valley: Esi Edugyan's *The Second Life of Samuel Tyne*

Different diasporic antecedents mark Esi Edugyan's first novel, *The Second Life of Samuel Tyne* (2004).[86] The opening setting is again Calgary, here the home of the civil service economist Samuel Tyne and his wife, Maud. They were born in Ghana, which they still refer to as the Gold Coast. Their conjugal challenges are complicated by the fact that "across the sea, their tribes had been deeply scornful of each other" (Edugyan 2004, 2).

While they met in Canada, their African past remains present in their lives in many other forms. Responding to the unsatisfactory way Samuel deals with their twin daughters' uncommunicative behaviour, for instance, Maud resorts to a geographically inflected proverb: "One does not ask a fool the way to Accra when one has a map in her pocket" (3). A curse by her abusive father is another part of her inheritance. It was uttered at the moment of her departure for Canada: "Abandon me and your mother's spirit will fell your husband and dry your insides to stone" (23). Although ineffective, the curse initially makes Maud's becoming pregnant seem "as likely as winning the Nobel Peace Prize" (22). The arrival of twins does not help: "Both Samuel and Maud were embarrassed to admit that not even an ocean could distance them from their superstition. For twins were a kind of misfortune"; considered "a freak occurrence," they "scared people. Only some awful wrongdoing could produce the same person twice" (24). Finally, Samuel's Canadian life has been determined by a family constellation in Africa that still shapes his present: to make amends for betraying Samuel's father, his uncle Jacob has Samuel educated in England and then takes him to Canada. His uncle's last, surprising gift is Samuel's inheritance of his house in the previously all-black settlement of Aster, a few hours away from Calgary.

Samuel is ready for a move. Stultified by his job and puzzled by his family, he spends his free time fixing mechanical devices in a shed where he feels – mistakenly – that "life could not find him" (8). Just after his uncle's death, his inane superiors reprimand him for his first mistake in fifteen years, providing the final push for him to quit: "Samuel Tyne was alive again" (13). Samuel's rebirth – the second life of Samuel Tyne – begins in Aster in 1968. He opens an electronics store, hoping to build the prototype of a computer (50, 65). The machine is the perfect embodiment of control that has been so absent from his life in Canada. He feels that "after fifteen years of the leash he'd finally seized it" (33); renting a shop in Aster appears to him like a "lease on his own little piece of the world" (65).

Based on one of the historical black settlements on the prairies, Amber Valley, Edugyan's Aster signifies "star" in Latin. As Karina Vernon points out, the novel thus relates Samuel's move to "the tradition of following the North Star" (2008, 204).[87] This particular journey, however, implies a complex substitution. Like Jacob before him – and like Harris's narrator or Foggo's parents' generation – Samuel has no desire to return to his origins. Instead, he searches for a black community in Canada: "Between Samuel and Jacob there had been a silent agreement that neither would return to Gold Coast … Aster, with its black origins, became a surrogate homeland, a way of returning without returning" (Edugyan 2004, 306).[88] As Vernon comments, in the encounter between an African immigrant family with the history of the Oklahoma settlers, Edugyan "'diasporizes' first-wave prairie history," confirming in the process "the continued importance of places like Amber Valley as locuses [*sic*] of black-inflected memory on the prairies" (2008, 204).[89]

Edugyan indeed builds on black prairies history. Aster is introduced as the "first black hamlet in Alberta" (2004, 35), and the novel rehearses part of the Oklahoma migration history. It also reminds readers of the white racist and state reaction to the arrival of such "strange pilgrims" (35): "As more blacks migrated from Oklahoma to set up lives on the prairies," the resistance from "the locals, folk who had themselves migrated little earlier" uses everything "from petitions to newspapers to name-calling" to "cure the province of its newcomers." Eventually, the government stops further black immigration (35); yet the community of blacks who have already claimed land persists.

Against this historical background, the novel begins to mythologize the town of Aster. The Tyne house appears from the beginning as a liminal space, sitting on the boundary between "Aster proper" and "the country" (42, 61). It is located on Stone Road, named after a stone wall collectively built by the black families of Aster whose contributions appear "like a patch in a stone quilt," but that was never finished and has now been reduced by erosion to "scarcely two inches" (36).[90] Like so many of the symbolic houses in the fictions of the Americas,[91] the Tyne house has its own story to tell (Cuder-Domínguez 2014, 439–40): it "radiated not only another era, but another world" (Edugyan 2004, 49). Built by a black settler, it has been further "diasporized" and seen occupants from many different cultures before the arrival of Jacob and then the Tynes (37–8). Aster is no longer predominantly black, and even the black population is no longer exclusively Oklahoma-descended (Vernon 2008, 210–13). In Edugyan's novel, the enigmatic Saul Porter, the last of the original Oklahoma immigrants and now neighbour of the Tynes, is married to another immigrant from Ghana, Akosua.

The town increasingly reveals itself as a liminal space of uncertainty. Samuel welcomes the "inspiring mix of people this town has," but his wife opines that "village life in a white man's country is poison, even if that village used to be a black one" (52). The subsequent events will give much support to her belief. While Samuel finally lives in his own house and the store begins to flourish, he too begins to realize that unpredictable events have relentlessly compromised Aster's promise as a refuge. The family's new white friends, Ray and Eudora Frank, as well as the Porter family next door, are puzzling in many ways. His shop landlord and the mayor seem to be racists (65, 91), and the behaviour of his twin daughters, Yvette and Chloe, is disturbing. Samuel, warned about an arsonist in Aster, responds lightheartedly: "My whole family was born by firelight … There is no reason to fear it now" (40). But when a local diner goes up in flames, he cannot avoid thinking that "Ray had brought him to this diner the day they'd found him the shop … Everything seemed connected in some dark and meaningful way" (90). This sense of foreboding is reinforced when he learns that the twins had eluded Maud and were unsupervised at the time of the fire. They had gone out for a stroll with Ama, the Métis girl Samuel had invited to join the family for the first summer (93–9). We also learn that, in the diner in question, people had stared at Ama and Yvette in a way that had left Yvette trembling: "I hate that … Even though this town used to be all black, everywhere you go they stare at you" (96). While Ama thinks that she had watched the outbreak of the fire together with Yvette from a diner across the street, she finds herself wondering later "if it really had been Yvette the whole time in that diner, or if she had been the victim of one of the twins' jokes" (101). More generally, the twins leave Ama afraid of the "drastic things she believed them capable of" (104).

Rife with increasingly horrifying possibilities, the text thus creates discomfort and suspense, and signals ever new irruptions of the uncanny (see Brydon 2008). Edugyan has suggested that the novel shows "definitely a hint of the gothic or the magic realistic" (in W. Compton 2005), in particular with regard to the twins, who boast miraculous abilities, such as speaking when six days old (17) or playing the piano without ever having practised (111). The twins isolate themselves and play tricks that become increasingly vicious; they leave Ama by herself on a raft on the Athabasca, where she almost drowns or freezes (160–5). When Maud falls off a ladder, Samuel suspects the twins may have had a hand in it (193). In another incident, they hand him codeine instead of the requested aspirin, seriously endangering him because of his allergies (241).

Like the town of Aster, the twins are based on historical precedent. Edugyan cites the Californian twin girls Poto and Cabengo and the Welsh "Silent Twins," "all of whom invented a language between them and refused to speak to anyone else" (in W. Compton 2005). As Andrea Davis has discussed, the second case concerns twins born to parents of Barbadian descent. These children responded to isolation and racism by "develop[ing] a private language combining Barbadian Creole and English." They were medically treated, convicted of arson, and locked away in an institution, where one of them died (A. Davis 2007, 43–4). Edugyan's twins follow a similar trajectory. Reacting to racism in Calgary, Yvette is overheard saying she "is tired of being black" (30). While linguistically extremely accomplished, the twins develop their own idiosyncratic communication. They become "unpredictable" even to their mother (165) and are accused of setting a second fire, which has destroyed the Porter's home. As the community turns against them and vandalizes Samuel's shop, Samuel takes the advice of Ray (261)[92] and institutionalizes the twins (276). As Davis comments, in the novel "it is Yvette and Chloe who are made to bear the scars of cultural displacement and racism" (2007, 44).

Edugyan's literary transformation of these case studies creates suspense and a sense of horror, but it also makes the twins signify in other ways. As with Chariandy and Harris, another cultural background intervenes here in Western (Canadian) time-spaces and epistemologies. Edugyan connects the uncanny, disruptive aura that surrounds the twins with African beliefs that remain active in the lives of the Tynes in Canada. The text offers a significant hint of this connection with a seeming non-sequitur. Samuel's dismissal of the arsonist warning, his assertion that there "is no reason to fear" firelight now, is followed by the seemingly unrelated information in the next sentence that he "had suppressed his guilt for not holding the Forty Days Ceremony" for his uncle. In what comes to look like an act of hubris, Samuel rationalizes that Jacob, isolating himself as a recluse, "had given up the privilege of being remembered"; Samuel assures himself that he "was not going to make himself uneasy by dragging past traditions into his life" (40). The havoc perpetrated by the twins, however, may be a consequence of Sam's disregard of African burial rituals, as Diana Brydon suggests (2008, 6). This possibility is supported by the accusations made by Akosua, "the African nationalist in the novel" (A. Davis 2007, 46–7). As Eudora reports to the Tynes, Akosua "didn't *see* them, but she's certain they did it. If not physically, then – and we don't all agree with this – through some magic or curse." For Akosua, the cause is directly related to Samuel's breach of his spiritual obligations: "She says you never had a proper burial for your uncle … She says he's causing madness in your children because of it" (259).

Brydon points out that "the mysteries embodied in the twins are never penetrated" (2008, 5). Indeed, the truth of Akosua's claims remains undecidable. She is often portrayed negatively, and her husband has ulterior motives with regard to the Tyne family's land. (As it turns out, so do the Franks, who have substantial influence on the community.) On the other hand, a number of factors support at least the claim that the twins are arsonists. One of Akosua's children may have seen the twins with a lighter before the fire was set (260), and Ama reports their return with it, reeking of smoke (265). The novel generally appears to support Akosua's wider contention that these upheavals are caused by disregard for spiritual obligations. When Samuel accepts his own guilt and responsibility, subsequent events seem to reward him, at least somewhat, for doing that.

Samuel thus follows his uncle's example: "I finally come to understand Jacob. For what you cannot change, you make amends" (277). Accused of madness by his wife, he admits a possible responsibility, conceding that "perhaps I passed it to our daughters" (277). He fulfills his traditional spiritual obligations when his wife dies, making "offerings of yams and whisky to God, with prayers for the well-being of the dead who were at the mercy of being forgotten" (296). Further, he includes a picture of Jacob and other deceased relatives in his private, traditional ceremony. Forty days after his wife's death, he performs the required ceremony together with the Porters, again including his uncle. As a result, "Jacob could finally stop wrestling and be blessed by his angel" (298).

Burying Maud next to Jacob with Ghanaian rituals affords Samuel a dual affirmation. The act puts him at peace with his ancestors and his African spirituality, but also confirms his own sense of Canadianness. He feels that their "citizenship had been finalized; their flesh, his kin, cold in the ground, were now inseverable from Alberta" (296). Edugyan makes the point that Samuel experiences, in this moment of personal tragedy, a profound sense of belonging in Alberta while at the same time recognizing his traditional Ghanaian spirituality and the powerful presence of his African antecedents. In fact, one sense of belonging seems only possible because he is at peace with the other.

Other circles are completed in the novel as well. The house that Samuel agreed to share with the Porters after the fire "belonged to him again" (302); Ama comes back to look after him in his old age (302); and a "lone twin" is seen returning to the house after his death.[93] There is the suggestion that Samuel's disregard of traditional beliefs may indeed have caused his calamities. His recognition of his hubris, which leads him to make amends like his uncle before him, seems to restore a certain balance in the novel's universe.

For Edugyan, by dramatizing the twins "at a distinct point in history within a certain geography, one is saying something very different about the racial experience in a given locale than if those same characters were placed into a different society. And that to me is an uncomfortable prospect" (in W. Compton 2005). The twins magnify the possible consequences of displacement and racism in the complex African Western Canadian time-space of Edugyan's novel. In responding to disruptive experiences, they themselves become agents of disruption. Their psychosis can be seen as a second-generation response to racism, displacement, and the cultural disorientation of their parents (Brydon 2008, 5; A. Davis 2007, 42–3). Adding a horrifying dimension to the novel, their dramatic reactions explode the tensions inherent in their lives. Their blackness, finally, positions them and their parents as the perfect targets of a witch hunt – even in the once-black town of Aster.

The novel, however, shows further pressures in this diasporic context. It is the African traditionalist and nationalist Akosua who most successfully provides some of the best arguments that help the Tyne family's false friends, the Franks, to stoke community opinion against the Tynes. The Franks manage to cite Akosua's African beliefs in support of their own goals while voicing some minor reservations about their non-Western aspects.

They successfully unleash the force of these beliefs on the community of Aster and the Tynes. Samuel himself finally accepts some of this reasoning. His "Western" response leads him to commit his twins to a "facility." At the same time, he heeds the healing aspects of his re-found traditional beliefs and accepts his obligations concerning them. His acceptance of the reality and power of ancestral knowledge appears to balance aspects of his diasporic life.

The African Canadian time-space of Edugyan's black prairies includes the possibility of causalities that may seem uncanny to Western understanding but that function as a critique of Western modernity from African perspectives (see Brydon 2008, 6). At the same time, the novel looks critically at some of these perspectives themselves. Akosua's beliefs lead to a demonizing of the twins. They are considered a disturbing anomaly in the cultural background she shares with Samuel and Maud, in which twins are seen to threaten concepts of identity, hierarchy, and anteriority – and thus even the principle of "primogeniture" (24). In the novel, they appear as perpetrators of cruel and horrible acts, but they are also victims who respond to prairies racism and are harshly judged by both Western and traditional Ghanaian beliefs. Eudora *and* Akosua thus collude in a process of characterization that will come to define the twins as evil (165, 259).[94] Influenced by this dual condemnation, Samuel prevails over Maud's objections and delivers them to a "facility" that seems a Kafkaesque nightmare in its denial of humanity. In Edugyan's novel, the consequences of that demonizing of what are, after all, children play out inexorably. As a result, aspects of both Western and traditional African beliefs are shown to fail the twins and their parents in their diasporic negotiations of the prairies.

With the cultural resources from either side of the Atlantic compromised, Samuel cannot "go home" to any safety presumably granted by the past. He cannot "return" to what may appear to be the "pure" kernel of his African past by following the star of Aster and the promise of black solidarity it signals through history and myth. Whatever peace and belonging is possible he can only find by forging a new present and future out of the past. Samuel qualifies his decision to move to Aster later "as a fool's dream, this ridiculous belief in the living perfection of the past." As he has come to realize, there "is no place in the world untouched by time" (283). The utopian aspect of Aster and its erstwhile exclusively black settler community does not deliver on its promise.[95] And as Saul Porter, the only surviving member of the original community in the novel, reveals in his own narrative of the community's settler experience (183–7), the hardships and betrayals suffered by that community are comparable in many ways to those experienced by Samuel. The ideal past never existed, it seems, in any form resembling the shape that captivated Samuel.

The Tyne house on the prairies does not offer the refuge and haven Samuel had sought in the mythic dimension of Aster. It is haunted by the various aspects of its past: a homestead in a black settler community, temporary home to transient migration experiences, Jacob's final destination after his own departure from Ghana, and, finally, the often inhospitable home of Samuel's dreams. Despite all this, the house becomes the place of his remembrance of things *only seemingly* past. In this place, he finds peace with regard to his uncle and his ancestors, and here he will have lived, in the end, what he accepts as a life of his own making, in both a tragic and a more positive sense.

For Edugyan, herself a second-generation prairies Canadian whose African parents met in Canada (in Mengiste 2013, 50), the "discovery of Amber Valley's existence … was the novel's main spur … Having grown up in 1970–80s Alberta, in which there seemed to be very few black people, I was fascinated to discover the existence of these black settlements" (in W. Compton 2005). Edugyan's novelistic exploration intervenes creatively in the historical record; concerned as it is not only with the consequences of the black Oklahoman migration north but also with later African immigration on the prairies, it takes liberties such as inserting, for example, "a family of Ghanaian immigrants into a historical community" (Vernon in W. Compton 2005).

In a three-way conversation with Edugyan and Wayde Compton, Vernon – also a second-generation black Albertan whose groundbreaking study on the black prairies was undertaken to undo a "damaging sense of unbelonging" – raises important questions about writers' responsibilities to the historical record. She suggests that Compton and Edugyan's works are "strikingly self-confident in their use of history" and engaged, to some extent, in "re-writing history" (in W. Compton 2005).[96] She also underlines that Edugyan's novel brings the earlier black prairies archive "into the consciousness of the present moment … by re-visiting an important site of first-wave history and re-imagining it from a contemporary, second wave perspective" (2008, 205). What unites Edugyan with Vernon and – as we will see in the next section – Wayde Compton is a sense of wonder and necessity. They are engaged in rediscovering marginalized black histories that have sunk beneath the surface of a black Atlantic that includes Western Canada and is part of its present and the future. In Vernon's inventive formulation, "when I found out about these historic black communities they seemed to me like buried, mythical places. The Black Atlantis" (in W. Compton 2005).

BLACK BRITISH COLUMBIA: WAYDE COMPTON AND ROOTED TRANSCULTURAL IMPROVISATION

The Canadian black Atlantis does not end at the Rockies. The (re)discovery and visibility of black British Columbian writing has been decisively advanced by Wayde Compton, who has "profoundly transformed our inherited understanding of British Columbia by recovering it as a black space" (Vernon 2012). As anthologist, editor, theorist, activist, and artist, he has helped to excavate the archive, nurtured and contributed to its current production, and drawn attention to the stakes of writing in the province. Partially inspired by George Elliott Clarke's anthology of black Nova Scotian writing, Compton's own anthology, *Bluesprint: Black British Columbian Literature and Orature* (2001), brings together texts from the nineteenth century and later and contemporary work. Together with Karina Vernon and David Chariandy, he has founded Commodore Books – "Western Canada's black literary press" – which has reissued Crawford Kilian's important history of British Columbia's black pioneers, *Go Do Some Great Thing* (2008); its list also includes Addena Sumter-Freitag's play *Stay Black & Die* (2007; see Vernon 2004, 69–76) and Fred Booker's admirable short-story collection *Adventures in Debt Collection* (2006).[97] A member of the Hogan's Alley Memorial Project (like the erstwhile Vancouver resident Vernon), Compton further collects and channels historical information about the earlier black community that existed near the Vancouver train station, another black community setting destroyed in the context of so-called urban renewal around 1970 and that today is the site of a highway overpass. In his own poetic work in *49th Parallel Psalm* (1999) and *Performance Bond* (2004), in his performances, and finally in his critical work, Compton draws upon the black British Columbian corpus and past in innovative ways. At the same time, he explores the relation between his own second-generation experience and black British Columbian history, as well as the possibilities of what he describes as his "Halfrican" (2004, 15) mixed-race identity.[98]

Compton locates important possibilities in black British Columbia's multiple marginalities. Like Peter Hudson, another black BC critic, who notes that "the fact of blackness in British Columbia" is marked by "both geographic isolation and demographic deficit" (2007),[99] Compton is more than aware of the province's "relatively small population of African descent" whose "history has barely penetrated the national or international consciousness" (2010, 11). In his essay collection *After Canaan: Essays on Race, Writing, and Region* (2010), however, he also highlights some opportunities arising from this marginality even within black culture. While black British Columbia is situated "outside the diasporic master narratives"[100] and on the "outer rim of black centres," this positionality also suggests that "we are, to some degree, in charge of our own enculturation" (14). For Compton, this cultural location signals an opportunity to sample and select – or to create and invent – articulations of identity out of available discourses and in proximity with other communities, in an artistic and theoretical practice he calls "an assertive Afroperipheralism" (15). The rediscovery and claiming of black British Columbian history is one of the foundations of this practice; another hallmark is reading and referencing this past creatively and making it part of the present from Compton's own generational and Halfrican perspective.

Black British Columbia began in 1858 with the arrival in Victoria of six hundred free black settlers from San Francisco. Fleeing increasingly hostile racist Californian laws (Winks 1997, 272; Kilian 2008, 11–19), these pioneers accepted an invitation from James Douglas – British Columbia's first governor and himself of mixed race – who wanted to stabilize the population of his young colony in the face of the Fraser River gold rush. As Compton's anthology reveals, among the first black writers of British Columbia were Douglas himself[101] and the businessman and newspaper editor Mifflin Wistar Gibbs, author of *Shadow and Light: An Autobiography with Reminiscences of the Last and Present Century* (1902).[102] The anthology also contains two slave narratives: a selection from William H.H. Johnson's account and the transcription of Sylvia Stark's recollections (see chapter 3), both produced in British Columbia. Another important segment from a later period consists of five transcribed testimonies by residents of Hogan's Alley.[103] Among the later and contemporary authors are musician Fred Booker and a host of younger writers, including the previously discussed Lorena Gale,[104] Peter Hudson, Karina Vernon, and Compton himself.

Compton innovatively references the history and earlier writing of black British Columbia in his own creative work. In this last part of chapter 5, I want to turn to his context-specific use of musical improvisation and hip hop as a model for textual production and performance in *49th Parallel Psalm* and *Performance Bond*. My main interest is to explore Compton's deployment of turntablism and remixing as metaphors for a practice of making a specifically located black historical context part of the present. As we have seen, Mairuth Sarsfield's *No Crystal Stair* references improvisational jazz practice to show how innovative black art can draw on a variety of resources in performances that nonetheless mediate historically specific forms of experience. Adjusting a long tradition of literary references to jazz and blues, Compton relies on hip hop – turning transformative textual "lit hop" – to articulate historical conditions and possible futures of black British Columbian diasporic subjectivity and performance.

Social Aesthetics and Transcultural Improvisation: Turntablism in *49th Parallel Psalm* and *Performance Bond*

The improvisational crossroads that allow Compton to combine transcultural and migrant resources in a rooted, historical, and social aesthetics, require a brief musicological preface regarding the global displacements of diasporic sounds that are facilitated by recording technologies. How can sounds and signs – transposed into new contexts from the original circumstances of their making, and fragmented, mixed, and reconfigured by turntablism, for instance – yield a new, socially mediated, and historically rooted aesthetics elsewhere? The very techniques of sampling and postmodern citation that drive Compton's artistic practice have been accused, after all, of betraying historical depth and the social relatedness of signs that undergo substantial transformation in improvisational performance and redeployment.

Interlude: Improvisation, Sound Writing Technologies, and the Displacements of Diasporic Sound

Improvisation often proves to be an effective practice in the contact zones of diasporic and transnational cultures. Transcultural improvisation can adapt and appropriate existing archives, materials, and techniques, and combine them through inventive sampling to produce new effects and solutions in a present defined by local circumstance. While such "dis–location" of erstwhile differently used ingredients is arguably the hallmark of invention generally, the increasing re-circulation of entire entities and sequences of artistically or otherwise produced artifacts has also been considered a defining feature of postmodern intertextual and often parodic re-articulation of earlier materials (e.g., Hutcheon 1988b). Employing a term from audiovisual culture in this respect, the cultural theorist and curator

Nicolas Bourriaud speaks of "postproduction" – the manipulation of previously recorded material – as an increasingly relevant form of artistic practice (Bourriaud 2000).[105]

But to what extent do DJing and other intertextually resourced forms of performance and improvisation – such as Compton's – either convey or "eradicate" the earlier contexts of their presumably "raw" materials in this process of "dis-location" and recontextualization? Do they leave the social dimension connected to these contexts entirely behind? Do they elide, recognize, sublate, assimilate, or otherwise mediate them? And how does this question relate to the status of "the social" not only of the resources, but of the performance itself?[106] With reference, for instance, to George Lewis's distinction between Afrological and Eurological perspectives on improvisation that I mentioned earlier,[107] Jesse Stewart calls for more scholarship that brings "the culturally specific aspects of Afrological engagements with postmodernism" into view. Stewart posits an "Afro-postmodernism" that "denotes the kind of fragmentation, plurality, and intertextuality normally associated with postmodernism, but locates these processes with the cultural matrix of the African diaspora wherein they often function in unique ways." In particular, Stewart suggests, they operate here "as strategies of identity formation that remember and honor the cultural past, while at the same time working to construct visions of a better future" (2010, 340–1). Stewart's reflections are made specifically with reference to DJing and turntablism, and thus they concern intertextual or intersonic practices of mixing and transforming mechanically transcribed "written sound" that often migrates across cultures and locations.

The transmission of sound and popular culture based on the oral – and on black – englishes and music was profoundly altered by the consequences of technological advances. The availability of mechanical sound transcription with Edison's 1877 invention of the phonograph contributed to the later dissemination and migration of blues, jazz, and eventually hip hop sounds. This development intensified dramatically first with new transmission technologies – from electromagnetic radiotelegraphy to television – and then with digitization and its attendant possibilities of dissemination. In the words of Georgina Born, "If music notation and recording were the means by which musical ideas, and then sounds, became spatially mobile – released, or alienated, from both place and co-presence – then digital media have accelerated those processes" (2005, 25). Mechanical sound writing thus opened the way for a secondary orality (Ong 2002) increasingly released from limits of time and space, but also from communities based on face-to face-contact – a necessary local condition of oral cultures that distinguished them from print cultures (see B. Anderson 1983). Following Edison's invention, the media facilitated what Paul Gilroy calls "translocal solidarities" (2000, 8), which rely on mediated nodes of exchange or appropriation of past-produced resources and thus unsettle the time flows and circulation patterns of "traditional" rooted cultures. The channels of conveyance and circulation signified by the agrarian metaphors of "root" and "culture" are opened to the chance of trades in other traditions.

These openings, however, can seem a mixed blessing. George Lipsitz suggests that "like other forms of contemporary mass communication, popular music simultaneously undermines and reinforces our sense of place. Music that originally emerged from concrete historical experiences in places with clearly identifiable geographic boundaries now circulates as an interchangeable commodity marketed to consumers all over the globe" (1994, 4). Yet while "consumption" might connote a certain passivity and absence of agency, it can also suggest a highly strategic and active practice of everyday life. This is the case in certain styles and practices of musical consumption. Gilroy argues that through performance in "black diaspora styles … the basic units of commercial consumption in which music is fast frozen and sold have been systematically subverted by the practice of racial politics." As he points out, such consumption as performance turns object into event (1993, 105). With reference to Michel de Certeau, he calls for "an enhanced understanding of 'consumption' that can illuminate its inner workings and the relationships between rootedness and displacement, locality and dissemination that lend them vitality in this countercultural setting" (105). Indeed, for de Certeau consumption channels agency "through its *ways of using* the products imposed by the dominant economic order" (de Certeau 1988, xii–xiii). Of course Bourriaud later highlights "a scrambling of boundaries between consumption and production" (2000, 13) that is typical of postmodernism, and notes that "in our daily lives, the gap that separates production and consumption narrows each day" (33). But what interests de Certeau more specifically – and what seems relevant with respect to Compton's artistic practice – is "the tactics of consumption, the ingenious ways in which the weak make use of the strong" (de Certeau 1988, xvii; qtd in Gilroy 1993, 103).

Gilroy sees such tactics of consumption at work in the "montage" strategies that musical innovators like Kool DJ Herc (aka Clive Campbell) operated by cutting and mixing available record tracks to produce what became hip hop. Such montage, however, and the transcultural and transnational migrations of hip hop and its commercialization draw attention to the relationships between what Gilroy calls "rootedness and displacement, locality and dissemination." Commercialization is certainly part and parcel of a nonetheless socially and historically specific aesthetics of hip hop. As the sociologist Herman Gray puts it, "Hip Hop is a commercial form fashioned from a specific confluence of social, cultural, and historical articulations that brought together different subjects, traditions, and narratives, recombining them so that they spoke to the specific local circumstances out of which they were fashioned. At the same time, as a popular commercial form, Hip Hop travels widely – across different social, geographic, media, and discursive spaces – adapting as it is adapted, recombining as it is itself recombined, to speak to local and specific conditions at the same time as it continues to signal identification and belonging to a global imagined community" (2003, 205).

Hip Hop in the Boondocks?

Wayde Compton's use of hip hop as literary metaphor and performance practice to channel black British Columbian voices is a case in point. Compton has emphasized hip hop as one of the factors intervening in his usage of black englishes: "For black writers in North America, these conditions constitute a new relationship to the old and treasured orality of our collective memory. While writers like Langston Hughes and Amiri Baraka looked to blues and jazz as their sources for memory and form in both poetry and prose (blues and jazz were received as much live as they were from recordings), black writers today have hip hop as their musical concomitant, their living extension of orality" (2003b). Compton is aware that hip hop, like any form and medium, comes with its own historical and cultural weight and logic. The relationship "between rootedness and displacement" evoked by Gilroy and Gray is one of Compton's concerns when he reflects on the mediated nature of this orality in hip hop and on the mediation of place that determines some of the meanings of consuming – and performing – hip hop in British Columbia: "Ironically, it is a type of music that is never quite completely live, but is plugged into a vast media machine that extends into every home and every ear individually more than communally. In the small culturally isolated black communities of western Canada, this individualization is exacerbated" (2003b). In his later *Performance Bond* (2004), Compton thus speaks of "hip hop / in the boondocks, / the relief package /

drop zone. I echo New York back / like a code cracker. / Reality hacker" (2004, 108). Yet he will also claim (via Chuck D): "Hip Hop is black Canada's CNN. / Talk stops for no border cop …" (2004, 102).

While Compton reflects critically on the mediated, transcultural, and potentially colonizing effects of hip hop "in the boondocks," he effectively consumes and practises hip hop in de Certeau's sense and in keeping with the claims to the style's adaptability to local circumstance. Compton employs hip hop as literary structural metaphor and practised improvisational form. The result is a border-crossing and intermedial social and historical aesthetics that adapts a number of historical and symbolic "tracks" to make these tracks answerable to the needs of a black British Columbian here and now.

History as Present (1): Legba's Technological Tidalectics

Compton's remixing of borders and histories for local consumption is coded under the sign of Legba, the voodoo trickster at the crossroads who controls traffic between humanity and the loa – the spirits of voodoo – who preside here over numerous other crossroads. Compton's text crosses the borders not only between the written and the spoken (black) word, music, and various other modes of conveyance, but also between the present and the past. Consider the opening poem of *49th Parallel Psalm*:

MC

conductor, conductor,
this is over
ture. I sure
foot halfstep
to drums splayed for you. does rum

conduct electricity? drop a dram
on the ground to be grounded,
to be landed,
so we can dig the sound
of the switches and the channels.
Shango flows into the amp.
the tubes warm up.
the filaments erupt.

go fourth and multiply,
go north and fly
to each cardinal point,
and us just
the forth generation from slavery. (1999, 12)

The book opens under the sign of the MC – in hip hop also called "move the crowd" and designating the rapper addressing the audience. Here, the MC leads a "cast" that is introduced in the first section, including, among others, Sam, the voodoo loa of Baron Samedi; JD, the initials of the first governor of British Columbia, James Douglas; and, at the end, DJ – the disk jockey as modern-day *griot*, and as Papa Labas or Legba at the crossroads.

The opening doubled invocation of a "conductor" replays and mixes musical and electronic references with historical tracks that point to the legacies of slavery, black disenfranchisement, and diaspora. The conductor, as Underground Railroad guide across borders and towards freedom of oppression, takes on multiple references and overtones – first in musical terms as a kind of orchestral DJ and then in electronic terms as a channelling device.

These doublings of the first line are replayed and complicated by the line break with its remix of the word "overture." In terms of doubled content, the break signals historical pastness (for instance, of the Underground Railroad and of the following history of black British Columbia) *together with*, or as a form of, a new beginning as "over" becomes "overture" – a musical and historical opening – but also "overture" as "proposal," whose meaning links the past of "over" to future possibilities.

In addition, the line break shows Compton in conversation with some of his acknowledged inspirations, such as Black Mountain–influenced Vancouver *TISH* poetics but also Edward Kamau Brathwaite's poetic trilogy *The Arrivants* (1973; see W. Compton 2003a, 492–7; H.N. Thomas 2006, 60)[108] and his concept of "tidalectics," with its emphasis on repetition. In the introduction to his 2001 anthology *Bluesprint: Black British Columbian Literature and Orature*, Compton describes the larger emphasis on repetition in tidalectics as "an Africanist model for thinking about history … In contrast to Hegel's *dialectics* … *tidalectics* describes a way of seeing history as a palimpsest, where generations overlap generations, and eras wash over eras like a tide on a stretch of beach … Repetition, whether in the form of ancestor worship or the poem-histories of the *griot*, informs black ontologies more than does the Europeanist drive for perpetual innovation, with its concomitant disavowals of the past. In a European framework, the past is something to be gotten over, something to be improved upon; in tidalectics, we do not *improve upon* the past, but are ourselves *versions* of the past" (2001, 17).

Commenting again on Brathwaite's tidalectics in a discussion of the connection between poetry and hip hop turntablism, "The Reinventing Wheel," Compton applies similar ideas of repetition and variation to small-scale decisions of utterance and re-articulation in black and electronic orality (here especially through remixing): "I think he means that each person, each beat, each stage of culture is a version of the last one, and is not a progressive disjuncture. If this is the case, then the orality of temporally – and spatially – removed Africa can also be this new electronic orality. The idea is not to break, or even to preserve, but to repeat; and to celebrate repetition, knowing that you will mis-duplicate – and that the mis-duplications are the closest achievable thing to an actual you" (2003b). This sense of connection and repetition also plays out, on a smaller scale, in the sound repetitions and connections that modulate meanings and overlays as "MC" continues its remixing of historical tracks, personal identity, electronic circuitry, and voodoo mythologies. From the narrator's *dance* we come to *drums*, associated with the voodoo loa Shango, and then – guided again by the sound pattern – to a *dram* of *rum*. Rum is often associated with Baron Samedi, the loa of death but also of sex and resurrection (and the subject of the following poem). The poem first evokes the possibility of rum as "conductor" in the various senses of that word (material, spiritual, historical), then recommends a small sacrifice of rum – a feeding of the loa – "to be grounded / to be landed" as immigrant in this enabling tidalectic mixing of voodoo mythology, black history, and electronics. This circuitry continues as Shango, the loa associated with thunder – and hence with the African resistance to enslavement – and with drums and music, dance and art, is amplified by the old-school, heat-radiating, conducting technology of tubes and filaments. The remix, here, is part of a historical and social aesthetics, replaying and mis-duplicating in the next lines Noah's post-deluge command to "go forth and multiply" (which is also urban slang for "get lost") as the misspelling doubled double "go *fourth* and multiply" (emphasis added), and finally leading to the direct connection ("go north … and us / just the forth generation from slavery") between the speaker's here and now and earlier generations as they fled from slavery and disenfranchisement to Canada.

At the Border of History and the Present (2): Legba's Turntables, James Douglas and the DJ

The enabling figure of Legba is omnipresent in Compton's improvisational tidalectics. This voodoo trickster at the crossroads, who is here also the gatekeeper at the border, appears later in "MC" and again in two poems connected as inverted doubles by their titles, "JD" and "DJ." The first title evokes James Douglas, the mixed-race first governor of British Columbia, who invited a founding group of blacks from San Francisco to cross the border to his province in 1858. The inversion of his initials as the title of a poem a few pages later, "DJ," relates him to the manipulator of tracks and hip hop. The time-crossing remix of the two signals – or what Compton calls "the temporal conflation of past, present and future (synchronic narrative)" that he associates with voodoo syncretism (W. Compton 2003a, 484) – channels again a historical and social aesthetics through tidalectic voodoo poetics and electronic media. Compton's James Douglas, apostrophized as "our own quadroon Moses," is a Legba at the crossroads:

> you held the keys
> like a lesser Legba – laughing, shuffling passports,
> passing
> in your black and white
> archival stance … (W. Compton 1999, 18)

Here again, chains of alliteration and assonance tidalectially replay and remix sounds, leading from a "lesser Legba" to "laughing" and "shuffling" (and thus card-playing and chance), and from "passports" to James Douglas's own "passing" and mixed race. This "black and white" is then remixed as the signifier of print and of the vagaries of historiography and the written archive.

The later, doubling poem "DJ" calls on "Papa Labas / [to] open the doors / straddle the roles," after invoking the DJ as the conductor at the crossroads of contemporary narratives, secondary orality, and knowledge:

> a hand on the texts and tomes   the keeper
> spins limbs   the griot
> holds in his collection the keys to corporeal
> wisdom   this body of texts
> these twelve-inch tables of counterclockwiseness …

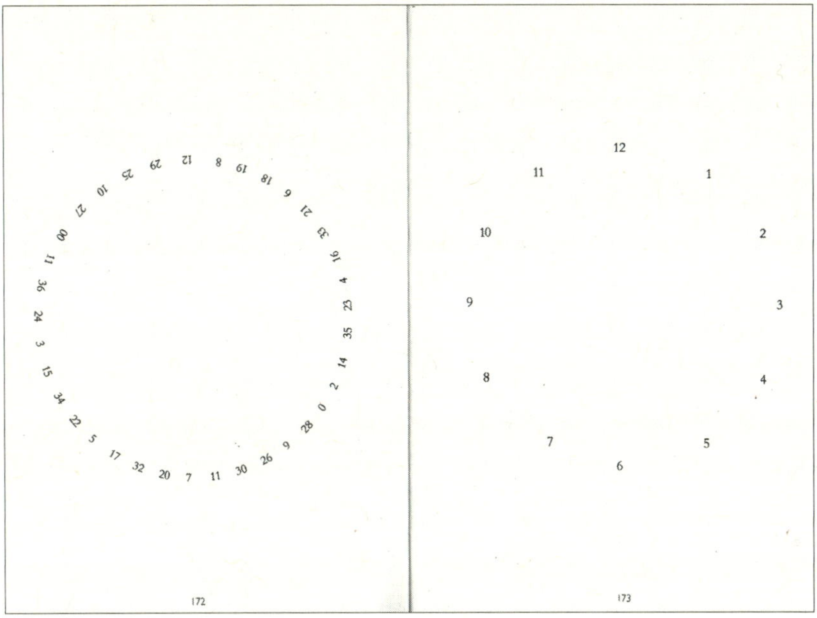

Reprinted from *49th Parallel Psalm* by Wayde Compton (Arsenal Pulp Press, 1999) with permission of the publisher and the author

> ...
> more singles in the crates than scrolls in the ancient library
> of Alexandria (1999, 25)

Compton's *49th Parallel Psalm* closes with the section "Hear," a counterpart in the present to the earlier "Their" and equally predicated on the oral. The very last poem is "49th Parallel Psalm," which invokes again the DJ with two "parallel" circles inserted after the line "living on the weals of steal." Concrete poetry here remixes the wheels of steel – or turntables – themselves as the conjunction of time and chance, with a DJ-Legba controlling the crossfader between the two "reinventing wheels."

The clock of the right circle is doubled by the American roulette wheel of the left (which, in contrast to the single-zero French wheel, includes both 0 and 00 for the bank – increasing its statistical advantage). Compton makes a few substitutions: number 1, the sign of beginning, has been replaced by two numbers 11: a doubled double. One of these numbers takes up the place of the numbers 1 and 13, with the latter thus also missing, as is its inversion, 31. Note that in roulette, the croupier or dealer spins the wheel and the ball in opposite directions, like the DJ when scratching the "twelve-inch tables of counterclockwiseness" (1999, 25).

Turntablism thus becomes the sign and medium of the DJ-Legba and of tidalectics: two circles doubling, mixing time at the crossroads between past and present, turning horizontal progression and dialectics into vertical repetition and counter-clockwiseness. The remixing of the tracks of history and time thus envisions the past as accessible resource of the present, suggesting agency and another chance.

Vèvè

Compton includes a performance of turntablism and MCing on a CD that is part of his second volume, *Performance Bond* (2004). Entitled, significantly, "The Reinventing Wheel," it offers examples of a secondary orality as remix of history, opening up to crossroads of past and future[109] at the fault lines and interstices of its reiteration. As one line states, "The rupture is the inscription, the brokenness the tradition" (2004, 103). The corresponding printed section directly precedes the section "Rune," which features Vancouver's former black neighbourhood, Hogan's Alley. It was erased by urban planning and a road viaduct around 1970. One of the first poems in this section, "Vèvè," articulates in other ways the interventionist tidalectics of "The Reinventing Wheel."

"Vèvè" is the sign in voodoo that *invokes* Legba as the master of the crossroads. The poem "Vèvè" is followed by further historical remixes and border crossings in the section "Rune," which includes a photo essay entitled "Lost-Found Landmarks of Black Vancouver" that fictively re-envisions doors under the signs of a reinvented black community: a "Coloured Benevolent Society," a Muslim temple, a black newspaper, and the "Pacific Negro Working Men's Association." Another remix supplements oral histories with black Vancouver residents – originally recorded by Daphne Marlatt and Carole Itter (*Opening Doors*) and reprinted in Compton's *Bluesprint* – with oral testimonies attributed to a fictive volume, *Portals*: *East Vancouver Oral Histories* (1972).[110] These inventive invocations can be read in light of the preceding, prefatory "Vèvè," a dialogue taking place "beside the Georgia Viaduct," the former site of Hogan's Alley. Two characters, Digital and Analogue, named after modes of recording and conveyance, discuss Brathwaite's poem equally entitled "Vèvè" and his evocation of Legba at the end of *The Arrivants* (1973). Brathwaite here evokes Legba's sign as the ground of writing – albeit a broken one.[111]

Analogue uses trail mix to pour a version of Legba's "Vèvè" on the broken ground of Hogan's Alley. It is eaten up by pigeons – an evanescence that prompts Digital to inquire about more permanent materials such as ink. A coyote – another incarnation of the trickster – walking by unnoticed (2004, 120), however, signals the efficacy of the Vèvè despite its subsequent erasure. Analogue later suggests that "maybe an ephemeral language that can drift away in the wind or be eaten by birds would be able to say things we can't think of" (2004, 121). The writing of the Vèvè is ephemeral, an evocative performance in real time. Yet if the passing coyote is any indication, the vanishing trace of this writing performance has the power to invoke Legba. Analogue remarks, "It's more than language, it's sorcery or worship. It's a portal between worlds" (2004, 118). He adds later, "I don't think it's quite right to call it writing. I think what Brathwaite means is that it's the *beginning* of writing or the urge to make a new kind of language, one unique to the New World" (2004, 119).

It is no coincidence that Brathwaite's poem appears at the very end of a trilogy in a section called "Beginning." Compton's "Vèvè" similarly comes in the last section, prefacing his remixed "portals" of Hogan's Alley. The Vèvè thus serves as sign of a "concluding" preface to a new, transformative beginning, invoking Legba to grant the remix of history, passage at the border, and conveyance to the loa. As the title of Compton's poem, "Vèvè" is both descriptive and performative. Writing the sign is itself an act of conjuring that invokes a new language with transforming powers. It performs and invokes a border-crossing language that renegotiates past elisions of black histories and creates portals for a new history and a future mediated by acts of tidalectic writing.

Many of the signs and materials of this performance and social aesthetics belong to far-flung diasporic archives and displacements, such as voodoo, Caribbean (here Bajan) exilic writing, or hip hop with far-away origins. But they are adopted and adapted here to speak to the (re-)rooting of a local history and culture. Not only the history and culture of black British Columbia is tidalectically re/cognized by Compton's lit-hop portals, but also a transcultural and transnational diasporic Canada. Compton creates figures of the reinventing and recording storyteller. His texts cross geographical borders of the African diaspora, reconfiguring the borders between histories of forgetting and storytelling histories that validate black diasporic experience. Compton's acts of writing come with the performative power of invocations, foreshadowing new kinds of speaking and seeing the New World.

6

Coda: Other Canadas, Other Americas, the Black Atlantic Reconsidered

Listening and responding tidalectically to Brathwaite through repetition and revision, Wayde Compton himself channels and finally performs a re-iteration of the Vèvè as sign/ature that invokes another new beginning. Like so many of the authors I have discussed, Compton finds resources locally and in other diasporic times and spaces, recirculating antecedents in his own, particular "remix." Re/cognized in textual practice and performance, this archive of recovered signs, narratives, and earlier scripts and "tracks" is actively reworked to enable a locally situated vision and perspective. These resources are made to support cultural identities in a process of "becoming" that – to recall Stuart Hall's words – "belongs to the future as much as to the past" (1990, 225). Another wave of Compton's interventionist tidalectics, his recent volume *The Outer Harbour* (2014), creates new portals in stories that explicitly move from the past and present to the future. The text combines fictive documentary and histories with the inventive possibilities of speculative fiction. Compton offers extended meditations on space, migrancy, and displacement, as well as indigeneity and race, together with thoughts on transformation and the co-presence of multiple realities. These virtualities include absented histories and futures in contest with simulacra and co-optive technologies created to perpetuate the dominant and protect the status quo. The opening story's main character suggests some of the transformative dimensions of the text, evoking relations between blackness, mixed race, indigeneity, and displacement. Riel, a black man with the name of the historical leader of the mixed-race Métis (12), is inspired by a "Mystery Migrant" and her performance of "Illegal Migration" (23). At the end of the story, he leaves his past contexts behind and is "commuting to the future" (30). This is what the stories do themselves, reaching from 2001 – and the turning point of 9/11 (30) – to the year 2025.

Several stories feature the *terra nova* of a volcanic island that has arisen in Vancouver's outer harbour. It is named Pauline Johnson Island (after the Mohawk writer who adopted Vancouver as her home) and is claimed by a First Nations activist and his friends, among them Jean, who "is pretty much black" (34). Suggestive of relations between First Nations and black diaspora displacements and of commonalities in their relation to state-sponsored geographies and space, their trip to the forbidden island makes them "illegal by being there" (43). Like the Mystery Migrant in the opening story, they experience "being people where they shouldn't be" (43). The state's violent response to their transgression leads to the first death in the island's new world. The killed person, however, is not effaced from what remains real in the text, signalling Compton's interest in the potentiality of alternative histories that are not written by the winners; instead, the character reappears later as "the insurgent." He exists on the island together with other "migrants" who transcend time and space. Though corralled in the "Pauline Johnson Island Special Detention Facility," they often "blink out" and are found outside of the facility, demonstrating "ICDP" or "Individual and Collective Displacement Phenomenon" (167–9). In opposition to masks of subjectivity projected by the state apparatus,[1] the ontological realities of these figures are transversal to the spaces and temporalities ordained by dominant definitions of the real. The future "will surely include a protracted campaign of clashing imaginations" (189); this statement sums up what is at stake in these speculative and transgressive alter-realities grounded in local yet also transnational circumstances. Further demonstrating the investments of Compton's fiction in contemporary struggles, this apt comment appears in an interpolated fictive document whose title references the turntablist counter-temporalities and wisdom discussed earlier, "Counter Clockwise and the G25 Riots: Fighting Fabulism with Fabulism?" (185).

Compton's speculative fiction joins other black Canadian artists' projects that explicitly address future dimensions in connection with their locally anchored worlds. Camille Turner's *Hush Harbour* is one of the examples that come to mind, an Afrofuturist sonic walk that remaps Toronto space via some of its black history (Turner 2012b). Listeners are guided through Toronto's Victoria Memorial Square and learn about Afronauts – guided by signals from the CN Tower – who transcend time and space; they accompany their forbear Samuel through the square in 1793 Toronto where he courts Peggy Pompadour, the historically documented slave of corrupt

Family Compact politician Peter Russell.[2] Like many of the other black Canadian works we have encountered, Turner's Afrofuturist re-visioning of Toronto finds sustenance in events of the past and makes them real and present for contemporary audiences.

Before reflecting further on the different ways in which audiences are engaged by these works, I want to recall some aspects of this vast archive of possible resources. It contains times and spaces that are reclaimed, revalued, and re-articulated, but also texts, artistic styles, and forms of performance that are both honoured and transformed by later works that employ them as usable resources for the present and the future. Compton's black British Columbia thus emerges as a remix of the local past, cross-border US and transnational connections, and speculative projections into the future; but some of these textual spaces are also nourished by African and Afro-Caribbean religious cosmologies and sustained by contemporary black music, mostly birthed in black urban spaces south of the border before being re-articulated in his work for local purposes. Related patterns appear in many other texts. Sarsfield's *No Crystal Stair* digs deep into local history, but the novel's black anglophone Montreal also arises out of musical connections, literary antecedents, and transnational networks that include the United States, the Caribbean, and Europe. Montreal appears through Haitian eyes in Agnant's *La dot de Sara*, and other francophone versions of the city are revealed in the palimpsestic time-spaces of works by Ollivier and numerous other Haitian Québécois authors. Anglophone Caribbean Canadian writers – Foster, Silvera, Austin Clarke, Brand, Philip, Alexis, Chariandy, and so many others I have not been able to discuss in detail – likewise reveal a Caribbean that often "takes place" in Toronto or elsewhere in Ontario. The Caribbean is alive – if not always well – in composite or hybrid spaces we still call Caribbean Canadian, although they are now part of Toronto or Montreal as signifiers of important Caribbean cities.

Black prairies texts also signal a rich network of black diasporic relations, including the African, Caribbean, and US connections articulated in the complex times and spaces created by Edugyan, Harris, and Foggo. The Canada-US nexus, present in Sarsfield and prominent in Compton's *49th Parallel Psalm*, marks Edugyan's *The Second Life of Samuel Tyne* through the Oklahoma migration, explored in more detail in Foggo's *Pourin' Down Rain*. Lawrence Hill's *Any Known Blood* makes the Canada–US border central, shifting back and forth across the line and moving from a present-day Ontario present backwards through the black Canadian nineteenth century to pre–Civil War US slavery and the event of Harpers Ferry.

In *The Book of Negroes*, these spatial and historical vectors of diaspora further extend to earlier British North American/United States times and spaces and, beyond that, to a black Atlantic dimension that includes African locations and the middle passage. Hill's novel links eighteenth-century Nova Scotia to the new-born United States, England, and various sites in Africa, but it also shows Nova Scotia as a site of slavery in what is now Canada. This theme is explored in more detail in George Elliott Clarke's *Beatrice Chancy* – set not much later in Nova Scotia – and Gale's *Angélique*.

In these texts, then, Canada is an important site for a substantial exploration of slavery and the black Atlantic and their foundational role in the development of modernity. Many of the other works make related connections. They show the long shadow of slavery in the unresolved and accumulated time experienced by post-slavery subjectivities. In Philip's *Zong!* or works by Brand – such as *A Map to the Door of No Return* and her many other texts discussed earlier – slavery and the middle passage are not only past but also present. Austin Clarke's *The Polished Hoe* and Agnant's *The Book of Emma* work through the difficult simultaneity of difference and equation that relates past and present in the accumulated temporalities of the black Atlantic.

In the earlier texts of nineteenth-century black Canada, slavery is an immediate presence. Autobiographical witnessing and retrospective accounting structure the time of slave narratives. But even there time is also perceived with an intense emphasis on the present and the future. In this context, it is striking to observe the cosmopolitan outlook in many of the nineteenth-century Canadian and earlier Nova Scotian writers of the black Atlantic. Their texts show black individuals trying to make a home for themselves in what is now Canada, revealing fiercely local interests in belonging; they also look at time and space, however, as dimensions of potential freedom and black possibility. David George, while on the ship from Nova Scotia to Sierra Leone, shared with Thomas Clarkson his desire to go England – which was later realized. Josiah Henson, Samuel Ringgold Ward, and many others crossed the border into Canada but also traversed the Atlantic. Mary Ann Shadd draws a strategic map of anti-slavery emigration and black freedom that includes Latin America and the Canadian Pacific coast. Martin Delany, finally, less intent upon Canada yet an influential Chatham resident, not only had Cuba, the wider Caribbean, and Central and Latin America on his mind, but also led an expedition to Africa.

In keeping with such diasporic perspectives, the time-spaces that are re/cognized and articulated in many black Canadian texts, past and present, come with very large horizons. Most of these writings are anchored in what is now Canada but continually relay its times and places via other diasporic histories and routings. Contemporary texts also mediate and "detour" subjectivities through local and global hauntings and re-memberings, which they rework as so many resources and enabling signs of community and commonality. Making wide-ranging connections across time and space, and bringing these diasporic histories and geographies into the here and now, black Canadian writing significantly contributes to the rewriting of circum-Atlantic and hemispheric modernity, repositioning Canada and our present in this context. Redefining modernity with reference to the foundational role of the black Atlantic, many of these texts re–present the unspeakable sufferings of dislocated and enslaved Africans as well as their extraordinary contributions to the Americas, emphasizing the decisive offerings of free black workers, entrepreneurs, visionaries, artists – and witnesses. The temporalities of these perspectives often span centuries; the spatial horizon of the black Atlantic implies not only Canada, the United States, and the Caribbean, but all of the Americas. Just as Glissant once remarked that "I speak and above all write in the presence of all languages of the world,"[3] these texts place readers in the presence of extensive spatial and temporal horizons.

To be "in the presence of" these times and spaces has multifaceted implications. What are some of the consequences that the presence of this work might have for readers, pedagogy, and scholarship? What does its presence mean in relation to other areas of writing, within and beyond Canada, and with respect to the nation itself? Such questions imply a range of critical problems that remain challenges in the future.

To begin, how do these horizons implicate readers, and how are different kinds of subjects and audiences interpellated by black Canadian texts? As Stuart Hall has suggested, black diasporic identities are produced in various ways with reference to the past. Both the past and this very process of identity-creation are the subject of many of the texts we have encountered. They either show or offer resources for the kind of affirmative or critical engagement with identities and scripts that Hall considers and that Anthony Appiah has also described (1996, 97–105; Siemerling 2005, 147–54). Detailed accounts of the communicative strategies of black Canadian texts, the positioning of their implied readers, and studies of actual reception, however, might make further use of these theoretical accounts. In addition, these issues of diasporic identity and identification are joined by questions of how non-black readers might respond to these works in the context of their own experiences, horizons of expectation, or limitations.[4] Some writers have suggested that they do not write with such issues in mind[5] or, by contrast, that their writing is meant to address and critique stereotypes typically present among non-black audiences. A number of writers offer a clear awareness of particular reader responses. Austin Clarke has suggested that when he "began writing, the reviewers at the time, all White, could not separate my work from their own views of blackness. There was nothing in their seeing me – or rather seeing my characters – that they would link to their own experience" (in H.N. Thomas 2006, 16). His comment seems to call for readings in more connective terms but does not appear to express a desire for excluding some of his potential audience. Some works, on the other hand, may be written primarily with certain readers in mind, such as black, diasporic, or regionally defined audiences. Yet most authors, once they have decided to publish a text, would seem interested in a wide readership – albeit certainly not at any cost.[6]

To the extent that black texts constitute public practices of witnessing, they require that their readers, as Derrida points out, be able to testify, in some way or other, to the fact that they have been in the presence of such witnessing.[7] Possible outcomes may include shared knowledge, the dismantling of stereotypes, transracial and translocal solidarities, the weakening of racism, and the extension of equitable principles and democracy. When black suffering is evoked in such testimony, however, not only issues of ethics, empathy, and political partiality are at stake, but also the additional problematic of what Saidiya Hartman has called the "spectacle of suffering" (1997, 19). Hartman declines to reproduce Frederick Douglass's account of his childhood witnessing of his aunt's beating.[8] She raises the question of how readers respond to such scenes: "Are we witnesses who confirm the truth of what happened in the face of the world-destroying capacities of pain, the distortions of torture, the sheer unrepresentability of terror, and the repression of the dominant accounts? Or are we voyeurs fascinated with and repelled by exhibitions of terror and sufferance?" (3).[9] She continues: "Or does the pain of the other merely provide us with the opportunity of self-reflection? At issue here is the precariousness of empathy and the uncertain line between witness and spectator" (3–4).

A related set of questions has been raised with respect to sentimentality. Paul Gilroy evokes James Baldwin's condemnation of sentimentality and "the ostentatious parading of excessive and spurious emotion" in *Uncle Tom's Cabin* (Baldwin 1965, 10; qtd in Gilroy 2010, 64). Gilroy himself censures any "immoral substitution of the comfortable reader or perverse spectator for the vulnerable victim" (65), and expresses concern over racial stereotypes in the novel (67). But he maintains that "the outright dismissal of any useful outcome from familiarity with the suffering of others should itself be questioned" (65). With reference to Luc Boltanski's *Distant Suffering* (1999; Gilroy 2010, 64), Gilroy emphasizes the "number of ways in which strategies premised upon emotional communication, psychological identification, and the formation of moral communities might open up possibilities for change achieved through social and political mobilization" (65). Work by Jane Tompkins on Stowe's novel (1985)[10] or by Martha Nussbaum on empathy[11] would support Gilroy's views in this regard. Despite his concerns about *Uncle Tom's Cabin*, Gilroy stresses the effective power of "heterophatic identification" (2010, 66), the role of the novel in mobilizing energies against slavery, and the novel's contribution to "a tradition of cosmopolitan reflection on racial hierarchy and injustice" (that, as he reminds us, also relates to nineteenth-century "struggles to defend indigenous peoples" [67]). While black Canadian writing is hardly exclusively concerned with black suffering, the questions raised by these issues suggest that more work on the communicative dimensions of black Canadian writing and its reception in different periods and by various groups of readers will be useful.

These concerns include the mediation of black Canadian writing by the literary institution, on both national and international levels, and its relation to other contexts of reception. Reviews and revisions of literary history are due in this regard. Given that Canadian literary and cultural history has been slow to give black writing appropriate consideration,[12] the ways in which black Canadian writing is inflected in national narratives needs re-examination. Despite recent improvements, the task of rewriting Canadian literary history to include black writing from all periods in an integral fashion remains incomplete.

Another unfinished critical task consists in examining representations of black characters in non-black writing, and the role of such representations for the constitution of whiteness. In the studies by Phanuel Antwi, George Elliott Clarke, and Jade Ferguson that I have cited, significant work has been done on the representation of blackness in white nineteenth-century Canadian writing. In chapters 3 and 5, I have discussed aspects of the role of blackness in Susanna Moodie's work and Morley Callaghan's *The Loved and the Lost* (1951). A more systematic analysis of the role of blackness in non-black Canadian writing would cover texts from Thomas Chandler Haliburton's writings to such later works as Louis Dantin's *Les enfances de Fanny* (1951), Donat Coste's *L'enfant noir* (1950), Ethel Wilson's *The Innocent*

Traveller (1949), Margaret Laurence's African writings, Hubert Aquin's *Trou de mémoire* (1968), Margaret Atwood's *Bodily Harm* (1981), Lori Lansens's *Rush Home Road* (2002), and many others.[13]

The use of black Canadian literary antecedents in non-black Canadian writing seems to have been little studied (in contrast to the Henson-Stowe file).[14] The question of how and why, conversely, black Canadian writing references other Canadian literary antecedents is also a relevant one. As Henry Louis Gates points out, black writers like Ralph Ellison or Ishmael Reed create texts "that are double-voiced in the sense that their literary antecedents are both white and black novels, but also modes of figuration lifted from the black vernacular tradition" (1988, xxiii). George Elliott Clarke cites this passage to signal a similar condition for black Canadian texts (2002a, 74). Elucidation of the strategic, ironic, or counter-discursive citations and appropriations of non-black Canadian writing through black intertextuality remains an intriguing and relevant critical endeavour.

The relation between black diasporic writing and indigeneity raises another set of important considerations in regard to both national spaces (as we have seen in Compton's *The Outer Harbour*) and the hemispheric aspects of the black Atlantic. Discussing the Canadian context, Christine Kim, Sophie McCall, and Melina Baum Singer suggest that "diaspora and nation are interdependent and mutually constituting, just as indigeneity and nation are reciprocally contingent and responsive" (2012, 2). With reference to the black prairies archive, Karina Vernon provides an extended discussion of the frequent use of metaphors of indigeneity that "enable critics to powerfully counter the sense of blackness as only a recently-arrived phenomenon by pointing out black presences that are so old and deeply rooted as to seem virtually indigenous" (2008, 141). There are, indeed, substantial gains to be had from using the concept of indigeneity to highlight "the special, but under-recognized, interrelationships of black Canadians to particular geographies that have evolved over generations despite the metaphorical and actual attempts on the part of the nation to remove them" (147). On the other hand, Vernon underlines not only the implicit potential for divisiveness between different black writers generated by this distinction, but also the necessity of considering "indigenizing metaphors from a postcolonial or First Nations' perspective" (143).

Citing Taiaiake Alfred's insistence on the primacy of First Nations (1999), Vernon critiques the recourse to claims of indigeneity in Canada by groups other than First Nations (2008, 148–9). She reminds us of pertinent analyses by Margery Fee (1987) and Terry Goldie (1989) about white settler fantasies of indigeneity and further evokes Marlene NourbeSe Philip's statement that the "only peoples who be(truly)long here – who be long here (I use 'be' in the African American vernacular sense), are the Native peoples" (Philip 1992, 22; qtd in Vernon 2008, 150). In a later interview, Philip is adamant that she does not see "Canada as a neutral space. I see it as a space that is still contested in terms of First Nations people … We come in; we buy houses on their land. We do what most immigrants do, but with little regard for their struggles" (in P. Saunders 2005, 208–9).[15] Vernon agrees with Philip's insistence on "coming face to face with the fact of black Canadians' non-aboriginality"; she notes, however, that "this does not mean that she also gives up trying to reclaim a sense of our belonging to Canada" (2008, 151). Bucknor and Coleman recognize Philip as one of the writers who "have insisted upon the importance of addressing and redressing the injustices perpetrated against aboriginal people as part and parcel of the assertion of Caribbean Canada as a culturally significant dynamic" (2005, xvi–xvii). Indeed, Philip is joined in this concern by Claire Harris, who states that "the First Nations are up against formidable forces … They need their elders, not colonizers. We must never forget that this civilization was born in blood" (in H.N. Thomas 2006, 127). The relation of black Canadian writing to indigeneity and First Nations has received some critical comment, but more systematic work like Vernon's is necessary to address this subject both nationally and in wider North American and hemispheric contexts.

The contextual relations of black Canadian writing as part of the black Atlantic and its hemispheric dimension further invite linguistic perspectives that often go beyond standard English or French. An array of englishes and Creoles – and sources and texts in Spanish and Portuguese – are relevant to contextual perspectives, which in many cases may require transdisciplinary collaboration. This is especially the case if slavery and post-emancipation subjectivities are to be understood as hemispheric conditions and thus take the Caribbean and Latin America in account. In addition, African cultural, religious, and linguistic knowledges are often immediately relevant with regard to black Canadian writing. For disciplines that have traditionally focused on geographically circumscribed national fields, relations with transnational and hemispheric studies can be challenging and difficult. Given its relatively recent disciplinary emergence, the study of Canadian literature is sometimes perceived to be threatened by the facile dismissal of nation as a relevant category of cultural mediation or by a preponderance of US perspectives in hemispheric studies.[16] But the fact that black Canadian writing, defined by specific locations and historical situatedness, frequently works through diasporic connections and locations invites productive crossings of disciplinary boundaries.

This challenge is one of the opportunities presented by black Canadian cultural studies. The field connects local and wider transnational horizons and facilitates cross-cultural and transdisciplinary engagement between readers, writers, and scholars both in Canada and abroad. The necessity and aptness of such connective perspectives is inherent in Glissant's idea of a "Poetics of Relation," which posits that "each and every identity is extended through a relationship with the Other" (1997b, 11). Narratives in related national and transnational, diasporic, and postcolonial fields can only benefit, in this perspective, from being rerouted through the extended black Atlantic articulated by black Canadian voices and accounts.

Questions of nation and national belonging have produced considerable debate within the diasporic field of black Canadian cultural studies. Andrea Davis proposes that black Canadian literature "may best be understood not as a set of 'coherent' national narratives but as a complex engagement of the multiple diasporic experiences that inform and influence understandings of Canadian-ness," but she also asserts that black Canadian literature articulates "a deliberately transgressive Canadian-ness" (2007, 31). While a writer like Dionne Brand has declared that she has "giv[en] up on land to light on" (1997, 45, 47) and critiqued the emphasis on national belonging,[17] a good number of the texts and writers that I have discussed valorize and (re)claim the nation or the nation-state. Marlene NourbeSe Philip dedicates her collection of essays, *Frontiers*, to Canada, albeit as a country that still has a long way to go.[18] The aforementioned extended debate between George Elliott Clarke and Rinaldo Walcott has provided an important dynamic in black Canadian cultural criticism and illustrates the tension between cultural nationalist positions and diasporic orientations. While Clarke emphasizes the necessity of having a strong position within the nation in order to combat erasure, Walcott sees diasporic sensibilities as antidotes to the foreclosures of the nation's "dominating narratives of collective belonging" and as a means for "overcoming the problem of locating oneself solely within national boundaries" (2003, 22). I think the merit of both views is undeniable, but they are needed in conjunction. Re-examining these positions, Vernon values aspects of Walcott's stance, which sees diasporic sensibilities address the nation's limits and actively interrupt Canadianness (2008, 29–32). Still, she is critical of his dismissal of Clarke's cataloguing and archival recovery of black writing as "regressive localism" (R. Walcott 2003, 22; Vernon 2008, 29).[19] Vernon maintains that there "are aspects of *both* the diasporic and national/archival approaches that are valuable" (2008, 31).

Clarke's critique of Gilroy's *The Black Atlantic* speaks to related issues. He takes Gilroy's seminal work to task for the elision of Canadian texts and contexts and for its tendency towards a transnationalist homogenization of the diasporic. For Clarke, this tendency needs to be counteracted by "cultural nationalism," as he states at the end of the essay "Must All Blackness Be American?" (Clarke 2002a, 71–85; see Vernon 2008, 23). As his title suggests, he also espies in Gilroy's selection of authors a concentration on US contexts that he decries elsewhere as "A Model Blackness."[20] I fully agree, of course, with Clarke's critique of the elision of black Canadian writing from both Canadian cultural history and narratives of the black Atlantic. If the impact and implications of black Canadian writing are not to be diminished, however, this writing's relational significance for multiple perspectives and its potential for overlapping and even conflicting reading strategies need to be seen among the assets to be emphasized. Neither a blithe disregard for its local contexts from exclusively transnational perspectives nor its enclosure in an unreconstructed national perspective will do. An exclusively transnational perspective risks to remain cut off from the localized contexts and resources of black Canadian writing; Cynthia Sugars reminds us that, in the context of postcolonial studies, "it is important to remember that the national is one site of the local" (Sugars 2010, 34). For a poetics that concentrates on national or more specific contexts, on the other hand, the full force of these texts is often only available with reference to the transnational networks and implications that they reference and that nourish them.

While purely national identification underdetermines black Canadian writing, bypassing the national comes at the cost of missed communalities, continued erasure from national histories, and exclusion from state-sponsored channels of recognition and conveyance. Historically, transnational and diasporic orientations have often coexisted with the struggle for full civic and cultural participation in local and national time-spaces and institutions.[21] Rinaldo Walcott fittingly suggests that it is necessary to think "contrapuntally within and against the nation" (2003, 22). Above all, it seems crucial to multiply the contexts in which black Canadian writing will be read, appreciated, and vigorously discussed, and to relate its full critical potential to other relevant areas of cultural production, conveyance, and reception. Black Canadian writing – a national designation that implies transnational routings – can successfully challenge and relativize national cultural history by relating it to diasporic, black Atlantic, and hemispheric perspectives. Conversely, black Canadian writing provides exceptional opportunities for other transnational, comparative, and period fields of scholarship to reflect on the possibilities and implications of a black Atlantic reconsidered. Marginalizing this rich and transformative corpus is not an option in the future.

APPENDIX: TIMELINE

The following timeline provides further context for the titles and authors mentioned in this study. It also seeks to give a sense of the development of black Canadian writing. It is not, however, an exhaustive inventory. The most complete bibliographic effort to date has been George Elliott Clarke's 110-page "Africana Canadiana: A Select Bibliography of Literature by African-Canadian Authors, 1785–2001" (G.E. Clarke 2002a, 338–448). Other resources include the website *African Canadian Online* (http://www.yorku.ca/aconline). It is important to note that many works have been inserted in the timeline to suggest the extent of an author's oeuvre; not all of them are discussed in the text (and thus appear in "Works Cited").

Part I covers early works and documents, the subject of chapters 2 and 3. Part II, which contains works dated from the 1960s, has a dual structure: works are listed year by year in a column on the left, while authors and their works are listed alphabetically on the right. While Part I contains documents of various kinds, only books have been included in Part II, with the exception of unpublished plays and some films and audio recordings. Unpublished plays are listed by the date of their first performance and identified parenthetically as "produced." Non-print media as well as anthologies, essays, and other expository or non-fiction texts are also identified parenthetically. Film credits for a number of writers have been incorporated, but a systematic inclusion of black Canadian cinema is beyond the scope of this timeline (see Greg Tourino's website "African Canadian Cinema" (http://africancanadiancinema.wordpress.com/african-canadian-cinema).

Some texts published and testimonies given before their authors' arrival in Canada have been included in the left column (slightly indented). In Part I, this is the case for the statements transcribed in the "Book of Negroes" and for some of the texts by John Marrant, Moses Roper, and Mary Ann Shadd. In Part II, it is notably the case for texts by Gérard Étienne before

1964, Lorna Goodison before the early 1990s, Pamela Mordecai before 1994, Anthony Phelps before 1964, Olive Senior before the early 1990s (although she studied in Canada in the 1960s), and Frederick Ward before 1970. The compilations by Benjamin Drew, Samuel Gridley Howe, and William Still in Part I and by Daphne Marlatt and Carole Itter in Part II have been included because they contain extensive black Canadian testimony (not because these editors and compilers themselves belong to a black Canadian corpus). Finally, I have included in Part I only those works by John Marrant and Martin Delany that seem relevant in this context. In Part II, I have occasionally added a note when a fiction writer (such as Wayne Grady, Melchior Mbonimpa, or Émile Ollivier) is also a science writer or professor who has published further works in his or her respective fields.

TIMELINE PART I: EARLIER WORKS AND DOCUMENTS (CHAPTERS 2 AND 3)

1734 Interrogations of Marie Joseph Angélique (Juridiction Royale de Montréal, "Procedure Criminel de Marie Joseph Angelique – Negresse – Incendiere, 1734" [orig. spelling])

1783 Guy Carleton's "Book of Negroes" (in Guy Carleton, 1st Baron Dorchester: Papers, The National Archives, Kew, PRO 30/55/100)

1785 John Marrant, *A Narrative of the Lord's Wonderful Dealings with John Marrant, a Black, (Now Going to Preach the Gospel in Nova-Scotia) Born in New-York, in North-America. Taken Down from His Own Relation, Arranged, Corrected by the Rev. Mr. Aldridge*

1790 John Marrant, *A Journal of the Rev. John Marrant, from August 18th, 1785, to the 16th of March, 1790. To Which Are Added, Two Sermons; One Preached on Ragged Island on Sabbath Day, the 27th of October, 1787; The Other at Boston in New England, on Thursday, the 24 of June 1789*

1798 Boston King, "Memoirs of the Life of Boston King, a Black Preacher, Written by Himself during His Residence at Kingswood School"

1793 David George, "An account of the life of Mr. David George, from Sierra Leone in Africa; given by himself in a conversation with Brother Rippon of London, and Brother Pearce of Birmingham"

1837 Moses Roper, *A Narrative of the Adventures and Escape of Moses Roper, from American Slavery. With an Appendix, Containing a List of Places Visited by the Author in Great Britain, Ireland and the British Isles, and Other Matter*

1845 Lewis Clarke, *Narrative of the Sufferings of Lewis Clarke, During a Captivity of More than Twenty-Five Years, Among the Algerines of Kentucky, One of the So Called Christian States of North America, Dictated by Himself*

1846 Lewis and Milton Clarke, *Narratives of the Sufferings of Lewis and Milton Clarke, Sons of a Soldier of the Revolution, During a Captivity of More than Twenty Years among the Slaveholders of Kentucky, One of the So Called Christian States of North America, Dictated by Themselves*

1846 Israel Lewis, *Crisis in North America: Slavery, War, Balance of Power, and Oregon*

1849 Mary Ann Shadd, *Hints to the Colored People of the North*

1849 Josiah Henson, *The Life of Josiah Henson, Formerly a Slave, Now an Inhabitant of Canada, as Narrated by Himself*

1849 Henry Bibb, *Narrative of the Life and Adventures of Henry Bibb, an American Slave, Written by Himself*

1851 Thomas Smallwood, *A Narrative of Thomas Smallwood (Coloured Man:) Giving an Account of His Birth – The Period He Was Held in Slavery – His Release – And Removal to Canada, etc., Together with an Account of the Underground Railroad. Written by Himself*

1851–53 *Voice of the Fugitive* (newspaper, published in Sandwich, Canada West [1851–52] and Windsor [1852–53])

1851 "Proceedings of the North American Convention" (Proceedings of the North American Convention of Colored Freemen in Toronto, published in the *Voice of the Fugitive,* 24 September 1851)

1852 Martin Robison Delany, *The Condition, Elevation, Emigration, and Destiny of the Colored People of the United States*

1852 Mary Ann Shadd, *A Plea for Emigration; or, Notes of Canada West, in Its Moral, Social and Political Aspect: With Suggestions Respecting Mexico, West Indies and Vancouver's Island, for the Information of Colored Emigrants*

1853–60? *The Provincial Freeman* (newspaper, published in Windsor [1853–54], Toronto [1854–55], and Chatham [1855–]; last extant issue June 1859)

1854 Mahommah Gardo Baquaqua, *An Interesting Narrative. Biography of Mahommah G. Baquaqua, A Native of Zoogoo, In the Interior of Africa. (A Convert to Christianity.) With a Description of That Part of the World; Including the Manners and Customs of the Inhabitants …*

1854 John William Robertson, *The Book of the Bible against Slavery*

1855 Samuel Ringgold Ward, *Autobiography of a Fugitive Negro; His Anti-Slavery Labours in the United States, Canada, and England*

1856 Benjamin Drew, ed., *A North-Side View of Slavery. The Refugee: or The Narratives of Fugitive Slaves in Canada. Related by Themselves, with an Account of the History and Condition of the Colored Population of Upper Canada* (compilation of accounts by self-emancipated former slaves residing in Canada)

1857 Austin Steward, *Twenty-Two Years a Slave, and Forty Years a Freeman: Embracing a Correspondence of Several Years, While President of Wilberforce Colony, London, Canada West*

1858 Josiah Henson, *Truth Stranger than Fiction: Father Henson's Story of His Own Life*

1859 Jermain Wesley Loguen, *The Rev. J.W. Loguen, as a Slave and as a Freeman: A Narrative of Real Life*

1859/1861–62 Martin Robison Delany, *Blake; or The Huts of America: A Tale of the Mississippi Valley, the Southern United States, and Cuba* (published serially)

1861 Osborne P. Anderson, *A Voice from Harper's Ferry: A Narrative of Events at Harper's Ferry; with Incidents Prior and Subsequent to its Capture by Captain Brown and His Men*

1861 Martin Robison Delany, *Official Report of the Niger Valley Exploring Party*

1861 William Troy, *Hair-Breadth Escapes from Slavery to Freedom*

1861 Lavina Wormeny, "Narrative of the Escape of a Poor Negro Woman from Slavery"

1864 Samuel Gridley Howe, *The Refugees from Slavery in Canada West: Report to the Freedman's Inquiry Commission* (contains relevant narratives)

1870s–1913 Anderson Ruffin Abbott, newspaper articles and unpublished writings, including notebooks from 1898(?)–1913

1872 William Still, ed., *The Underground Railroad: A Record of the Facts, Authentic Narratives, Letters, etc., Narrating the Hardships, Hair-breadth Escapes and Death Struggles of the Slaves in Their Efforts for Freedom and Related by Themselves, and Others, or Witnessed by the Author; Together with Sketches of Some of the Largest Stockholders, and Most Liberal Aiders and Advisers, of the Road* (contains relevant narratives and accounts)

1876 Josiah Henson, *"Uncle Tom's Story of His Life": An Autobiography of the Rev. Josiah Henson (Mrs. Harriet Beecher Stowe's "Uncle Tom"), from 1789 to 1876* (ed. John Lobb; two further editions covering additional years in 1878 and 1879)

1881 Josiah Henson, *An Autobiography of the Rev. Josiah Henson ("Uncle Tom"), from 1789 to 1881* (ed. John Lobb, first Canadian edition)

1883–97(?) *The British Lion* (newpaper, Hamilton)

1889 Jim Henson, *Broken Shackles*

1901 William H.H. Johnson, *The Horrors of Slavery*

1902 Mifflin Gibbs, *Shadow and Light: An Autobiography with Reminiscences of the Last and Present Century*

1903–04 *Neith* (newspaper, Saint John, NB)

1905–12 Alfred Schmitz Shadd, articles in *The Melfort Moon* and *Carrot River Journal*

1914–19 *Canadian Observer* (newspaper, Toronto)

1915–20 *Atlantic Advocate* (newspaper, Halifax)

1923– *The Dawn of Tomorrow* (newspaper, London, ON)

1928 Long Sylvester Lance, *Long Lance: The Autobiography of a Blackfoot Indian Chief*

1934–41 *The Free Lance* (newspaper, Montreal)

1946–56 *The Clarion* (newspaper, New Glasgow, NS, appearing temporarily as *The Negro Citizen*)

1949–80 (?) *Africa Speaks* (newspaper, Toronto)

1953–56 *The Canadian Negro* (newspaper, Toronto)

TIMELINE PART II: SELECTED WORKS AFTER 1960

Chronological

1960

Gérard Étienne, *Au milieu des larmes*

Gérard Étienne, *Plus large qu'un rêve*

Anthony Phelps, *Été*

1961

Gérard Étienne, *La raison et mon amour*

Anthony Phelps, *Présence*

1962

Gérard Étienne, *Essai sur la négritude* (non-fiction)

Anthony Phelps, *Éclats de silence*

1963

Gérard Étienne, *Gladys*

1964

Austin Clarke, *The Survivors of the Crossing*

Gérard Étienne, *Le nationalisme dans la littérature haïtienne*

Alphabetical by Author

Marie-Célie Agnant

1994 *Balafres*

1995 *La dot de Sara*

1997 *Le silence come le sang*

1999 *Alexis d'Haïti*

1999 *Le Noël de Maïté*

2000 *Alexis, fils de Raphaël*

2001 *Le livre d'Emma*

2003 *Vingt petits pas vers Maria*

2003 *La légende du poisson amoureux*

2003 *L'oranger magique: Conte d'Haïti*

2007 *Un alligator nommé Rosa*

2008 *La nuit du Tatou*

2009 *Et puis parfois quelquefois …*

André Alexis

1994 *Despair and Other Stories of Ottawa*

1998 *Childhood*

1999 *Lambton Kent*

2005 *Ingrid and the Wolf*

2008 *Asylum*

2010 *Beauty and Sadness: Or, the Intermingling of Life and Literature*

Frederick Ward, *Poems*

1965

Austin Clarke, *Among Thistles and Thorns*

1966

Gérard Étienne, *Lettre à Montréal*

Anthony Phelps, *Points cardinaux*

Marie Stark Wallace, "Notes made by Marie Albertina Stark (afterwards Mrs Wallace) from the recollections of her mother, Sylvia Stark, who was born a slave in Clay County, Missouri, and settled on Salt Spring Island with her husband, Louis Stark, and family in the year 1860, as homesteaders" (first published in Compton 2002)

Frederick Ward, ed., *Anthology of Nine Baha'I Poets* (anthology)

1967

Austin Clarke, *The Meeting Point*

1968

Anthony Phelps, *Le conditionnel*

Anthony Phelps, *Mon pays que voici*, suivi de *Les dits du fou-aux-cailloux*

1971

Austin Clarke, *When He Was Free and Young and Used to Wear Silks*

1972

Gérard Étienne, *Dialogue avec mon ombre*

Frederick Ward, ed., *Present Tense* (anthology)

1973

Austin Clarke, *Storm of Fortune*

2013 *A*

2014 *Pastoral*

Lillian Allen

1982 *Rhythm an' Hardtimes*

1983 *Dub Poet: The Poetry of Lillian Allen* (audio recording)

1984 *The Teeth of the Whirlwind* (with Dionne Brand, Clifton Joseph, Charles C. Smith)

1985 *Curfew Inna BC* (audio recording)

1986 *Revolutionary Tea Party* (audio recording)

1987 *If You See the Truth*

1987 *Let the Heart See* (audio recording)

1988 *Conditions Critical* (audio recording)

1991 *Why Me?*

1992 *Nothing but a Hero: Poetry for Children and Young People*

1993 *Women Do This Every Day: Selected Poems Of Lillian Allen*

1998 *(We Shall Take Our) Freedom and Dance* (audio recording)

1999 *Psychic Unrest*

2012 *Anxiety* (audio recording)

Maxine Bailey

1998 with Sharon Lewis, *Sistahs*

Robert Berrouët-Oriol

1986 *Lettres urbaines: poèmes;* suivi de *Le dire-à-soi (du rapport à la langue)*

2005 *Thòraya, d'encre le champ*

2010 *En haute rumeur des siècles* (illustrations Frankétienne)

2010 *Poème du décours*

Camille Haynes, ed., *Black Chat: An Anthology of Black Poets*

Anthony Phelps, *Et moi, je suis une île*

Anthony Phelps, *Moins l'infini: Roman haïtien*

1974

Gérard Étienne, *Le nègre crucifié* (1974/1994)

Harold Head (as Morena Kirchwa), *Bushman's Brew*

Frederick Ward, *Riverlisp: Black Memories*

1975

Austin Clarke, *The Bigger Light*

Liz Cromwell, *Canadian Jungle Tea: Poems*

Liz Cromwell, ed., *One Out of Many* (anthology)

Headley Tulloch, *Black Canadians: A Long Line of Fighters* (non-fiction)

1976

Liz Cromwell, *Awake Sweet Agony*

Harold Head, *Canada in Us Now* (anthology)

Anthony Phelps, *Mémoire en colin-maillard*

Anthony Phelps, *Motifs pour le temps saisonnier*

1977

Carrie Best, *That Lonesome Road: The Autobiography of Carrie M. Best*

Austin Clarke, *The Prime Minister*

Émile Ollivier, *Paysage de l'aveugle*

Frederick Ward, *Nobody Called Me Mine: Black Memories*

2013 *Découdre le désastre* suivi de *L'île anaphore*

Carrie Best

1977 *That Lonesome Road: The Autobiography of Carrie M. Best*

Ayanna Black

1986 *No Contingencies*

1990 *Linked Alive: Sets of Renga* (with Dôre Michelut, Anne-Marie Alonzo, Paul Savoie)

1992 ed., *Voices: Canadian Writers of African Descent* (anthology)

1994 ed., *Fiery Spirits: A Collection of Short Fiction and Poetry by Canadian Writers of African Descent* (anthology)

2000 ed., *Fiery Spirits & Voices: Canadian Writers of African Descent* (anthology)

Fred Booker

2006 *Adventures in Debt Collection*

Walter Borden

1986 *Tightrope Time: Ain't Nuthin' More than Some Itty Bitty Madness Between Twilight & Dawn*

George Elroy Boyd

1988 *Shine Boy* (produced)

1996 *Two, By George* [*Consecrated Ground* and *Gideon's Blues*]

1999 *Consecrated Ground*

2005 *Wade in the Water*

2009 *Le Code Noir* (produced)

Dionne Brand

1978 *'Fore Day Morning*

1979 *Earth Magic*

1978

Dionne Brand, *'Fore Day Morning*

1979

Dionne Brand, *Earth Magic*

Gérard Étienne, *Un ambassadeur macoute à Montréal*

Daphne Marlatt and Carole Itter, comps and eds, *Opening Doors: Vancouver's East End* (narratives by Nora Hendrix, Rosa Pryor, Austin Phillips, Leona Risby, and Dorothy Nealy)

1980

Austin Clarke, *Growing up Stupid under the Union Jack: A Memoir*

Lorna Goodison, *Tamarind Season*

Pamela Mordecai, ed., with Mervyn Morris, *Jamaica Woman: An Anthology of Fifteen Jamaican Women Poets* (anthology)

Anthony Phelps, *La bélière caraïbe*

Marlene NourbeSe Philip, *Thorns*

1981

Paul Fehmiu Brown, *Ces canadiens oubliés*

Paul Fehmiu Brown, *En commençant par la fin: Récit biographique*

Harry Gairey, *A Black Man's Toronto 1914–1980: The Reminiscences of Harry Gairey*

Daniel G. Hill, *The Freedom-Seekers: Blacks in Early Canada Conditions* (non-fiction)

Frederick Ward, *A Room Full of Balloons*

1982 *Primitive Offensive*

1982 *Winter Epigrams & Epigrams to Ernesto Cardenal in Defense of Claudia*

1984 *Chronicles of the Hostile Sun*

1986 *Rivers Have Sources, Trees Have Roots: Speaking of Racism* (non-fiction, with Krisantha Sri Bhaggiyadatta)

1988 *Sans Souci and Other Stories*

1989 *Older Stronger Wiser* (film)

1990 *No Language is Neutral*

1991 *No Burden to Carry: Narratives of Black Working Women in Ontario 1920s–1950* (oral histories)

1991 *Sisters in Struggle* (film)

1993 *Long Time Comin'* (film)

1994 *Bread out of Stone: Recollections, Sex, Recognitions, Race, Dreaming, Politics* (non-fiction)

1994 *We're Rooted Here and They Can't Pull Us Up: Essays in African Canadian Women's History* (with Peggy Bristow, coord., et al; non-fiction)

1996 *Listening for Something … Adrienne Rich and Dionne Brand in Conversation* (film)

1996 *In Another Place, Not Here*

1997 *Land to Light On*

1999 *At the Full and Change of the Moon*

2001 *A Map to the Door of No Return: Notes to Belonging*

2002 *Thirsty*

2005 *What We All Long For*

2006 *Inventory*

2009 *Fierce Departures: The Poetry of Dionne Brand*

2010 *Ossuaries*

1982

Lillian Allen, *Rhythm an' Hardtimes*

Dionne Brand, *Primitive Offensive*

Dionne Brand, *Winter Epigrams & Epigrams to Ernesto Cardenal in Defense of Claudia*

Lorris Elliott, *Coming for to Carry*

Gérard Étienne, *Cri pour ne pas crever de honte*

1983

Lillian Allen, *Dub Poet: The Poetry of Lillian Allen* (audio recording)

George Elliott Clarke, *Saltwater Spirituals and Deeper Blues*

Afua Cooper, *Breaking Chains*

Gérard Étienne, *Une femme muette*

Clifton Joseph, *Metropolitan Blues*

Émile Ollivier, *Mère-Solitude*

Anthony Phelps, *Même le soleil est nu*

Marlene NourbeSe Philip, *Salmon Courage*

Makeda Silvera, ed., *Silenced: Talks with Working Class West Indian Women about Their Lives and Struggles as Domestic Workers in Canada* (non-fiction)

Frederick Ward, *The Curing Berry*

David Woods, *For Elsie Dorrington* (produced)

1984

Dionne Brand, *Chronicles of the Hostile Sun*

Claire Harris, *Fables from the Women's Quarters*

Claire Harris, *Translation into Fiction*

2011 *Chronicles: Early Works*

2014 *Love Enough*

Paul Fehmiu Brown

(Brown has published several other works as a historian)

1981 *Ces canadiens oubliés*

1981 *En commençant par la fin: Récit biographique*

1998 *Appel du sang: Roman*

1998 *Marie-Josèphe-Angélique, Montréal, Québec, 21 juin 1734*

2011 *Les cahiers de Sicka: Roman historique*

Rosemary Brown

1989 *Being Brown: A Very Public Life* (memoir)

Christian Campbell

2010 *Running the Dusk*

David Chariandy

2007 *Soucouyant*

Austin Clarke

1964 *The Survivors of the Crossing*

1965 *Among Thistles and Thorns*

1967 *The Meeting Point*

1971 *When He Was Free and Young and Used to Wear Silks*

1973 *Storm of Fortune*

1975 *The Bigger Light*

1977 *The Prime Minister*

1980 *Growing up Stupid under the Union Jack: A Memoir*

1985 *When Women Rule*

1986 *Nine Men Who Laughed*

Charles Smith, ed., *The Teeth of the Whirlwind: Poems by Allen, Brand, Joseph, Smith* (anthology)

Carol Talbot, *Growing Up Black in Canada* (memoir)

David Woods, *Voices* (produced)

1985

Lillian Allen, *Curfew Inna BC* (audio recording)

Austin Clarke, *When Women Rule*

Lorris Elliott, *Other Voices: Writings by Blacks in Canada* (anthology)

Dany Laferrière, *Comment faire l'amour avec un nègre sans se fatiguer*

Dany Laferrière, *Haïti (Québec)* (narrator, film)

Anthony Phelps, *Haïti, Haïti*

Olive Senior, *Talking of Trees*

Charles Smith, ed., *sad dances in a white field* (anthology)

David Woods, *The Dream Continues …* (produced)

1986

Lillian Allen, *Revolutionary Tea Party* (audio recording)

Robert Berrouët-Oriol, *Lettres urbaines: poèmes*; suivi de *Le dire-à-soi (du rapport à la langue)*

Ayanna Black, *No Contingencies*

Walter Borden, *Tightrope Time: Ain't Nuthin' More than Some Itty Bitty Madness between Twilight & Dawn*

Dionne Brand, *Rivers Have Sources, Trees Have Roots: Speaking of Racism* (non-fiction, with Krisantha Sri Bhaggiyadatta)

Austin Clarke, *Nine Men Who Laughed*

Austin Clarke, *Proud Empires*

1986 *Proud Empires*

1992 *In This City*

1992 *Public Enemies: Police Violence and Black Youth* (non-fiction)

1993 *There Are No Elders*

1994 *A Passage Back Home: A Personal Reminiscence of Samuel Selvon* (memoir)

1997 *The Origin of Waves*

1999 *Pigtails 'n' Breadfruit: The Rituals of Slave Food, A Barbadian Memoir*

1999 *The Question*

2002 *The Polished Hoe*

2003 *Choosing His Coffin: The Best Stories of Austin Clarke*

2004 *Love and Sweet Food: A Culinary Memoir*

2008 *More*

2013 *They Never Told Me: And Other Stories*

2013 *Where the Sun Shines Best*

George Elliott Clarke

1983 *Saltwater Spirituals and Deeper Blues*

1990 *Whylah Falls*

1991–92 ed., *Fire on the Water: An Anthology of Black Nova Scotian Writing* (anthology)

1993 *Provençal Songs*

1994 *Lush Dreams, Blue Exile*

1997 ed., *Eyeing the North Star: Directions in African-Canadian Literature* (anthology)

1997 *Provençal Songs II*

1999 *Whylah Falls: The Play*

1999 *Beatrice Chancy*

Lorris Elliott, *The Bibliography of Literary Writings by Blacks in Canada* (bibliography)

Lorna Goodison, *I Am Becoming My Mother*

Claire Harris, *Travelling to Find a Remedy*

Émile Ollivier, *La discorde aux cent voix*

Olive Senior, *Summer Lightning*

Makeda Silvera, ed., *Fireworks: The Best of Fireweed* (anthology)

1987

Lillian Allen, *If You See the Truth*

Lillian Allen, *Let the Heart See* (audio recording)

Joël des Rosiers, *Métropolis Opéra*

Gérard Étienne, *La reine soleil levée: Récit*

Dany Laferrière, *Eroshima*

Pamela Mordecai, ed., *From Our Yard: Jamaican Poetry since Independence* (anthology)

Pamela Mordecai, *Grandma's House* (illustrations Annabel Spenceley)

Pamela Mordecai, *Storypoems: A First Collection*

Anthony Phelps, *Orchidée nègre*

Charles Smith, *Partial Lives*

H. Nigel Thomas, *Spirits in the Dark*

Maxine Tynes, *Borrowed Beauty*

1988

Lillian Allen, *Conditions Critical* (audio recording)

George Elroy Boyd, *Shine Boy* (produced)

2000 *Gold Indigoes*

2001 *Execution Poems*

2001 *Blue*

2002 *Odysseys Home: Mapping African-Canadian Literature* (non-fiction)

2003 *Québécité: A Jazz Fantasia in Three Cantos*

2005 *George & Rue*

2005 *Illuminated Verses* (with photography by Ricardo Scipio)

2006 *Black*

2007 *Trudeau: Long March, Shining Path*

2008 *Blues and Bliss: The Poetry of George Elliott Clarke*

2009 *I & I*

2011 *Red*

2012 *Directions Home: Approaches to African-Canadian Literature* (non-fiction)

2013 *Illicit Sonnets: Poetry*

2013 *Lasso the Wind: Aurelia's Verses and Other Poems* (illustrations Susan Tooke)

2014 *Traverse*

2014 *Settling Africville* (produced)

Wayde Compton

1999 *49th Parallel Psalm*

2002 *Bluesprint: Black British Columbian Literature and Orature* (anthology)

2004 *Performance Bond*

2010 *After Canaan: Essays on Race, Writing, and Religion* (non-fiction)

2014 *The Outer Harbour*

Dionne Brand, *Sans Souci and Other Stories*

Lorris Elliott, *Literary Writings by Blacks in Canada: A Preliminary Survey* (bibliography)

Lorna Goodison, *Heartease*

Stanley Péan, *La plage des songes*

Marlene NourbeSe Philip, *Harriet's Daughter*

H. Nigel Thomas, *From Folklore to Fiction: A Study of Folk Heroes and Rituals in the Black American Novel* (non-fiction)

Frederick Ward, *Crossroads: Three Jazz Pianists* (narrator and script, film)

Frederick Ward, *Somebody Somebody's Returning*

1989

Dionne Brand, *Older Stronger Wiser* (film)

Rosemary Brown, *Being Brown: A Very Public Life* (memoir)

Afua Cooper, *The Red Caterpillar on College Street*

Afua Cooper, *Sunshine* (audio recording)

Bernadette Dyer, *Of Earth and from The Sky*

Bernadette Dyer, *PEJ and Other Poems*

Lorna Goodison, *Poems: Lorna Goodison*

Sylvia Hamilton, *Black Mother, Black Daughter* (film)

Claire Harris, *The Conception of Winter*

Dany Laferrière, *Comment faire l'amour avec un nègre sans se fatiguer* (*How to Make Love to a Negro without Getting Tired*) (scriptwriter, film)

Afua Cooper

1983 *Breaking Chains*

1989 *Sunshine* (audio recording)

1989 *The Red Caterpillar on College Street*

1990 *Poetry Is Not a Luxury* (audio recording)

1992 *Memories Have Tongue: Poetry*

1994 *We're Rooted Here and They Can't Pull Us Up: Essays in African Canadian Women's History* (with Peggy Bristow et al.; non-fiction)

1999 ed., *Utterances and Incantations: Women, Poetry and Dub* (anthology)

2002 *The Underground Railroad: Next Stop, Toronto!* (with Adrienne Shadd, Karolyn Smardz Frost)

2002 *Worlds of Fire* (audio recording)

2006 *The Hanging of Angélique: The Untold Story of Canadian Slavery and the Burning of Old Montréal* (non-fiction)

2006 *Copper Woman and Other Poems*

2009 *Love and Revolution* (audio recording)

2009 *My Name Is Henry Bibb: A Story of Slavery and Freedom*

2009 *My Name Is Phillis Wheatley: A Story of Slavery and Freedom*

Archie Crail

1990 *Archie Crail's Exile*

1992 *The Bonus Deal*

Liz Cromwell

1975 ed., *One Out of Many* (anthology)

1975 *Canadian Jungle Tea: Poems*

Pamela Mordecai, ed., with Betty Wilson, *Her True-True Name: An Anthology of Women's Writing from the Caribbean* (anthology)

Pamela Mordecai, *Journey Poem*

Marlene NourbeSe Philip, *She Tries Her Tongue, Her Silence Softly Breaks*

Gwendolyn Robinson and John W. Robinson, *Seek the Truth: A Story of Chatham's Black Community* (non-fiction)

Olive Senior, *The Arrival of the Snake-Woman and Other Stories*

Makeda Silvera, *Growing Up Black: A Resource Manual for Black Youths* (non-fiction)

Makeda Silvera, ed., with Nila Gupta, *The Issue Is 'ism: Women of Colour Speak Out (anthology)*

Dorothy Williams, *Blacks in Montreal, 1628–1986: An Urban Demography* (non-fiction)

1990

Ayanna Black, *Linked Alive: Sets of Renga* (with Dôre Michelut, Anne-Marie Alonzo, Paul Savoie)

Dionne Brand, *No Language Is Neutral*

George Elliott Clarke, *Whylah Falls*

Afua Cooper, *Poetry Is Not a Luxury* (audio recording)

Archie Crail, *Archie Crail's Exile*

Joël des Rosiers, *Tribu*

Cheryl Foggo, *Pourin' Down Rain* (memoir)

Lorna Goodison, *Baby Mother and the King of Swords*

Clifton Joseph, *Oral / Trans / Missions* (audio recording)

Djanet Sears, *Afrika Solo*

1976 *Awake Sweet Agony*

Joël des Rosiers

1987 *Métropolis Opéra*

1990 *Tribu*

1993 *Savanes*

1996 *Théories caraïbes: Poétique du déracinement* (non-fiction)

1999 *Vétiver*

2007 *Un autre soleil*

2007 *Caïques*

2009 *Lettres à l'indigène*

2010 *Gaïac*

2013 *Métaspora: Les patries intimes* (non-fiction)

Max Dorsinville

1995 *James Wait et les lunettes noires* (transl. *Erzulie Loves Shango*)

Bernadette Dyer

1989 *Of Earth and from the Sky*

1989 *PEJ and Other Poems*

2000 *Villa Fair: Stories*

2004 *Waltzes I Have Not Forgotten*

2007 *Abductors*

Esi Edugyan

2004 *The Second Life of Samuel Tyne*

2007 *Diese Fremden: Kurzgeschichten*

2011 *Half-Blood Blues*

2014 *Dreaming of Elsewhere: Observations on Home* (non-fiction)

Lorris Elliott

1982 *Coming for to Carry*

1985 *Other Voices: Writings by Blacks in Canada* (anthology)

Maxine Tynes, *Woman Talking Woman*

Frederick Ward, *Oliver Jones in Africa* (narrator and script, film)

David Woods, *Native Song: Poetry and Paintings*

David Woods, *Nova Scotia Black Reality Song* (produced)

1991

Lillian Allen, *Why Me?*

Dionne Brand, *No Burden to Carry: Narratives of Black Working Women in Ontario 1920s–1950* (oral histories)

Dionne Brand, *Sisters in Struggle* (film)

George Elliott Clarke, ed., *Fire on the Water: An Anthology of Black Nova Scotian Writing*, vol. 1 (anthology)

Gérard Étienne, *La pacotille*

Cheryl Foggo with Clem Martini, *Playing Fair: Carol's Mirror* (script, film)

Cecil Foster, *Distorted Mirror: Canada's Racist Face* (non-fiction)

Cecil Foster, *No Man in the House*

Dany Laferrière, *L'odeur du café*

Suzette Mayr, *Zebra Talk*

Émile Ollivier, *Passages*

Stanley Péan, *Le tumulte de mon sang*

Marlene NourbeSe Philip, *Looking for Livingstone: An Odyssey of Silence*

Althea Prince (as Althea Trotman), *How the East Pond Got Its Flowers*

Makeda Silvera, ed., *Piece of My Heart: A Lesbian of Colour Anthology* (anthology)

Makeda Silvera, *Remembering G and Other Stories*

Maxine Tynes, *Save the Word for Me*

1986 *The Bibliography of Literary Writings by Blacks in Canada* (bibliography)

1988 *Literary Writings by Blacks in Canada: A Preliminary Survey* (bibliography)

Gérard Étienne

1960 *Au milieu des larmes*

1960 *Plus large qu'un rêve*

1961 *La raison et mon amour*

1962 *Essai sur la négritude* (non-fiction)

1963 *Gladys*

1964 *Le nationalisme dans la littérature haïtienne* (non-fiction)

1966 *Lettre à Montréal*

1972 *Dialogue avec mon ombre*

1974/1994 *Le nègre crucifié*

1979 *Un ambassadeur macoute à Montréal*

1982 *Cri pour ne pas crever de honte*

1983 *Une femme muette*

1987 *La reine soleil levée: Récit*

1991 *La pacotille*

1993 *La charte des crépuscules: Oeuvres poétiques (1960–1980)*

1995 *La question raciale et raciste dans le roman québécois* (non-fiction)

1998 *Le Bacoulou*

1998 with François Soeler, *La Femme noire dans le discours littéraire haïtien: Éléments d'anthroposémiologie* (non-fiction)

1998 *L'injustice, la désinformation, le mépris de la loi* (non-fiction)

2000 *La romance en do mineur de Maître Clo*

2001 *Vous n'êtes pas seul*

Ann Wallace, ed., *Daughters of the Sun, Women of the Moon: An Anthology of Canadian Black Women Poets* (anthology)

David Woods, *Part of the Deal* (radio play)

1992

Lillian Allen, *Nothing But a Hero: Poetry for Children and Young People*

Ayanna Black, ed., *Voices: Canadian Writers of African Descent* (anthology)

Austin Clarke, *In This City*

Austin Clarke, *Public Enemies: Police Violence and Black Youth (non-fiction)*

George Elliott Clarke, ed., *Fire on the Water: An Anthology of Black Nova Scotian Writing*, vol. 2 (anthology)

Afua Cooper, *Memories Have Tongue: Poetry*

Archie Crail, *The Bonus Deal*

Lorna Goodison, *Selected Poems*

Sylvia Hamilton, *Speak It! From the Heart of Black Nova Scotia* (film)

Claire Harris, *Drawing Down a Daughter*

Claire Harris, ed., with Edna Alford, *Kitchen Talk: Contemporary Women's Prose and Poetry* (anthology)

Lawrence Hill, *Some Great Thing*

Dany Laferrière, *Le goût des jeunes filles*

Pamela Mordecai, *Don't Ever Wake a Snake: Poems and Stories for Children*

Stanley Péan, *Sombres allées et autres endroits peu hospitaliers: Treize excursions en territoire de l'insolite*

Marlene NourbeSe Philip, *Frontiers: Essays and Writings on Racism and Culture, 1984–1992* (non-fiction)

2002 *Au cœur de l'anoréxie*

2004 *Au bord de la falaise*

2006 *Un cauchemar en plein midi d'été*

2006 *Hervé Lebreton et la poétique de la femme* (non-fiction)

2008 *Monsieur le président*

2008 *Natania*

2009 *Le Créole une langue …* (non-fiction)

Minister Faust (Malcolm Azania)

2004 *The Coyote Kings, Book One: Space-Age Bachelor Pad*

2007 *From the Notebooks of Dr. Brain* (re-published as *Shrinking the Heroes* in 2013)

2011 *The Alchemists of Kush*

2011 *Journey to Mecha: Eight Visionary SF, Fantasy, Philosophical and Satirical Tales*

2012 *E-Force: Sixteen Stories of Ultra-Freaking Awesomeness*

2012 *War & Mir*, vol. 1: *Ascension*

2013 *A Bad Bad Beat Was Brewing: An Africentric Scroll of Bizarre, Brutal, Inspiring and Supernatural Tales*

2013 *The Wonderful Wizard Wangari* (produced)

2014 *War & Mir*, vol. 2: *The Darkold*

Cheryl Foggo

(Foggo is also a journalist and screenwriter)

1990 *Pourin' Down Rain* (memoir)

1991 with Clem Martini, *Playing Fair: Carol's Mirror* (script, film)

1997 *One Thing That's True*

Althea Prince (as Althea Trotman), *How the Starfish Got to the Sea*

David Woods, *Black Journey* (radio play)

1993

Lillian Allen, *Women Do This Every Day: Selected Poems Of Lillian Allen*

Dionne Brand, *Long Time Comin'* (film)

Austin Clarke, *There Are No Elders*

George Elliott Clarke, *Provençal Songs*

Joël des Rosiers, *Savanes*

Gérard Étienne, *La charte des crépuscules: Oeuvres poétiques (1960–1980)*

Lorna Goodison, Olive Senior et al., *A Quartet of Stories: Maya Angelou, Lorna Goodison, Olive Senior, Alice Walker*

Lawrence Hill, *Trials and Triumphs: The Story of African-Canadians* (non-fiction)

Dany Laferrière, *Cette grenade dans la main du jeune nègre est-elle une arme ou un fruit?*

Stanley Péan, *L'emprise de la nuit*

Marlene NourbeSe Philip, *Showing Grit: Showboating North of the 44th Parallel* (non-fiction)

Althea Prince, *Ladies of the Night and Other Stories*

George Seremba, *Come Good Rain*

Karen Shadd-Evelyn, *I'd Rather Live in Buxton* (memoir)

Makeda Silvera, ed., *The Other Woman: Women of Colour in Contemporary Canadian Literature* (non-fiction)

Maxine Tynes, *The Door of My Heart*

2001 *I Have Been in Danger* (illustrations Aries Cheung)

2011 *Dear Baobab* (illustrations Qin Leng)

2014 *John Ware Reimagined* (produced)

Cecil Foster

1991 *Distorted Mirror: Canada's Racist Face* (non-fiction)

1991 *No Man in the House*

1995 *Caribana, the Greatest Celebration* (non-fiction, photography Chris Schwarz)

1995 *Sleep On, Beloved*

1996 *A Place Called Heaven: The Meaning of Being Black in Canada* (non-fiction)

1998 *Island Wings* (memoir)

1998 *Slammin' Tar*

2001 *Dry Bone Memories*

2005 *Where Race Does Not Matter: The New Spirit of Modernity* (non-fiction)

2007 *Blackness and Modernity: The Colour of Humanity and the Quest for Freedom* (non-fiction)

2014 *Genuine Multiculturalism: The Tragedy and Comedy of Diversity*

2014 *Independence*

Harry Gairey

1981 *A Black Man's Toronto 1914–1980: The Reminiscences of Harry Gairey*

Lorena Gale

1995 *What Colour Is Black? Art, Politics and Racial Identity* (produced)

2000 *Angélique*

David Woods, *The Aunt Jemima Story* (radio play)

1994

Marie-Célie Agnant, *Balafres*

André Alexis, *Despair and Other Stories of Ottawa*

Ayanna Black, ed., *Fiery Spirits: A Collection of Short Fiction and Poetry by Canadian Writers of African Descent* (anthology)

Dionne Brand, *Bread out of Stone: Recollections, Sex, Recognitions, Race, Dreaming, Politics* (non-fiction)

Peggy Bristow, Dionne Brand, Linda Carty, Afua Cooper, Sylvia Hamilton, and Adrienne Shadd, *We're Rooted Here and They Can't Pull Us Up: Essays in African Canadian Women's History* (non-fiction)

Austin Clarke, *A Passage Back Home: A Personal Reminiscence of Samuel Selvon* (memoir)

George Elliott Clarke, *Lush Dreams, Blue Exile*

Lorna Goodison, *A Quartet of Poems: Alice Walker, Lorna Goodison, Maya Angelou, Grace Nichols*

Sylvia Hamilton, *Against the Tides: The Jones Family* (film, part 2 of *Hymn to Freedom*)

Dany Laferrière, *Chronique de la dérive douce*

Stanley Péan, *La mémoire ensanglantée*

Rosemary Sadlier, *Leading the Way: Black Women in Canada* (non-fiction)

Olive Senior, *Gardening in the Tropics*

Adrienne Shadd, ed., with Carl E. James, *Talking about Difference: Encounters in Culture, Language, and Identity* (non-fiction)

2001 *Je me souviens: Memories of an Expatriate Anglophone Montréalaise Québécoise, Exiled in Canada*

2005 "The Darwinist" (dissertation)

2008 *The Voice* (produced)

Lorna Goodison

1980 *Tamarind Season*

1986 *I Am Becoming My Mother*

1988 *Heartease*

1989 *Poems: Lorna Goodison*

1990 *Baby Mother and the King of Swords*

1992 *Selected Poems*

1993 *A Quartet of Stories: Maya Angelou, Lorna Goodison, Olive Senior, Alice Walker*

1994 *A Quartet of Poems: Alice Walker, Lorna Goodison, Maya Angelou, Grace Nichols*

1995 *To Us, All Flowers Are Roses*

1999 *Turn Thanks*

2000 *Guinea Woman: New and Selected Poems*

2001 *Travelling Mercies*

2005 *Controlling the Silver*

2005 *Fool-Fool Rose Is Leaving Labour-in-Vain Savannah: Short Stories*

2006 *Goldengrove: New and Selected Poems*

2007 *From Harvey River: A Memoir of My Mother and Her People*

2011 *By Love Possessed: Stories*

2013 *Supplying Salt and Light*

2013 *Oracabessa*

Makeda Silvera, *Her Head a Village and Other Stories*

Ernest Tucker, *Underworld Dwellers*

1995

Marie-Célie Agnant, *La dot de Sara*

Max Dorsinville, *James Wait et les lunettes noires* (transl. *Erzulie Loves Shango*)

Gérard Étienne, *La question raciale et raciste dans le roman québécois* (non-fiction)

Cecil Foster, *Caribana, the Greatest Celebration* (non-fiction, photography Chris Schwarz)

Cecil Foster, *Sleep On, Beloved*

Lorena Gale, *What Colour Is Black? Art, Politics and Racial Identity* (produced)

Lorna Goodison, *To Us, All Flowers Are Roses*

Suzette Mayr, *Moon Honey*

Pamela Mordecai, *De Man: A Performance Poem*

Pamela Mordecai, *Ezra's Goldfish and Other Story Poems*

Emile Ollivier, *Les urnes scellées*

Stanley Péan, *L'automne sauvage*

Anthony Phelps, *Les doubles quatrains mauves*

Rosemary Sadlier, *Mary Ann Shadd: Publisher, Editor, Teacher, Lawyer, Suffragette* (non-fiction)

Robert Sandiford, *Winter, Spring, Summer, Fall: Stories*

Olive Senior, *Discerner of Hearts*

George Seremba, ed., with Yvette Nolan and Betty Quan, *Beyond the Pale: Dramatic Writing from First*

Wayne Grady

(Grady has published many other books as a literary science writer and translated over a dozen novels from French)

2010 *Breakfast at the Exit Café: Travels through America* (with Merilyn Simonds)

2013 *Emancipation Day*

Sylvia Hamilton

(Hamilton is best known as a film director)

1989 *Black Mother, Black Daughter* (film)

1992 *Speak It! From the Heart of Black Nova Scotia* (film)

1994 *Against the Tides: The Jones Family* (film, part 2 of *Hymn to Freedom: The History of Blacks in Canada*)

1994 *We're Rooted Here and They Can't Pull Us Up: Essays in African Canadian Women's History* (with Peggy Bristow et al.; non-fiction)

2000 *Portia White: Think on Me* (film)

2007 *The Little Black School House* (film)

2011 *We Are One* (film)

2014 *And I Alone Escaped to Tell You*

Claire Harris

1984 *Fables from the Women's Quarters*

1984 *Translation into Fiction*

1986 *Travelling to Find a Remedy*

1989 *The Conception of Winter*

Nations Writers and Writers of Colour (anthology)

Makeda Silvera, ed., with C. Allyson Lee, *Pearls of Passion: A Treasury of Lesbian Erotica* (anthology)

H. Nigel Thomas, *How Loud Can the Village Cock Crow? and Other Stories*

David Woods, *Nova Scotia Suite* (produced)

1996

George Elroy Boyd, *Two, By George* [*Consecrated Ground* and *Gideon's Blues*]

Dionne Brand, *In Another Place, Not Here*

Dionne Brand, *Listening for Something … Adrienne Rich and Dionne Brand in Conversation* (film)

Joël des Rosiers, *Théories caraïbes: Poétique du déracinement* (non-fiction)

Cecil Foster, *A Place Called Heaven: The Meaning of Being Black in Canada* (non-fiction)

Claire Harris, *Dipped in Shadow*

Lawrence Hill, *Women of Vision: The Story of the Canadian Negro Women's Association, 1951–1976* (non-fiction)

Dany Laferrière, *Pays sans chapeau*

Rachel Manley, *Drumblair: Memories of a Jamaican Childhood* (memoir)

Stanley Péan, *Treize pas vers l'inconnu*

Stanley Péan, *Zombi Blues*

Marlene NourbeSe Philip, *Caribana: African Roots and Continuities – Race, Space and the Poetics of Moving* (non-fiction)

Frederick Ward, *The Road Taken* (narrator and script, film)

1992 ed., with Edna Alford, *Kitchen Talk: Contemporary Women's Prose and Poetry* (anthology)

1992 *Drawing Down a Daughter*

1996 *Dipped in Shadow*

2000 *She*

Camille Haynes

1973 ed., *Black Chat: An Anthology of Black Poets*

Harold Head

1974 (as Morena Kirchwa) *Bushman's Brew*

1976 *Canada in Us Now* (anthology)

Daniel G. Hill

(Hill published further titles as a sociologist and human rights expert)

1981 *The Freedom-Seekers: Blacks in Early Canada Conditions* (non-fiction)

Lawrence Hill

1992 *Some Great Thing*

1993 *Trials and Triumphs: The Story of African-Canadians* (non-fiction)

1996 *Women of Vision: The Story of the Canadian Negro Women's Association, 1951–1976* (non-fiction)

1997 *Any Known Blood*

2001 *Black Berry, Sweet Juice: On Being Black and White in Canada* (memoir)

2004 *Seeking Salvation: A History of the Black Church in Canada* (script, film)

2007 *The Book of Negroes*

2013 *Blood: The Stuff of Life* (non-fiction)

1997

Marie-Célie Agnant, *Le silence comme le sang*

Dionne Brand, *Land to Light On*

Austin Clarke, *The Origin of Waves*

George Elliott Clarke, ed., *Eyeing the North Star: Directions in African-Canadian Literature* (anthology)

George Elliott Clarke, *Provençal Songs II*

Cheryl Foggo, *One Thing That's True*

Lawrence Hill, *Any Known Blood*

Dany Laferrière, *La chair du maître*

Dany Laferrière, *Le charme des après-midi sans fin*

Andrew Moodie, *Riot*

Stanley Péan, *L'Appel des loups*

Stanley Péan, *Quand la bête est humaine*

Marlene NourbeSe Philip, *A Genealogy of Resistance and Other Essays* (non-fiction)

Rosemary Sadlier, *Harriet Tubman: Freedom Seeker, Freedom Leader* (non-fiction)

Robert Sandiford, *Attractive Forces* (illustrations Justin Norman, graphic story collection)

Mairuth Sarsfield, *No Crystal Stair*

Djanet Sears, *Harlem Duet*

Rinaldo Walcott, *Black Like Who? Writing Black Canada* (non-fiction)

Dorothy Williams, *The Road to Now: A History of Blacks in Montreal* (non-fiction)

David Woods, *Once* (radio play)

2013 *Dear Sir, I Intend to Burn Your Book: An Anatomy of a Book Burning* (non-fiction)

Nalo Hopkinson

1998 *Brown Girl in the Ring*

2000 *Midnight Robber*

2000 ed., *Whispers from the Cotton Tree Root: Caribbean Fabulist Fiction* (anthology)

2001 *Skin Folk*

2003 ed., *Mojo: Conjure Stories* (anthology)

2003 *The Salt Roads*

2004 ed., with Uppinder Mehan, *So Long Been Dreaming: Postcolonial Fiction & Fantasy* (anthology)

2005 ed., with Geoff Ryman, *Tesseracts Nine* (anthology)

2007 *The New Moon's Arms*

2012 *The Chaos*

2012 *Report from Planet Midnight*

2013 *Sister Mine*

Clifton Joseph

(Joseph is best known as a dub poet)

1983 *Metropolitan Blues*

1990 *Oral / Trans / Missions* (audio recording)

Dany Laferrière

1985 *Comment faire l'amour avec un nègre sans se fatiguer*

1985 *Haïti (Québec)* (narrator, film)

1987 *Eroshima*

1989 *Comment faire l'amour avec un nègre sans se fatiguer* (*How to Make Love to a Negro without Getting Tired*) (scriptwriter, film)

1998

André Alexis, *Childhood*

Lillian Allen, *(We Shall Take Our) Freedom and Dance* (audio recording)

Maxine Bailey and Sharon Lewis, *Sistahs*

Paul Fehmiu Brown, *Appel du sang: Roman*

Paul Fehmiu Brown, *Marie-Josèphe-Angélique, Montréal, Québec, 21 juin 1734*

Gérard Étienne, *Le Bacoulou*

Gérard Étienne with François Soeler, *La Femme noire dans le discours littéraire haïtien: Éléments d'anthroposémiologie* (non-fiction)

Gérard Étienne, *L'injustice, la désinformation, le mépris de la loi* (non-fiction)

Cecil Foster, *Island Wings* (memoir)

Cecil Foster, *Slammin' Tar*

Nalo Hopkinson, *Brown Girl in the Ring*

Tessa McWatt, *Out of My Skin*

Suzette Mayr, *The Widows*

Andrew Moodie, *Oui* (produced)

Andrew Moodie, *Wilbur County Blues* (produced)

David Odhiambo, *diss/ed banded nation*

Stanley Péan, *Un petit garçon qui avait peur de tout et de rien*

David Woods, *Choices in the Skin* (produced)

1999

Marie-Célie Agnant, *Alexis d'Haïti*

Marie-Célie Agnant, *Le Noël de Maïté*

André Alexis, *Lambton Kent*

1991 *L'odeur du café*

1992 *Le goût des jeunes filles*

1993 *Cette grenade dans la main du jeune nègre est-elle une arme ou un fruit?*

1994 *Chronique de la dérive douce*

1996 *Pays sans chapeau*

1997 *La chair du maître*

1997 *Le charme des après-midi sans fin*

2000 *Le cri des oiseaux fous*

2000 *J'écris comme je vis: Entretien avec Bernard Magnier* (non-fiction)

2000 *Je suis fatigué*

2004 *Comment conquérir l'Amérique en une nuit* (director and scriptwriter, film)

2004 *Le goût des jeunes filles* (*On the Verge of a Fever*) (scriptwriter, film)

2005 *Les années 80 dans ma vieille Ford*

2006 *Je suis fou de Vava*

2006 *Vers le sud*

2008 *Je suis un écrivain japonais*

2009 *L'énigme du retour*

2009 *La fête des morts*

2010 *Conversations avec Dany Laferrière (with* Ghila Sroka)

2010 *Tout bouge autour de moi*

2011 *L'art presque perdu de ne rien faire*

2013 *Le baiser mauve de Vava*

2013 *Journal d'un écrivain en pyjama*

Didier Leclair

2000 *Toronto, je t'aime*

2003 *Ce pays qui est le mien*

2007 *Un passage vers l'Occident*

Lillian Allen, *Psychic Unrest*

George Elroy Boyd, *Consecrated Ground*

Dionne Brand, *At the Full and Change of the Moon*

Austin Clarke, *Pigtails 'n' Breadfruit: The Rituals of Slave Food, A Barbadian Memoir*

Austin Clarke, *The Question*

George Elliott Clarke, *Beatrice Chancy*

George Elliott Clarke, *Whylah Falls: The Play*

Wayde Compton, *49th Parallel Psalm*

Afua Cooper, *Utterances and Incantations: Women, Poetry and Dub* (anthology)

Joël des Rosiers, *Vétiver*

Lorna Goodison, *Turn Thanks*

Andrew Moodie, *A Common Man's Guide To Loving Women*

Émile Ollivier, *Mille eaux*

Stanley Péan, *Noirs désirs*

Stanley Péan, *Le temps s'enfuit*

Stanley Péan, *Toute la ville en jazz* (non-fiction)

Marlene NourbeSe Philip, *Coups and Calypsos*

H. Nigel Thomas, *Moving through Darkness: Poems*

2000

Marie-Célie Agnant, *Alexis, fils de Raphaël*

Ayanna Black, ed., *Fiery Spirits & Voices: Canadian Writers of African Descent* (anthology)

George Elliott Clarke, *Gold Indigoes*

Bernadette Dyer, *Villa Fair: Stories*

2010 *Le soixantième parallèle*

2012 *Le complexe de Trafalgar*

2014 *Un ancien d'Afrique: Les chiens de Kigali*

Sharon Lewis

(Lewis is also a director, actor, and on-air host)

1998 with Maxine Bailey, *Sistahs*

Tessa McWatt

1998 *Out of My Skin*

2000 *Dragons Cry*

2004 *There's No Place Like …*

2004 *This Body*

2009 *Step Closer*

2011 *Vital Signs*

2013 *The Taste of Marmalade*

Rachel Manley

(Manley also published a number of books as Rachel Manley Drummond before moving to Canada)

1996 *Drumblair: Memories of a Jamaican Childhood* (memoir)

2000 *Slipstream: A Daughter Remembers* (memoir)

2008 *Horses in Her Hair: A Granddaughter's Story* (memoir)

Valery Mason-John and Kevan Anthony Cameron

2013 eds, *The Great Black North: Contemporary African Canadian Poetry* (anthology)

Suzette Mayr

1991 *Zebra Talk*

1995 *Moon Honey*

Gérard Étienne, *La romance en do mineur de Maître-Clo*

Lorena Gale, *Angélique*

Lorna Goodison, *Guinea Woman: New and Selected Poems*

Sylvia Hamilton, *Portia White: Think on Me* (film)

Claire Harris, *She*

Nalo Hopkinson, *Midnight Robber*

Nalo Hopkinson, ed., *Whispers from the Cotton Tree Root: Caribbean Fabulist Fiction* (anthology)

Dany Laferrière, *Le cri des oiseaux fous*

Dany Laferrière, *J'écris comme je vis: Entretien avec Bernard Magnier* (non-fiction)

Dany Laferrière, *Je suis fatigué*

Didier Leclair, *Toronto, je t'aime*

Tessa McWatt, *Dragons Cry*

Rachel Manley, *Slipstream: A Daughter Remembers* (memoir)

Andrew Moodie, *The Lady Smith*

Stanley Péan, *La nuit démasque*

Stanley Péan, *Pl@nète culture* (non-fiction)

Anthony Phelps, *Immobile voyageuse de Picas et autres silences*

Djanet Sears, ed., *Tellin' It Like It Is: A Compendium of African Canadian Monologues for Actors* (anthology)

Djanet Sears, ed., *Testifyin': Contemporary African Canadian Drama*, vol. 1 (anthology)

George Seremba, ed., with Carmen Aguirre and Ann Lambert, *Along Human Lines: Dramas from Refugee Lives*

1998 *The Widows*

2001 *Tale* (illustrations Geoff Hunter)

2004 *Venous Hum*

2011 *Monoceros*

Melchior Mbonimpa

(Mbonimpa, a professor of Religious Studies, has published several volumes on African politics)

2001 *Le totem des Baranda*

2003 *Le dernier roi faiseur de pluie*

2006 *Les morts ne sont pas morts*

2008 *La terre sans mal*

2012 *La tribu de Sangwa*

2014 *Diangombé, l'immortel*

Jospeh Mensah

(Mensah, a professor of geography and international development, has published several other volumes)

2002 *Black Canadians: History, Experiences, Social Conditions* (non-fiction)

Andrew Moodie

1997 *Riot*

1998 *Oui* (produced)

1998 *Wilbur County Blues* (produced)

1999 *A Common Man's Guide to Loving Women*

2000 *The Lady Smith*

2006 *The Real McCoy*

2010 *Toronto the Good*

Pamela Mordecai

1980 ed., with Mervyn Morris, *Jamaica Woman: An Anthology of Fifteen Jamaican Women Poets* (anthology)

Karen Shadd-Evelyn, Joyce Shadd Middleton, and Bryan Prince, *Something to Hope For: The Story of the Fugitive Slave Settlement, Buxton, Canada West* (non-fiction)

Makeda Silvera, ed., with Stephanie Martin, *Sapodilla: The Sister Vision Book of Lesbian Poetry* (anthology)

Rinaldo Walcott, ed., *Rude: Contemporary Black Canadian Cultural Criticism* (non-fiction)

2001

Marie-Célie Agnant, *Le livre d'Emma*

Dionne Brand, *A Map to the Door of No Return: Notes to Belonging*

George Elliott Clarke, *Blue*

George Elliott Clarke, *Execution Poems*

Gérard Étienne, *Vous n'êtes pas seul*

Cheryl Foggo, *I Have Been in Danger* (illustration Aries Cheung)

Cecil Foster, *Dry Bone Memories*

Lorena Gale, *Je me souviens: Memories of an Expatriate Anglophone Montréalaise, Québécoise, Exiled in Canada*

Lorna Goodison, *Travelling Mercies*

Lawrence Hill, *Black Berry, Sweet Juice: On Being Black and White in Canada* (memoir)

Nalo Hopkinson, *Skin Folk*

Suzette Mayr, *Tale* (illustrations Geoff Hunter)

Melchior Mbonimpa, *Le totem des Baranda*

Pamela Mordecai, *Certifiable*

Pamela Mordecai with Martin Mordecai, *Culture and Customs of Jamaica* (non-fiction)

1987 ed., *From Our Yard: Jamaican Poetry since Independence* (anthology)

1987 *Grandma's House* (illustrations Annabel Spenceley)

1987 *Storypoems: A First Collection*

1989 ed., with Betty Wilson, *Her True-True Name: An Anthology of Women's Writing from the Caribbean* (anthology)

1989 *Journey Poem*

1992 *Don't Ever Wake a Snake: Poems and Stories for Children*

1995 *De Man: A Performance Poem*

1995 *Ezra's Goldfish and Other Story Poems*

2001 *Certifiable*

2001 with Martin Mordecai, *Culture and Customs of Jamaica* (non-fiction)

2005 *The True Blue of Islands*

2006 *Pink Icing and Other Stories*

2012 *Subversive Sonnets*

Donna Bailey Nurse

2003 *What's a Black Critic to Do? Interviews, Profiles and Reviews of Black Writers* (non-fiction)

2006 ed., *Revival* (anthology)

2011 *What's a Black Critic to Do II: Interviews, Profiles and Reviews of Black Writers* (non-fiction)

David Odhiambo

1998 *diss/ed banded nation*

2003 *Kipligat's Chance*

2010 *The Reverend's Apprentice*

Émile Ollivier, *Regarde, regarde les lions*

Émile Ollivier, *Repérages* (non-fiction)

Stanley Péan, *Le cabinet du Docteur K*

Stanley Péan, *Cette étrangeté coutumière*

Althea Prince, *Being Black: Essays*

Althea Prince, *Loving This Man*

H. Nigel Thomas, *Behind the Face of Winter*

Verna Thomas, *Invisible Shadows: A Black Woman's Life in Nova Scotia* (memoir)

2002

Dionne Brand, *Thirsty*

Austin Clarke, *The Polished Hoe*

George Elliott Clarke, *Odysseys Home: Mapping African-Canadian Literature* (non-fiction)

Wayde Compton, *Bluesprint: Black British Columbian Literature and Orature* (anthology)

Afua Cooper, *Worlds of Fire* (audio recording)

Gérard Étienne, *Au cœur de l'anoréxie*

Joseph Mensah, *Black Canadians: History, Experiences, Social Conditions* (non-fiction)

Oscar Peterson, *A Jazz Odyssey: The Life of Oscar Peterson*

Robert Sandiford, *Stray Moonbeams* (illustrations Justin Norman, graphic story collection)

Adrienne Shadd, Afua Cooper, Karolyn Smardz Frost, *The Underground Railroad: Next Stop, Toronto!* (non-fiction)

Makeda Silvera, *The Heart Does Not Bend*

Émile Ollivier

(between 1976 and 1992, Ollivier has also published six volumes on sociology and pedagogy)

1977 *Paysage de l'aveugle*

1983 *Mère-Solitude*

1986 *La discorde aux cent voix*

1991 *Passages*

1995 *Les urnes scellées*

1999 *Mille eaux*

2001 *Regarde, regarde les lions*

2001 *Repérages* (non-fiction)

2004 *La brûlerie*

2011 *Repérages 2* (non-fiction)

Stanley Péan

1988 *La plage des songes*

1991 *Le tumulte de mon sang*

1992 *Sombres allées et autres endroits peu hospitaliers: Treize excursions en territoire de l'insolite*

1993 *L'emprise de la nuit*

1994 *La mémoire ensanglantée*

1995 *L'automne sauvage*

1996 *Treize pas vers l'inconnu*

1996 *Zombi Blues*

1997 *L'appel des loups*

1997 *Quand la bête est humaine*

1998 *Un petit garçon qui avait peur de tout et de rien*

1999 *Noirs désirs*

1999 *Le temps s'enfuit*

1999 *Toute la ville en jazz* (non-fiction)

2000 *La nuit démasque*

2000 *Pl@nète culture* (non-fiction)

2001 *Le cabinet du Docteur K*

David Woods, *Home* (radio play)

2003

Marie-Célie Agnant, *La Légende du poisson amoureux*

Marie-Célie Agnant, *L'Oranger magique: Conte d'Haïti*

Marie-Célie Agnant, *Vingt petits pas vers Maria*

Austin Clarke, *Choosing His Coffin: The Best Stories of Austin Clarke*

George Elliott Clarke, *Québécité: A Jazz Fantasia in Three Cantos*

Nalo Hopkinson, ed., *Mojo: Conjure Stories* (anthology)

Nalo Hopkinson, *The Salt Roads*

Didier Leclair, *Ce pays qui est le mien*

Melchior Mbonimpa, *Le dernier roi faiseur de pluie*

Donna Bailey Nurse, *What's a Black Critic to Do? Interviews, Profiles and Reviews of Black Writers* (non-fiction)

David Odhiambo, *Kipligat's Chance*

Rosemary Sadlier, *The Kids Book of Black Canadian History* (non-fiction)

Robert Sandiford, *Sand for Snow: A Caribbean-Canadian Chronicle* (memoir)

Djanet Sears, *The Adventures of a Black Girl in Search of God*

Djanet Sears, ed., *Testifyin': Contemporary African Canadian Drama*, vol. 2 (anthology)

2004

Austin Clarke, *Love and Sweet Food: A Culinary Memoir*

Wayde Compton, *Performance Bond*

Bernadette Dyer, *Waltzes I Have Not Forgotten*

2001 *Cette étrangeté coutumière*

2004 *Taximan: Propos et anecdotes recueillis depuis la banquette arrière* (non-fiction)

2006 *Jazzman: Chroniques et anecdotes autour d'une passion* (non-fiction)

2007 *Autochtones de la nuit*

2011 *Bizango*

Oscar Peterson

2002 with Richard Palmer, *A Jazz Odyssey: The Life of Oscar Peterson*

Anthony Phelps

1960 *Été*

1961 *Présence*

1962 *Éclats de silence*

1966 *Points cardinaux*

1968 *Le conditionnel*

1968 *Mon pays que voici*, suivi de *Les dits du fou-aux-cailloux*

1973 *Et moi, je suis une île*

1973 *Moins l'infini: roman haïtien*

1976 *Mémoire en colin-maillard*

1976 *Motifs pour le temps saisonnier*

1980 *La bélière caraïbe*

1983 *Même le soleil est nu*

1985 *Haïti, Haïti*

1987 *Orchidée nègre*

1995 *Les doubles quatrains mauves*

2000 *Immobile voyageuse de Picas et autres silences*

2004 *Femme Amérique*

2005 *Une phrase lente de violoncelle*

2006 *La contrainte de l'inachevé*

2011 *Une plage intemporelle*

2012 *L'araignée chiromancienne*

Esi Edugyan, *The Second Life of Samuel Tyne*

Gérard Étienne, *Au bord de la falaise*

Minister Faust (Malcolm Azania), *The Coyote Kings, Book One: Space-Age Bachelor Pad*

Lawrence Hill, *Seeking Salvation: A History of the Black Church in Canada* (script, film)

Nalo Hopkinson, ed., with Uppinder Mehan, *So Long Been Dreaming: Postcolonial Fiction & Fantasy* (anthology)

Dany Laferrière, *Comment conquérir l'Amérique en une nuit* (director and scriptwriter, film)

Dany Laferrière, *Le goût des jeunes filles* (*On the Verge of a Fever*) (scriptwriter, film)

Tessa McWatt, *There's No Place Like ...*

Tessa McWatt, *This Body*

Suzette Mayr, *Venous Hum*

Émile Ollivier, *La brûlerie*

Stanley Péan, *Taximan: Propos et anecdotes recueillis depuis la banquette arrière* (non-fiction)

Anthony Phelps, *Femme Amérique*

Althea Prince, ed., with Susan Silva-Wayne, *Feminisms & Womanisms: A Women's Studies Reader* (anthology)

Bryan Prince, *I Came as a Stranger: The Underground Railroad* (non-fiction)

David Woods, *Witness* (radio play)

2005

André Alexis, *Ingrid and the Wolf*

Robert Berrouët-Oriol, *Thòraya, d'encre le champ*

George Elroy Boyd, *Wade in the Water*

2012 *Nomade je fus de très vieille mémoire*

Marlene NourbeSe Philip

1980 *Thorns*

1983 *Salmon Courage*

1988 *Harriet's Daughter*

1989 *She Tries Her Tongue, Her Silence Softly Breaks*

1991 *Looking for Livingstone: An Odyssey of Silence*

1992 *Frontiers: Essays and Writings on Racism and Culture, 1984–1992* (non-fiction)

1993 *Showing Grit: Showboating North of the 44th Parallel* (non-fiction)

1996 *Caribana: African Roots and Continuities – Race, Space and the Poetics of Moving* (non-fiction)

1997 *A Genealogy of Resistance and Other Essays* (non-fiction)

1999 *Coups and Calypsos*

2008 *Zong! As Told to the Author by Setaey Adamu Boateng*

Althea Prince

1991 *How the East Pond Got Its Flowers* (as Althea Trotman)

1992 *How the Starfish Got to the Sea* (as Althea Trotman)

1993 *Ladies of the Night and Other Stories*

2001 *Being Black: Essays*

2001 *Loving This Man*

2004 ed., with Susan Silva-Wayne, *Feminisms & Womanisms: A Women's Studies Reader* (anthology)

2009 *The Politics of Black Women's Hair* (non-fiction)

Dionne Brand, *What We All Long For*

George Elliott Clarke, *George & Rue*

George Elliott Clarke, *Illuminated Verses* (with photography by Ricardo Scipio)

Cecil Foster, *Where Race Does Not Matter: The New Spirit of Modernity* (non-fiction)

Lorena Gale, "The Darwinist" (dissertation)

Lorna Goodison, *Controlling the Silver*

Lorna Goodison, *Fool-Fool Rose Is Leaving Labour-in-Vain Savannah: Short Stories*

Nalo Hopkinson, ed., with Geoff Ryman, *Tesseracts Nine* (anthology)

Dany Laferrière, *Les années 80 dans ma vieille Ford*

Pamela Mordecai, *The True Blue of Islands*

Anthony Phelps, *Une phrase lente de violoncelle*

Robert Sandiford, *The Tree of Youth and Other Stories*

Olive Senior, *Over the Roofs of the World*

2006

Fred Booker, *Adventures in Debt Collection*

Dionne Brand, *Inventory*

George Elliott Clarke, *Black*

Afua Cooper, *Copper Woman and Other Poems*

Afua Cooper, *The Hanging of Angélique: The Untold Story of Canadian Slavery and the Burning of Old Montréal* (non-fiction)

Gérard Étienne, *Un cauchemar en plein midi d'été*

2012 ed., *In the Black: New African Canadian Literature* (anthology)

2013 ed., *Beyond the Journey: Women's Stories of Settlement and Community Building in Canada*

2013 ed., *So the Nailhead Bend, So the Story End: An Anthology of Antiguan and Barbudan Writing* (anthology)

Bryan Prince

2000 with Karen Shadd-Evelyn and Joyce Shadd Middleton, *Something to Hope For: The Story of the Fugitive Slave Settlement, Buxton, Canada West* (non-fiction)

2004 *I Came as a Stranger: The Underground Railroad* (non-fiction)

Gwendolyn Robinson and John W. Robinson

1989 *Seek the Truth: A Story of Chatham's Black Community* (non-fiction)

Rosemary Sadlier

1994 *Leading the Way: Black Women in Canada* (non-fiction)

1995 *Mary Ann Shadd: Publisher, Editor, Teacher, Lawyer, Suffragette* (non-fiction)

1997 *Harriet Tubman: Freedom Seeker, Freedom Leader* (non-fiction)

2003 *The Kids Book of Black Canadian History* (non-fiction)

2009 *Black History: Africa, the Caribbean, and the Americas* (non-fiction)

Robert Sandiford

1995 *Winter, Spring, Summer, Fall: Stories*

Gérard Étienne, *Hervé Lebreton et la poétique de la femme (non-fiction)*

Lorna Goodison, *Goldengrove: New and Selected Poems*

Dany Laferrière, *Je suis fou de Vava*

Dany Laferrière, *Vers le sud*

Melchior Mbonimpa, *Les morts ne sont pas morts*

Andrew Moodie, *The Real McCoy*

Pamela Mordecai, *Pink Icing*

Donna Bailey Nurse, ed., *Revival* (anthology)

Stanley Péan, *Jazzman: Chroniques et anecdotes autour d'une passion* (non-fiction)

Anthony Phelps, *La contrainte de l'inachevé*

H. Nigel Thomas, ed., *Why We Write: Conversations with African Canadian Poets and Novelists* (non-fiction)

Ernest Tucker, *Lost Boundaries*

2007

Marie-Célie Agnant, *Un alligator nommé Rosa*

David Chariandy, *Soucouyant*

George Elliott Clarke, *Trudeau: Long March, Shining Path*

Joël des Rosiers, *Un autre soleil*

Joël des Rosiers, *Caïques*

Bernadette Dyer, *Abductors*

Esi Edugyan, *Diese Fremden: Kurzgeschichten*

Minister Faust (Malcolm Azania), *From the Notebooks of Dr. Brain*

Cecil Foster, *Blackness and Modernity: The Colour of Humanity and the Quest for Freedom* (non-fiction)

1997 *Attractive Forces* (illustrations Justin Norman, graphic story collection)

2002 *Stray Moonbeams* (illustrations Justin Norman, graphic story collection)

2003 *Sand for Snow: A Caribbean-Canadian Chronicle* (memoir)

2005 *The Tree of Youth and Other Stories*

2010 *Great Moves* (illustrations Geof Isherwood, graphic story collection)

2013 *And Sometimes They Fly: A Novel*

Mairuth Sarsfield

1997 *No Crystal Stair*

Djanet Sears

1990 *Afrika Solo*

1997 *Harlem Duet*

2000 ed., *Tellin' It Like It Is: A Compendium of African Canadian Monologues for Actors* (anthology)

2000 ed., *Testifyin': Contemporary African Canadian Drama*, vol. 1 (anthology)

2003 *The Adventures of a Black Girl in Search of God*,

2003 ed., *Testifyin': Contemporary African Canadian Drama*, vol. 2 (anthology)

Olive Senior

(Senior has also published several non-fiction volumes about Jamaica and the Caribbean)

1985 *Talking of Trees*

1986 *Summer Lightning*

Lorna Goodison, *From Harvey River: A Memoir of My Mother and Her People*

Sylvia Hamilton, *The Little Black School House* (film)

Lawrence Hill, *The Book of Negroes*

Nalo Hopkinson, *The New Moon's Arms*

Didier Leclair, *Un passage vers l'Occident*

Stanley Péan, *Autochtones de la nuit*

Olive Senior, *Shell*

Addena Sumter-Freitag, *Stay Black & Die*

H. Nigel Thomas, *Return to Arcadia*

2008

Marie-Célie Agnant, *La nuit du Tatou*

André Alexis, *Asylum*

Austin Clarke, *More*

George Elliott Clarke, *Blues and Bliss: The Poetry of George Elliott Clarke*

Gérard Étienne, *Monsieur le président*

Gérard Étienne, *Natania*

Lorena Gale, *The Voice* (produced)

Dany Laferrière, *Je suis un écrivain japonais*

Rachel Manley, *Horses in Her Hair: A Granddaughter's Story* (memoir)

Melchior Mbonimpa, *La terre sans mal*

Marlene NourbeSe Philip, *Zong! As Told to the Author by Setaey Adamu Boateng*

2009

Marie-Célie Agnant, *Et puis parfois quelquefois …*

George Elroy Boyd, *Le Code Noir* (produced)

Dionne Brand, *Fierce Departures: The Poetry of Dionne Brand*

1989 *The Arrival of the Snake-Woman and Other Stories*

1993 *A Quartet of Stories: Maya Angelou, Lorna Goodison, Olive Senior, Alice Walker*

1994 *Gardening in the Tropics*

1995 *Discerner of Hearts*

2005 *Over the Roofs of the World*

2007 *Shell*

2011 *Dancing Lessons*

2012 *Birthday Suit* (illustrations Eugenie Fernandez)

2013 *Anna Carries Water* (illustrations Laura James)

George Seremba

1993 *Come Good Rain*

1995 ed., with Yvette Nolan and Betty Quan, *Beyond the Pale: Dramatic Writing from First Nations Writers and Writers of Colour* (anthology)

2000 ed., with Carmen Aguirre and Ann Lambert, *Along Human Lines: Dramas from Refugee Lives*

Adrienne Shadd

1994 ed., with Carl E. James, *Talking about Difference: Encounters in Culture, Language, and Identity* (non-fiction)

1994 *"We're Rooted Here and They Can't Pull Us Up": Essays in African Canadian Women's History* (with Peggy Bristow et al.; non-fiction)

2010 *The Journey from Tollgate to Parkway: African Canadians in Hamilton* (non-fiction)

Karen Shadd-Evelyn

1993 *I'd Rather Live in Buxton* (memoir)

George Elliott Clarke, *I & I*

Afua Cooper, *Love and Revolution* (audio recording)

Afua Cooper, *My Name Is Henry Bibb: A Story of Slavery and Freedom*

Afua Cooper, *My Name Is Phillis Wheatley: A Story of Slavery and Freedom*

Joël des Rosiers, *Lettres à l'indigène*

Gérard Étienne, *Le créole une langue ...* (non-fiction)

Dany Laferrière, *L'énigme du retour*

Dany Laferrière, *La fête des morts*

Tessa McWatt, *Step Closer*

Althea Prince, *The Politics of Black Women's Hair* (non-fiction)

Rosemary Sadlier, *Black History: Africa, the Caribbean, and the Americas* (non-fiction)

Addena Sumter-Freitag, *Back in the Days*

2010

André Alexis, *Beauty and Sadness: Or, the Intermingling of Life and Literature*

Robert Berrouët-Oriol, *En haute rumeur des siècles* (illustrations Frankétienne)

Robert Berrouët-Oriol, *Poème du décours*

Dionne Brand, *Ossuaries*

Christian Campbell, *Running the Dusk*

Wayde Compton, *After Canaan: Essays on Race, Writing, and Religion* (non-fiction)

Joël des Rosiers, *Gaïac*

Wayne Grady, with Merilyn Simonds, *Breakfast at the Exit Café: Travels through America*

2000 with Joyce Shadd Middleton and Bryan Prince, *Something to Hope For: The Story of the Fugitive Slave Settlement, Buxton, Canada West* (non-fiction)

Makeda Silvera

1983 ed., *Silenced: Talks with Working Class West Indian Women about Their Lives and Struggles as Domestic Workers in Canada* (non-fiction)

1986 ed., *Fireworks: The Best of Fireweed* (anthology)

1989 *Growing up Black: A Resource Manual for Black Youths* (non-fiction)

1989 ed., with Nila Gupta, *The Issue Is 'ism: Women of Colour Speak Out* (anthology)

1991 ed., *Piece of My Heart: A Lesbian of Colour Anthology*

1991 *Remembering G and Other Stories*

1993 ed., *The Other Woman: Women of Colour in Contemporary Canadian literature* (non-fiction)

1994 *Her Head a Village and Other Stories*

1995 ed., with C Allyson Lee, *Pearls of Passion: A Treasury of Lesbian Erotica* (anthology)

2000 ed., with Stephanie Martin, *Sapodilla: The Sister Vision Book of Lesbian Poetry* (anthology)

2002 *The Heart Does Not Bend*

Charles Smith

1984 ed., *The Teeth of the Whirlwind: Poems by Allen, Brand, Joseph, Smith* (anthology)

1985 ed., *sad dances in a white field* (anthology)

Dany Laferrière *with* Ghila Sroka, *Conversations avec Dany Laferrière*

Dany Laferrière, *Tout bouge autour de moi*

Didier Leclair, *Le soixantième parallèle*

Andrew Moodie, *Toronto the Good*

David Odhiambo, *The Reverend's Apprentice*

Robert Sandiford, *Great Moves* (illustrations Geof Isherwood, graphic story collection)

Adrienne Shadd, *The Journey from Tollgate to Parkway: African Canadians in Hamilton* (non-fiction)

H. Nigel Thomas, *Lives: Whole and Otherwise*

2011

Dionne Brand, *Chronicles: Early Works*

Paul Fehmiu Brown, *Les cahiers de Sicka: Roman historique*

George Elliott Clarke, *Red*

Esi Edugyan, *Half-Blood Blues*

Minister Faust (Malcolm Azania), *The Alchemists of Kush*

Minister Faust (Malcolm Azania), *Journey to Mecha: Eight Visionary* SF, *Fantasy, Philosophical and Satirical Tales*

Cheryl Foggo, *Dear Baobab* (illustrations Qin Leng)

Lorna Goodison, *By Love Possessed: Stories*

Sylvia Hamilton, *We Are One* (film)

Dany Laferrière, *L'art presque perdu de ne rien faire*

Tessa McWatt, *Vital Signs*

Suzette Mayr, *Monoceros*

1987 *Partial Lives*

Addena Sumter-Freitag

2007 *Stay Black & Die*

2009 *Back in the Days*

Carol Talbot

1984 *Growing Up Black in Canada* (memoir)

Lyle Talbot, with Carol Talbot

2013 *Memoir of a Black Canadian Activist* (non-fiction)

H. Nigel Thomas

1987 *Spirits in the Dark*

1988 *From Folklore to Fiction: A Study of Folk Heroes and Rituals in the Black American Novel* (non-fiction)

1995 *How Loud Can the Village Cock Crow? and Other Stories*

1999 *Moving through Darkness: Poems*

2001 *Behind the Face of Winter*

2006 ed., *Why We Write: Conversations with African Canadian Poets and Novelists* (non-fiction)

2007 *Return to Arcadia*

2010 *Lives: Whole and Otherwise*

2014 *When the Bottom Falls Out and Other Stories*

Verna Thomas

2001 *Invisible Shadows: A Black Woman's Life in Nova Scotia* (memoir)

Ernest Tucker

1994 *Underworld Dwellers*

2006 *Lost Boundaries*

Donna Bailey Nurse, *What's a Black Critic to Do II: Interviews, Profiles and Reviews of Black Writers* (non-fiction)

Émile Ollivier, *Repérages 2* (non-fiction)

Stanley Péan, *Bizango*

Anthony Phelps, *Une plage intemporelle*

Olive Senior, *Dancing Lessons*

2012

Lillian Allen, *Anxiety* (audio recording)

George Elliott Clarke, *Directions Home: Approaches to African-Canadian Literature* (non-fiction)

Minister Faust (Malcolm Azania), *E-Force: Sixteen Stories of Ultra-Freaking Awesomeness*

Minister Faust (Malcolm Azania), *War & Mir*, vol. 1: *Ascension*

Nalo Hopkinson, *The Chaos*

Nalo Hopkinson, *Report from Planet Midnight*

Didier Leclair, *Le complexe de Trafalgar*

Melchior Mbonimpa, *La tribu de Sangwa*

Pamela Mordecai, *Subversive Sonnets*

Anthony Phelps, *L'araignée chiromancienne*

Anthony Phelps, *Nomade je fus de très vieille mémoire*

Althea Prince, ed., *In the Black: New African Canadian Literature* (anthology)

Olive Senior, *Birthday Suit* (illustrations Eugenie Fernandez)

2013

André Alexis, *A*

Robert Berrouët-Oriol, *Découdre le désastre* suivi de *L'île anaphore*

Headley Tulloch

1975 *Black Canadians: A Long Line of Fighters* (non-fiction)

Maxine Tynes

1987 *Borrowed Beauty*

1990 *Woman Talking Woman*

1991 *Save the Word for Me*

1993 *The Door of My Heart*

Rinaldo Walcott

1997 *Black Like Who? Writing Black Canada* (non-fiction)

2000 ed., *Rude: Contemporary Black Canadian Cultural Criticism* (non-fiction)

Ann Wallace

1991 ed., *Daughters of the Sun, Women of the Moon: An Anthology of Canadian Black Women Poets* (anthology)

Marie Stark Wallace

1966 "Notes made by Marie Albertina Stark (afterwards Mrs Wallace) from the recollections of her mother, Sylvia Stark, who was born a slave in Clay County, Missouri, and settled on Salt Spring Island with her husband, Louis Stark, and family in the year 1860, as homesteaders" (first published in Compton 2002)

Frederick Ward

1964 *Poems*

1966 ed., *Anthology of Nine Baha'I Poets* (anthology)

1972 ed., *Present Tense* (anthology)

1974 *Riverlisp: Black Memories*

Austin Clarke, *They Never Told Me: And Other Stories*

Austin Clarke, *Where the Sun Shines Best*

George Elliott Clarke, *Illicit Sonnets: Poetry*

George Elliott Clarke, *Lasso the Wind: Aurelia's Verses and Other Poems* (illustrations Susan Tooke)

Joël des Rosiers, *Métaspora: Les patries intimes* (non-fiction)

Minister Faust (Malcolm Azania), *A Bad Bad Beat Was Brewing: An Africentric Scroll of Bizarre, Brutal, Inspiring and Supernatural Tales*

Minister Faust (Malcolm Azania), *The Wonderful Wizard Wangari* (produced)

Lorna Goodison, *Oracabessa*

Lorna Goodison, *Supplying Salt and Light*

Wayne Grady, *Emancipation Day*

Lawrence Hill, *Blood: The Stuff of Life* (non-fiction)

Lawrence Hill, *Dear Sir, I Intend to Burn Your Book: An Anatomy of a Book Burning* (non-fiction)

Nalo Hopkinson, *Sister Mine*

Dany Laferrière, *Le baiser mauve de Vava*

Dany Laferrière, *Journal d'un écrivain en pyjama*

Tessa McWatt, *The Taste of Marmalade*

Valerie Mason-John and Kevan Anthony Cameron, eds, *The Great Black North: Contemporary African Canadian Poetry* (anthology)

Althea Prince, ed., *Beyond the Journey: Women's Stories of Settlement and Community Building in Canada* (anthology)

1977 *Nobody Called Me Mine: Black Memories*

1981 *A Room Full of Balloons*

1983 *The Curing Berry*

1988 *Crossroads: Three Jazz Pianists* (narrator and script, film)

1988 *Somebody Somebody's Returning*

1990 *Oliver Jones in Africa* (narrator and script, film)

1996 *The Road Taken* (narrator and script, film)

Dorothy Williams

1989 *Blacks in Montreal, 1628–1986: An Urban Demography* (non-fiction)

1997 *The Road to Now: A History of Blacks in Montreal* (non-fiction)

David Woods

1983 *For Elsie Dorrington* (produced)

1984 *Voices* (produced)

1985 *The Dream Continues …* (produced)

1990 *Native Song: Poetry and Paintings*

1990 *Nova Scotia Black Reality Song* (produced)

1991 *Part of the Deal* (radio play)

1992 *Black Journey* (radio play)

1993 *The Aunt Jemima Story* (radio play)

1995 *Nova Scotia Suite* (produced)

1997 *Once* (radio play)

1998 *Choices in the Skin* (produced)

2002 *Home* (radio play)

2004 *Witness* (radio play)

Althea Prince, ed., *So the Nailhead Bend, So the Story End: An Anthology of Antiguan and Barbudan Writing* (anthology)

Robert Sandiford, *And Sometimes They Fly: A Novel*

Olive Senior, *Anna Carries Water* (illustrations Laura James)

Lyle Talbot with Carol Talbot, *Memoir of a Black Canadian Activist* (non-fiction)

2014

André Alexis, *Pastoral*

Dionne Brand, *Love Enough*

George Elliott Clarke, *Settling Africville* (produced)

George Elliott Clarke, *Traverse*

Wayde Compton, *The Outer Harbour*

Esi Edugyan, *Dreaming of Elsewhere: Observations on Home* (non-fiction)

Minister Faust (Malcolm Azania), *War & Mir*, vol. 2: *The Darkold*

Cheryl Foggo, *John Ware Reimagined* (produced)

Cecil Foster, *Genuine Multiculturalism: The Tragedy and Comedy of Diversity*

Cecil Foster, *Independence*

Sylvia Hamilton, *And I Alone Escaped to Tell You*

Didier Leclair, *Un ancien d'Afrique: Les chiens de Kigali*

Melchior Mbonimpa, *Diangombé, l'immortel*

H. Nigel Thomas, *When the Bottom Falls Out and Other Stories*

NOTES

CHAPTER ONE

1 The phrase "in what is now Canada" is a reminder of the fact that "Canada" is an imprecise term of convenience with respect to earlier periods. A *Canadien* was originally an inhabitant of New France. Prior to joining Confederation, "the inhabitants of colonial New Brunswick, Newfoundland, Nova Scotia, and Prince Edward Island certainly did not think of themselves as Canadian. Canada was a colony, then a pair of colonies, up the St. Lawrence" (Mackey 2010, 11).

2 I use the term "black Canadian" to refer to black African-descended individuals and populations in what is now Canada. Common critical usage also employs the term "African Canadian." Wilson Tettey and Korbla Puplampu, however, remind us that it can hardly be said that all African Canadians are black. In fact, only about 30 per cent of those who self-identified as African in the 1996 Canadian census were black, while 27 per cent were white and 20 per cent South Asian (Tettey and Puplampu 2005, 8–9). Canadian scholar Rinaldo Walcott prefers the term "black" over hyphenated terms (and presumably also unhyphenated versions of them) because he feels that a phrase like "Jamaican-Canadian," for example, draws "on multicultural narratives that are concerned with origin" for which "black identities must be rooted elsewhere ... outside Canada" (1997, 5). For a discussion of the term "black" in a Canadian context, see also George Elliott Clarke (2002a, 15–17) and Mensah (2010, 22–5). I am aware that "race" is not a scientifically valid term (see Gates 1988, 1–20; Appiah 1986; Jacquard 1996; L. Hill 2001; Rotman 2003) but a socially constructed reality contingent on historical and geographical variation (e.g., Hall 1996, 254; Vernon 2008, 12). As Anthony Appiah has pointed out, however, "the label works despite the absence of an essence" (1996, 81) and can also help to shape positive identifications and scripts that people use (and vary) in their lives (see Siemerling 2005, 145–54, and 2010, 148–52; George Elliott Clarke 2002a, 16–17). Paul Gilroy, the author of *Against Race* (2000), thus speaks nonetheless of "racial and ethnic minorities who did not appreciate

having their particularity deconstructed or made to appear absurd" (2010, 80).

3 One exception is Sophia Pooley, who was brought to Canada as a slave in 1778. She was sold to Mohawk chief Joseph Brant, then to the English immigrant Samuel Hatt. Her testimony can be found among the slave narratives collected by Benjamin Drew (Drew 2000, 192–5).

4 I will return at the end to Paul Gilroy's foundational study, which has been repeatedly criticized for its elision of Canadian contexts. Gilroy mentions Canada mainly with reference to Martin Delany (1983, 20, 23) but never discusses the rich implications of this location. For an example of fruitful inclusion of such connections in recent hemispheric work, see R. Adams (2009, 61–99).

5 Slavery ended formally with abolition in the British Empire in 1834, while courts made it impracticable earlier (see chapter 3); the last known advertisements for sales appear in 1820 in Halifax and 1821 in Quebec, while some later wills still mention slaves as property (Winks 1997, 110).

6 For an account of slave narratives in the context of hemispheric studies, see Siemerling (2014).

7 Upper and Lower Canada become Canada West and Canada East in the United Province of Canada in 1840. With Canadian Confederation in 1867, they are named Ontario and Quebec and are joined by Nova Scotia and New Brunswick to form the Dominion of Canada (New Brunswick is part of Nova Scotia until 1784). Manitoba becomes a province in 1870 and British Columbia joins in 1871, followed by Prince Edward Island in 1873 and Alberta, Saskatchewan, Newfoundland, and Nunavut in the twentieth century.

8 In addition to the volumes dedicated to Peterson and Jones (see chapter 5), standard works on jazz in Canada are the relevant volumes by Mark Miller (1982, 1989, 1997, 2001). Jazz and other black musics in Canada were notably the subject of a conference convened by Leslie Sanders and Natasha Smith at York University in 2003 (http://www.yorku.ca/aconline/music_conference/schedule.html). Rinaldo Walcott focuses on Canada in chapter 2 of his PhD dissertation, "Performing the Postmodern: Black Atlantic Rap and Identity in North America" (1996), and, in *Black Like Who?* (1997/2003), discusses examples of black Canadian film and musics, including hip hop and the work of groups like the Dream Warriors (2003, 141–4 and passim). Substantial research on black Canadian hip hop, for example, is underway in the work of Mark V. Campbell, who curated *T-Dot Pioneers* in 2010, an exhibition on Toronto hip hop history.

9 See Tourino's 2010 MA project thesis, "Online Representations of African Canadian Cinema: An Ethnographic and Archival Analysis," which is available at the valuable website associated with his project, http://africancanadiancinema.wordpress.com. Other information is provided in the section on "African Canadian Film" by African Canadian Online, at http://www.yorku.ca/aconline/film.html.

10 This work is finally available in English, translated by George Tombs (Trudel 2013).

11 Often referred to as the Massey Commission (after its chair, Vincent Massey), the Royal Commission on National Development in the Arts, Letters and Sciences was created in 1949 to investigate the relation between the state and culture, initially prompted by the question whether Canada's public broadcasting system should be extended to television. The commission's report (1951), however, covered a wide range of cultural issues and was instrumental in drawing attention to Canadian cultural dependency on the United States. In its wake, the National Library was established in 1953 and the Canada Council for the Arts in 1957, which later began to administer literary prizes and writers' grants (see Litt 2007, 38–40; Robert 1989, 138–40).

12 These developments have been amply documented and analysed in Canadian literary criticism. I offer a comparative analysis of narratives of cultural emergence in this period in *The New North American Studies: Culture, Writing, and the Politics of Re/Cognition*, especially chapter 6 (2005, 116–44).

13 The White Paper was retracted in 1971, and its policy recommendations never implemented (see Dickason 2002, 377–9). Cree lawyer Harold Cardinal rejects the White Paper in his influential 1971 volume *The Unjust Society: The Tragedy of Canada's Indians*, heralding an increased production of First Nations writing in Canada in its wake. The Royal Commission on Aboriginal Peoples, reporting in 1996, called for substantive changes in the treatment of First Nations and recognition of the Métis in Canada. In 2008 the government of Canada apologized for the suffering inflicted by the residential school system and the history of attempted forced assimilation. For a recent personal account that includes First Nations history in Canada, see Thomas King's *The Inconvenient Indian: A Curious Account of Native People in North America* (2012).

14 A Redress Agreement and an apology were offered by the Canadian government in 1988; see Miki and Kobayashi (1991) and Miki (2004).

15 Dorothy Sterling and Victor Ullman publish important volumes on Delany in 1971, with chapters on his time in Canada. Delany and the emigration of blacks to Canada are also an important subject in Floyd J. Miller's *The Search for a Black Nationality* (1975). Still a standard resource on black nationalism, this volume also discusses other mid-nineteenth-century black leaders in Canada, such as Henry and Mary Bibb and Mary Ann Shadd.

16 For a discussion of the belated emergence of race in the discussion of Canadian literature, see Coleman and Goellnicht (2002).

17 On the congress, see Austin (2007, 521–8; 2013, 16–26), D.W. Williams (1997, 119), and Mills (2007, 184–91); on Burnley "Rocky" Jones, see Sylvia Hamilton's 1994 documentary *Against the Tides: The Jones Family* (part 2 of *Hymn to Freedom: The History of Blacks in Canada*); on the Sir George Williams Affair, see Austin (2013, 129–56), Williams (1997, 118–38), and Mills (2007, 191–8).

18 Earlier scholarship on black Canadians includes Montreal mayor Jacques Viger's *De l'esclavage en Canada* (completed and published by Louis-Hippolyte

LaFontaine in 1859), Thomas Watson Smith's *The Slave in Canada* (1899), William Renwick Riddell's *The Slave in Canada* (1920), and Fred Landon's many articles on black Canadian history, which appeared for over forty years after the end of the First World War (see Landon 2009). In 1960, Daniel G. Hill completed his thesis on "Negroes in Toronto: A Sociological Study of a Minority Group" at the University of Toronto, and in 1963 William and Jane Pease's *Black Utopia: Negro Communal Experiments in America* appeared, a volume that also discussed the black nineteenth-century settlements in Canada. Victor Ullman's *Look to the North Star: A Life of William King* (1969) detailed the life of the white reformer who founded the Elgin Settlement, or Buxton, in 1849 in Canada West, and in 1971 Donald G. Simpson completed an unpublished thesis at the University of Western Ontario entitled "Negroes in Ontario from Early Times to 1870." Yet as Robin Winks claims in a 1969 article announcing his subsequent book, the "only general studies of the Negro in Canada published by the 1960's were Ida Greaves, 'The Negro in Canada,' McGill University Economic Studies, whole no. 16 (Orillia, Ont., 1930), and Harold H. Potter, 'Negroes in Canada,' *Race: The Journal of the Institute of Race Relations*, III (Nov., 1961), 39–56" (1969, 15n5).

19 This story is fleshed out in Lawrence Hill's *The Book of Negroes* (discussed here below and in chapter 4). In his acknowledgments, Hill mentions reading his parents' copy of the study by Walker, a good friend of theirs (481–2).

20 George Elliott Clarke lists those by Camille Haynes in 1973, Liz Cromwell in 1975, and Harold Head in 1976 (2002, 430–1); for comments on the latter, see also Chariandy (2001), and Bucknor and Coleman (2005, viii–ix).

21 Austin Clarke's Toronto trilogy consists of *The Meeting Point* (1967), *Storm of Fortune* (1973), and *The Bigger Light* (1975). His other early texts are the novel *The Survivors of the Crossing* (1964) and the short story collections *Among Thistles and Thorns* (1965) and *When He Was Free and Young and Used to Wear Silks* (1971). Clarke's later novel *The Polished Hoe* is discussed in chapter 4.

22 See the discussion in chapter 5. Ward's first poetry collection is *Poems* (1964). *Riverlisp* is followed by two further novels, *Nobody Called Me Mine* (1977) and *A Room Full of Balloons* (1981), the poetry collection *The Curing Berry* (1983), his play *Somebody Somebody's Returning* (1988), and his collaboration in the documentaries *Oliver Jones in Africa* (1990), *The Road Taken* (1997), and *Crossroads: Three Jazz Pianists* (1998).

23 Brand's first collections of poetry are *'Fore Day Morning* (1978) and *Earth Magic* (1979), followed by *Primitive Offensive* in 1982; much of her work is considered in detail in chapter 4.

24 Surveying course offerings in the literatures of Canada at a substantial number of Canadian universities in the academic year 1997–98, Paul Martin's study of the teaching of Canadian literature, *Sanctioned Ignorance: The Politics of Knowledge Production and the Teaching of the Literatures of Canada* (2013), even then finds only one course dedicated to black Canadian writing (see his Appendix 1, 193–220). In a much more recent assessment, Charmaine Nelson

notes that "there is a decided absence of Black or African-Canadian Studies programs in Canadian academia" (2010, 11).

25 Silvera's collection is discussed in chapter 4. In addition, Daniel G. Hill published *The Freedom Seekers: Blacks in Early Canada* in 1981. Together with Donna Hill, he founded the Ontario Black History Society in 1978.

26 This period saw the publication of his memoir *Growing Up Stupid under the Union Jack* (1980), the short story collections *When Women Rule* (1985) and *Nine Men Who Laughed* (1986), and the novel *Proud Empires* (1988).

27 Further first works include Lorris Elliott's novel *Coming to Carry* (1982), Afua Cooper's collection of poetry *Breaking Chains* (1984), and Nigel Thomas's novel *Spirits in the Dark* (1987). Lorna Goodison's first collection of poetry, *Tamarind Season* (1980), appeared when she still lived in Jamaica.

28 Her early albums include *Dub Poet: The Poetry of Lillian Allen* (1983) and the Juno Award–winning *Revolutionary Tea Party* (1986) and *Conditions Critical* (1988). Her volumes of poetry include *Women Do This Every Day: Selected Poems of Lillian Allen* (1993) and *Psychic Unrest* (1999).

29 As Greg Tourino observes (with reference to Gittings 2002), the "foundation of an African Canadian cinema essentially begins with National Film Board Studio D documentaries of the 1970s and 1980s that as a result of Canada's official multiculturalism policy provided the first real opportunities for visible minority filmmakers" (2010, 19).

30 The Writing and Publication Program was launched in 1977–78 as a result of the multiculturalism policy announced by Pierre Elliott Trudeau in 1971, which became law with Bill C 93, the Canadian Multiculturalism Act, in 1988. Canadian state multiculturalism has been contentious and critiqued for, among other things, upstaging the importance of the francophone fact in Quebec, reinforcing essentialized identities, camouflaging asymmetrical power relationships, diverting attention from class, and conflating issues of ethnicity and race; for discussions, see, for example, Bannerji (2000), Davey (1995), Hutcheon and Richmond (1990), Kamboureli (2000), Siemerling (1996), Huggan and Siemerling (2000). For a defence of multiculturalism policies and a discussion of the impact of the WPP, see Young (2001). Besides Elliott's bibliography and Brand's *Sans Souci and Other Stories*, the WPP also supported, for instance, George Elliott Clarke's *Fire on the Water* and Rosemarie Sadlier's *Leading the Way: Black Women in Canada* (1994).

31 Virgo's other features are *Lie with Me* (2005) and *Poor Boy's Game* (2007). He also has numerous television credits and is the director of a television mini-series adaptation of Hill's *The Book of Negroes*.

32 Several of these authors and a few who began publishing after 2000 are discussed in more detail below, such as Hill, Chariandy, Alexis, Foster, Gale, and Agnant in chapter 4 and Sarsfield, Mayr, Compton, and Edugyan in chapter 5.

33 George Elliott Clarke won the Governor General's Award for poetry for his *Execution Poems* in 2001. Subsequent notable awards included the Giller Prize in 2002 and the Commonwealth Writers Prize in 2003 for Austin Clarke's *The*

Polished Hoe, the Commonwealth Writers Prize for Lawrence Hill's *The Book of Negroes* in 2008, and the Griffin Poetry Prize for Dionne Brand's *Ossuaries* in 2011. Also in 2011, Esi Edugyan's *Half-Blood Blues* won the Giller Prize and was short-listed for the Man Booker Prize.

34 After important earlier essays, the first book-length studies dedicated specifically to black Canadian writing were Walcott (1997/2003), G.E. Clarke (2002a), and collections of essays edited by Walcott (2000) and Maureen Moynagh (2005, on black Canadian theatre). Important book-length contributions by historians were Bristow (1994) and Williams (1997). Among relevant conferences, I have already mentioned the black Canadian musics conference organized by Sanders and Smith in 2003; the "Caribbean Migrations" conference organized by Hyacinth Simpson at Ryerson University in 2005 occasioned many papers on Caribbean Canadian writers; and the first MLA session dedicated to "Black Writing in Canada" was convened by Siemerling in Washington, DC, also in 2005. A conference on Dionne Brand was organized by Rinaldo Walcott and Katherine McKittrick in Toronto in 2008. This incomplete list suggests only some of the scholarly activities in that period.

35 An excellent summary of that debate – which began with Clarke's response in 1997 to Walcott's *Black Like Who?* – has been offered by Karina Vernon (2008, 22–33). Walcott offers his perspective in the introduction to the second edition of *Black Like Who?* (2003), while Clarke returns to the debate in the introduction of *Directions Home* (2012). I revisit this exchange briefly in chapter 6.

36 As Herb Wyile has observed, while "the writers of the 60s were obsessed with the here and now, contemporary Canadian historical novelists have been engaged in coming to terms with both the present and the past" (2002, xi). It is interesting to consider possible parallels with his observation that historical fiction increases *after* the initial "flourishing of Canadian literature in the 1960s" (2002, xi); he cites Margaret Atwood's comment that writers at that point "were taken up by the momentous discovery that we ourselves existed, in what was then the here and now, and we were busily exploring the implications of that" (Atwood 1997, 15; qtd in Wyile 2002, xi).

37 Two prominent examples are Hutcheon (1988a, 61–77) and Wyile (2002, 2007).

38 Two well-known sites in this regard are the Uncle Tom's Cabin historic site in Dresden, Ontario, and the Buxton National Historical Site and Museum, a tribute to Rev. William King's Elgin Settlement (see chapter 3). The latter offers excellent pedagogical material adapted to the Ontario school curriculum, as well as on-site classes in a period classroom (http://www.buxtonmuseum.com/education/education.html).

39 Deconstructive notions of radical alterity offer one form of caveat, as does Glissant's insistence on a certain *opacité* (1995, 54) that would withstand a universalizing gaze; other aspects of this problematic are evoked, for example, by Sommer (1999) and – discussed here below – McBride (2001) and Austen (2011).

40 I take this phrase from the title of Ingrid Monson's study of improvisatory practice in jazz (1996).

41 I will return to the questions of practice and improvisation with respect to turntablism and de Certeau's notion of consumption in chapter 5. For now, let me just evoke Anthony Appiah's discussion of how individuals negotiate identity with reference to available "scripts." Appiah elaborates on such processes of identification in particular with reference to Ian Hacking's work (Appiah 1996, 78–9; Appiah 2005, 21–3, 65–6; Hacking 1986; see also Siemerling 2005, 147–54). I will reference these ideas again in chapters 4 and 5.

42 The extensive scholarly discussion of Du Bois's concept defies summary here; see Siemerling (2005, 31–8).

43 I have been inspired here by Daniel Coleman's useful discussion of melancholia with reference to two Canadian texts (2012; see here below and chapter 4).

44 To explicate this internalization, Freud invokes Otto Rank and speculates that the ego, faced with disappointment, regresses to narcissism and "wants to incorporate this object into itself … by devouring it" (1917, 249). The advantage is that "in spite of the conflict with the loved person [or "loss of a more ideal kind" (244)] the love-relation need not be given up" (248). This explains, though, how "the shadow of the object fell upon the ego, and the latter could henceforth be judged by a special agency"; here, object-loss becomes an "ego-loss" (248).

45 In "Theses on the Philosophy of History," Benjamin notes in Thesis V: "The true picture of the past flits by. The past can be seized only as an image which flashes up at the instant when it can be recognized and is never seen again" (1968, 255); in Thesis VI, he adds: "To articulate the past historically … means to seize hold of a memory as it flashes up at a moment of danger" (1968, 255).

46 In a very perceptive reading of two important texts by Dionne Brand with reference to theories of melancholia, Maureen Moynagh (2008) suggests that it is not on the level of the text itself that melancholia holds out hope, but at the level of the audience. The reader is in the position of the psychoanalyst who understands the incapacitating circumstances of melancholic subjects in the text (2008, 71–2). This explanation is a useful qualification in this context, but it paints aggrieved subjects themselves as entirely powerless and without agency.

47 Cheng references Werner Sollors's discussion of "Indian Melancholy" in *Beyond Ethnicity* (Sollors 1986, 115–30). In the context of Canadian First Nations' history, the assimilationist politics of Duncan Campbell Scott, Confederation poet and high-ranking civil servant in the Department of Indian Affairs, comes readily to mind, as exemplified in his much-anthologized poem "The Onondaga Madonna."

48 The interiorization of potentially antagonistic perspectives is explored perhaps more productively in Du Bois's concept of double consciousness, where it is conscious and can offer a productive edge (Siemerling 2005).

49 Coleman summarizes: "Ironically, then, this theory which provides a powerful criticism of the status quo, can too easily become a powerful re-citation of

the status quo … We come to understand the disavowing systems of heterosexism, neo-colonialism, or whiteness, but the theory does very little to liberate homosexuals, colonized, or racialized groups from its power" (2012, 59).

50 With reference to the Holocaust, Giorgio Agamben opens his chapter on "The Witness" with the observation that in "the camp, one of the reasons that can drive a prisoner to survive is the idea of becoming a witness" (1999, 15).

51 In Zilpha Ellis's translation, "The Route of the Big Boats" (Agnant 2006, 195).

52 I discuss further aspects of her statement that her life is "a ghost story" (Hill 2007a, 4) in chapter 4. She also haunts London and the empire that has forced her into slavery.

53 In his essay "'A Self-Unsealing Poetic Text': Poetics and the Politics of Witnessing" (2000), Derrida distinguishes between these three aspects in the context of his discussion of Paul Celan's poem "Aschenglorie."

54 Baucom thus inquires "about the witness testari, the witness who calls into being a body of executors charged with the task of assuming and transmitting the property she has taken in the event as its observer/survivor?" For Derrida, he suggests, "that witness exists for the nonwitness," who is called upon to engage with what has been witnessed (Baucom 2005, 176–7).

55 Other responses include J.M.W. Turner's painting *Slavers Throwing Overboard the Dead and the Dying, Typhoon Coming On* (1840; for detailed discussion, see Wood 2000, 41–77; Baucom 2005, 245–96) and Fred D'Aguiar's novel *Feeding the Ghosts* (1997).

56 The exact number seems uncertain; according to Schama, 122 slaves were thrown overboard while 10 others decided to jump themselves, with one managing to climb back on board (2008, 160); Fisch and Baucom count 133 (Fisch 2007, xv; Baucom 2005, 129), while Hodges et al. mention 130 (1996, xxix).

57 Sharp played a crucial role already in the 1772 *Sommerset* case that was a prelude to later abolitionism in England (see chapter 2), also presided over by Lord Mansfield.

58 The text of that decision to order a second trial, known as *Gregson v. Gilbert*, has survived. While some sources claim that a second trial resulted in a reversal of the original decision, there seems to be no evidence. As Geoffrey Clark notes, the "outcome of the second trial, if one was in fact ever held, is lost to history since it was not reported" (2010, 56). No criminal charges were ever laid against the captain of the ship.

59 Sharp was also a co-founder of Freetown in Sierra Leone, one of the sites in Hill's novel.

60 In an interview, Hill places the main emphasis on plausibility: "I have taken several liberties with dates and places and so forth, but I wanted the novel to be realistic … And I wouldn't like it if a historian came behind me and said, 'This is preposterous. The things that Hill is having take place in this novel are utterly impossible, never happened and never could have happened.' It doesn't so much matter if they never happened, but I would like them to be plausible and to make sense" (in Sagawa 2008, 316).

61 For Hirsch, "postmemory describes the relationship of the second generation to powerful, often traumatic, experiences that preceded their births but that were nevertheless transmitted to them so deeply as to seem to constitute memories in their own right" (2008, 103; see also Hirsch 1997).

62 Hirsch continues: "Thus less-directly affected participants can become engaged in the generation of postmemory, which can thus persist even after all participants and their familial descendants are gone" (2008, 111).

63 As Derrida remarks later, "There are several times of the specter. It is a proper characteristic of the specter, if there is any, that no one can be sure if by returning it testifies to a living past or to a living future" (2006, 123).

64 Baucom builds his "Theory of Melancholy Sentiment" (the subtitle of his chapter 9) with reference to Adam Smith's "experimental melancholy," developed in his *Theory of Moral Sentiments* (1759). For Smith, it is an attempt to put ourselves in the situation of the dead. Baucom describes melancholia in this context "not as a result of the traumas that have happened to us but as a way of making ourselves happen within the space of the traumatic, not as a way of lodging the past within the present but as a way of lodging the present (and ourselves) in the deathly afterlife of past historical situations" (2005, 259). These eloquent formulations, while trying to articulate an interactive temporality, elide the incapacitating and often self-destructive side of melancholia. For other relevant discussions of Smith's theory in this context, see Wood (2002, 100–93) and Boltanski (1999).

65 Glissant refers here to the work of Gilles Deleuze and Félix Guattari, linking this concept with the notion of the rhizome, which "maintains … the idea of rootedness but challenges that of a totalitarian root" (2007, 11).

66 Baucom later acknowledges that the idea of melancholy testimony is largely negated by Glissant's poetics. He suggests nonetheless that this "does not mean that Glissant utterly dismisses the eighteenth and nineteenth-century project of sympathy I have traced. Though the relational politics of errancy may seek to put an end to such a liberal project, Glissant discovers in precisely such a dead end of political attachment the first stirring of a more promising beginning" (2005, 314).

67 Glissant occasionally uses the term "melancholic," but not in the sense of mental separation, disavowal, or absent knowledge of the causes.

68 Medovarski poses the related if somewhat different question of what it means "in the current global capitalist conjuncture that a novel about the slave trade has generated so much money?" (2013, 9). Her analysis focuses on what she perceives to be the contrast between "Hill's sophisticated economic critiques" and "the ways the novel is circulated as a material commodity" and promoted, so that "the novel's text and paratext are sometimes troublingly contradictory" (22).

69 Morrison continues: "So if I'm looking to find and expose a truth about the interior life of people who didn't write it … if I'm trying to fill in the blanks

that the slave narratives left – to part the veil that was so frequently drawn, to implement the stories that I heard – then the approach that's most productive and most trustworthy for me is the recollection that moves from the image to the text" (1995, 93–4). On the idea of fiction as a form of truth-telling, see Duff (2011, 238–41).

70 Rushdy locates the beginnings of the neo-slave narrative in the 1960s shift from civil rights movement politics to black nationalism and the attendant debates over the representation of slavery. He points in particular to the response of black writers and intellectuals to the publication of William Styron's *The Confessions of Nat Turner* in 1967: "Black Power Intellectuals challenged Styron's novel on … its representation of a nonheroic slave rebel, its presumption of assuming the voice of a slave, its uninformed appropriation of African American culture, its deep, almost conservative allegiance to the traditional historiographical portrait of slavery" (Rushdy 1999, 4). Early examples of neo-slave narratives include Margaret Walker's *Jubilee* (1966), Ernest Gaines's *The Autobiography of Miss Jane Pittman* (1971), Ishmael Reed's *Flight to Canada* (1976), and Octavia Butler's *Kindred* (1979). For a succinct discussion of the genre, see V. Smith (2007).

71 I will return to this idea and musical improvisation in the discussion of turntablism and the work of Wayde Compton in chapter 5.

72 I use the notation "re/cognition" to designate the ambivalent and contradictory duality by which cognitive change ("re–cognition") inevitably draws on available values, categories, and narratives ("recognition"). Recognition often implies identification or acceptance under dominant standards. In this sense, "recognition" limits "re–cognition" because the former assimilates potential difference to known and accepted patterns. I have developed this heuristics elsewhere in the context of "New" World paradigms and of W.E.B. Du Bois's elaboration of "double consciousness" as a framework to study North American cultures comparatively and as the ongoing results of conflicted articulations of cultural emergence (Siemerling 2005).

73 Neither are they limited to one racially identified tradition. In *The Signifying Monkey*, Henry Louis Gates observes that "anyone who analyses black literature must do so as a comparativist, by definition, because our canonical texts have complex double formal antecedents, the Western and the black" (1988, xxiv). This otherwise appropriate observation would barely begin to describe the multiplicity of major traditions in several languages that are antecedents for black Canadian writing.

74 Gilroy points out that "the history of Europe's colonial crimes and of the applied raciology that warranted them cannot stand outside the genealogy we create for human rights … The development of human rights cannot … either be plausibly or usefully narrated as a tidy sequence of waves that corresponds to the American, French, and Russian revolutions and the U.N.'s Declaration of Human Rights" (2010, 58).

CHAPTER TWO

1 As mentioned earlier, the one exception is the short narrative by Sophia Pooley.

2 According to Trudel, the first indigenous slaves were offered by the Iroquois to the French governor in 1671 (2004, 21); as indigenous slaves became more numerous, they were named "Panis" (30n15); they accounted for approximately two-thirds of the slave population of New France (2004, 90).

3 Afua Cooper cites the 1731 Montreal census by the Sulpician fathers, according to which "the servile class consisted of 142 slaves, both Panis and African" (2006, 144). African slavery in New France was authorized by Louis XIV in 1689, shortly after the Code Noir regulated slavery in the West Indies in 1685. The authorization had no direct impact, however, because of intervening wars and perhaps for reasons of insufficient capital (Trudel 2004, 34–48; Winks 1997, 5–23).

4 I agree with George Elliott Clarke's suggestion that such transmissions should be read as slave narratives (2005c, 17–18).

5 Juridiction royale de Montréal, "Procedure Criminel contre Marie Joseph Angélique negresse – Incendiere, 1734." I have used here the transcriptions and translations made available by the website "Torture and the Truth: Angélique and the Burning of Montreal," *Great Unresolved Mysteries in Canadian History* (http://www.canadianmysteries.ca/sites/angelique/accueil/indexen.html).

6 There were six interrogations in all, including two during which the accused was placed under more intimidating conditions "in the criminal seat"; in addition, various meetings were recorded where Angélique was confronted with witnesses.

7 The merchant François Poulin de Francheville is listed by Trudel as holding ten slaves. While this number seems small by comparison with slavers elsewhere, it made him one of the more important owners in New France (Trudel 2004, 140–2).

8 Mackey's work also offers a detailed critique of Trudel's findings and numbers (2010, 95–107). As Mackey points out, Trudel's trailblazing work was undertaken in the age of index cards and the absence of many microfilm and archive centres, a situation that required his predecessor "to trudge from church to church" in his quest for some of his records (97).

9 In 1799 and again in 1800, slave owners petitioned for legislative support to quell the increasing numbers of absconding slaves, after several of them secured their freedom through the courts (Mackey 2004, 4; Trudel 2004, 304–12).

10 These copies now reside in the Public Record Office, Kew Gardens, London, and in the Papers of the Continental Congress in the National Archives, Washington. The British version was copied in 1884 – presumably by a copyist in London – at the behest of Nova Scotia's commissioner of public records from 1857 to 1891, Thomas Beamish Akins (see also note 15).

11 On John Laurens, the instigator of this last-minute addition to Article 7, see Pybus (2006, 60–1) and Schama (2008, 56, 136–8).

12 The book details ten different hearings, one of which involved two children and another that concerned a woman with three children, bringing the number of individuals to fourteen.

13 The "Cases" of the "Book of Negroes" are not included in his edition.

14 The case thus does not seem to be directly about embarkation for Nova Scotia, as neither Nancy nor Flora Bartram nor their father appear in the "Book of Negroes"; there are numerous entries listed simply under the first name Nancy, however, and there is an entry for a Toney Bartram (Hodges et al. 1996, 205). Shortly after this case was heard, the board sent a letter to Brigadier General Birch to clarify that it felt responsible only for cases of impending embarkation (5).

15 Page references are to the British version of the ledger at the British National Archives at Kew, available as page photographs with transcription of the Inspection Roll on the site of the Public Archives of Nova Scotia (PANS) at http://novascotia.ca/archives/virtual/africanns/BN.asp and at http://blackloyalist.info/sourcedetail/display/15 (pages 7–8 are missing in the latter; the transcriptions of the "Cases" below are mine). My transcriptions have been checked against those by Ruth Whitehead. I would like to thank her for making her unpublished transcription of the ledger available to me.

16 The name is spelled Dobson in the transcription of Hodges et al. (1996, xviii).

17 In the "Book of Negroes," these passes are often referenced in abbreviated form as GBC, and GMC for the equivalent General Musgrave Certificates.

18 "Carleton's interpretation of the Provisional Agreement … was that blacks who are already with the British before 30 November 1782 and who claimed freedom by the proclamations were technically free and therefore could not be considered as American property on that date. Only confiscated slaves and those who came after the agreement were covered by article VII" (Walker 1992, 10–11).

19 Another woman and her three children were re-enslaved on 7 August 1783; in her case, the proclamations of freedom were deemed inapplicable because she was a slave within British lines and was thus not considered to have joined the British: "The Board are of Opinion that while the Claimant remained within the British Lines under the Protection of the British Army his Negroes were not entitled to the Benefit of the Proclamations respecting Negroes and as the Wench was not sent out of the Lines with him She never became entitled to the Benefit of those Proclamations and therefore are of Opinion that the Wench and her Children ought to be delivered to the Claimant to be disposed of as he may think proper" (15).

20 The research website www.blackloyalist.info by Cassandra Pybus et al. dedicates the following entry to her: "Judith Jackson 53 is in the Royal Artillery Department and travels without a partner alone in the BON. She is said to have run for years before but other evidence makes it clear she defected to Lord

Dunmore in 1775–6. She is alone in the Birchtown muster. Her owner is given as Clain but there was no such person. Her owner might be John McLean, who was a British merchant and suspect Loyalist charged with treason" (accessed 20 September 2013). The entry also notes that Jackson waited until the last British ship out, unsuccessfully seeking to recover her daughter, whom Eilbeck illegally had sent back to Virginia (see also Pybus 2006, 70). Hodges also identifies John MacLean as her former owner: "Judith Jackson fled from her master, John MacLean of Norfolk, Virginia, in 1773 … Shortly after this, MacLean left for Great Britain, leaving his affairs in the hands of Eilbeck, Ross & Company. Jackson remained at large in Norfolk … After Dunmore's proclamation, she joined his regiment, working as a laundress. Eight years later, she received a certificate from General Birch, entitling her to passage to Nova Scotia. Unexpectedly, Eilbeck, now a loyalist, arrived to demand possession of Jackson and her children. By her testimony to the board, Jackson revealed that she had joined the troops in Virginia, traveled with them to South Carolina, then voyaged to New York in 1782. Despite Eilbeck's claim as a loyal subject of His Majesty, the board referred Jackson's case to Carleton, who determined that her eight years of service outweighed her old master's property rights" (Hodges et al. 1996, xviii; see also Schama 2008, 152). By contrast, as noted earlier, Walker suggests that the cases involving Loyalist claimants were forwarded to Birch, not Carleton (1992, 12).

21 Port Roseway was settled by four hundred families that became known as the "Port Roseway Associates," and lists enumerating these families show substantial numbers of "servants" accompanying them (e.g., Szick et al.). Honouring General Birch, Black Loyalists named their settlement on the northwest side of the harbour Birchtown. On Shelburne and Birchtown more generally, see Walker's chapters "Freedom Denied" and "Black Society in Loyalist Nova Scotia" (1992, 40–93).

22 These protocols are perhaps more comparable to the Brazilian Inquisition hearings described by Krueger (2002).

23 An earlier board was set up by General Leslie during the evacuation of Charleston in 1782 (Pybus 2006, 59; Schama 2008, 134–5). No record was kept, but Pybus estimates "that between 7,000 and 8,000 blacks left Charlestown. The great majority of these were people enslaved to departing Loyalists, with about 15 percent, some 1,500 people, going as free people in one capacity or another, be it indenture servant, cook, soldier, seaman, or free settler" (Pybus 2006, 60).

24 These reports are preserved by the Public Records Office as part of the British Parliamentary Papers and can be found in the documents of the Colonial Office, CO 116/138–42, CO 116/143–53, CO 116/156, CO 116/157–63 (see Lean and Burnard 2002, 122n7). Slaves were able to complain to these officials about brutal punishments and lack of food and clothing. These sources reveal over a thousand slave testimonies from the beginning of the nineteenth century, mostly transcribed in the first person (Lean and Burnard 2002, 122).

25 This investigation, following James Williams's 1837 apprenticeship narrative *A Narrative of Events, since the First of August, 1834*, produced testimony from over 120 apprentices (British Parliamentary Papers 1837–38, 49:159–263; partially rendered in J. Williams 2001). In Diana Paton's words, the proceedings offer "the most substantial collection of first-person accounts of their experiences by Caribbean slaves or former slaves" (Paton 2001, xiii).

26 In addition black testimony was also recorded by the Spanish in Florida. As Jane Landers notes in her *Black Society in Spanish Florida*, "the archive of the second Spanish Government known as the East Florida papers has survived virtually intact. This remarkable source contains a truly vast array of … records, and the history of black Floridians is found throughout, much of it generated in their own words, and often their own hand" (Landers 1999, 5). Interrupted by British possession, Spanish control over Florida was from 1565–1763 and 1784–1821. When Florida was transferred to the United States in 1821, "most of the free black community, like their predecessors in 1763, joined in a mass exodus to Cuba. Others fought on with the Seminoles and shared their fate" (Landers 1999, 3).

27 It is not mentioned as such in Hodges and Cook's discussion of the columns, which precedes their transcription of the US version of the document (Hodges et al. 1996, xlix–l). The actual transcription offers its content nonetheless in parentheses, although Hodges and Cook, in their brief note on the text, associate information in these parentheses with the "Claimant" category (Hodges et al. 1996, l).

28 According to Hodges and Cook, the third book is written in paragraph form (Hodges et al. 1996, xlix). This claim is not accurate with regard to the British version as it is reproduced on the site of the Public Archives of Nova Scotia.

29 See his discussion in this respect of the work of Robin Winks (1971), James Walker (1992), Ellen Wilson (1976), Graham Russell Hodges et al. (1996), Gary Nash (1981), Sylvia Frey (1983, 1991), Simon Schama (2008), and Cassandra Pybus (2006) (Whitfield 2007, 1981–2).

30 Among the reasons for this neglect, Whitfield cites the fact that the subject of Loyalist slaves did not fit into the popular pattern that contrasted American enslavement with Canadian freedom (2007, 1982) and problems with documentary evidence: "For example, the Loyalists regularly referred to their slaves as servants, and without another piece of evidence such as a will or runaway advertisement it is nearly impossible to know definitively if they were actually enslaved. Also, as Maritime Canada remained a society with slaves as opposed to a slave society, newspapers rarely commented on the scope or extent of enslavement" (2007, 1982–3).

31 Less clear is the relationship between the Reverend Dr Sayre, who travelled on the *Cyclops*, bound for Port Roseway, with Phillis and Rosanna, identified as "Formerly the property of the Reverend Dr. Sayre." Perhaps he had manumitted his slaves. There is also a Molly listed aboard the *Grand Duchess of Russia*, also bound for Port Roseway, in the possession of John Menshall but "Free as per certificate from the Reverend Dr. Sayre."

32 In addition to the writers on slavery in New France and Lower Canada already mentioned (Trudel, Winks, Gay, Mackey), see also Donovan (1995) and Whitfield (2006, 12–14) on slavery in French Nova Scotia and Ile Royal [Cape Breton] under the French Regime.

33 The group was organized by Loyalists in New York who wanted to relocate to Port Roseway (see Whitfield 2009, 62) and consisted of approximately four hundred families. They were the first to arrive in Shelburne, in the spring of 1783 (Walker 1992, 21–2), and thus ahead of the ships enumerated in the "Book of Negroes." Several of the associates, however, did not travel with this first group, often because their land grants had not been confirmed; some of them seem to have travelled with their "servants" or slaves registered in the "Book of Negroes." On Shelburne's later development, see Wetherell and Roetger (1989).

34 The source is available in searchable form from Collections Canada; Taylor's entry can be found at http://www.bac-lac.gc.ca/eng/discover/military-heritage/loyalists/loyalist-port-roseway/Pages/item.aspx?IdNumber=449&.

35 My own search produced eighteen individuals; Hodges et al. list twenty-nine (1996, Table 6, 222).

36 The Loyalist Claims Commission was established by the British government in 1783 to compensate Loyalists for their losses.

37 For another interpretation of the "Possession" rubric, however, see Pybus, who sees many of these individuals as travelling "under the protection of departing Loyalists" (2006, 66). See also Anne Yarbrough's entry "Black Pilots' Connection to Henry Mowatt" in her blog "Nova Scotia Island Journal," where she discusses four black pilots on the ship *Ann* sailing to Port Roseway and their relationship to Henry Mowatt; in the entry "The Black Pilots Who Went to Sierra Leone from Birchtown," she writes about the decision of two of them to move to Sierra Leone later (Yarbrough 2010a, 2010b). These four black pilots are also briefly discussed by Walker (1992, 31).

38 Discussing Ukawsaw Gronniosaw's *Narrative*, Henry Louis Gates writes that by the time of its appearance in 1770, "only four black people are thought to have published books in Western languages (Juan Latino, Jacobus Capitein, Wilhelm Amo, and Briton Hammon)" (1988, 138).

39 In addition, Equiano's friend and leader of the London "black poor," Ottobah Cugoano, published his *Thoughts and Sentiments* in 1787 (see Gates 1988, 146–52).

40 The 1783 arrivals were preceded by black evacuees from Charlestown in late 1782 and followed by a group of Jamaican Maroons in 1796 and the Black Refugees after the war of 1812.

41 Marrant's volume saw twenty editions by 1835 (Gates 1988, 142) and almost forty by 1850 (Gould 2007, 21); on the publication history, see Helen Thomas (2000, 309–10n65).

42 As George Elliott Clarke points out, Africadian literature as orature began with song, story, and sermon (1991, 1:11).

43 Gould emphasizes that "unlike the antebellum slave narrative, eighteenth-century narratives were more generically fluid. They were published and read as many things at once. The generic field includes spiritual autobiography, the conversion narrative, the providential tale, criminal confession, Indian captivity narrative, sea adventure story, and the picaresque novel" (2007, 13).

44 As Pierce writes, "these captivity narratives are religious documents, modeled along conversion and spiritual narrative forms, replete with Puritan and Calvinist theology." In showing Natives as savages and enemies of God, she points out, these narratives strengthened the settler self in opposition to the fully othered "Indians" and justified their removal, thus morally supporting brutal colonization and the doctrine of manifest destiny (2007, 85).

45 Gates explains that the "trope of the Talking Book is the ur-trope of the Anglo-African tradition. Bakhtin's metaphor of double-voiced discourse … comes to bear in black texts through the trope of the Talking Book … making the white written text speak with the black voice is the initial mode of inscription of the metaphor of the double-voiced" (1988, 131).

46 In the preface to the second edition, Aldridge reads Marrant's narrative strictly in terms of divine intervention: "Were the power, grace, and providence of God ever more eminently displayed than in the conversion, success, and deliverances of *John Marrant*?" (Marrant 2002, 48). While he denies having shaped the content, he admits to altering the language: "I have always preserved Mr. *Marrant's* ideas, tho' I could not his language; no more alterations, however, have been made than were thought necessary" (Marrant 2002, 49).

47 With reference to Alan Richardson's essay "Romantic Voodoo: Obeah and British Culture, 1797–1807," Helen Thomas suggests that "the 'contact zone' between Romanticism and black writing had clearly been established by the end of the century" (2000, 172).

48 François Crouzet speaks of "the decisive stage of the Industrial Revolution, the 20 years which followed the peace of 1783" (1980, 82).

49 Again, George shows himself as an active, enterprising agent in this context: "On the voyage from Halifax to Sierra Leone, I asked the Governor if I might not hereafter go to England? and some time after we arrived there, I told him I wished to see the Baptist brethren who live in his country" (George 2002, 189).

50 Accounts of the Sierra Leone experience include Walker (1992, 145–403), Pybus (2006, 139–55, 169–202), and Schama (2008, 201–397). According to Walker, George died in 1810 (Walker 2000a), while Schama indicates 1802 (2008, 395). King died as an agent of the Sierra Leone Company in Sherbro, south of Freetown, in 1802 (Walker 2000b).

51 As Pybus points out, many of those travelling to Sierra Leone were actually born in Africa (2006, 150).

52 On the reception of slave narratives in England, see also Fisch (2000), especially chapter 3, "'Repetitious Accounts so Piteous and so Harrowing': The Ideological Work of American Slave Narratives in England" (Fisch 2000, 52–68).

53 See for instance the inclusion of Boston King's "Memoirs" in Sugar and Moss (2009, 1:147–53). These authors appeared in the anthology of black Nova Scotian literature edited by George Elliott Clarke in 1991.

54 The equally important *Narrative* by David Thompson, based on diary entries written in the 1780s and 90s, is not published before 1916; John Franklin's *Journey* appears in 1823.

55 As Marrant's *Journal* reveals, for instance, he converts Cherokees to Christianity, and Natives are part of his congregation.

56 In his summary of Williams's argument and the subsequent debate, Brown notes that Williams puts less weight on "the skirmishes in Parliament that traditionally received greatest attention from British and Imperial historians" and insists that the abolitionist cause picked up speed "when it became economically convenient to do so. The value of the British sugar colonies, he argued, declined appreciably after the American Revolution" and the attack on the slave system "was, at heart, an attack on monopoly, on the exclusive right of British Caribbean sugar producers to meet the demand of British consumers," conducted in the name of free trade (C.L. Brown 2006, 13). While Brown suggests that Williams's "decline thesis," though preventing later historians from returning to humanitarian accounts, "fell from favor" (16), others see validity in his account (see Blackburn 1997; Solow and Engerman 1987; and note 60 on Brown and Blackburn below).

57 In the British reception of slave narratives, as Fisch demonstrates, the emphasis "is not on the presence in the narratives merely of violence and cruelty; the emphasis is on the violence of American slave society and the cruelty of the United States" (2000, 60). Such perspectives highlight "the dark prison-house of American society" (61); in one review of the narrative of John Brown, "England, more than slavery or John Brown, ends up being the subject and hero." Summarizing the usefulness of the slave narrative for British imperial purposes, Fisch writes: "Thus enlisted to do the work of Empire, the slave narrative is constructed … as an indictment of America and as a vindication of English superiority" (63).

58 Ottabah Cugoano (who called himself John Stewart in England), friend of Equiano and one of the leaders of the London Black Poor, expresses grave doubts about the wisdom of returning to West Africa, the place of original enslavement. In his *Thoughts and Sentiments on the Evil and Wicked Traffic of the Slavery and Commerce of the Human Species* (1787), he emphasizes that the slave factory of Bance Island was operated by Liverpool merchants close to the site of the Sierra Leone settlement (Pybus 2006, 111–12).

59 This perspective is undermined by Williams, who points to duplicity and ambiguity in British actions.

60 Brown thus shows that in the view of Victorian and Edwardian historians the "regrettable years of avarice and exploitation, 'the old commercialism,' thankfully lay in the past" (C.L. 2006, 8). Yet Blackburn sides with Eric Williams and those historians who suggest a direct relation between that disavowed

past and the present before and after the turn of the century. They claim that "the profits of Britain's 'triangular trade' with Africa and the West Indies lent a major impulse to the Industrial Revolution" (Blackburn 1997, 517, 542; for the debate, see Solow and Engerman 1987). Slavery is here a constitutive factor of modernity. Plantation economies, while representing an agrarian mode of production, provided raw materials and export markets for advanced economies and, together with the slave trade, involved forms of credit and modes of trust typical of capital accumulation (Baucom 2005, esp. 80–112). As agrarian modes of production, they constituted an "accumulation of stock" that for Adam Smith preceded "the division of labor" (A. Smith 1976, 277; qtd in Blackburn 1997, 512) and that Marx calls "primitive accumulation" (in opposition to "capitalist accumulation"). In the case of the British trade, however, for Blackburn "this was 'primitive accumulation' conceived of not as an episode but as an ongoing aspect of the Metropolitan accumulation process – what might be termed 'extended primitive accumulation'" (1997, 515). Marx identifies primitive accumulation mostly with the British enclosures, but also includes imperial control over colonies and slavery in the list of practices: "The discovery of gold and silver in America, the extirpation, enslavement and entombment in mines of the indigenous population of that continent, the beginnings of the conquest and plunder of India, and the conversion of Africa into a preserve for the commercial hunting of blackskins, are all things which characterize the dawn of the era of capitalist production. These idyllic proceedings are the chief moments of primitive accumulation … The different moments of primitive accumulation can be assigned in particular to Spain, Portugal, Holland, France, and England, in more or less chronological order. These different moments are systematically combined together at the end of the seventeenth century in England; the combination embraces the colonies, the national debt, the modern tax system, and the system of protection. These methods depend in part on brute force, for instance the colonial system. But they all employ the power of the state, the concentrated and organized force of society, to hasten, as in a hothouse, the process of transformation of the feudal mode of production into the capitalist mode, and to shorten the transition" (Marx, *Capital*, qtd in Blackburn 1997, 514).

CHAPTER THREE

1 Related studies of race in the work of white nineteenth-century Canadian authors include Jade Ferguson's analysis of race and value in Haliburton's "The White Nigger" (J. Ferguson 2013) and Phanuel Antwi's dissertation "Hidden Signs, Haunting Shadows: Literary Currencies of Blackness in Upper Canadian Texts" (2011). Antwi offers detailed analyses of Richardson's *Wacousta* and *The Canadian Brothers* and the work of the Strickland sisters Catharine Parr Traill and Moodie.

2 Besides the texts I discuss here, further Canadian slave texts and reported or transcribed testimony include those in the Canadian volume of *The Black Abolitionist Papers* (Ripley 1986, vol. 2). The volume contains a former slave's letter to his erstwhile owner (65–7), an unsuccessful petition by a Nelson Hackett to Lord Sydenham to prevent his extradition to the United States (84–6), a black victim's warning against false friends who were black but in the pay of slave catchers (99–100), or a speech by the escaped slave of Senator Henry Clay, Lewis Richardson (101–3). We find here also an editorial by Henry Bibb on the already mentioned case of Frederick "Shadrach" Wilkins (130–2), a letter by a former slave writing from Saint John, New Brunswick in 1854 (133–5), and a text sent to Mary Ann Shadd by the Amherstburg True Band – one of the many similarly named black self-help organizations in Canada West and mostly composed of former slaves (306–9). Blassingame's *Slave Testimony* also contains a letter from Robert Brown, a resident of Chatham, written in the hope of buying his wife and child from their owner, Mr Brown, for $750 (1977, 29), and the slave narrative of James Curry, who later lived twenty-seven years in Canada (128–44).

3 As in the American Revolutionary War, the British sought to attract black support, this time with the 1814 Proclamation by Vice-Admiral Alexander Cochrane (see Whitfield 2006, 30–4).

4 As George Elliott Clarke has observed, "in Nova Scotia ... between 1798 and the 1960s, black 'writers' published mainly a few religious works" (2003, 78). For further black Nova Scotian writing from the nineteenth century, see volume 1 of Clarke's anthology *Fire on the Water* (1991, 57–112); this section includes the "Petition of Colored People at Preston" (1841) to the lieutenant governor of Nova Scotia; the slave narrative by John William Robertson, printed in Halifax and entitled *The Book of the Bible against Slavery* (1854); and Peter Evander McKerrow's "A Brief History of the Coloured Baptists of Nova Scotia," which renders the arrival of Richard Preston. A former slave from Virginia, Preston assumed his last name after discovering his Black Refugee mother in Preston, and he went on to organize numerous Baptist churches that united in 1854 in the African Baptist Association of Nova Scotia (G.E. Clarke 1991, 14; Winks 1997, 139; Whitfield 2006, 92–8; Walker 1976, 393).

5 Peggy Bristow writes about slaves near Amherstburg, Canada: "All sixty slaves on Matthew Elliot's farm near Amherstburg knew what the ring driven into the black locust tree at the front of the house meant. Anyone could be tied to the ring and flogged. Some fled across the border to Ohio" (1994b, 72). Ohio joined the Union as a free state in 1803. Vermont abolished slavery for all women over eighteen and all men over twenty-one in its constitution of 1777; in New York, the slave trade was banned in 1788, and an Act for the Gradual Abolition of Slavery was passed in 1799. In 1827, all slaves born before 4 July 1799 were also finally freed.

6 As a consequence, US attempts to recover runaway slaves from the British in New York in 1783 and in Canada in the nineteenth century ironically found

their reverse and perverse counterpart in this period: "By 1807 slave-owners in the Western District of Upper Canada had suffered such losses to Detroit, in the territory of Michigan … that ten of the owners petitioned the Lieutenant-Governor" to keep their property safe. Yet although "Britain made representations to the United States, nothing could be done, since extradition arrangements had elapsed" (Winks 1997, 99).

7 Mackey points out that Chief Justice William Osgoode, often cited as an important actor in these developments, in fact no longer held office in 1803 and had already left the province (2010, 70).

8 See the summary of cases and legislation provided by Ripley (1986, 4–6).

9 "Beginning in the 1820s and continuing well into the 1840s," Ripley writes, "the social, economic, and political status of blacks in northern cities began to decline. Violence and segregation increased; voting rights and economic opportunity diminished. Northern urban centers became home for thousands of immigrants from Europe who competed for jobs, trades, and professions that had traditionally belonged to blacks" (1986, 9).

10 Lewis, appointed as agent to solicit support, was dismissed several times from his functions and eventually charged with embezzling funds (Winks 1997, 155–60; Mackey 2004, 120–6); he died in Montreal.

11 The pamphlet is reprinted in Mackey (2004, 200–3); in it, Lewis unrealistically calls for petitioning the queen for a meeting of "100,000 Coloured Men … to assemble at Niagara for the purpose of putting an end to Slavery" (200). For a more detailed discussion, see "Bad News Lewis" (Mackey 2004, 120–6).

12 Like most of the other slave narratives discussed in this chapter, Steward's account is available at the website *Documenting the American South*, at http://docsouth.unc.edu/fpn/steward/steward.html. An escaped former Virginia slave, Steward ran a successful grocery store in Rochester in the 1820s but was recruited to help run the Wilberforce settlement in 1831. In 1837, because of infighting and the difficulties with Israel Lewis, he returned, financially ruined, to Rochester.

13 When two of his horses died inexplicably, one after the other, Steward only later deduced that they must have been poisoned. At the very moment he pondered how to overcome this potentially ruinous loss, he was offered a considerable sum out of the money collected for the colony, presumably to buy his complicity as well as his silence.

14 Steward's interest in storytelling and in the form of the literary sketch is also visible in his story of a smuggler's escape (chapter 22), his rendering of the Quaker abolitionist Benjamin Lundy's account of the setting up of a black settlement in Haiti (chapter 24), or his description of a fugitive slave's attempted suicide (chapter 28).

15 Her name is also transcribed in various sources as Ruthie (Frost 2007, xxi) or Rutha (Ripley 1986, 5).

16 As Karolyn Smardz Frost points out, abolitionist hopes for a gradual demise of slavery had faded by the 1830s: "The expansion of cotton-growing territories into the West and Southwest and the proposed removal of the Indians

from still more lands under President Andrew Jackson's administration meant that more slaves would be needed and their prices would rise. Accordingly, reformers who earlier subscribed to the 'gradualist' school turned to a more 'immediatist' stance." William Lloyd Garrison thus founded *The Liberator* in 1831, calling for immediate abolition in the first issue (Frost 2007, 87).

17 As William Andrews points out, the 1832 *Memoir of Mrs. Chloe Spear* "extols the piety of Spear, a 'faithful servant' while enslaved in Massachusetts, but offers few specifics about the conditions of her enslavement, while Gilbert Vale's 1835 *Fanaticism* … introduces 'the woman who would become Sojourner Truth to the American reading public as Isabella Van Wegenen'" but is "concerned solely with Isabella's role in the cult" (2003, xxxvii).

18 Ifeoma Nwanwko emphasizes this dimension when she discusses Prince's narrative in terms of black cosmopolitan consciousness (2005).

19 Wedderburn, the son of a Scottish plantation owner and slave dealer and a slave mother, was freed at birth.

20 The 1853 Jamaican slave narrative of Archibald Monteath has only recently received sustained critical attention (see Warner-Lewis 2007).

21 Turner and nineteen of his followers were hanged. Incidentally, in the same year G.W.F. Hegel was laid to rest, the philosopher who in his *Philosophy of History* denied Africans any form of transcendence or history.

22 Important critical comment includes Gates (1987), M. Ferguson (1992 and 1987/1997), Paquet (1992), Sharpe (1996), Whitlock (2000), McBride (2001), Nwankwo (2005), Simmons (2009), and Antwi (2011).

23 With reference to a phrase by Harriet Jacobs, Sharpe argues "that Prince relied on her sexual relations with free men for establishing 'something akin to freedom' from her owners" (1996, 46).

24 As Sharpe explains, the "antislavery movement did not condone practices that went against the Protestant ideals of obedience, self-discipline, hard work, and moderation. Its definition of freedom was also racially coded … The slave that had to be freed … was not only an enslaved body over which the master had absolute control but also an African body bound to 'heathenism' and savagery. The antislavery position, like its proslavery counterpart, articulated a racial hierarchy, but one that was culturally rather than biologically determined" (1996, 33).

25 Clare Midgley makes a similar point: "Prince's own testimony at the libel action brought by Wood against Pringle shows that Strickland omitted the information Prince had given her about living for seven years with a Captain Abbott prior to her marriage, about whipping another woman she found in bed with the captain, and about living with another man out of wedlock. Stressing instances of Prince's sexual victimization, Strickland thus suppressed instances of her attempts to exercise control over her intimate life for fear they would undermine her support from the 'respectable'" (Midgley 1992, 91).

26 Mrs Pringle, having been asked to verify the marks on Prince's body (added in the third addition, see Whitlock 2000, 22; Sharpe 1996, 38), confirmed that Prince's skin was "lacerated with gashes" in many places, adding: "I beg to add

to my own testimony that of Miss Strickland (the lady who wrote down in this house the narratives of Mary Prince and Ashton Warner)" (Prince 1997, 131).

27 Sharpe adds in a note that "one English traveler to St. Vincent reports that she 'could comprehend little or nothing of what they [slaves] said; for though it was English … it was almost as unintelligible as if they had spoken in any of their native African tongues'" (Sharpe 1996, 54). The citation is from Mrs Carmichael's *Domestic Manners and Social Condition of the White, Coloured, and Negro Population of the West Indies* (1833).

28 The transcriber of James Williams's apprentice narrative, Archibald Palmer, actually makes such an attempt, furnishing us with an exception to normal transcription practice in the nineteenth century; for a discussion that also references Prince's *History* in this context, see Paton (2001, xxxiii–xxxiv).

29 Paton in her discussion of Williams's narrative wisely weighs aspects of control over the result in such collaboration: on the one hand, she cites Andrews's comment about the "power relationship that gave the supposed passive amanuensis ultimate control over the fate of the manuscript and considerable influence over the immediate future of the narrator" (Andrews 1986, 21; qtd in Paton 2001, xxxi), a comment that is here directly applicable to Pringle but also pertains to some extent to Strickland; on the other hand, Paton also refers us to scholarship demonstrating "the narrator's ability to exert control over the writing process despite inequalities of power" (xxxii).

30 Despite her straightforward attack on any reader sitting on the fence with regard to slavery, Moodie sought to win her audience over by presenting her own conversion and earlier lack of concern as a model and, in the process, offering her own theory of reader response and empathy: "Thinking that the same means which had operated so effectually upon my own mind might produce a favourable result in other persons who had been accustomed to view the case in the same careless and prejudiced manner, it occurred to me that I might publish, with some small advantage to the cause, the following little history, taken down from the narration of a young negro, who had recently made his escape from slavery in the West Indies, and had come over to England on purpose to establish his claims to freedom" (Warner 1831, 11–12).

31 "The Vanquished Lion" appeared originally in 1831 in *Ackerman's Juvenile Forget Me Not: A Christmas, New Year's, and Birthday Present for 1832* (reprinted in Moodie 1991, 31–42). Written in the context of Moodie's potential emigration to the Cape Colony (and mentioning Pringle as a former settler there), the story describes emigration from England and the overcoming of a child's racial prejudice concerning the slave owned by a relative. Saved from a snake by the slave, the child successfully requests the slave's freedom. As in some of her later, post-emigration texts, Moodie employs here abolitionist rhetoric together with a stereotyped portrayal of the slave that includes, in contrast to her transcribed slave narratives, the use of the vernacular.

32 The intervening abolition of slavery in the British Empire perhaps made it a less pressing concern for Moodie as a British subject, yet slavery was in fact

now a much closer reality for her, given Canada's adjacency to the United States and the effects of the Underground Railroad.

33 In the afterword to her collection of poems *The Journals of Susanna Moodie: Poems* (1970), Atwood describes Moodie's "violent duality": "If the national mental illness of the United States is megalomania, that of Canada is paranoid schizophrenia. Mrs. Moodie is divided down the middle: she praises the Canadian landscape but accuses it of destroying her; she dislikes the people already in Canada but finds in people her only refuge from the land itself … She claims to be an ardent Canadian patriot while all the time she is standing back from the country and criticizing it as though she were a detached observer, a stranger" (Atwood 1970, 62). Moodie is also imagined in a television play by Atwood, *The Servant Girl* (1974), and appears in her novel *Alias Grace* (1996). Atwood comments further on the subject in the film *The Enduring Enigma of Susanna Moodie* (1997).

34 As Whitlock writes with reference to Thurston, "the Traills, Moodies and Stricklands emigrated because of impoverishment in England and Scotland. Genteel poverty preceded emigration. However, as pioneers they faced a life of degradation, hardship and humiliation previously unknown" (Whitlock 2000, 51).

35 The Moodies arrived too late in the year to start farming and had to live on John Dunbar Moodie's limited capital; he subsequently sold his commission as half-pay officer to invest in a steamboat but lost three-quarters of his investment (Thurston 1996, 67–9).

36 For a critical discussion of that claim, see Antwi (2011, 181–2).

37 In her discussion of Haliburton's sketch "The White Nigger" in *The Clockmaker*, Jade Ferguson refers to a similar incident in Mark Twain's 1897 short story "Tom Sawyer's Conspiracy" (2013, 256–7).

38 In a subplot, a young woman named Marcella considers suicide when her impoverished mixed-race mother and her brother, to support themselves, try to bully her into marrying a wealthy white planter. In this subplot Moodie equates a certain type of marriage with slavery, a theme evoked in the late eighteenth century by Mary Wollstonecraft (H. Thomas 2000, 86–9). Interestingly, Moodie also thematizes black-on-black slavery, presenting this mother, despite her poverty, as still owning an old slave whom she exploits ruthlessly. Moreover, Moodie portrays the exploitation of children in terms of slavery; the mother, for example, resists Marcella's adoption, saying that "she could not afford to purchase an additional slave to supply the child's place, and perform the never-ending tasks required of her" (Moodie 1854b, 194). On the theme of the tragic mulatto more generally, see Sollors (1997, 220–45).

39 Midgley, for example, writes of the Strickland-Prince collaboration: "Despite the campaigning intention of her autobiography, white middleclass women activists thus treated Prince not as a fellow-activist but rather as a victim of slavery, as a possibly unreliable individual whose account needed authentication, and as a working-class servant. Given this, it is hardly surprising that

they did not think to recruit her as a member of one of their ladies' anti-slavery associations" (1992, 89).

40 Andrew Lesk writes that Moodie "was a product of a time when anti-Semitism ran rampant" but rightly objects to this passage being glossed over in the Gray biography of the Strickland sisters (Lesk 2001, 212; Gray 1999, 173).

41 In *Race, Slavery, and Liberalism in Nineteenth-Century American Literature*, Arthur Riss delineates the rise of race theory and points out that "by the time *Uncle Tom's Cabin* was published [in 1852], racial difference was considered a permanent and self-evident fact" also among reformers (2006, 66); he thus questions "the assumption that essentialist conceptions of the Negro were always in the service of a pro-slavery position" (62).

42 Thurston notes the existence of an 1854 poem explicitly about slavery in the United States, entitled "Freedom for the Slave," in the Patrick Hamilton Ewing Collection at the National Library of Canada (1996, 191n36).

43 The main character Rachel becomes the eponymous Flora Lindsay in the later text, while the slave Cesar is renamed Hector.

44 The charivari, originally a French custom of making noise with pots and pans at weddings, in this Canadian version became a means of enforcing social norms, with participants seeking to extract money in exchange for peace from couples whose marriage was deemed socially offensive. In *The Journals of Susanna Moodie*, Atwood dedicates her poem "Charivari" to this chapter (Atwood 1970, 37).

45 For an extended discussion of "The Charivari" that focuses on race, see Antwi (2011, 198–259).

46 In "The Charivari," Moodie writes that "of all follies, that of taking out servants from the old country is one of the greatest … They no sooner set foot upon the Canadian shores than they become possessed with this ultra-republican spirit. All respect for their employers, all subordination, is at an end; the very air of Canada severs the tie of mutual obligation which bound you together. They fancy themselves not only equal to you in rank, but that ignorance and vulgarity give them superior claims to notice. They demand in terms the highest wages, and grumble at doing half the work, in return, which they cheerfully performed at home. They demand to eat at your table, and to sit in your company; and if you refuse to listen to their dishonest and extravagant claims, they tell you that 'they are free; that no contract signed in the old country is binding in "Meriky"; that you may look out for another person to fill their place as soon as you like; and that you may get the money expended in their passage and outfit in the best manner you can'" (Moodie 2007, 133). Another version of this passage can be found in "Trifles," where Moodie articulates perhaps even more clearly the dissolution of hierarchy but uses language that equates this process with emancipation from slavery: "When we look upon this as the reaction rising out of their former miserable and slavish state, we cannot so much blame them; but are obliged to own that it is the natural result of a sudden emancipation from their former bondage … The master before

whom they lately bowed in reverence, and whose slightest word was a law, now degenerates into the *man*; and their mistress, the *dear lady*, whom they strove by every attention to please, is the *woman* – while persons in their own rank are addressed as ma'am and sir" (Moodie 1991, 191–2).

47 See Thomas's discussion of the connections between the former slave-trade captain John Newton's *Authentic Narrative* (1764), Robert Southey's "The Sailor Who Had Served in the Slave Trade" (1790), and Coleridge's "The Rime of the Ancient Mariner" (1798), which she also relates to the Zong massacre (2000, 93–4). Her comment on Wordsworth's sonnet "To Toussaint L'Ouverture" is equally pertinent; for her, it "provides an important example of the appropriation and concealment of abolitionist discourse contained within Romantic poetry, via its gradual withdrawal from its original focus, the great slave rebel, and its subsequent prioritization of the symbolic emblem of Romanticism – the power of 'man's unconquerable mind,' the imagination" (110); see also her section "Wordsworth and the Slaves" (109–14).

48 There are some further references to abolitionism and representations of blackness in Moodie's later writing. In an 1858 letter, she describes Pringle addressing her in a séance in the previous year: "'You will not live to see the abolition of slavery in the United States. It will end in blood and great political changes must take place … God will prepare the mind of the slave, for the great moral change that awaits his condition.'" Her only comment is: "Since obtaining this communication I have watched with great interest the Kansas question" (Moodie 1985, 181). In 1871, she published the racist story "Washing the Black-A-Moor White: A Page from Life" in the *Canadian Literary Magazine* (Moodie 1991, 253–6).

49 Finseth argues that "the text is largely free of the sort of stylistic embellishing that can generate uncertainty about who is really telling the story. Nonetheless, in several places one senses that the hand of someone other than Roper himself has taken the pen. These are passages in which richly efflorescent commentary breaks through the earthy, matter-of-fact tone of the story" (2003, 27).

50 The report recommends emigration as the only viable option in the face of oppression in the United States, but it also "represents one of the few instances when black abolitionists publicly endorsed the concept of revolution as an alternative to slavery and racial oppression" (Ripley 1986, 270).

51 One example is an added opening paragraph in which the speaker, employing repeatedly Latinate expressions and now thoughtfully looking back upon his life, employs biblical typology and evokes the figure of Moses. The different editions are available at http://www.docsouth.unc.edu.

52 Four more teachers arrived in 1844 and the school had seventy students in 1845 (D.G. Hill 1981, 72–3).

53 On King and the Elgin settlement, see Winks 1997, 208–8; D.G. Hill 1981, 76–89.

54 Among others, Hill mentions also James T. Rapier, the American congressman, and William Parker, a Raleigh Township counsellor (D.G. Hill 1981, 86).

55 In a manuscript from about 1906 entitled "Niagara Movement & Booker T. Washington," Abbott indeed sides with "the Niagara Movement of W.E.B. Du Bois in opposition to Booker T. Washington's manual training school" (Winks 1997, 330; Abbott Papers, Notebook V).

56 "The law also ordered state and federal authorities to cooperate in capturing fugitives, and it imposed a $1,000 fine or six-month jail sentence on anyone that aided a runaway. Most important, the law made the slave certification hearing an administrative, and not a judicial, procedure. Blacks could not testify on their own behalves and had no right to counsel or to a habeas corpus hearing; free blacks regarded the law as a severe threat to their freedom" (Ripley 1986, 116–17).

57 Later revised as *Harriet, the Moses of her People* (1886).

58 Ripley et al. note that free blacks "held nine national conventions between 1830 and 1848. The various convention agendas shared the goal of ending slavery, elevating the status of all blacks, and providing a national focus for black reform. During the 1830s, influenced by William Lloyd Garrison and other white reformers, delegates pursued a wide range of reforms while diluting their uniquely black perspective … During the 1840s, black national conventions became more militant and independent, emphasizing black priorities. Beginning with the North American Convention (1851) in Toronto, the movement focused on black nationalism and emigration" (Ripley 1986, 140n2).

59 This group included Martin Delany, who would nonetheless move to Canada a few years later (see below). Frederick Douglass did not attend the convention because of "his anti-emigrationist stance, at least at this point in his career" (Frost 2007, 291).

60 I am referring here to F.O. Matthiessen's foundational *The American Renaissance* (1941), the basis of much revisionism in subsequent US literary criticism and discussed below in the context of Mary Ann Shadd's work. William Andrews refers to the critical attitudes that writers of the American Renaissance such as Melville and Hawthorne evinced towards their own culture and nation to contextualize the radicalization of black autobiographers after the 1850 Fugitive Slave Act. He rightly states that during "a parallel renaissance in Afro-American letters of the 1850s, figures like [Frederick] Douglass sought answers to the problem of America by undertaking similar critiques of mainstream thinking, written from the perspective of marginal observers … To signify and interpret the shadowy borders of other-consciousness became increasingly the central concern of black autobiography in the crisis leading up to the Civil War" (1986, 169).

61 In her article "The Contestation over National Identity: Nineteenth-Century Black Americans in Canada," Jane Rhodes, the biographer of Mary Ann Shadd, explores the "formation of a continental diaspora" (2000, 175) and suggests that Mary Ann's father, Abraham Shadd, for instance, "seems to have successfully produced a transnational identity through which he could continue to be an 'American' at the same time that he established strong roots in

Canada" (182). As her title suggests, however, she views her subject mostly from a US perspective. Nancy Kang's discussion of border-crossing slave narratives warns repeatedly against appropriating these texts exclusively on behalf of either US ("American") or Canadian letters (2005). Heike Paul more recently discusses many of these texts in the "disciplinary context of contemporary transnational American studies" (2011, 166) and suggests that the "Canada-US border in the nineteenth century produced transnational and diasporic black subjects" who nonetheless considered the border a "life-saving barrier" (167–9).

62 The so-called Confederation Poets – Charles G.D. Roberts, Bliss Carman, Archibald Lampman, and Duncan Campbell Scott – were all born in the 1860s shortly before Canadian Confederation in 1867 but began publishing only in the 1880s. The term "Confederation Poets" was conferred upon this group by critic Malcolm Ross in a 1960 anthology of work by these writers.

63 Shadd's relevance has been stressed by other researchers in Canada. The contributors to the volume *"We're Rooted Here and They Can't Pull Us Up": Essays in African Canadian Women's History* thus state: "A Black Feminist Historiography would begin with the writings of newspaper editor and publisher Mary Ann Shadd" (Bristow et al. 1994a, 4). Rinaldo Walcott, who uses the passage containing this statement as a chapter epigraph, suggests that Shadd can help us "to think about Blackness in Canada" and "inform our contemporary discussions and dialogues" (2000b, 33).

64 The family home was a station on the Underground Railroad (Bearden and Butler 1977, 12–13). Shadd received a Quaker education in Wilmington, Delaware (Ripley 1991, 4:34n4), where she "would have received instruction in religion and philosophy, literature, writing, basic mathematics, Latin and French, and the mechanical arts. Mary Ann was also exposed to the values of the Society of Friends, who believed in the brotherhood of man and in education as the means for moral and social uplift" (Rhodes 1998, 17). Her father, Abraham D. Shadd, was an early member of the American Anti-Slavery Society, a subscription agent for Garrison's *Liberator*, and an important participant in the black convention movement (Ripley 1991b, 4:33–4n4; Bearden and Butler 1977, 15; Rhodes 1998, 4–18). From 1835 on, he was involved in the American Moral Reform Society, guided by the wealthy black Philadelphia leaders James Forten, William Whipper, and Robert Purvis. The values articulated by this group are recognizable in many of Shadd's later positions; they include the "avoidance of color distinction in their social and political activities" as well as an "insistence on identifying with a universal concept of mankind rather than any racial identity, which was criticized by many black activists. The American Moral Reform Society also vocally supported the ability of women to have an equal role in reform and abolition organizations" (Rhodes 1998, 18).

65 In Shadd's letter, which appeared in the *North Star* on 23 March, her opening words agree with remarks by Henry Highland Garnet on the situation of blacks in New York in an earlier letter to the *North Star* (12 January 1849).

Garnet, a respected black reformer, was also known for his 1843 Buffalo "Address to the Slaves of the United States," which was "generally perceived as a call for slave violence" (Ripley 1991a, 3:336–7n9).

66 On Shadd as a "figure of the in-between," see Walcott (2000b, 32–5).

67 This aversion was underlined by her later claim to have left the American Methodist Episcopal Church (AME) "because it was intentionally segregated" (Rhodes 1998, 22). Her lack of religious affiliation, however, made her subsequent dealings with supporting institutions such as the American Missionary Association more difficult (letter from Shadd in 1851 to George Whipple, Ripley 1986, 2:185; see also Rhodes 1998, 38). Rhodes observes that "her arguments echoed the work of Lewis Woodson, a black minister from Pittsburgh, considered by many the ideological forebear of 19th-century black nationalism. In the 1830s Woodson wrote a series of articles for *The Colored American* in which he criticized disunity among blacks and complained about the influence of the clergy on African-American thought. Mary Ann Shadd shared his disdain" (Rhodes 1998, 22).

68 Anthony Appiah thus notes that Du Bois "was unable to escape the notion of race he explicitly rejected," and suggests that "his life's work was, in a sense, an attempt at just this impossible project" (1992, 46). For an analysis of this conjuncture, see Siemerling (2005, 147–54).

69 In the 1830s and 1840s, Lewis Woodson proposed agriculture and rural settlement as a means towards greater economic autonomy, especially for blacks unemployed in the cities (F.J. Miller 1975, 98–100). Despite Rhodes's claim to the contrary, Shadd would have been diametrically opposed to Woodson's insistence on black churches as necessary means to black betterment (F.J. Miller 1975, 97–8; Rhodes 1998, 22).

70 Shadd's attack on the church as disempowering also has many parallels in Marx, whose qualification of religion as "the opiate of the masses" appears in his earlier 1843/44 introduction to his *A Contribution to the Critique of Hegel's Philosophy of Right*.

71 The pamphlet was excerpted by a correspondent signing JBY in the *North Star*, 8 June 1849.

72 Cuffe actually transported thirty-eight settlers to Sierra Leone in 1815, but the project came to an end with his death two years later (Park 2001, 10).

73 On the heterogeneous composition of the society, see also Park 2001, 11–12.

74 Douglass wrote in the *North Star* of 8 June 1849: "It is idle – worse than idle, ever to think of our expatriation, or removal" (qtd in Rhodes 1998, 28).

75 Larwill tried to prevent William King from buying land for the Elgin Settlement in 1849 and ran successfully for the Legislative Assembly in the 1854 election. He was twice defeated, however, with the help of the black vote, first in 1853 and then in 1857 (Winks 1997, 212–14).

76 See G.E. Clarke (2005c, 11–14) for a survey of these omissions.

77 See Sundquist 1989.

78 After the 1839 successful slave revolt on board the *Amistad*, "Benito Cereno" deals with the widespread fear of slave revolts; see Sundquist's chapter "Melville, Delany, and New World Slavery" (1993, 135–221).

79 On the tensions in Whitman, see for instance Martin Klammer's *Whitman, Slavery, and the Emergence of Leaves of Grass* (1995).

80 See, for instance, Michaels and Pease (1989); Pease theorizes that Matthiessen's canon-forming inclusions and exclusions and the homogenizing effects of his choices were partially underwritten by "the political demands of WW II" (xi, 113–55).

81 Stowe's text seems to have increased traffic on the Underground Railroad, as a passage from a letter to the *Provincial Freeman* by William Stills, one of its most active agents, demonstrates. He states that "there is not the least room to doubt but that the underground Railroad will do this year, according to what has already been done since the year set in, just double the amount of business that was done last year. In this respect that mischievous book Uncle Tom's Cabin, may be charged with helping the underground largely; for but few of the intelligent 'articles' there are in the south, who have not read, or heard it read, and consequently have at once 'fired up' to strike for Canada" (William Still, "For the Provincial Freeman," *Provincial Freeman*, 6 May 1854).

82 Ironically, in her *Key to Uncle Tom's Cabin*, Stowe identifies not only Lewis Clarke – who, as we have seen, indeed emigrated to Canada – but also Frederick Douglass – the most visible opponent to emigration – as one of the real-life examples to illuminate the character of George Harris (Stowe 1853, 13–19). In addition to having George Harris and his family move to Liberia, Stowe at the end of *Uncle Tom's Cabin*, in the paragraphs immediately following George's long letter explaining his decision, tells us that Topsy will go as a missionary to Africa as well.

83 Stowe's novel appeared in the *National Era* from 5 June 1851 to 1 April 1852 (Levine 2003, 184).

84 Delany's comment suggests that there might have already been an exchange with Shadd at this point: "Mary Ann Shadd, a very intelligent young lady, peculiarly eccentric, published an excellent pamphlet, issued from the press in Wilmington, Delaware, in 1849, on the elevation of the colored people. The writer of this work, was favored with an examination of it before publication, which he then highly approved of, as an excellent introduction to a great subject, fraught with so much interest. Miss Shadd has traveled much, and now has charge of a school in Sandwich, Canada West" (Delany 2004, 145). Sterling claims the two met during Delany's 1849 visit to Wilmington for the *North Star* (1971, 161). When Shadd composed her *Plea*, she might well have been aware of Delany's *Condition*. Delany sent out copies to black papers in April and May 1852 (Sterling 1971, 148). It was reviewed by Oliver Johnson in the *Pennsylvania Freeman* on 29 April, with a subsequent response by Delany, and then by William Lloyd Garrison in the *Liberator* on 7 May, again with a response by Delany on 14 May (Sterling 1971, 148; Ullman 1971, 146–9). Given

the role and connectedness of the Shadd clan in abolitionist contexts, it is likely that Shadd at least knew of Delany's text by May 1852.

85 This chapter is absent in Robert S. Levine's Delany reader (Levine 2003); I cite another edition (Delany 2004). Delany's fear is well-founded. He appropriately references William Lyon Mackenzie, who after the defeat of the Upper Canada Rebellion – against which both Moodie's husband and Josiah Henson fought (according to a later version of his narrative) – flees to the United States and later seeks to invade Upper Canada with the help of volunteers from the United States. In the late 1850s Mackenzie openly calls for United States annexation of Canada. There is also an "Annexation Manifesto" by Montreal business people in 1849. Overall, however, Ullman points out that there is little realistic chance for a United States annexation of Canada at that point, partially because the "South knew that any annexed Canadian province would be another 'free' state and another threat, like the Pacific Northwest, to their political domination the country" (1971, 129).

86 I follow the original 1852 edition, available at http://www.canadiana.org/view/47542/0007; a widely available print edition with Canadianized spelling has been edited and prefaced by Richard Almonte (M.A. Shadd 1998).

87 See Almonte in M.A. Shadd (1998, 105n5) and Gerson (2009, 87–8).

88 Later in *A Plea for Emigration*, Shadd reviews political rights in Canada: "There is no legal discrimination whatever affecting colored emigrants in Canada, nor from any cause whatever are their privileges sought to be abridged" (1852, 26). Her next sentence, however, evokes *ex negativo* another reality while marking the decisive difference with the United States: "On taking proper measures, the most ample redress can be obtained" (26).

89 The Separate School Act of 1850 made separate black schools possible but also encouraged whites to ask for them. Rhodes notes that at that time "most black children attended schools in the planned settlements like Elgin and Dawn or those supported by the A.M.A., or they obtained no education at all. Canada's black leaders, as well as the A.M.A., generally condemned separate schooling in principle, but in reality that was the only educational opportunity available for the swelling black population" (1998, 37). See also Winks (1997, 365–9).

90 Shadd points out in particular that not only whites, but also free blacks were prohibited from settling on the society's lands, although they often arrived in Canada destitute as a consequence of the Fugitive Slave Act. Shadd actually accuses the society of entrenching the slaveholders' ideology that sought to sow contempt for free blacks among slaves, charges it with dividing the black community, and identifies it as a tough competitor for poor free blacks in search of cheap land (1852, 24).

91 Writing about the black Canadian population, Shadd notes that they "have a paper conducted by the Rev. Henry Bibb, and other able men, white and colored, are laboring among them" (1852, 31).

92 On the relation between the Bibbs and Shadd after the publication of her pamphlet, see Rhodes (1998, 47–69) and Bearden and Butler (1977, passim).

On Mary and Henry Bibb and the *Voice of the Fugitive*, see also Cooper (1994, 2000).

93 Apart from the Fugitive Slave Act and the Compromise, another reason for Delany's abandoning hope for black "elevation" in the United States might have been his experience of not being allowed to complete his medical studies at Harvard when the medical faculty cowed to some of its racist students. Delany was one of the first three blacks to be admitted to Harvard's medical school (Sterling 1971, 122–35; Ullman 1971, 115–21).

94 He remarks in a footnote: "The native language of these countries, as well as the greater part of South America, is *Spanish*, which is the easiest of all foreign languages to learn … And we earnestly entreat all colored persons who can, to study, and have their children taught Spanish. No foreign language will be of such *import* to colored people, in a very short time, as the Spanish. Mexico, Central and South America, importune us to speak their language; and if nothing else, the silent indications of Cuba, urge us to learn the Spanish tongue" (Delany 2004, 193). Delany began his own study of Spanish at age twenty-one in Pittsburgh in 1833, but he failed to convince his reading club to follow his example (Sterling 1971, 44–5).

95 Delany, "Call for a National Emigration Convention of Colored Men," *Provincial Freeman*, 25 March 1845 (in Levine 2003, 240–2).

96 Shadd's objections proved justified. Delany's speech at the 1854 Cleveland convention was invoked, for instance, by a United States House Committee when Lincoln favoured emigration of free US blacks in 1862.Yet Lincoln's plan for a black settlement in Chiriquí (in today's Panama) "fizzled largely because Central Americans objected to the use of their territory as dumping ground for people the United States considered undesirable" (Sterling 1971, 228–9). Similarly, Delany's plans for a black settlement in Africa's Niger Valley failed because of a renounced land treaty in 1861 (Sterling 1971, 222–3; Ullman 1971, 233).

97 Shadd concludes the editorial: "What will you do, or what your women say, for they must go along, when surrounded by big spiders, lizzards, snakes, centipedes, scorpions, and all manner of creeping and biting things? Do you want to be sun-struck? Do you court yellow fever and laziness, haughty employers, and contemptible black prejudice? If you do, go in peace."

98 Rhodes's comments reflect Shadd's complex, to some extent contradictory, positioning that I identified earlier: "Shadd's nationalism blended these two impulses: blacks could not hope to possess and control Canada, but could claim their rightful place within a nation-state that promised them equality and citizenship. At the same time, she believed that the political, social, and cultural unification of black people was essential for their survival. Shadd shared Martin Delany's advocacy of an autonomous black political force that could fight white supremacy from beyond the borders of the United States. But she was fundamentally at odds with Delany's romance with Africa as the 'Fatherland,' and his assertions of black hegemony" (Rhodes 1998, 87).

99 Heather Murray suggests that "the *Provincial Freeman* was rushed into print" (2002, 69) shortly after the *Voice of the Fugitive*, under the headline "A Deed of Blood," reported, on 8 March 1853, on a murder outside the place where a meeting of Shadd supporters was held (Murray 2002, 66–9).

100 Shirley Yee points out that during "the 1850s black men in at least two states continued to thwart black women's attempts to obtain an equal voice with men in the conventions on both the state and national level. In 1855 … delegates at the National Convention of Colored Men [in Philadelphia] excluded women from membership when they voted 23 to 3 against admitting Mary Ann Shadd as a member, although they allowed her to deliver an address. Frederick Douglass had been one of the three men who favored admitting Shadd" (1992, 146).

101 Yee remarks: "While some black women struggled to meet middle-class standards of respectable womanhood in their daily lives and in their activism, others, such as [Sojourner] Truth, Harriet Tubman, and Mary Ann Shadd Cary, essentially did what they pleased, abandoning any kind of sexual stereotypes and ignoring prevailing expectations of ladylike behavior" (1992, 156).

102 Ward was accused after his implication in the Syracuse "Jerry" case in October 1851 (see the next section below).

103 Both Douglass and Delany attacked Ward in the *North Star* of 27 June 1850. Delany regretted "to learn that in you the cause of our downtrodden people has recently experienced a sad and mortifying damper" (in Levine 2003, 175); Ward's seeming acquiescence in segregated seating arrangements during an anti-slavery meeting in Philadelphia was here essentially the pretext for a charged exchange between Douglass and Delany (see Levine 2003, 175–9).

104 Newman, a former slave from Richmond, Virginia, briefly led the British-American Institute at Dawn from 1845 to 1846 and resumed work there in 1850–52. He later joined the *Provincial Freeman* (Ripley 1986, 302–3). From 22 August 1855 onward, Newman appeared as editor and Mary Ann's brother Isaac D. Shadd as publishing agent on the masthead.

105 Later in her life, Shadd pursued women's rights and suffragist activities in the United States (Ripley 1986, 192; Streitmatter 1994, 31–2; Rhodes 1998, 168–70, 191–7).

106 See, for instance, the following articles: "Woman's Rights" (6 May 1854, 12 August 1854); "Miscellaneous" on "Employment of *Women* in France" (2 September 1854); "Power of Women in Turkey" (7 April 1855); "Female Education" (7 June 1856); "Praiseworthy Example" (19 April 1856); "Speech of Lucy Stone Blackwell" (19 April 1856); "Miss Watkins …" (11 July 1857); "Women in America" (15 August 1857).

107 After travelling with Shadd in the United States to raise funds for the *Freeman*, H. Ford Douglas, later a co-editor of the *Freeman*, critiques United States blacks for their "ignorance and deplorable indifference" and complains about their willingness to buy from white racists while not supporting black enterprises. For Douglas, "that government has stamped its peculiarities upon

their individual character producing an anomaly impossible to describe. They ... present a combination of incongruities resulting from the local influences which surround them; for there is nothing more apparent among the colored people in the States, than want of an individuality, without which, it is morally impossible for them ever to rise politically and socially, in the scale of being" ("The Colored People and Slavery," *Provincial Freeman*, 17 May 1856).

108 See Jason Silverman's study of fugitive slaves in Canada, *Unwelcome Guests; Canada West's Response to American Fugitive Slaves, 1800–1865*. Silverman writes: "That Canadians gave refuge to thousands of fugitive blacks is undeniable; but that they did so because of philanthropic and humanitarian reasons is not. As the number of blacks entering Canada multiplied, so did Negrophobia on the part of white Canadians. This sentiment manifested itself in educational, social, and religious discrimination and segregation that permeated all levels of black life. In the end, the ostensible Canadian Canaan strangely resembled the antebellum North or the Jim Crow South" (1985, viii).

109 Other examples are the texts written or compiled by Benjamin Drew (1856), William Wells Brown (1861), and Samuel Gridley Howe (1864), and William Still's later *The Underground Railroad* (1872) (see below).

110 Leaving later in 1853 on a fundraising tour, Ward stayed in England for over two years; he did not return to Canada, settling instead in Jamaica (Ripley 1986, 292–3n7).

111 On Haliburton and racism, see Clarke (1997b).

112 The Boston reverend Nehemiah Adams originally opposed slavery, but after a trip to the South he portrays it as benign in his *South-Side View of Slavery*.

113 The text is also available at http://docsouth.unc.edu/neh/drew/drew.html.

114 The narrative of his Toronto interviewee William Howard corroborates that of William Grose cited above. Howard states, "I expected to work for a living, go where I would. I could not be stopped from working. Canada is the best place that ever I saw: I can make more money here than anywhere else I know of. The colored people, taken as a whole, are as industrious as any people you will find. They have a good deal of ambition to go forward, and take a good stand in the community. I know several who own houses and lands. They are a very temperate people" (112).

115 The narrative of Alfred T. Jones, who kept an "apothecary shop on Rideout street," offers a glimpse of the obstacles well-to-do blacks might have faced. Jones states that there "are colored people employed in this city in almost all the mechanic arts; also in grocery and provision stores, etc. Many are succeeding well, are buying houses, speculating in lands, and some are living on the interest of their money" (152). However, he was compelled "to go to England shortly on a suit at law involving my title to a large property on Dundas street, valued at $45,000. The case has been through chancery in the provincial court, and I have now appealed to the House of Lords. I am winding up my business preparatory to leaving" (152–3).

116 This section contains the only known narrative of slavery experienced in Canada by Sophia Pooley (192–5), who was brought to Canada as a slave and sold to Mohawk chief Joseph Brant and then to the English immigrant Samuel Hatt. Pooley was freed in 1813.

117 On the Elgin settlement at North Buxton, see D.G. Hill (1981, 76–89); Winks (1997, 209–18); Pease and Pease (1963).

118 On the development and failure of Dawn, see D.G. Hill (1981, 71–4); Winks (1997, 179–81, 195–204); Pease and Pease (1963).

119 Howe's report is deeply concerned with the health of the settlers in Canada and with the medical opinion that blacks were incompatible with cold climates. The report also seeks to allay fears of amalgamation, reporting that from Canadian evidence, "there need be no anxiety upon the score of amalgamation of races in the United States" (1864, 33; see also Edelstein, 2004, xvii–xviii). The black narratives include discussions of the weather, white prejudice, the experience at Buxton, and a longer account of a black tobacco manufacturer in Hamilton.

120 The free son of a slave father and a free black woman, Troy moved to Canada West in 1851. He lived first in Amherstburg and then in Windsor, where he is mentioned in Brown's description of black Canadian settlements as "an educated and enterprising man … building a fine church, for his congregation, which is of the Baptist order" (W.W. Brown 1986, 477–8). Troy eventually returned to his native Virginia.

121 From 1852 on, Still was the chairman of the Philadelphia General Vigilance Committee, which had "aided almost eight hundred fugitive slaves by the beginning of the Civil War" (Ripley 1986, 205).

122 Around 1790, the Brazilian slave population is estimated at 1.5 million and was thus larger than that of the French and British Caribbean together (Bergad 2007, 63). In total, it is estimated to have comprised between 3.5 and 6 million slaves (Krueger 2002, 170).

123 Robert Krueger identifies roughly 700 pages of text by over 140 Brazilian slaves or former slaves. While the largest part comes from the Portuguese Inquisition or trial transcripts (Krueger 2002, 172), the corpus also contains an 1982 interview with one of the last surviving former slaves, Mariano Pereira dos Santos, and twenty-six letters and 350 pages of dictation by Brazil's first black female writer, the prolific Santa Rosa Egipcíaca. She escaped forced prostitution to become a "pious church woman" and successful preacher before being interrogated by the inquisition (Krueger 2002, 175–7; Mott 1983).

124 Baquaqua wrote to Gerrit Smith on 25 May 1854 from Chatham, asking that return mail be sent there. He wrote again to Smith on 4 July 1854, this time from Detroit where he says he had gone to arrange for the publication of his narrative, which he had paid an English man (Samuel Moore) to write for him (Law and Lovejoy 2003, 247–50).

125 Three years of residence were normally required at that time to obtain Canadian citizenship. Baquaqua reports in his narrative "being so well pleased

with the reception I there met with, I at once determined to become the subject of her Majesty, for which purpose I attended at the proper office, gave the oath of allegiance, and procured my papers of naturalization without any difficulty" (Law and Lovejoy 2003, 191).

126 As Baquaqua's letters illustrate, he was literate, though expressed himself at times in ungrammatical English (see Law and Lovejoy 2003, 233–50).

127 Baquaqua closes his narrative by expressing his wish to eventually return to Africa and be "useful in the regeneration of my own loved country" (192). He moved to Britain in 1855, looking for ways to fulfill this wish, but there is no further trace of him after 1857 (Law and Lovejoy 2003, 1–2, 75).

128 As Ullman points out, the "organization of the National Board of Commissioners was revised so that all officers on the Central Board could reside within a 60 mile radius of its new headquarters in Chatham, Canada West. This allowed continuation of Delany as president, with four of its eight other members from Chatham, two from Detroit, and one from London, Canada West" (1971, 182–3).

129 Miller, however, sees it as a more definite positional change by Shadd, leading from her "initial hostility of any form of black separatism" to a "nationalist-emigrationist position" (1975, 157). This reading is not supported by Shadd's July 1856 editorial, which endorses the Cleveland convention as facilitating a "broad platform of free discussion and inquiry, without bickering, animosity or jealousy" and states that "Emigrationists hold that political elevation … can be obtained by removal to foreign and more liberal governments" ("The Emigration Convention," *Provincial Freeman*, 5 July 1856; repr. in Ripley 1986, 339–42).

130 These decisions are contained in the "Abstract of the Minutes of the Cleveland National Convention," *Provincial Freeman*, 25 November 1856 (see also Ullman 1971, 182; F.J. Miller 1975, 166). Mary E. Bibb, at this point widowed, was also named to the Board of Publication; the *Repository* would never appear, however.

131 Delany helped in Archie McKellar's eventually successful campaign against Edwin Larwill, a racist who failed to prevent the establishment of King's Elgin settlement, debating with him publicly in Chatham in 1849.

132 In what is known as the Pottawatomie Massacre, Brown responded to pro-slavery violence against the town Lawrence, Kansas by leading a raid that killed five active supporters of slavery. Violent incidents were frequent at the time as a result of the 1854 Kansas-Nebraska Act, which left the decision of whether these newly created territories would allow slavery in the hands of the settlers.

133 Under the pseudonym Frank A. Rollin, *Life and Public Services of Martin R. Delany* was published in Boston in 1868.

134 Delany states that Brown would not offer details about his planned fortifications; Osborne Anderson, who will participate in the eventual attack on Harpers Ferry (discussed below), also makes it clear that even the participants in the raid remained in the dark until the last moment about the specific nature of their undertaking.

135 Winks paraphrases Delany's claim and notes that Brown's host in Chatham, the poet James Madison Bell, was also left unaware of such plans, though he suggests that others might have known more (Winks 1997, 267–7). Both Ullman and Sterling accept Delany's claim (Ullman 1971, 200; Sterling 1971, 167–8); Levine, by contrast, suggests that Delany's account came "at a time when he would have been loath to reveal his past insurrectionist activities" and claims that the "evidence suggests that Brown had called the Chatham convention with the intention of gaining the support of black leaders for a plan to organize and lead a rebellion of the slaves of the United States" (1997, 287n10).

136 The "Journal of the Provisional Constitutional Convention, held on Saturday May 8, 1858" and the "Provisional Constitution" appear as Appendix 2 and 3 respectively in the *United States Senate Select Committee Report on the Harper's Ferry Invasion*, also known as the Mason Report (United States of America 1860, 45–7, 48–50). The report is available at http://www.wvculture.org/history/jbexhibit/masonreport.html.

137 In fact, only one person also present at the Chatham meetings, Osborne Anderson, would participate in the eventual raid (see the discussion of Anderson below).

138 Thomas M. Kinnard, for example, declined, and J.W. Loguen's nomination was "withdrawn, Mr. Loguen not being present, and it being announced that he would not serve, if elected" ("Journal," in United States of America 1860, 47).

139 Levine suggests that Blake "may be regarded as a surrogate for Delany himself (1997, 191); Carla L. Peterson sees him as a "fictional projection of the author, recast as a picaresque hero who contemplates the possibilities of black revolution" (1995, 169–70; qtd in Levine 1997, 291n30). A number of episodes in the text also have equivalences in Delany's own travels.

140 Twenty-six chapters of the novel appeared in the *Anglo-African Magazine* from January to July 1859 (F.J. Miller 1970, xi); of the 80 announced chapters, 74 were subsequently published in the *Weekly Anglo-African* from November 1861 to May 1862, breaking off, for unknown reasons, just as the hero is implicated in an armed revolt in Cuba (Sundquist 1993, 184).

141 Levine argues that the "numerous 'authenticating' footnotes on Africa in the novel's second part … suggest that Delany had reconceived aspects of the novel during 1861 to bring it more into accord with his hopes to 'regenerate' Africa" (1997, 179) and that the "references later in part 1 to the condition of blacks in Canada … would suggest that Delany did his main work on *Blake* sometime between 1856 and 1859" (1997, 177).

142 Perhaps the most important of these is Levine's extended analysis in his 1997 study *Martin Delany, Frederick Douglass, and the Politics of Representative Identity*; see also Ernest (1995), Clymer (2003), Nwankwo (2005), Chiles (2008), Doolen (2009), and Cole (2011).

143 Sundquist calls the text prophetic in many ways: "Appearing almost without notice on the eve of the Civil War and strangely apocalyptic in its narrative

inconclusion, *Blake* is the most appropriate final account of New World slavery – and of the antebellum world of slaves and masters alike – at the moment of its revolutionary cataclysm" (1993, 221).

144 For instance, Delany draws on his views of Cuba, expressed earlier in a series of essays on the threat of US annexation of Cuba in the *North Star* in 1849 (F.J. Miller 1970, xxii); furthermore, a number of the poems in *Blake* (250, 259–60, 286, 308) are taken – without attribution – from James M. Whitfield, "whose writings had appeared in the *North Star*" (Sundquist 1993, 203n).

145 Ernest, for example, shows the difference between "Stowe's idealized cabins" and Delany's much more realistic "huts," and points to scenes of direct revision, such as the Jim Crow performance of little Harry for Shelby and Haley in Stowe's novel that contrasts with a similar yet finally fatal scene in *Blake* (Ernest 1995, 110-11; Delany 1970, 67–8).

146 Douglass's story is based on an actual slave revolt in 1841 on the *Creole*, while Melville's story draws on the *Amistad* revolt in 1839 (see Sundquist 1993, 115–24, 177–8).

147 With reference to Stepto's discussion of the relationship between Stowe and Douglass in "Sharing the Thunder" (Stepto 1986), Levine notes that he "argues that Stowe took Turner as a subject of her second novel in response to Douglass's 'The Heroic Slave,' his revisionary celebration, in response to Stowe's Uncle Tom, of black revolutionary violence. Thus *Dred* must be viewed, in part, as the result of Stowe's creative exchanges with Douglass (and, by extension, with Delany) on the question of black leadership in a slave culture" (1997, 155).

148 Miller demonstrates that *Blake* shows a familiarity with the slave narratives by Henry Bibb and others (1970, xxi–xxii).

149 Sterling seems to make a direct connection between Delany's hero's plans and those of John Brown (although the grassroots multiplication of insurrection envisioned in *Blake* seems quite different from Brown's top-down, military-style operation): "Martin, who was still waiting to hear from John Brown, was careful not to reveal the details of Henry's plan for a slave rebellion" (Sterling 1971, 180).

150 Sundquist points out that "American slavers flying under a Spanish or Portuguese flag could not be searched by American cruisers; and ships under American flag could not be searched by British cruisers," with the consequence that "flags became transparent conveniences in a political charade" (Sundquist 1993, 200); as a result, in Du Bois's words, "the American slave trade finally came to be carried on principally by United States capital, in United States ships, officered by United States citizens, and under the United States flag" (Du Bois 1986b, 163; qtd in Sundquist 1993, 200–1).

151 While Stowe's kind senator cannot bear the human consequences of his own law-making and engages in an act of Underground Railroad "conducting" that is entirely illegal under the law he has just voted for, in another striking contrast between the two novels, Delany's northern judge will soon turn even

more actively to the slave trade, illustrating Delany's conviction that economic logic takes precedence over moral concerns and suasion.

152 The protagonist is originally called Henry Holland (Delany 1970, 26, 27, 81) and emerges as Blake in part 2 of the novel, in a scene that reveals him also as Henrico Blacus (193). As Gilroy points out, Blake "assumes various names in the different locations he visits, but his English appellation is surely significant in that it offers an echo of an earlier, explicitly Atlanticist radicalism" (1993, 27).

153 Sundquist observes that "the historical characters and events to which Delany alludes lay several spheres of action upon one another … the Dred Scott decision of 1857, the Fugitive Slave Law of 1850, and Cuban political events of the 1840s all seem to be telescoped into the much shorter timeframe of the novel" (1993, 184). The connection to Placido, to whom are ascribed a number of poems taken from elsewhere, has been analysed in more detail by Sundquist (1993, 199–210), Levine (1997, 203–5), and especially Nwankwo (2005, 54–80).

154 See Levine for a reading of the ending that speculates about a continuation of non-violence in the missing last chapters (1997, 215–16).

155 Josiah Henson describes his arrival in Canada in the first edition of his narrative with these words: "When I got on the Canada side, on the morning of the 28th of October, 1830, my first impulse was to throw myself on the ground, and giving way to the riotous exultation of my feelings, to execute sundry antics which excited the astonishment of those who were looking on. A gentleman of the neighborhood, Colonel Warren, who happened to be present, thought I was in a fit, and as he inquired what was the matter with the poor fellow, I jumped up and told him *I was free*. 'O,' said he, with a hearty laugh, 'is that it? I never knew freedom make a man roll in the sand before.' It is not much to be wondered at, that my certainty of being free was not quite a sober one at the first moment; and I hugged and kissed my wife and children all round, with a vivacity which made them laugh as well as myself" (1849, 58–9).

156 See Delany's earlier reference in *Condition*, discussed above, to the leader of the 1837 Upper Canada Rebellion, William Lyon Mackenzie (2004, 190). On black militia service from 1793 onward, including participation in the war of 1812 and the 1837 uprising, see Winks (1997, 150–3).

157 See Jason Silverman's study, *Unwelcome Guests: American Fugitive Slaves in Canada, 1830–1860*.

158 In the concluding chapter of part 1, Henry renames himself Gilbert Hopewell "to prevent all traces of himself out of Canada, wither he was known to have gone" (Delany 1970, 157). Canada serves here as a place of identity transformation and regeneration of hope – as suggested by the new name. In chapter 40, Canada appears again briefly as a safe house and base for further travel, again with the help of "Rev. W. Mon—" who has already appeared in chapter 33; he has been identified by Miller as Delany's old friend William C. Monroe (Delany 1970, 318n21).

159 Here Delany asserts that these plans were originally conceived in his twenties (Delany 2004, 38); in the later *Official Report* – in what Levine calls "a blatant

effort at historical revisionism" (1997, 183) – Delany claims that African emigration, explicitly excluded in the "Call" for the 1854 Cleveland convention (Delany 2004, 230), was the subject of "Secret Sessions" during the meeting (Delany 2004, 237–8). According to Ullman, Delany already had plans for Africa in 1854: "Right after the Cleveland convention, too, Delany began to question the once glorious game of hemispheric black unity as a plan for both refuge and the abolition of American slavery. He returned more and more, as president of the National Board of Commissioners, to his earliest concept of Africa as the sole hope for a black Israel" (1971, 175).

160 The report was published in 1861 but according to Levine perhaps drafted while Delany sailed from Africa to England in 1860 (Levine 2003, 336). According to Ullman, Delany prepared the *Official Report* for the printer after his return on 29 December 1861 to Chatham (1971, 247). On the African expedition and the London visit, see F.J. Miller (1975, 170–231) and (Levine 1997, 183–9).

161 Though not directly implicated in the attack, Frederick Douglass was among those who fled – at least temporarily – to Canada to elude the furious backlash (Winks 1997, 268).

162 It is not clear whether even then the participants were aware of the details of John Brown's plans. As Frederick Douglass renders Anderson's account in *Life and Times of Frederick Douglass*, "Anderson further told me that Captain Brown was careful to keep his plans from his men, and that there was much opposition among them when they found what were the precise movements determined upon; but they were an oath-bound company and like good soldiers were agreed to follow their captain wherever he might lead" (Douglass 1881b, 326); Libby points out that in the sentence preceding this passage Douglass confuses Jeremiah and Osborne Anderson but means the latter (1979, 149).

163 See also Bearden and Butler (1977, 195–7, 201–2, 206) and D.G. Hill (1981, 21, 23, 214).

164 Villard claims that Anderson's account contains "many erroneous statements" (1910, 685): "Osborn [*sic*] P. Anderson … the colored raider from Canada, subsequently wrote a misleading and exaggerated account of their escape from the armory, in which he states that they remained at their posts until the final capture of Tuesday. This is, however, incredible" (1910, 445–6). Libby suggests that Villard equates the moment of Anderson's leaving with the moment of Brown's actual capture, while Anderson may have thought Brown was captured on Monday when, just prior to his decision to escape, he witnessed "the charge upon the engine house with the ladder, which resulted in the opening of the doors to the marines" (O.P. Anderson 1861, 45; Libby 1979, 153–4).

165 Libby points out that Anderson's text uses omissions and asterisks to protect others, such as in his description of the Chambersburg meeting between Brown and Douglass (1979, 73).

166 See Bearden and Butler (1977, 203), Rhodes (1998, 131), and Libby (1979, 183–4). Hallie Q. Brown writes in *Homespun Heroines and Other Women of Dis-*

tinction that Shadd "compiled the notes of Osborn [*sic*] P. Anderson" (1926, 95).

167 William Wells Brown later suggested that Mary Ann Shadd would have joined had she been allowed to (Rhodes 1998, 131), but Brown did not admit women even at the Chatham convention. The one exception was "General" Harriet Tubman, who was involved in planning the raid but was ill, failing to arrive in time to intervene (Libby 1979, 147–8).

168 Chapter 2, for example, contains the minutes of the Chatham convention, which were public at this point anyway.

169 Anderson writes in chapter 3: "During the sojourn at Chatham, the commissions to the men were discussed, &c. It has been a matter of inquiry, even among friends, why colored men were not commissioned by John Brown to act as captains, lieutenants, &c. I reply, with the knowledge that men in the movement now living will confirm it, that John Brown did offer the captaincy, and other military positions, to colored men equally with others, but a want of acquaintance with military tactics was the invariable excuse" (1861, 14–15).

170 Anderson cites a Harpers Ferry citizen who estimated "at least seventy killed, besides wounded"; Anderson continues: "Hazlett had said there must be fifty, taking into account the defense of the three strong positions. I do not know positively, but would not put the figure below thirty killed, seeing many fall as I did, and knowing the 'dead aim' principle upon which we defended ourselves. One of the Southern published accounts, it will be remembered, said twenty citizens were killed, another said fifteen. At last it got narrowed down to five, which was simply absurd, after so long an engagement" (O.P. Anderson 1861, 48).

171 Slavery in the United States was abolished only with the Thirteenth Amendment in 1865. Lincoln's 1862 announcement and the 1863 Emancipation Proclamation were not general. They were a result of military necessity rather than principle, and guided by available possibilities of saving the Union. In August 1862 Lincoln still declared that "If I could save the Union without freeing any slave, I would do it; and if I could do it by freeing all the slaves, I would do it; and if I could do it by freeing some and leaving others alone, I would do that also" (qtd Ullman 1971, 268–7). In September 1862 Lincoln announced emancipation in Confederate states that would refuse to return to the Union by the beginning of 1863; but although none of them returned, the proclaimed emancipation in those states required victory of the Union; it also did not concern the "border states," which held slaves but were not part of the Confederacy (Missouri, Kentucky, Maryland, or Delaware).

172 See also Levine (1997, 224–37) on Douglass and Delany in this period and later.

173 Her narrative is rendered – that is, not in her own words – in the *Montreal Gazette* of 31 January 1861; it is reprinted in Mackey (2004, 162–6).

174 Reprinted as *The Life of Wm. H.H. Johnson: From 1839–1900, and The New Race* (1904).

175 Selections from Johnson, Stark, Gibbs, and others can be found in W. Compton (2001).

176 On Abbott, see Winks (1997, 328–32), D.G. Hill (1981, 206–8), Newby (1998), Murray (2002, 65, 152–4), and O. Thomas (1998).

177 She refers to the *Census of Canada*, 1931, for these figures.

178 The manuscript census of 1861 shows that there were 17,053 blacks in Canada West, as opposed to the "11,000 quoted in the published report" (Wayne 1995, 467). Howe's estimates for 1863 are between 15,000 and 20,000 (468).

179 Even Winks, whom we have seen question white British American perceptions that equated *all* blacks in Canada with fugitives, assumed that "three-quarters" of his estimated 40,000 blacks in Canada West "had been or were fugitive slaves or their children" (1997, 240); for another author who refers to the numbers arrived at by Winks and Wayne, see A. Shadd (1994, 64n14).

180 While the *Brown vs Topeka Board of Education* Supreme Court decision of 1954 abolished school segregation, other segregationist legislation required the 1964 Civil Rights Act and the 1965 Voting Rights Act to be overruled.

181 Mathieu reports near-lynchings in Canada (16), and the Ku Klux Klan entered Canada in the 1920s (Winks 1997, 320–5). The image of Canada as promised land, however, would remain powerful for many blacks in the United States.

182 It is no coincidence that in this period W.E.B. Du Bois wrote many of the pieces that would form *The Souls of Black Folk* (1903), a book that vehemently protests Booker T. Washington's politics of compromise and deplores the "disfranchisement of the Negro," the "legal creation of a distinct status of civil inferiority for the Negro" (i.e., *Plessy vs Ferguson*), and "the steady withdrawal of aid from institutions for the higher training for the Negro" (Du Bois 1986a, 399).

183 See chapter 5 (below), Mathieu (2010, 22–60), Winks (1997, 300–13), and Vernon (2008, 48–57).

184 See the discussion of Caribbean domestic and farm workers in chapter 4.

185 For instance, George Elliott Clarke comments on the role of the black church in Nova Scotia (1991, 1:11–29; 2002, 113–15), highlighting the genre of the "African-Canadian church history" (2012, 46–57; here, 46); the documentary *Seeking Salvation: A History of the Black Church in Canada* was scripted by Lawrence Hill (2004), also the author of *Women of Vision: The Story of the Canadian Negro Women's Association, 1951–1976* (1996); Union United Church and the Universal Negro Improvement Association (UNIA) in Montreal are examined in detail by Bertley (1976, 1983); and Marano (2010) provides a wider discussion of the Universal Negro Improvement Association in Canada and its social functions.

CHAPTER 4

1 "Africadian" is a neologism coined by Clarke to designate black Nova Scotian writing and culture.

2 *Moins l'infini: Roman haïtien* (1973), *Mémoire en colin-maillard* (1976), *Haïti, Haïti* (1985), and later *La contrainte de l'inachevé* (2006).

3 See *Métropolis Opéra* (1987), *Tribu* (1990), *Savanes* (1993), *Vétiver* (1999), and *Caïques* (2007); des Rosiers also published the essay *Théories caraïbes* (1996).

4 See the more detailed discussion below of Agnant, Étienne, Ollivier, and Laferrière.

5 In his introduction to the excerpt, Elliott introduces the title of the play as *Who All Was There* (1985, 56). It remains unpublished, like his *How Now Black Man* (produced at the Montreal Centaur Theatre and adopted as the inaugural play of the Black Theatre Workshop) and his other plays. Elliott is the author of the *Bibliography of Literary Writings by Blacks in Canada* (1986) and was commissioned by Multiculturalism Canada to establish a bibliography of black Canadian literature, which appeared in 1988. He had previously published the novel *Coming for to Carry* (1982).

6 Hill has produced significant documentary work on black Canadian history. *Trials and Triumphs: The Story of African-Canadians* (1993), addressed primarily to young readers, illustrates the most important developments of black Canadian history and culture. I have already mentioned *Women of Vision: The Story of the Canadian Negro Women's Association, 1951–1976* (1996), which retraces the association's activities and political interventions, and Hill's script for the documentary *Seeking Salvation: A History of the Black Church in Canada*, which premiered in 2004.

7 Mahatma barely avoids being named "Euripides Homer," proposed by his father, who sees him obviously destined for "some great thing," yet objected to by his mother, whose veto extends to both Greek and "Negro pride names" but fails to include other great race leaders (L. Hill 1992, 49–50).

8 His name evokes Langston Hughes and the author of *Cane* (1923), Jean Toomer, two Harlem Renaissance authors who also reflected on mixed race.

9 *The Book of Negroes* appeared in the United States, New Zealand, and Australia as *Someone Knows My Name*, following the decision by the United States publisher to avoid the original title because of an anticipated reader discomfort with the word "Negro." Indeed the Dutch translation, *Het negerboek*, provoked the threat of a book burning by a group objecting to the title's terminology, leading to a burning of a copy of the title page on 22 June 2011 in Amsterdam. Hill has discussed the title in an article in the *Guardian* on 20 May 2008. He responded to the book burning threat in the *Toronto Star* on 20 June 2011, in an article in the *New Yorker* on 22 June 2011 (all available online), and his subsequent volume *Dear Sir, I Intend to Burn Your Book: An Anatomy of a Book Burning* (2013).

10 With reference to George Handley, Maureen Moynagh highlights the importance of family history to the post-slavery narrative in general and works like Hill's *Any Known Blood* in particular (2010, 136; Handley 2000, 3). See Flagel (2005) for an excellent discussion of *Any Known Blood* with respect to genre, the family saga, and the family memoir, as well as to the relationship of the embedded neo-slave narrative in chapter 22 to the rest of the novel.

11 The first epigraph comes from the Swedish economist Gunnar Myrdal's *An American Dilemma: The Negro Problem and Modern Democracy* (1944): "Everybody having a known trace of Negro blood in his veins – no matter how far back it was acquired – is classified as a Negro. No amount of white ancestry, except one hundred percent, will permit entrance to the white race." The second epigraph sounds Langston's name and filiation by citing Langston Hughes' poem, "Cross": "My old man died in a fine big house / My ma died in a shack / I wonder where I'm gonna die, / Being neither white nor black?"

12 The following pages rely on an earlier article on *Any Known Blood* (Siemerling 2010) that elaborates further on processes of identification (Fuss 1995), passing (Sollors 1997), racial and other identity "scripts" (Appiah 1996), and Hill's own *Black Berry, Sweet Juice: Growing Up Black and White in Canada* (2001).

13 These include the loss not only of employment but also of his marriage. His family research allows the family to come together, and when he crosses back into Canada at the end of the novel, he is accompanied by a relative, a friend, and a lover. Cuder-Domínguez calls *Any Known Blood* "a bildungsroman, centered on the voyage of self-discovery of a young man who must come to terms with his racial and cultural roots" (2003, 57); although the protagonist is thirty-eight in this case, the characterization seems apt.

14 One might also consider here a concept by Diana Fuss, who speaks of "disidentification." With reference to what Judith Butler calls disavowed identities, she writes: "What at first may appear to be refused identification, Butler proposes, might in some cases more accurately be termed a disavowed one – an identification that has already been made and denied in the unconscious. A disidentification, in other words, may actually represent 'an identification that one fears to make only because one has already made it'" (Fuss 1995, 7; quoting Butler 1993, 112).

15 Passing may evoke that "feeling of elation and exultation" that Werner Sollors ascribes to "an experience of living as a spy who crosses a significant boundary and sees the world anew from a changed vantage point, heightened by the double consciousness of his subterfuge. Thus persons who pass may enjoy their roles as tricksters who play, as does [James Weldon Johnson's] 'ex-colored man,' a 'capital joke' on society" (1997, 253; see also 268).

16 On the same day his father discovers his passing, he gets himself fired as a speech writer by inserting comments that are applauded by black journalists but do not render the views of the minister, who reads them unwittingly.

17 His wish to be clearly recognized as black, however, proves a challenge at times. He has to contend with comments like "You're pushing white, son. Pushing awful hard (123)" or "Ain't there enough white churches where you all come from?" (125).

18 Alexis also refers to one of the most cited exchanges on the question of race and nation when he remarks parenthetically: "Of course, the question whether 'black experience tout court' exists at all is the question. The disagreements between Léopold Senghor and Richard Wright at the first conference on Negritude are a challenge to the idea that a shared race is enough to overcome

differences of language, culture and history" (Alexis 1995). See also Fanon's "On National Culture" (1963, 206–48, especially 215–16).

19 "Historiographic metafiction" – a phrase coined by Linda Hutcheon – refers to works "that are not quite historical novels in the traditional sense, for they are also very metafictional in their attention to the processes of writing, reading, and interpreting. They are both self-consciously fictional but also overtly concerned with the facts (and consequences) of the reading and writing of history as well as fiction. In other words, the aesthetic and the social, the present and the past, are not separable discourses in these novels" (Hutcheon 1988a, 13–14). Elsewhere Hutcheon qualifies as "historiographic metafiction" "novels which are both intensely self-reflexive and yet paradoxically also lay claim to historical events and personages" (Hutcheon 1988b, 5). See also Wyile (2002, 140–1).

20 While Hill omits the middle name in the acknowledgments, Aberdeen is also a character in the novel. He provides the protagonist with historical information about earlier Langston Canes, including the Oakville trial of Langston Cane I for bigamy. Hill makes it clear, however, that "this novel is a novel. Family stories have been altered or exaggerated, and almost all of this book is invented" (1997, 507). Hill also invokes the historical Oakville ship captain and UGRR conductor Robert Wilson, but he insists that in the novel "specific events, dialogue, and diary entries involving Wilson are invented" (1997, 512).

21 The date of the speech is moved to 15 June 1879 when it is summarized in a diary entry by Langston Cane II's adoptive father, Nathan Shoemaker (L. Hill 1997, 419).

22 By contrast, Langston Cane IV tries to hide the past of his sister, an earlier prostitute, from his son.

23 A similar episode about the insights to be gained from the master's interdiction of learning how to read appears in *Life and Times of Frederick Douglass* (it had already appeared in *Narrative of the Life of Frederick Douglass, an American Slave, Written by Himself* in 1845): "This was a new and special revelation, dispelling a painful mystery against which my youthful understanding had struggled, and struggled in vain, to wit, the white man's power to perpetuate the enslavement of the black man. 'Very well,' thought I. 'Knowledge unfits a child to be a slave.' I instinctively assented to the proposition, and from that moment I understood the direct pathway from slavery to freedom. It was just what I needed, and it came to me at a time and from a source whence I least expected it … Wise as Mr. Auld was, he underrated my comprehension, and had little idea of the use to which I was capable of putting the impressive lesson he was giving to his wife … That which he most loved I most hated; and the very determination which he expressed to keep me in ignorance only rendered me the more resolute to seek intelligence. In learning to read, therefore, I am not sure that I do not owe quite as much to the opposition of my master as to the kindly assistance of my amiable mistress. I acknowledge the benefit rendered me by the one, and by the other, believing that but for my mistress I might have grown up in ignorance" (Douglass 1881b, 71).

24 "I would fain pray; but doubts arising, partly from my neglect of the means of grace, and partly from the sham religion which everywhere prevailed, cast in my mind a doubt upon all religion, and led me to the conviction that prayers were unavailing and delusive" (Douglass 1881, 131).

25 Axe in hand and ready to "strike the fatal blow," Henson pulls back in the name of Christianity and because "I was about to lose the fruit of all my efforts at self-improvement, the character I had acquired, and the peace of mind that had never deserted me" (Henson 2003, 53–4).

26 Hill signals another possible source when he reveals that Cane's fellow fugitive Paul Williams is related to Aberdeen Williams, whose great-grandfather's first name, as mentioned above, is the same as Hill's historian-informant Alvin B. Aberdeen Duncan's middle name.

27 Moynagh suggests that "Cane refuses the Loyalist work ethic directed at black settlers, which emphasizes homesteading, sobriety, and churchgoing as a means to self-reliance and independence" because he is critical "of what he reads as black submission to white expectations" (2010, 142).

28 The scene is rendered from the point of view of both Wilson and later Cane I (381–3, 470–3).

29 For Langston Cane I, the decision to leave comes earlier than in the case of Anderson and does so as a consequence of a clear rejection of one of Brown's decisions (L. Hill 1997a, 489).

30 Douglass writes: "I told him [Brown], and these were my words, that all his arguments, and all his descriptions of the place, convinced me that he was going into a perfect steel-trap, and that once in he would never get out alive; that he would be surrounded at once and escape would be impossible" (1881, 324).

31 For these and other differences between Cane I and Anderson, see also Flagel (2005, 261–4).

32 Ordered by his father to guard an abandoned schoolhouse outside Harpers Ferry in order to arm insurgent slaves – although he knows they will not come – he finally acts against one of his father's instructions: to keep silent about Douglass's refusal to mobilize support for the raid (Banks 1998, 741–2). When his companions decide to disclose this information to the other raiders, Owen neither stops nor joins them. He obeys what he is convinced is the will of his father, who "does not want me to save him" (744).

33 Hill concludes his review: "*Cloudsplitter* … illustrates that people of great accomplishments are not necessarily great people. Banks deftly dramatizes John Brown's commitment to unshackling African-Americans, and at the same time laments that, in the process, [Brown] destroyed the lives of those around him."

34 Flagel points out a number of further similarities between Cane I and Cane V; as she observes, "only Langston Canes I and V control their autobiographical narratives of self-discovery in the first person voice" and "[c]hronologically and stylistically they are bookends of their family"; finally, they are "the two who chew over their past mistakes and shape their own stories" (2005, 256).

35 This pattern begins with Langston Cane II, who withholds his father's narrative from his family and replaces it with a more palatable version: "I have kept the matter from my own family and have simply said that my father was rumored to have died a hero's death at Harpers Ferry" (427).

36 Langston's Aunt Millicent (Mill) Cane returns to Canada to rejoin her childhood friend Aberdeen and her own brother, re-crossing a line she had drawn with respect to Langston Cane IV's mixed race marriage. Aberdeen had left Oakville after his interest in a white woman triggered a Ku Klux Klan incident (based on an actual event in Oakville in 1930); Mill is left heartbroken and "convinced that she had lost her best friend because he had been seeing a white woman, and nobody could change her mind" (L. Hill 1997a, 326). Her nephew's family history project thus meets an initially cold reception on her part. Yet Rinaldo Walcott points out that Mill's role is central because from a certain point onward she provides support and much of the family documentation; it is thus "through her that Cane V is able to complete his investigation" (2003, 69–70). In *Black Berry*, Hill devotes a chapter to the "emotionally charged issue of black men loving white women" (115–49).

37 Hill's title is part of an intertextual web that also includes John Howard's *Black Like Me* (1961), Rinaldo Walcott's *Black Like Who?* (1997/2003), and Hill's review of Walcott, "Black Like Us, Eh?" Hill again addresses here the relationship between African Canadian and African American experience, and he identifies as one of Walcott's main arguments that "part of what makes African-Canadian society unique is the way it plays off black cultures in other countries." Hill comments on the title: "It seems ironic but fitting that Rinaldo Walcott's collection of essays about black culture in Canada features cover art and a title taken from the American experience. *Black Like Who?*, which emphasizes the distinctiveness of the black Canadian experience and urges black artists in this country to celebrate their identities more profoundly, draws its title from the American classic *Black Like Me*. Written by the late John Howard Griffin and published in 1961, *Black Like Me* was a best-selling autobiographical account of a white American who underwent a series of medical treatments to change his skin colour temporarily in order to write a first-person account about American racism. Borrowing from Griffin's book to create the title *Black Like Who?* seems to be Walcott's playful way of saying that room remains for new definitions of the black experience in Canada." Walcott discusses other responses to his book, in particular that of George Elliott Clarke, in his introduction to the second edition (2003, 11–23).

38 Historically, this attempt proved successful in 1807, though the abolition of slavery itself had to wait until 1834.

39 Most of the existent slave narratives begin with slavery in the New World, with the exception of texts like those by Baquaqua (see above) or Equiano. Hill mentions the importance of Equiano in interviews (in Sagawa 2008, 315; in Siemerling 2013, 17; see also note 42 below); he also acknowledges to have repeatedly read the family saga *Roots* (in Siemerling 2013, 20).

40 Bamanankan is spoken today mostly in Mali; Fulfulde is the language spoken by Fula and other groups in West Africa.

41 Hill attributes some of his knowledge about coffles to texts like Mango Park's *Travels in the Interior Districts of Africa: Performed in the Years 1795, 1796, and 1797* (1816): "He is watching slave coffles go by, observing what people look like, and it is this kind of text that literally allows me to see how the captives are being managed physically as they are being shepherded, and driven, and forced to the coast and into slavery" (Siemerling 2013, 18).

42 Duff provides a brief discussion of Euquiano's narrative as an intertext in Hill's novel (2011, 250–1), while Yorke stylistically compares Equiano's slave narrative with Hill's text (2010).

43 It is ironic that the title words of *The Book of Negroes* itself will not be allowed to stand by several publishers, as mentioned above.

44 John Clarkson, the brother of the more famous abolitionist Thomas Clarkson, organized and led the exodus of black Nova Scotians to Sierra Leone in 1792 and plays a substantial role in the corresponding sections of the novel.

45 See Medovarski on Lindo's "economics lesson" to Aminata (2013, 9), on her relation to the practices and theories of economic exchange at the time (15–21), and on Hill's portrayal of "alternate economies" (20) in the novel. Hill's interest in economics goes back to his university education. He studied economics (in Siemerling 2013, 6), graduating "from Laval with a B.A. honours in Economics in 1980," and as a reporter covered "national economic issues for the *Globe and Mail* and the *Winnipeg Free Press*" (personal interview, 3 December 2007).

46 The role of Solomon Lindo in the novel speaks to Hill's interest in creating complex figures. While he seeks to convince Aminata that because of his Jewishness "you and I are both outsiders" (188), and while he procures numerous advantages for Aminata and saves her later from re-enslavement in New York, Aminata wonders why he does not set her free (202, 209). See Hill's comments in Siemerling (2013, 22–3) and Casteel (2014).

47 Aminata will later meet Queen Charlotte, King George III's wife, in London (463–4); she has been previously informed that "they call her the Black Queen" because she "got some African in her" (194).

48 The original entry runs: "David, 10, likely boy, residence of claimant, Germany. (M. Gen. Kospoth) The boy goes with the General who got him at Philadelphia; the boy can give no account with whom he formerly lived." The American version by Hodges transcribes the claimant's name as "Kosporth" instead, as Ruth Whitehead's comparative analysis shows (Whitehead n.d.). I would like to thank the author for giving me access to this invaluable document.

49 David was perhaps one of the "black Hessians" recruited by Hessian soldiers who fought on the British side. His age seems to fit the description by George Jones: "Since most of the black Hessians were drummers, they tended to be very young, mostly in their teens or early twenties … Slavery was, of course, a major factor in black recruitment. Though seldom stated in the Hessian

records, many of the blacks, certainly most of those recruited in the Southern colonies, had been slaves" (Jones 1982, 293). In addition to drummers, "a good number were Knechte (servants or laborers)" (295). While the "records of the troops from Hesse-Cassel show that one-hundred and thirty-one clearly identifiable Blacks enlisted" (Hoffman 1981, 82), it seems many others were more informally associated with the troops. Hoffman quotes one of the German captains describing the situation in the army of Cornwallis and the Hessian Jäger Corps: "Each officer had four to six horses, three to four Negroes, and sometimes one or two Negresses as cook or mistress" (Hoffman 1981, 82). Jones concludes that "some thirty-one black Hessians are said to have accompanied their units to Europe and been baptized with German names" (Jones 1982, 302). Besides Hesse-Cassel (Hessen Kassel), the city of Brunswick (Braunschweig) also received black soldiers from the War of Independence (Hoffman 1981, 82).

50 This event in the novel is based on English Canada's first race riots in 1784; Hill sets it in 1787, as he points out in his note on history at the end of the novel.

51 In the novel, one of these is a labourer named Ben Johnson (2007a, 239). Hill, in a rather sobering fashion, thus brings to life a painting by W. Booth, "A Black Woodcutter at Shelburne, Nova Scotia 1788," partially reproduced at the beginning and in full later in the illustrated edition of *The Book of Negroes* (2009, viii, 348), where Hill comments on the connection between the painting and the writing of the scene in which Ben Johnson is killed (2009, ix, 349).

52 His fate has much in common with that of David George, who also loses the use of his legs (in his case due to frostbite) and repeatedly suffers severe oppression and prosecution at the hand of white opponents.

53 Thomas Peters was a self-emancipated former slave from North Carolina who served with the Black Pioneer Brigade before settling in Nova Scotia and then in Saint John, New Brunswick. In 1791, he travelled to England to represent the grievances of black settlers. His mission found the support of Granville Sharp. John Clarkson, at the beginning of his journal for the years 1791–92, *Clarkson's Mission to America*, attributes his decision to support the Nova Scotia Black Loyalists to a petition by Thomas Peters that is copied in his diary (Clarkson 1971, 31–2); Hill has Aminata write the conclusion of Peters's second petition, which explains that free Nova Scotian blacks "cannot conceive that it is really the Intention of the British Government to favour Injustiçe, or tolerate Slavery in Nova Scotia" (L. Hill 2007a, 353; see also Walker 1999).

54 Wetherell and Roetger enumerate a number of other factors, but they acknowledge the departure of a substantial black labour force as one of the reasons for Shelburne's decline (1989, 81).

55 *L'esclavage au Canada français: Histoire et conditions de l'esclavage* was published in 1960, followed by his 1990 *Dictionnaire des esclaves et de leurs propriétaires au Canada français.* In 2004, the follow-up edition, *Deux siècles d'esclavage au Québec; suivi du: Dictionnaire des esclaves et de leurs propriétaires au Canada français sur* CD-ROM appeared. As mentioned earlier, Mackey

offers a detailed discussion and some revision of Trudel's numbers (2010, 95–107). Paul Femiuh Brown, who has studied the subject for decades, mentions a certain resistance to this kind of historical work of recovery in Quebec in the twentieth century (phone conversation, 11 August 2011).

56 At the Centre d'histoire de Montréal, the exhibit "Qui a mis le feu à Montréal. 1734. Le procès d'Angélique" ran from October 2006 to December 2008, while an exhibit of the Musée du Château Ramezay, "La Justice en Nouvelle-France: Crimes et châtiments," October 2006 to March 2007, also dealt with the subject. On 6 November 2007, Radio-Canada offered a radio documentary on Angélique in its series "De Remarquables Oubliés" (http://www.radio-canada.ca/radio/profondeur/RemarquablesOublies/angelique.htm). The Web project *Les grands mystères de l'histoire canadienne/Great Unresolved Mysteries in Canadian History* provides a rich resource for historical documentation on Angélique in "La torture et la verité: Angélique et l'incendie de Montréal/Torture and Truth: Angélique and the Burning of Montreal" (http://www.canadianmysteries.ca/sites/angelique/accueil/indexen.html).

57 This statement is rendered by Gale in Act II, Scene xi: "But I cannot, in all honesty, suspect the negress because there were no fires in my chimneys that day" (61).

58 Gale was also a successful actress with a strong presence in theatre, film, and TV. Her other well-known work as a playwright is *Je me souviens*, published in 2001. It is a vigorous reaction by a former black anglophone Quebecker (she had moved to Vancouver at that point) to Jacques Parizeau's infamous post-referendum remarks about "ethnics." Gale, who died in 2009, also wrote "The Darwinist" and "The Voice" (see Nestruck 2009).

59 The play appeared in almost final form in *Canadian Theatre Review* 100 (1998) and as a volume was published by Playwrights Canada Press (2000). It was reprinted in Djanet Sears's anthology *Testifyin'* (2003).

60 It was also produced in Detroit and New York in 1999.

61 Her age is indicated as twenty-nine, which somewhat contradicts her own statement in the play that she was born "around 1710" (11), which would make her around 24 at the time of the Montreal fire.

62 As a leitmotif, the sound of drums is also related to Angélique's memories of Madeira and the practice there of festive celebrations of the past: "Everyone would gather round. And to the beating of a drum, they would tell the stories of our ancestors" (32). Drumming is evoked again during the rapprochement between Angélique and Claude (45), another (failed) alliance.

63 Her statement on 14 April 1734 is rendered by the court clerk and translated on *Canadian Mysteries* as follows: "The Said Negress entered the home of the said francheville And Came out as quickly and returned to She who is deposing And told Her, 'You just don't want to laugh; there is Madame francheville who is Laughing Well with Madame duvivier, Who will not long Be in Her Home and will not Sleep there,' And Went back; that she saw Her three or four times in the Street Looking Towards the Roof of the House of the said deceased

Sieur de francheville; that she had the Daughter of Sieur De Couagne of Isle Royal and the daughter of Sieur desrivieres Enter into the Said House; And that one quarter hour later, a fire alert was shouted out" (Juridiction royale de Montréal, "Deposition of Marie dit Manon, April 14, 1734").

64 In the scene, Angélique asks, "Claude, you didn't start that fire?" (65).

65 During that first interrogation, Angélique attested that she had contradicted her owner's accusation with the following words: "Madame, quoique Je soit Mechante, Je ne Suis pas assez Malheureuse pour faire une action Comme Cella" ("Madame, although I may be Miserable, I Am not Wretched enough to do an act Like That") (Juridiction royale de Montréal).

66 *Beatrice Chancy* was published in 1998 as a libretto in four acts in *Canadian Theatre Review* and as a verse drama by Polestar Book Publishers in 1999. Clarke details the relationship between the two works in his "Embracing *Beatrice Chancy*, or In Defence of Poetry" (2000a); for a stage production history up to the premiere of the opera in June 1998, see G.E. Clarke 1999, 155–7.

67 Nova Scotian slavery predates the influx of 1783; see, for example, Hamilton (1994, 14–19); Winks (1997, 27–8); Donovan (1995).

68 Applying Clarke's comment on Derek Walcott's "ways of blackening English" via incorporation of the Western canon to Clarke's own work, Diana Brydon comments that "as a metaphor describing Clarke's art, 'cannibalizing the Canon,' captures the aggression, the fraught politics, the edgy humour and the exuberant excess of his achievement, turning one of the more potent justifying metaphors for imperial racism back on itself and enabling appropriation, digestion, transformation and elimination to replace direct protest against the injustices of the world" (2004, 192).

69 Lydia Jackson is remembered in George Elliott Clarke's poem "Hammonds Plains African Baptist Church" in *Saltwater Spirituals and Deeper Blues*: "i think of Lydia Jackson, / slave madonna, pregnant with child, / whose Nova Scotian owner, distinguished Dr. Bulma / kicked her hard in the stomach, / struck her viciously with fire tongs, / and then went out / upon the ocean / in his dory / to commune with God" (1983, 24).

70 She thus utters the following creed after the second killing: "White men, you took away my freedom / And gave me religion. / So be it: I became a devout killer" (G.E. Clarke 1999, 140). Anne Compton thus remarks in her interview with Clarke that "there's metaphysical grief in *Beatrice Chancy* in spite of its intense physicality. In … *Beatrice Chancy*, they're beyond faith" (1998, 151).

71 In "Racing Shelley," Clarke reads Shelley's verse tragedy of 1820 as a "gothic slave narrative" (2000c); he enumerates a host of other texts dealing with this figure in the acknowledgments for his play, and he cites numerous other literary Beatrices (1999, 152–3); in "Embracing Beatrice Chancy," he writes that he "fell into a metaphorical Italy, *via* Dante, Shelley, and Pound … and sought to create a triple Beatrice – the warrior-martyr of Shelley and the passive saint of Dante, but also the sexual odalisque of Pound" (2000a, 17).

72 See also Donna Heiland's essay "George Elliott Clarke's *Beatrice Chancy*: Sublimity, Pain, Possibility" on the connection between the Gothic and Clarke's play.

73 Famously, this distinction is also made by Sartre in *Being and Nothingness* (1956, 561; see Siemerling 1994, 70).

74 Referring to Gérard Genette's terminology, Larson thus distinguishes between paratext, peritext, and epitext: "The paratext operates as a 'vestibule' (Genette, *Seuils* 8), a permeable area that facilitates a reader's approach to a text. This liminal zone exists largely within the text itself, in what Genette dubs the peritext, namely the title, author name, publication information, chapter headings, dedications, epigraphs, preface, introduction, illustrations, afterword, or notes. The paratext also includes elements beyond the physical boundaries of a work that nonetheless influence a reader. This 'epitext' includes reviews, interviews with the author, letters, and editorial remarks. These peripheral elements, both peritextual and epitextual, assume a force that Genette likens to the performative impact of speech acts. They can impart information, relay authorial intention and interpretation, or signal a text's engagement within or against a particular genre" (2006, 104).

75 Clarke's opening epigraphs about women and resistance are examples of peritextual elements guiding the reader; they offer a clear indication of how the author views Beatrice's role in the play that follows: "'The abolition of slavery … is emphatically the duty and privilege of women' – BOURNE / 'La femme a le droit de monter sur l'échafaud; elle doit également avoir celui de monter à la tribune' – GOUGES (9)."

76 See Moynagh (2002, 109–10) on the mulatto/a in this context.

77 In Robert Plant Armstrong's description of the difference between synthesis in progress and syndetic accretion, "in so far as successive phases grow out of prior ones, the synthetic work is linear … The syndetic … growth is through repetition of the same inventory of similar units" (1981, 13; qtd in Pavlić 1996, 168).

78 In chapter 5, we will see a similar model evoked by Wayde Compton in his reference to Edward Brathwaite's Caribbean, anti-dialectical modelling of history that he terms "tidalectics."

79 A film that deals with such interrupted genealogies is the documentary *Loyalties*, where black Nova Scotian Carmelita Robinson discovers some of the missing pieces in the puzzle of her ancestry and other black Nova Scotians talk about the silences surrounding their past (Patten 1999).

80 "Burning cross ignites racial tension in Nova Scotia," *Globe and Mail*, 24 February 2010, available at http://www.theglobeandmail.com/news/national/burning-cross-ignites-racial-tension-in-nova-scotia/article1480350.

81 Some of the notable exceptions here are Canadian First Nations accounts and Japanese Canadian writing related to the incarceration of Japanese Canadians during the Second World War (G.E. Clarke 2002b, 53).

82 See Reems (2008, 13–14).

83 Graham Cromwell [or Graham Jarvis] was shot in 1985 in Weymouth Falls, NS, at point blank range by a white person who was later acquitted by an all-white jury on the grounds of self-defence. Clarke describes his own involvement in the campaign to repeal the judgment in "The Birmingham of Nova Scotia: The Weymouth Falls Justice Committee vs. The Attorney General of Nova Scotia" (G.E. Clarke 1992).

84 "*Whylah Falls* was for me a kind of falling into consciousness, not merely a racial consciousness, which was always there, but a poetic consciousness, and understanding finally that while there was a great world of Anglo-American poetry out there, there was this Black Nova Scotian, 'Africadian' poetry that was rooted in the voice and in these shared jokes, stories, proverbs. If I really wanted to be a stronger poet, I felt that's the material I had to work with" (in A. Compton 1998, 139–40). Clarke offers a similar comment about language for his subsequent novel *George & Rue*: "In drafting *George & Rue*, I tried, really, to incorporate Black Maritime (Africadian) and white rural speech. Its English could not be standard – or monarchical, but closer to the earth, I mean, to the world" (Kyser 2007, 865).

85 See also Clarke's interviews with Wyile (Wyile 2007, esp. 136–8), A. Compton (1998, 139), Fee and Gunew (2000); on the Shakespearean intertext, see Sanders (1999, 115) and Brydon (2004).

86 It seems that by 2000 Clarke had already finished a first draft of the novel as well, which he rewrote in 2002 (Kyser 2007, 870).

87 As David Steeves comments in a thesis on law and literature that looks in particular at contextual arguments in law, "Clarke's novel … is intended to place the Hamiltons' murderous act in both a cultural and historical context. Furthermore, Clarke's contextual approach references a model for adjudication that has recently received judicial consideration" (2009, 99).

88 "*Geo*: No, we needed money, / so you hit the So-and-So, / only much too hard. / Now what?" (35).

89 Clarke cites Hustak (1987) and N. Boyd (1988); see also Backhouse (1999) and, with direct reference to *George & Rue*, Steeves (2009).

90 "Crypt" opens with a photograph of a grave with a handsome headstone and a bust, though half of the face is missing. The photograph remains cryptic and without caption, but the split face of *memoria* seems to announce the split response to the brothers, adumbrated in the two sections of "Crypt," to consign their lives to oblivion or to "read and reread" (214) in a process of future re-inscription.

91 Cohen discusses out-migration from the African Caribbean as a case of a "deterritorialized diaspora," a term by which he designates groups that "can be thought of as having lost their conventional territorial reference points, to have become in effect mobile and multi-located cultures" (2008, 124). He makes the point that "Indo-Caribbeans did not go back to India, while African-Caribbeans did not return to Africa" (125).

92 Black Caribbean Canadian writing is part of a West Indian diasporic production that extends to many other parts of the world. As a result of indenture following slavery, that diasporic corpus comprises many writers of Indian descent, including, to name a few authors in Canada, Neil Bissoondath, Cyril Dabedeen, Shani Mootoo, and Harold Sonny Ladoo.

93 Glissant formulates elsewhere a *right* not to be recognized only in universalizing terms of sameness: "Le droit à l'opacité serait aujourd'hui le signe le plus évident de la non-barbarie" (1995, 54; "The right to opacity would be today the most evident sign of non-barbarism"). See also Walter Mignolo's work on Occidentalism and what he calls the "*geopolitics of epistemology*" (2005, 44) in the opening chapter of his *The Idea of Latin America* (2005, 1–50) or Alberto Moreiras's reflections on theorizing Latin America as a region in his *The Exhaustion of Difference* (2001).

94 "Le Divers … signifie la relation de l'esprit humain vers une relation transversale, sans transcendance universaliste" (Glissant 1997a, 327). Dash's translation narrows the phrase "relation transversale" to "cross-cultural" (which comes with its own, often symmetrical, connotations): "Diversity … means the human spirit's striving for cross-cultural relationship, without universalist transcendence" (Glissant 1989, 99).

95 This is my own, more literal rendering of the passage, which Dash translates as follows: "Caribbeanness … tears us free from the intolerable alternative of the need for nationalism and introduces us to the cross-cultural process that modifies but does not undermine the latter" (Glissant 1989, 139).

96 The titular chapter was originally published in Spanish in 1985, then translated in Gustavo Pérez Frimat's collection *Do the Americas Have a Common Literature?* (1990). The interconnection between these Spanish, French, and English conceptualizations of the Caribbean deserves more elucidation than I can provide in this context, as does the question of translation here (see, for example, Edwin Gentzler's chapter "Border Writing and the Caribbean" in his *Translation and Identity in the Americas*, 143–79).

97 Glissant's passage reads in the original: "la crispation du temps … une chronologie qui s'est embuée, quand elle n'a pas été oblitérée pour toutes sortes de raisons, en particulier coloniales. Le romancier américain … se trouve, se débat, dans un temps éperdu" (1997a, 435–6).

98 "Nous ne le voyons pas s'étirer dans notre passé … mais faire irruption en nous par blocs, charroyés dans des zones d'absence où nous devons difficilement, douloureusement, tout recomposer si nous voulons nous rejoindre et nous exprimer" (Glissant 1997a, 436–7).

99 "Ce temps éclaté, souffert, est lié à des espaces 'transportés' … L'espace du roman américain … me semble ouvert, éclaté, irrué" (1997a, 436–7).

100 A continuation of this work on creolization and creoleness in Caribbean language and culture can be found in the reflections by Jean Bernabé, Patrick Chamoiseau, and Raphaël Confiant in *Éloge de la Créolité* (bilingual ed. 1993; French orig. 1989).

101 As Mensah points out, Canada had earlier recruited black labour from the Caribbean when it was economically convenient or necessary – for instance, to work in Nova Scotia coal mines or as domestic workers in the early 1900s (2010, 70).

102 I have mentioned Lillian Allen briefly in chapter 1. Afua Cooper, a historian, writer, and dub poet, has produced four collections of poetry, from *Breaking Chains* (1983) and *The Red Caterpillar on College Street* (1989) to *Copper Woman and Other Poems* (2006); two narratives for children, about Henry Bibb and Phillis Wheatley (both 2009); and three albums (1989, 2002, 2009). Lorna Goodison, a painter and writer, has published numerous collections of multi-accented poetry, including *Tamarind Season* (1980), *Travelling Mercies* (2001), and her more recent collections *Supplying Salt and Light* and *Oracabessa* (both 2013), as well as three volumes of short stories, including *Fool-Fool Rose Is Leaving Labour-in-Vain Savannah* (2005) and *By Love Possessed* (2011). Speculative fiction writer and editor Nalo Hopkinson has authored short story collections and novels, beginning with *Brown Girl in a Ring* (1998) and including *Salt Roads* (2003) and *Sister Mine* (2013). The collections of poetry by Pamela Mordecai, who also writes for children and is a prodigious anthologist, range from *Journey Poem* (1989) to *Subversive Sonnets* (2012); she has also written a book of short fiction, *Pink Icing and Other Stories* (2006). Antigua-born Althea Prince is the author of two children's books (as Althea Trotman), the collection *Ladies of the Night and Other Stories* (1993), and the novel *Loving This Man* (2001); her non-fiction titles include *Being Black* (2001) and *The Politics of Black Women's Hair* (2009). Olive Senior, since arriving in Canada at the beginning of the 1990s, has published the collections of poetry *Gardening in the Tropics* (1994), *Over the Roofs of the World* (2005), and *Shell* (2007); the short story collection *Discerner of Hearts* (1995); and the *Encyclopedia of Jamaican Heritage* (2003). St Vincent native Nigel Thomas – briefly mentioned in chapter 5 – has authored poems, short stories, and the novels *Spirits in the Dark* (1987), *Behind the Face of Winter* (2001), and *Return to Arcadia* (2007).

103 His first novels – *No Man in the House* (1991), *Sleep On, Beloved* (1995), and *Slammin' Tar* (1998) – were joined by *Dry Bone Memories* (2001), his memoir *Island Wings* (1998), and his examinations of racism and race in *A Place Called Heaven* (1996), *Where Race Does Not Matter* (2005), and *Blackness and Modernity* (2007). Other works include *Distorted Mirror: Canada's Racist Face* (1991) and *Caribana, the Greatest Celebration* (1995). Foster has also worked as a reporter in Barbados and Canada.

104 The Temporary Foreign Worker Program (TFWP) – which among other relevant categories lists agricultural workers and live-in caregivers – brought 338,189 individuals to Canada in 2012 (Curry 2013). See also http://www.hrsdc.gc.ca/eng/jobs/foreign_workers/index.shtml.

105 The character Smokie makes the connection more explicit in explaining the presence of his sneakers on the Canadian farm where he and his colleagues

perform hard labour, most of them to support family in Barbados: "Not just shoes but shoes for runnin' … 'Cause everybody would done know that with these shoes gone, I'm burnin' up the road, smoking it down, slammin' tar. Runnin' like hell" (Foster 1998, 237). See also McCallum and Olbey (1999, 163) on the role of flight in Brand's *In Another Place, Not Here.*

106 Albert Jones, for example, follows all the rules in his application for landed immigrant status, hoping to be rewarded "by the Canadians for his dedication" (36). In the end, this hope will be disappointed (341).

107 We witness Johnny thinking "that it has been a long two months at home, if that is what you can still call this island where he was born" (7). Johnny is so out of place at "home" that he gets mugged by "people he doesn't know and couldn't even identify" but who have been "born and raised" on his street at home "since he joined the Program" (156). He carries a scar that reminds "him of what can happen when he doesn't know the lay of his so-called native land anymore" (156). As well, Johnny "pretends not to notice" when his wife and the cab driver taking him to the airport exchange "glances in the rearview mirror" (23).

108 According to a traditional Anancy story, he first receives his stories from the Akan skygod Nyame. In Foster's novel, the god appears in female form and Brer Anancy is in her crosshairs for having focused his earlier reporting too exclusively on Marcus Garvey, thereby entirely missing the importance of Du Bois (93–110, 259–61).

109 He has indeed been in a physical contest with the diaries from the beginning. As a spider in Johnny's travel luggage, he has "to scramble for my life as the books in the bag tumble in my direction" (26). Otherwise, he endorses the reporting of events: "If people … only knew the true Anancy story, then perhaps they could own and possess their own history. If only he, and all the others listening, could find a way to tune in to what we are reporting, what we have narrated all these centuries, everybody would be wiser and better off generally" (41). Most worrisome to him, it seems, is the appearance of a female story teller who opposes him by focusing on young Winston as the centre of the story. She is furthermore part of a move towards "nation language," which catches Brer Anancy by surprise (287–92) but marks Foster's novel itself, beginning with the title.

110 Overhearing the remark "This ain't no foolish Anancy story … You think I's a comedian or something?," he reacts: "Now the blood is truly rushing to my head … There is nothing funny about our work" (40).

111 The narrator invokes Garvey here with the following words: "This is the Prophet at his best on this miscegenation nonsense, saying so boldly, if even some now say so foolishly: *The White American Society, Anglo-Saxon Clubs, and Ku Klux Klan have my full sympathy in fighting for a pure white race, even as we are fighting for a pure Negro race*" (216–17).

112 See also Gairey's brief mention of his role in the domestic workers program's origin (1981, 35) and the discussions by Ruth L. Harris (1989, 71–131) and Linda Carty (1994, 217–20).

113 Henry notes in 1968 that 2,250 have arrived since 1955, "at a quota of 280 per year" (1968, 83).

114 It consisted of the acquaintances and their acquaintances of a West Indian nurse with training in sociology who worked for the author (1968, 84). In her later study, *The Caribbean Diaspora in Toronto: Learning to Live with Racism*, Henry discusses a middle-class bias in the sample for that study that was noticed and corrected (1994, 279).

115 In addition to being granted landed immigrant status upon arrival, after one year they were "free to pursue other careers or continue their education and training. They may also send for close members of their family and fiancés" (F. Henry 1968, 83).

116 Makeda Silvera arrived in Canada from Jamaica in 1967 and was one of the founders of Sister Vision Press. Her work includes short stories in *Remembering G and Other Stories* (1991) and *Her Head a Village* (1994), her anthologies *Piece of My Heart: A Lesbian of Colour Anthology* (1991) and *The Other Woman: Women of Colour in Contemporary Canadian Literature* (1993), and her novel *The Heart Does Not Bend* (2003). For a discussion of intergenerational relations between women and issues of queer sexuality in the novel, see Kim (2006).

117 Silvera objects to the standard requirement for distance and disinterestedness on the part of the interviewers, arguing that her own feminist approach, which reveals her point of view to interviewees, made the interviews in *Silenced* possible (ix–x). As we will see below, this issue appears in a different form in the narrator's reflections on translation in Agnant's *Le livre d'Emma*, while that author's first novel, *La dot de Sara*, is based on work that correlates with Silvera's call for further oral history work, such as on "Caribbean women and ageing in Canada" (x).

118 As Silvera points out, even landed immigrant status does not always lift the threat of deportation. She recounts her involvement as a journalist and activist in the "Seven Jamaican Mothers Case," in which women claimed they had been encouraged by both Canadian and Jamaican officials to withhold any information about their children. They were accused – when economic need diminished in Canada – of having submitted fabricated information and were marked for deportation, but ultimately they won in the courts (1989, vi–vii).

119 A black woman from Antigua, Julie, reported a breach of regulations to Immigration. She was never able to find another position and had protracted and difficult dealings with the authorities until she was forced to return to Antigua (25–31).

120 Silvera reveals, for instance, that more than sixteen thousand such visas were issued in 1982, "despite the fact that unemployment in Canada had been rising at an alarming rate" (1998, 9). In 2013, John Ibbitson revealed in the *Globe and Mail* that the "number of temporary foreign workers – from those brought in to harvest crops, to workers in tourist industries, to factory workers, to highly skilled professionals – swelled to 446,847 in 2011 from an estimated 186,753 in 2001" (Ibbitson 2013).

121 Casteel (2005) and Chariandy (2005) also comment in particular on Jewish-black relations in Clarke's work; see also Craig (1987, 88–94).

122 Barbados gained independence in 1966. As Clarke points out in an interview with Linda Richards, Bimshire "is another name for Barbados. Anyone who knows the West Indies would know if you said Bimshire" (Richards 2002).

123 In receiving the prestigious Giller Prize, the book was honoured as exceptional Canadian fiction. As David Chariandy points out, an "anxious debate … emerged after Clarke won the 2002 Giller Prize … for a novel told almost entirely in Caribbean vernacular and set wholly outside of Canada itself" (2005, 143). Rinaldo Walcott rightly asks, "Why must Clarke's great novel be set in Canada?," pointing to "assumptions that place a limit on what being Canadian is imagined to be" (2003, 12). Such debate signals anxiety concerning national definitions of literature and the fact that various national times and spaces belong to each other in transnational and diasporic contexts and perspectives.

124 Clarke's biographer Stella Algoo-Baksh cites a 1962 letter by Collymore to his former student Clarke: "The dialogue or the story should not be too West-Indianized, especially as to spelling – this would cause the non-West Indian reader to find it too much like a foreign language. The best thing is to try to suggest most of it in speech rhythms. Of course, you must bring in the misspelt word here and there, but not too often … and of course the ignored auxiliary and the floating participle – all these make for the raciness of the speech" (1994, 51). Clarke discusses this passage and the use of nation language in his later interview with fellow Caribbean Canadian author Nigel Thomas (H.N. Thomas 2006, 31–3).

125 "*It is better, if the will of God be so, that a man suffer for well-doing, than for evil-doing*" (A.C. Clarke 2002, 9).

126 An example is John Donne's use of the pun in "A Hymn to God the Father": "that at my death Thy Son / Shall shine as he shines now."

127 Bellfeels himself is partly black: "Mr. Bellfeels, as white as he looks today, it's really not pure white. He mixed. He doesn't like to be in the sun too long" (112); see also her later reference to him "being not pure-blood" (367).

128 Percy thus expresses his amazement when she recounts her history after Bellfeels's death, "with the way she speaks, using the Village dialect" (87).

129 After the brief encounter, the sun/son returns on this Easter morning: "And then, all of a sudden, the sun that had-went suddenly behind a cloud came out again, and was shining more brighter, and the light had-changed the same way, as in the story we listened to in Sunday school from *Bible Stories for Children*. Like a miracle of light, this brightness … and in this brightness cut short, there was this darkness; and in this blackness, Mr. Bellfeels disappeared" (12).

130 Austin Clarke describes this predicament in a conversation with Donna Bailey Nurse: "Mary made tremendous accommodations. She gave up her dignity, a large slice of her pride, to accommodate Mr. Bellfeels. But this was not something of her own initiative. Her mother had told her from the beginning that if she decided not to be involved with Mr. Bellfeels there would be ten other

women in the village who would do it. Her mother knew that Mary had the best qualifications for being Bellfeels's mistress. She was pretty and of the right complexion. This, to me, was a very pragmatic view of the situation" (Nurse 2003, 137).

131 See David Steeves's discussion of the requirements of "doing contextualism" or "contextual adjudication" in legal sentencing (especially chapter 4; Steeves 2009, 92–157). His thesis on law and literature deals more specifically with George Elliott Clarke's *George & Rue*, but it can also be fruitfully applied to *The Polished Hoe.*

132 One passage of the novel explicitly plays on the homophony of the two words in vernacular registers: Mary-Mathilda, with reference to her hoe and the status of a harlot or whore, says that they "are both the same, and sound the same" (118). In his interview with Linda Richards, however, Clarke denies awareness of the pun at the moment of writing (Richards 2002).

133 Harrison College, founded in 1733, is a prestigious secondary school in Bridgetown, Barbados.

134 Clarke suggests that his work "can not be called a historical novel because my uses of time [are] more psychological than historical" (Richards 2002).

135 "She only told me about the blood. Blood on the walls. Blood on their bodies. Blood on their clothes … Blood on the ground. Ma standing in this blood covering her two feet, and having to mop it up" (345).

136 Mary-Mathilda later repeats her uncertainty about this ancestor's travels: "And Ma never really found out if Gran came straight from Elnina-Africa, or was transship from Waycross-Georgia, and then here'" (366). In another version, however, Mary-Mathilda offers: "Ma says that her grans on the mother and father side come from a place in Africa call Elmina; was haul-off ship in Amurca; and then was transship here to Bimshire" (389). At some point she links the birth year of one of her great-grandmothers to the publication of Nat Turner's *Confessions* in 1831, "The year my great-gran born!" (393–4). Another evocation, finally, of either that or of the following generation occurs when Mary-Mathilda remembers how, during a hurricane, "Gran sitting by the table … and mumbling words I couldn't understand. Ma it was who told me later that it was her native language Gran was talking in, asking the spirits for mercy; and all the time Gran pleading to her African gods in her African dialect …" (202).

137 Educated in Trinidad and Jamaica, Philip arrived in Canada in 1968, becoming a lawyer and practising law before turning to writing. Her earlier works are the volumes of poetry *Thorns* (1980) and *Salmon Courage* (1983) and a novel for adolescents, *Harriet's Daughter* (1988). Her volumes of essays include *Frontiers: Essays and Writings on Racism and Culture* (1992), *Showing Grit: Showboating North of the 44th Parallel* (1993), *Caribana: African Roots and Continuities – Race, Space and the Poetics of Moving* (1996), and *Genealogy of Resistance and Other Essays* (1997).

138 I take these phrases from Wayde Compton's discussion of James Snead's essay "Repetition as a Figure of Black Culture" (Snead 1990). Compton suggests that Snead "assesses the particular value placed on perpetual immanence in Black expression. Defined against the Western interpretation of repetition as valuable only if it is innovative (what is known as 'progress,' or as Snead calls it, the 'not yet there' model), Snead suggests a Black cultural paradigm he calls the 'always already there' model, or simply a model that embraces repetition" (W. Compton 1997, 156–7).

139 The manuscript version of the volume won the prestigious Casa de las Americas Prize in 1988.

140 "The Absence of Writing or How I almost Became a Spy" (1989, 10–25).

141 Philip suggests that language "succeeded in pushing the African further away from the expression of her experience, and, consequently, the meaning of it" (1989, 15).

142 These are the ECNELIS, the SINCEEL, the LENSECI, the CESLIENS, and the NEECLIS. As Dorothy Jones points out, "each group's name is an anagram of the word silence, except for one, the CESLIENS, whose name represents the plural, silences" (2004, 200). One could add that CESLIENS also means "those links" or "those connections" in French, suggesting the function of relation that silence has in Philip's work.

143 "*She Tries Her Tongue* … has taken me a long way towards the goal of decentring the language. This is not the same thing as destroying a language, which is a far harder thing to do" (1989, 22).

144 Given the existence of some other accounts of the incident (e.g., Granville Sharp's), Philip admits that this claim is relative, but it seeks to convey the official nature of the court case account (Austen 2011, 76).

145 This is admittedly my own extrapolation of a passage from her notebook that reads slightly differently in the original: "I separate subject from verb, verb from object – create semantic mayhem, until my hands bloodied, from so much killing and cutting, reach into the stinking, eviscerated innards, and like some seer, sangoma, or prophet who, having sacrificed an animal for signs and portents of a new life, or simply life, reads the untold story that tells itself by not telling" (193–4). "Sangoma," she explains in a note, is "a Zulu word meaning healer of both physical and spiritual ailments" (2008, 208n13).

146 A journal note in Philip's text, for example, states that "certain words leap out at me, asking me to choose them" (2008, 195); with reference to such passages, Austen observes that, her various techniques of fragmentation notwithstanding, Philip "still casts the formation of her poetry as a product of some mystical happenstance, or even as an ancestral voice – Setaey Adamu Boateng – using her as a conduit" (2011, 65).

147 Philip sometimes invites audiences to read passages collectively (e.g., at the University of Waterloo on 26 May 2012).

148 While "Os" is the Latin word for bone or bones, the equally Latinate section titles "Ratio" and "Dicta" refer to legal procedure, while "Ebora" means

"underwater spirits" in Yoruba (Dowling 2011, 54). Some of the epigrams are discussed below.

149 The only description beyond "negro man" or "negro woman" she finds is "Negro girl (meager)." The absence of recognition of the slaves' humanity leaves Philip shaken: "The African men, women, and children on board the *Zong* were stripped of all specificity, including their names. Their financial value, however, was recorded and preserved for insurance purposes" (2008, 194).

150 Tyrone Williams points out that these are "largely Shona and Yoruba," and he provides some further discussion of what he calls Philip's "anxiety about the lost 'names' of the victims" (2009, 786).

151 Philip explains that "it is totally subversive in the face of the kind of broad-brush brutalizing where people just get reduced to Negro man, Negro woman, and ditto, ditto, ditto. You pay attention to one, and it is such an amazing act – and one that spills over to all the other dittos – paying attention and taking care with just the one … And that's why it is so important for me to name these lost souls in the footnotes to the early poems" (in P. Saunders 2008, 78).

152 The subsequent "Ebora" uses superimposed text and is equally fragmented.

153 Dowling suggests that the names are placed "in the middle of the page and rendered in a font resembling handwritten cursive script. Centred on the page, caressed by the stroke of the pen, the twenty-two names and twenty-two people to whom they refer are no longer mere 'dicta'" (2011, 54).

154 Literally, "the presence of the past." In *Confessions* 11, 20, St Augustine also speaks of "preasens de praeteritis" as memory.

155 The poem "*Zong!* #14" appears on page 173 of *Specters*, #24 on 195, #22 on 213, #4 on 242, #20 on 265, and #17 on 297.

156 On these works, see, for instance, Forster (2002), Mason (2006), Brydon (2007), Härting (2007), Lousley (2008), Fabre (2013–14), and Bernabei (2013–14).

157 Brand made these remarks during an event organized by Winfried Siemerling and Graham Huggan, "US/Canadian Writers' Perspectives on the Multiculturalism Debate: A Symposium at Harvard University," 10 May 1997. Said explains in *Orientalism* that the second part of Gramsci's passage is not available in the 1971 translation *The Prison Notebooks: Selections* but can be found in Gramsci's original *Quaderni del Carcere* (Said 1978, 329–30n16). Diana Brydon mentions that Brand told her that she "kept this excerpt from Said pinned above her desk as she wrote the poem [*Ossuaries*]" (2007, 994).

158 In an interview with Pauline Butling (2005), Brand mentions – among others – Eric Williams and C.L.R. James, the Trinidadian pro-independence movement, Kamau Brathwaite, George Lamming, V.S. Naipaul, Derek Walcott, Frederick Douglass, W.E.B. Du Bois, Langston Hughes, Frantz Fanon, the American civil rights and black power movements, Sonia Sanchez, Nikki Giovanni, Don Leome, Amiri Baraka, Pan-Africanism and Nkrumah, the Toronto Black Education Project, and Toronto black authors Makeda Silvera, Ayanna Black, Clifton Joseph, Lillian Allen, Roger McTair, Marlene NourbeSe

Philip, and Claire Harris. Diana Brydon observes: "Brand's social poetics derives from the cultural traditions of the black Atlantic in dialogue with black Marxisms and global anti-racist, social justice, and environmental activism. It has never been simply nation-based" (2007, 993). To these lists one has to add Brand's engagements in feminist and lesbian struggles and her collaborations to produce historical and documentary work about women, such as the oral histories in *Rivers Have Sources, Trees Have Roots: Speaking of Racism* (1986); *No Burden to Carry: Narratives of Black Working Women in Ontario 1920s–1950* (1991); the volume of historical research *"We're Rooted Here and They Can't Pull Us Up": Essays in African Canadian Women's History* (1994, with Peggy Bristow, Linda Carty, Afua P. Cooper, Sylvia Hamilton, and Adrienne Shadd); and her films *Older Stronger Wiser* (1989), *Sisters in the Struggle* (1991), and *Long Time Comin'* (1993).

159 For comment on Brand's use of the demotic, see Zackodnik (1996), Wiens (2000), Forster (2002, 163–4).

160 It was feared and forbidden by white authorities; its practitioners were often prosecuted (de Barros).

161 Tracing several "textual interactions" that show Brand's "resistant reading of Walcott" (Gingell 1994, 44), Gingell affirms that the latter "has proved a central but largely antithetical literary ancestor for Brand" (43). While "Walcott felt he could not take sides," the "corollary of the recognition that 'no language is neutral' for Brand is that each speech or writing act is necessarily marked by race, gender, the historical moment of its articulation … and by the audience to which it is addressed" (51).

162 Another version of the trope appears in "St Mary's Estate": "This must have been the look toward the sea that slaves saw as they pulled oxen … This must have been a look of envy" (1988, 45).

163 For example, *In Another Place, Not Here* (Brand 1996, 23).

164 Heliconia is the generic name for a type of beautiful flower common in the tropical Americas and pollinated mostly by hummingbirds. The name evokes perhaps also the helicon, Greek seat of the gods and related to Poseidon Helikonios (of Helike).

165 The Manzanilla is a beach in Trinidad.

166 The phrase "then even being born to her was temporary" (22) seems to suggest this but is not unequivocal.

167 The past that occasions her trembling contains also a gender-specific "blood-stained blind of race and sex" (27) that continues after slavery.

168 The grandmother's photograph is not the only one in the story; other pictures, of her mother and of the narrator herself, prove equally misleading.

169 As Brydon suggests, "'Blues Spiritual' is a poem about agency, about acting and being acted upon, about acting in history and in art. The poem is prompted into life by the act of looking" (1992, 83).

170 Such poetic practice has affinities with the work of Toni Morrison, who in "The Site of Memory" remarks about her grandparents' generation: "these people are my access to me; they are my entrance into my own interior life"

(1995, 95). Morrison also quotes Zora Neale Hurston in this context: "'I have memories within me that came out of the material that went to make me'" and comments: "But memories and recollection won't give me total access to the unwritten interior life of these people. Only the act of the imagination can help me" (1995, 92).

171 She touches on it very briefly in her Governor General's Award–winning *Land to Light On* (1997, 46).

172 Brand describes her personal experience during the invasion in Grenada in her essay "Nothing of Egypt" (Brand 1994, 137–40); see Dalleo (2010) for Brand's treatment of Grenada, and Corr (2009) for a discussion of the relationship between the romantic and the revolutionary in the novel; see also Dickinson (1999) and Cook (2005).

173 McCallum and Olbey cite Brand's interview with Dagmar Novak in this context (McCallum and Olbey 1999, 163; Novak 1990).

174 Brand switches here to a third-person point of view and another register, clearly insisting on a multiple linguistic order that moves in and out of particular registers. The demotic here renders mainly the dying woman's account of Adela's slave life.

175 This passage stages an interpersonal conjuring of the past that recalls Faulkner's Shreve and Quentin imagining Sutpen in *Absalom, Absalom*. But while Faulkner is concerned with a cursed male genealogy descending from Southern slave owners, Brand pointedly pursues the unrecorded female genealogy of the descendants of slaves. One can also reference here passages in Morrison's *Beloved* that similarly seem to abolish the boundary between individuals (such as the related monologues of Sethe and Beloved, 1987, 200–17). Yet comparisons such as these come with a certain danger of reductionism. While a comparison with Faulkner may look like praise, it also suggests a dependency on another writer, although Faulkner in fact also shares "black" influences himself. For a discussion of such comparisons, see the comment by Rushdy, who cites Morrison's statement "I am not *like* James Joyce … I am not *like* Thomas Hardy; I am not *like* Faulkner" (Rushdy 1999, 11–12). Comparisons between two black women writers such as Morrison and Brand can be similarly reductive if they seek likeness rather than connectedness. For a discussion of Morrison's "rememory" together with Brand's "unforgetting," see Johnson (2009, 110–11).

176 During an assault, Verlia jumps off a cliff called "Morne des sauteurs" ("Leapers' Hill"), a historical reference to the 1652 communal act of suicide by Caribs to avoid enslavement by French invaders. In addition to Elizete and Verlia, another central character in the novel is Albena, a political organizer in Toronto and the lover first of Verlia and then Elizete.

177 Walcott speaks here of an interstitial "post-national black lesbian feminist space/place" (2003, 52). See also Dickinson (1999, 156–72).

178 Definitions of the term "neo-slave narrative" have varied. For Ashraf Rushdy, neo-slave narratives are "contemporary novels that assume the form, adopt the

conventions, and take on the first-person voice of the antebellum narrative" (1999, 3). As Pilar Cuder-Domínguez observes, however, "Pamela McCallum and Christian Olbey have … argued that [Brand's novel] can also be read as a neo-slave narrative because it is 'concerned with the representation of the profound and deep-rooted physical and physiological effects of slavery as they persist in contemporary forms of superexploitative labour practices endemic to the contemporary process of capitalist globalization'" (2003, 68; McCallum and Olbey 1999, 164).

179 McCallum and Olbey note: "Although born the citizen of a free country in the second half of the twentieth century, Verlia – like Elizete and her ancestor Adela before her … – is marked by the persistent psychological scars of slavery. And it should come as no surprise that, like many slaves, her longing is to run, to take flight (the figure of "flying," in various forms, is associated with Verlia throughout the novel)" (McCallum and Olbey 1999, 163).

180 Maroonage was the practice of escaped slaves throughout the Americas of hiding in inaccessible places such as forests and mountains in order to survive.

181 Together with the nuns, "the nineteen slaves exist now only in several imaginations. Even there, every day, washing, digging, weeding, their movements are infected with the nuns' hovering" (41).

182 The name of "Terre Bouillante," the maroon settlement that Kamena looks for in a torrent of rain and where descendants later live, designates another liminal space between land and water; the way there is, in fact, also associated with mud.

183 It is interesting to speculate on the reasons for Brand's decision to use the name Marie Ursule instead of the name of the slave-revolt leader who inspired her own character, Thisbe, which Brand finds in V.S. Naipaul's *The Loss of El Dorado* (Brand 1999, 301–2). Given the context, another inspiration may have been the voodoo loa Erzulie, often associated with the Virgin Mary, valued for protecting women and children. Brand comments: "When I read Gabriel García Márquez's *One Hundred Years of Solitude* many years ago, it suggested to me just how much could be said … I saw such possibilities of speech, how you could move in and out of an idea as well as in and out of various voices. I remember reading it and thinking I could write anything" (Butling 2005, 80).

184 See McCallum and Olbey (2008), who point to differences from other famous literary family trees but do not evoke García Márquez's novel.

185 "'*Pain c'est viande beque, vin c'est sang beque, nous va mange pain beque nous va boir sang beque.*' Bread is the flesh of the white man, wine is the blood of the white man, we will eat the white man's flesh, we will drink the white man's blood" (11).

186 See also Goldman (2004) for a discussion of water imagery and "drifting" as counter-imagery to imperial mappings in Brand.

187 Elaine Savory writes: "Tidalectics can be expressed (or, as Brathwaite would put it, xpressed) as the ways in which ideas flow together and separate like the edges of waves on a coral beach. They weave together, reshape, separate, flow

back, and come forward again. This is more accurate as an image of Caribbean intellectual traditions than are such Euro-American oppositional models as dialectics, on which tidalectics is obviously a play" (1994, 754).

188 McCallum and Olbey make the important point that the "last chapter, which repeats the title of the novel," evokes "the ebb and flow of tides and Brathwaite's 'tidalectics'" (2008, 28).

189 For the lyrics, see http://letras.terra.com/celia-cruz/1555580/.

190 Yemaya is, for example, associated with the amniotic fluid as the beginning of life, and during Bola's birth "the gush of afterbirth followed like an ocean" that "sailed Bola away from the hands of Marie Ursule" (8). Marie Ursule sees "Bola swimming into the future" (46–7), and Bola "left like a going river. She would live for ever and ever … She will hike to towns, bringing necessary rains and floods" (71).

191 Yemaya is said to be the mother of fifteen orishas, while Bola has fourteen children.

192 The passage that narrates her longing has often been cited: "I would like one single line of ancestry, Mama. One line from you to me and farther back, but a line that I can trace … One line like the one in your palm with all the places where something happened and is remembered. I would like one line full of people who have no reason to forget anything, or forgetting would not help them or matter because the line would be constant, unchangeable. A line I can reach for in my brain when I feel off kilter" (246–7; see also Cuder-Domínguez 2003, 68; Moynagh 2001, 195; Laramee 2008, n.p., para 8).

193 Similarly, Eula has not opened most of the letters from her furious sisters (251).

194 The drawing appears earlier as a piece of contention among Bola's descendants (252). For further discussion of the drawing, see McCallum and Olbey (2008, 27–8), Laramee (2008, para 6).

195 The phrase is from David Turnbull's *Maps Are Territories: Science Is an Atlas: A Portfolio of Exhibits* (1994). One of Brand's entries on this phrase can indeed be taken as a description of *At the Full and Change of the Moon*. Under the headline "Forgetting," Brand notes: "'We need a cognitive schema …' This door is really the door of dreams. This existence in the Diaspora is like that – dreams from which one never wakes. Then what here can be called cognition let alone a schema? A set of dreams, a strand of stories which never come into being, which never coalesce. One is not in control of dreams; dreams take place, the dreamer is captive, even though it is the dreamer who is dreaming" (2001, 28–9).

196 Brand has described her project in an interview with Paolo Da Costa in the following terms: "I wanted to write a piece of work that meandered around that image taken from the historical moment when blacks were taken from Africa to the so-called New World. I wanted to contemplate that moment, as it seemed to me that it existed still, hovered over the lives of blacks of the Diaspora … I wanted to think about how it still worked as a metaphor for how

we were taken, in the lives that we lived in the contemporary, how we were uprooted. I wanted to go beyond the historical fact of the door, or slavery, etc., because that we know and agree to. My guess was that it still functioned, that it was the great metaphor; it functions as a quadrant, in the way that the world found us, or we found the world" (Da Costa 2001, n.p.).

197 Albert Johnson was shot on 26 August 1979. See Blatchford (1980) and Mason (2006, 786).

198 In *What We All Long For*, Brand's diasporic list-making will also emphasize in some cases the transformative dynamic of the immigrant city: "In this city there are Bulgarian mechanics, there are Eritrean accountants, Columbian café owners, Latvian book publishers, Welsh roofers, Afghani dancers, Iranian mathematicians, Tamil cooks in Thai restaurants, Calabrese boys with Jamaican accents, Fushen deejays, Filipina-Saudi beauticians; Russian doctors changing tires, there are Romanian bill collectors, Cape Croker fishmongers, Japanese grocery clerks, French gas meter readers, German bakers, Haitian and Bengali taxi drivers with Irish dispatchers" (2005, 5). Analyses of the transnational, diasporic spaces of Brand's city include Dobson (2006), Brydon (2007), Smyth (2008), Fellner (2010), and Ty (2011).

199 Brand has explored the situation of a black second generation in Canada in her earlier essay "Brownman, Tiger …" (1994, 101–21). She suggests that the promises of the civil rights movement that motivated their parents often seem meaningless to their children, as they face continued prejudice and discrimination. As David Chariandy has pointed out, Brand's later take on this generation in *What We All Long For* "portrays different attitudes and degrees of agency" (Chariandy 2007a, 826).

200 Indeed, Brand repeats the moment from Jackie's perspective: "He was not what Jackie had in mind. I control my shit, 'brother'" (91).

201 Oku also appears childlike in the presence of Jackie (160), and he infantilizes her lover as "boy," a term racially used to deny a black man's personhood.

202 Brand's subsequent novel, *Love Enough* (2014), is still haunted by a character with the nickname "Ghost." His real name is here Germain, while his sister is called Lia; their mother, Mercede, comes again from an Italian background. The provenance of the nickname is here linked with the title – in this case, an inappropriate kind of selfish love bestowed by Mercede on the children (49–50) – and with the novel's recurrent motif of suddenly being someone else. To their troubled mother, "they were practically like twins, and like ghosts" (51). While Lia dislikes the idea "of turning into someone else, or turning into nothing" (51), Germain adopts Ghost as his name. As is the case with Carla in the earlier novel, Lia's life is largely determined by a family context she seems unable – or unwilling – to leave behind: "Tied to her brother, Germain, and her strange mother, Mercede" (22). As in the earlier novel, Ghost's presence conjures the weight of a seemingly inescapable socio-economic past (although the provenance of that fate is not explicitly connected here with race, and the father is absent and unremembered [53]). Ghost also prolongs and

perpetuates the forever unresolved ending of *What We All Long For*, where, with a friend, he drives his father's Audi to Forest Hill to steal a BMW – the Beamer X5 – and leaves its occupant lifeless by the roadside (2005, 315–17). In *Love Enough* – which combines several lightly interconnected narratives but was originally titled for the object of their uncertain longing, *Beamer* (Medley 2014) – it still remains uncertain whether their victim is dead. Fate remains unreadable and undecidable: "They beat a man to death. Maybe" (11). Having abandoned the stolen car and continuing in the Audi, they seem to be endlessly cruising in the city, forever on the move like the diasporic urban descendants of Kamena that Brand had described in *A Map to the Door of No Return*. As the Audi "gains flight" – a recurrent term of escape and transformation in Brand's work that I have discussed earlier – on Toronto's Don Valley Parkway, the narrator asks: "Who wants to live in the lives they have in the present?" (165), and then, imagining the two friends still obsessed with movement and speed later in their lives, the narrator comments: "They work on making things run faster, or diagnosing what makes systems slow down" (166).

203 For Lai, Quy "embodies Agamben's *homo sacer*, in the sense of a 'bare life' that does not belong to the realm of the (socialized) human, even as it founds this realm, and therefore can be killed without being sacrificed" (2014, 209).

204 The ending of the novel highlights that idea. Brand gives voice to the silence and invisibility of this character during and after the camp of Bidong, as she has given voice to the silences of the middle passage. Quy, however, is left for dead at the roadside at the moment he seems to have found some form of "home." Brand then continues the pattern of disruption and connection by giving the very last sentence of the novel to a thought about the artist character Tuyen and her never-ending work of producing a *lubaio*, an artwork and signpost for human wishes in the city (Brand 2005, 150, 307–8, 318).

205 Discussions about the end of the novel can be found in Brydon (2006, 105–6, 109–10), Blair (2012, 47–8, 59–62), Smyth (2008, 287), and Dobson (2006, 101; 2009, 196).

206 Chariandy cites, in particular, interviews with Donna Bailey Nurse (2000) and Michael Redhill (1999).

207 Alexis's other works include a collection discussed below, *Despair and Other Stories of Ottawa* (1994); Brechtian parody and inversion in his play about Southern Ontario, *Lambton Kent* (1999); his children's novel *Ingrid and the Wolf* (2005); a quirky treatment of the Brian Mulroney–era Ottawa in his novel *Asylum* (2008); and his collection of fiction, memoir, and criticism, *Beauty and Sadness* (2010).

208 Chariandy himself seems to be "genuinely intrigued about the question of whether or not *Soucouyant* is a Canadian novel, and what any answer to this question might imply about our individual understandings of Canada and its culture(s)" (in Tancock 2008, 3). He thus observes that he is "not an authority on Caribbean culture per se, but the 'Caribbean-ness' of my novel was deeply

important to me … Maybe my novel is fully Canadian and Caribbean, but in ways that all of us haven't quite yet been able to recognize" (3).

209 Chariandy suggests that the task is to understand "how these second-generation writers imagine the Caribbean and … what complex and ambivalent attitudes these writers might harbour (and inscribe) with respect to their parents' cultural heritage" (2004, 80). Elsewhere, he asks, "What, if anything, do we owe to the memories of others?" (Tancock 2008, 1).

210 The novel's narrator offers this explanation: "A soucouyant is something like a female vampire … She disguises herself by dressing up in the skin of an old woman, but at night she'll shed her disguise and travel across the sky as a ball of fire. She'll hunt out a victim and suck his blood as he sleeps, leaving him with little sign of her work except increasing fatigue, a certain paleness, and perhaps, if he were to look closely on his body, a tell-tale bruise or mark on his skin" (135). See also Giselle Liza Anatol's feminist reading of the figure of the soucouyant and La Diablesse in works by Nalo Hopkinson (Anatol 2004).

211 The connection between the female soucouyant and sexuality is suggested by the reverse male "biting" in the song by Calypso singer Sparrow, heard at the wedding: "One a de women started to beg. He bite she on the chest. He bite she on the leg" (16).

212 I'm improvising here over a title by Linda and Michael Hutcheon (1996) on related connections in opera; it is noteworthy, however, that a similar constellation also pertains to Morley Callaghan's use of black jazz in *The Loved and the Lost* (discussed below).

213 His opening of chapter 3, "Two words forward, one word back" (20), seems to adapt Dorothy Livesay's "one step forward / two steps back" in her well-known poem "Day and Night" (lines 9–10).

214 The narrator does make it clear that racism plays a role when he reminisces about his mother, Katarina: "Mrs. Martin was wary of a certain tendency in Negroes, a tendency that was sure to show itself, however good Katarina might appear on the surface. Katarina was even darker than Edna, and look at Edna … she had hoodwinked people into treating her white, and no good came of that" (39). The same Mrs Martin, the narrator reports, "never really accepted Katarina. She was even less sympathetic now that Katarina showed clear signs of being Black: keeping her own hours, neglecting her schoolwork" (48).

215 On the role of the Trinidadian housekeeper in the novel, Mrs Williams, see Sanders (2000, 179–80) and Hudson (2000, 197–8).

216 The unexpected intrusion of memory is one of the signs of trauma. In her discussion of *Soucouyant*, Jennifer Bowering Delisle, citing Susan J. Brison, suggests that "traumatic memories 'are experienced by the survivor as inflicted, not chosen' … and therefore disrupt one's sense of oneself as made up of continuous memories, and ongoing narrative" (Delisle 2011, 3, citing Brison 1999, 41).

217 In a profile of Chariandy, Donna Bailey Nurse notes that he was "haunted by Toni Morrison's *Beloved*, in which a spirit representing a dark history returns" (2011, 32).

218 See my discussion of melancholia and Coleman's essay in chapter 1.

219 In a "downward interpretation," soucouyants can be rationally explained as inventions – for instance, as "scapegoats of people who fear or despise elderly women, and the legend of their bloodsucking powers rationalizes people's desire for their lands and properties" (Coleman 2012, 62).

220 Nurse reports that Chariandy consulted, among other works, Michael Ondaatje's *The English Patient* in his search for technical solutions to the time structure of his own novel (2011, 31–2). With regard to the bruise, however, there seems to be a more direct equivalent in Ondaatje's *In the Skin of Lion*, where a character awakes to an injury – a broken arm – he sustained during what might have been a dream (Siemerling 1994, 169).

221 Chariandy discusses Hall's "Cultural Identity and Diaspora," which I have considered in chapter 1 and returned to earlier here in chapter 4, in his own "Postcolonial Diasporas" (Chariandy 2006).

222 This last sentence suggests again Ondaatje's *In the Skin of a Lion* as possible intertext, a novel that closes with the syntactically identical sentence: "'Lights,' he said" (1987, 244). This sentence takes us back to the opening of the novel and the beginning of a long drive in the night during which the story we have just read will be told, conjoining historical and personal pasts as they emerge from darkness.

223 In a 2004 article in *Canadian Woman Studies*, "Écrire pour tuer le vide du silence," she describes having witnessed, in Haiti, a house being burnt to the ground with the residents inside.

224 After her 1994 volume of poetry, *Balafres*, she went on to write two novels, *La dot de Sara* (1995) and *Le livre d'Emma* (2001), as well as the collection of stories *Le silence comme le sang* (1997). She has also produced four children's books and has transcribed Haitian legends in *L'oranger magique* (2003b) and *La légende du poisson amoureux* (2003a).

225 I have discussed this work elsewhere in the context of issues of ethics, identification, and cross-cultural communication (Siemerling 2007). Agnant's work has received attention in francophone criticism (e.g., Lequin 2002, Bernier 2002, Naudillon 2005, Ndiaye 2004, Selao 2010); it has been discussed in English by Proulx (2004, 2005), Lyngaas (2011), and in some reviews of the translated *Book of Emma* (e.g., Hulan 2009).

226 Agnant states, "C'est un pays où l'écriture se conjugue au masculin … Comparativement au nombre d'hommes qui font ce métier d'écrivain, on dénombre très peu de femmes et lorsqu'elles arrivent à le faire, il y a toutes sortes de moyens mis en place pour qu'elles se taisent; que ce soit par l'entourage ou par les hommes qui écrivent … Haïti est un pays où les femmes assurent la transmission orale, mais où, de manière concrète, très peu d'entre elles arrivent à écrire" (Boucher 2005, 204; "It is a country where literature is the domain

of men … In comparison to the number of male writers, there are very few women who manage to write, and there are all kinds of obstacles put in their way to silence them, be it by their environment or by the men who write … Haiti is a country where women look after the oral transmission but where, in practical terms, very few of them manage to write" [my translation]). Agnant is certainly not alone in making these claims (see, for instance, Condé 1993, 83; qtd in Boucher 2005, 198).

227 "Un jour, grand-maman, j'écrirai ton histoire, l'histoire de ta vie. Elle sera belle, tu verras … le monde entier la lira cette histoire, alors elle ne finira jamais, elle sera éternelle, belle et éternelle" (1995, 25–6; "One day, grandmother, I will write your story, the story of your life. It will be beautiful, you will see … the whole world will read that story, so it will never end, it will be timeless, beautiful and timeless"). All translations from *La dot de Sara* are mine.

228 Agnant published her versions of some of these stories (2003a, 2003b); for a more general discussion of folklore in francophone Caribbean literature, see Laroche (1997).

229 "Giselle a beau être née tout comme moi aux Mombins, elle n'est pas de là-bas. Ces histoires farfelues, comme elle les appelle, occupent une part importante de l'enfance chez nous. Qu'aurions-nous fait … sans nos contes et notre univers de légendes" (1995, 60; "Giselle may be born like me in Mombins, but she is not from down there. These weird stories, as she calls them, are an important part of our childhood. What would we have done … without our tales and our world of legends … ?").

230 "Elle lutte, on dirait, contre un désir irrésistible de prendre part à ce monde, notre monde de femmes et de légendes comme elle l'appelle … On dirait que cette complicité entre Sara et moi la ravit et la dérange en même temps" (67; "She fights, it seems, against an irresistible desire to take part in this world, our world of women and legends as she calls it … It seems that this complicity between Sara and myself enchants and disturbs her at the same time").

231 For Agnant's comments on Creole in the novel and in her own life, see Boucher (2005, 210–13).

232 Despite his anglophone name, Ian MacLeod, it is clear that the doctor speaks French (7). The choice of an anglophone name for a character who here represents the repressive norm adds a further level of potential meaning to a text that thus references an at least tricultural repertoire.

233 Flore's willingness to assist the white doctor and her light skin colour (24, 36) initially trigger the aggression of Emma (22–4), who has been rejected by her own light-skinned mother (55–63, 122; see Naudillon 2005, 79, 85). Flore must also contend with the possibility that Emma murdered her child. Emma's suspected deed is never explicitly stated as a fact, yet it is suggested in several passages (107) and more or less assumed in most critical readings (see Ndiaye 2004, 56; Naudillon 2005, 77–8).

234 Emma announces this trajectory early, seen here as an almost inevitably predetermined space of her subjectivity, grounded in slavery: "Écrivez, docteur

MacLeod … Emma nous est venue d'une colonie de morts vivants. Lambeau de chair pourrie sur le chemin des bateaux, elle a dérivé jusqu'ici. Mais ce n'est qu'une escale, un jour, elle reprendra le chemin des bateaux" (27; "Write, Dr. MacLeod … 'Emma came to us from a colony of the living dead. A scrap of rotten flesh on the path of the ships, she was blown off course to this place. But it's just a stop; one day she will return to the path of the ships'" [2006, 33–4]).

235 In chapter 1, see my explanation of this term as designating the often ambivalent and contradictory duality by which cognitive change ("re-cognition") inevitably draws on available values, categories, and narratives ("recognition").

236 This and all subsequent translations of passages from this novel are those of Zilpha Ellis (Agnant 2006).

237 Agnant's text thus moves from an understanding and seemingly "transparent translation" according to host society–sanctioned norms to identification with another reference system. In terms of translation theory, this could be considered a "foreignizing translation" (Venuti 1995), one that does not seek to hide the qualities of the translated source text behind what seems a perfectly transparent target language, but rather alerts the recipient of the translation to the fact of difference by importing qualities of the source into the target language. This is one of the desiderata expressed by Walter Benjamin in "The Task of the Translator" (in Benjamin 1968, 69–82).

238 The doctor "écrit tout dans son cahier" (26; "writes all in his notebook" [2006, 32]). Emma challenges this account: "Quand tu auras tout noté, tu écrira un autre livre … à dépecer les négresses, et dans lequel tu écriras tout à travers" (32; "When you have taken all your notes, you will write another book … dismembering black women, and in which everything you write will be wrong" [2006, 39]).

239 "Tu es là, à répéter pour ces Blancs tous mes mots … Tu ne sais rien de la vraie histoire … Tu dois tout avoir appris dans ces livres qu'ils ont eux-mêmes écrits pour te conter ta propre histoire … Ainsi, eux seuls continueront à écrire pour nous, pour qu'on ne sache pas que déjà sur les bateaux, ils nous volaient et notre corps et notre âme. Ça, Poupette, tu ne l'as pas lu dans leurs grands livres, hein?" (22–3; "You are here, repeating all my words for these whites … You know nothing of the real story. … You must have learned everything from those books that they themselves have written to tell you your own history … So that they alone will continue to write for us, so that people will not know that already on the slave ships they stole both our bodies and our souls. You didn't read that in your big books, did you, Dollie?" [2006, 28–9]).

240 "Je ne suis plus une simple interprète. Petit à petit, j'abandonne mon rôle, je deviens une partie d'Emma, j'épouse le destin d'Emma" (18; "I am not simply an interpreter. Little by little, I abandon my role; I become a part of Emma; I embrace Emma's destiny" [2006, 21]).

241 The story begins with the abduction of Emma's forebear Kilima from Africa that separates her from her mother, Malayika, whose name means "ange gardien" (133; "guardian angel" [2006, 164]). Later the medical woman and mid-

wife Cécile makes good on her threat (144) to use violence if Kilima, whom she has adopted in place of her own lost daughter, is touched. She stabs the plantation owner, whose friends then mutilate her along with Kilima. Kilima sets fire to the plantation and flees with the other slaves into maroonage, where she tries to kill both her child and herself.

242 Emma thus compares Mattie's storytelling with the process of writing, and she compares her own listening to reading: "Vivre avec Mattie, c'était comme vivre dans un grand livre, un livre qu'elle construisait chaque jour, page après page, et dans lequel je découvrais les arabesques et les méandres de l'âme des humains. C'est dans ce livre que je découvris des vies étonnantes" (109; "Living with Mattie was like living in a big book, a book that she constructed each day, page after page, and in which I discovered the arabesques and the meanderings of human souls. It's in this book that I discovered some amazing lives" [2006, 136–7]).

243 The translations in the remainder of this chapter are mine.

244 François Duvalier was president from 1957 to 1971. After his death, his son Jean-Claude Duvalier took over until ousted in an uprising in 1986; in 2011, he returned from exile in France and was arrested but lived under house arrest in Port-au-Prince until his death in 2014.

245 Lyngaas comments on the difficulty of translating the word "mouroir": the "terms 'nursing home,' 'twilight home,' and 'hospice' do not effectively convey the idea that this is a place where people are left to die" (2011, 976).

246 After an earlier incarceration at age fifteen for participating in activities against the Magloire government, Étienne is again imprisoned and tortured after participating in a coup against François Duvalier in 1961. He leaves for Montreal, offering his lyrical greeting to the city in his long poem *Lettre à Montréal* (1966).

247 All page references are to the third edition from 1994. Translations are mine.

248 Étienne notes that "écrit sur un terre d'exil, le NÈGRE constituait pour moi un lieu … de parole et de délivrance" and developed "une thématique qui marquera désormais mon oeuvre littéraire, celle de l'impuissance" (Étienne 1994, 9; "written in exile, NÈGRE offered me a space … of speaking and deliverance" … "a theme that has marked my subsequent work, that of powerlessness").

249 Étienne prefaces the novel with the following rather unusual but unequivocal remark: "Toute resemblance avec des personages réels, vivants ou connus, n'est ni coïncidence ni effet du hasard" (1979, 8; "Any resemblance to real, living or known persons is neither a coincidence nor unintended").

250 In Étienne's own autobiography, voodoo is associated with destructive tendencies in his own family and with the separation of his parents, while on a national level Duvalier used voodoo to intimidate large parts of the Haitian population. It is only with his later novel, *La romance en do mineur de Maître Clo* (2000), that Étienne begins to look at voodoo, not from the perspective

of his own childhood experience, but in terms of its own merits (see his comments in Dumontet 2003, 214).

251 See also Étienne's subsequent novel, *La reine soleil levée* (1987), and his essay *La femme noire dans le discours littéraire haïtien: Éléments d'anthroposémiologie* (1998).

252 His name evokes the words "mal à vie," which could be translated as "poorly alive."

253 The translations in this section are mine. Ollivier writes: "Je me regarde vivre deux tonalités qui parfois cheminent parallèlement, d'autres fois s'enchevêtrent et même harmonisent" (qtd in Gauvin 2012, 82; "I watch myself living two tonalities that sometimes run parallel, at other times get entangled and even harmonize").

254 On this work, see in particular Coleman (1998, 52–81). The title was first translated as *How to Make Love to a Negro* (1987) by David Homel, who also translated other works by Laferrière. To mention just a few more works by Laferrière that are not discussed here, one could cite *Eroshima* (1987), *Le goût des jeunes filles* (1992), *La chair du maître* (1997), *Le charme des après-midi sans fin* (1997), *Le cri des oiseaux fous* (2000), *Vers le sud* (2006), and *Je suis un écrivain japonais* (2008).

255 The narrator's mother thus observes: "On a l'impression d'être déjà mort, ici … Les tueurs ne sont pas plus vivants que les tués. Nous sommes tous déjà morts" (102; "One feels already dead here … The killers are no more alive than the killed. We are all already dead").

256 As Angela MacLellan points out, this division references Édouard Glissant's poem *Pays rêvé, pays réel* (1985) and its reflection on a complex, multiple, and intermediary state between two worlds (2012, 23).

257 For a reading of *Pays sans chapeau* and *L'énigme du retour* in terms of Glissant's notion of "detour" and Homi Bhabha's "third space," see MacLellan (2012).

CHAPTER 5

1 A few examples of further contexts that deserve consideration – in addition to those constituted by other black Canadian art forms, as I have briefly suggested in the introduction – include black francophone writing in Ontario, such as the work of Didier Leclair and Melchior Mbonimpa. Leclair was born in Montreal, grew up in Africa, and is now a resident of Toronto; he is the author of *Toronto, je t'aime* (2000, Trillium Award), *Ce pays qui est le mien* (2003), *Un passage vers l'Occident* (2007), and *Le soixantième parallèle* (2010). Mbonimpa, born in Burundi and now a professor at the University of Sudbury, has published a number of non-fiction volumes and the novels *Le totem des Baranda* (2001), *Le dernier roi faiseur de pluie* (2003), *Les morts ne sont pas morts* (2006), and *La terre sans mal* (2008). Mbonimpa is thus part of the African diaspora in Canada in the more restricted sense of direct immigration from Africa, the subject of *The African Diaspora in Canada: Negoti-*

ating Identity and Belonging (2005), edited by Wisdom J. Tettey and Korbla P. Puplampu. Other relevant sites include the protest over the renaming of Negro Creek Road in Holland Township, evoked in Djanet Sears's *The Adventures of a Black Girl in Search of God* (see Leslie Sanders's introduction to the play in Sears's anthology of black Canadian theatre, *Testifyin'*, vol. 2 [Sanders 2003]), or the continuing discussions about "Nigger Rock," possibly a black cemetery in Quebec on the Vermont border (see Back 2005; Mackey 2010, 78, 445n148).

2 The centre was closed in 1989 owing to lack of funding. Before moving to its present location on Coursol Street in what is now Little Burgundy, the Negro Community Centre (NCC), renamed later the NCC/Charles H. Este Cultural Centre in honour of its long-time minister, was located in the basement of Union United Church, a black Montreal landmark institution founded by railroad porters in 1907 (see Bertley 1976).

3 My translation.

4 Volume 5 of the final report of the Royal Commission on Bilingualism and Biculturalism reiterates its mandate to "recommend what steps should be taken to develop the Canadian confederation on the basis of an equal partnership between the two founding races, taking into account the contribution made by the other ethnic groups" (3). But it also states, "We repeat that we accept the words 'race' and 'people' in their traditional sense – meaning a national group, with no biological significance – and we prefer to emphasize the facts of language and culture rather than the concepts of 'race,' 'people,' or even 'ethnic group'" (7).

5 See especially "Tout Montréal 1: Les Deux Saint-Laurent." Mary Jean Green observes, "In *Bonheur d'occasion* … the multiethnic city she described in 1941 has disappeared, replaced by a bipolar city divided between rich and poor, anglophone and francophone, where the only 'immigrants' are Roy's impoverished French-Canadian characters, who have migrated into the city from nearby farms. In its form, which is shaped by the destiny of a large French-Canadian family, Roy's first novel is reminiscent of the familiar structure of the traditional Québécois *roman de la terre*, reflecting as well its representation of the city as a site of English domination. Although *Bonheur d'occasion* broke new literary ground by placing its French-Canadian characters in an urban setting, it did not go so far as to integrate Roy's early vision of the city as a place of hybridity" (2004, 13).

6 The park is named after Sir George-Étienne Cartier (1814–1873), a participant in the 1837 Lower Canada Rebellion and later one of the "Fathers of Confederation."

7 "A savage blast of music, with saxophones blaring, filled the room" (Roy 1969, 88). Like all further translations from *Bonheur d'occasion*, this is taken from Hannah Josephson's translation of the novel, *The Tin Flute*.

8 "A dealer in religious objects, ornaments and church wines" (Roy 1969, 86).

9 "'Is that some new Negro dance?' asked M. Létourneau" (Roy 1969, 89).

10 Sherry Simon points out that *The Loved and the Lost* and Roy's *Bonheur d'occasion* are among the few novels that "have used the vertical drop between mountain and river as dramatic material to be exploited"; many other works have concentrated instead on the east–west linguistic split (2009, 4).

11 David Leahy argues that "given the semiotic field of blacks in the novel it is difficult to imagine that predominantly white readerships in the early 1950s would not have presumed Peggy's murderer was black" (1994, 37).

12 As Dorothy Williams specifies in her history of Montreal's black community, "The current dimensions of section [*sic*] that was the St. Antoine district includes Little Burgundy and St. Henri. Little Burgundy runs from Atwater avenue east to Peel street, from the Lachine Canal north to the Ville Marie expressway. St. Henri extends along St. Antoine, from Atwater west to Glen Road" (D.W. Williams 1997, 36–7). Originally, Williams explains, the Saint Antoine district designated the entire eastern administrative part of Montreal.

13 As Collison remarks, "By moving to Mountain Street Shadrach Minkins put himself in the center of the most dynamic area of the city" (1997, 204). Tulchinsky (1977) and Day (1864) illustrate this claim. For a history of Saint-Henri, see Société historique de Saint-Henri.

14 Hence the name of the Lachine Canal: "Upon arriving in New France, Cavelier de La Salle … dreamed of discovering this very route [to China]. Later, his seigneury, located near the rapids, was mockingly dubbed "La Chine" – the name in French for China" (Desloges and Gelly 2002, 9).

15 Sealy won a Juno Award in 2000 for *Africville Suite*, partially inspired by his Africville-born father. Sealy still performs actively and is a co-owner of the jazz record label Triplet Records, established in 1989.

16 Mark Miller notes, "His only recorded solo of any consequence, an 84-bar improvisation on *Now's The Time*, was made at Parker's side and issued 40 years later on the CD *Charlie Parker, Montreal, 1953* (Uptown)" (2001, 207).

17 Marrelli points out that "The Corner" was "close to where the black community lived, and to the trains where many blacks worked as porters. At 'The Corner' black entertainment was the drawing card, but both black and white audiences were welcome" (Marrelli 2004, 100).

18 For example, Bertley (1976, 1980) and Hostesses of Union United Church (1982).

19 Sarsfield's book was a finalist in the CBC's 2005 "Canada Reads" competition.

20 The novel brings up, for instance, the disenfranchisement of French Canadian women during that period and features characters from Italian, Russian, and other backgrounds, as well as a fully multicultural wedding that combines Russian Orthodox ceremony with the temptations of Creole cooking.

21 The church is located on Delisle Street on the west side of Atwater Avenue and thus is technically just outside present-day Little Burgundy. But by referring to Little Burgundy as "a 'salt and pepper' district on the eastern fringes of St. Henri" (43), Sarsfield retains, like Oliver Jones's personal geography, the

historical unity of a wider Saint-Henri that stretched further east than today's administrative boundaries.

22 "The Coloured Ladies Club" in the novel corresponds to the Coloured Women's Club of Montreal, which was founded in 1902. Initially, it was "an exclusive club of only fifteen women – all wives of American porters" that assisted the black community and its newly arrived immigrants (D.W. Williams 1997, 50–1); on the important role of women in the UNIA, see D.W. Williams (1997, 60–1).

23 Randolph "advocated a grand alliance between blacks and the trade union movement … Many blacks regarded organized labor as an enemy of racial integration, because blacks were barred from most of labor's craft unions. Randolph relentlessly attacked unions that excluded black workers" (George Meany Memorial Archives).

24 For Canada, see Calliste (1987, 1988).

25 Williams writes: "Countering Garvey's segregationism was the integrationism of Asa Philip Randolph, a prominent black American union organizer and civil rights activist. His aim was to unite all workers regardless of race" (1997, 58).

26 As already mentioned, the association of Montreal's black community with jazz, drinking, and gambling was seen, naturally, with distaste by many of its members; the novel reflects this sentiment: "Rockhead's, the jazz cabaret on lower Mountain Street, was the 'den of iniquity,' Otis explained, that Prohibition had made irresistible to American sportsmen and gamblers … it marked the halfway point on the streetcar run along St. Antoine. When the last streetcar before morning arrived at Mountain Street, how many of those Black musicians, who wore mysterious dark glasses while entertaining white folks at Rockhead's, would climb aboard for the long ride home to their own families in the respectable working-class districts St Henri and Verdun?" (14–15).

27 Lou Hooper was born in North Buxton and became a successful recording artist in New York before arriving in Montreal in 1933 (Gilmore 1988, 48). He played piano in Myron Sutton's Canadian Ambassadors (M. Miller 1982, 8), and became one of Peterson's teachers. Maynard Ferguson played trumpet with Peterson in the Johnny Holmes Orchestra before becoming an orchestra leader himself (Gilmore 1988, 110–14). Paul de Marky was the Hungarian-born teacher of Oscar Peterson's sister Daisy and eventually of Oscar Peterson himself.

28 On at least one known occasion, Holmes had to fend off racism before Peterson could become one of the first black musicians to play with the Holmes Orchestra at the Montreal Ritz-Carleton (see Marrelli 2004, 86; Gilmore 1988, 103–5; Lees 1988, 51–2, 59).

29 Writing about his legendary trio with bassist Ray Brown and guitarist Herb Ellis (who replaced Barney Kessel), Peterson comments, "It may seem un-

likely, but I honestly believe that the question of a single white person between two Negroes in a group on stage never came up amongst us until the subject was broached in a newspaper interview. If I recall correctly, when Herbie was asked how he felt playing in such a group, I believe his answer was something like, 'I can't answer that because I really hadn't noticed who I was playing with racially.' Herbie's attitude remained this way throughout his entire six years in the group, and it's still true for all of us today" (Peterson and Palmer 2002, 80).

30 As a child, Peterson was expected to perform on the piano when Marcus Garvey visited Montreal; he describes his impressions of Garvey and the UNIA: "He drove home that it would only be with the courage and determination to create and sustain our very own black industries, grocery stores, taxis, airlines, and even shipping lines that we would at last be truly free from the economic bondage that we endured. Intriguingly, if we thrust that form of thinking forward to today's world, Marcus Garvey was dead on the mark … When I think back to those countless Sunday afternoons, I realize that I got more from those [UNIA] meetings than I was aware of at the time. Not only did the repeated public performances in the hall increase my musical confidence, but – more importantly – I learned from Marcus Garvey and others the need for dedication and devotion to any cause that one sincerely believes in. Many of the young Montreal blacks of today may not even have heard of the UNIA; nevertheless, it served their forebears as a place of spiritual sustenance and personal reconstruction" (Peterson and Palmer 2002, 28–9).

31 "Realizing that the material was original, [Norman Ganz] asked me what the title should be and I decided, due to the predominance of Martin Luther King, Jr. at the time, and the intense focus on the Civil Rights Movement taking place, that it should be called 'The Hymn to Freedom'" (Peterson, "Musical Moments," oscarpeterson.com).

32 Gilmore's description of Peterson's hiring differs slightly from Sarsfield's account. While Sarsfield writes that "Holmes never hesitated" (135), Gilmore suggests an artistically more complex moment (100–1).

33 In his autobiography, Peterson himself remembers how his former teacher Paul de Marky "always insisted on relating my playing to that of Franz Liszt, of whom he was a descendant" (Peterson and Palmer 2002, 47). When his old teacher heard him play again after many years, he exclaimed, "Liszt … Liszt! You are indeed a modern reincarnation" (49).

34 For Fiske, whiteness exercises power through "exnomination" as "the means by which whiteness avoids being named and thus keeps itself out of the field of interrogation and therefore off the agenda for change" (1994, 42; qtd in Lewis 1996, 140).

35 The debate in the novel has its counterpart in musicology. In an influential discussion of "Afrological" and "Eurological" perspectives, for instance, the trombonist and music scholar George Lewis highlights the paradoxical status of boundaries in John Cage's statements about experimental music, which turn on notions of "indeterminacy" and "chance operations" but entirely dis-

miss jazz (136–8). This is all the more surprising given the influence of bebop on the New York school of which Cage was a member (139). With respect to Cage's elision of Black traditions, Lewis writes that "despite such declarations as 'the world is one world now' … it is clear that Cage has drawn very specific boundaries, not only as to which musics are relevant to his own musicality but as to which musics suit his own taste" (1996, 138).

36 Tessa McWatt moved with her family from Guyana to Toronto as a small child in the early 1960s. Living now in London, England, she still identifies as a Canadian writer. Like the early *Out of My Skin*, her most recent novel, *Vital Signs* (2011), is set in Canada. She has published five novels and a collection of short stories.

37 Personal communication, 30 January 2010.

38 Of particular interest here is francophone Haitian Montreal jazz buff Stanley Péan, whose considerable oeuvre includes his personal tour of jazz, *Jazzman* (2006).

39 "Africadian" is Clarke's coinage, assembled from the words "Africa" and "Acadia." The latter term once referred to what is now Nova Scotia and New Brunswick (G.E. Clarke 1991–92, 2:9).

40 The main body of black writing in this period, Clarke suggests, is made up of church-related texts and meeting minutes (2002a, 109).

41 Clarke writes that, unfortunately, "in the early 1960s, it didn't sound racist and it didn't seem wrong" to demand the destruction of Africville. "Many – Black and white – thought it was all for the best that Africville was broken into rubble and its people dispersed to public housing, where they would have access to city services" (G.E. Clarke 2003b, 393). The withholding of these services, the erasure of the community by city planning that ruthlessly declared its site to be part of an industrial zone, and the encroachment upon its location by undesired public sites like the city dump had been part of the deteriorating public image of Africville to begin with. For detailed accounts of Africville and the process leading to relocation, see Clairmont and Magill (1987), Clairmont (2010a), Clairmont ([1992] 2010b; I cite the second edition), and Nelson (2009). See also the video clips available by searching for "Africville" on the website of the Canadian Broadcasting Corporation (CBC) Digital Archives (http://www.cbc.ca/archives/).

42 Ward is the scriptwriter and narrator of Selwyn Jacob's documentary about Canadian railroad porters, *The Road Taken* (1997, with music by Joe Sealy). He has also contributed to the jazz documentaries *Oliver Jones in Africa* (1990) and *Crossroads: Three Jazz Pianists* (1998).

43 Clarke calls the work "only conditionally a novel and not a poem" (2012, 199) and "a series of prose-poems *cum* sound poetry" (201). Ward encountered Africville stories first when, on his way from Detroit to Denmark, he was "stranded by a dockworkers' strike in Halifax" and met "exiles from the recently bulldozed … village of Africville" (198). Clarke suggests that Ward "uses Africville as a touchstone for scenes and characters out of African America" (199).

44 The Africville school opened in 1883 and operated until 1953, when "it was closed and the children transferred to integrated schools elsewhere in Halifax" (Clairmont 2010a, 36).

45 Ward's other works include anthologies, an earlier collection, *Poems* (1964), the novels *Nobody Called Me Mine: Black Memories* (1977) and *A Room Full of Balloons* (1981), and a number of plays and screenplays.

46 See also "Africville Is My Name" and "Africville Spirit" in *Woman Talking Woman* (1990). Her other volumes are *Borrowed Beauty* (1987), *Save the Word for Me* (1991), and *Door of My Heart* (1993); for detailed discussions of Tynes's work, see Stone (1997), Fuller (1999), G.E. Clarke (2012, 164–75).

47 Hamilton's oeuvre includes a number of films about black Nova Scotia: *Black Mother, Black Daughter* (1989), *Speak It! From the Heart of Black Nova Scotia* (1992), *Against the Tides: The Jones Family* (1994, Part 2 of *Hymn to Freedom*), *Portia White: Think on Me* (2000), and *The Little Black School House* (2007), which deals with racially segregated schools in both Nova Scotia and Ontario.

48 Bernard is anthologized in volume 2 of Clarke's *Fire on the Water* (1991, 126–34), and she composed the music for *Black Mother, Black Daughter* by Sylvia Hamilton.

49 These included "Mary Sparling, the director of the Art Gallery … Shelagh Mackenzie, a national Film Board Producer, Bridglal Pachai, the director of the Nova Scotia Black Cultural Society … Henry Bishop, Curator of the Black Cultural Centre, and Don Clairmont, a Dalhousie University sociologist" (Kimber 2010, 83).

50 In the same year and with a number of explanatory endnotes, it was also reprinted in volume 2 of Clarke's *Fire on the Water* (1992, 53–65).

51 In an August 1962 meeting, though, with "local politicians and some one hundred Africville residents and supporters" in Seaview Church prior to the October 1962 city council meeting that made the decision on the relocation, "the Africvilleans strongly rejected relocation and urged that they be allowed to stay in Africville and develop it according to City specifications" (Clairmont 2010b, 63).

52 The church was "bulldozed at the unlikely hour of 3:30 a.m. in 1967" (AGS 2010, 121).

53 Wedderburn repeats the phrase "I did not see the flowers" (in Kimber 2010, 98), referring to "a photograph of Africville on the cover of the catalogue" of the 1989 exhibition, which he "held up as he reiterated his failure to see Africville in such romantic terms when he visited it prior to its destruction" (Moynagh 1998, 29).

54 Out of this failure, Clarke sees the rebirth of an Africadian nationalism in secular form in the 1970s, symbolized by insurgent "intellectuals like Burnley 'Rocky' Jones" and "Nova Scotia's own Black Consciousness Movement [which] began, it seems, just as the last vestiges of Africville were being reduced to rubble" (2002a, 295). Jones appears in the documentary mentioned

in note 47, *Hymn to Freedom*, Part 2: Nova Scotia, "Against the Tides: The Jones Family" (Almeta Speaks Production 1994, dir. Sylvia Hamilton).

55 Another account of the history of Africville can be found in James W. St G. Walker's contribution to the "Special Africadian Issue" of the *Dalhousie Review* (Walker 1997), which contains – besides other essays – poetry, fiction, and drama by Sylvia Hamilton, David Woods, Walter Borden, and Frederick Ward.

56 Moynagh suggests that this literary production participates in an anti-modernist response to modernization that is otherwise the idiom of a white Nova Scotian self-fashioning that privileges "rural life as a place of moral, psychic, and social regeneration" (1998, 16). As Wyile highlights, the razing of Africville "represents within the Folk paradigm" – explored by Ian McKay (1994) and referenced by Moynagh – "a substantial irony … as a community, Africville more closely approximated the touted virtues of the folk paradigm than did the mainstream culture that effectively destroyed it in the name of modernization" (2011, 115–16). See also "Mapping Africadia's Imaginary Geography: An Interview with George Elliott Clarke" (Moynagh 1996) and Leslie Sanders's "Anti/Modern Spaces: African Canadians in Nova Scotia (1999), in which she makes the troubling claim that "despite Nova Scotia's official policy regarding 'the folk,' modernity leaves us few options for their representation without romanticism, condescension, yearning and retreat" (1999, 120).

57 See "Summons" in Woods's *Native Song: Poetry and Paintings* (1990). His poems "Mood Indigo" (named after a composition by Duke Ellington, who had in-laws in Africville) and "The Spirit of Africville" are included as "Poem #1" and "Poem #2" on Sealy's *Africville Suite*, to which he also contributed the cover painting.

58 The play was first published in *Two by George* (1996), which also included *Gideon's Blues*. Other plays by Boyd include *Shine Boy* (produced at the Neptune Theatre in Halifax in 1988), *Wade in the Water* (2005), and *Le Code Noir* (produced by Montreal's Black Theatre Workshop in 2009). Boyd has also worked for radio, television, and film.

59 In an introduction to the play, Clarke observes that his name "suggests he is 'minor'" (G.E. Clarke 2003b, 394). His historical counterpart would have been the aforementioned Charles Coleman.

60 His historical counterpart was a forty-year-old "trained social worker employed by the province, Peter MacDonald" from Cape Breton, who "exhibited some empathy with Africvilleans and appreciated their long struggle, and he was able to win the trust of most residents" (Clairmont 2010b, 68, 69).

61 In discussing the play, Wyile suggests that Clancy is a key figure in the play not only because he acts as intermediary between the city and the community, but also "because Boyd portrays him as the repository of the divergent and contradictory impulses of white authority," speaking "the language of liberal improvement and racial reconciliation" that masks "whites' arrogant

presumption of the authority to tell Blacks how to live their lives even after restricting their opportunities to live otherwise" (2011, 117).

62 Other writers contributing to the Africadian Renaissance are not mainly concerned with Africville; in the words of one of the characters of Walter Borden's *Tightrope Time* (2005), originally published in 1986 and also excerpted in Clarke's anthology (1991, 2:31–42), this extraordinary one-person play is "not so much an historical documentation of the quest by a people for a place in the Nova Scotian or indeed the Canadian mosaic, as it is an illumination of the resilience of the human spirit" (Borden 2005, 17).

63 Prior to the opening, controversy erupted over the hiring of a white Anglican priest, Carole Nixon, as executive director of the Africville Historical Trust, overseeing further implementation of the Africville plans (Warnica 2011). Nixon has since been replaced by Sunday Miller.

64 There are pertinent connections between the memory work and the cultural and communal present-building around Africville, the reactivation of the Montreal Charles Este/Negro Community Centre, and, as we will see, the memorialization of Hogan's Alley in Vancouver.

65 At the same time, the Oklahoma transition from territory to state in 1908 came with legislation against the black vote and in favour of segregation. Canadian authorities were advertising in the United States around the same time for new settlers. Canadian public reaction to black arrivals, however, was hostile (Winks 300–6; Vernon 2008, 48–57; Mathieu 2010, 22–60).

66 Vernon also mentions, among others, Ian Samuels, Archie Crail, Tololwa Mollel, Nigel Darbasie, Trevor Lawrence, Minister Faust, Kaie Kellough, Selwyn Davis, and Troy Burle Bailey; their "work is connected to the prairies, either because they currently live and write there, or because they have spent some time on the prairies" (2008, 16). Vernon herself was part of this second wave; her family moved from Honduras to Alberta in 1981, and at school she was one of two black students in her class (Vernon 2008, 189–90). Because she took her PhD at the University of Victoria, some of her poetry is published in Wayde Compton's anthology of black British Columbian writers, *Bluesprint* (2001, 282–90). She now lives in Toronto.

67 Suzette Mayr also uses humour to approach race and gender, together with the theme of metamorphosis, in her novels *Moon Honey* (1995) and *Venous Hum* (2004) (see Brydon 2008; Mayr in T.H. Thomas 2006, 164–77). In 2011, she published the novel *Monoceros*, which won the 2012 ReLit Award and the City of Calgary W.O. Mitchell Award.

68 In addition to Winks's study of black Canadian history, Vernon cites the alternative histories by Palmer (1982), Shepard (1997), Utendale (1985), and Waiser (2005) (Vernon 2008, 47).

69 The narrator notes that the Queen's English is used for the benefit of white society, while black American speech establishes black community credentials (1990, 17–18). She comes to understand that the latter is used "to entertain one another, and to affirm their 'Blackness.' They were people with ambivalent feelings about their isolation from other Blacks. They had no desire to return

to the America that their parents had fled, nor did they wish to be completely swallowed by the white society in which they all lived" (18).

70 Foggo offers here a brief account of A. Philip Randolph's role in the organization of black railroad worker unions (60–1), which we have encountered in the earlier discussion of black anglophone Montreal. In Lawrence Hill's *Some Great Thing*, the father is a former Winnipeg railroad employee.

71 The narrator remembers "the intoxicating music of Sam and Dave, the Temptations, Joe Tex, Ben E. King, and Solomon Burke" (38). She is confirmed in her blackness by James Brown (52), and she rebukes her relatives for listening to country gospel records instead of black gospel (65–6). Her white friend, who, much to her amusement, renounces her whiteness (49), listens to James Taylor's "Sweet Baby James" and "Fire and Rain" (48).

72 As the epilogue reveals, the narrator reneged on her earlier commitment not to engage in the practice (118).

73 Claire Harris arrived from Trinidad in 1966 and moved to Calgary. Beginning with *Fables from the Women's Quarters* (1984), she problematizes language and gives voice to silenced subjects, critiquing racism, sexism, and the consequences of colonialism. After publishing further poetry and *Drawing Down a Daughter* (1992), Harris portrays in *She* (2000) a West Indian woman's multiple personality disorder that is related to historical contexts.

74 Zackodnik points out that the speaker's "renegotiation of identity … frequently turns on ambivalent feelings for her unborn child, her husband, the Caribbean, and her own mother" (1999, 163).

75 The passage is perhaps also a comment on publishing in the Caribbean (see G.E. Clarke 2012, 116–31), echoing the concerns about women's access to writing opportunities there that are thematized by Agnant (Boucher 2005, 204).

76 The story was published separately as "A Matter of Fact" (C. Harris 1988).

77 This, however, is before the man introduces himself to her father as "Burri," inciting the interest of the narrator, who has heard his name years earlier in her great-aunt's story. Is the "memory" of thinking of introducing herself to him as "La Diablesse in waiting" *before* that moment, then, editorializing by a later self? This idea is supported by the next sentence, which seems to suggest that she did not actually have the thought at the time: "Well … not really" (59) and a subsequent comment about fact and fiction (see below). On the other hand, such an inexplicable anticipation would correspond to the non-linear temporality suggested by the text generally.

78 The time sequence is questioned further in a sequel, in which a police report and a retired officer indicate 1959 as the date of the mysterious accident (63–6), not three years prior to Armstrong's 1954 visit to her father (62), that is, 1951, or four years earlier when the old woman tells the story (i.e., 1947).

79 As Zackodnik observes, "throughout this collection, Harris resists … resolving what is problematic and contradictory" (1999, 176).

80 Beckford suggests that the "old storyteller's tale is based on the West African tradition of storytelling, and the belief in 'nommo,' *the word*, a belief that utterance breathes life" (Beckford 2011, 199).

81 Rudy refers here to an account by Ian Sowton (1995) of a reading by Harris at York University in 1993.

82 As Rudy's discussion rightly emphasizes, in its self-reflexive speculations about fact and fiction, Harris's text is an example of the theory-fictions produced by other feminist writers at the time, like Daphne Marlatt and Nicole Brossard.

83 Harris ironizes even this somewhat essentializing view of "African" storytelling when she discusses the great-aunt's performance: "There is something of the ancestral, of Africa in this" (52), commenting later, "I am sure the story was written as I have written it because that is how the books say Afro-Caribbean tales are told. Your books, I mean" (58–9). She then, somewhat misleadingly, continues: "But this is not really about style. This is about plot" (59).

84 The old storyteller chastises the small boy, aligning his desire for a linear narrative and "progress" of the story with patriarchal trust in evidence only: "You is man, all you don't have no real sense. Is not only what you see that there" (54).

85 See E.A. Williams (2004), Blumenthal (2006), and Austen (2009), who offers a valuable analysis of Harris's use of the visual space on the page. On the difficulties of the diasporic subject in *She*, Austen comments: "While migrancy may broaden the term 'home' to apply to multiple spaces, it simultaneously complicates one's ability to claim a space of belonging" (2009, 183).

86 Edugyan later authors the Giller Prize–winning *Half-Blood Blues* (2011), about a black German and other jazz musicians in Germany and France under the Nazi regime.

87 Vernon mentions a number of other prairie "communities settled by the black pioneers – Amber Valley, Brooks, Junkins (Wildwood), Clyde, Campsie, Keystone, Maidstone, Rosetown, Eldon, Turtleford County, and the Swan River Valley" (8–9).

88 In her lecture *Dreaming of Elsewhere: Observations on Home* (2014), Edugyan reflects further on the notion of return and "the problem of belonging, of *home*, both as a place and as an idea" (2014, 5–6). Although a second-generation Canadian who "had never set foot in Africa in my life," she "knew" her first trip there "would be, in some ways, a kind of return" (19). She is promptly asked when she and her siblings will "move back" (22). As Edugyan narrates how they are presented with the possible privileges but also obligations, ingrained opinions, and prejudices towards others that would await them, she makes a point of repeating the words of a song playing in the background that would also seem to speak to Samuel and Jacob's situation: "Are you free from the curses of your ancestors?" and "Are you free from the curses of the past?" (22–3). Edugyan concludes her lecture with the idea that home is not "a place, only" but "a way of thinking, an *idea* of belonging, which matters more to us than the thing itself" (32).

89 "Just as Samuel inherits a house in Aster, so too Edugyan, a black prairies author, inherits the whole historic and cultural legacy of the black prairies;

it is hers to work with, her novel announces, and to imaginatively inhabit" (Vernon 2008, 204).

90 As Vernon observes, "Edugyan's legend is richly allusive, even allegorical" (2008, 208); on the one hand, it points to the original black settlers' need to keep the bigoted earlier settlers, who resent their presence, at bay; on the other hand, the incomplete wall may allegorize "the pioneers' incomplete attempts at self-isolation" (209) and the subsequent effacement of their all-black status.

91 I am thinking, for instance, of Faulkner's *Absalom, Absalom*, García Márquez's *One Hundred Years of Solitude*, and certainly of Toni Morrison's *Beloved*.

92 Ray and Eudora Frank evince extremely reactionary ideas (149–53), including hostility to immigration, a belief in eugenics – including "doctor-approved marriages" and ending the lives of those "who would have died in an older society" (152–3) – and approval of the forced institutionalization of handicapped people (153).

93 That there is only one surviving twin may be a reference to the Welsh case or perhaps signals the end of the pernicious power associated with twins in the novel.

94 The twins themselves toy with that image when they hand Ama a book entitled *The Devils* in lieu of a Bible (69).

95 Aster is also named as the setting in two of the stories in Edugyan's translated collection *Diese Fremden* (2007), which has been published so far only in German. In the story, "Joe," a Ghanaian Canadian immigrant, discovers that his son's refusal of a traditional African meal has been caused by racist slurs in school. When he visits the school, which at this point is identified as being in Aster (112), and forces his son to punch the perpetrator, the principal of the school intervenes. The father's immigrant experience and the child's initially enigmatic behaviour in response to racism have a number of parallels in Edugyan's novel. In "Francis," a kind of magic realist ghost story, the titular character has to tell his wife when she returns after an absence that she has died several weeks ago, her gravestone being one of the largest in the town of Aster (2007, 40). This story finds a parallel in the novel's emphasis on Maud's resting place in Aster's Canadian soil.

96 Vernon points out that "until recently many black authors, at least those in Canada, felt that part of their job was to be historians, so that black Canadian history wouldn't get erased from the public imagination" (in W. Compton 2005).

97 Booker is also a musician and has lived in Canada since 1966.

98 Compton elaborates on his understanding of discourses on race, mixed race, and passing in his essay "Pheneticizing versus Passing" (2010, 19–59).

99 According to the 2001 census, Hudson writes, "black people make up 0.6 per cent of the population of the province" (2007, 154) or 24,465 individuals (173n4).

100 Compton points out that "our communities developed beyond the sites of slavery; interracial families are our standard experience rather than an excep-

tional or suspect one; our dialect is the same as the dominant society" (2010, 14).

101 Compton describes Douglas elsewhere as "a rampaging colonizer who used gunboats to blast local First Nations people into compliance on occasion" and Gibbs as "an arch-capitalist who eventually advocated that B.C. be annexed by the United States." Compton pursues, "I don't regard these forebears as people to emulate. Nevertheless, I'm glad to have their writing" (2005). On Gibbs, see also Kilian (2008, passim).

102 For a more detailed analysis of Gibbs's elaborate style, see Compton (2010, 61–81).

103 These testimonies by Nora Hendrix (the paternal grandmother of Jimi Hendrix), Rosa Pryor, Austin Phillips, and Dorothy Nealy were originally transcribed and published by Daphne Marlatt and Carole Itter in *Opening Doors: Vancouver's East End* (1979).

104 As mentioned earlier, Gale lived her later life in Vancouver. Her "expatriate" status from Quebec is suggested by the title of her second play, *Je me souviens: Memories of an Expatriate Anglophone Montréalaise Québecoise Exiled in Canada* (2001).

105 For Bourriaud, "emblematic figures" in this context are not only the DJ but also the programmer (Bourriaud 2000, 29). They are producers of the "emergence of a new cultural configuration" that seems to answer the demands of Guy Debord's 1956 situationist "Methods of Detournement" (Debord 1981). Debord demanded that the "literary and artistic heritage of humanity should be used for partisan propaganda purposes … Any elements, no matter where they are taken from, can serve in making new combinations" (qtd in Bourriaud 2000, 29).

106 In this respect, Bourriaud's *Postproduction* (2000) re-articulates aspects of a postmodern aesthetics that emphasizes the active role of the audience and interaction to the point of blurring the line of producing and consuming art. Yet the "cultural" itself is marginalized here to the extent of its disappearance: any aesthetics of the transcultural that one might find here seems socially fairly indeterminate. While his aesthetics of the "encounter" puts a premium on sociability, the social dimensions mediated in this "contact zone" (to use Pratt's 1991 phrase) point mainly in the direction of de-scripting and defamiliarization.

107 Lewis makes it clear that for "African-American improvisers … sonic symbolism is often constructed with a view toward social instrumentality as well as form" (Lewis 2004, 133). Any elision of social specificity would radically underdetermine such forms of improvisation. Or as Walter M. Muyumba puts it, "Studying how musicians communicate in jazz performance is a way of developing a more cultural music theory and a more musical culture theory" (2009, 18).

108 For a recent extended discussion of Compton's relation to Brathwaite, see Smyth (2014).

109 See the sound sample available in Compton (2003b), "The Reinventing Wheel," at http://www.horizonzero.ca/flashsite/issue8/issue8.html?lang=en&section=compton. Compton discusses his developing performances of "The Reinventing Wheel" in "Turntable Poetry, Mixed Race, and Schizophonophilia" (W. Compton 2010, 183–201); see also Leow (2012, 50–64).

110 The year 1972 is, incidentally, Compton's year of birth. For his alterations of historical fact, see his conversation with Vernon and Edugyan in which he states that the section "Lost-Found Landmarks" is "a satire on Afrocentrism"; aware of the potential problems given that there is "so little awareness of actual black histories," he adds, however, that he is "probably rebelling a little against the representative status that lands on any minority writer" (in W. Compton 2005). Compton offers a full historical account of Hogan's Alley, together with comment on his own poetic sequence "Rune," in his substantial essay "Seven Routes to Hogan's Alley and Vancouver's Black Community" (2010, 83–144).

111 "So on this ground, / write; / within the sound / of this white limestone *vèvè*, / / talk / of the empty roads, / vessels of your head, / claypots, shards, ruins. / [...] / the Word becomes / again a god and walks among us / look, here are his rags, / here is his crutch and his satchel / of dreams; here is his hoe and his rude implements / / on this ground / on this broken ground" (Brathwaite 1973, 265–6).

CHAPTER 6

1 In stories literally involving projectors but also gaming and fantasy, Compton speculates about forms of virtuality that are co-opted for state counter-insurgency.

2 Afrofuturism is a term usually attributed to Mark Dery (1993); an inspiration for Turner's project, it "draws from non-Western cosmologies, mythology, fantasy, science, technology and history to posit new possible futures" (Turner 2012a, 47). Futuristic dimensions are also presented by other black Canadian writers working in speculative fiction, such as Nalo Hopkinson and Minister Faust (the pen name of educator, activist, and former NDP candidate Malcolm Azania). Hopkinson's *Brown Girl in the Ring* (1998) offers a post-economic-meltdown vision of downtown Toronto in which its remaining core is described as a doughnut hole: "That's what they call it when an inner city collapses and people run to the suburbs … Just a little bit of history. You like it?" (1998, 10–11). Faust's science fiction novel *The Coyote Kings, Book One: Space-Age Bachelor Pad* (2004) features characters of African descent, Africentric and science fiction themes, and the search for ancient African technology in the Edmonton inner-city neighbourhood of Kush, also the setting of his subsequent *The Alchemists of Kush* (2011).

3 "Je parle et surtout j'écris en présence de toutes les langues du monde" (Glissant 1994, 31).

4 See my exploration of this aspect with regard to the first two novels by Agnant (Siemerling 2007).

5 Dionne Brand has stated that, in her own use of the demotic, she "didn't care who understood it or not. I never do anyway. That's one thing I decided about audience a long time ago. That the audience would simply have to walk in if they could and if they couldn't, well, they could go read something else" (in Butling 2005, 73).

6 Brand's comment in the previous note is an example of the limits of such a desire. Doris Sommer is among those theorists who have studied intentional textual obstacles to universalizing reader assumptions (1999). In an interview with Maureen Moynagh, George Elliott Clarke offers the following "map" of readers he has in mind: "I'm writing for anyone who reads English, although I do have certain audiences in mind. I am very interested in being read by my own fellow Black Nova Scotians, or to use my word, Africadians. I'm very interested in having some standing within my own community as a writer people know, and as a writer they may enjoy reading or hearing. I'm also interested in the larger community of people in Nova Scotia, and in the Maritimes in general, because part of my project is to make them more aware of our contributions and our historical presence in this part of Canada. Then there is the even larger audience of English Canadians, who often are unaware of our existence in this area. And then there is the United States, particularly African Americans, who many of us are descended from and who represent our major 'ethnic connection,' and so I feel that we have a bond, or a potential bond with them that ought to be further developed" (in Moynagh 1996, 72).

7 To recall Derrida's point: "At the end of the day the judge, the arbiter, or the addressee do have to be *also* witnesses; they do have to be able to testify, in their turn, before their conscience or before others, to what they have attended, to what they have been present at, to what they happened to be in the presence of: the testimony of the witness in the witness box" (Derrida 2000, 200; cf. Baucom 2007, 177).

8 For an extended discussion of Hartman's gesture, see Fred Moten's *In the Break: The Aesthetics of the Black Radical Tradition* (2003).

9 Similar questions are raised by Marcus Wood in *Slavery, Empathy, and Pornography* (2002). He examines, for example, John Stedman's *Narrative, of a Five Years' Expedition, against the Revolted Negroes of Surinam, in Guiana, on the Wild Coast of South Africa; From the Years 1772, to 1777* (1796). Wood also comments on the illustrations produced by William Blake and other engravers for this work, especially in the context of the consumption of pornography at the end of the eighteenth and the beginning of the nineteenth century. On Stedman, see also H. Thomas (2000, 125–66).

10 Tompkins has interpreted the exceptional success of Harriet Beecher Stowe's *Uncle Tom's Cabin* in the US pre–Civil War context in this perspective. By presenting individuals subjected to slavery as members of families first and racially marked others second, Stowe successfully appealed to American read-

ers' strong sentiments about family and belonging, showing black children brutally separated from parents, and husbands from wives. Readers were thus made to transfer their "familiar" emotions to those held in slavery. Tompkins explains in this way the "Sentimental Power" of the novel to affect social change (1985, 122–46), and Stowe's novel is often credited with having effectively influenced American history. It is important, however, to understand that the novel achieves these goals by itself relying heavily on stereotypical portrayals. As this example demonstrates, the side effects of such hermeneutics include almost certainly an aspect of projection rather than a purely Levinasian recognition of the other. This very aspect of projection allows for the transference of emotion, with all its positive and problematic implications.

11 In *Poetic Justice*, Nussbaum maintains that novels have the power of bridging distance and facilitating empathy across social divides. She argues that the resulting "ability to imagine the concrete ways in which people different from oneself grapple with disadvantage" is so valuable that it should serve in economic and legal decision-making (1995, xvi).

12 I have suggested some reasons for this circumstance in the introduction. For another discussion and a survey of omissions in relevant materials, see G.E. Clarke (2005c, 11–14).

13 See, for example, Peter Hudson's comment on Wilson's novel (Hudson 2007) or George Elliott Clarke's writing on Dantin (Eugène Seers) (2002a, 163–80) and Haliburton (2002, 86–106; 1994; 1997b).

14 As Ishmael Reed writes, *Uncle Tom's Cabin* "borrowed so liberally from Josiah Henson's 1849 autobiography that ... Martin Delany proposed, in a letter to Frederick Douglass, that Stowe's publisher pay Henson five thousand dollars" (2009, 381).

15 Philip was a founder of Vision 21, a coalition-building attempt interested, as she states, "in creating a space and place for art by African, Asian, and First Nations artists" (in P. Saunders 2005, 210)

16 For several full discussions of these issues, see Siemerling and Casteel (2010, 3–84).

17 In *A Map to the Door of No Return*, she writes, "I know many nationalists along this journey. Each square foot of the Americas has its nationalism. And probably the most powerful of these nationalisms can be experienced in the U.S. But Jamaica, Brazil, Antigua, even the volcanic Montserrat are no less virulent. There are flags and anthems, even a real love for each place – the ways and objects and events which collect into nations. But the Door of No Return opens all nationalisms to their imaginative void" (2001, 49).

18 "For Canada, / in the effort of becoming a space / of true true be/longing" (1992, 5). Philip expresses the complexity of that relation in an interview with Patricia Saunders: "I am more than a little wary of the thrust in this country to lay claim to people's histories and cultures under the rubric of multiculturalism and subsume them under the brand of Canada. I have just argued that I believe that the configuration of Canada allowed me a certain space to create

something. Does that make the work Canadian? Perhaps. But it is a more complex and problematic definition of Canadian. Because it has to do with writing up against a new space that threatened to overwhelm and erase" (in P. Saunders 2005, 212).

19 Walcott speaks of "the regressive localism of Clarke's melancholic cataloguing" (2003, 22). Vernon comments, "But dismissing the archival method as regressively local and melancholic, as Walcott does, seems a dangerously dehistoricising move, one that does nothing to address the nation's historical amnesia when it comes to black history" (2008, 29).

20 Clarke vehemently critiques Gilroy's *The Black Atlantic* in the introduction to *Odysseys Home* (2002a, 8–9); in the same volume, he offers another defence of cultural nationalism in "Treason of the Black Intellectuals?" (182–210).

21 As Hortense Spillers reminds us in the context of the United States, "the internationalist dimension … already constitutes the horizon of black consciousness" long before Du Bois, while at the same time the "African-American community has waged a constant struggle to achieve national belonging; to gain access to the protective mechanisms and constitutional guarantees of the nation-state, and to be allowed to express the dimensions of juridical personality that distinguishes the citizen in the dignity of the public square" (2012, 3).

WORKS CITED

Abbott, Anderson Ruffin. Abbott Papers. Baldwin Room, Toronto Reference Library

Adams, Nehemiah. 1854. *A South-Side View of Slavery; or Three Months at the South in 1854*. Boston: T.R. Marvin. http://utc.iath.virginia.edu/proslav/presnaat.html

Adams, Rachel. 2009. *Continental Divides: Remapping the Cultures of North America*. Chicago: University of Chicago Press

Africville Genealogical Society (AGS). 2010. *The Spirit of Africville*. With contributions by Donald Clairmont, Stephen Kimber, Bridglal Pachai, and Charles Saunders. 2nd ed. Halifax: Formac Publishing

Agamben, Giorgio. 1999. *Remnants of Auschwitz: The Witness and the Archive*. Translated by Daniel Heller-Roazen. New York: Zone Books

Agnant, Marie-Célie. 1995. *La dot de Sara*. Montreal: Éditions du Remue-ménage

– 1997. *Le silence comme le sang*. Montreal: Éditions du Remue-ménage

– 2001. *Le livre d'Emma*. Montreal: Éditions du Remue-ménage

– 2002. "Écrire en marge de la marge." In *Reconfigurations: Canadian Literatures and Postcolonial Identities/Littératures canadiennes et identités postcoloniales*, edited by Marc Maufort and France Bellarsi, 15–20. Brussels: Peter Lang

– 2003a. *La légende du poisson amoureux*. Montreal: Mémoire d'encrier

– 2003b. *L'oranger magique: Conte d'Haïti*. Montreal: 400 Coups

– 2004. "Écrire pour tuer le vide du silence." *Canadian Woman Studies/Les Cahiers de la Femme* 23, no. 2 (Winter): 86–91

– 2006. *The Book of Emma*. Translated by Zilpha Ellis. Toronto: Insomniac Press

– 2007. *Un alligator nommé Rosa*. Montreal: Éditions du Remue-ménage

Alexis, André. 1994. *Despair and Other Stories of Ottawa*. Toronto: Coach House Press

– 1995. "Borrowed Blackness." *This Magazine* 28, no. 8 (May): 14–20. LexisNexis. 1 August 2003. http://lexis-nexis.com

– 1998. *Childhood: A Novel*. New York: Henry Holt

– 1999. *Lambton Kent: A Play*. Toronto: Gutter Press

Alfred, Taiaiake. 1999. *Peace, Power, Righteousness: An Indigenous Manifesto*. Don Mills, ON: Oxford University Press

Algoo-Baksh, Stella. 1994. *Austin C. Clarke: A Biography*. Toronto: ECW Press
Anatol, Giselle Liza. 2004. "A Feminist Reading of Soucouyants in Nalo Hopkinson's *Brown Girl in the Ring* and *Skin Folk*." *Mosaic* 37, no. 3: 33–50
Anderson, Benedict. 1983. *Imagined Communities: Reflections on the Origin and Spread of Nationalism*. London: Verso
Anderson, Osborne Perry. 1861. *A Voice from Harper's Ferry*. Boston: Printed for the author
Andrews, William L. 1986. *To Tell a Free Story: The First Century of Afro-American Autobiography, 1760–1865*. Urbana: University of Illinois Press
– 1998. "Narrating Slavery." In *Teaching African American Literature*, edited by Maryemma Graham and Sharon Pineault-Burke, 12–30. New York: Routledge
– 2003. *Classic African American Women's Narratives*. Oxford: Oxford University Press
Antwi, Phanuel. 2011. "Hidden Signs, Haunting Shadows: Literary Currencies of Blackness in Upper Canadian Texts." In *Open Access Dissertations and Theses*. http://oatd.org
Appiah, K. Anthony. 1986. "The Uncompleted Argument: Du Bois and the Illusions of Race." In *'Race,' Writing, and Difference*, edited by Henry Louis Gates Jr, 21–37. Chicago and London: University of Chicago Press
– 1992. *In My Father's House: Africa in the Philosophy of Culture*. New York: Oxford University Press
– 1996. "Race, Culture, Identity: Misunderstood Connections." In *Color Conscious: The Political Morality of Race*, by K. Anthony Appiah and Amy Gutmann, 30–105. Princeton, NJ: Princeton University Press
– 2005. *The Ethics of Identity*. Princeton and Oxford: Princeton University Press
Armstrong, Robert Plant. 1981. *The Powers of Presence: Consciousness, Myth, and Affecting Presence*. Philadelphia: University of Pennsylvania Press
Assmann, Aleida. 2006. *Der Lange Schatten der Vergangenheit: Erinnerungskultur und Geschichtspolitik*. München: Beck
Atwood, Margaret. 1970. *The Journals of Susanna Moodie: Poems*. Toronto: Oxford University Press
– 1997. *In Search of Alias Grace: On Writing Canadian Historical Fiction*. Charles R. Bronfman Lecture in Canadian Studies. Ottawa: University of Ottawa Press
Audet, Francis-J. 1932. "William Brown (1737–1789). Premier Imprimeur, Journaliste et Libraire de Québec. Sa Vie et Ses Oeuvres." In *Mémoires de la Société Royale Du Canada*, 97–112. Third series, vol. 26, section 1
Austen, Veronica. 2009. "Inhabitable Spaces in Claire Harris's *She*." *Studies in Canadian Literature* 34, no. 2: 178–93
– 2011. "*Zong!*'s 'Should We?' Questioning the Ethical Representation of Trauma." *English Studies in Canada* 37, nos 3–4: 61–81
Austin, David. 2007. "All Roads Led to Montreal: Black Power, the Caribbean, and the Black Radical Tradition in Canada." *Journal of African American History* 92, no. 4: 516–39

– 2013. *Fear of a Black Nation: Race, Sex and Security in Sixties Montreal*. Toronto: Between the Lines

Back, Francis. 2005. "Autour du 'Nigger Rock': Rapport de Recherche sur la Communauté Noire dans la Région de Saint-Armand/Philipsburg et sur la Famille Luke." Rapport présenté au Ministère de la Culture et de la Communication, Direction générale de la Montérégie

Backhouse, Constance. 1999. *Colour-Coded: A Legal History of Racism in Canada, 1900–1950*. Toronto: published for the Osgoode Society for Canadian Legal History by University of Toronto Press

Baldwin, James. 1965. "Everybody's Protest Novel." In *Notes of a Native Son*, by James Baldwin. London: Corgi

Banks, Russell. 1998. *Cloudsplitter*. Toronto: Vintage

Bannerji, Himani. 2000. *The Dark Side of the Nation: Essays on Multiculturalism, Nationalism, and Gender*. Toronto: Canadian Scholars' Press

Baucom, Ian. 2001. "Specters of the Atlantic." *South Atlantic Quarterly* 100, no. 1: 61–82

– 2005. *Specters of the Atlantic: Finance Capital, Slavery, and the Philosophy of History*. Durham, NC: Duke University Press

Bayne, Clarence S. 2004. "The Origins of Black Theatre in Montreal." *Canadian Theatre Review* 118: 34–40

Bearden, Jim, and Linda Jean Butler. 1977. *Shadd: The Life and Times of Mary Shadd Cary*. Toronto: New Canada Publications

Beckford, Sharon Morgan. 2011. *Naturally Woman: The Search for Self in Black Canadian Women's Literature*. Toronto: Inanna

Benítez-Rojo, Antonio. (1996) 2001. *The Repeating Island: The Caribbean and the Postmodern Perspective*, 2nd ed. Translated by James E. Maraniss. Durham and London: Duke University Press

Benjamin, Walter. 1968. *Illuminations*. Edited by Hanna Arendt and translated by Harry Zohn. New York: Schocken

– 1999. *The Arcades Project*. Translated by Howard Eiland and Kevin McLaughlin. Cambridge, MA: Harvard University Press

Bergad, Laird W. 2007. *The Comparative Histories of Slavery in Brazil, Cuba, and the United States*. Cambridge and New York: Cambridge University Press

Bernabei, Franca. 2013–14. "Shaking Up the Subject in *Ossuaries*: Dionne Brand's Lyrical Anti-Lyric." *MaComère* 14, nos 1–2: 204–20

Bernabé, Jean, Patrick Chamoiseau, and Raphaël Confiant. 1993. *Éloge de la Créolité/In Praise of Creoleness*. Translated by M.B. Taleb-Khyar. Paris: Gallimard

Bernier, Silvie. 2002. *Les heritiers d'Ulysse*. Outremont, QC: Lanctôt

Bertley, L. 1976. *Montreal's Oldest Black Congregation: Union Church*. Pierrefonds: Bilongo Publishers

– 1980. "UNIA of Montreal 1917–97." PhD thesis, Concordia University

Bhabha, Homi K., ed. 1990. *Nation and Narration*. London and New York: Routledge

Bibb, Henry. (1849) 2005. *Narrative of the Life and Adventures of Henry Bibb, an American Slave*. With an introduction by Lucius C. Matlack. Mineola, NY: Dover. http://docsouth.unc.edu/neh/bibb/bibb.html

Black, Ayanna, ed. 1992. *Voices: Canadian Writers of African Descent*. Toronto: HarperCollins

Blackburn, Robin. 1997. *The Making of New World Slavery: From the Baroque to the Modern, 1492–1800*. London and New York: Verso

Blair, Jennifer. 2012. "The Queer Racing of Children in Dionne Brand's *What We All Long For*." *Studies in Canadian Literature/Études en littérature canadienne* 37, no. 1: 47–65

Blassingame, John W., ed. 1977. *Slave Testimony: Two Centuries of Letters, Speeches, Interviews, and Autobiographies*. Baton Rouge: Louisiana State University Press

Blatchford, Christie. 1980. "Johnson Shot While Kneeling or Crouching, Pathologist Says." *Toronto Star*, 28 October

Blumenthal, Anna S. 2006. "Claire Harris's *She*: The MPD Metaphor and the Post-Colonial Caribbean Woma." *Dalhousie Review* 86, no. 3: 359–71

Boltanski, Luc. 1999. *Distant Suffering: Morality, Media and Politics*. Translated by Graham Burchell. Cambridge Cultural Social Studies. Cambridge and New York: Cambridge University Press

Borden, Walter. (1986) 2005. *Tightrope Time: Ain't Nuthin' More than Some Itty Bitty Madness between Twilight & Dawn*. Toronto: Playwrights Canada Press

Born, Georgina. 2005. "On Musical Mediation: Ontology, Technology, and Creativity." *Twentieth-Century Music* 2, no. 1: 7–36.

Boucher, Colette. 2005. "Québec-Haïti. Littérature transculturelle et souffle d'oralité: Une entrevue avec Marie-Célie Agnant." *Ethnologies* 27, no. 1: 195–221

Boucher, Colette, and Thomas C. Spear, eds. 2013. *Paroles et silences chez Marie-Célie Agnant: L'oublieuse mémoire d'Haïti*. Paris: Karthala

Bourriaud, Nicolas. 2000. *Postproduction: Culture as Screenplay: How Art Reprograms the World*. New York: Lukas & Sternberg

– 2002. *Relational Aesthetics*. Translated by Simon Pleasance and Fronza Woods and with the participation of Mathieu Copeland. Collection Documents sur l'art. Dijon: Les presses du réel

Boyd, George Elroy. 2003. "Consecrated Ground." In *Testifyin': Contemporary African Canadian Drama*, edited by Djanet Sears, 2:391–483. Toronto: Playwrights Canada Press

Boyd, Neil. 1988. *The Last Dance: Murder in Canada*. Scarborough, ON: Prentice-Hall Canada

Bradley, David. 1981. *The Chaneysville Incident: A Novel*. New York: Harper & Row.

Brand, Dionne. 1988. *Sans Souci and Other Stories*. Stratford, ON: Williams-Wallace

– 1990. *No Language Is Neutral*. Toronto: Coach House Press

– 1991. *No Burden to Carry: Narratives of Black Working Women in Ontario, 1920s–1950s*. Toronto: Women's Press

– 1994. *Bread out of Stone: Recollections, Sex, Recognitions, Race, Dreaming, Politics*. Toronto: Coach House Press

– 1996. *In Another Place, Not Here*. Toronto: A.A. Knopf Canada
– 1997. *Land to Light On*. Toronto: McClelland & Stewart.
– 1999. *At the Full and Change of the Moon*. Toronto: Vintage
– 2001. *A Map to the Door of No Return: Notes to Belonging*. Toronto: Doubleday Canada
– 2002. *Thirsty*. Toronto: McClelland & Stewart.
– 2005. *What We All Long For: A Novel*. Toronto: A.A. Knopf Canada
– 2006. *Inventory*. Toronto: McClelland & Stewart
– 2010. *Ossuaries*. Toronto: McClelland & Stewart
– 2014. *Love Enough: A Novel*. Toronto: Knopf Canada.
Brathwaite, Edward. 1973. *The Arrivants: A New World Trilogy*. Oxford: Oxford University Press
Braziel, Jana Evans, and Anita Mannur. 2003. "Nation, Migration, Globalization: Points of Contention in Diaspora Studies." In *Theorizing Diaspora: A Reader*, edited by Braziel and Mannur, 1–22. Malden, MA, and Oxford: Blackwell
Brecht, Bertolt. 1964. *Brecht on Theatre: The Development of an Aesthetic*. Translated by John Willett. London: Methuen
Brison, Susan J. 1999. "Trauma Narratives and the Remaking of the Self." In *Acts of Memory: Cultural Recall in the Present*, edited by Jonathan Crewe, Mieke Bal, and Leo Spitzer, 39–54. Hanover: Dartmouth College
Bristow, Peggy, ed. 1994a. *"We're Rooted Here and They Can't Pull Us Up": Essays in Canadian Women's History*. Toronto: University of Toronto Press
– 1994b. "'Whatever You Raise in the Ground You Can Sell It in Chatham': Black Women in Buxton and Chatham, 1850–60." In *"We're Rooted Here and They Can't Pull Us Up": Essays in Canadian Women's History*, edited by Peggy Bristow, 69–142. Toronto: University of Toronto Press
Brooks, Joanna. 1999. "John Marrant's *Journal:* Providence and Prophecy in the Eighteenth Century Atlantic." *The North Star: A Journal of African American Religious History* 3, no. 1: 1–21
Brooks, Joanna, and John Saillant, eds. 2002. *Face Zion Forward: First Writers of the Black Atlantic, 1785–1798*. Boston: Northeastern University Press
Brown, Christopher Leslie. 2006. *Moral Capital: Foundations of British Abolitionism*. Chapel Hill: University of North Carolina Press
Brown, Hallie Q. 1926. *Homespun Heroines and Other Women of Distinction*. Xenia, OH: Aldine Publishing. http://docsouth.unc.edu/neh/brownhal/menu.html
Brown, William Wells. (1861) 1986. "The Colored People of Canada." In *The Black Abolitionist Papers*, edited by C. Peter Ripley, 2:461–98. Chapel Hill and London: University of North Carolina Press
Brydon, Diana. 1992. "Reading Dionne Brand's 'Blues Spiritual for Mammy Prater.'" In *Inside the Poem: Essays and Poems in Honour of Donald Stephens*, 81–7. Toronto: Oxford University Press
– 2004. "George Elliott Clarke's Othello." *Canadian Literature* 182: 188–94
– 2006. "'A Place on the Map of the World': Locating Hope in Shani Mootoo's *He Drown She in the Sea* and Dionne Brand's *What We All Long For*." *MaComère* 8: 94–111

– 2007. "Dionne Brand's Global Intimacies: Practicing Affective Citizenship." *University of Toronto Quarterly* 76, no. 3: 990–1006

– 2008. "Global Friction, Alberta Fictions." *English Quarterly* 40, nos 1–2, special issue: *The Prairies in 3-D: Disorientations, Diversities, Dispersals*, 3–9

Bucknor, Michael A., and Daniel Coleman. 2005. "Introduction: Rooting and Routing Caribbean-Canadian Writing." *Journal of West Indian Literature* 14, nos 1–2: i–xliii

Butler, Judith. 1990. *Gender Trouble: Feminism and the Subversion of Identity*. New York and London: Routledge

– 1993. *Bodies That Matter: On the Discursive Limits of "Sex."* New York and London: Routledge

– 1997. *The Psychic Life of Power: Theories in Subjection*. Stanford, CA: Stanford University Press

Butling, Pauline. 2005. "Dionne Brand on Struggle and Community, Possibility and Poetry." Interview with Dionne Brand in *Poets Talk: Conversations with Robert Kroetsch, Daphne Marlatt, Erin Mouré, Dionne Brand, Marie Annharte Baker, Jeff Derksen, and Fred Wah*, edited by Pauline Butling and Susan Rudy, 63–87. Edmonton: University of Alberta Press

Callaghan, Morley. 1983. *The Loved and the Lost*. 1951. Toronto: Macmillan

Calliste, Agnes. 1987. "Sleeping Car Porters in Canada: An Ethnically Submerged Labour Market." *Canadian Ethnic Studies* 19, no. 1: 1–20

– 1988. "Blacks on Canadian Railways." *Canadian Ethnic Studies* 20, no. 2: 36–52

Campbell, Mark V. 2010. "Remixing Relationality: 'Other/Ed' Sonic Modernities of Our Present." PhD diss., University of Toronto

Cartwright, Keith. 2006. "'To Walk with the Storm': Oya as the Transformative 'I' of Nora Neale Hurston's Afro-Atlantic Callings." *American Literature* 78, no. 4: 741–67

Carty, Linda. 1994. "African Canadian Women and the State: 'Labour Only, Please.'" In *"We're Rooted Here and They Can't Pull Us Up": Essays in Canadian Women's History*, edited by Peggy Bristow, 193–229. Toronto: University of Toronto Press

Caruth, Cathy. 1996. *Unclaimed Experience: Trauma, Narrative, and History*. Baltimore: Johns Hopkins University Press

Casteel, Sarah Phillips. 2005. "Experiences of Arrival: Jewishness and Caribbean-Canadian Identity in Austin Clarke's *The Meeting Point*." *Journal of West Indian Literature* 14, nos 1–2: 113–40

– 2014. "Port and Plantation Jews in Contemporary Slavery Fiction of the Americas." *Callaloo* 37, no. 1: 112–29

Chamberlin, J. Edward. 1993. *Come Back to Me My Language: Poetry and the West Indies*. Toronto: McClelland & Stewart

Chamoiseau, Patrick, and Jean Bernabé. 1989. *Éloge de la Créolité*. Paris: Gallimard

Chariandy, David. 2001. "'Canada in Us Now': Locating the Criticism of Black Canadian Writing." *Essays on Canadian Writing* 75: 196–216

– 2004. "Haunted Diasporas: The Second Generation Stories of André Alexis." *Journal of West Indian Literature* 12, nos 1–2: 79–89

– 2005. "'That's What You Want, Isn't It?' Austin Clarke and the New Politics of Recognition." *Journal of West Indian Literature* 14, nos 1–2: 141–65
– 2006. "Postcolonial Diasporas." *Postcolonial Text* 2, no. 1. http://postcolonial.org/index.php/pct/article/view/440/159
– 2007a. "'The Fiction of Belonging': On Second-Generation Black Writing in Canada." *Callaloo* 30, no. 3: 818–29
– 2007b. *Soucouyant: A Novel of Forgetting*. Vancouver: Arsenal Pulp Press
Cheng, Anne Anlin. 2001. *The Melancholy of Race: Psychoanalysis, Assimilation, and Hidden Grief*. New York: Oxford University Press
Chiles, Katy. 2008. "Within and Without Raced Nations: Intratextuality, Martin Delany, and *Blake; or the Huts of America*." *American Literature* 80, no. 2: 323–52
Cho, Lily. 2011. "Affecting Citizenship: The Materiality of Melancholia." In *Narratives of Citizenship: Indigenous and Diasporic Peoples Unsettle the Nation State*, edited by Aloys N.M. Fleischmann, Nancy Van Styvendale, and Cody McCarroll, 107–27. Edmonton: University of Alberta Press
Clairmont, Donald. 2010a. "Africville: An Historical Overview." In Africville Genealogical Society, *The Spirit of Africville*, 35–56. Halifax: Formac Publishing
– 2010b. "Moving People: Relocation and Urban Renewal." In Africville Genealogical Society, *The Spirit of Africville*, 57–78. Halifax: Formac Publishing
Clairmont, Donald H., and Dennis William Magill. 1987. *Africville: The Life and Death of a Canadian Black Community*. Toronto: Canadian Scholars' Press
Clark, Geoffrey. 2010. "The Slave's Appeal: Insurance and the Rise of Commercial Property." In *The Appeal of Insurance*, edited by Geoffrey Clark and Greg Anderson, 52–74. Toronto: University of Toronto Press
Clarke, Austin C. 1964. *The Survivors of the Crossing*. Toronto: McClelland & Stewart
– 1965. *Amongst Thistles and Thorns*. Toronto: McClelland & Stewart
– 1967. *The Meeting Point*. Toronto: Macmillan of Canada
– 1971. *When He Was Free and Young and He Used to Wear Silks: Stories by Austin Clarke*. Toronto: Anansi
– 1986. *Nine Men Who Laughed*. Markham, ON: Penguin Books
– 1992. *In This City*. Toronto: Exile Editions
– 2002. *The Polished Hoe*. Toronto: Thomas Allen
Clarke, George Elliott. 1983. *Saltwater Spirituals and Deeper Blues*. Porters Lake, NS: Pottersfield Press
– 1990. *Whylah Falls*. Winlaw, BC: Polestar Press
–, ed. 1991. *Fire on the Water: An Anthology of Black Nova Scotian Writing*. 2 vols. Lawrencetown Beach, NS: Pottersfield Press
– 1992. "The Birmingham of Nova Scotia: The Weymouth Falls Justice vs. The Attorney General of Nova Scotia." In *Toward a New Maritimes*, edited by Ian McKay and Scott Milsom, 17–24. Charlottetown: Ragweed Press
– 1994. "White Niggers, Black Slaves: Slavery, Race, and Class in T.C. Haliburton's *The Clockmaker*." *Nova Scotia Historical Review* 14, no. 1: 13–40
–, ed. 1997a. *Eyeing the North Star: Directions in African-Canadian Literature*. Toronto: McClelland & Stewart

- 1997b. “Must We Burn Haliburton?” In *The Haliburton Bi-Centenary Chaplet: Papers Presented at the 1996 Thomas Raddall Symposium*, edited by Richard A. Davies, 1–40. Wolfville, NS: Gaspereau Press
- 1998a. “*Beatrice Chancy*: A Libretto in Four Acts.” *Canadian Theatre Review* 96: 62–77
- 1998b “Contesting a Model Blackness: A Meditation on African Canadian African Americanism, or the Structures of African-Canadianité.” *Essays on Canadian Writing* 63: 1–55 (repr. in G.E. Clarke, *Odysseys Home,* 2002a, 27–70)
- 1999. *Beatrice Chancy*. Victoria: Polestar
- 2000a. “Embracing Beatrice Chancy, or In Defence of Poetry.” *New Quarterly* 20, no. 3: 15–24
- 2000b. “An Interview with George Elliott Clarke (September 2000).” With Margery Fee and Sneja Gunew. *Canadian Literature*. http://canlit.ca/interviews.php?interview=9
- 2000c. “Racing Shelley, or Reading *The Cenci* as a Gothic Slave Narrative.” *European Romantic Review* 11, no. 2: 168–85
- 2001a. *Blue*. Vancouver: Polestar
- 2001b. *Execution Poems: The Black Acadian Tragedy of “George and Rue.”* Wolfville, NS: Gaspereau Press
- 2002a. *Odysseys Home: Mapping African-Canadian Literature*. Toronto: University of Toronto Press
- 2002b. “Raising Raced and Erased Executions in African-Canadian Literature: Or, Unearthing Angélique.” *Essays on Canadian Writing* 75: 30–61
- 2003a. “Inking BC in Black and Blue.” *Essays on Canadian Writing* 79: 76–82
- 2003b. “Making the ‘Damn’ Nation the Race’s ‘Salvation’: The Politics of George Elroy Boyd’s *Consecrated Ground*.” In *Testifyin’: Contemporary African Canadian Drama*, edited by Djanet Sears, 2:393–6. Toronto: Playwrights Canada Press
- 2003c. *Québécité: A Jazz Fantasia in Three Cantos*. Kentville, NS: Gaspereau Press
- 2005a. “Does (Afro-)Caribbean-Canadian Literature Exist? In the Caribbean?” *Journal of West Indian Literature* 14, nos 1–2: 260–304
- 2005b. *George & Rue*. Toronto: HarperCollins
- 2005c. “‘This Is No Hearsay’: Reading the Canadian Slave Narrative.” *Papers of the Bibliographical Society of Canada* 43, no. 1: 7–32. Proquest
- 2006. Foreword to *The Hanging of Angélique: The Untold Story of Canadian Slavery and the Burning of Old Montréal*, by Afua Cooper, xi–xviii. Toronto: HarperCollins
- 2007. *Trudeau: Long March, Shining Path*. Kentville, NS: Gaspereau Press
- 2008. “In Memory of Dr. Lorris Elliott, Ph.D. (1932–99): A Founding Author and Critic of African-Canadian Literature.” *Kola*. http://www.thefreelibrary.com/In+memory+of+Dr.+Lorris+Elliott,+Ph.D.+%281932-99%29%3A+a+founding+author...-a0180798289
- 2012. *Directions Home: Approaches to African-Canadian Literature*. Toronto: University of Toronto Press

Clarke, Lewis, and Milton Clarke. 1846. *Narratives of the Sufferings of Lewis and Milton Clarke: Sons of a Soldier of the Revolution*. Boston: Bella Marsh. http://docsouth.unc.edu/neh/clarkes/clarkes.html

Clarkson, John. 1971. *Clarkson's Mission to America*, edited and with an introduction by Charles Bruce Fergusson. Halifax: Public Archives of Nova Scotia

Clymer, Jeffory A. 2003. "Martin Delany's Blake and the Transnational Politics of Property." *American Literary History* 15, no. 4: 709–31

Cohen, Robin. (1997) 2008. *Global Diasporas: An Introduction*. London and New York: Routledge

Cole, Jean Lee. 2011. "Theresa and Blake: Mobility and Resistance in Antebellum African American Serialized Fiction." *Callaloo* 34, no. 1: 158–75

Coleman, Daniel. 1998. *Masculine Migrations: Reading the Postcolonial Male in 'New Canadian' Narratives*. Theory/Culture. Toronto: University of Toronto Press

– 2012. "Epistemological Cross-Talk: Melancholia, Historical Trauma, and Spiritual Cosmology." In *Crosstalk: Canadian and Global Imaginaries in Dialogue*, edited by Diana Brydon and Marta Dvořák, 53–72. Waterloo, ON: Wilfrid Laurier University Press

Coleman, Daniel, and Donald Goellnicht. 2002. "Introduction: 'Race' into the Twenty-First Century." *Essays on Canadian Writing* 75: 1–29

Collison, Gary. 1997. *Shadrach Minkins: From Fugitive Slave to Citizen*. Cambridge and London: Harvard University Press

Compton, Anne. 1998. "Standing Your Ground: George Elliott Clarke in Conversation." *Studies in Canadian Literature/Études en littérature canadienne* 23, no. 2: 138–64

Compton, Wayde. 1997. "'Even the Stars Are Temporal': The Historical Motion of George Elliott Clarke's *Saltwater Spirituals* and *Deeper Blues*." *North: New African Canadian Writing*, special issue edited by Peter Hudson. *West Coast Line* 22, no. 31.1: 156–63

– 1999. *49th Parallel Psalm*. Vancouver: Advance Editions

–, ed. 2001. *Bluesprint: Black British Columbian Literature and Orature*. Vancouver: Arsenal Pulp Press

– 2003a. "Culture at the Crossroads: Voodoo Aesthetics and the Axis of Blackness in Literature of the Black Diaspora." In *A Pepper-Pot of Cultures: Aspects of Creolization in the Caribbean*, special issue of *Matatu* (27–8), edited by Gordon Collier and Ulrich Fleischmann, 481–513

– 2003b. "The Reinventing Wheel: On Blending the Poetry of Cultures through Hip Hop Turntablism." *HorizonZero*. http://www.horizonzero.ca/flashsite/issue8/issue8.html?lang=en&section=compton

– 2004. *Performance Bond*. Vancouver: Arsenal Pulp Press

– 2005. "Black Writers in Search of a Place: A Three Way Conversation about History, Role Models, and Inventing 'The Black Atlantic.'" With Esi Edugyan and Karine Vernon. *The Tyee*. http://www.thetyee.ca/Life/2005/02/28/BlackWriters

– 2010. *After Canaan: Essays on Race, Writing, and Region*. Vancouver: Arsenal Pulp Press

– 2014. *The Outer Harbour: Stories*. Vancouver: Arsenal Pulp Press
Condé, Maryse. 1993. *La parole des femmes: Essai sur les romancières des Antilles de langue française*. Paris: L'Harmattan
Cook, Méira. 2005. "In Between: Dionne Brand's Poetics of Love and Resistance." In *Writing Lovers: Reading Canadian Love Poetry by Women*, 79–107. Montreal and Kingston: McGill-Queen's University Press
Cooper, Afua. 1994. "Black Women and Work in Nineteenth Century Canada West: Black Woman Teacher Mary Bibb." In *"We're Rooted Here and They Can't Pull Us Up": Essays in Canadian Women's History*, edited by Peggy Bristow, 143–70. Toronto: University of Toronto Press
– 2000. "'Doing Battle in Freedom's Cause': Henry Bibb, Abolitionism, Race Uplift, and Black Manhood 1842–1854." PhD diss., University of Toronto
– 2006. *The Hanging of Angélique: The Untold Story of Canadian Slavery and the Burning of Old Montréal*. With a foreword by George Elliott Clarke. Toronto: HarperCollins
Corr, John. 2009. "Affective Coordination and Avenging Grace: Dionne Brand's *In Another Place, Not Here*." *Canadian Literature* 201: 113–29
Craig, Terrence. 1987. *Racial Attitudes in English-Canadian Fiction: 1905–1980*. Waterloo, ON: Wilfrid Laurier University Press
Crouzet, François. 1980. "Toward an Export Economy: British Exports during the Industrial Revolution." *Explorations in Economic History* 17: 48–93
Cuder-Domínguez, Pilar. 2003. "African Canadian Writing and the Narration(s) of Slavery." *Essays on Canadian Writing* 79: 55–75
– 2014. "Transnational Memory and Haunted Black Geographies: Esi Edugyan's *The Second Life of Samuel Tyne*." In *Canadian Literature and Cultural Memory*, edited by Cynthia Sugars and Eleonor Ty, 432–43. Don Mills, ON: Oxford University Press
Curry, Bill. 2013. "Employers Nervous about Ottawa's Rush to Reform Foreign-Worker Program." *Globe and Mail*. http://www.theglobeandmail.com/news/politics/employers-fret-ottawas-rush-to-reform-foreign-worker-program/article11299146
Da Costa, Paulo. 2001. "An Interview with Dionne Brand." http://www.ciberkiosk.pt/brand.html. Now available as "Dionne Brand – A Map to the Door of No Return." Interview with Paulo Da Costa. 4 April 2013. http://www.paulodacosta.ca/a-map-to-the-door-of-no-return
Dalleo, Raphael. 2010. "Post-Grenada, Post-Cuba, Postcolonial: Rethinking Revolutionary Discourse in Dionne Brand's *In Another Place, Not Here*." *Interventions: International Journal of Postcolonial Studies* 12, no. 1: 63–74
Dash, Michael J. 1998. *The Other America: Caribbean Literature in a New World Context*. Charlottesville: University Press of Virginia
Davey, Frank. 1995. "The Literary Politics of Canadian Multiculturalism." In *Multiculturalism in North America and Europe: Social Practices – Literary Visions*, edited by Hans Braun and Wolfgang Klooss, 103–14. Trier: Wissenschaftlicher Verlag Trier

Davidson, Joyce, and Christine Milligan. 2004. Editorial: "Embodying Emotion Sensing Space: Introducing Emotional Geographies." *Social and Cultural Geography* 3, no. 4: 523–32

Davis, Andrea. 2004. "Diaspora, Citizenship and Gender: Challenging the Myth of the Nation in African Canadian Women's Literature." *Canadian Woman Studies* 23, no. 2: 64–9

– 2005. "Sex and the Nation: Performing Black Female Sexuality in Canadian Theatre." In *African Canadian Theatre*, edited by Maureen Moynagh, 107–22. Toronto: Playwrights Canada Press

– 2007. "Black Canadian Literature as Diaspora Transgression: *The Second Life of Samuel Tyne*." *Topia* 17: 31–49

Davis, David Brion. 1966. *The Problem of Slavery in Western Culture*. Ithaca, NY: Cornell University Press

– 1975. *The Problem of Slavery in the Age of Revolution, 1770–1823*. Ithaca, NY: Cornell University Press

Day, Samuel Phillips. 1864. *English America, or, Pictures of Canadian Places and People*. London: T Cauthley Newby

De Barros, Juanita. 2004. "'Setting Things Right': Medicine and Magic in British Guiana, 1803–38." *Slavery and Abolition* 25, no. 1: 28–50

Debord, Guy. 1981. "Methods of Detournement." In *Situationist International Anthology*. Edited and translated by Ken Knabb. Berkeley: Bureau of Public Secrets

de Certeau, Michel. (1984) 1988. *The Practice of Everyday Life*. Translated by Steven Rendall. Berkeley: University of California Press

Delany, Martin R. 1970. *Blake; or The Huts of America*. With an introduction by Floyd J. Miller. Boston: Beacon Press

2004. *The Condition, Elevation, Emigration, and Destiny of the Colored People of the United States; and, Official Report of the Niger Valley Exploring Party*. With an introduction by Toyin Falola. Classics in Black Studies. Amherst, NY: Humanity Books

Delisle, Jennifer Bowering. 2011. "'A Bruise Still Tender': David Chariandy's *Soucouyant* and *Cultural Memory*." *Ariel* 41, no. 2: 1–21

Derrida, Jacques. 2000. "'A Self-Unsealing Poetic Text': Poetics and the Politics of Witnessing." In *Revenge of the Aesthetic: The Place of Literature in Theory Today*, edited by Michael P. Clark, 180–207. Berkeley and Los Angeles: University of California Press

– (1994) 2006. *Specters of Marx: The State of Debt, the Work of Mourning and the New International*. Translated from the French by Peggy Kamuf, with an introduction by Bernd Magnus and Stephen Cullenberg. New York and London: Routledge

Dery, Mark. 1993. "Black to the Future: Interviews with Samuel R. Delaney, Greg Tate and Tricia Rose." *South Atlantic Quarterly* 92, no. 4: 735–78

Desloges, Yves, and Alain Gelly. 2002. *The Lachine Canal: Riding the Waves of Industrial and Urban Development, 1860–1950*. Translated by Donald Kellough. Sillery, QC: Septentrion

Dickason, Olive Patricia. 2002. *Canada's First Nations: A History of Founding Peoples from Earliest Times*. Don Mills, ON: Oxford University Press
Dickinson, Peter. 1999. *Here Is Queer: Nationalisms, Sexualities, and the Literatures of Canada*. Toronto: University of Toronto Press
Dobson, Kit. 2006. "'Struggle Work': Global and Urban Citizenship in Dionne Brand's *What We All Long For*." *Studies in Canadian Literature/Études en littérature canadienne* 31, no. 2: 88–104
– 2007. "Spirits of Elsewhere Past: A Dialogue on Soucouyant." *Callaloo* 30, no. 3: 808–17
– 2009. *Transnational Canadas: Anglo-Canadian Literature and Globalization*. Waterloo, ON: Wilfrid Laurier University Press
Donovan, Kenneth. 1995. "Slaves and Their Owners in Ile Royale, 1713–1760." *Acadiensis* 25, no. 1: 3–32
Doolen, Andy. 2009. "Be Cautious of the Word 'Rebel': Race, Revolution, and Transnational History in Martin Delany's *Blake; or, The Huts of America*." *American Literature* 81, no. 1: 153–79
Douglass, Frederick. 1881a. *John Brown. An Address by Frederick Douglass, at the Fourteenth Anniversary of Storer College, Harper's Ferry, West Virginia, May 30, 1881*. Dover, NH: Morning Star Job Printing House
– 1881b. *Life and Times of Frederick Douglass*. Hartford, CT: Park Publishing
Dowling, Sarah. 2011. "Persons and Voices: Sounding Impossible Bodies in M. NourbeSe Philip's *Zong!*" *Canadian Literature* 210/211: 41–58
Drew, Benjamin. (1856) 2000. *The Refugee; or The Narratives of Fugitive Slaves in Canada. Related By Themselves, with An Account of the History and Condition of the Colored Population of Upper Canada*. Reprint: Toronto: Prospero
Du Bois, W.E.B. (1903) 1986a. *The Souls of Black Folk*. In *Writings*, edited by Nathan Huggins, 357–548. New York: Library of America
– 1986b. *The Suppression of the African Slave-Trade*. In *Writings*, edited by Nathan Huggins, 1–356. New York: Library of America
– (1909) 2001. *John Brown*. Edited and with an introduction by David Roediger. New York: Modern Library
Duff, Christine. 2011. "Where Literature Fills the Gaps: *The Book of Negroes* as a Canadian Work of Rememory." *Studies in Canadian Literature/Études en littérature canadienne* 36, no. 2: 129–44
Dumontet, Danielle, ed. 2003. *L'esthetique du choc: Gérard Étienne ou l'écriture haïtienne au Québec*. Frankfurt: Peter Lang
Edelstein, Tilden G. 2004. Introduction to the Dover edition. In *Refugees from Slavery: Autobiographies of Fugitive Slaves in Canada*, by Benjamin Drew, ix–xxi. Mineola, NY: Dover Publications
Edugyan, Esi. 2004. *The Second Life of Samuel Tyne: A Novel*. Toronto: Vintage Canada
– 2007. *Diese Fremden: Kurzgeschichten*. Translated by Bettine Obrecht. Stuttgart: Merz & Solitude
– 2011. *Half-Blood Blues*. Toronto: Thomas Allen Publishers

– 2014. *Dreaming of Elsewhere: Observations on Home*. Edmonton: University of Alberta Press, Canadian Literature Centre/Centre de littérature canadienne

Elgersman, Maureen G. 1999. *Unyielding Spirits: Black Women and Slavery in Early Canada and Jamaica*. New York: Garland Publishing

Eng, David L. 2000. "Melancholia in the Late Twentieth Century." *Signs: Journal of Women in Culture and Society* 25, no. 4: 1275–81

Eng, David L., and David Kazanjian, eds. 2003. *Loss: The Politics of Mourning*. With an afterword by Judith Butler. Berkeley: University of California Press

Ernest, John. 1995. *Resistance and Reformation in Nineteenth-Century African-American Literature: Brown, Wilson, Jacobs, Delany, Douglass, and Harper*. Jackson: University Press of Mississippi

Étienne, Gérard. 1979. *Un ambassadeur macoute à Montréal*. Montreal: Nouvelle Optique

– 1983. *Une femme muette*. Montreal: Nouvelle Optique

– 1987. *La reine soleil levée: Récit*. Montreal: Guérin Littérature Collection/Roman

– 1991. *La pacotille: Roman*. Montreal: L'Hexagone

– 1994. *Le nègre crucifié: Récit*. Montreal: Éditions Balzac

–, with the collaboration of François Soeler. 1998. *La femme noire dans le discours littéraire haïtien: Éléments d'anthroposémiologie*. Littératures à l'Essai. Montreal: Éditions Balzac

– 2000. *La romance en do mineur de Maître Clo*. Montreal: Éditions Balzac

– 2001. *Vous n'êtes pas seul*. Montreal: Éditions Balzac

– 2004. *Au bord de la falaise*. Montreal: CIDIHCA

Fabre, Cara. 2013–14. "From Cultural Transformation to Systemic Resistance through Dionne Brand's *Thirsty* and *Inventory*." *MaComère* 14, nos 1–2: 101–23

Fanon, Frantz. 1963. *The Wretched of the Earth*. Translated by Constance Farrington. New York: Grove Press

Faust, Minister. 2004. *The Coyote Kings, Book One: Space-Age Bachelor Pad*. New York: Del Rey

Fee, Margery. 1987. "Romantic Nationalism and the Image of Native People in Contemporary English-Canadian Literature." In *The Native in Literature*, edited by Cheryl Calver Thomas King and Helen Hoy, 15–33. Toronto: ECW Press

Fee, Margery, and Sneja Gunew. 2000. "An Interview with George Elliott Clarke (September 2000)." *Canadian Literature* website, http://canlit.ca/interviews/9

Fellner, Astrid M. 2010. "'Translating Toronto on a Bicycle': Dionne Brand's *What We All Long For* and the Challenges of Urbanity." In *REAL: The Yearbook of Research in English and American Literature* 26: 231–44

Ferguson, Jade. 2009. "From Dixie to the Dominion: Violence, Race, and the Time of Capital." PhD diss., Cornell University

– 2013. "Discounting Slavery: The Currency Wars, Minstrels, and 'The White Nigger' in Thomas Chandler Haliburton's *The Clockmaker*." In *Parallel Encounters: Culture at the Canada–US Border*, edited by Gillian Roberts and David Stirrup, 243–59. Waterloo, ON: Wilfrid Laurier University Press

Ferguson, Moira. 1992. *Subject to Others: British Women Writers and Colonial Slavery, 1670–1834*. New York: Routledge

– 1997. Introduction to Mary Prince, *The History of Mary Prince: A West Indian Slave*. Rev. ed. University of Michigan Press

Figueroa, Victor. 2006. "The Kingdom of Black Jacobins: C.L.R. James and Alejo Carpentier on the Haitian Revolution." *Afro-Hispanic Review* 25, no. 2: 55–71

Filewood, Alan. 2001. "'From Twisted History': Reading Angélique." In *Siting the Other: Revisions of Marginality in Australian and English-Canadian Drama*, edited by Marc Maufort and Franca Bellarsi, 279–90. Brussels: Peter Lang

Finseth, Ian Frederick. 2003. Introduction to *A Narrative of the Adventures and Escape of Moses Roper*, in *North Carolina Slave Narratives: The Lives of Moses Roper, Lunsford Lane, Moses Grandy, and Thomas H. Jones*, edited by William L. Andrews, 24–34. Chapel Hill and London: North Carolina University Press

Firmat, Gustavo. 1990. "Introduction: Cheek to Cheek." In *Do the Americas Have a Common Literature?*, edited by Firmat Gustava, 1–6. Durham, NC: Duke University Press

Fisch, Audrey A. 2000. *American Slaves in Victorian England: Abolitionist Politics in Popular Literature and Culture*. Cambridge and New York: Cambridge University Press

–, ed. 2007. *The Cambridge Companion to the African American Slave Narrative*. Cambridge and New York: Cambridge University Press

Fiske, John. 1994. *Media Matters: Everyday Culture and Political Change*. Minneapolis: University of Minnesota Press

Flagel, Nadine. 2005. "Resonant Genres and Intertexts in the Neo-Slave Narratives of Caryl Phillips, Octavia Butler, and Lawrence Hill." PhD diss., Dalhousie University

Foggo, Cheryl. 1990. *Pourin' Down Rain*. Calgary: Detselig Enterprises

Forster, Sophia. 2002. "'Inventory Is Useless Now but Just to Say': The Politics of Ambivalence in Dionne Brand's *Land to Light On*." *Studies in Canadian Literature/Études en littérature canadienne* 27, no. 2: 160–82

Foster, Cecil. 1995. *Caribana: The Greatest Celebration*. Photographs by Chris Schwarz. Toronto: Ballantine Books

– 1996. *A Place Called Heaven: The Meaning of Being Black in Canada*. Toronto: HarperCollins

– 1998. *Slammin' Tar: A Novel*. Toronto: Random House of Canada.

Freud, Sigmund. 1953–74. "Mourning and Melancholia." In *The Standard Edition of the Complete Psychological Works of Sigmund Freud, Volume XIV (1914–1916): On the History of the Psycho-Analytic Movement, Papers on Metapsychology and Other Works*, general editor James Strachey, 237–58. London: Hogarth Press and the Institute for Psycho-Analysis

Frey, Sylvia R. 1983. "Between Slavery and Freedom: Virginia Blacks in the American Revolution." *Journal of Southern History* 49, no. 3: 375–98

– 1991. *Water from the Rock: Black Resistance in a Revolutionary Age*. Princeton, NJ: Princeton University Press

Frost, Karolyn Smardz. 2007. *I've Got a Home in Glory Land: A Lost Tale of the Underground Railroad*. Toronto: Thomas Allen

Fuller, Danielle. 1999. "'Raising the Heart': The Politics of the Popular and the Poetics of Performance in the Work of Maxine Tynes." *Essays on Canadian Writing* 67: 76–112

– 2004. *Writing the Everyday: Women's Textual Communities in Atlantic Canada*. Montreal and Kingston: McGill-Queen's University Press

Fuss, Diana. 1995. *Identification Papers*. New York and London: Routledge

Gairey, Harry. 1981. *A Black Man's Toronto 1914–1980: The Reminiscences of Harry Gairey*. Edited and with an introduction by Donna Hill. Toronto: Multicultural History Society of Ontario

Gale, Lorena. 2000. *Angélique*. Toronto: Playwrights Canada Press

– 2001. *Je me souviens: Memories of an Expatriate Anglophone Montréalaise Québécoise Exiled in Canada*. Vancouver: Talonbooks

– 2003. "Angélique." In *Testifyin': Contemporary African Canadian Drama*, edited by Djanet Sears, 2:1–71. Toronto: Playwrights Canada Press

Garvey, Johanna. 2003. "'The Place She Miss': Exile, Memory, and Resistance in Dionne Brand's Fiction." *Callaloo* 26, no. 2: 486–503

Gates, Henry Louis, Jr, ed. 1986. *"Race," Writing, and Difference*. Chicago and London: University of Chicago Press

–, ed. 1987. *The Classic Slave Narratives*. New York: Signet

– 1988. *The Signifying Monkey: A Theory of Afro-American Literary Criticism*. New York: Oxford University Press

Gauvin, Lise. 2012. *Émile Ollivier: Un destin exemplaire*. Montreal: Mémoire d'encrier

Gay, Daniel. 2004. *Les noirs du Québec, 1629–1900*. Cahiers des Amériques. Sillery, QC: Septentrion

Genette, Gérard. 1987. *Seuils*. Paris: Éditions du Seuil

Gentzler, Edwin. 2008. *Translation and Identity in the Americas: New Directions in Translation Theory*. Abingdon and New York: Routledge

George, David. (1793) 2002. "An account of the life of Mr. David George, from Sierra Leone in Africa; given by himself in a conversation with Brother Rippon of London, and Brother Pearce of Birmingham." Repr. in Brooks and Saillant (2002, 177–90)

George Meany Memorial Archives. Accessed 25 October 2007. "A. Philip Randolph, 1889–1979, Trade Union Leader." http://www.georgemeany.org/archives/leader.html

Gerson, Carole. 2009. "Literature of Settlement." In *The Cambridge History of Canadian Literature*, edited by Coral Ann Howells and Eva-Marie Kröller, 87–103. Cambridge and New York: Cambridge University Press

Gilmore, John. 1988. *Swinging in Paradise: The Story of Jazz in Montréal*. Montreal: Véhicule Press

Gilroy, Paul. 1993. *The Black Atlantic: Modernity and Double Consciousness*. Cambridge, MA: Harvard University Press

– 2000. *Against Race: Imagining Political Culture beyond the Color Line*. Cambridge: Belknap Press of Harvard University Press
– 2010. *Darker than Blue: On the Moral Economies of Black Atlantic Culture*. W.E.B. Du Bois Lectures. Cambridge: Belknap Press of Harvard University Press
Gittings, Christopher E. 2002. *Canadian National Cinema: Ideology, Difference and Representation*. London and New York: Routledge
Gingell, Susan. 1994. "Returning to Come Forward: Dionne Brand Confronts Derek Walcott." *Journal of West Indian Literature* 6, no. 2: 43–53
Gleason, Judith. 1987. *Oya: In Praise of an African Goddess*. Boston: Shambhala
Glémaud, Michèle. 1996. "La littérature des femmes Haïtiennes migrantes: Le cas du Canada." In *Multi-culture, multi-écriture: La voix migrante au feminin en France et au Canada*, edited by Lucie Lequin and Maïr Verthuy, 123–30. Paris and Montreal: Harmattan
Glissant, Édouard. 1989. *Caribbean Discourse: Selected Essays*. Translated and with an introduction by J. Michael Dash. Charlottesville: University Press of Virginia
– 1990. *Poétique de la relation*. Paris: Gallimard
– 1995. *Introduction à une poétique du divers*. Montreal: Presses de l'Université de Montréal
– (1981) 1997a. *Le discours Antillais*. Paris: Gallimard
– 1997b. *Poetics of Relation*. Translated by Betsy Wing. Ann Arbor: University of Michigan Press
– 2007. *Mémoires des esclavages: La fondation d'un centre national pour la mémoire des esclavages et de leurs abolitions*. Paris: Gallimard
Goldie, Terry. 1989. *Fear and Temptation: The Image of the Indigene in Canadian, Australian and New Zealand Literature*. Montreal and Kingston: McGill-Queen's University Press
Goldman, Marlene. 2004. "Mapping the Door of No Return: Deterritorialization and the Work of Dionne Brand." *Canadian Literature* 182: 13–28
Goldman, Marlene, and Joanne Saul. 2006. "Talking with Ghosts: Haunting in Canadian Cultural Production." *University of Toronto Quarterly* 75, no. 2: 645–55
Gould, Philip. 2007. "The Rise, Development, and Circulation of the Slave Narrative." In *The Cambridge Companion to the African American Slave Narrative*, edited by Audrey Fisch, 11–27. Cambridge and New York: Cambridge University Press
Government of Canada. 1969. *Statement of the Government of Canada on Indian Policy (The White Paper, 1969)*. http://www.aadnc-aandc.gc.ca/eng/1100100010189
Gramsci, Antonio. 1971. *Selections from the Prison Notebooks of Antonio Gramsci*. Edited and translated by Quintin Hoare and Geoffrey Nowell Smith. New York: International Publishers
– 1975. *Quaderni del Carcere*. Edited by Valentino Gerratana. Torino: G. Einaudi
Gray, Charlotte. 1999. *Sisters in the Wilderness: The Lives of Susanna Moodie and Catharine Parr Traill*. Toronto: Viking
Gray, Herman. 2003. "Transcommunality: Politics, Culture, and Practice." In *Transcommunality: From the Politics of Conversion to the Ethics of Respect*, edited by John Brown-Childs, 197–210. Philadelphia: Temple University Press

Green, Mary Jean. 2004. "Transcultural Identities: Many Ways of Being Québécois." In *Textualizing the Immigrant Experience in Contemporary Quebec*, edited by Susan Ireland and Patrice J. Proulx, 11–22. Westport and London: Praeger

Grizzle, Stanley G. 1998. *My Name's Not George: The Story of the Brotherhood of Sleeping Car Porters: Personal Reminiscences of Stanley G. Grizzle*. Toronto: Umbrella Press

Gunew, Sneja. 2004. *Haunted Nations: The Colonial Dimensions of Multiculturalism*. New York and London: Routledge

Hacking, Ian. 1986. "Making up People." In *Reconstructing Individualism: Autonomy, Individuality and the Self in Western Thought*, edited by Morton Sousa, Thomas Heller, and David Wellbery. Stanford, CA: Stanford University Press

Halbwachs, Maurice. 1980. *The Collective Memory*. Translated from the French by Francis J. Ditter and Vida Yazdi Ditter. New York: Harper & Row

Halifax Regional Municipality. 2010. "Apology." http://halifax.ca/Africville/apology.html

Hall, Stuart. 1990. "Cultural Identity and Diaspora." In *Identity: Community, Culture, Difference*, edited by Jonathan Rutherford, 222–37. London: Lawrence & Wisehart

– 1996. "New Ethnicities." In *Stuart Hall: Critical Dialogues in Cultural Studies*, edited by David Morley and Kuan-Hsing Chen, 441–9. London: Routledge

Hamilton, Sylvia. 1994. "Naming Names, Naming Ourselves: A Survey of Early Black Women in Nova Scotia." In *"We're Rooted Here and They Can't Pull Us Up": Essays in Canadian Women's History*, edited by Peggy Bristow, 13–40. Toronto: University of Toronto Press

Handley, George. 2000. *Postslavery Literature in the Americas*. Charlottesville: University of Virginia Press

Hannan, Jim. 2013–14. "'The Beamer's Silver Skin': Global Literature and the Impossible Object of Desire in Dionne Brand's *What We All Long For*." *MaComère* 14, nos 1–2: 82–100

Harel, Simon. 2005. *Les passages obligés de l'écriture migrante*. Montreal: XYZ éditeur

Harris, Claire. 1984. *Fables from the Women's Quarters*. Toronto: Williams-Wallace

– 1986. "Poets in Limbo." In *A Mazing Space: Writing Canadian Women Writing*, edited by Shirley Newman and Smaro Kamboureli, 115–25. Edmonton: Longspoon Press/NeWest Press

– 1988. "A Matter of Fact." In *Imagining Women*, edited by the Second Story Collective, 101–17. Toronto: Women's Press

– 1992. *Drawing Down a Daughter*. Fredericton, NB: Goose Lane

– 2000. *She*. Fredericton, NB: Goose Lane

Harris, Jennifer. 2004. "Ain't No Border Wide Enough." *Journal of American Culture* 27, no. 4: 367–74

Harris, Ruth L. 1989. "The Transformation of Canadian Policies and Programs to Recruit Foreign Labor: The Case of Caribbean Female Domestic Workers, 1950's–1980's." PhD diss., Michigan State University

Härting, Heike. 2007. "The Politics of Vulnerability: Diaspora, Race, and Global Citizenship in A.M. Klein's *The Second Scroll* and Dionne Brand's *Thirsty*." *Studies in Canadian Literature/Études en littérature canadienne* 32, no. 2: 177–99

Hartman, Saidiya V. 1997. *Scenes of Subjection: Terror, Slavery, and Self-Making in Nineteenth-Century America*. New York: Oxford University Press

Henry, Frances. 1968. "The West Indian Domestic Scheme in Canada." *Social and Economic Studies* 17, no. 1: 83–91

– 1994. *The Caribbean Diaspora in Toronto: Learning to Live with Racism*. Toronto: University of Toronto Press

Henry, Jeff. 2004. "Black Theatre in Montreal and Toronto in the Sixties and Seventies: The Struggle for Recognition." *Canadian Theatre Review* 118: 29–33

Henson, Josiah. 1849. *The Life of Josiah Henson, Formerly a Slave, Now an Inhabitant of Canada, as Narrated by Himself*. Boston: Arthur D. Phelps. http://docsouth.unc.edu/neh/henson49/menu.html

– (1881) 2003. *Autobiography of Josiah Henson. An Inspiration for Harriet Beecher Stowe's Uncle Tom*. With an introduction by Robin Winks. Mineola, NY: Dover

Hill, Daniel G. 1981. *The Freedom-Seekers: Blacks in Early Canada*. Agincourt: Book Society of Canada

Hill, Lawrence. 1992. *Some Great Thing*. Winnipeg: Turnstone Press

– 1993. *Trials and Triumphs: The Story of African-Canadians*. Toronto: Umbrella Press

– 1994. "Zebra: Growing Up Black and White in Canada." In *Talking about Difference: Encounters in Culture, Language and Identity*, edited by Carl James and Adrienne Shadd, 41–7. Toronto: Between the Lines

– 1996. *Women of Vision: The Story of the Canadian Negro Women's Association, 1951–1976*. Toronto: Umbrella Press

– 1997a. *Any Known Blood*. Toronto: HarperCollins

– 1997b. "Black Like Us, Eh?" *Toronto Star*, 25 October, J20

– 1998. "Gory, Gory, Hallelujah." Review of *Cloudsplitter*, by Russell Banks. *Maclean's* 111, no. 15: 64

– 2001. *Black Berry, Sweet Juice: On Being Black and White in Canada*. Toronto: HarperFlamingo

– 2007a. *The Book of Negroes*. Toronto: HarperCollins

– 2007b. "Freedom Bound." *Beaver* 87, no. 1: 16–23

– 2009. *The Book of Negroes: Illustrated Edition*. Toronto: HarperCollins

– 2013. *Blood: The Stuff of Life*. CBC Massey Lectures Series. Toronto: House of Anansi Press

Hindmarsh, D. Bruce. 2005. *The Evangelical Conversion Narrative: Spiritual Autobiography in Early Modern England*. Oxford and New York: Oxford University Press

Hirsch, Marianne. 1997. *Family Frames: Photography, Narrative, and Postmemory*. Cambridge, MA: Cambridge University Press

– 2008. "The Generation of Postmemory." *Poetics Today* 29, no. 1: 103–28

Hodges, Graham Russell, Susan Hawkes Cook, and Alan Edward Brown. 1996. *The Black Loyalist Directory: African Americans in Exile after the American Revolution*. New York: Garland

Hoffman, Elliott W. 1981. "Black Hessians: American Blacks as Germans Soldiers." *Negro History Bulletin* 44, no. 4: 81–2, 91

Hopkinson, Nalo. 1998. *Brown Girl in the Ring*. New York: Grand Central Publishing

Hostesses of Union United Church. 1982. *Memory Book: Union United Church, 75th Anniversary 1907–1982*. Montreal: Hostesses of the United Church

Howe, Samuel Gridley. 1864. *The Refugees from Slavery in Canada West: Report to the Freedman's Inquiry Commission*. Boston: Wright and Potter

Hudson, Peter. 2000. "The Last Days of Blackness: André Alexis Gets Over." In *Rude: Contemporary Black Canadian Cultural Criticism*, edited by Rinaldo Walcott, 189–99. Toronto: Insomniac Press

– 2007. "'The Lost Tribe of a Lost Tribe': Black British Columbia and the Poetics of Space." In *Black Geographies and the Politics of Place*, edited by Katherine McKittrick and Clyde Woods, 154–76. Toronto and Cambridge, MA: Between the Lines, South End Press

Huggan, Graham, and Winfried Siemerling, eds. 2000. "U.S./Canadian Writers' Perspectives on the Multiculturalism Debate: A Round-Table Discussion at Harvard University." With Nicole Brossard, Clarke Blaise, George Elliott Clarke, Paul Yee, and Geeta Patel. *Canadian Literature* 164: 82–111

Hulan, Shelley. 2009. "Total Recall." *Canadian Literature* 200:122–3

Hustak, Alan. 1987. *They Were Hanged*. Toronto: James Lorimer

Hutcheon, Linda. 1988a. *The Canadian Postmodern: A Study of Contemporary English-Canadian Fiction*. Toronto: Oxford University Press

– 1988b. *A Poetics of Postmodernism: History, Theory, Fiction*. New York and London: Routledge

Hutcheon, Linda, and Michael Hutcheon. 1996. *Opera: Desire, Disease, Death: Texts and Contexts*. Lincoln: University of Nebraska Press

Hutcheon, Linda, and Marion Richmond. 1990. *Other Solitudes: Canadian Multicultural Fictions*. Toronto: Oxford University Press

Ibbitson, John. 2013. "Ottawa's New Rules for Foreign Workers Program." *Globe and Mail*. http://www.theglobeandmail.com/news/politics/ottawas-new-rules-for-foreign-workers-program/article11601857

Jacquard, Albert. 1996. "An Unscientific Notion." *UNESCO Courier* 49, no. 3: 22–5

Jacobs, Diane. 1996. "On Becoming a Black Canadian." *Kola* 8, no. 2: 71–2

Jakobson, Roman. 1987. "Linguistic and Poetics." In *Language in Literature*, edited by Krystyna Pomorska and Stephen Rudy, 62–94. Cambridge, MA: Belknap Press of Harvard University Press

JBY. 1849. "Miss Shadd's Pamphlet." *North Star*, 8 June 1849

Johanson, Reg. 2005. "Review of Wayde Compton, *Performance Bond*." *The Rain* 3, no. 3 (August–October): 1

Johnson, Erica L. 2009. "Unforgetting Trauma: Dionne Brand's Haunted Histories." In *Caribbean Ghostwriting*, 109–30. Madison, NJ: Fairleigh Dickinson University Press

Jonassaint, Jean. 1986. *Le pouvoir des mots, les maux du pouvoir: Des romanciers haïtiens de l'exil.* Paris: Éditions de l'Arcantère; Montreal: Presses de l'Université de Montréal

Jones, Dorothy. 2004. "Writing the Silence." *Kunapipi* 26, no. 1: 196–206

Jones, George Fenwick. 1982. "The Black Hessians: Negroes Recruited by the Hessians in South Carolina and Other Colonies." *South Carolina Historical Magazine* 83, no. 4: 287–302

Joseph, Maia. 2007. "Wondering into Country: Dionne Brand's *A Map to the Door of No Return*." *Canadian Literature* 193: 75–92

Juridiction royale de Montréal. 1734. "Procedure criminel contre Marie Joseph Angélique negresse – incendiere." Archives nationales du Québec, Centre de Montréal (see transciptions and translations at http://www.canadianmysteries.ca/sites/angelique/proces/indexen.html)

Jurney, Florance Ramon. 2003. "Entretien avec Marie-Célie Agnant." *French Review* 79, no. 2: 384–94

Kagawa, Jessie. 2008. "Projecting History Honestly: An Interview with Lawrence Hill." *Studies in Canadian Literature/Études en littérature canadienne* 33, no. 1: 307–22

Kamboureli, Smaro. 2000. *Scandalous Bodies: Diasporic Literature in English Canada.* Toronto: Oxford University Press

Kang, Nancy. 2005. "'As If I Had Entered a Paradise': Fugitive Slave Narratives and Cross-Border Literary History." *African American Review* 39, no. 3: 431–58. Proquest

Kilian Crawford. (1978) 2008. *Go Do Some Great Thing: The Black Pioneers of British Columbia.* Burnaby: Commodore Books

Kim, Christine. 2006. "Postcolonial Romance, Ghostly Love Stories, and *The Heart Does Not Bend*." *Mosaic* 39, no. 2: 57–73

Kim, Christine, Sophie McCall, and Melina Baum Singer, eds. 2012. *Cultural Grammars of Nation, Diaspora, and Indigeneity in Canada.* Waterloo, ON: Wilfrid Laurier University Press

Kimber, Stephen. 2010. "The Africville Experience: Lessons for the Future." In Africville Genealogical Society, *The Spirit of Africville*, 79–104

King, Boston. (1798) 2002. "Memoirs of the Life of Boston King, a Black Preacher. Written by Himself, During His Residence at Kingswood-School." Repr. in Brooks and Saillant (2002, 209–32)

King, Thomas. 2012. *The Inconvenient Indian: A Curious Account of Native People in North America.* Toronto: Doubleday Canada

Klaus, Peter. 2012. "Mémoire individuelle et histoire collective: Les premier romans d'Émile Ollivier." In *Émile Ollivier: Un destin exemplaire*, edited by Lise Gauvin, 39–50. Montreal: Mémoire d'encrier

Kolodny, Annette. 1984. *The Land before Her: Fantasy and Experience of the American Frontiers, 1630–1860.* Chapel Hill: University of North Carolina Press

Krauter, Joseph F., and Morris Davis. 1978. *Minority Canadians: Ethnic Groups.* Toronto: Methuen

Krueger, Robert. 2002. "Brazilian Slaves Represented in Their Own Words." *Slavery and Abolition* 23, no. 2: 169–86

Krupat, Arnold. 1983. "The Indian Autobiography: Origin, Type, and Function." In *Smoothing the Ground: Essays on Native American Oral Literature*, edited by Brian Swann, 261–82. Berkeley: University of California Press

Kyser, Kristina. 2007. "George and Ruth: An Interview with George Elliott Clarke about Writing and Ethics." *University of Toronto Quarterly* 76, no. 3: 861–73

Laferrière, Dany. 1985. *Comment faire l'amour avec un Nègre sans se fatiguer: Roman*. Montreal: VLB

– 1987. *How to Make Love to a Negro: A Novel*. Translated by David Homel. Toronto: Coach House Press

– 1991. *L'odeur du café*. Montreal: VLB

– 1993. *Cette grenade dans la main du jeune nègre est-elle une arme ou un fruit?* Montreal: VLB

– 2006. *Pays sans chapeau: Roman*. Montreal: Boréal Compact

– 2009. *L'énigme du retour: Roman*. Montreal: Boréal

– 2010. *Tout bouge autour de moi*. Montreal: Mémoire d'encrier

Lai, Larissa. 2006. "The Cameras of the World: Race, Subjectivity, and the Multitude in Dionne Brand's *What We All Long For*." Paper presented at the conference "No Language Is Neutral: A Conference on Dionne Brand," 4 October

– 2014. *Slanting I, Imagining We: Asian Canadian Literary Production in the 1980s and 1990s*. Waterloo, ON: Wilfrid Laurier University Press

Landers, Jane. 1999. *Black Society in Spanish Florida*. With a foreword by Peter H. Wood. Urbana: University of Illinois Press

Landon, Fred. 2009. *Ontario's African-Canadian Heritage: Collected Writings by Fred Landon, 1918–1967*. Edited by Karolyn Smardz Frost et al. Toronto: Natural Heritage Books

Laramee, Michael. 2008. "Maps of Memory and the Sea in Dionne Brand's *At the Full and Change of the Moon*." *Anthurium: A Caribbean Studies Journal* 6, no. 2

Laroche, Maximilien. 1997. "Littérature et folklore dans la Caraïbe francophone." In *Ethnologies francophones de l'Amérique et d'ailleurs*, edited by Anne Marie et Laurier Turgeon Desdouits, 225–38. Quebec: Presses de l'Université Laval

Larson, Katherine. 2006. "Resistance from the Margins in George Elliott Clarke's *Beatrice Chancy*." *Canadian Literature* 189: 103–18

Law, Robin, and Paul E. Lovejoy, eds. 2007. *The Biography of Mahommah Gardo Baquaqua: His Passage from Slavery to Freedom in Africa and America*. Princeton, NJ: Markus Wiener Publisher

Leahy, David. 1994. "Race, Gender and Class Enigmas in *The Loved and the Lost* and *Au Milieu, La Montagne*." *Textual Studies in Canada* 5: 32–45

Lean, John, and Trevor Burnard. 2002. "Hearing Slave Voices: The Fiscal's Reports of Berbice and Demerara-Essequebo." *Archives: Journal of the British Records Association* 27:120–33

LeBreton, Mireille. 2011. "Un ambassadeur macoute à Montréal de Gérard Étienne ou l'expression exorcisante des démons duvaliéristes du passé." In *L'oeuvre roman-*

esque de Gérard Étienne: É(cri)ts d'un révolutionnaire, edited by Najib and Ivette Bénayoun-Szmidt Redouane, 57–90. Paris: L'Harmattan

Leclair, Didier. 2000. *Toronto, je t'aime: Roman*. Ottawa: Éditions du Vermillon

– 2003. *Ce pays qui est le mien: Roman*. Ottawa: Éditions du Vermillon

– 2007. *Un passage vers l'Occident*. Ottawa: Vermillon

Lees, Gene. 1988. *Oscar Peterson: The Will to Swing*. Toronto: Lester & Orpen Dennys

Leow, Joanne. 2012. "Mis-Mappings and Mis-Duplications: Interdiscursivity and the Poetry of Wayde Compton." *Canadian Literature* 214:47–66

Lequin, Lucie. 2002. "Marie-Célie Agnant: Une écriture de la mémoire et du silence." In *Reconfigurations: Canadian Literatures and Postcolonial Identities/ Littératures Canadiennes et Identités Postcoloniales*, edited by Marc and Bellarsi Maufort, Franca, 21–32. Brussels: Peter Lang

Lesk, Andrew. 2001. "Private and Public Domiciles." *Canadian Literature* 170/171: 211–13

Levine, Robert S. 1997. *Martin Delany, Frederick Douglass, and the Politics of Representative Identity*. Chapel Hill: University of North Carolina Press

–, ed. 2003. *Martin R. Delany: A Documentary Reader*. Chapel Hill and London: University of North Carolina Press

Lewis, George. 2004. "Improvised Music after 1950: Afrological and Eurological Perspectives." In *The Other Side of Nowhere: Jazz, Improvisation, and Communities in Dialogue*, edited by Daniel Fischlin and Ajay Heble, 131–72. Middletown, CT: Wesleyan University Press

Libby, Jean. 1979. *Black Voices from Harpers Ferry: Osborne Anderson and the John Brown Raid*. Palo Alto, CA: published by the author

Lipsitz, George. 1994. *Dangerous Crossroads: Popular Music, Postmodernism and the Poetics of Place*. London and New York: Verso

Litt, Paul. 2007. "The State and the Book." In *History of the Book in Canada*, edited by Carole Gerson and Jacques Michon, 3:34–44. Toronto: University of Toronto Press

Loguen, Jermain Wesley. 1859. *The Rev. J.W. Loguen, as a Slave and as a Freeman: A Narrative of Real Life*. Syracuse, NY: J.G.K. Truair & Co.

Lousley, Cheryl. 2008. "Lousley, Cheryl." *Canadian Poetry: Studies, Documents, Reviews* 63: 37–58

Lyngaas, Scott W. 2011. "Confronting Haitian History in the Novels of Marie-Célie Agnant." *French Review* 84, no. 5: 967–77

McBride, Dwight A. 2001. *Impossible Witnesses: Truth, Abolitionism, and Slave Testimony*. New York: New York University Press

McCallum, Pamela, and Christian Olbey. 1999. "Written in the Scars: History, Genre, and Materiality in Dionne Brand's *In Another Place, Not Here*." *Essays on Canadian Writing* 68: 159–82

– 2008. "'Standing in the Middle of the World Cracking': Class, Cultural Memory, and Collectivity in Dionne Brand's *At the Full and Change of the Moon*." In

Beyond the Canebrakes: Caribbean Women Writers in Canada, edited by Emily Allen Williams, 11–35. Trenton: Africa World

McKay, Ian. 1994. *The Quest of the Folk: Antimodernism and Cultural Selection in Twentieth-Century Nova Scotia*. Montreal and Kingston: McGill-Queen's University Press

Mackey, Frank. 2004. *Black Then: Blacks and Montreal 1780s–1880s*. Montreal and Kingston: McGill-Queen's University Press

– 2010. *Done with Slavery: The Black Fact in Montreal, 1760–1840*. Montreal and Kingston: McGill-Queen's University Press

McKittrick, Katherine. 2006. *Demonic Grounds: Black Women and the Cartographies of Struggle*. Minneapolis: University of Minnesota Press

MacLellan, Angela. 2012. "Le retour et le détour glissantiens chez Dany Laferrière." MA thesis, Département d'études françaises, University of Waterloo

MacLennan, Hugh. (1945) 1993. *Two Solitudes*. Toronto: Stoddart

McWatt, Tessa. 1998. *Out of My Skin: A Novel*. Toronto: Riverbank Press

Mannette, J.A. 1990. "'Revelation, Revolution, or Both': Black Art as Politics." Lecture presented at the conference "400 Years: African Canadian History," Multicultural History Society of Ontario, Toronto, June

Maracle, Lee. 2002. *Daughters Are Forever*. Vancouver: Polestar

Marano, Carla. 2010. "'Rising Strongly and Rapidly': The Universal Negro Improvement Association in Canada, 1919–1940." *Canadian Historical Review* 91, no. 2: 233–59

Marlatt, Daphne, and Carole Itter, comp. and ed. 1979. *Opening Doors: Vancouver's East End*. Victoria: Aural History Program

Marrant, John. (1790) 2002a. *A Journal of the Rev. John Marrant, from August 18th, 1785, to the 16th of March, 1790*. Repr. in Brooks and Saillant (2002, 93–160)

– (1785) 2002b. *A Narrative of the Lord's Wonderful Dealings with John Marrant, a Black (Now Going to Preach the Gospel in Nova-Scotia), Born in New-York, in North-America. Taken Down from His Own Relation, Arranged, Corrected by the Rev. Mr. Aldridge. The Fourth Edition, Enlarged by Mr. Marrant, and Printed (with Permission) for His Sole Benefit, with Notest Explanatory*. Repr. in Brooks and Saillant (2002, 47–75)

Marrelli, Nancy. 2004. *Stepping Out: The Golden Age of Montreal Night Clubs, 1925–1955*. Montreal: Véhicule Press

Martin, Paul. 2013. *Sanctioned Ignorance: The Politics of Knowledge Production and the Teaching of the Literatures of Canada*. Edmonton: University of Alberta Press

Marx, Karl. 1976. *Capital: A Critique of Political Economy*. With an introduction by Ernest Mandel and translated by Ben Fowkes. Harmondsworth, UK: Penguin

Mason, Jody. 2006. "Searching for the Doorway: Dionne Brand's *Thirsty*." *University of Toronto Quarterly* 75, no. 2: 784–800

Mason-John, Valerie, and Kevan Anthony Cameron, eds. 2013. *The Great Black North: Contemporary African Canadian Poetry*. Calgary: Frontenac House Poetry

Mathieu, Sarah-Jane. 2010. *North of the Color Line: Migration and Black Resistance in Canada, 1870–1955*. Chapel Hill: University of North Carolina Press

Matthiessen, F.O. 1941. *American Renaissance*. New York: Oxford University Press
Mauss, Marcel. (1922) 1987. *The Gift: Forms and Functions of Exchange in Archaic Societies*. London: Routledge
Mayr, Suzette. 1995. *Moon Honey*. Nunatak Fiction. Edmonton: NeWest Press
– 1998. *The Widows*. Edmonton: NeWest Press
– 2004. *Venous Hum*. Vancouver: Arsenal Pulp Press
– 2011. *Monoceros: A Novel*. Toronto: Coach House Books
Mbonimpa, Melchior. 2001. *Le totem des Baranda: Roman*. Sudbury, ON: Prise de parole
– 2003. *Le dernier roi faiseur de pluie: Mémoires de Dagano: Roman*. Sudbury, ON: Prise de parole
– 2006. *Les morts ne sont pas morts: Roman*. Sudbury, ON: Prise de parole
Medley, Mark. 2014. "Watching Toronto in the Rear-View Mirror in Love Enough." *Globe and Mail Sunday*, 5 October. http://www.theglobeandmail.com/arts/books-and-media/watching-toronto-in-the-rear-view-mirror-in-love-enough/article20917850/
Medovarski, Andrea. 2013. "Currency and Cultural Consumption: Lawrence Hill's *The Book of Negroes*." *Studies in Canadian Literature/Études en Littérature Canadienne* 38, no. 2: 9–30
Mengiste, Maaza. 2013. "The Place in Between: An Interview with Esi Edugyan." *Callaloo* 36, no. 1 (Winter): 46–51
Mensah, Joseph. 2010. *Black Canadians: History, Experiences, Social Conditions*, 2nd ed. Halifax: Fernwood
Michaels, Walter Benn, and Donald E. Pease, eds. (1985) 1989. *The American Renaissance Reconsidered*. Baltimore: Johns Hopkins University Press
Midgley, Clare. 1992. *Women against Slavery: The British Campaigns, 1780–1870*. London and New York: Routledge
Mignolo, Walter. 2005. *The Idea of Latin America*. Oxford: Blackwell
Miki, Roy. 2004. *Redress: Inside the Japanese Canadian Call for Justice*. Vancouver: Raincoast Books
Miki, Roy, and Cassandra Kobayashi. 1991. *Justice in Our Time: The Japanese Canadian Redress Settlement*. Vancouver: Talonbooks
Miller, Floyd J. 1970. Introduction to *Blake; or The Huts of America*, by Martin R. Delany. Boston: Beacon Press
– 1975. *The Search for a Black Nationality: Black Emigration and Colonization 1787–1863*. Urbana: University of Illinois Press
Miller, Mark. 1982. *Jazz in Canada: Fourteen Lives*. Toronto: University of Toronto Press
– 1989. *Cool Blues: Charlie Parker in Canada, 1953*. London, ON: Nightwood Editions
– 1997. *Such Melodious Racket: The Lost History of Jazz in Canada, 1914–1949*. Toronto: Mercury Press
– 2001. *The Miller Companion to Jazz in Canada and Canadians in Jazz*. Text and photographs by Mark Miller. Toronto: Mercury Press

Mills, Sean William. 2007. "The Empire Within: Montreal, the Sixties, and the Forging of a Radical Imagination." PhD diss., Queen's University

Miraglia, Anne Marie. 2011. "Le retour à la terre et l'absence du père dans *Pays sans chapeau* et *L'Énigme du Retour* de Dany Laferrière." *Voix et Images* 36, no. 2: 81–92

Moisan, Clément, and Renate Hildebrand. 2001. *Ces étrangers du dedans: Une histoire de l'écriture migrante au Québec (1937–97)*. Quebec: Nota Bene

Monson, Ingrid. 1996. *Saying Something: Jazz Improvisation and Interaction*. Chicago: University of Chicago Press

Moodie, Susanna. 1853. *Life in the Bush versus the Clearings*. New Canadian Library. London: R. Bentley

– 1854a. *Flora Lyndsay, or, Passages in an Eventful Life*. London: R. Bentley

– 1854b. *Matrimonial Speculations*. London: R. Bentley

– 1985. *Letters of a Lifetime*. Edited by Carl Ballstadt, Elizabeth Hopkins, and Michael Peterman. Toronto: University of Toronto Press

– 1991. *Voyages: Short Narratives of Susanna Moodie*. Edited and with an introduction by John Thurston. Ottawa: University of Ottawa Press

– (1852) 2007. *Roughing It in the Bush; or, Life in Canada*. Edited by Michael Peterman.. A Norton Critical Edition. New York and London: Norton

Moreiras, Alberto. 2001. *The Exhaustion of Difference: The Politics of Latin American Cultural Studies*. Durham, NC: Duke University Press

Morrison, Toni. 1987. *Beloved*. New York: Knopf

– 1990. *Playing in the Dark: Whiteness and the Literary Imagination*. New York: Vintage

– 1995. "The Site of Memory." In *Inventing the Truth: The Art and Craft of Memoir*, edited by William Zinser, 85–102. Revised and expanded 2nd ed. Boston and New York: Houghton Mifflin

Moten, Fred. 2003. *In the Break: The Aesthetics of the Black Radical Tradition*. Minneapolis: University of Minnesota Press

Mott, L. 1983. *Rosa Egipcíaca. Uma Santa Africa No Brasil*. Rio de Janeiro: Bertrand

Moynagh, Maureen. 1996. "Mapping Africadia's Imaginary Geography: An Interview with George Elliott Clarke." *Ariel* 27, no. 4: 71–94

– 1998. "Africville, an Imagined Community." *Canadian Literature* 157: 14–34

– 2001. "Uses of Cultural Memory." *Canadian Literature* 170/171: 193–5

– 2002. "'This History's Only Good for Anger': Gender and Cultural Memory in *Beatrice Chancy*." *Signs* 28, no. 1: 97–124

–, ed. 2005. *African-Canadian Theatre*. Vol. 2 of *Critical Perspectives on Canadian Theatre in English*. Toronto: Playwrights Canada Press

– 2008. "The Melancholic Structure of Memory in Dionne Brand's *At the Full and Change of the Moon*." *Journal of Commonwealth Literature* 43, no. 1: 57–75

– 2010. "Eyeing the North Star? Figuring Canada in Postslavery Fiction and Drama." In *Canada and Its Americas: Transnational Navigations*, edited by Winfried Siemerling and Sarah Phillips Casteel, 135–47. Montreal and Kingston: McGill-Queen's University Press

Murray, Heather. 2002. *Come, Bright Improvement: The Literary Societies of Nineteenth-Century Ontario*. Toronto: University of Toronto Press

Muyumba, Walton M. 2009. *The Shadow and the Act: Black Intellectual Practice, Jazz Improvisation, and Philosophical Pragmatism*. Chicago and London: University of Chicago Press

Nash, Gary B. 1981. "Thomas Peters: Millwright and Deliverer." In *Struggle and Survival in Colonial America*, edited by David G. Sweet and Gary B. Nash, 69–85. Berkeley: University of California Press

Naudillon, Françoise. 2005. "Le continent noir des corps: Représentations du corps féminin chez Marie-Célie Agnant et Gisèle Pineau." *Études françaises* 41, no. 2: 73–85

NCC/Charles H. Este Cultural Centre. "Our History." http://www.nccmontreal.org/ncc-eng-history.htm

Ndiaye, Christiane. 2004. "Récit des origines chez quelques écrivaines de la francophonie." *Études françaises* 40, no. 1: 43–63

Nelson, Charmaine A., ed. 2010. *Ebony Roots, Northern Soil: Perspectives on Blackness in Canada*. Newcastle upon Tyne: Cambridge Scholars

Nelson, Jennifer J. 2008. *Razing Africville: A Geography of Racism*. Toronto: University of Toronto Press

Nepveu, Pierre. 2004. *Lectures des lieux: Essais*. Collection Papiers Collés. Montreal: Boréal

Nepveu, Pierre, and Gilles Marcotte. 1992. *Montréal imaginaire: Ville et littérature*. Montreal: Fides

Nestruck, J. Kelly. 2009. "Jerry Wasserman: Je me souviens de Lorena Gale." *Globe and Mail*, online

Newby, M. Dalyce. 1998. *Anderson Ruffin Abbott: First Afro-Canadian Doctor*. Canadian Medical Lives. Markham, ON: Associated Medical Services and Fitzhenry & Whiteside

Novak, Dagmar. 1990. "Interview." In *Other Solitudes: Canadian Multicultural Fictions*, edited by Linda Hutcheon and Marion Richmond, 271–7. Toronto: Oxford University Press

Nurse, Donna Bailey. 2000. "Writing through Race: Black Writers on Being Edited, Published, and Reviewed in Canada." *Quill & Quire* 66, no. 5 (May): 18–19

– 2003. *What's a Black Critic to Do? Interviews, Profiles, and Reviews of Black Writers*. Toronto: Insomniac Press

–, ed. 2006. *Revival: An Anthology of Black Canadian Writing*. Toronto: McClelland & Stewart

– 2011. *What's a Black Critic to Do II: Interviews, Profiles and Reviews of Black Writers*. London, ON: Insomniac Press

Nussbaum, Martha. 1995. *Poetic Justice: The Literary Imagination and Public Life*. Boston: Beacon Press

Nwankwo, Ifeoma C.K. 2005. *Black Cosmopolitanism: Racial Consciousness and Transnational Identity in the Nineteenth-Century Americas*. Philadelphia: University of Pennsylvania Press

Ollivier, Émile. 1977. *Paysage de l'aveugle: Roman*. Montreal: P. Tisseyre
- 1983. *Mère-Solitude: Roman*. Paris: Albin Michel
- 1986. *La discorde aux cent voix: Roman*. Paris: A. Michel
- 1995. *Les urnes scellées: Roman*. Paris: A. Michel
- 1999. *Mille eaux: Récit*. Haute Enfance. Paris: Gallimard
- 2001. *Regarde, regarde les lions: Nouvelles*. Paris: Albin Michel
- (1991) 2002. *Passages: Roman*. Montreal: Typo
- 2004. *La brûlerie: Roman*. Montreal: Boréal

Ondaatje, Michael. 1978. "García Márquez and the Bus to Aracataca." In *Figures in a Ground: Canadian Essays on Modern Literature. Collected in Honor of Sheila Watson*, edited by Diane Bessai and David Jackel, 19–31. Saskatoon: Western Producer Prairie Books
- 1987. *In the Skin of a Lion*. Toronto: McClelland & Stewart

Ong, Walter J. 2002. *Orality and Literacy: The Technologizing of the Word*. London: Routledge

Page, Kezia. 2011. *Transnational Negotiations in Caribbean Diasporic Literature: Remitting the Text*. New York: Routledge

Palmer, Howard. 1982. *Patterns of Prejudice: A History of Nativism in Alberta*. Toronto: McClelland & Stewart

Paquet, Sandra Pouchet. 1992. "The Heartbeat of a West Indian Slave: 'A History of Mary Prince.'" *African American Review* 26: 131–45

Park, Eunjin. 2001. *"White" Americans in "Black" Africa: Black and White American Methodist Missionaries in Liberia, 1820–1875*. New York: Routledge

Paton, Diana. 2001. Introduction to *A Narrative of Events, Since the First of August, 1834, by James Williams, an Apprenticed Labourer in Jamaica*, by James Williams, xiii–lv. Durham, NC, and London: Duke University Press

Patten, Leslie Ann, director. 1999. *Loyalties*. With Carmelita Robertson and Ruth Whitehead. National Filmboard of Canada (NFB)

Paul, Heike. 2011. "Out of Chatham: Abolitionism on the Canadian Frontier." *Atlantic Studies* 8, no. 2: 165–88

Pavlić, Edward. 1996. "Syndetic Redemption: Above-Underground Emergence in David Bradley's *The Chaneysville Incident*." *African American Review* 30, no. 2: 165–84

Pease, Donald E. 1985. "*Moby Dick* and the Cold War." In *The American Renaissance Reconsidered*, edited by Walter Benn Michaels and Donald E. Pease, 113–55. Baltimore: Johns Hopkins University Press
- 1986. "Melville and Cultural Persuasion." In *The American Renaissance Reconsidered*, edited by Sacvan Bercovitch, and Myra Jehlen, 384–417. Cambridge: Cambridge University Press

Pease, William Henry, and Jane H. Pease. 1963. *Black Utopia: Negro Communal Experiments in America*. Madison: Madison State Historical Society of Wisconsin

Perez, Elizabeth. 2010. "The Virgin in the Mirror: Reading Images of a Black Madonna through the Lens of Afro-Cuban Women's Experiences." *Journal of African American History* 95, no. 2: 202–28

Peterman, Michael A. 1983. "Susanna Moodie (1803–1885)." In *Canadian Writers and Their Works: Fiction Series 1*, edited by Jack David, Robert Lecker, and Ellen Quigley, 63–104. Downsview, ON: ECW Press

Peterson, Carla L. 1995. *Doers of the Word: African-American Women Speakers and Writers in the North (1830–1880).* New York: Oxford University Press

Peterson, Oscar, and Richard Palmer, ed. and consultant. 2002. *A Jazz Odyssey: The Life of Oscar Peterson.* London and New York: Continuum

Philip, Marlene NourbeSe. 1988. *Harriet's Daughter.* Toronto: Women's Press

– 1989. *She Tries Her Tongue: Her Silence Softly Breaks.* Charlottetown: Ragweed

– 1991. *Looking for Livingstone: An Odyssey of Silence.* Stratford, ON: Mercury Press

– 1992. *Frontiers: Essays and Writings on Racism and Culture.* Stratford, ON: Mercury Press

– 1997. *A Genealogy of Resistance and Other Essays.* Toronto: Mercury Press

– 2008. *Zong! As Told to the Author by Setaey Adamu Boateng.* Toronto: Mercury Press

Pierce, Yolanda. 2007. "Redeeming Bondage: The Captivity Narrative and the Spiritual Autobiography in the African American." In *The Cambridge Companion to the African American Slave Narrative*, edited by Audrey Fisch, 83–98. Cambridge and New York: Cambridge University Press

Port Roseway Associates. 1782–83. "Minute Book of Proceedings: Musterbook of Free Black, Settlement of Birchtown, 1784." Reference MG 9 B9-14, microfilm reel H-984. Library and Archives Canada, Ottawa. http://www.bac-lac.gc.ca/eng/discover/military-heritage/loyalists/loyalist-port-roseway/Pages/port-roseway-associates-loyalists.aspx

Prince, Mary. 1997. *The History of Mary Prince: A West Indian Slave.* Edited by Moira Ferguson. University of Michigan Press

Proulx, Patrice J. 2004. "Migration and Memory in Marie-Célie Agnant's *La dot de Sara* and Abla Faroud's *Le bonheur a la queue glissante*." In *Textualizing the Immigrant Experience in Contemporary Quebec*, edited by Susan Ireland and Patrice J. Proulx, 127–36. Westport: Praeger

– 2005. "Bearing Witness and Transmitting Memory in the Works of Marie-Célie Agnant." *Quebec Studies* 39: 35–53

Pybus, Cassandra. 2006. *Epic Journeys of Freedom: Runaway Slaves of the American Revolution and Their Global Quest for Liberty.* Boston: Beacon Press

Quarles, Benjamin. (1974) 2001. *Allies for Freedom: Blacks and John Brown.* Boston and New York: Da Capo Press

Redhill, Michael. 1999. "An Interview with André Alexis." *Brick* 62: 50–6

Redouane, Najib. 2003. "Écrivains haïtiens au Québec: Une écriture du dépassement identitaire." *Globe: Revue internationale d'études québécoises* 66, no. 1: 43–64

Redouane, Najib, and Ivette Bénayoun-Szmidt, eds. 2011. *L'oeuvre romanesque de Gérard Étienne: É(cri)ts d'un révolutionnaire.* Paris: L'Harmattan

Reed, Ishmael. 2009. "Mark Twain's Hairball." In *A New Literary History of America*, edited by Greil Marcus and Werner Sollors, 380–4. Cambridge: Harvard University Press

Reems, Carmen. 2008. "In Black and White: Subverting the Racial Stereotypes of Historical Mainstream News Media in Black Canadian Literature." MA thesis, Dalhousie University

Rhodes, Jane. 1998. *Mary Ann Shadd Cary: The Black Press and Protest in the Nineteenth Century*. Bloomington: Indian University Press

– 2000. "The Contestation over National Identity: Nineteenth-Century Black Americans in Canada." *Canadian Review of American Studies* 30, no. 2: 175–86

Richards, Linda. 2002. "Austin Clarke." *January Magazine*. http://januarymagazine.com/profiles/aclarke.html

Richardson, Alan. 1993. "Romantic Voodoo: Obeah and British Culture, 1797–1807." *Studies in Romanticism* 32, no. 1: 3–28

Riley, Sandra. 2000. *Homeward Bound: A History of the Bahamas to 1850 with a Definitive Study of Abaco in the American Loyalist Plantation Period*. Miami: Riley Hall Publishers

Ripley, C. Peter, ed. 1986. *The Black Abolitionist Papers*. Vol. 2: *Canada, 1830–1856*. Chapel Hill: University of North Carolina Press

– 1991a. *The Black Abolitionist Papers*. Vol 3: *United States 1830–1846*. Chapel Hill: University of North Carolina Press

– 1991b. *The Black Abolitionist Papers*. Vol. 4: *United States 1847–1858*. Chapel Hill: University of North Carolina Press

Riss, Arthur. 1994. "Racial Essentialism and Family Values in *Uncle Tom's Cabin*." *American Quarterly* 46: 513–44

– 2006. *Race, Slavery, and Liberalism in Nineteenth-Century American Literature*. Cambridge: Cambridge University Press

Robbins, Bruce. 1994. "Upward Mobility in the Postcolonial Era: Kinkaid, Mukherjee, and the Cosmopolitan Au Pair." *Modernism/Modernity* 1, no. 2: 133–51

Robert, Lucie. 1989. *L'Institution du littéraire au Québec*. Quebec City: Presses de l'Université Laval

Rollin, Frank A. 1868. *Life and Public Services of Martin R. Delany: Sub-Assistant Commissioner, Bureau Relief of Refugees, Freedmen, and of Abandoned Lands, and Late Major 104th U.S. Colored Troops*. Boston: Lee and Shepard

Roper, Moses. (1837) 1848. *A Narrative of the Ventures and Escape of Moses Roper, from American Slavery. With an Appendix Containing a List of Places Visited by the Author in Great Britain, Ireland and the British Isles, and Other Matter*. London: printed for the author. http://docsouth.unc.edu/neh/roper/roper.html

Roth, Leah. 2012. "Une parole libératrice." *Voix plurielles* 9, no. 1: 197–209

Rotman, David. 2003. "Genes, Medicine, and the New Race Debate." *Technology Review* 106, no. 5 (June): 41–7

Roy, Gabrielle. 1941. "Tout Montréal 1: Les deux Saint-Laurent." *Le bulletin des acriculteurs* 37, no. 6: 8–9, 37, 40

– (1955) 1967. "Les deux nègres." In *Rue Deschambault*, 8–28. Montreal: Beauchemin

– 1969. *The Tin Flute*. Translated by Hannah Josephson. Toronto: McClelland & Stewart

– 1993. *Bonheur d'occasion*. 1945. Montreal: Boréal

Royal Commission on Bilingualism and Biculturalism. 1969. *Final Report of the Royal Commission on Bilingualism and Biculturalism*. Vol. 4. Ottawa: Queen's Printer

Rudy, Susan. 1996. "'What There Is Teasing beyond the Edges': Claire Harris's Liminal Autobiography." *Essays on Canadian Writing* 60: 78–99

Rushdy, H.A. Ashraf. 1999. *Neo-slave Narratives: Studies in the Social Logic of a Literary Form*. Oxford and New York: Oxford University Press

Sadlier, Rosemary. 1994. *Leading the Way: Black Women in Canada*. Toronto: Umbrella Press

– 1995. *Mary Ann Shadd: Publisher, Editor, Teacher, Lawyer, Suffragette*. Signature series. Toronto: Umbrella Press

– 2012. *Harriet Tubman: Freedom Seeker, Freedom Leader*. A Quest Biography. Toronto: Dundurn Press

Sagawa, Jessie. 2008. "Projecting History Honestly: An Interview with Lawrence Hill." *Studies in Canadian Literature/Études en Littérature Canadienne* 33, no. 1: 307–22

Said, Edward. 1978. *Orientalism*. New York: Vintage

Sanders, Leslie. 1999. "Anti/Modern Spaces: African Canadians in Nova Scotia." In *Floating the Borders: New Contexts in Canadian Criticism*, edited by Nurjehan Aziz, 106–21. Toronto: TSAR

– 2000. "Impossible to Occupy: André Alexis's *Childhood*." In *Rude: Contemporary Black Canadian Cultural Criticism*, edited by Rinaldo Walcott, 169–87. Toronto: Insomniac Press

– 2003. "History at Negro Creek; Djanet Sears' *The Adventures of a Black Girl in Search of God*." In *Testifyin': Contemporary African Canadian Drama*, edited by Djanet Sears, 2:487–9. Toronto: Playwrights Canada Press

– 2009. Introduction to *Fierce Departures: The Poetry of Dionne Brand*, by Dionne Brand, ix–xv. Waterloo, ON: Wilfrid Laurier University Press

Sanders, Leslie, and Rinaldo Walcott. 2000. "At the Full and Change of CanLit: An Interview with Dionne Brand." *Canadian Women Studies* 20, no. 2: 22–6

Sansregret, Marthe. 2005. *Oliver Jones, le musicien et l'homme*. Outremont, QC: Stanke

Sarsfield, Mairuth. 1997. *No Crystal Stair*. Toronto: Moulin Publishing

Sartre, Jean-Paul. 1956. *Being and Nothingness*. Translated by Hazel E. Barnes. New York: Washington Square Press

Satyre, Joubert. 2009. "Fantômes du passe chez Émile Ollivier et Gérard Étienne: De l'écriture comme exorcisme." *Canadian Literature* 200: 90–104

– 2012. "La rumeur dans *La Discorde aux cent voix*: Lieux et thèmes, narrativité et baroque." In *Émile Ollivier: Un destin exemplaire*, edited by Lise Gauvin, 51–61. Montreal: Mémoire d'encrier

Saunders, Charles. 1992. "A Visit to Africville, Summer 1959." In *Fire on the Water*, edited by George Elliott Clarke, 2:53–65. Lawrencetown Beach, NS: Pottersfield Press

Saunders, Patricia. 2005. "Trying Tongues, E-Raced Identities, and the Possibilities of Be/Longing: Conversations with NourbeSe Philip." *Journal of West Indian Literature* 14, nos 1–2: 202–19

– 2008. "Defending the Dead, Confronting the Archive: A Conversation with M. Nourbese Philip (Interview)." *Small Axe* 26: 63–79

Savory, Elaine. 1994. "Wordsongs & Wordwounds/Homecoming: Kamau Brathwaite's *Barabajan Poems*." *World Literature Today* 68, no. 4: 750–7

Schama, Simon. (2005) 2008. *Rough Crossings: Britain, the Slaves, and the American Revolution*. Toronto: Penguin

Sears, Djanet, ed. 2000–03. *Testifyin': Contemporary African Canadian Drama*. Toronto: Playwrights Canada Press

Selao, Ching. 2010. "Les mots/maux de l'exil/ex-île: Les romans de Marie-Célie Agnant." *Canadian Literature* 204: 11–25

Sernett, Milton C. 2007. *Harriet Tubman: Myth, Memory, and History*. Durham, NC: Duke University Press

Shadd, Adrienne. 1994. "'The Lord Seemed to Say "Go"': Women and the Underground Railroad Movement." In *"We're Rooted Here and They Can't Pull Us Up": Essays in Canadian Women's History*, edited by Peggy Bristow, 41–68. Toronto: University of Toronto Press

– 2001a. "'Where Are You Really From?' Notes of an 'Immigrant' from North Buxton, Ontario." In *Encounters in Race, Ethnicity, and Language*, edited by Carl E. James and Adrienne Shadd, 10–16. Toronto: Between the Lines

– 2001b. "'Why Are Black People So Angry?' The Question of Black Rage." In *Encounters in Race, Ethnicity, and Language*, edited by Carl E. James and Adrienne Shadd, 291–300. Toronto: Between the Lines

– 2010. *The Journey from Tollgate to Parkway: African Canadians in Hamilton*. With a foreword by the Hamilton Black History Committee. Toronto: Natural Heritage Books

Shadd, Adrienne, Afua Cooper, and Karolyn Smardz Frost. 2002. *The Underground Railroad: Next Stop, Toronto!* Toronto: Natural Heritage Books

Shadd, Mary A. 1852. *A Plea for Emigration, or, Notes of Canada West, in Its Moral, Social and Political Aspect: With Suggestions Respecting Mexico, West Indies and Vancouver Island, for the Information of Colored Emigrants*. Detroit: George W. Pattison

– (1852) 1998. *A Plea for Emigration, or, Notes of Canada West*. Edited and with an introduction by Richard Almonte. Toronto: Mercury Press

Sharpe, Jenny. 1996. "'Something Akin to Freedom': The Case of Mary Prince." *Differences: A Journal of Feminist Cultural Studies* 8, no. 1: 31–56

– 2013. "The Archive and Affective Memory in M. Nourbese Philip's Zong!" *Interventions: International Journal of Postcolonial Studies* 16, no. 4: 465–82

Shepard, R. Bruce. 1997. *Deemed Unsuitable: Blacks from Oklahoma Move to the Canadian Prairies in Search of Equality in the Early 20th Century Only to Find Racism in Their New Home*. Toronto: Umbrella Press

Siemerling, Winfried. 1994. *Discoveries of the Other: Alterity in the Work of Leonard Cohen, Hubert Aquin, Michael Ondaatje, and Nicole Brossard*. Toronto: University of Toronto Press

– 1996. *Writing Ethnicity: Cross-Cultural Consciousness in Canadian and Québécois Literature*. Toronto: Essays on Canadian Writing Press

– 2005. *The New North American Studies: Culture, Writing, and the Politics of Re/Cognition*. New York and London: Routledge

– 2007. "Ethics as Re/Cognition in the Novels of Marie-Célie Agnant: Oral Knowledge, Cognitive Change, and Social Justice." *University of Toronto Quarterly: A Canadian Journal of the Humanities* 76, no. 3 (Summer): 838–60

– 2010. "'May I See Some Identification?' Race, Borders, and Identities in *Any Known Blood*." In *Canada and Its Americas: Transnational Navigations*, edited by Winfried Siemerling and Sarah Phillips Casteel, 148–70. Montreal and Kingston: McGill-Queen's University Press

– 2013. "A Conversation with Lawrence Hill." *Callaloo* 36, no. 1 (Winter): 5–26

– 2014. "Slave Narratives and Hemispheric Studies." In *The Oxford Handbook of the African American Slave Narrative*, 344–61. Oxford University Press

Siemerling, Winfried, and Sarah Phillips Casteel, eds. 2010. *Canada and Its Americas: Transnational Navigations*. Montreal and Kingston: McGill-Queen's University Press

Silvera, Makeda. 1983. *Silenced: Talks with Working Class West Indian Women about Their Lives and Struggles as Domestic Workers in Canada*. Toronto: Williams-Wallace

– 1989. *Silenced: Talks with Working Class Caribbean Women about Their Lives and Struggles as Domestic Workers in Canada*. 2nd ed., with a new introduction. Toronto: Sister Vision Press

Silverman, Jason. 1985. *Unwelcome Guests: Canada West's Response to American Fugitive Slaves, 1800–1865*. Millwood, NY: Associated Faculties

Simmons, Merinda. 2009. "Beyond 'Authenticity': Migration and the Epistemology of 'Voice' in Mary Prince's *History of Mary Prince* and Maryse Condé's *I, Tituba*." *College Literature* 36, no. 4: 75–99

Simon, Sherry. 2006. *Translating Montreal: Episodes in the Life of a Divided City*. Montreal and Kingston: McGill-Queen's University Press

– 2009. "The Post-Industrial South-West." In *Used/Goods*, edited by Gisele Amantea, Lorraine Oades, and Kim Sawchuk. Montreal: Cut Rate Collective

Simpson, Donald G. 1970. "Negroes in Ontario from Early Times to 1870." PhD diss., University of Western Ontario

Smith, Adam. 1976. *An Inquiry into the Nature and Causes of the Wealth of Nations*. Oxford: Clarendon Press

Smith, Valerie. 2007. "Neo-slave Narratives." In *The Cambridge Companion to the African American Slave Narrative*, edited by Audrey A. Fisch, 168–85. Cambridge and New York: Cambridge University Press

Smyth, Heather. 2008. "'The Being Together of Strangers': Dionne Brand's Politics of Difference and the Limits of Multicultural Discourse." *Studies in Canadian Literature/Études en littérature canadienne* 33, no. 1: 272–90

– 2014. "The Black Atlantic Meets the Black Pacific: Multimodality in Kamau Brathwaite and Wayde Compton." *Callaloo* 37, no. 2: 389–403

Snead, James A. 1990. "Repetition as a Figure of Black Culture." In *Black Literature and Literary Theory*, edited by Henry Louis Gates Jr, 59–79. New York: Routledge

Société historique de Saint-Henri. "Histoire de Saint-Henri: Saint-Henri, avant, pendant et après le canal." http://www.saint-henri.com

Sollors, Werner. 1986. *Beyond Ethnicity: Consent and Descent in American Culture*. New York and Oxford: Oxford University Press

– 1997. *Neither Black nor White Yet Both: Thematic Explorations of Interracial Literature*. New York: Oxford University Press

Solow, Barbara L., ed. 1991. *Slavery and the Rise of the Atlantic System*. Cambridge: Cambridge University Press

Solow, Barbara L., and Stanley L. Engerman, eds. 1987. *British Capitalism and Caribbean Slavery: The Legacy of Eric Williams*. Cambridge: Cambridge University Press

Sommer, Doris. 1999. *Proceed with Caution, When Engaged by Minority Writings in the Americas*. Cambridge: Harvard University Press

Sowton, Ian. 1995. "An Autobiography. Of Sorts (Reading Claire Harris, *Drawing Down a Daughter*)." *Open Letter*, 9th series, no. 3: 25–34

Spillers, Hortense J. 2012. "Interlocutions: American Transnationalism and the African Diaspora." Conference paper, Futures of American Studies Institute, Dartmouth College

Stanton, Susan Marion. 2001. "*Voice of the Fugitive:* Henry Bibb and 'Racial Uplift' in Canada West, 1851–1852." MA thesis, University of Victoria

Steeves, David L. 2009. "A Novel Approach to the Law: The Case for an Expanded Study of Canadian Law and Literature." MA thesis, Dalhousie University

Stepto, Robert B. 1986. "Sharing the Thunder: The Literary Exchanges of Harriet Beecher Stowe, Henry Bibb, and Frederick Douglass." In *New Essays on "Uncle Tom's Cabin,"* edited by Eric J. Sundquist, 135–53. New York: Cambridge University Press

Sterling, Dorothy. 1971. *The Making of an Afro-American: Martin Robison Delany, 1812–1885*. Garden City, NY: Doubleday

Steward, Austin. 1857. *Twenty-Two Years a Slave, and Forty Years a Freeman: Embracing a Correspondence of Several Years, While President of Wilberforce Colony, London, Canada West*. Rochester, NY: William Alling. http://docsouth.unc.edu/fpn/steward/menu.html

Stewart, Jesse. 2010. "DJ Spooky and the Politics of Afro-Postmodernism." *Black Music Research Journal* 30, no. 2 (Fall): 337–61

Stewart, Maria W. 1987. *Maria W. Stewart, America's First Black Woman Political Writer: Essays and Speeches*. Edited and with an introduction by Marilyn Richardson. Bloomington: Indiana University Press

Still, William. 1872. *The Underground Railroad*. New York: Arno Press and New York Times

Stone, Marjorie. 1997. "The Poet as Whole-Body Camera: Maxine Tynes and the Pluralities of Otherness." *Dalhousie Review* 77, no. 1: 227–58

Streitmatter, Rodger. 1994. *Raising Her Voice: African-American Women Journalists Who Changed History*. Lexington: University of Kentucky Press

Sugars, Cynthia. 2010. "Worlding the (Postcolonial) Nation: Canada's Americas." In *Canada and Its Americas: Transnational Navigations*, edited by Winfried Siemerling and Sarah Phillips Casteel, 31–47. Montreal and Kingston: McGill-Queen's University Press

Sugars, Cynthia, and Laura Moss. 2009. *Canadian Literature in English: Texts and Contexts*. Toronto: Pearson Longman

Sugars, Cynthia, and Gerry Turcotte, eds. 2009. *Unsettled Remains: Canadian Literature and the Postcolonial Gothic*. Waterloo, ON: Wilfrid Laurier University Press

Sundquist, Eric J. (1985) 1989. "Slavery, Revolution, and the American Renaissance." In *The American Renaissance Reconsidered*, edited by Walter Benn Michaels and Donald E. Pease. Baltimore: Johns Hopkins University Press

– 1993. *To Wake the Nations: Race in the Making of American Literature*. Cambridge and London: Belknap Press of Harvard University Press

Szick, Lark, Randal Oulton, and Gail Facini. 1998 (updated by Rick Roberts 2013). "Names Submitted To Be Part Of The PORT ROSEWAY ASSOCIATION Group Of Loyalists." *The Global Gazette: Canada's Online Family History Magazine*. http://globalgenealogy.com/globalgazette/List001/list38.htm

Talbot, Carol. 1984. *Growing Up Black in Canada*. Toronto: Williams-Wallace

Tancock, Kat. 2008. "Interview with Author David Chariandy." *Canadian Living*. http://www.canadianliving.com/life/community/interview_with_author_david_chariandy.php

Tettey, Wisdom J., and Korbla P. Puplampu, eds. 2005. *The African Diaspora in Canada: Negotiating Identity and Belonging*. Calgary: University of Calgary Press

Thomas, H. Nigel. 2001. *Behind the Face of Winter*. Toronto: TSAR Publications

–, ed. 2006. *Why We Write: Conversations with African Canadian Poets and Novelists: Interviews*. Toronto: TSAR Canada

Thomas, Helen. 2000. *Romanticism and Slave Narratives: Transatlantic Testimonies*. Cambridge: Cambridge University Press

Thomas, Owen. 1998. "Abbott, Anderson Ruffin." In *Dictionary of Canadian Biography*. Vol. 14. Toronto and Quebec: University of Toronto/Université Laval. http://www.biographi.ca/en/bio/abbott_anderson_ruffin_14E.html

Thurston, John. 1991. Introduction to *Voyages: Short Narratives of Susanna Moodie*, by Susanna Moodie, vii–xxix. Ottawa: University of Ottawa Press

– 1996. *The Work of Words: The Writing of Susanna Strickland Moodie*. Montreal and Kingston: McGill-Queen's University Press

Thwaites, Reuben Gold. 1897. *The Jesuit Relations and Allied Documents*. Vol. 5. Cleveland: Burrows Bros Co.

Tompkins, Jane. 1985. *Sensational Designs: The Cultural Work of American Fiction, 1790–1860*. New York: Oxford University Press

Tourino, Kevin Gregory. 2010. "Online Representations of African Canadian Cinema: An Ethnographic and Archival Analysis." MA thesis, Simon Fraser University

Troy, William. 1861. *Hair-Breadth Escapes from Slavery to Freedom*. Manchester: Bremner. http://docsouth.unc.edu/neh/troy/menu.html

Trudel, Marcel, with the collaboration of Micheline d'Allaire. 2004. *Deux siècles d'esclavage au Québec; Suivi du Dictionnaire des esclaves et de leurs propriétaires au Canada français sur CD-ROM*. Montreal: Hurtubise HMH

– 2013. *Canada's Forgotten Slaves: Two Centuries of Bondage*. Translated by George Tombs. Montreal: Véhicule Press

Tucker, Ernst. 2006. *Lost Boundaries*. Bloomington, IN: Authorhouse

Tulchinsky, Gerald J.J. 1977. *The River Barons: Montreal Businessmen and the Growth of Industry and Transportation, 1837–53*. Toronto: University of Toronto Press

Turnbull, David. 1994. *Maps Are Territories: Science Is an Atlas: A Portfolio of Exhibits*. Chicago: University of Chicago Press

Turner, Camille. 2012a. "Evoking a Site of Memory: An Afrofuturist Sonic Walk That Maps Historic Toronto's Black Geographies." Project report. Toronto: York University. http://yorkspace.library.yorku.ca/xmlui/handle/10315/20829

– 2012b. "Hush Harbour." Sonic Walk, MP3 audio file. http://camilleturner.com/?project=hush-harbour

Ty, Eleanor. 2011. "Representing 'Other' Diasporas in Recent Global Canadian Fiction." *College Literature* 34, no. 8: 98–114

Tynes, Maxine. 1987. *Borrowed Beauty*. Porters Lake, NS: Pottersfield Press

– 1990. *Woman Talking Woman*. Lawrencetown Beach, NS: Pottersfield Press

– 1991. *Save the World for Me*. Porter's Lake, NS: Pottersfield Press

– 1993. *The Door of My Heart*. Lawrencetown Beach, NS: Pottersfield Press

Ullman, Victor. 1971. *Martin R. Delany: The Beginnings of Black Nationalism*. Boston: Beacon Press

United States of America. 1860. *Senate Select Committee Report on the Harper's Ferry Invasion*. 36th Congress, 1st Session. Senate. Rep. Com. No. 278

Utendale, Kent. 1985. "Race Relations in Canada's Midwest: A Study of the Immigration, Integration and Assimilation of Black Minority Groups." PhD diss., Pacific Western University

Venuti, Lawrence. 1995. *The Translator's Invisibility: A History of Translation*. London and New York: Routledge

Vernon, Karina. 2004. "Writing a Home for Prairie Blackness: Addena Sumter Freitag's *Stay Black and Die* and Cheryl Foggo's *Pourin' Down Rain*." *Canadian Literature* 182: 67–83

– 2008. "The Black Prairies: History, Subjectivity, Writing." PhD diss., University of Victoria

– 2012. "*After Canaan: Essays on Race, Writing, and Region* by Wayde Compton. Review." *BC Studies* 174. http://www.bcstudies.com/reviews.php?id=838669

Villard, Oswald Garrison. 1910. *John Brown, 1800–1859: A Biography Fifty Years After*. London and New York: Constable, Houghton Mifflin

von Frank, Albert J. 2006. "John Brown, James Redpath, and the Idea of Revolution." *Civil War History* 52, no. 2: 142–60

Waiser, Bill. 2005. *Saskatchewan: A New History*. Calgary: Fifth House

Walcott, Derek. 1979. *The Star-Apple Kingdom*. New York: Farrar, Straus, and Giroux
Walcott, Rinaldo. 1996. "Performing the Postmodern: Black Atlantic Rap and Identity in North America." PhD diss., University of Toronto
– 1997. *Black Like Who? Writing Black Canada*. Toronto: Insomniac Press
–, ed. 2000a. *Rude: Contemporary Black Canadian Cultural Criticism*. Toronto: Insomniac Press
– 2000b. "'Who Is She and What Is She to You?' Mary Ann Shadd Cary and the (Im)Possibility of Black/Canadian Studies." In *Rude: Contemporary Black Canadian Cultural Criticism*, edited by Rinaldo Walcott, 27–47. Toronto: Insomniac Press
– 2003. *Black Like Who? Writing Black Canada*. 2nd rev. ed. Toronto: Insomniac Press
Walcott-Hackshaw, Elizabeth. 2006. Review of *The Polished Hoe*. *Callaloo* 29, no. 2: 680–2
Walker, James W. St G. 1984. *The West Indians in Canada*. Canada's Ethnic Groups, no. 6. Ottawa: Canadian Historical Association
– (1976) 1992. *The Black Loyalists: The Search for a Promised Land in Nova Scotia and Sierra Leone 1783–1870*. Toronto: University of Toronto Press
– 1997. "Allegories and Orientations in African-Canadian Historiography: The Spirit of Africville." *Dalhousie Review* 77, no. 2: 155–78
– 1999. "Myth, History and Revisionism: The Black Loyalists Revisited." *Acadiensis* 29, no. 1: Web
– 2000a. "George, David." In *Dictionary of Canadian Biography Online*. Toronto: University of Toronto Press. http://www.biographi.ca/009004-119.01-e.php?&id_nbr=2489&&PHPSESSID=ufcrenq7uck2fq4epnbt3m1922
– 2000b. "King, Boston." In *Dictionary of Canadian Biography Online*. Toronto: University of Toronto Press. http://www.biographi.ca/009004-119.01-e.php?&id_nbr=2489&&PHPSESSID=ufcrenq7uck2fq4epnbt3m1922
Walvin, James. 2011. *The Zong: A Massacre, the Law and the End of Slavery*. New Haven, CT: Yale University Press
Ward, Frederick. 1974. *Riverlisp: Black Memories*. Plattsburgh, NY: Tundra Books
– 1983. *The Curing Berry*. Toronto: Williams-Wallace
Ward, Samuel Ringgold. 1855. *Autobiography of a Fugitive Negro; His Anti-Slavery Words and Labors in the United States, Canada, and England*. London: J. Snow. http://docsouth.unc.edu/wards/menu.html
Warner, Ashton. 1831. *Negro Slavery Described by a Negro: Being the Narrative of Ashton Warner, a Native of St. Vincent's. With an Appendix Containing the Testimony of Four Christian Ministers, Recently Returned from the Colonies, on the System of Slavery as It Now Exists*. Edited by S. Strickland. London: Samuel Maunder. http://docsouth.unc.edu/neh/warner/menu.html
Warner-Lewis, Maureen. 2007. *Archibald Monteath: Igbo, Jamaican, Moravian*. Kingston: University of the West Indies Press
Warnica, Richard. 2011. "Africville Can't Escape Racial Divide: The Choice of a New Halifax Museum's Executive Director is Stoking Old Tensions." *Maclean's*, 26 Sep-

tember. http://www.macleans.ca/news/canada/africville-cant-escape-racial-divide

Wayne, Michael. 1995. "The Myth of the Fugitive Slave: The Black Population of Canada West on the Eve of the American Civil War: A Reassessment Based on the Manuscript Census of 1861." *Histoire sociale/Social History* 56: 465–85

Wegmann-Sánchez, Jessica. 2001. "Rewriting Race and Ethnicity across the Border: Mairuth Sarsfield's *No Crystal Stair* and Nella Larsen's *Quicksand and Passing*." *Essays on Canadian Writing* 74: 136–66

Wetherell, Charles, and Robert W. Roetger. 1989. "Another Look at the Loyalists of Shelburne, NS, 1783–95." *Canadian Historical Review* 57, no. 1: 76–91

Whitehead, Ruth. N.d. "The Black Loyalists of South Carolina 1775–1785." Unpublished manuscript

Whitehead, Ruth, and Carmelita A.M. Robertson, eds. 2003. *The Life of Boston King, Black Loyalist, Minister, and Master Carpenter 1760?–1802*. Halifax: Nimbus Publishing and the Nova Scotia Museum

Whitfield, Harvey Amani. 2006. *Blacks on the Border: The Black Refugees in British North America, 1815–1860*. Burlington: University of Vermont Press

– 2007. "Black Loyalists and Black Slaves in Maritime Canada." *History Compass* 5, no. 6: 1980–97

– 2009. "The American Background of Loyalists Slaves." *Left History* 14, no. 1: 58–87

Whitlock, Gillian. 2000. *The Intimate Empire: Reading Women's Autobiography*. London and New York: Cassell

Wiens, Jason. 2000. "'Language Seemed to Split in Two': National Ambivalence(s) and Dionne Brand's *No Language Is Neutral*." *Essays on Canadian Writing* 70: 81–102

Williams, Dorothy W. 1997. *The Road to Now: A History of Blacks in Montreal*. Montreal: Véhicule Press

– 2005. "Print and Black Canadian Culture." In *History of the Book in Canada*. Vol 2: *1840–1918*, edited by Yvan Lamonde, Patricia Fleming, and Gilles Gallichan, 40–3. Toronto: University of Toronto Press

Williams, Emily Allen. 2004. "Triadic Revelations of Exilic Identity: Claire Harris's *Fables from the Women's Quarters, Dipped in Shadow*, and *She*." *Studies in the Literary Imagination* 32, no. 2: 53–75

Williams, Eric. (1944) 1964. *Capitalism and Slavery*. Introduction by D.W. Brogan. London: A. Deutsch

Williams, James. 2001. *A Narrative of Events, Since the First of August, 1834, by James Williams, an Apprenticed Labourer in Jamaica*. Introduction by Diana Paton. Durham, NC, and London: Duke University Press

Williams, Tyrone. 2009. "Marlene Nourbese-Philip, *Zong!*" *African American Review* 43, no. 4: 785–7

Wilson, Ellen Gibson. 1976. *The Loyal Blacks*. New York: Capricorn

Winks, Robin W. 1969. "The Canadian Negro: A Historical Assessment: The Problem of Identity: Part II." *Journal of Negro History* 54, no. 1: 1–18

– (1971) 1997. *The Blacks in Canada: A History*. 1971. Montreal and Kingston: McGill-Queen's University Press
– 2003. Introduction to *Autobiography of Josiah Henson: An Inspiration for Harriet Beecher Stowe's Uncle Tom*. Mineola, NY: Dover Publications
Wood, Marcus. 2000. *Blind Memory: Visual Representations of Slavery in England and America 1780–1865*. New York: Routledge
– 2002. *Slavery, Empathy, and Pornography*. Oxford and New York: Oxford University Press
Woods, David. 1990. *Native Song: Poetry and Paintings*. Lawrencetown Beach, NS: Pottersfield Press
Wormeny, Lavina. 1861. "Narrative of the Escape of a poor Negro Woman from Slavery." *Montreal Gazette*, 31 January. Reprinted in *Black Then: Blacks and Montreal, 1780s–1880s*, by Frank Mackey, 162–6. Montreal and Kingston: McGill-Queen's University Press, 2004
Wyile, Herb. 2002. *Speculative Fictions: Contemporary Canadian Novelists and the Writing of History*. Montreal and Kingston: McGill-Queen's University Press
– 2007. *Speaking in the Past Tense: Canadian Novelists on Writing Historical Fiction*. Waterloo, ON: Wilfrid Laurier University Press
– 2011. *Anne of Tim Hortons: Globalization and the Reshaping of Atlantic-Canadian Literature*. Waterloo, ON: Wilfrid Laurier University Press
Yarbrough, Anne. 2010a. "Black Pilots' Connection to Henry Mowatt." In *Nova Scotia Island Journal*. http://novascotiaisland.blogspot.com/2010/04/black-pilots-connection-to-henry-mowatt.html
– 2010b. "The Black Pilots Who Went to Sierra Leone from Birchtown." In *Nova Scotia Island Journal*. http://novascotiaisland.blogspot.com/2010/10/black-pilots-who-went-to-sierra-leone.html
Yee, Shirley J. 1992. *Black Women Abolitionists: A Study in Activism, 1828–1860*. Knoxville: University of Tennessee Press
Yorke, Stephanie. 2010. "The Slave Narrative Tradition in Lawrence Hill's *The Book of Negroes*." *Studies in Canadian Literature/Études en littérature canadienne* 35, no. 2: 129–44
Young, Judy. 2001. "No Longer 'Apart'? Multiculturalism Policy and Canadian Literature." *Canadian Ethnic Studies* 33, no. 2: 88–116
Zackodnik, Teresa. 1996. "'I'm Blackening in My Way': Identity and Place in Dionne Brand's *No Language Is Neutral*." In *Writing Ethnicity: Cross-Cultural Consciousness in Canadian and Québécois Literature*, edited by Winfried Siemerling, 194–211. Toronto: ECW Press
– 1999. "'Writing Home': Claire Harris's *Drawing Down a Daughter*." *Ariel* 30, no. 3: 163–90
Zamir, Shamoon. 1995. *Dark Voices: W.E.B. Du Bois and American Thought, 1888–1903*. Chicago: University of Chicago Press

INDEX